Foundation Flash 8

Sham Bhangal and Kristian Besley

friendsof

DESIGNER TO DESIGNER™

an Apress® company

Foundation Flash 8

ISBN-13 (pbk): 978-1-59059-542-8

ISBN-10 (pbk): 1-59059-542-4

Printed and bound in the United States of America 9 8 7 6 5 4 3 2

Distributed to the book trade worldwide by Springer-Verlag New York, Inc., 233 Spring Street, 6th Floor, New York, NY 10013. Phone 1-800-SPRINGER, fax 201-348-4505, e-mail orders-ny@springer-sbm.com, or visit www.springeronline.com.

For information on translations, please contact Apress directly at 2560 Ninth Street, Suite 219, Berkeley, CA 94710. Phone 510-549-5930, fax 510-549-5939, e-mail info@apress.com, or visit www.apress.com.

The source code for this book is freely available to readers at www.friendsofed.com in the Downloads section.

Credits

Lead Editor
Chris Mills

Technical Reviewer
Todd Yard

Editorial Board
Steve Anglin, Dan Appleman,
Ewan Buckingham, Gary Cornell,
Tony Davis, Jason Gilmore,
Jonathan Hassell, Chris Mills,
Dominic Shakeshaft, Jim Sumser

Project Manager
Beth Christmas

Copy Edit Manager
Nicole LeClerc

Copy Editors
Damon Larson and Liz Welch

Assistant Production Director
Kari Brooks-Copony

Production Editor
Linda Marousek

Compositor and Artist
Katy Freer

Proofreader
Patrick Vincent

Indexer
Present Day Indexing

Cover Image Designer
Corné van Dooren

Interior and Cover Designer
Kurt Krames

Manufacturing Director
Tom Debolski

Case study illustrations courtesy of Gareth Southwell at www.woodpig.com

CONTENTS AT A GLANCE

CONTENTS

Chapter 18: Futurescape **519**

ABOUT THE AUTHORS

Sham Bhangal began on the route to web design in 1991, designing and specifying information screens for safety critical computer systems, as used in places like nuclear power plant control rooms. He soon discovered that more conventional interface design, animation, and multimedia tools were available, such as SoftimageXSI, Photoshop, and Flash. He has been writing books and articles on them since the turn of the century.

As well as being an author by night, Sham works as a Flash developer for an e-learning company during the day, creating online testing applications, simulations, and other web-based teaching applications using lots of class-based ActionScript and a fair bit of user interface and content design. He is also known to engage in copious amounts of freelance web design work.

Like all professional web designers, he never sleeps because new ideas and old clients have a habit of keeping him awake. You can catch up with him at boy@futuremedia.org.uk, or through his weblog, http://weblog.motion-graphics.org/.

Kristian Besley is a Flash/web developer currently working in an educational establishment and specializing in interactivity and dynamic-driven content (using ASP and PHP). He is also a lecturer in multimedia.

He has written a number of books, including *Flash MX Video*, *Learn Programming with Flash MX*, and the Foundation Flash series. He was a contributor to *Flash Math Creativity*, *Flash MX Games Most Wanted*, and *Flash Video Creativity*. He is also a contributor to *Computer Arts* magazine and has produced freelance work for numerous clients, including the BBC.

Kristian was born and currently resides in Swansea, Wales. He is a fluent Welsh speaker and is the creator of the first ever Welsh translation search plug-in for Firefox and Mozilla (available from http://mycroft.mozdev.org).

Portrait image courtesy of Simon James at www.thefresh.co.uk.

ABOUT THE TECHNICAL REVIEWER

Todd Yard is a lead Flash developer at Brightcove (www.brightcove.com) in Cambridge, Massachusetts, and has contributed as an author or technical editor on 11 other friends of ED Flash books, including *Flash 8 Essentials* and *Extending Flash MX 2004*.

ABOUT THE COVER IMAGE DESIGNER

Corné van Dooren designed the front cover image for this book. Having been given a brief by friends of ED to create a new design for the Foundation series, he was inspired to create this new setup combining technology and organic forms.

With a colorful background as an avid cartoonist, Corné discovered the infinite world of multimedia at the age of 17—a journey of discovery that hasn't stopped since. His mantra has always been "The only limit to multimedia is the imagination," a mantra that is keeping him moving forward constantly.

After enjoying success after success over the past years— working for many international clients, as well as being featured in multimedia magazines, testing software, and working on many other friends of ED books—Corné decided it was time to take another step in his career by launching his own company, *Project 79*, in March 2005.

You can see more of his work and contact him through www.cornevandooren.com or www.project79.com.

If you like his work, be sure to check out his chapter in *New Masters of Photoshop: Volume 2*, also by friends of ED (ISBN: 1-59059-315-4).

INTRODUCTION

This book aims to give you a solid foundation in the most essential skills you need to use Flash 8—both the Basic and Professional versions. By the end of the book, you'll understand how the components of a Flash movie fit together, you'll have used all of the key tools, and you'll have integrated all your learning in a series of detailed creative exercises. Our mission is to launch you into orbit around planet Flash, equipped with all the tools and knowledge you need to make a safe landing.

Flash is one of the hottest content-creation technologies on the Web. From its origins as an animation package, Flash has grown stronger and planted deep roots. It is already used to create all kinds of content, such as website front-ends, interactive games, animated cartoons, movie trailers, and PDA interfaces. Perhaps its most significant role, however, is in creating *interfaces* for all these different areas. Its ability to present a clean, friendly, and functional front-end to the user is coupled with its power behind the scenes. Designers love Flash for its speed, quality, ease of use, and clearly structured functionality, and at the same time, both programmers and designers can use its ActionScript programming language to produce phenomenal results. Whatever kind of interface you want to build, Flash has the answer. If you've never used Flash before, you're in for a real treat.

As the Internet has changed, Flash has moved with it, evolving into a two-tier system. The timeline-based animation is still there, but it is underpinned by a stronger emphasis on functionality that enables you to create the large, code-heavy sites required for today's e-commerce front-ends, e-learning applications, and other intelligent user interfaces. Don't worry if you are not a heavy-duty programmer, though; you can still build Flash sites using many of the new features aimed directly at designers who are not programmers:

- If you are experienced in bitmap editing applications such as Adobe Photoshop, you will be able to leverage this experience in Flash, because Flash now supports many of the features seen in Photoshop, such as filters and blend modes.

- If you are more of an Illustrator/Freehand person, then you're also going to like Flash, because its new Object Drawing mode will make you feel right at home.

- If you are a video content producer, then Flash is also for you, because it is now one of the most powerful over-the-Web video-delivery systems.

- If you are a musician, then be prepared to learn a system that allows you to give your creations the web presence they deserve: 32-channel sound at the quality and format of your choosing!

- Finally, if you are a traditional web designer, then you are in for a treat, because Flash already supports many of the things you are already familiar with (ActionScript, a JavaScript-like scripting language; support for subsets of both CSS and HTML; and runtime import of most of the common bitmap formats you are already used to). It also seamlessly addresses some of the things you have always had trouble with, such as consistent color, one single plug-in for all multimedia types (sound, video, animation), embedded fonts, multilanguage localization, and of course, a good interactive web animation system. Flash also addresses areas in which you may have previously thought Flash was weak, such as accessibility and security.

This book will take you step by step through every aspect of designing your own Flash interface, building your knowledge and skills with each chapter. We'll also look at the pitfalls and practicalities that every Flash web designer faces, teach you how to make your designs web friendly, and ensure that you know how to get your hard work up on the Net. But before we dive into these complex issues, let's make sure you know the basics of how Flash works, and why it's such a capable authoring tool.

Flash—the big picture

When you create a Flash movie for the Web, you're pulling together images, sound, video, text, and animation, and bundling them in a file that gets posted up on a website.

The Flash software you install on your computer is the authoring environment in which you create your masterpiece. The work in progress is stored in a file with the extension .fla. Once you're happy with your movie and you want to publish it to the Internet, Flash will convert the FLA file into a playable file with the extension .swf—pronounced "swiff" in the Flash community. The SWF file is then linked to an HTML file on the server that hosts your site:

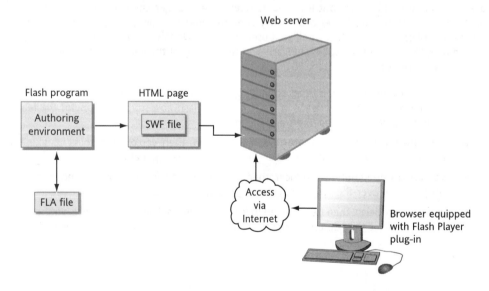

When a user visits your site, the SWF file is downloaded into their browser and your movie is played back. All the viewer needs is the Flash Player installed on his machine. This player is a reasonably compact download, and the vast majority of the world's browsers are equipped to play back Flash content.

One of the reasons that Flash is such a popular tool is that it uses **vector graphics** technology. There are two main graphic standards on the Internet: **raster** (bitmaps) and **vector**. The majority of static images that you see on the Web are raster images, composed of files in formats such as BMP, GIF, and JPG. Raster images do a good job, but a big raster image usually requires a large file size, and a large file size means a long download time. And on the Web, download time is *everything*. Internet users are picky—if a site's packed with raster images and is taking too long to load, they'll just skip it and go somewhere else. This is where vectors come in. They're small, fast, and funky.

> *Vector images describe the image in terms of coordinates and mathematical transformations. That sounds complicated, but it's really as simple as saying, "Put a dot here, put a dot there, and draw a line between them." This compares with the raster technique of describing the color and position of every single pixel in the image.*

Vector graphic files are much more compact and efficient compared to rasters, and Flash is the main tool for delivering vector graphics and vector-based animations on the Web. The files that Flash creates are therefore comparatively small, which is one of the reasons for Flash's success.

A well-constructed Flash file will also **stream** onto the user's computer. That means it will load the first part of the animation and start playing it back while the rest of the animation loads in the background. Streaming a file correctly is an important technique for a Flash designer because it means that visitors are presented with something visual and enticing almost immediately—removing the danger that they will get bored and go elsewhere instead of waiting for the site to download.

Another disadvantage of raster images is that they're *display dependent*, meaning that if you create them to look just right on one particular display, the image could come out significantly altered if someone uses a different display resolution to view it. In addition, if you *zoom in* on a raster image, the pixels just get bigger and bigger until you end up with a screen full of squares of color that are completely unrecognizable as the source image. Vector images, though, can work independently of the display because the line will always be the same relative length and clarity no matter what resolution you use to view it. Also, no matter how far you zoom into a vector, the image will still stay crisp and at full resolution.

Why would you ever want to use a raster? Raster formats are good for images with thousands of different colors. Can you imagine trying to describe a photograph in terms of vectors? It would be horribly complicated, and you'd wind up with a far bigger file size compared to the raster equivalent. Luckily, Flash has the best of both worlds: the vast majority of its drawings and animations are vector-based, but when you need the extra richness that you can only get with a raster, Flash will allow you to import a bitmap and use it in conjunction with the dominant vectors.

Despite the fact that Flash is normally associated with vectors, Flash 8 now also includes many features normally associated with bitmaps, and this feature makes Flash much more accessible to people who are coming to Flash from more traditional digital art disciplines (especially graphic design and traditional web design).

What's significant about Flash 8

If you've used a previous version of Flash, the first thing you'll notice is. . .er. . .that it appears like nothing much has changed! Looks can be deceptive, though, because a whole lot has changed—so much so that many well-known and well-respected Flash designers are already calling Flash 8 *the* most significant Flash release in years!

Most of the new features do not involve the look and feel of the interface, but the things you can do with it.

For the designer or digital artist looking to create a web presence with Flash, there is a whole lot of new stuff. First, you now have lots of little tweaks to the tools and general interface that make it all easier to work with. Changes to gradient production, tweens (custom easing), the way vectors are drawn (Object Drawing), and tabbed panels are some examples of this.

Second, there are totally new features such as filters and other effects that will revolutionize your workflow. Stuff you would normally have had to do in a separate application, or do manually (such as adding drop shadows or bevels to buttons, or creating logos) can be done quickly and easily within Flash. Better still, doing them in Flash results in effects that are very bandwidth friendly. Further, all the new visual effects can be animated, allowing you to create animated content that was just not possible with previous versions of Flash. If you've ever used Photoshop layer blend and filter effects, you are in for a happy surprise—Flash 8 supports them, and—get this—you can animate these effects in real time! Not only can you apply these effects to bitmaps and vectors (including vector animations), but you can also apply most of them to video as well!

Third, there is now an updated scripting help system, called Script Assist. This helps nonprogrammers to write ActionScript, Flash's scripting language. ActionScript is the doorway to many of Flash's high-end visual effects, as well as the thing that allows you to add that all-important ingredient, interactivity, to your Flash content. Script Assist is one way of getting through that doorway with the minimum of fuss (and more importantly, without a lot of programming knowledge!).

One of the most significant subsets of the new enhancements for designers are those enhancements that are within the Flash Player itself.

The Flash 8 Player has several optimizations that allow you to create animations and user interfaces that run much faster than previous Flash content. This allows you to create more complex effects, bigger and better sites, or just simply smoother, more fluid animations. The Flash 8 Player now lets you import PNG files at runtime, allowing you to import images with embedded alpha channels on the fly. The Flash 8 Player also has much improved video facilities, a better sound engine, and a better text rendering engine that results in clearer, sharper text.

Of course, because the new features in Flash 8 are not obvious, it makes having a guide to help you along all the more important. That's where this book comes in!

Our aims and philosophy in this book

As its title suggests, the aim of this book is to give you a solid, extensible foundation in Flash design, implementation, and programming. We believe that Flash is too complex a tool to cover definitively from scratch in 1,000 pages, let alone 600-odd. We want to provide a rock-steady foundation: an in-depth treatment of the core aspects of using Flash rather than an overview of each and every feature.

We believe in creating a reliable foundation so you can understand Flash more fully and absorb and internalize the material we cover. We're not going to list every menu option and cover every single ActionScript command in immense detail. We're going to concentrate on the core of learning Flash successfully, taking you from a zero knowledge of Flash to being able to put up a website you can be proud of.

Everyone knows that the best way to learn is to play and practice. It's no good if someone just *tells* you what to do—to master Flash, you have to *use* it. This book follows that philosophy by providing examples and tutorials in every chapter, and on every topic we cover. It's another well-known fact that although small examples are fun and can help you learn, it's difficult to apply those examples in the real world when you've finished the book. So, at the end of each chapter, you'll be able to apply the things you've just learned to the **case study project**. Each case study is an opportunity for you to put the information you learn in each chapter into building a complete and fully functional website that you can use as your online portfolio:

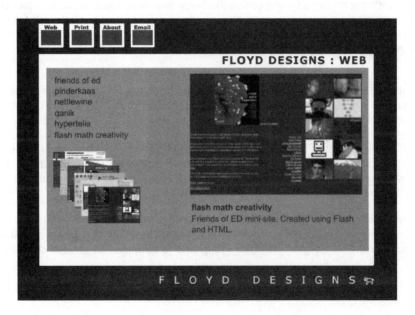

The website you'll create will have a full navigation menu and animated content, and it will dynamically load in images and text files using ActionScript. As it's created, this real-world example will reinforce the core skills you learn in this book.

We believe that by learning the Flash skills you need in context, you'll build the knowledge and mental adaptability to fit your expanding knowledge and specialization into a structured and reliable framework.

How to use this book

To use this book, all you'll need is a copy of Macromedia Flash 8 and a computer to run it on. This book is written for either Flash Basic or Flash Professional. Most of the book can be completed using only Flash Basic, but a small subset of the features we will discuss are specific to Flash Professional. If you have Flash Basic installed, we recommend that you revisit the Flash Professional specific sections using the 30-day Flash 8 trial available at www.macromedia.com (the trial version allows you to trial either Flash Basic or Flash Professional).

If you want to publish your Flash movies onto the Internet, you'll also need a connection and some web space to publish them to. Your Internet service provider (ISP) will be able to sort this out for you if you have any problems.

The case study you'll create contains an animated introduction, interactive buttons, and examples of dynamic masking using ActionScript, and it will be fully optimized for publishing to the Web. Its modular nature means that you can easily go back and find the specific functionality that you're looking for and modify it or replace it with something completely different. If, for example, you want to use the buttons in a different website or reuse any of the animated effects, you can easily flip to the relevant chapter for a recap on how to do it, and then just pull the desired part out of the one movie and incorporate it in the other.

You don't have to download anything to use this book, but we've supplied support files containing the sounds and images that we've used to allow you to re-create the examples exactly as they are in the book. The case study files, and all support material, can be found available for download on this book's page at www.friendsofed.com. We'll point you to the relevant files in the chapters as necessary.

The case study project files are there so you can pick up the project at any stage in the book and work through it, or you can use them as backups if you've lost your files and don't want to have to re-create them all again. You may just want to check that your results are the same as ours. The files are arranged so that you have a pre-prepared project as the starting point for any chapter. For example, if you want to start from Chapter 5, you'd go into the appropriate folder and use the for chapter5.fla file, which contains all the work done on the case study from the beginning through to Chapter 4. Likewise, if you've just finished the Chapter 5 case study and want to check it against ours to make sure it looked right, you would use for chapter6.fla.

We also have some optional sound and video files that can be downloaded if you want to try your hand at the compression material we cover in Chapter 11. These (uncompressed) sound and video files are quite large, though, and could take a long time to download on some connections.

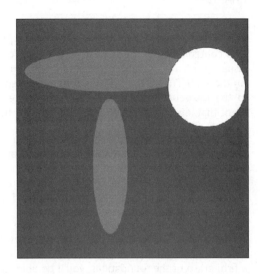

Chapter 1

FLASH MOVIE ESSENTIALS

What we'll cover in this chapter:

- Exploring the Flash stage, where you create movies in Flash
- Finding and using tool and object properties in the Properties panel that are guaranteed to make authoring in Flash easier
- Manipulating the size of the stage and changing your movie's overall background in the Document Properties dialog box
- Controlling the playback of your movie in the Timeline
- Using frames to create and arrange the content of your movie
- Making content move through animation
- Using layers to add depth to your movie and keep track of complex content
- Creating separate scenes that contain distinct chunks of your movie

Macromedia Flash is the gateway to state-of-the-art web content. Flash is the standard file format for delivering interactive, visually rich content and animation on the Web. (This is the SWF file format I talked about in the Introduction.) It's also the authoring environment that lets you create and publish the SWF files.

In this chapter, I'm going to introduce you to the authoring environment—the Flash interface—and take you through the essentials of creating visual content in Flash and making it move. In doing this, you'll start building a picture of the main components of a Flash movie and see how they fit together.

Taking time to understand the core elements at the heart of a Flash movie will pay off later. After you have a firm grasp of the foundations, you'll be able to build on them. So let's begin by looking at the first thing that almost everybody wants to do when they open their copy of Flash: create a movie and make interesting things happen on the screen.

The authoring environment

If you don't already have Flash up and running, start it now. When you first open Flash, you see an array of screen elements: icons, menus, toolbars, panels, and status bars.

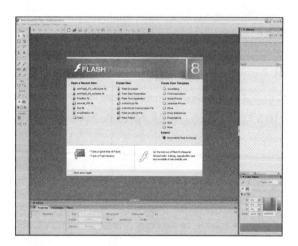

If you've already explored Flash a little, your screen setup might look a little different from the previous screenshot. The screen may also look slightly different if you are using Flash Basic. For the purposes of this book, it's best to reset to the default setup. Don't worry too much about this for now; I'll show you how to do that in a moment.

This is the feature-rich authoring environment (Flash's studio, workshop, and test track combined) that lets you create your Flash movies and export them so they can be published on the Web and accessed by the adoring multitudes.

If you've never used a Macromedia product before (and especially if you're coming to Flash from a programming background, where all you're used to is a code editor), you might be intimidated by the unfamiliar interface the first time you open Flash—don't be. Before long, you'll be navigating the interface with ease. And there's an added bonus to learning the Flash interface: Macromedia uses a common interface across all of its software, so once you're familiar with Flash, you'll have no trouble finding your way around other Macromedia programs, such as Dreamweaver.

There's a tremendous amount of detail and power tucked away in the Flash interface, and at first it can seem a little daunting if you're new to the software. To avoid a sense of clutter, and to turn down the volume a little, let's clear some of the elements out of the way. Then you can concentrate on the bare essentials. (Don't worry, you won't be missing a thing—I'll explain all the core features over the course of the book.)

Configuring the authoring environment

1. Select Create New ➤ Flash Document from the central window or File ➤ New ➤ Flash Document.

Flash 8 Professional users will see a number of avail-able document types in the center column of the startup screen. Discussion of most of these docu-ment types is beyond the scope of this book (although some of them are covered in the upcom-ing friends of ED book Foundation Flash 8 ActionScript, expected to be published in 2006). For all the exercises throughout this book, always select the Flash Document *type.*

2. If you've used Flash before picking up this book, reset the default setup by selecting Window ➤ Workspace Layout ➤ Default.

Panels are used to help you modify and manipulate the content of your Flash movie. This content can be graphic images, pieces of animation, text, or code. You can use the panels and menu options to alter their characteristics and the way they behave. All the panels are dockable; you can drag them around the screen and dock them to the other panels. Currently, the pan-els you can see are docked. An undocked panel is called a floating panel.

A lone floating panel has a slightly different appear-ance than a docked one. As shown in the following image, the floating panel (on the right) has an extra bar at the top that the docked panel (on the left) doesn't.

For the benefit of clarity, the panels in screenshots throughout the book are often shown as floating panels. This enables you to clearly focus on that single panel.

Now let's customize the authoring environment. If you decide at a later stage that Macromedia's preset Flash panel layout (Window ➤ Workspace Layout ➤ Default) isn't particularly to your liking, you have the option of saving your own customized layout (Window ➤ Workspace Layout ➤ Save Current).

Each element you create in your movie (such as pictures and text) is treated as a discrete object. Each element has its own attributes, such as color, transparency, and size, and you can use the panels to change these attrib-utes. Additionally, changing panel settings can alter the way an object behaves. You'll look at all of these attrib-utes as you progress through the book. At the moment, though, you don't have any content to work with, so let's move the panels out of the way.

Windows users: To minimize the panel, click the arrow button on the side of the panel or the panel title. To close/open a panel docking area, click the arrow to the side of the docking area as shown in the following image.

There are also two other docking areas to the left and top of the screen, which aren't often used. They contain the toolbar panel and Timeline panel, and they're sufficiently important that they should be left as they are, unless you have a really good reason to change them.

To redisplay the panels, click either of the arrow buttons. Although you've put them out of the way for now, you'll come back to them later.

Mac users: You can close floating panels (i.e., those that are not docked to one of the docking areas noted previously) by clicking the triangle in the upper-left corner of the panel.

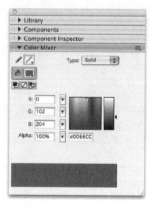

You can also click the arrow belonging to the panels on the bottom of the screen to hide the Properties and Actions panels. This hides the panels from view and provides you with a great deal more screen space to play with.

Note that the panels shown in the following screenshot are docked. A docked panel is one that's fixed in one of the docking areas. There are two docking areas that are most commonly used: the one at the bottom of the screen that shows the Actions and Properties panels, and the one to the far right of the screen that holds the Color and Library panels. Don't worry too much about these panels at the moment (although you should be able to pick them out by looking at their titles).

After you've hidden the Properties and right-hand panels, you're left with a white area in the middle of the main window. This area is called the stage, and it's what the end user will see when he or she views your finished Flash site or animation. Hopefully by then, the site will have lost some of its current minimalist appearance!

To the left of the screen is a toolbar containing all the Flash drawing tools. Toward the top of the screen is the Timeline. The Timeline is fundamental to the way Flash creates animation, and you'll examine it in detail later in this chapter.

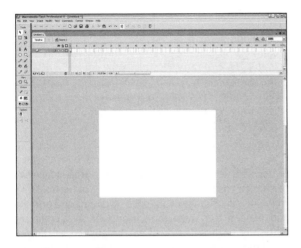

4. Click the Show Frame option.

The white area in the center of the screen should now be visible in its entirety.

As I've already mentioned briefly, the white area is called the stage, and it's where all the action in your movie takes place. The gray area around the stage is called the work area. Let's talk a little about these different areas.

On both platforms, you can close individual panels by right-clicking (CTRL-clicking on the Mac) the title bar and clicking Close Panel, *or choosing the* Close Panel *option from the drop-down menu (at the upper-right corner of each panel) when the panel is maximized.*

Alternatively, selecting Window ➤ Hide Panels *or pressing F4 will also close all onscreen panels (including the Tools panel). You can bring them back by selecting* Window ➤ Show Panels *or pressing F4 again. Most designers prefer the F4 route because it's the quickest way to clear everything out of sight. F4 is indeed one key to remember.*

Next, you want to make sure that you can see all of the stage area. Being able to fill the screen with the stage area is important because, as you've seen, it's where all your visual content will be created.

3. Click the Magnification drop-down box near the upper right of the screen above the Timeline.

The stage

The stage can be likened to what a movie director sees in the viewfinder of a camera. What the director sees in the viewfinder is what will appear onscreen when the audience views the finished product. In the motion picture world, the action takes place on the film set (the stage), while actors are waiting offstage, ready to make their entrance.

5

At various times in the movie, different people and objects will be visible on the stage, and consequently in the shot. The stage in Flash works on the same principle: at any given point in your Flash movie, the things that are on the stage are what the viewers will see when the movie is rendered in their browsers. Keep in mind that the movie set can be much larger than the camera's field of view, and the camera can move around and seek out previously hidden corners.

If you want end users to see something in the Flash movie that plays in their browser, that something has to be visible on the stage area when you create the movie. This also means that movie content can move onto the stage from the "wings." For example, an animated actor could enter stage left, walk across the stage, and exit stage right. In the Flash authoring environment, any visual element that moves beyond the boundaries of the stage winds up in the work area.

The work area

The work area surrounds the stage. You can place content in the work area, but usually only content that actually appears on (or moves across) the stage will show up in the finished movie. When you're designing your movie, you need to think about whether the visual elements it contains will spring into existence directly on the stage, or whether they're going to wait in the wings and then move onto the stage at a later time.

One example of this would be a car that starts its journey in the work area to the left of the stage, moves across the stage (and into the viewer's sight), and then accelerates off into the work area on the right.

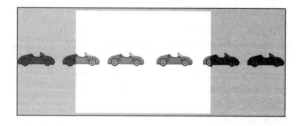

While the content is on the stage, the viewer sees it in the browser. When it's "in the wings," it's usually invisible to the viewer.

> *Although content outside the stage usually won't show up in the final Flash page (as seen on the Web), you can force Flash to show content outside the stage area by altering the HTML page that your Flash content is displayed within. For now, though, it's easier to assume that any content outside the stage won't be seen.*

So far, you've used the Magnification drop-down box to change your view of the stage *in the authoring environment*. Any changes you make by zooming in and out and making the stage look bigger or smaller in the authoring environment will *not* be applied to the finished movie seen by the end user. These magnification changes are just to help you see things more clearly when you're creating and modifying your movie.

To alter the size and proportions of the stage itself (and therefore your finished movie when it's displayed in the user's browser), you need to change the properties of the stage itself. Flash 8 has a resource that enables you to do that easily—it's called the Properties panel. Let's take a quick look at that now.

The Properties panel

The Properties panel makes working in Flash a whole lot easier, mainly because it's contextual (i.e., the options shown on it will change depending on what you're doing, and in a way such that most of the things you need to do or know are accessible directly from it). With the Properties panel, you can easily manipulate all your movie's contents from one place. You'll be using it frequently throughout this book, and it will come to be your best friend when creating movies in Flash.

By default, the Properties panel is positioned at the bottom center of the screen (you might recall minimizing it when you hid all the panels earlier using *F4*). If you've followed my lead and hidden it, you can retrieve it by clicking the arrow at the bottom center of the screen. You can also press *F4* again to bring all the docking areas and panels back.

If you don't already have it open, you can access the Properties panel by selecting the Window ➤ Properties menu option or by pressing *Ctrl+F3*. Once you have the Properties panel open, click the Properties tab if it isn't already selected.

You don't have any content on your stage yet, so the Properties panel should appear as shown in the following image. If it doesn't appear like this (e.g., if you have a tool selected by mistake or have been poking at something with your mouse), then select the Selection tool (the first tool on the upper left of the toolbar) and click once on the stage.

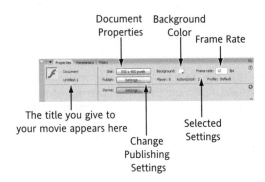

The Properties panel is split into two parts: the upper and lower sections. You'll see in the next chapter that when you use an item from the Tools panel, the upper section has properties specifically related to that tool, whereas the lower section is related to an item you've selected in your work area. The lower section can be opened and closed using the arrow in the lower-right corner.

Let's move on to see how you can use the Properties panel even though you have no content on your stage yet.

The size of the stage

When you're planning your Flash movie, you should consider how much browser space you want the finished movie to take up. You'll need to decide what size you want the movie's window to be, based on factors such as the kind of content you're displaying, what else will appear alongside the movie in the host page, and

so on. When you've made that decision, you can alter the size of the stage to match your plan.

You can view the stage's current dimensions and global characteristics by clicking the Size button in the Properties panel. This opens the Document Properties dialog box, in which you can make global changes to the properties (or characteristics) that affect the whole movie. You can also use it to create a title and comments about the movie.

You can also display the Document Properties dialog box by selecting the Modify ➤ Document *menu option, by right-clicking the stage and selecting* Document Properties *from the context-sensitive menu, or by double-clicking the box that displays* 12.0 fps *(located under the Timeline).*

The first thing you can add to the document properties is a title and description. Neither of these is used in the final movie at all—they're just there for you to keep track of what you've created. For now, give the movie a title of My first Flash movie and leave the description blank.

You can see that the default Dimensions of the stage are 550 pixels wide by 400 pixels high. When you change the dimensions of your stage, Flash will always measure them from the upper-left corner. For example, if you change the width of your movie to 750 pixels and the height to 600 pixels, Flash will simply add 200 pixels to the right side of the stage and 200 pixels to the bottom. Flash uses the upper-left corner as the place that the document grows from because this is the convention in print design—much of web design takes its inspiration from print-based graphic design.

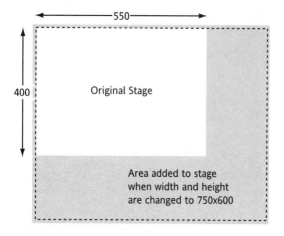

If your brain doesn't translate pixel-speak easily, you can always change the units of measurement that Flash uses throughout the entire movie by picking a different measurement option from the Ruler units drop-down box.

Whichever option you choose will be applied throughout the movie until you choose a different option.

> When you set the Dimensions of the stage in the Document Properties dialog box, you're directly affecting the size of the window in which your Flash movie will be displayed on the user's browser. It's good practice to think about this before you start creating your visual content on the stage. You can always change the size of the stage however and whenever you like—but the more advance planning you do, the smoother your movie-creation process is likely to be.

Note that the Match: Printer and Match: Contents options will automatically change the size of the stage if you select them. Match: Printer will set the stage size to reflect the default paper size for your default printer, and Match: Contents will change the stage so that it's large enough to contain all the content elements you've created (even those that spill over into the work area outside the stage). The Match: Contents option will probably be ghosted out at the moment because you don't have any content on the stage.

There are a number of other global properties that you can change for the whole movie. All the important properties are covered as they come up during the course of building the example movies in this book. At this stage, let's just observe that the Frame rate property influences the playback speed and smoothness of your movie. The default frame rate is 12 fps, which means that your movie will play back at a speed of 12 frames per second (fps). This default frame rate is a trade-off between computer speed and movie smoothness that seemed to work in the early days of Flash. Most designers today tend to set it a little higher, given that computers today can easily handle faster frame rates (and also because Flash itself is better written to optimize animations and can therefore play them faster). A good rule of thumb is 18 fps for new designs for which you want smoothness, although some designers opt for 24 or 30 fps. For now, stick to the default of 12 fps (but feel free to come back later and experiment when you've completed the chapter; the frame rate can be anything from 0.01 to 120 fps).

The next movie property you'll concentrate on is the Background color option. You use this option to set the background color your movie displays when shown in the user's browser.

The movie's background color

Again, the background color is something you should probably think about when you're *planning* your movie. The questions you might ask yourself include the following: What size will the display window be in the browser? Will the movie take up the whole display in the browser? Do I need to stick to a color scheme that matches the site in which my Flash movie will appear?

You can change the background color simply by clicking the Background box in the Properties panel and selecting a color.

The background color will remain the same throughout the entire movie. You can't change the color in different parts of the movie.

Another thing you need to think about in this context is the background color of the web page in which your movie will appear. If your finished movie is embedded in an HTML page, the choice you make for the background color of the movie is important. By default, Flash will take the background movie color you specify and use it as the background color of the HTML page in which your movie appears.

There are a number of options you can use when exporting your finished movie for publishing on the Web. I'll talk about the built-in publishing features of Flash in more depth in Chapter 14.

Let's start a little movie project that you'll be working on over the next couple of chapters. This is a simple movie that will get you started practicing your Flash skills, and it will also give you the chance to start expressing your creativity in the Flash authoring environment.

Creating the movie background

The test movie is set at night. The cicadas are doing their thing, there's a cool breeze, the moon is up, and there's the faint aroma of fresh mushrooms rising from a garden mushroom patch. You're going to start creating this scene in Flash.

The background for your little movie scenario is going to be the night sky, so you need to choose a suitable background color to reflect that.

1. If you don't already have it open, display the Properties panel (select Window ➤ Properties or press *CTRL+F3*) and select the Properties tab. Because mushrooms grow only at night, select a deep midnight blue from the color box in the Properties panel (revealed by clicking the Background color picker).

   If you don't see the document properties, it may be because you've selected something other than the stage. To get back on track, select the Selection tool (the top-left tool in the toolbar) and then click once on the stage.

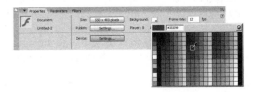

2. Clicking a color will adjust the color of the stage accordingly. You'll notice that when you move the cursor over each color, its identity is displayed with a pound sign (#) followed by a hexadecimal (hex) value (made up of numbers and letters). These hex values are the same ones that people use when writing HTML web pages, and each combination of numbers and letters represents a unique, universally recognized color. This makes it very easy for you to match your background and host web page colors.

Default movie settings

The values you set for this particular movie in the Properties panel are saved automatically. If you want these settings to be applied to all of your Flash movies in the future, go to the Document Properties dialog box (select Modify ➤ Document or press *Ctrl+J*) and click the Make Default button.

Flash assumes that you want to use these settings whenever you create a new movie. You can change these default settings as and when you need to.

Having set the global properties for the movie, your next step is to create some content. You're going to do this by walking through a basic creation/modification/animation scenario in the context of your movie. This will familiarize you with some essential techniques and give you the chance to stretch those creative muscles.

While introducing you to the creation/modification/animation process, I'll cover two absolutely critical features of the Flash authoring environment: the Timeline and frames.

The Timeline

The Timeline is one of the most important parts of the Flash interface, and it's one of the most important things to understand as you learn Flash.

When a web surfer visits your site and your movie starts to play, Flash plays a sequence of still frames. This produces animation in much the same way as Hollywood films you see at the movie theater, which are also a sequence of still images. The order of the images in a Hollywood blockbuster is defined by the film roll, and the order of the images in Flash is defined by the Timeline. If you look carefully at the Timeline, you'll see that it looks a bit like a film roll—each square in it represents one still image (or one frame in the movie).

The Timeline is thus the thing that controls the animation that the user sees. In short, the Timeline is a representation of how your animation will change over time, and it's literally what it says it is: a *line* representing the passage of *time*.

What the user sees in his or her browser between the start and end points of the movie is determined by the content you create in your movie and by how you use the Timeline to organize that content into a sequence of frames. The length of your movie's Timeline will determine how long the movie runs and how content changes in the movie over time. As the movie's author, you control all this by using the Flash Timeline in conjunction with the content you create and place on the stage.

To help you visualize this, picture a simple movie scenario: a time-lapse nature movie that shows a mushroom growing in slow motion. At the start of the movie, you have the tiny head of a mushroom poking up through the soil, and at the end of the movie, you see a full-grown mushroom standing tall above the grass.

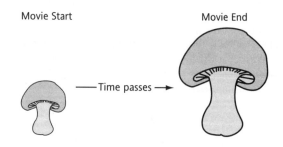

Clearly, your movie won't consist of only those two images, and your movie won't just jump from tiny stalk to full-grown mushroom instantaneously. In between the two points, time passes and your mushroom moves through the intermediate stages of growth until it attains its full-grown state. Between the start and end points of the time-lapse movie will be a whole series of images that represent the mushroom at the different stages of its development.

In the real world, mushrooms have a natural growth rate, which is determined by mushroom DNA or by divine guidance (depending on whom you ask). In a Flash movie, you have to *imitate* the effect of time passing—and that's where the Timeline comes in. To create the effect of time passing, you need a start point, an end point, and some space in between that represents the passage of time. The Timeline lets you do this and gives you complete control over the length of your movie, the speed at which it plays, and what you see on the screen at each point in time. How? By using those frames you saw on the Timeline.

Frames

Let's take a look at the Timeline in the Flash authoring environment. If your Timeline is closed, open it with the Window ➤ Timeline menu option. After it's open, you'll see the following:

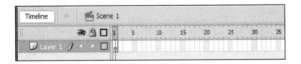

The white rectangle with the text Timeline *in it isn't just a title, but also a rather well-disguised button. Clicking it toggles the Timeline between maximized and minimized states, and it's a quick way to hide away the Timeline when you want to concentrate on the stage.*

Now take a look at the left part of the Timeline:

You can see that the top part of the Timeline (the solid gray part) is divided into numbered segments, and there are corresponding divisions in the lower part, consisting of groups of four white rectangles separated by single gray rectangles.

As briefly noted previously, each of these little boxes on the lower part represents a frame, and the numbers on the top part give you a frame number reference: frame 1 on the left through to frame 45 (and beyond) on the right. Your movie can be one frame long, or it can be thousands of frames long. The length of your movie is determined by the highest numbered frame that has content.

The red rectangle with the line coming out of it on the Timeline is called the playhead.

The playhead

The playhead indicates where you currently are in your movie. You can click the playhead and drag it back and forth along the Timeline, and the stage will change to show the contents in the selected frame. At the moment, of course, you don't have any images or objects on the stage, but as you start to add content, you'll see how you can spool through your movie using the playhead.

The playhead lets you anticipate what will be seen when the movie plays back in the browser. When you position the playhead over a frame, you see what will be displayed on the screen at that point during playback.

Your movie begins in frame 1. By default, when your movie loads into the user's browser, it will start at frame 1 and play through the rest of the frames in sequence until the end frame. At the moment, all the frames in the Timeline shown here are empty—that's because you haven't created any content yet. If you were to play your nighttime movie now (by pressing *F12*), you'd see just a block of color displayed in the browser window. This is Flash displaying the background color of the movie that you set using the Properties panel. To make your movie more interesting, you have to add content at various points along the Timeline that can play back in the browser, which is where frames come in.

By placing content in frames at different points along the Timeline, you imitate the passing of time, create animations, and generally make things happen in your movie. Just like that time-lapse mushroom movie mentioned earlier, you can create start and end points and show all the stages in between. When the movie plays, Flash looks at each frame on the Timeline and renders what it finds there in the user's browser. To achieve the effect of content appearing and disappearing, animating and morphing, Flash provides different types of frames.

To see the nature and effects of the different types of frames that Flash provides, you first have to get some content onto the stage. So without further ado, it's time to start drawing.

Making mushrooms

First, let's create a mushroom that will live out its life under the midnight sky that you created as your background.

1. Make sure the View ➤ Snapping ➤ Snap to Objects menu option is checked. If it isn't, select it.

> Windows users can also toggle the Snap to Objects option using the Magnet button in the Main toolbar at the top of the screen. This toolbar isn't visible by default, but you can display it by selecting the Window ➤ Toolbars ➤ Main menu option.

Turning on Snap to Objects invokes Flash's ability to help you make your drawings more precise. This feature automatically snaps the drawing cursor to certain points as Flash anticipates what you're trying to do. For example, when you activate Snap to Objects and draw with the Oval tool, the oval you are drawing jumps to become a perfect circle when you get close to the shape of it. However, with Snap to Objects off, the Oval tool will let you draw an oval with whatever dimensions you want. Whether you use Snap to Objects or not is entirely dependent on personal preference and what you're trying to achieve. If you're drawing perfect circles, it makes sense to leave it on, but for most freehand drawings, it's easier to leave it off. Experiment and see what works best for you in different circumstances.

Next, you need to select the drawing tool that you'll use to draw your mushroom. All the drawing tools are accessed in the Tools panel. I'll detail more aspects of the Tools panel and its contents in the next chapter, but you'll start using some of its features as you work through this example.

The Tools panel is located (by default) on the left side of the authoring environment. If you hover the mouse pointer over any of the tool buttons in the Tools panel, a tool tip will pop up with a description of what that the button does.

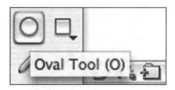

The letter in brackets next to each tool's name is the shortcut key for that tool. In this case, pressing O will select the Oval tool. Each of the tools will be covered in the next chapter, but you'll dip into them now as you set about creating some content.

2. Click the Oval tool. At the bottom of the Tools panel, you'll see some new icons appear under the heading Options. These icons represent the available options for drawing ovals. I won't go into them too much now, but you need to make sure that the leftmost one—Object Drawing—is selected. The option is selected when the icon is in the *in*, or *enabled*, position (as shown in the following image, in which both icons are selected).

Now you need to select a color for the outline of the shape you're going to draw.

3. If you're not already displaying it, bring up your Properties panel by pressing *CTRL+F3* (*CMD+F3* on the Mac). You'll notice that the Properties panel has changed since the last time you looked at it—it now reflects that you've selected the Oval tool.

Stroke Color

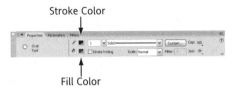

Fill Color

From here, you can pick a color for the outline (stroke color) of the object you're drawing. Similarly, the Fill Color box allows you to select the color you want to use to fill the area *inside* the outline. By default, many of the objects you draw using tools from the Tools panel have an outline and a filled interior. You can control and modify these outlines and fills to a very fine degree, as you'll see as you progress through this book.

4. Click the Stroke Color box and set the stroke color to a dark brown. (The Stroke Color box is the color block with a little pencil to its left.)

5. Click the Fill Color box and set the fill color to a lighter, mushroom-like brown. (The Fill Color box is the color block with a paint bucket to its left).

Notice that the two color blocks are shown on both the Properties panel and the Tools panel. You can select the colors from either panel. (Keep in mind that if you change the fill or stroke color in one panel, your change will be reflected in the other.)

6. Below the color blocks on the Tools panel, you'll see another section called Options. This section has two icons. Roll your mouse pointer over them and wait for the tool tips to appear to see what they are. The leftmost is labeled Object Drawing. Don't worry about exactly what this means now; you'll look at it in more detail in Chapter 2. All you have to do for now is make sure it's in the enabled position.

7. Now for the actual drawing. At the bottom of the stage, about halfway across, click and drag upward with the Oval tool to make a small stalk for your mushroom. Don't worry if you don't have the circle exactly where you want it on the stage. You'll see how to move things around soon.

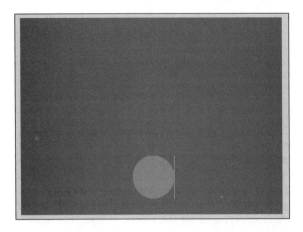

8. Using the same click-and-drag action, draw a flatter, larger oval just above the top edge of the stalk. If you're unhappy with either oval, press *CTRL/CMD+Z* (undo) and/or *CTRL/CMD+Y* (redo) and redraw to your heart's content.

This larger oval will be the cap of your baby mushroom.

You can, of course, fine edit the ovals rather than having to undo and redraw them. You don't know how to fine edit just yet, so using undo is a quick workaround that will get you started. Don't worry about the simplistic shapes you're creating at the moment—you'll have the ability to create fantastically finer fungi once you've learned a little more about editing shapes later on in the book.

9. If you look at the Timeline now, you'll notice that the first frame has changed, as shown in the following image:

If you look closely at the lower part, you'll see that this frame is now shaded a darker gray and it contains a little black circle. This is due to the fact that, in a new movie, Flash assumes you want the action to start in frame 1. When you started drawing on the stage, Flash assumed that the oval was the first piece of content you were creating for this movie, so it put the drawing in frame 1.

Flash created the starting point for your movie based on the drawing you made. This is the first fixed point in time for your movie—the first image in a sequence of images that you want to display changing over time. Flash uses a particular type of frame to store fixed points in time that hold visual (or other) content: a keyframe.

Keyframes

In the world of traditional animation, there are two types of animation frames. A keyframe denotes a major point in the animation, such as a main character turning to face a particular direction. In such a case, you would have two keyframes: one that shows the character in his starting position and another that shows him looking in the new direction. Think of keyframes as *frames* that show *key events* in the animation.

The remaining frames in the animation are those frames between keyframes. These in-between frames are usually called tween frames, or simply tweens. Obviously, animators spend so much time animating that they don't have time to say "in between"!

A keyframe in the world of Flash is very similar to an animator's keyframe. A keyframe indicates that something important happens at the point in the Timeline where the keyframe is located. For example, it indicates a point at which something new is displayed on the stage, a point at which something is made to disappear, or a transition from one piece of content to another. Keyframes are markers in time, indicating start and end points for the different transitions that make up an animation.

Think back to the time-lapse nature movie discussed earlier. Remember how I said that the start and end points of that movie would be the baby mushroom and the full-grown mushroom? In Flash, those start and end points are defined by "snapshots" of the stage contained in keyframes. You need a keyframe in frame 1, which contains the baby mushroom image, and a keyframe in a later frame (say frame 15), which contains the image of the fully developed mushroom.

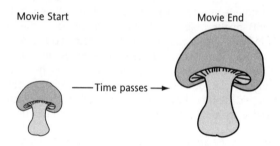

When you've set up these two keyframes, you can tell Flash to make your mushroom grow between the two keyframes. You'll end up with a smooth animation of a growing mushroom in between the two keyframes. There are two important concepts here:

- The duration of the growth animation is defined by the frame rate and the distance between the two keyframes.

- The amount the mushroom changes (how big it gets, how small it starts off as, etc.) is defined by the sizes of the two mushrooms you've drawn in the two keyframes.

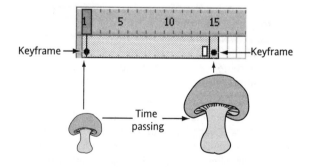

For the moment, remember that if something significant changes onscreen in your movie, there will probably be a keyframe involved. Keyframes are the keys to making things happen.

More on frames in a moment—but first, a bit of house-keeping.

Saving your movie

It's good practice to save your work often, just in case your dog eats it or your computer crashes and burns. The way to save your embryonic Flash movie is the same way you save files in most other programs.

1. Click File ➤ Save in the main menu.
2. You'll be prompted with a dialog box asking where you want to save the movie and what name you'd like to give it. Choose (or create) a suitably named folder to save your work in, type Mushroom in the File name box, and click Save.

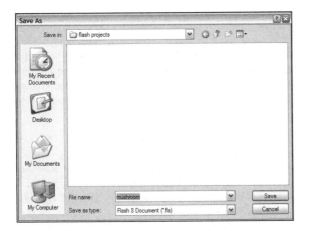

Flash automatically saves the movie as an FLA file (.fla is the extension used for Flash authoring files).

Remember that there's a distinction between the file that you work on in the authoring environment (the FLA file, which is pronounced "ef-el-a" and is short for Flash Authoring) and the file that's loaded and played when a surfer visits your site (the SWF file, which is pronounced "swiff" and is short for Shockwave Flash). As an author, you create and modify your content inside the FLA; the SWF is created when you publish your movie. The publishing process takes all the drawings and other content that you created in your FLA file and compresses and encodes them into the SWF format. The SWF file is much smaller and more compact than its parent FLA file, and it is thus much quicker and more efficient to download for the end user.

Now that you have your example movie safely saved, you can continue your exploration of frames. You've already drawn a couple of ovals in frame 1 that represent your baby mushroom—the starting point for your movie. If you were to play the movie now, you'd see a static image of your baby mushroom in the browser. (You can do this by pressing *F12*, which will open your default browser and render your movie.) You'll need to close the browser or click back into your Flash window after you've finished viewing your masterpiece. The reason you see this static image is that you've created only a single frame with any content in it—the movie has nowhere to go except this single keyframe.

Next, you're going to see how to add an end point for your "mushroom growth" movie, and how to create the sequence of images that imitates the passage of time and shows the mushroom growing. This means you'll have a proper movie to play rather than a single frame.

Animation

You've already seen that keyframes mark the beginning and end points of pieces of action in your movie. In this sense, Flash can be compared to traditional animated cartoons. In traditional cartoons, the animator plans out the action sequence that she wants to create—for example, a car driving from one side of the screen to the other. She creates the background for the action—maybe a desert setting with some distant mountains—and this background typically remains static.

Next, the animator creates her start and end images of the car—that is, the car on the left of the screen, and the car on the right of the screen. Clearly, she also needs to have a series of intermediate images that show the car in progress across the desert. Each image would be drawn onto a separate sheet of transparent acetate. The plan would be to use a movie camera to photograph the start, intermediate, and end images against the static background, to create a number of different frames of film. Running the frames in sequence would show the car in motion against the static background.

This is a time-consuming business, and cartoon production companies don't want to make their star animators slave over frame after frame of minutely changing action. The solution is to get the lead animators to create the key images—the start and end points and important transitional images—and then use apprentice animators called "in-betweeners" to draw the images that come in between the keyframes that the expert animator created. These in-between frames are critical to ensuring that the cartoon action is smooth and convincing.

In Flash, you do things similarly. You can create keyframes that define significant stages in the action that you want to show, and then you get Flash to generate the in-between frames that link the keyframes together. This saves you a lot of time and effort in creating the transitional frames, and it's an important factor in making Flash the successful animation package it has become. (Note that you can mimic the traditional animation method in Flash if you want, by hand-drawing each frame individually. This can be a powerful way to express yourself and create great animation, but it's too big a subject to tackle in this book. Maybe in another book . . .)

> Throughout this book I refer to animation in Flash as *tweening. As you might have guessed, this is short for* in-betweening, *or the process of creating the transitional frames that go in between the keyframes.*

Let's get back to your mushroom movie. Currently, you have that single starting keyframe containing the baby mushroom. Next, you want to create a keyframe that holds the full-grown version, and then get Flash to create all the in-between frames that show the mushroom growing over time. Let's work through that in an exercise now.

Working with frames

As I've said already, a keyframe marks a significant change in your movie. To create the image showing your mushroom when it's full-grown, you need to add a keyframe to the Timeline. This will tell Flash that you have some important new content that it needs to be aware of.

To insert a new keyframe into the Timeline, simply click the Timeline at the position where you want to add your keyframe. After you've selected the frame position, you can choose the Insert ➤ Keyframe menu option, or use the keyboard shortcut *F6*, and a new keyframe will appear.

You might wonder how far along the Timeline you should put your second keyframe. The answer to this depends on how long you want your piece of action to last. The thing to remember here is the frame rate setting that you saw in the Properties panel: 12 fps by default. This frame rate setting means that for every 12 frames your movie takes up on the Timeline, there will be one second of action when the movie plays back. The math is fairly simple: estimate how long you want the action to last in seconds, and multiply the number of seconds by the frame rate. You can always change the position of the keyframes later on if you need to tweak the timing of different pieces of action.

Let's make that mushroom grow.

1. Click frame 14—parallel to the first keyframe—of your mushroom movie and press *F6* to insert a keyframe. You'll see immediately that the Timeline has changed:

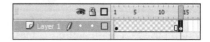

Frame 14 now has a black circle in it and a black border (note that the circle is white and the frame is black in the preceding image because the frame is selected), and all the frames between frames 1 and 14 have turned gray. Additionally, there's a small white rectangle in frame 13, and the playhead has jumped to frame 14. Let's take a look at what this all means:

- The black border around frame 14 indicates that it's a keyframe. You're going to use this keyframe to hold some content that's different from the frames that precede it.

- The white rectangle in frame 13 tells you that it's the last frame before a new keyframe, and that all the frames to the left of this rectangle contain the same content as the previous keyframe—in this case, frame 1. The frames are grayed out to show you that they contain the same content as frame 1. Every frame in the black-bordered box running from frame 1 through frame 13 contains the same image of the baby mushroom you created in frame 1. You can prove this to yourself by clicking and dragging the playhead (the red rectangle above the Timeline) left and right between frames 1 and 14.

- The black circle in the keyframe at frame 14 indicates that this frame contains some content. But why? You didn't add any content to this frame yet, did you? Flash has carried over the content from the previous keyframe (frame 1). This is the default behavior when you add a new keyframe. This feature can be very useful, as you'll see in a moment.

There's one other thing to note here: when you move the playhead backward and forward through your movie (click and drag the playhead directly to move it up and down the Timeline manually, and you'll see the stage change in real time), the current frame number is indicated in the area just underneath the Timeline.

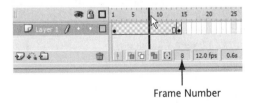

Frame Number

Flash allows you to click and drag the playhead around the Timeline. When you do this, you're performing what animators call *scrubbing*. By constantly scrubbing through the frames that you're working on as you create your animations, you can get a good impression of how your work is turning out.

So far, then, you have an opening keyframe (frame 1), followed by some intermediate frames (frames 2 through 13), and a new keyframe (frame 14) that will soon contain the image of your full-grown mushroom.

All the frames from 2 to 13 now "belong" to the keyframe in frame 1 and reflect what is in it. If you changed the image in frame 1, the slave frames (2 through 13) would change to reflect the new picture. Frame 14 would remain as it is, however, because you told Flash that you want this frame to be self-contained so it can contain new content.

2. Double-click anywhere on the Timeline between the two keyframes. You'll see that frames 1 through 13 turn black:

This shows you that these frames all hold the same content—they're all dependent on the content in the keyframe at frame 1. You can't alter the content in frames 2 through 13 by editing them directly, but you can change their contents *indirectly* by amending what's in frame 1. You can only directly edit content that's in a keyframe.

3. Deselect the black-highlighted frames by clicking away from them. Next, click anywhere between the keyframes. This time, only the frame you clicked is selected.

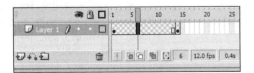

4. Use the Insert ➤ Timeline ➤ Frame menu option two times or press the *F5* key twice to insert two new frames into the Timeline at the position where you just clicked. These new frames will inherit the contents of the preceding keyframe (frame 1).

Using the playhead to move through your movie, you can see that it's now 16 frames long, and each of the frames contains the same picture of a mushroom. I promise that your mushroom will grow soon, but first there are a few more tricks I can show you with frames.

5. Click between the keyframes again to select a single frame. This time, rather than inserting slave frames, you're going to insert a blank keyframe. A blank keyframe is just what its name suggests: a keyframe that has no content in it. It is, however, independent of the content of the keyframe that precedes it.

6. Use the Insert ➤ Timeline ➤ Blank Keyframe menu option or press *F7* to convert one of the normal frames in your Timeline into a blank keyframe.

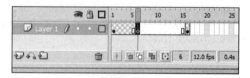

A blank keyframe is represented in a similar way as a keyframe except that it shows an unfilled circle in the Timeline. This is because it doesn't yet have any content. The remaining white frames are all dependent on the blank keyframe you just inserted.

If you now scroll through your movie using the playhead, you'll see that all the dependent frames after the blank keyframe are also blank, reflecting the fact that the keyframe before them is empty. Blank keyframes are useful for stopping animations or dividing different pieces of content that exist on the same layer. (Stay tuned—there's more on layers later.)

You'll also see that the keyframe at frame 16 still has the baby mushroom image in it. That's because it inherited the content of frame 1 when you created it. However, there's no link between the inherited image and the current (possibly amended) content of frame 1—frame 16's keyframe is completely independent.

You don't want half of the frames in your movie to be blank, so somehow you'll have to get rid of that blank keyframe and its dependent frames. There are two ways to do this: you can either delete the blank keyframe or convert it into a normal frame. Let's do the latter. The advantage of this approach is that the movie's length remains the same.

7. Click the blank keyframe and use the Modify ➤ Timeline ➤ Clear Keyframe menu option or press *SHIFT+F6*. The white frames become shaded again, and if you run the movie through now, you'll see that they've all been refilled with your baby mushroom picture.

You now have 16 frames in your movie, all filled with exactly the same mushroom image. You want the movie to last for 15 frames because it's a nice, round number, so you'll have to remove one of those frames now.

8. Click to select a single frame anywhere between the two keyframes and use the Edit ➤ Timeline ➤ Remove Frames menu option or press *SHIFT+F5* to delete the highlighted frame. You should now be left with two keyframes on your Timeline (in frames 1 and 15) and a set of identical normal frames between the keyframes that contain the same image of your mushroom you created in frame 1.

The normal frames that separate the keyframes may appear to be plain and boring at the moment, but don't dismiss them: they're the Flash equivalent of pawns on a chessboard or foot soldiers in an army. They're not as glamorous as the other elements, but they're just as important. You use them to define the time between your keyframes, and this has a big effect on how your animation plays back. The number of frames between keyframes defines how fast and how smoothly a tween will occur.

In Flash, you have three methods for adding, converting, and deleting frames, and each has its own advantages and disadvantages. The first and most formal method is to use the Timeline section of the Edit, Insert, and Modify menus. These menus contain all the manipulation actions associated with frames.

The second and probably most commonly used method is to use the keyboard shortcuts that mimic the menu options. The major problem with this is that you have to learn the shortcuts first, but most people pick them up quite quickly. Many Flash designers get to know them by heart and use them all the time (the text on my F5 and F6 keys has almost worn away through use!).

The third method involves right-clicking the relevant frame in the Timeline to highlight it, and then selecting the appropriate command from the context-sensitive menu that appears.

Throughout the tutorial sections of this book, I'll use a mixture of these methods. There's no single best method—whichever one you find easiest is the one you should use.

As promised, let's make your mushroom live and . . . well, breathe.

Making the mushroom grow

Frame 15 is going to be the final frame of your movie, which means that you need to populate it with the content that represents the final growth stage of your mushroom. Let's add the full-grown mushroom image to the keyframe in frame 15.

1. Click frame 15 in the Timeline. Notice that when you click the frame, the whole mushroom (the two ovals you drew earlier) is already selected. Remember, these ovals were inherited from the keyframe in frame 1, so they're identical in shape and position to the mushroom in frame 1. This in turn means that you don't have to worry about positioning the image of the mushroom in frame 15—it's in exactly the same place as it is in frame 1. This will make your animation easier to create.

A related and very useful feature in Flash is the ability to copy (or cut) and paste content into exactly the same location on the stage. This is particularly handy when you want to paste images or other components into other keyframes or other layers and still have them occupy the same coordinates on the stage as the original image. To achieve this, copy (or cut) the original component, and then use the Edit ➤ Paste in Place *menu option. This way, you're sure to place your object exactly where you want it. I guarantee that you'll find this feature immensely useful in your Flash career.*

2. Click the Selection tool in the top-left corner of the Tools panel, and then click the background of the stage to deselect the mushroom.

3. Click the middle of the cap of your mushroom. This will select it, and a light blue rectangle (the bounding box) will appear around the shape to signify the selection.

4. Click and hold the mushroom cap and drag it to where you want the cap of your full-grown mushroom to be. (Alternatively, holding down the *SHIFT* key and using the arrow keys makes your selection move in units of 10 pixels.)

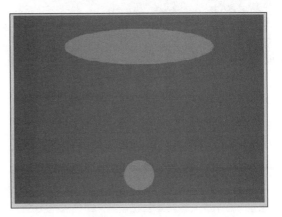

If you hold down the SHIFT key while you drag, Flash will help you drag the mushroom cap upward in a straight line. Also, you need to single-click to select a shape. If you inadvertently double-click instead, you'll enter inside the shape (you're actually in an edit mode) rather than select it. You'll know this has occurred if the shape you drag leaves its outline behind! To recover from this, press CTRL+Z twice to undo the move, and then double-click any blank space on the stage to get out of the edit mode.

5. Click the stalk (the lower oval) to select it, and then press BACKSPACE (or DELETE). This will delete the baby version of the stalk from frame 15 (although the old smaller stalk is still intact in frames 1 through 14).

Your next task is to create the full-grown version of the mushroom stalk.

6. Click the Oval tool in the Tools panel again, and draw a long, thin oval from the bottom of the cap of your mushroom down to the bottom of the stage. The stalk you just created is in front of the cap.

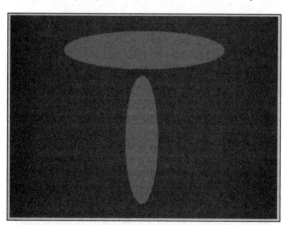

If you need to move your new stalk after you've drawn it, select the Selection tool, click the stalk, and drag it to the desired position. If things go wrong, you can always use the undo option by selecting Edit ➤ Undo from the menu bar or pressing CTRL+Z.

7. Press the ENTER key to preview your movie. Hmm, not *particularly* convincing, is it? You're getting the same picture for 14 frames and then a sudden jump to a full-grown fungus. What you really want is a smooth transition from baby mushroom to full-grown mushroom, and Flash can do that for you. You're about to see how Flash can perform as an underpaid, unappreciated in-betweener.

8. Double-click between the two keyframes on the Timeline to select the first keyframe and all the normal frames that depend on it.

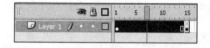

Now you're going to change the behavior of these frames. You'll tell Flash that you want to create an animation that smoothly transforms the small mushroom in frame 1 into the full-grown version that you just created in frame 15. Your ability to do this is entirely dependent on the existence of your two keyframes. The keyframes define the two different states of the mushroom, and you're asking Flash to create all the in-between frames that will represent the growth of the mushroom. Let's do that.

9. If you don't have your Properties panel open, open it with the Window ➤ Properties ➤ Properties menu option, and select the Properties tab. Then click the frames. The Properties panel now changes to reflect the fact that you have frames selected:

Now you're going to use the Properties panel to give these frames a label and create your growth animation.

10. Click inside the far left box (under the word Frame) in the Properties panel and give your frames a Name label that identifies them—in this case, Mushroom Growth. Then, using the Type drop-down, select Comment. This attaches the label to frame 1. Now if you look at your frames, you can see some text attached to the first keyframe to remind you of what is happening.

> Using labels makes it easier to identify specific bits of
> action inside a large and complex movie. They're also
> important when you come to use code to control your
> animations, but you'll look at code (ActionScript) in
> greater detail in Chapters 10 and 11.

11. Click the drop-down menu next to Tween and
select Shape.

This will automatically create a shape tween. Flash will
understand that you want the stalk in frame 1 to
morph into the stalk in frame 15, and that you want the
cap in frame 1 to morph into the cap in frame 15, and
it will automatically generate the in-between images in
frames 2 through 14 that will produce this effect.

12. Click and drag the playhead between frames 1 and
15, and notice that the tweened frames on the
Timeline have now been colored green by Flash,
indicating a shape tween. There's also an arrow
pointing from frame 1 to frame 15 that indicates
the length of the tween.

(For clarity, I've removed the label from subsequent
screenshots.)

13. Slowly drag (or, to use the proper animation terminology, *scrub*) the playhead back to frame 1, and
notice that Flash has automatically filled in all the
animation frames between 1 and 15. Press ENTER to
preview the movie, and you'll see the mushroom
steadily grow to its full size.

14. Save your happy-grow-lucky mushroom.

You've spent some time looking at frames in Flash,
and you've started to see how they can help you
achieve the effects that you're after in your movies.
Frames and tweens are covered in much more depth in
Chapters 6 and 7.

Next up in this whirlwind tour, I'll introduce you to
another vital element of Flash authoring files: layers.

Layers

Whereas the Timeline and its frames help you organize
and manipulate content over time, layers help you add
depth to the movie and allow you to separate out
pieces of content and action that would otherwise get
tangled up. If you had to place your entire movie content on a single layer, it would be horrendously difficult
to achieve anything complicated. By separating the
action onto different layers, you can create much more
convincing and complex movies, and make full use of
the flexibility and power that Flash's Timeline gives you.
Multiple layers mean that your movies can have a host
of different elements on the stage, all acting completely independently of each other.

A traditional animator would have a different set of
acetate sheets for each part of his cartoon. For example, the background forest would be on one set of
sheets, Little Red Riding Hood would be happily skipping on another set, and the Big Bad Wolf would be
stalking her on yet another set. By keeping the parts
separate, the animator has much greater control over
the individual aspects of his cartoon. If something
needed to be altered, the animator could change just
one set—say, adding an evil twinkle to the Wolf's eye—
without having to redraw the forest or Little Red Riding
Hood as well. Another benefit of having separate animations on different sets of acetate is that the sets can
be reused later in the cartoon, or indeed in a
completely different cartoon, so while Jack and Jill are
running up the hill in cartoon 2, cartoon 1's Little Red
Riding Hood can be happily skipping along below them
without having to be redrawn. The content on the
different layers is independent and portable.

In Flash, layers are shown to the left of the Timeline.
Each new Flash movie comes with a single layer by
default.

Insert Folder

Insert Layer ⟶   Delete Layer

This layer—Layer 1—is the default layer you've been working with in your mushroom movie so far.

In Flash, layers are the equivalent of those separate sheets of acetate containing different visual components. Layers make movies easier to alter and allow for much greater richness of content. Let's take a look at what layers allow you to do in your sample movie.

It's good practice to keep each element of your movie on a separate layer for ease of editing and for neatness. Let's see how this works in this exercise. The active layer in Flash is the highlighted layer with the pencil icon next to its name. This pencil icon indicates that this layer is currently selected.

1. Click the Insert Layer button. Flash will create a new layer above Layer 1 and call it Layer 2.

2. Notice that Flash has automatically made Layer 2 15 frames long to match the length of Layer 1. If you look at these frames, though, they will still all be empty.

Flash always calls a new layer Layer n, where n is the sequential number after the last layer you created. This means that even if you later delete a layer, Flash will still increment the next layer's number as if the deleted layer still exists. For example, if you delete Layer 2 and then add another layer, the new layer would be called Layer 3 even though there's no longer a Layer 2. Luckily, the good people at Macromedia understand just how confused you are at the moment, so instead of making you try to work out which layer is which, they've given you the ability to uniquely name each layer, which means that you can forget about the whole

numbers shebang and work with meaningful, descriptive layer names instead. Giving names to your movie's layers is another good habit to get into, and it will save you a lot of heartache.

3. Double-click Layer 1 in the Timeline. When you double-click it, the layer will become editable, allowing you to change the name of the layer.

4. Type Mushroom and press ENTER.

5. You want Layer 2 to contain a picture of the moon in front of your night-sky background, so double-click where it says Layer 2, type moon, and press ENTER. You now have your two layers meaningfully named, and you can instantly infer what's on each of them.

6. Click the Oval tool. Your moon will be a full one, so you'll use this tool to create the celestial body.

7. Click the Black and White button under the two color boxes at the bottom of the Tools panel. This button resets the colors to a black stroke with a white fill, Flash's defaults.

8. Still on the moon layer, use the playhead to go to the final frame of the movie, and then draw a circle (remember, you can hold down the SHIFT key to help you draw a perfect circle) over the top of the right side of your full-grown mushroom cap:

If you look at the Timeline, you'll notice that Flash automatically created a keyframe at frame 1 of the moon layer, and it also populated all the frames on this layer with the image of the moon. This is a handy effect, because you want the moon to be visible in the sky throughout your movie. If you'd wanted the moon to appear in the movie from frame 15 onward (but not before), you'd have needed to create a keyframe at frame 15 in the moon layer.

9. Press ENTER to play your movie. Flash zips through the Timeline and displays the content of both layers for you.

But something looks slightly wrong, doesn't it? The mushroom seems to be farther away than the moon, and bigger, too. If you're going to get the perspective right, you'll need to put the moon *behind* the mushroom. You need to get the layers' stacking order right.

The higher up a layer appears in the layer list on the left of the Timeline, the closer the contents of that layer appear to you on the screen. To get your mushroom in front of the moon, you just have to move its layer above the moon's layer in the layer list. Let's do that now.

10. Click the Mushroom layer in the layer list and drag it above the moon layer. You'll see a shaded bar appear while you're dragging the layer.

This bar indicates where the layer will go when you release the mouse.

11. Now when you play your movie, the mushroom will rise in front of the moon. Perspective has been returned, and the tale of the very big mushroom and the very small moon has been consigned once more to legend.

Deleting a layer is as easy as adding a layer—it takes just a click of a button. To delete a layer, click the layer to highlight it, and then click the Delete Layer button, which is indicated by the trash can icon underneath the layer listing. Note that Flash won't let you delete all the layers in a movie; there must always be at least one layer. If you're trying to delete everything from a movie

and start again, it's easier to close the current movie and start a new one.

> *As you've seen, layers are a useful way to manage and control your content. Flash has the added ability to use layer folders to bundle together similar layers for further ease of use. You'll learn more about these in Chapter 4.*

Layer modes

Layer modes define how you view and use specific layers in the authoring environment. There are three layer modes in Flash and, by default, they're all turned off. You control the three modes by clicking the icons in the columns after the layer name. The status of the modes for a particular layer is indicated by the two dots and the square next to that layer's name.

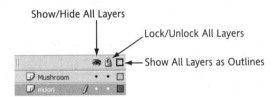

The first column controls showing and hiding a layer, the second controls locking and unlocking a layer, and the third column is used for viewing the contents of that layer as outlines. Let's take a look at how these different modes interact in the authoring environment and see what benefits they offer.

Working with layer modes

With all three of the layer mode selector icons in the off position, the authoring environment will behave exactly as it has so far. If you were to draw a circle with the Oval tool right now, it would appear as normal on the currently selected (active) layer. Let's see what happens when you start switching the layer modes on.

1. In the Mushroom layer, click the dot underneath the eye icon.

Three things happen:

- Because you hid the layer, its contents disappear from the stage in the authoring environment.

- A red "x" replaces the dot in the eye column, reminding you that this layer is currently hidden.

- The pencil icon gets a red line struck through it, indicating that the contents of the hidden layer cannot be edited. If you try to draw on the stage now (with any tool, such as the Oval tool, that draws shapes or lines on the stage), you'll find that the cursor has changed to a pencil with a warning circle next to it.

The warning circle tells you that the currently selected tool can't be used at the moment. The logic here is that if you were able to draw on the hidden layer, you'd be able to unwittingly draw all over the content that you've created so carefully already. Flash is protecting you from yourself.

If you were to click the stage with the Oval tool, you'd get an error prompt:

Hiding layers is very helpful when you need to concentrate on the content on a particular layer and you don't want the content of other layers to obstruct your view. For example, in the final frame of your mushroom movie, the mushroom covers part of the moon. If you wanted to draw a face on your moon, it would be hard to see what you were doing because the mushroom would be in the way. By hiding the Mushroom layer, you could see the whole of the moon, select the moon

layer, and draw to your heart's content. You could then click the "x" in the eye column and the Mushroom layer would be visible again.

2. Click the "x" in the eye column to return everything to normal. Then click the dot in the lock column. A small padlock replaces the dot, and the pencil again has a line through it. This time, though, although the layer is locked and you can't draw or select objects on it, the mushroom is visible.

Locking layers allows you to work with objects above or below them without accidentally selecting anything in the locked layers. This is useful when you're drawing or modifying on one layer and you want to see the content of the other layers to keep things in context. Locking the surrounding layers means you can draw and edit confidently, secure in the knowledge that you won't mess anything up on the other layers.

The final mode allows you to display all objects on a layer as outlines only, rather than as filled shapes.

3. Unlock the Mushroom layer by clicking the small padlock across from the layer name. Click the colored box to the right, and the mushroom is reduced to just an outline. The outline takes its color from the color of the box that you just clicked. Each layer will have its own dedicated outline color (automatically allocated by Flash, although you can alter it by double-clicking the colored box and using the color picker you see appear in the Layer Properties window), so you can easily make out which objects belong to which layer.

4. Click the outline button on the moon layer and (on your monitor, at least!) you'll see that the moon's outline is a different color than the mushroom's.

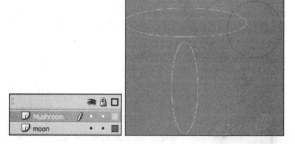

Outline mode helps you get a grip on exactly what's in your movie across all layers. Things start to get complicated when you have lots of different things on lots of layers and you can't quite see what is going on. Outline mode lets you step back from the jumble and get a clear view. Outline mode is also useful for previewing your movie, because it's easier for Flash to render outlines than filled shapes, meaning that the movie preview displays quicker.

You can easily change the layer mode for *all* the layers by using the icon at the top of each of the columns. To turn outline mode *off* for both of your movie's layers, just click the black box next to the eye and the lock. This will instantly return your mushroom and moon to their full-color glory.

If you're working with a lot of layers and want to lock every layer except the layer you're currently working on, it's easiest to click the Lock/Unlock All Layers button to lock every layer, and then click in the padlock column of the layer you want to use to unlock it. The same principle applies to the show/hide feature invoked via the eye icon.

Using layer folders (see Chapter 4), it's possible to lock or hide the content of a folder with one click. Locking or hiding the folder layer also affects all the content within the layer in the same way. This makes it easy to show/hide or lock/unlock similarly grouped elements while editing other content on the stage.

Layer modes affect only how you see the layers as you're constructing them. They have no effect on the final movie that you create, so layers that are hidden in the authoring environment will be visible in the final movie. Similarly, layers that are in outline mode will be seen in full color when they're rendered in the browser.

Before continuing, if you haven't done so already, test the movie. Notice that any layer modes you set don't affect the final output. The layer modes are there to help you in creating your content only; they have no effect on the final movie.

When creating a Flash movie, it's always a good idea to view the movie in the browser every so often. In most cases, the final Flash content will be viewed by the end user in a browser. To view your mushroom in the browser, select File ➤ Publish Preview ➤ HTML.

If you don't see the HTML option appear, Select File ➤ Publish Settings. *Select the* Formats *tab and check* HTML.

Now let's move on to the last Flash concept to be introduced in this chapter: scenes.

Scenes

You'll use scenes to organize your movie into sections that you can view as independent pieces of the whole movie. The ability to have a multiscene movie allows you to break up your content into logical chunks and helps you organize your movie efficiently.

Flash movies can be large or small, simple or complex. Small, simple movies can usually be contained in a single scene with no problem, but when you're creating a large movie that has long animations, multiple scenes can be the way to go.

Scenes in Flash are useful in the same way scenes in a theater production are useful: they split the story into easy-to-manage sections. Scenes are less useful when you add code into the mix.

You can think of scenes as an extension of your Timeline: they give you the ability to break up the action and continue from one scene to another. The benefit of scenes to you as an author is that your large animation projects can become more manageable. For one thing, you can create and plan them one scene at a time.

Each new Flash movie starts out with one default scene, named Scene 1. You can tell what scene you're currently in by looking at the scene name directly above your layers.

You can view, add, or delete scenes as you like by using the Scene panel (Window ➤ Other Panels ➤ Scene or *SHIFT+F2*).

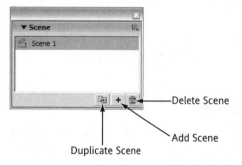

Delete Scene
Add Scene
Duplicate Scene

Here, you can use the buttons to manipulate scenes, and you can drag scenes to change the order of playback. You can also double-click any scene in the Scene panel and give it a meaningful name. Once again, this is useful for bringing clarity to your movie authoring files.

By default, Flash always plays the scenes in the sequence in which the scenes are listed in the Scene panel, so make sure you keep the scenes in the right order. You can also use Flash ActionScript to jump from scene to scene and play the scenes in different sequences.

Another way to switch between scenes in the authoring environment is to click the Scene button directly above the frames on the right, and click the scene you want to edit in the drop-down list.

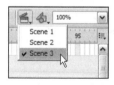

There's yet another way of navigating between your movie's scenes in the authoring environment: the Movie Explorer.

The Movie Explorer

The Movie Explorer gives you the ability to browse your way through your whole movie at different levels of detail. You can open the Movie Explorer by choosing the Window ➤ Movie Explorer menu option or by pressing *ALT+F3*.

The Movie Explorer window looks something like this:

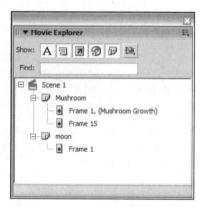

As you can see from this view, the Movie Explorer reveals the contents of your mushroom movie in depth, in terms of its component scenes, layers, and keyframes (provided that you've chosen the relevant options from the Show buttons along the top). You can click any node in this hierarchy and view that point in the movie. This is a powerful way of helping you navigate through your movies, especially as they grow in size and scope. You'll be seeing more of the Movie Explorer as you progress through the book.

For now, though, let's just recap what you've learned before moving on to the next chapter.

Summary

In this chapter, I introduced you to the Flash authoring environment and demonstrated some of the essential elements of Flash movie creation. You learned that

- You create movie content on the stage, which has a surrounding work area.

- You can use the Properties panel to change the global characteristics of your movie, such as its size and background color.

- You add content to the stage, and that content is displayed in the viewer's browser when the movie plays back.

- Your movie is a series of keyframes representing points in time. These are played back in sequence as the playhead moves along the Timeline.

- You use keyframes to hold new or changed content, and to indicate to Flash that something significant is happening. Keyframes are separated by normal frames that influence how long the transitions or gaps between keyframes last.

- You can create layers to add depth and manageability to your movies.

- You can use scenes to separate your animations into distinct chunks.

- You can use the Movie Explorer to navigate through your entire movie and browse its content.

In the next chapter, you'll look in more depth at the built-in Flash tools that enable you to create movie content. As you've already seen, these tools are found in the Flash Tools panel.

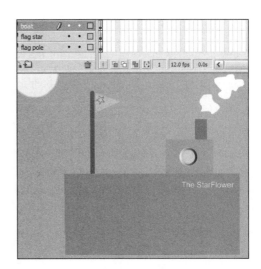

Chapter 2

THE FLASH TOOLS PANEL

What we'll cover in this chapter:

- Examining the Flash Tools panel, where Flash's integral drawing and manipulation tools are located
- Understanding the capabilities of the tools on the Tools panel
- Using the tools on the Tools panel to create and amend movie content (i.e., images and text)
- Precision drawing and fine-tuning with Bezier curves

In the previous chapter, you looked at the key structures contained in every Flash movie: the stage, the Timeline, keyframes, frames, and layers. In this chapter, you're going to start exploring Flash's built-in facilities for creating and manipulating movie content.

To do this, you'll examine each of Flash's drawing and editing tools in context by creating a Flash illustration. These tools are the integral means through which you draw pictures, create text, and manipulate visual elements on the stage in Flash. All these built-in content creation tools are accessed via the Flash Tools panel.

The Tools panel

The **Tools panel** is where you'll find all of Flash's drawing and editing tools. Using these tools in conjunction with Flash's Properties panel and other panels, you'll have at your disposal everything you need to design and manipulate the visual components and building blocks of your movie.

By default, the Tools panel is situated on the left side of the screen when you open Flash for the first time, but you can move it around or hide it, just like any other panel. The Tools panel itself is subdivided into four sections: Tools, View, Colors, and Options.

- The Tools section is where all the basic design and manipulation options are found. These tools can be used to draw pictures and create other graphics, create text elements, select objects, edit or transform graphics already on the stage, and reposition graphics around the stage.

- The View section contains tools for two main functions: zooming in and out on the stage, and changing the stage's position on the screen. These changes of view and position apply only to the screen display in the authoring environment where you're creating the movie; any changes you make to the view here don't have any effect on the way the finished movie itself is rendered in the user's browser. You might, for example, want to shift the stage around onscreen so that you can see other screen elements, such as open panels, more clearly.

- The Colors section is used to control the color of the stroke (line) or fill of an object. For instance, if you want to have a blue circle with a black outline, you choose those options in the Colors section. The top tool in the Colors section determines the stroke color, and the tool below it (the one with the paint bucket icon) controls the object's fill color. Reading from left to right, the three remaining tools in the Colors section are responsible for setting the stroke and fill colors to black and white, switching off the stroke or fill (depending on which of them is selected), and swapping back and forth between black stroke/white fill and white stroke/black fill. You can also assign your own colors to stroke and fill (more on that later).

- The Options section is where you can change some of the properties of the selected tool. For example, you can change the size and shape of the Brush tool to make different kinds of brushstrokes. Note that not every tool in the Tools panel has options that modify its characteristics, so don't worry if this section appears blank for some tools.

> You can customize the position of icons in the toolbar using Edit ➤ Customize Tools Panel on the PC and Flash Professional ➤ Customize Tools Panel on the Mac.

If you're working in Windows, you'll see that the modifiers in the Options section of the Selection tool are duplicated in the main toolbar at the top of the screen:

These options become visible on the main toolbar contextually and usually appear when you select a tool or object on the stage that has options associated with it. You'll look at how to use these options as you progress through the book.

Later in this chapter, you'll flex your muscles with the tools to create a vector drawing of a boat. By the end of this chapter, you'll have a working knowledge of all the basic tools as well as a sense of how to apply them to achieve the results you want.

Let's start our examination of the Tools panel tools with the Selection tool, which is used for manipulating the visual elements of a movie.

The Selection tool

The **Selection tool** is perhaps the most impor tant tool in Flash, and it's the one you'll use most often when creating and amending visual content on the stage. Here's what the Selection tool looks like in the Tools panel:

Essentially, the Selection tool is used to select objects on the stage for editing, and to move and place those selected objects just where you want them. The Selection tool has a few little quirks that are important to understand. Let's take a look at them now.

> *The Selection tool allows you to select whole objects, but if you want to select subparts of individual objects, such as the points that make up a stroke or fill outline, you would use the* **Subselection tool***. The Subselection tool is the white pointer next to the Selection tool on the toolbar. It looks sufficiently similar to the Selection tool for some of you to be wondering what it is—so now you know! You will look at the Subselection tool in more detail a little later in the chapter.*

Using the Selection tool

Let's examine the basics of using the Selection tool. For this exercise, you'll need something drawn on your stage.

1. Open a new movie and click the Oval tool in the Tools panel. In the Options section, make sure the Object Drawing option icon (the icon on the left that looks like a circle) is not selected.

Object Drawing mode is an important new feature of Flash 8, but to understand its usefulness, you'll first need to look at the normal (non-Object) drawing mode. Also worth noting is that the Options section in the toolbar is contextual: the available icons in the

Options section change depending on which tool you have selected.

2. Select a black stroke and a fill color of your choice from the Properties panel. To choose a color for strokes and fills, simply click the relevant color picker box to bring up the color palette and make your choice.

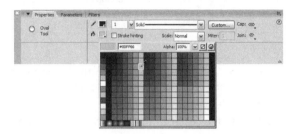

Note that you can also use the color picker in the toolbar to select your colors. If you change the colors using the Properties panel, you will see the toolbar change to reflect the new color.

> *Occasionally, you may find that the Properties panel doesn't change to reflect the tool you have just selected. If this occurs, click on the stage with your tool.*

3. Click the stage and hold down the mouse button, dragging the mouse so that you draw a nice big circle on the stage. (Remember that holding down the SHIFT key while you drag will result in a perfect circle.)

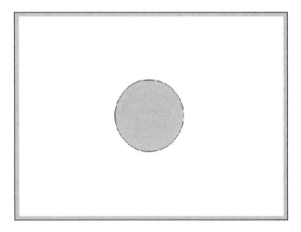

4. Select the Selection tool by clicking its icon in the Tools panel.

When you select the Selection tool, its three associated modifiers appear in the Options section of the Tools panel.

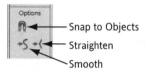

Snap to Objects

Straighten

Smooth

You can apply these modifiers to the objects that you select with the Selection tool—you'll learn how to use each of these later.

5. Point to the center of the big circle you've drawn.

Note that when you move the Selection tool over the center of the circle, a cross with arrows on each of its arms appears next to the mouse pointer. This indicates that you're hovering over an object that can be selected and moved simply by clicking and dragging.

6. Click the colored part of the circle (it will be highlighted as soon as you click it) and drag it off to the side. Then release the mouse button.

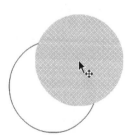

This action separates the fill part of the shape from its enclosing line (stroke), so that the circle becomes two separate objects.

> *Flash does not tie the fill and stroke together, giving you a single object. This may seem strange to some readers who have experience with other vector-based drawing programs. Not to worry, though: Flash does treat the stroke and fill as a single object when you have Object Drawing mode selected, something that I'll cover soon.*

Note that by default, the enclosed shapes you draw using the tools in the Tools panel consist of an outline and a fill. You can choose to have no outline or no fill by selecting the Stroke Color or Fill Color box in the Properties panel and then clicking the No Color selector.

7. Select the Oval tool from the Tools panel and click the Fill Color box. Above the palette of colors is a white box containing a red diagonal line. This is the No Color selector.

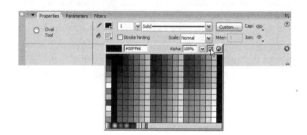

Clicking the No Color selector will put a red slash through the Fill Color box in the Properties panel, indicating that the color for that drawing element (stroke or fill) is switched off.

You can see from the following image that it's taken a bite out of the original stroke that used to surround the circle. (Dang!)

What's the solution to this? You can always undo the change you just made by pressing *Ctrl+Z*, and then try again. A less haphazard way to avoid separating an object into its component pieces is to make sure that you select both the colored fill and the surrounding stroke before moving the object. The way to achieve this is to double-click the object you want to move, which will select both its stroke and its fill. By double-clicking a shape like this, you ensure that you can drag it around as a single entity—except you have to remember to double-click every time you select the object!

Another solution is to group the components together so they're treated as a single shape. To do this, you can choose one of two methods: you can double-click the shape with the Selection tool (thus selecting both the fill and the stroke) and choose the Modify ➤ Group menu option or press *Ctrl+G* (*Cmd+G* on the Mac); or you can select the Selection tool and use it to draw a rectangle around the shapes that you want to group together.

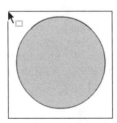

Again, this will select both the stroke and the fill, and you can use the same Modify ➤ Group option to group them. Whichever method you use, the result will be the same: your object's components (in this case, the circle's surrounding stroke and color fill) will be grouped together.

Grouped objects, when selected, are highlighted by a colored bounding box that indicates they're a group. The color of this line is determined by the global Highlight Color setting you choose via the General category of the Flash preferences (Edit ➤ Preferences on Windows; Flash Professional ➤ Preferences on the Mac).

To separate grouped items back into their component parts, select the group and then choose the Modify ➤ Ungroup menu option. You can also select Modify ➤ Break Apart to achieve the same effect.

Some other common mishaps can befall you when you use the Selection tool to select and move objects. For example, take a look at this:

Yes, it's that familiar circle, drawn once again using the Oval tool, but this time with a green fill (honest) and a black stroke.

Now, suppose you want to use the Selection tool to select the circle so you can move it. You remember that you need to select both the fill and the stroke, so you decide to use the Selection tool to draw a selection box. You click and drag the mouse to draw the box, as follows:

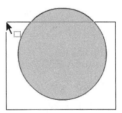

Sadly, it's easy to misjudge the starting position for the drag, and you can accidentally miss the top of the circle. If you decide to persevere, at the end of the drag, when you release the mouse button and click the center of the circle and try to drag it away to the right, you'll see something like the following:

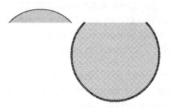

Hmm. Not quite right. Flash thinks that you want to carve up your circle rather than move it as a single entity. Again, this problem can be avoided by grouping the stroke and fill segments. Take care—those selection boxes can be sharp!

Select Edit ➤ Undo to undo your unfortunate circle-disfiguring accident. Draw another circle so that it overlaps the first as shown in the following image (on the left). Unselect everything by clicking with the Selection tool on a blank part of the stage. Finally, move either of the circles (remember to double-click to select both the fill and stroke). You'll see that the overlapping circle has cut a chunk out of the one below it (in the right image)!

The fact that one circle takes a bite out of the other is due to both circles trying to occupy the same space. Although this isn't a good thing in this example, it can come in handy at other times. Being able to carve one shape from another is a useful and quick way to create many irregular shapes, such as donuts and crescents.

Wouldn't it be nice if you could just tell Flash to treat all the shapes you draw as a single object, so that the stroke and fill are stuck together and can't be separated? Well, in Flash 8 you can.

8. You need to clear all the content on the stage before you try this next example. You *could* use the Selection tool to select everything on the stage and then press the DELETE key to delete it all, but there is a much easier way. Press CTRL+A (CMD+A on the Mac) to select all the content on the stage, and then press DELETE to delete it all.

9. Select the Oval tool. In the Options section of the Tools panel, make sure that Object Drawing mode is selected this time (the leftmost icon with the circle in it). Draw out a circle as you did in step 3. You will see a circle appear as before, except this time the circle looks much like a group because it has a bounding box around it.

10. Select the Selection tool and use it to move the circle you have just drawn by clicking and dragging the circle to a new location. Notice that you didn't have to double-click the circle (so that both the fill and stroke are selected) as you had to before.

11. Next, select the Oval tool and draw a new circle in a blank space on the stage. Using the Selection tool as you did in step 10 (remembering that you don't have to double-click), move the new circle so that it touches the old one. Drag the new circle back to its original position.

Notice that the new circle didn't take a bite out of the old circle!

If you ever need to draw ovals of an exact size, you can do so by selecting the Oval tool and then ALT-clicking on the stage. This also works for the rectangle tool.

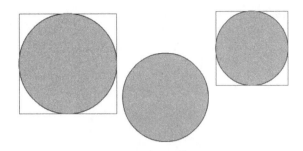

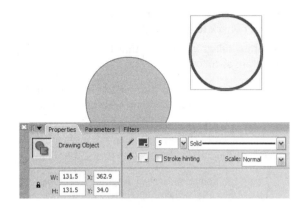

When you're in Object Drawing mode, anything you draw becomes a **Drawing Object** rather than a series of unconnected fills and strokes. A Drawing Object acts rather like a group, and the fill and stroke are grouped together so you can stop thinking of your circle as two separate elements. The previous way of drawing, where objects take bites out of each other, is called **merge drawing**.

OK, so now you're thinking, "Well, that's cool, but it's no different from a group!" When you're in Object Drawing mode, your shapes are better than groups in one significant respect: they remain editable.

12. Select either of the two Drawing Objects you currently have on the stage (i.e., the two circles) and look at the Properties tab of the Properties panel (Window ➤ Properties ➤ Properties). You'll see that information about both the fill and stoke are available to you. Let's look at how you can use this information to change the circle.

13. Select the fill color in the Properties panel and choose another color. You'll see that the circle fill color changes.

14. You can also change the stroke color. Next to the stroke color, you'll see a number. Either by selecting and changing the number directly in the box, or by using the drop-down menu to select a value, change this value to 5. You'll see the circle stroke change to reflect the new number.

15. Finally, unselect the Drawing Object by selecting the Selection tool and clicking a blank space on the stage. Still using the Selection tool, move the cursor so that it's over the stroke. You'll see the cursor change so that it has a little curve section below it.

Now click and drag away from the shape. You'll see that you can change the shape of the stroke in this way, and when you release the mouse button, the fill and stroke will update to reflect the new shape.

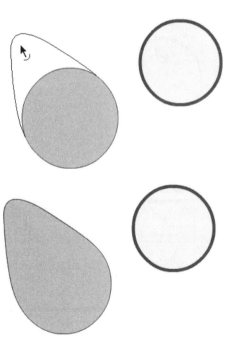

35

16. Undo (*Ctrl+Z* or Edit ➤ Undo) a few times until you're back to two circles.

Two other things you might want to do with drawing groups are as follows:

- Change the depth of drawing groups (so that, for example, the circle in front becomes the circle at the back).

- Make a set of shapes a drawing group or prevent a set of shapes from being a drawing group.

17. Using the Selection tool to drag one of the two circles, place the Drawing Objects so that they overlap. Select the object in front and then right-click (*Ctrl*-click on the Mac) and select Arrange ➤ Send Backward from the context menu that appears. The Arrange submenu can also be found in the Modify ➤ Arrange menu option.

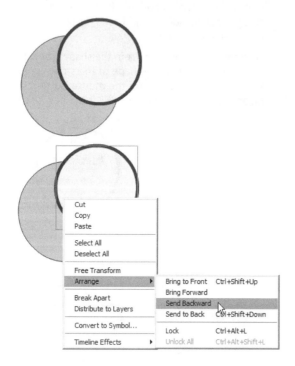

The object in front will move to the back.

18. Right-click the object again, and this time select Arrange ➤ Bring Forward (or use the Modify ➤ Arrange submenu). The circle will move to the front again.

The Bring to Front and Send to Back options are much the same as the two options you just tried, except that they move the circle to the topmost and lowest depth, respectively.

19. To change a Drawing Object to raw shapes, ungroup it as you would a grouped object (i.e., use the Modify ➤ Ungroup menu option or press *Ctrl+B*). Do this now with one of the two circles by selecting it with the Selection tool and then pressing *Ctrl+B*.

> When you ungroup multiple Drawing Objects, make sure the Drawing Objects aren't overlapping; otherwise, they'll start taking bites out of each other once they're ungrouped.

20. To make the shape you just ungrouped a Drawing Object again, simply select it (remember that you have to double-click this time because the shape is now raw fills and strokes, and you want to select them both), and then select Modify ➤ Combine Objects ➤ Union.

You've looked at how to select and move objects, both here and in the last chapter when you constructed your first mushroom-oriented Flash movie. The Selection tool has one other important use, though: it can help you change the shape of objects by dragging their outlines. Let's take a look at this functionality next.

Extending your mushroom's cap

Let's modify the mushroom-based movie you started working on in the previous chapter.

1. Open your `mushroom.fla` file from the end of the last chapter.

2. Click the keyframe in frame 15 of the Mushroom layer.

3. Choose the Selection tool from the Tools panel.

4. Click the stage, away from the drawn shapes, to ensure that nothing is selected.

5. Position the point of the arrow on the edge of the mushroom cap—that is, touching the line around the filled shape. You'll notice that when the arrow point touches the line, the mouse pointer changes to an arrow with a curved line underneath it.

This change of mouse pointer indicates that you are now in a position to click and drag a *point* on a line, thus changing the shape of that line. A mouse pointer with a right angle underneath the pointer, like this:

means that you are in a position to drag a *corner*.

6. Click the line and drag it upward to create a domed, more natural-looking cap for your mushroom. Notice that when you release the mouse button, the fill expands to flood the modified shape with color.

7. Play the movie. You'll see that Flash has automatically modified all the frames between the keyframes so that the animation shows the smooth growth of your newly amended mushroom cap. Flash is great at making life easy for you in this respect. If you change the start or end points of your animation—the keyframes—Flash will recalculate all the in-between images without even asking you.

Next, let's take a look at a tool that lets you see objects in fine detail: the Zoom tool.

The Zoom tool

The following images show the **Zoom tool** in the Tools panel (left image), along with its related modifiers in the Options section (right image).

The Zoom tool is very easy to use. Clicking the screen with the Enlarge option selected will zoom in on the screen, and clicking with the Reduce option selected will zoom out. Simple.

You can also go immediately to the Zoom tool with the keyboard. Holding down *CTRL*+spacebar gives you the Zoom tool with the Enlarge option, and holding down *CTRL*+*ALT*+spacebar gives you the Zoom tool with the Reduce option. These keyboard shortcuts are useful because they don't deselect your current tool. For example, if you want to select something small with the Selection tool, holding down *CTRL*+spacebar and clicking the stage allows you to zoom in on your object. When you release the keys, you're back to the Selection tool.

After you've selected your zoom in or out mode, you can temporarily switch from one state to the other by holding down the *ALT* key in Windows or the *OPTION* key on the Mac. When you click the screen with this key pressed, the zoom will operate in the opposite direction from what's selected in the Options section. This saves you from having to keep changing the mode in the Options box whenever you want to zoom in and out.

With the Zoom tool selected, you can also drag a box around an area, and Flash will enlarge that area to fill the screen.

A feature related to the Zoom tool is the **Pixel Zoom**. When you zoom in beyond 400%, a pixel grid appears that allows you to draw shapes and objects more precisely. For this feature to work, you need to select the View ➤ Snapping ➤ Snap to Pixels menu option. You can see the pixel grid here when you zoom in to 1600% at the bottom of your mushroom movie:

Bottom of Mushroom Stalk

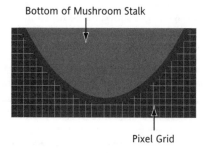

Pixel Grid

Zooming in and out

1. Still in your mushroom.fla file, hide the Mushroom layer by clicking the dot in the eye column next to its name.

2. Use the Zoom tool to enlarge the moon until it fills the screen. Look at the edge of the moon and notice that the quality of the image doesn't degrade as you zoom in, no matter how much you increase the magnification. This is one of the wonders of working with vector graphics—you never lose any detail.

   Also, note that any changes in magnification you make inside of the FLA file don't affect the finished movie. The zoom features are just there to help you when you're creating your movie.

The next tool you're going to look at is also a relatively simple one: the Hand tool.

The Hand tool

The **Hand tool** is used for moving around the segment of the stage that's displayed on your screen. It's most useful when you're zoomed in and not able to see the entire movie all at once. Remember that any changes in view you make in the authoring environment won't have any effect on the display of your finished movie.

Using the Hand tool, move the stage around in the window, making sure that you finish up with the moon in the middle again. You can achieve the same effect using the scrollbars below and to the right of the stage, but the Hand tool feels somehow more controlled and intuitive.

Holding down the spacebar selects the Hand tool. Like the Zoom keyboard shortcuts, releasing the spacebar brings you back to whatever tool you were using before you pressed the spacebar.

The Tools panel's drawing and modification tools

In this section, you're going to use Flash's drawing and modification tools to create a picturesque scene of a colorful fishing boat out on the ocean. The beauty of this exercise is that it familiarizes you with all the tools in the Tools panel, and what's more, it doesn't require you to be van Gogh.

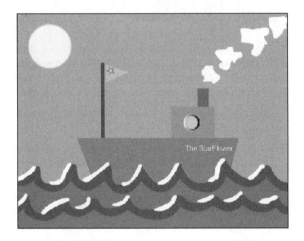

You'll start by creating the boat's hull using the Rectangle tool. Before you begin, close the mushroom.fla file because you no longer need it.

Ahoy, Matey!

The Rectangle tool

The **Rectangle tool**, as its name suggests, is used for drawing squares and rectangles.

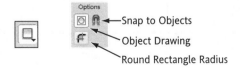

To draw a rectangle, select the Rectangle tool and simply click and drag a shape to the required size. Pressing the *SHIFT* key while drawing will snap the rectangle to a perfect square.

As you can see in the preceding image, the Rectangle tool has a couple of modifiers in the Options section of the Tools panel. The second modifier, the grandly named Round Rectangle Radius, controls the extent to which the corners of the rectangle you're drawing are rounded.

Let's put the Rectangle tool to use by creating the hull of your boat.

Making your boat

You're going to make the skeleton of your boat with three rectangles.

1. Open a blank Flash document.

2. Open the Document Properties window. The quickest way to do this is to press *CTRL+J* or double-click the Frame rate number (currently 12 fps) below the Timeline and change the background color to a light blue (#66CCFF).

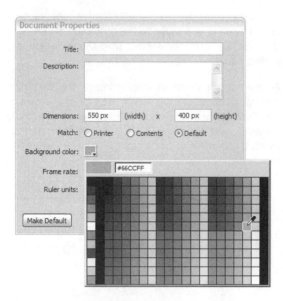

3. Rename the existing layer boat.

4. Click the Rectangle tool, and select a red fill and no stroke outline color using the color pickers on either the toolbar or the Properties panel (I've used the toolbar here).

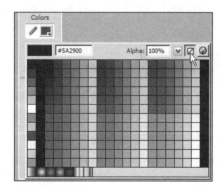

Make sure you're in Object Drawing mode by clicking the circle icon in the Options section.

5. Draw a large red rectangle for the hull of the boat. Unselect the rectangle by clicking a blank area of the stage with the Selection tool.

Next, you'll draw the boat's control room on the same layer. Because you're going to draw this on the same layer, you need to switch on the Snap to Objects feature for the Rectangle tool. This will enable you to draw the control room without overlapping the hull.

6. With the Rectangle tool still selected, click the magnet icon in the tool's list of Options (if it isn't already selected). This switches on Snap to Objects.

7. Draw a green (#33CC66) rectangle with no stroke outline color above the hull, stretching the square until the mouse pointer snaps to the top of the hull. The snapping here makes the possibility of overlapping smaller because the mouse pointer is attracted to—and sticks to—the existing line.

8. After you've finished, draw a smaller rectangle in a dark green so that your boat looks something like this:

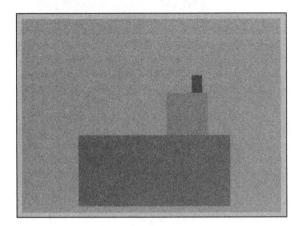

At the moment, your boat is a little blocky and LEGO-tastic, but you'll enhance it using other tools later. For now, that's all you require of the Rectangle tool. The next thing to add to the boat is the porthole for the cap'n to watch the storms a-coming. You'll do this with the Oval tool.

The Oval tool

You've already used the **Oval tool** a couple of times.

The Oval tool allows you to draw oval shapes naturally and circles when holding down the *SHIFT* key. Let's use it to add a porthole to your boat.

Making a porthole with the Oval tool

1. Create a new layer above the boat layer and name it porthole.

2. Use the Zoom tool to zoom in on the control room. This will allow a little more precision when drawing the porthole.

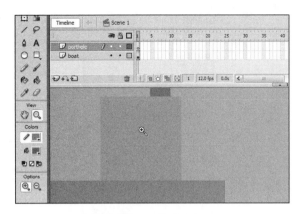

Let's start by creating the shiny porthole frame.

3. Select the Oval tool in Object Drawing mode, click the Fill Color selector in the Tools panel, and choose the leftmost gradient fill (it's at the bottom-left corner of the color picker).

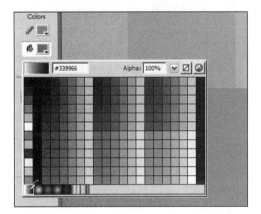

Chapter 5 covers gradients and colors in detail.

4. Select a gray stroke color.

5. Make sure you have selected the porthole layer in the Timeline (you may want to lock the boat layer so you're unable to inadvertently draw in it). Place your mouse pointer directly in the center of the control room, and click and drag to start drawing an oval.

You'll notice that the Oval tool draws shapes from the top corner down.

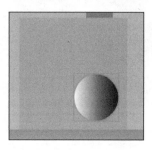

This isn't much good if you want your porthole centered in the rectangle, but luckily there is a way to get the Oval tool to work in your favor: by using the mouse pointer as the center of the circle. Press *Ctrl+Z* (*Cmd+Z* on the Mac) to undo the circle you just drew.

6. This time, while drawing the oval, hold down the *Alt* key. The oval will now be drawn using the initially clicked point as its center. Remember to hold down the *Shift* key for a perfect circle.

7. When you're happy with your circle, release the mouse button.

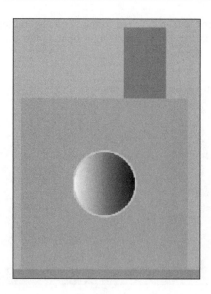

Now you need to draw another oval for the window.

8. Unselect the circle you just drew by choosing the Selection tool and clicking an empty part of the stage. Select the Oval tool again, choose a light blue color fill, and keep the same gray stroke color.

9. This time, click the center of the window frame, and hold down *Alt* and *Shift* while you draw your window.

You now have a porthole, and the boat's captain can look out for any giant calamari on the horizon. Before you look at the next tool, let's add some sunshine.

10. On a new layer called sun, draw a circle in the top-left corner and give it a yellow fill and no stroke.

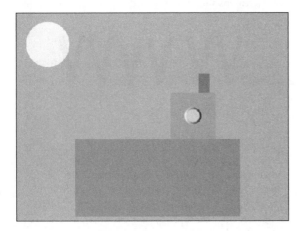

That's it for the Oval tool for now. Let's move on to the next tool.

The Line tool

The **Line tool** is used for drawing lines; it really is as easy as it sounds. Lines have a number of attributes, though, so you can have quite a few options when drawing lines in Flash. Since these settings are common to all path-drawing tools (the Line, Pen, and Pencil tools) and the shape-drawing tools (the Rectangle and Oval tools), let's break off a little and look at all the available settings.

Here's the Line tool icon in the Tools panel:

To use the Line tool, select it, click (and hold) the starting point of your line, and then drag the mouse and release at the end point. To help you work with the Line tool more effectively, the Properties panel will let you closely control the characteristics of the lines you draw.

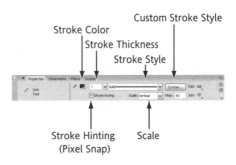

As with the other tools you've used (e.g., the Oval and Rectangle tools), you can set the stroke color (with the color box) and stroke thickness (by entering a number in the Stroke Thickness box).

If you want sharp lines, you should select the Stroke hinting option. This forces Flash to snap the points in your lines to the nearest whole pixel, resulting in sharper graphics.

As a general rule, you should always have Stroke hinting *checked for low line thicknesses when creating website interfaces; otherwise, the lines may appear blurry and dull. If you want all your content to snap to the nearest pixel (recommended), you should get used to working with both* View ➤ Snapping ➤ Snap to Pixels *and the* Stroke hinting *check box checked. Using these options will usually result in your site's vector-based graphics having a much sharper look (they will have more effect on horizontal/vertical edges and a lesser or no effect on diagonal lines).*

There are times when blurry and dull lines are a good thing, for example:

- *You're using the Line tool to create artwork rather than to draw website interfaces.*

- *You're laying vectors over bitmaps and don't want the user to be able to differentiate between the two. Blending the lines into the bitmap background by forcing Flash to anti-alias heavily is one way of doing this, and unchecking the* Stroke hinting *check box is one way to make Flash anti-alias.*

43

You'll look at stroke styles and custom stroke styles in the next exercise, when you create a flag pole for your ship.

The Scale drop-down controls how your strokes will change thickness as the graphics they're part of are also scaled. For example, setting Stroke to None means that a 2-pixel-thick stroke will always be 2 pixels thick, irrespective of how the graphic it is in is scaled, whereas setting Scale to Normal makes the stroke thickness scale in proportion to the main graphic. Scaling is only really useful when you use symbols, so I won't discuss it further here.

As well as controlling the look of the appearance of the line lengths that form your strokes, you can control the way your strokes look and behave at the ends.

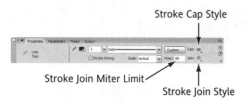

Stroke Cap Style

Stroke Join Miter Limit

Stroke Join Style

The Cap drop-down allows you to define what the ends (caps) of the stroke will look like. You can have either no cap (the stroke ends right at the second point in the line, with a squared-off end), rounded cap (the cap is rounded off with a half circle), or square cap (the stroke ends with a square; this looks much like the None option for no cap, except that the squared-off end is half the line thickness beyond the end of the stroke).

None (No cap)

Rounded Cap

Square Cap

Flash also allows you to change the way that joins between lines are made. This is done via the Join drop-down. The Join drop-down allows you to select one of three options: Miter, Round, or Bevel.

The Round and Bevel options are fairly straightforward—they force Flash to add rounded or beveled end caps to the ends of your strokes. The Miter options

allow you to set how far the corner point extends, and you enter the Miter limit in the Miter requester (valid values are between 0 and 60). The following image shows Miter values of 1 to 4, and you can see from this that the Miter value is how far the corner point is allowed to extend, and it's measured in pixels. If you want a Miter value of 0, select the Bevel option instead.

Round Bevel 1 2 3 4

> Speakers of the Queen's English might not recognize the word "miter," as it isn't a commonly known term (unless, of course, you've taken a woodworking class or you're a fashion designer). The corresponding British English word is "mitre."
>
> The Join and Miter options work only for strokes when you aren't in Object Drawing mode. In Object Drawing mode, you're drawing separate rather than joined lines, so Join and Miter have no relevance. The Join setting will affect a rectangle's corner points irrespective of the drawing mode you're currently in.

The Miter value is really only appropriate for either thick lines or for very acute angles.

Also, although the Cap and Join drop-downs appear on most drawing tools that allow you to create strokes (the Line, Pen, Oval, and Rectangle tools), they aren't really appropriate for the Oval tool. This is because they relate to cap and corner points, and of course a circle has neither by default. They do become important even for an oval if you cut parts of the oval away using other tools, so the addition of cap and corner points to ovals is still necessary.

That's all the theory out of the way. Stay sharp at the back, because here comes the test!

Making a flag pole with the Line tool

1. Make sure that the Properties panel is open (Window ➤ Properties ➤ Properties).

2. Choose the Line tool from the Tools panel. Make sure you are in Object Drawing mode. The Properties panel is updated to display the current properties for the Line tool, showing line color, thickness, and style, as well as a button that allows you to further customize your line, as you've just seen.

As you know, these modifiers work in conjunction with the other drawing tools, which means that you can always alter the characteristics of the outlines of your ovals and rectangles after you've drawn them.

3. Click the Stroke Color box to bring up the Properties panel's standard color palette, and select a dark woody brown for the flag pole. Select a rounded cap.

4. Click the down-pointing arrow to the right of the Stroke Height box.

5. A slider pops up that you use to control the height of your line. (You can also type a precise height into the box if you prefer; the maximum size is 200.)

6. Set the stroke thickness to 8 by moving the slider up. To fix your size choice, release the mouse button.

7. To preview the line, click the Custom button. In the Stroke Style window that appears, a simple preview is displayed on the left.

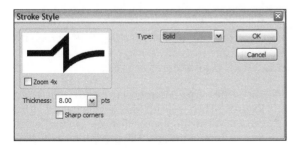

Don't worry about the rest of this window for now; you'll take another look at it shortly. Click OK to close the Stroke Style window.

8. In the Line tool's options (on the toolbar), click the Snap to Objects option (indicated by the magnet icon).

The Snap to Objects feature ensures that when your line gets close to a vertical or horizontal orientation, the line will automatically snap to a perfectly straight position. As you draw your line, you'll see a small circle at the end of the line, and when the line snaps into place, this circle grows bolder to signal that you've reached the desired angle. When you're in Snap to Objects mode, you can also hold down the *Shift* key while you're dragging to snap your line in 45-degree angle increments.

9. Insert a new layer called flag pole. Make sure this layer is below the boat layer.

10. Draw a flag pole at the front of the boat by clicking and dragging a line. Make the pole a little taller than the smokestack. When you're happy with its length, snap the line to vertical, and release the mouse button to fix the line.

Now that you have a pole, it needs a flag.

11. Unselect Object Drawing mode. On the same layer (flag pole), draw an unfilled red triangle outline an inch or two away from the pole using the Line tool with a thickness of 1 (the other options don't matter). You'll finish the flag shortly.

Even though the Line tool in Flash isn't **rubber-banded**—that is, it doesn't continue the next line from where you drew the last one—because you have the Snap to Objects option selected, Flash will automatically snap to any previously drawn line, making continuous drawing easy. Remember, though, you have to turn Object Drawing mode off if you want your lines to use the Join settings.

12. When you're done, save the movie as boat.fla.

Earlier on, you got a quick look at the Stroke Style window when you used it to preview the height and color of your line. Let's take a closer look at it now.

Creating custom stroke styles

If you don't want all your lines to be perfectly straight, you can create a **custom stroke style**. Flash allows you to easily change contents of the stage, including more than just changing the color and size of your stroke. Let's see how it works in practice.

1. Open a new, blank Flash document.

2. Using the options in the Tools panel, draw a simple line of any color with a stroke thickness of 10 and a rounded cap using the Line tool (with Object Drawing mode off, so you're in Merge Drawing mode). Draw two connected lines as shown here:

3. Choose the Selection tool and click the first stroke. Notice that only the first stroke is selected. To select both strokes, double-click either stroke (if this doesn't work, you most likely have two unconnected lines and need to draw your lines again). When either one or both strokes are selected, the Properties panel changes to show the properties of the stroke. Notice that you can change the stroke color or styles (stroke style, color, join, and cap) of your line by changing the appropriate values in the Properties panel. As an example, make sure both lines are still selected, and then change the cap from rounded to square. Notice that the line caps are now square.

4. Click the Custom button in the Properties panel. The Stroke Style window opens with some stroke options visible.

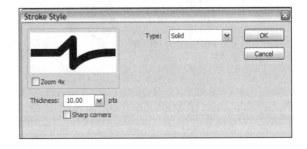

The preview on the left shows possible variations of the line, from perfectly straight to a variety of curves and edges. This shows you how your line will look in almost any situation.

Next, you're going to make the line look rickety and old from many years of wear by creating a customized stroke style that is textured and rough.

5. Click the Type drop-down menu and select Ragged. When you do this, a number of other drop-down menus appear that you can use to further customize the line. The preview pane displays these options as you select them.

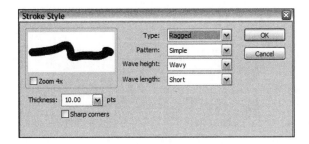

I won't go through all the possibilities here, but there are a variety of menu options for each Type style. Have some fun and experiment with the other options later on. Let's change the line a little so you get a ragged effect.

6. Select Solid from the Pattern drop-down menu, Very Wavy from the Wave height drop-down menu, and Short from Wave length drop-down menu. Uncheck the Sharp corners check box (below the preview pane). The line in the preview pane of the Stroke Style window should now look like this:

The stroke looks much more natural and expressive, but there is a problem: the stroke has lost its corners. If you ever encounter this problem, you can fix it by checking the Sharp corners check box. Do it now to see the effect. The line will still be Ragged, but it will follow the original a lot more closely.

Uncheck the Sharp corners check box before continuing.

7. Click OK and take a look at your stroke on the stage (click a blank area of the stage to unselect the stroke so you can see its final appearance). It looks like a twisted branch right now.

Some of the Custom options will give you some pretty wacky results, and others will help you to quickly achieve some useful effects, such as the creation of a dotted line. Flash also has a number of preset line styles, all of which are accessible from the Stroke Style drop-down in the Properties panel.

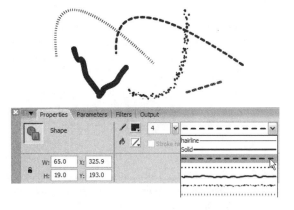

Before we move on, it's worth noting some points that will lead to efficient use of the Line tool and stroke styles in general (remember that you can change the stroke of lines around ovals and rectangles as well as just drawing lines):

- Some of the more complex line styles can increase the file size of your SWF considerably if overused. They can also slow down your animations because they take longer to draw. Use complex line styles only when you really need to.

- The hairline style is particularly useful; it's a stroke of 0 thickness. Flash draws it at a width of 1 pixel regardless of any scaling or other transformation. Flash is also able to draw this line style much faster than any of the other styles and thicknesses, so if you're a speed demon and want the smoothest animation or fastest website design, use hairlines whenever possible.

That's all for the Line tool—you can close the current FLA. Let's move on and make some more modifications to your scene, this time using the Paint Bucket tool.

The Paint Bucket tool

The **Paint Bucket tool**, more commonly known as the **Fill tool**, is used for filling in empty shapes or changing the fill color of existing shapes.

I'll talk about the following modifiers later in the book when you come to use them "in anger." For the moment, let's stick with the core functionality of the Paint Bucket tool.

The Paint Bucket tool is used in conjunction with the Properties panel's color palette (or the one in the Tools panel). You select the Paint Bucket tool, pick a color from the color palette, and then click the area that you want to fill with that color. Let's do that now in the context of your boat.

Filling the flag with color

In this exercise, you're going to fill in your flag.

1. Go back to your `boat.fla` file and click the Paint Bucket tool.

2. In the Properties panel, select a bright green color.

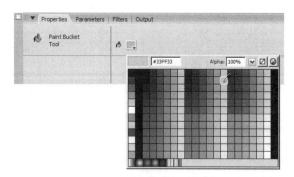

3. Click inside the flag triangle to fill it instantly with the color you selected.

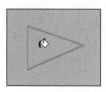

4. Using the Selection tool, double-click the red stroke so that all your lines are selected. Then press the *DELETE* key to leave a triangular fill only. Move the flag so that it touches the flag pole.

5. Once you have a fill, you don't need to use the Paint Bucket tool if you want to change the fill. You can simply select the flag (with the Selection tool) and change the fill color in the toolbar or Properties panel if you want to experiment with different shades of green or if you're a rebel and want a pirate's black flag instead.

> Note that you made your flag outline using raw shapes (i.e., you didn't draw the flag outline in Object Drawing mode), the Paint Bucket tool fills the area enclosed by an outline of line shapes and doesn't accept a shape composed of separate drawing objects.

Now that you've seen a couple of ways to apply changes to different objects on your stage, let's look at how you can copy characteristics from one object to another. You'll use the Eyedropper tool to do this.

*Every mouse pointer has a point called a **hotspot** that tells the computer exactly where you're clicking the screen. The hotspot for the Paint Bucket tool is the end of the paint spilling out of the can.*

You've quickly made your flag—not bad for a minute's work! Later in the book, you'll take a closer look at the Fill Transform tool, which is closely related to the Paint Bucket tool. For now, though, let's move on and investigate the Ink Bottle tool.

The Ink Bottle tool

The **Ink Bottle tool** works hand in hand with the Paint Bucket tool. Whereas the Paint Bucket tool changes *fills*, the Ink Bottle does the same for *lines* and *strokes*. The Ink Bottle tool has no options.

If a fill does not have a stroke outline, the Ink Bottle tool can be used to give it one. This is where the Ink Bottle tool comes in handy.

The hotspot for the Ink Bottle is at the tip of the spilled ink. Let's use it to give your sun a thick, glowing orange outline.

Adding a stroke to a fill

1. Select the Ink Bottle tool and ensure that the Properties panel is open (Window ➤ Properties ➤ Properties).

2. In the Properties panel, select an orange stroke color.

3. Change the Stroke Thickness to 4.

You're making these selections to specify the stroke color and thickness that will outline the sun. Now, let's apply these settings.

4. With the Ink Bottle tool still selected, click the sun. The orange stroke has now been applied to the yellow fill.

The Eyedropper tool

The **Eyedropper tool** is used to copy the colors and styles of fills (or lines) from objects that you've already created.

When you use the Eyedropper tool to copy an object's attributes, Flash automatically switches to the tool you use to apply these attributes to another object. That is, if you copy a *fill* style, Flash will switch to the Paint Bucket tool, and if you copy a *line/stroke* style, Flash will switch to the Ink Bottle tool.

The Eyedropper tool can also be used to copy bitmaps and gradients, and you'll look at that in more detail later. Let's now apply the Eyedropper tool to your example movie.

Copying colors from lines and fills

Bad memory? Can't remember what color you used for the sun or its stroke outline? Use the Eyedropper tool to retrieve the colors.

1. Click the Eyedropper tool and move it over the flag's fill. Notice that a little paintbrush icon appears next to the mouse pointer. This indicates that if you click that spot, you can copy a fill style. If you move the mouse pointer over a stroke, you will see a pencil appear next to the pointer.

2. Click the sun's fill. The Eyedropper tool switches to the Paint Bucket tool. Notice that the fill color in the Tools panel has changed to the color you just selected.

This selected color—inherited by the Tools panel—can be used by any of the other tools.

Let's hoist the flag!

The PolyStar tool

The **PolyStar tool**'s curious name is a fusion of the shapes that it creates: polygons and stars. In essence, the PolyStar tool is two tools, but because each one is a little obscure, Macromedia bundled them together.

If you're having trouble finding the PolyStar tool, that's because it's hidden under the Rectangle tool. To select it, click and hold the Rectangle tool icon until the menu appears, and then select PolyStar Tool.

If you intend to use the PolyStar tool regularly, and you find its hiding place unintuitive, you can move it to its own place by customizing the Tools panel (Edit ➤ Customize Toolbars _on Windows;_ Flash Professional ➤ Customize Tools panel _on the Mac)._

The PolyStar tool works in a very similar way to the other shape tools. To draw a shape, just click and drag until you're satisfied with the result, and then release the mouse button. The only major difference with the PolyStar tool is the option to set the number of sides on the star and polygon shapes. Let's see how this works.

Adding a star to the flag using the PolyStar tool

In this exercise, you're going to add a star to your flag. It might not be as cool as a skull and crossbones, but this is a friendly vessel.

1. Select the layer flag pole.

2. Using the Zoom tool, draw a box around the flag to zoom in on that specific area. This will make your flag decorating a little easier.

3. Select the PolyStar tool and choose a red outline and an orange fill. Select the Solid Stroke style and a thickness of 1.

4. In the Properties panel, select a rounded cap and join, and then click Options. (Note that the PolyStar tool doesn't have any options in the Tools panel; they appear via the Options button in the Properties panel.)

The Tool Settings box displays the settings for the PolyStar tool. Here, you can create a star or a polygon using the Style drop-down menu. The settings in this dialog box also allow you to customize the number of sides on your shape and the star point size (or thickness). The default star point size is 0.5.

Star Point Size   0.1   0.5   1

5. Make sure that layer flag pole is selected. Select star from the Style drop-down menu and leave the other options as they are. Click OK to close the Tool Settings dialog box.

6. Draw a star on the flag with Object Drawing mode turned off (hint: start dragging from the center of the flag to get a good-sized star that fits on the flag).

7. The flag consists of raw shapes at the moment, and now is a good time to make it a Drawing Object. To do this, double-click anywhere on the flag. This will select all the shapes and strokes in the flag. Next, select the Modify ➤ Combine Objects ➤ Union menu option. When you do this, there is a chance that the flag may suddenly appear in front of the flag pole, as shown here:

If this happens to your flag, right-click the flag and choose Arrange ➤ Send Backward from the context menu that appears.

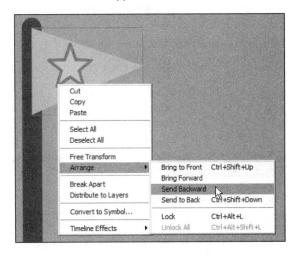

The flag looks a little stiff and starchy. A real flag would blow in the wind, and you'll fix that later using the Envelope tool.

8. Use the Zoom tool to zoom out and view your handiwork. When you're happy with your star, you'll move on to cover something completely different . . .

The Pencil tool

The **Pencil tool** is used to draw freeform lines.

You use the Properties panel to set the Pencil tool's characteristics, such as stroke height, style, and color. The Pencil tool also has one modifier in the Options section of the Tools panel (apart from the Object Drawing toggle that all drawing tools have): the Pencil mode modifier. This modifier is an important one, as it controls how the line behaves when you draw by clicking and dragging with the mouse.

Clicking this modifier reveals that there are three Pencil modes to choose from.

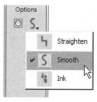

Let's see how these work in a short exercise.

Using the Pencil tool

1. Save your boat movie and create a new movie by choosing the File ➤ New menu option or by pressing CTRL+N (CMD+N on the Mac) and selecting Flash Document. This will open a fresh, blank movie in Flash.

> *When working with more than one Flash file, you'll notice that a tab at the top of the Flash interface represents each Flash document. This speeds up any Flash work dramatically because it lets you quickly switch between FLAs.*
>
>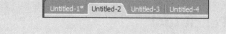

2. Using the Pencil tool, draw a series of similar lines with the different Pencil modes and notice the results.

■ **Straighten mode** will flatten some of the curves in your line. This tool will also automatically complete simple shapes that you draw. For example, if you draw a rough circle with Straighten mode on, Flash will snap it to a perfect circle:

■ **Smooth mode** will refine the curves in your hand-drawn shapes, *rounding* out kinks and generally softening awkward shapes. It's a good mode to use if your freehand drawing is a little shaky (or if you're using a mouse).

■ **Ink mode** is the basic Pencil mode. If you want to draw something on the screen and have it appear *exactly* the way you drew it, this is the mode to use. In this mode, you'll notice that Flash seems to smooth the lines a little bit—this is just a result of the process of converting the line from the bitmap line that Flash uses while you're drawing to the vector version that Flash will store and render. When you use the Pencil tool in Ink mode, it's usually a good idea to have the Stroke hinting check box (in the Properties panel) selected. This ensures your lines are sharp and not blurry, especially if you're using a low thickness setting.

3. Close the movie that you've been using to experiment with the Pencil modes. Don't save it (unless you really like it), and your original boat movie will be displayed again.

Now we'll take a look at the Pencil tool's larger sibling, the Brush tool.

The Brush tool

The **Brush tool** is very similar to the Pencil tool, but instead of drawing lines, you paint fills with it. Every time you use the Brush tool on your movie, you're simply painting a fill with no enclosing borderline.

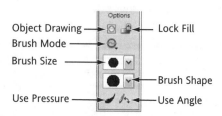

The Brush tool has six options (not including the Object Drawing icon):

- The Brush Mode option controls the way that your brush strokes are painted. This option has five modifiers:

  - Paint Normal paints over anything else that's on the screen (provided it's on the same layer as the one you're drawing on, of course).

  - Paint Fills paints fills and leaves lines in place and visible through the fill that you just painted. This option (and the Paint Behind and Paint Inside options) assumes all the graphics you have drawn are *not* Drawing Objects. If you are using Drawing Objects, you can, of course, use Modify ➤ Break Apart to make the offending Drawing Object a shape, and then use the Modify ➤ Combine Objects submenu to get back to Drawing Objects when you're done.

  - Paint Behind paints only on blank areas of the current layer—any objects on that layer won't be painted over.

  - Paint Selection paints only on areas of the screen that have been highlighted with the Selection tool.

  - Paint Inside paints only inside the lines. This is the tool you needed when you had those coloring books as a kid. When you start painting, Flash will ignore any marks you paint when your brush crosses a line (note that Flash will fill to the side of the line you start painting from):

- The Brush Size option changes the width and spread of the brushstrokes.

- The Brush Shape button opens a menu containing a selection of shapes to paint with: round, flat, and so on.

- The Use Pressure and Use Angle options allow you to use the Pressure and Angle values used by a graphics tablet if you're using one as an input device. If you have such a device connected and have used it before in something like Photoshop, then these options should be self-explanatory.

- The Lock Fill button works in the same way as the Lock Fill button for the Paint Bucket tool. Its use is covered in the "Locking fills" section of Chapter 5.

Drawing with the Brush tool

Here you'll add some waves to your scene. You're setting sail at last!

1. Select the Brush tool and pick a dark blue fill color from the Properties panel. Deselect Object Drawing mode. Remember that the Brush tool draws fills, not strokes.

2. Choose a mid-size brush from the Tools panel options, and ensure that the Brush Mode is set to Paint Normal.

3. In the Properties panel, set the Smoothing option to 100.

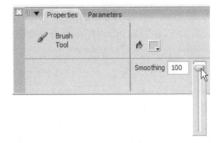

The Smoothing value determines the amount that drawings with the brush are smoothed and sharpened. This is very much like the Pencil tool's Smooth mode. If this setting is low, the result will be rough edges. A setting that's too high, however, will remove the curves from your drawings.

4. Create a new layer, name it waves, and place it above all the other layers.

5. Use the Brush tool to draw two lines of waves across the body of the boat. Make sure your waves run off the stage on either side.

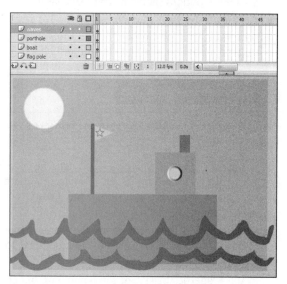

> *Don't worry about drawing off the edge of the stage. Remember that viewers see only the contents of the stage.*

6. Draw a line on either side of the waves, connecting them to make a closed shape.

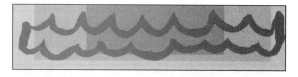

The reason you're connecting the waves is so that you can fill the gap between the waves with a lighter blue. Let's do that now.

7. Select the Paint Bucket tool and choose a medium blue fill color (#0099FF).

8. Click the space between the waves to fill the area.

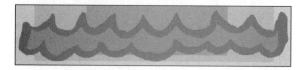

Now you need to create a space for filling below the bottom wave because at the moment you can't fill the space at the bottom of the screen. You can do this by creating a closed shape around the wave.

9. Select the Brush tool and choose the wave color (you can use the Eyedropper tool to select this color directly if you don't remember which color it is from the color picker).

10. Draw a line off the bottom of the stage parallel to the waves.

11. Connect the new line to the side of the waves above it. This creates another closed space, ready to fill with the Paint Bucket tool.

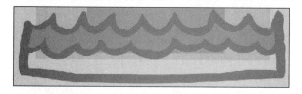

12. Use the Fill tool to fill in the space with the same fill color as before (#0099FF).

You've almost completed your waves. Almost? Well, they look a little dull, don't they? Before you move on to the next tool, let's give the waves a little detail: some white foam.

13. With the Brush tool selected, choose a white fill color.

14. Select a smaller brush size from the Tools panel's Options section.

15. Draw some highlights on the left side of each wave. This will give the illusion of the sun reflecting off the sea.

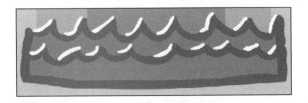

That's about it for your waves. Simple and fast! Now that you've seen how to paint, next up you'll learn how to erase any mistakes you might have made.

The Eraser tool

The **Eraser tool** is similar to the Brush tool, except it erases rather than paints.

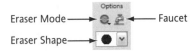

Eraser Mode ——— Faucet

Eraser Shape ———

It has three modifiers:

- The Eraser Mode button has five modifiers. These are the same as those for the Brush Mode button on the Brush tool, and they behave in the same ways.

- The Eraser Shape button lets you change the shape of the eraser's "footprint."

- The Faucet button changes the Eraser tool so that it will erase an entire fill or line at once. In this mode, you just touch the Eraser tool hotspot to the target line or fill, and the whole thing is erased.

Next, let's take a look at the Text tool.

The Text tool

The **Text tool** is used in conjunction with the Properties panel. Together, they allow text entry and editing in your Flash movie. In Flash, text fields can also be used as hyperlinks (more on this later).

For now, though, it's time to name the boat.

Using the Text tool

First, you'll define how your text should look.

1. Create a new layer above boat and name it text.

2. Click the Text tool in the Tools panel. This will open the Text tool properties in the Properties panel. Make sure that the drop-down menu on the far left is set to Static Text.

The options displayed in the Properties panel are similar to those in a word processing program, and many of them will probably be familiar to you. For now, let's concentrate on the top section of the Properties panel. If the lower section is visible, close it by using the arrow at the bottom right of the Properties panel. The options in the top section are as follows:

- **Text Type**: This is the type of text box you're creating (more about this later).

- **Font**: This is the font you want to use. Note that Flash previews the fonts when you open the font list.

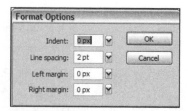

■ **Font Size Position**: This is where you can choose to display the font as subscript or superscript.

■ **Auto Kern**: This check box is in the lower part of the Properties inspector, so you may have to click the triangle at the bottom right of the panel to see it. **Kerning** is the gap between pairs of characters. Most fonts have built-in kerning so that the gaps between certain characters will be different sizes. For example, the gap between an "A" and a "D" will be larger than that between an "A" and a "V." The default is to use the font's built-in kerning, and in most cases you'll want to leave this setting at the default.

■ **Font Rendering Method**: This determines whether or not the text is anti-aliased (i.e., smoothed out). If you want anti-aliased text, you can select one of the presets: Anti-alias for read-ability, which gives better quality anti-aliasing but is slower for animation, or Anti-alias for animation, which gives a lower quality anti-aliasing that results in smoother animation. You can also define your own anti-aliasing parameters by selecting the Custom anti-alias option.

■ **Format**: This provides increased control over the format of individual lines of text. This includes the amount of the indent, line spacing, and the left and right margins of each line. Individual lines of text are given their own settings here:

■ **Text modifiers**: The Bold and Italic modifiers make the text bold and italic, respectively, and the Color button opens the standard Flash color palette so that you can choose the text color.

Note that in Flash, there's no text modifier that will underline text. If you want to have underlined static text in Flash, you'll have to manually draw a line underneath it.

3. Select the Text tool and click near the stern of the boat.

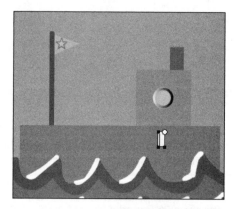

A small text box appears with a blinking cursor at the text insertion point. Don't worry if your insertion point isn't in exactly the right place—you'll be able to position the text precisely later.

4. In the Properties panel, choose a font that you like the look of (I used Arial Black), and choose a font size that will fit nicely. Notice that as you move the Font Size slider up and down, the text box on your stage is automatically resized. This guide will help you to choose a text size that fits on your boat.

5. Set the color of your font to white.

6. Type some text into your text box. Feel free to call your boat what you like. I called mine "The StarFlower."

7. Click the Selection tool. The box around the text disappears and is replaced with a thin, colored highlight (this is the color that you've set as your default Highlight Color on the General section of the Edit ➤ Preferences menu). You can now pick up this text with the Selection tool's mouse pointer and move it around until you're happy with its position. You can also change its size by clicking one of the little boxes on the corner points of the outline.

8. To go back and edit the text again, click the text with the Text tool (or you can double-click it with the Selection tool).

Save the boat movie before you move on to the next exercise.

Checking spelling

Flash has a spell checker that can check all text in your FLA. Let's see how it works.

1. Open a new Flash document.

2. Use the Text tool to type the following text (or something equally riddled with errors!):

My spellin is prety awful

Before you can ask Flash to correct your spelling, you have to set a few options.

3. Select Text ➤ Spelling Setup and you'll see a great number of options and a selection of dictionary languages. You want the default options, which are as shown in the following image. Check that yours are the same, and then click OK.

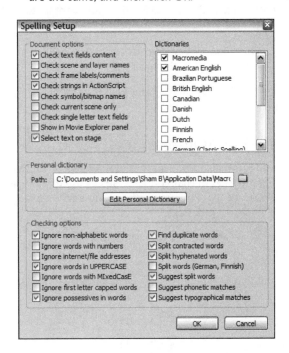

4. Select Text ➤ Check Spelling to run the spell checker. Flash's spell checker will run through all the text fields and check for any spelling errors.

It's no surprise, then, that Flash has found an error (or two). From here onward, the procedure will most likely seem familiar to you, as it's similar to all the other applications with spell-checking functionality. The most important thing you did here was to switch the spell checker on and notify Flash that you want it to do some work.

5. When you've finished correcting your spelling, save and close the Flash movie.

Next up is an extremely useful tool: the Free Transform tool.

The Free Transform tool

The **Free Transform tool** is used to manipulate different properties of your content. You can use it to resize, rotate, and perform some pretty impressive tasks on elements on your stage.

Clicking this option reveals four different options in the Tools panel. They are as follows (going top left, top right, bottom left, and bottom right):

- **Rotate and Skew**: This option limits the function of the Free Transform tool exclusively to rotating and skewing objects.

- **Scale**: This option allows the Free Transform tool to scale your objects.

- **Distort**: This option allows scaling from each point, giving maximum flexibility and, as the name suggests, distortion.

- **Envelope**: This option uses Bezier curves (more on these later) to manipulate simple shapes. Like the Distort option, Envelope cannot be used on grouped objects.

By default, none of the options is selected, and the tool allows you to rotate, scale, and skew. Let's give it a try.

Using the Free Transform tool

In this exercise, you're going to modify a simple square using the Free Transform tool.

1. Open a new Flash movie.

2. Select the Rectangle tool using Object Drawing mode. (If you just worked through the previous exercise, its icon will be hidden beneath the PolyStar tool.) Draw a square with a red fill and a black stroke. Give it a stroke height of 5. If you still have rounded corners set from earlier and want a straighter rectangle, click the Round Rectangle Radius button in the Options section of the Tools panel. This brings up the Rectangle Settings window. To draw a rectangle with no rounded corners, enter 0 in the Corner Radius box.

3. With the rectangle still selected, select the Free Transform tool in the Tools panel.

4. A number of anchor points will appear around the shape. You can move these points to manipulate the scale of the shape in different directions. Let's make your square a rectangle.

5. Place your mouse pointer over the top-center point. When you do this, the mouse pointer changes to a double-ended arrow, indicating that you can resize your selection.

6. While the mouse pointer is a double-ended arrow, click and drag upward. You'll notice that Flash shows you a ghostly outline preview of your target shape. This affects none of the other sides; only the side you're dragging will change.

When you release the mouse, the shape is updated and you now have a rectangle.

You resized the square in one direction only—if you had chosen any of the corner anchor points, the square would be resized in both height and width. Let's give that a try.

7. Move your mouse pointer over the top-right corner anchor point. Your mouse pointer changes into a two-headed diagonal arrow. Click and drag to manipulate the shape in both width and height.

If you look at the square on the stage, you'll probably notice that it isn't centered. You can center it by putting your mouse pointer over the square so that it turns into the familiar arrow with which you can drag the shape.

One of the other default actions of the Free Transform tool is rotation. Let's experiment a little with it.

8. It would help if your square had an identifier for your rotations. Choose the Text tool with a yellow text fill color and place a large N at the top center—you'll use this as your north indicator:

At this point you'll need to *group* your objects so that they act as a unit; otherwise, your north will remain north while your square goes south.

> *A Drawing Object can contain only shapes, so you can't add the text to the Drawing Object. You have to use a group, which can contain anything.*

9. Click the Selection tool and select all the objects on the stage by drawing a box around them. Choose the Modify ➤ Group menu option or press *CTRL*+*G* to bundle the objects together as one unit. Now that your objects are grouped, you can manipulate them all at once.

10. Select the grouped objects with the Selection tool and then click the Free Transform tool. The familiar anchor points should appear, so place your mouse pointer just outside any of the corner points and notice that it's been replaced with a circular mouse pointer:

11. Click and drag right to rotate the square 90 degrees. Again, if you hold down the *SHIFT* key, Flash gives you a helping hand and snaps in increments of 45 degrees:

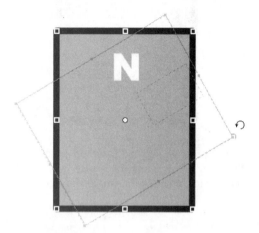

An extra feature of the Free Transform tool is the ability to adjust the center pivot of your rotation. When the square is selected, you'll see a small white circle in the center—that's the pivot for the rotation. You can move that white circle anywhere you like and the shape will still rotate around it, even if the pivot is off the stage.

Let's take a look at the final basic function of the Free Transform tool: the *skew*.

12. Make sure the group is selected and place the mouse pointer over the perimeter of the square between any of the anchor points.

You'll notice that the mouse pointer turns into a peculiar shape that on closer inspection is two arrows pointing in different directions.

13. Click and drag to see the skew in action:

Let's now take a look at the Distort modifier option. This can be applied only to simple elements (i.e., shapes or Drawing Objects) and not grouped objects.

14. Return your skewed square back to its original square shape by pressing *CTRL+Z*. Select the square using the Selection tool. To ungroup the object so that you can use the Distort option, choose the Modify ➤ Break Apart menu option twice. This will turn your entire rectangle (the text and rectangle itself) into raw shapes, which the Free Transform tool works best with.

15. Select the square and text again, click the Free Transform tool, and then select the Distort modifier from the Options section at the bottom of the Tools panel:

16. When your square is selected, you'll see those familiar anchor points again. Placing the mouse pointer over the anchor points will change the mouse pointer to a small white chevron. Select the top-left corner anchor point and drag it toward the center of the square:

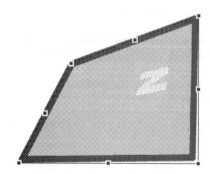

The shape now reflects the new location of the anchor point.

To conclude your look at the Free Transform tool, you'll now quickly use the Envelope modifier option. Like the Distort option, Envelope can't be used on grouped objects.

17. Return your shape to its original square by pressing *CTRL+Z* to undo the distortion.

18. Select the square by double-clicking it (to select all parts of it at once), and with the Free Transform tool selected in the Tools panel, click the Envelope modifier option.

You'll notice that when you select the square with the Envelope modifier option, many more anchor points appear around the perimeter of the shape.

19. Drag as many anchor points as you like in whatever directions you want.

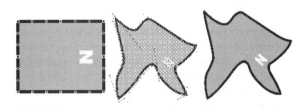

Some experimentation with the last two options of the Free Transform tool will enable you to create some wild shapes, as well as some subtle shapes.

20. Close the current Flash document without saving the changes.

If you're feeling really creative, you might want to make your flag look like it's flapping around in the breeze using your newfound tools. If you wish to do this, simply select your flag, and then select the Free Transform tool and use the Envelope modifier to create an envelope roughly as shown in the following image. Note that when you're using the Envelope tool with a complex shape (i.e., a shape containing a large number of separate strokes and fills), your end result can get a little strange looking unless you keep the amount of envelope-based distortion sensible!

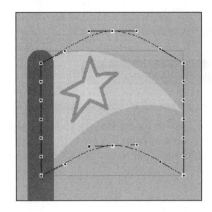

What's next? The mighty Pen tool, that's what!

The Pen tool

The principles embodied in the **Pen tool** are an example of how science and math can have unforeseen spin-offs.

Bezier curves

The space race gave us microprocessors and nonstick pans, but a lesser-known spin-off comes from the automobile industry of the 1970s. Designers had just started using CAD/CAM packages to design cars, but there was a problem: the computers couldn't draw squiggly lines. They could do straight lines and simple curves, but they couldn't come up with a way to draw squiggles. Squiggly lines are difficult because the equations that define them—unlike those for straight lines or regular curves—are extremely complex.

The solution to this problem was a special kind of curve called a **Bezier**, named after a mathematician by the name of Pierre Bezier. Monsieur Bezier's curve is used in all sorts of computer applications today, from designing curved cars to displaying PostScript fonts.

The difference between a Bezier and a normal curve is that a normal curve is made up of points. A Bezier curve, on the other hand, is made up of points that include two additional pieces of data that we will call *direction* and *speed*.

Bezier curves are drawn using the Pen tool. Let's see how the Pen tool works in practice.

Working with Bezier curves

1. Open a fresh Flash movie to experiment with.

2. Select the Pen tool, and make sure you have the fill color and line color selected. The mouse pointer changes into a pen nib with a little "x" next to it:

   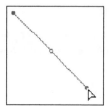

3. Drag in the general direction you want the curve to go:

   A line starts to appear as you drag. This line consists of three points—one at the center and one on each end—so there's a kind of "bow tie" look to the line. The center point of the line is where your finished curve will start.

4. Don't let the bow tie get too big—once you're happy with it, release the mouse button. You've now created the starting point of the curve.

5. Position the mouse pointer at another point on the screen where you want your curve to pass through. In the same way you did before, drag out another bow tie, keeping the mouse button pressed as you position the bow tie:

Notice that as you drag the second bow tie around, the curve between the two center points of the bow ties changes in real time. The way it changes is pretty difficult to explain, but once you've seen it, it somehow looks totally natural. The direction of the bow tie defines what *direction* the curve goes in, and the *length* of the bow tie affects its curvature.

A good way to think of it is that the bow ties represent the position (via the center point of the bow tie) and the speed (via the length of the bow tie) of a car trying to move in a straight line between the two points. As it gets faster (the bow ties get bigger) the car travels in a curved path. Some of you may recognize the bow tie as the car's *velocity vector*, but the rest of us will be having fun making the squiggle dance to care too much about the math. In fact, practicing drawing the curves using the bow ties is the best way to get the feel of what's happening.

6. Keep adding bow ties to form a roughly puddle-shaped squiggle as shown here:

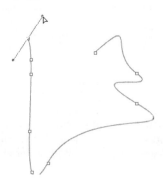

As you put the Pen tool near the original starting point of the first bow tie (or near *any* point on a line that would make a closed area), the Pen tool changes to show an "o" where it was previously an "x":

This is Flash's way of saying that the next point you add will create a closed shape. This sounds a little complicated, but try it. As with most everything associated with Beziers, it's easier to do than it is to explain!

Sometimes when you're constructing shapes with the Pen tool, you don't want a shape composed completely of curves; rather, you want a mixture of curves and sharp corners. If you want to create a corner rather than another curve, you simply click the stage with the Pen tool rather than clicking and dragging. This will give you a mix of curves and straight lines:

7. Close the movie without saving it.

Now that you've had a little experience with the Pen tool, let's enhance your scene.

Making smoke with the Pen tool

Even though the Pen tool has some really beneficial uses for illustrations and high graphics work, you're just going to create a few clouds of smoke with it.

1. Return to your boat movie and create a new layer called smoke.

2. Select the Pen tool, and choose a white fill and stroke.

3. Use the Zoom tool to zoom in on the boat's smokestack, and use the Pen tool to create a sequence of simple curves on the stage. Remember to click and drag to shape a curve, and release the mouse button when you're happy with it.

4. When you have a few decent curves, close the shape by clicking the starting point. (The mouse pointer will change to show an "o" when your mouse pointer is over the start point.) When you do this, the shape will be closed and filled. Now you have some smoke emanating from the boat's smokestack.

5. Draw smoke clouds up to the top of the screen.

6. Save your movie.

If any of your clouds are less than perfect, you can edit them with the Subselect tool.

The Subselect tool

The **Subselect tool** is certainly worth getting to know. It allows you to select and alter specific points on a curve, which means you can control how you modify the curves that you created.

When you choose the Subselect tool from the Tools panel and click a Bezier stroke, a skeleton-like structure appears inside your shape. This shows you the start and end points of the curves, and the shape of the curves that underlie the displayed drawing.

> *You might have to zoom right in to see this clearly—it's easier to see if you have a big fat line like the one in the preceding image.*

And there's more: if you click one of the little nodes on the skeleton, the Bezier bow ties will appear, allowing you to modify the curves with precision and confidence.

There's another application of the Subselect tool that's extremely useful: you can use it to modify shapes that weren't drawn with the Pen tool.

Modifying shapes with the Subselect tool

1. In the boat movie, choose the Subselect tool, and then click any of the smoke clouds.
2. The same skeleton and node structure appears. Click a node, and those familiar bow ties spring into view again:

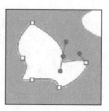

This reveals that all the shapes you've drawn using Flash's drawing tools are composed of Beziers that you can modify. By dragging the bow ties, you can rework shapes:

This tool is very useful for reforming shapes.

Shaping the boat using the Subselect tool

Until now, your boat has been a square mass. It would never carve through the water! It's time to shape the hull.

1. Hide the waves layer from view so you can work with the boat a little more easily.

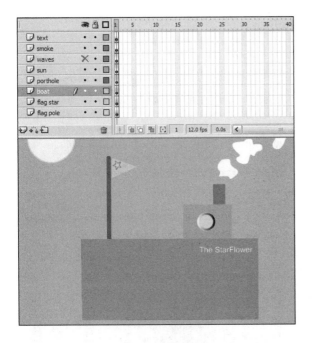

2. Select the Subselect tool and click a corner of the hull. The four corner points of the boat appear.

3. Click and drag the bottom-left point to create a slight angle. Then release the mouse button to apply it.

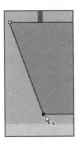

4. Repeat the same process for the bottom right point.

The boat scene is now finished! From here, you can use the tools to add more detail or alter what is already in the scene.

Beziers and animation

One thing about Bezier curves that doesn't become apparent until you play around with them is that they're not just a fancy drawing tool: they can be used to simulate real-world movements much better than standard curves. For example, imagine a tennis ball hitting a net. When the ball makes contact with the net, the ball's weight and momentum will drag the net with it, changing the net's shape. If you draw your net with Beziers, the fine control you have with the bow ties lets you regulate a significant parameter—the *tension* of the net:

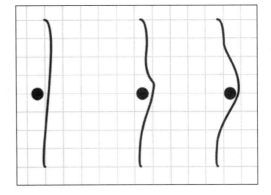

As you'll learn in detail later in this book, these images could be animated with a **shape tween**. The Bezier curve bow ties can be used to set the tension of the net, and therefore show its acceleration. Acceleration is a fundamental attribute of good animation because it's the direct result of forces acting on the shape—which is what animation should try to express. With Beziers you can animate the effects of these forces more easily.

The use of Beziers used for *animation* rather than just for shape creation opens up a whole new facet to expressive animation. If you stop thinking "tennis net" and start thinking "eyebrows and mouths" for example, you can begin to see how these curves could help you animate a face as its expression changes.

In this chapter, you've taken a long look at some of the more important aspects of Flash's integral tools. You haven't covered every single option, but you'll see more as you progress through this book.

Case study

In this exercise, you're going to set up the layout and begin to create the basic interface for your portfolio website. You'll be using this portfolio website throughout the book to implement the ideas we discuss in each chapter, and this will help you see the Flash components you're learning about in context.

Creating background and base elements

Let's start by creating the background for your movie. First, you'll set up your movie's global properties.

1. Open a new Flash document. Open the Document Properties dialog box using Modify ➤ Document and change the dimensions of the movie's stage to 550 (width) × 400 (height) pixels. (It should be this size already, because this is the default.) Change the Title to Floyd Design and in the Description field enter Foundation Flash book example, followed by today's date.

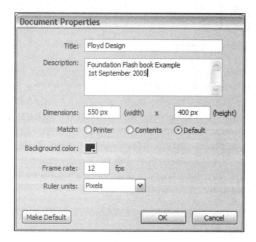

It's always a good idea to date every FLA you create. At the moment, you most likely have fewer than ten FLAs on your hard drive, but after only a few months of web design, you'll have hundreds! Just adding the date to everything will help immensely when it comes time to sift through those files, because it will allow you to track when each FLA was started (the date it was last modified will be the date your operating system gives when you look at the FLA in your file explorer).

2. Select a dark blue color (#003366) for the movie background color and click OK.

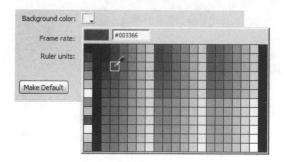

3. Change the name of the movie's default single layer to white rectangle.

4. Before you proceed, save your movie with a suitable name, such as FoundationSite.

5. Use the Rectangle tool with Object Drawing enabled to draw a large white rectangle with a white fill and stroke color roughly in the center of the stage. Don't be too fussy about its location; you'll correctly center it later.

6. Open the Properties panel (Window ➤ Properties ➤ Properties) and select the white rectangle. The Properties panel displays the rectangle's width and height, shown as W and H, respectively. Typing in these text fields will allow you to change the size of the rectangle.

7. Make sure the little padlock icon does not have a line that connects the H and W fields. If it does, click the padlock to make the connecting line go away. Click the W text field (width), type 485, and press *ENTER*. Change the value in the H text field (height) to 300 and press *ENTER* again.

The rectangle changes to the size you specified. If your rectangle is now outside the stage area, drag it back in (using the Selection tool) so that it's roughly in the center again. Specifying a particular size will allow you to work with the same settings I'm using, and it will make the case study creation easier throughout the book.

This will act as your main viewing area or page:

8. Create a new layer called colored rectangles and select the Rectangle tool.

9. Set no stroke color and a fill color of #66CC00. To select this color, click the color picker in the Properties panel, click the text field at the top, and type in #66CC00.

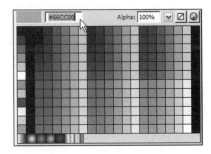

Note that you can also use the color picker in the toolbar to do the same thing.

10. Draw a single tall rectangle and change the size of the shape to a width of 113 and a height of 258 using the Properties panel.

11. With the rectangle still selected, copy and paste it three times. You can copy and paste via the options in the Edit menu or by using the normal *CTRL+C/CTRL+V* keyboard combinations.

> If you're using Windows, using the copy/paste options on the right-click menu might be quicker. To do so, right-click the rectangle and select Copy, and then right-click where you want to paste and select Paste.

When you make your copies, make sure to move each rectangle into its own space, so it doesn't overlap another rectangle. Use the Selection tool to position the copies roughly in their own space within the white rectangle. Don't worry too much about their precise alignment for the moment—you'll place them correctly later.

12. Select each of the rectangles individually and change the fill colors to #99FF00, #FF9933, and #00CC66.

In the final site, these four rectangles will expand to show your four pages.

13. Insert a new layer called logo + text.

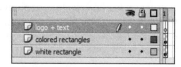

14. With the Text tool, add your name or company name below the white rectangle. Set the font to Verdana, its size to 12, and its color to white. Change the character spacing of the text to 14 and position the text roughly at the bottom-right edge.

15. Zoom in and draw a symbol or icon for your company alongside the text with the Pencil tool. (I've drawn a dog.)

Here's how it looks in context:

16. Create a new layer called buttons. Not surprisingly, this layer will house all your buttons.

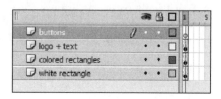

17. On the buttons layer, use the Rectangle tool to draw a small square with a white stroke and fill in the top-left corner.

18. Select the square and resize it to a width and height of 34 pixels using the Properties panel. This will form the basis of your button.

19. To finish the button, draw a smaller red rectangle—30 pixels wide by 22 pixels high—away from the white square.

20. Drag this rectangle into the white square. Leave a bit of white space above it, where you'll put the text later (you can use the arrow keys to fine tune the placement of the red rectangle).

In the next chapter, you'll convert this shape into a navigational button.

That's all for the case study in this chapter. This project might seem simple so far, but as you work through the case study exercises at the end of each chapter, you'll see the concepts and content build bit by bit. This is the way any Flash movie is built: first you have an idea, then you create the building blocks that you need for your movie, and finally you splice them all together.

Summary

In this chapter, you worked through some of the main features of the Tools panel and used different tools to add and amend movie content. You'll continue to do this throughout the book.

You learned that

- Drawn shapes in Flash consist of strokes and fills that can be moved and modified separately. They can also be shapes, Drawing Objects, or groups.

- Flash's drawing tools have modifiers that control how drawn elements look and behave.

- You can use tools (such as the Ink Bottle and Paint Bucket tools) with their modifiers to change the attributes (color, height, etc.) of strokes and fills.

- You can use the Properties panel to change the characteristics of drawn objects.

- You can create text fields and customize them using the Properties panel.

- The Pen tool allows you to draw precise and amendable Bezier curves.

- You can select and alter the curves and lines that make up any drawn shape in Flash with the Subselect tool.

Now that you've seen how to create simple shapes and text in Flash, let's look at how you can convert them into components that you can reuse. These reusable content components are the subject of the next chapter.

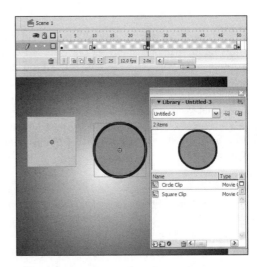

Chapter 3

FLASH SYMBOLS AND LIBRARIES

What we'll cover in this chapter:

- Understanding what symbols are, why they're useful, how to create them, and how to store and reuse movie content elements in the Library:
    - Graphic symbols contain simple moving content and are the cornerstone of cartoon animation in Flash.
    - Button symbols are the easiest method to achieve interactivity.
    - Movie clip symbols are independent, self-contained movie components that free you from the linear tyranny of your movie's main Timeline. They can contain as much interactivity as buttons and are the most powerful of Flash's symbols.

In Macromedia Flash, a **symbol** is a particular kind of movie content component—a piece of self-contained content that you can save and reuse time and time again. Symbols add life and richness to your movies by allowing you to break free of a rigid, static timeline. Now that you know how to get around the stage and main Timeline, and you have a working knowledge of the Tools panel, you can begin to really make Flash come to life.

Symbols are a vital part of making great Flash movies.

Typically, you create symbols when you know that you're going to have particular elements that you'll use repeatedly in a movie or in a number of movies, or when you want to encapsulate a little piece of action or animation and use it independently of what's going on in the rest of the movie. And you can share the saved symbols from one movie with your other movies, too.

Using stored symbols rather than uniquely created content for every element in your movie has at least three advantages. First, symbols allow you to create far more interesting, flexible, and extensible movies. Second, they give you the benefits of mass production and reusable components. Third, symbols help you keep your movie file size small, which in turn keeps end users happy and attentive to your site.

In this chapter, you'll learn about the three symbol types that Flash employs, and you'll create and use an example of each. Here, you'll get a solid grounding in the basics of symbols that will stand you in good stead, and in later chapters you'll examine the more complicated aspects of critical symbols in more detail.

Symbol essentials

A symbol at its most basic level is something in Flash that you can use time and time again. That something could be a simple picture, an interactive button, or even an entire mini-movie that runs within your main movie. You can convert your existing movie content into symbols, or you can create symbols from scratch.

Either way, you save the completed symbol so that you can use it again later.

Symbol Creation

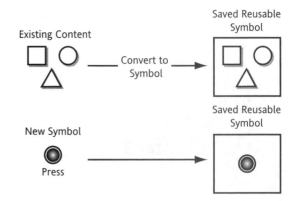

Every time you create a new symbol in Flash, it's added to a library that is attached to your FLA authoring file. The **Library** is where all the reusable symbols are stored for the movie that you're working on.

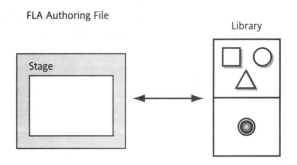

To use one of the saved symbols in your movie, open the Library, select the symbol that you want to add, and drag it onto your stage. The original symbol remains in the Library; however, Flash creates a copy of the stored symbol and renders it on the stage for you. The stored symbol kept in the Library is like a template that Flash uses to create a brand-new copy of the saved symbol. When you create a new, individual copy of a stored symbol on your stage, it's known as an **instance** of that stored symbol.

Each new instance is a unique object—an exact copy of the stored symbol that the instance is based on. There's also a link between the symbol and its instances. If you amend the underlying symbol, the amendments ripple through to the instances, too. However, you can change the properties (tint, size, and so on) of individual instances without affecting the original symbol.

One way of picturing the relationship between the stored symbol and the copy (or copies) of it that you create on the stage is to think about that familiar kitchen tool, the cookie cutter. A cookie cutter is designed to turn out multiple copies of cookies that are the same size and shape—it's essentially a template for mass production of identical objects.

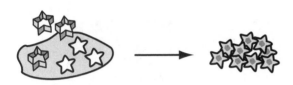

You apply the cookie cutter to cookie dough and produce identical cookies every time. In Flash, the stored symbol is the cookie cutter, and the instance copied onto the stage is the identical individual cookie derived from the cookie cutter. With cookies, you can add toppings to specific instances, and in Flash you can change the characteristics of individual instances via the Properties panel.

> As you'll see later, in Flash, if you change the shape of the cookie cutter (the stored symbol) after baking cookies (instances), *every single cookie will immediately change to the new shape!*

One of the nice things about creating instances of symbols is that you can customize each instance on the stage individually. For example, suppose you need a series of buttons in your movie that the user clicks to navigate through your website. Rather than create the same button 15 times, you can create just one button symbol in your Library and then customize each instance of the button on your main movie stage.

Let's start creating some symbols and see how to implement them in practice.

Symbol types

When you create symbols in Flash, you have three basic types to choose from:

- Graphic symbols
- Button symbols
- Movie clip symbols

Each symbol type has different capabilities and levels of complexity, and your choice of symbol will be based on what you want that symbol to do—that is, how you want it to *behave*. For example, if you just want to reuse a static graphic that's essentially inanimate, the graphic symbol is the best fit. For a symbol that has some animation and maybe some sound, you would choose to create a movie clip symbol. Each of the different symbol types has its own range of possible behaviors, from the simple graphic symbol to the potentially very complex movie clip symbol.

All three symbol types are created by one of two methods. You can either convert an existing drawing or other object (such as a text field) into a symbol, or you can create a new symbol from scratch. You'll use both methods to construct symbols in the following examples.

Let's begin with the simplest kind of symbol: the graphic symbol.

Graphic symbols

Although graphic symbols are not as feature-rich as button or movie clip symbols, they're no less important. They're used for static images throughout your movie, so if you know that you're going to use an object over and over again, and you don't need it to be interactive or animated, a graphic symbol is your best bet.

Let's create a simple graphic symbol now.

Creating a graphic symbol

1. Open Flash and create a new blank movie by clicking the File ➤ New menu option.

2. Select the Text tool from the Tools panel, ensure that you have Static Text selected in the left side of the Properties panel, and click the stage. In the text field that appears, type the words Graphic Symbol. Click the Selection tool so that you can select the text you've just placed on the stage, and then choose the Modify ➤ Convert to Symbol menu option (or press *F8*). The Convert to Symbol dialog box appears.

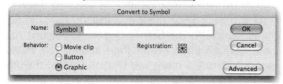

This is where you choose the *type* of symbol you want to create. Notice that Flash labels the categories of symbols using the term Behavior because each type of symbol has its own repertoire of behaviors.

3. If it's not selected already, change the behavior of the symbol to a graphic by clicking the radio button next to the word Graphic.

4. Change the name by deleting Symbol 1 in the Name field and typing Graphic Symbol.

5. Also in this dialog box, you'll see the Registration matrix, a grid composed of nine small squares, one of which is black. You can click any of the squares to define the point that Flash will consider the center of your symbol. If it's not already selected, click the center square because you want the **registration point** to be in the very center of your symbol. Finally, click OK.

Your text field now has a registration point—a small cross—in the center:

So far you've created a new graphic symbol, assigned it a registration point, and given it a symbol name. This is the name that the symbol will be stored under in the Library.

6. Double-click the Graphic Symbol text field. When you do this, Flash opens a separate editing window. You're no longer looking at the main stage—instead, you're in the Edit Symbols window for your graphic symbol. Flash indicates this to you by highlighting the name of your symbol above the Timeline, next to the name of your movie's default first scene:

The blue arrow on the left is Flash's equivalent of the ubiquitous Back button; it gives you a shortcut to move back a level from wherever you are. In your current scene, the Back button will take you to the main Timeline in Scene 1.

When you're editing a symbol, it's very important to realize that you're no longer on the main Timeline; rather, you're inside the symbol you're editing.

> Even though the timeline you see when you're editing a symbol sometimes looks much the same as the main Timeline, it's important to realize it is a different timeline altogether. Perhaps even more important than the differences between the main Timeline and the symbol Timeline are their similarities. The main Timeline and symbol Timeline contain the same basic features: frames, keyframes, and a playhead. The symbol Timeline has its own frames/keyframes, and this Timeline is played through by the symbol's own playhead, which can be doing something totally different from what the main Timeline's playhead is doing.

This symbol was created by converting content using the Modify ➤ Convert to Symbol menu option. However, you can also create a symbol from scratch by choosing the Insert ➤ New Symbol menu option.

When you create a symbol from scratch using Insert ➤ New Symbol, rather than converting existing content, Flash automatically starts **Edit Symbols** mode. The contents of a symbol created in this way aren't modified on the main stage; you can alter the symbol's content only in Edit Symbols mode.

You'll see that in Edit Symbols mode, the Timeline and layer list are displayed. This is very important: it shows you that *each symbol has its own internal layers and Timeline*. If you add extra layers while inside Edit Symbols mode, this would affect only that one symbol, not the entire movie.

> *It can sometimes be a bit confusing to see whether you're in Edit Symbols mode or normal editing mode. The only way to really be sure is to check above the Timeline to see if the symbol name appears there. If it does, you're definitely in Edit Symbols mode, and if it doesn't, you're not. Additionally, creating symbols from scratch in Edit Symbols mode prevents you from seeing the rest of your movie. You're more likely to achieve the continuity you want by designing your symbol on the main stage and converting it after you're satisfied that it fits with the rest of your movie.*
>
> *A quick way to get out of Edit Symbols mode is to double-click a blank area on the current stage with the Selection tool. Flash equates this action with pressing the Back button and will go back to the main Timeline. If Flash is already at the main Timeline, it can go back no farther, so it will stay there. Thus, a quick way to make sure that you're on the main Timeline is to furiously click a blank part of the stage with the Selection tool a few times.*

7. Click the Back button or the Scene 1 button to return to the main Timeline. (These buttons are to the left of your graphic symbol name, just above the main Timeline.) You're now back in normal edit mode, and you're looking at the stage and the main Timeline.

8. Select the text field with the Selection tool and delete it. Your symbol disappears—to see it again, you must open the Library. Flash automatically created a place to store your new symbol in the Library that's associated with this FLA authoring file.

9. Open the Library by using the Window ➤ Library menu option, and take a look at the window that pops up.

10. The entry for your new graphic symbol is in the white box in the lower half of the window. The small icon with the circle, square, and triangle on it next to the name is the identifying tag for a graphic symbol.

11. Double-click the icon next to your new symbol's name in the Library window. This will redisplay Edit Symbols mode, where you can work on the content of your symbol.

12. Back in Edit Symbols mode (you'll see a blank screen containing your graphic symbol with the registration point in the center), select the Text tool from the Tools panel.

13. Using the text properties in the Properties panel, change the symbol's font color. Then click the blue Back arrow or the Scene 1 button to return to the Timeline and normal editing mode.

Although there's no text anywhere on the stage because you deleted it earlier, if you look in the Library and click your graphic symbol, you'll see the changes you made to your symbol in the preview pane of the Library. To put the symbol back on the stage, you can simply click and drag it out to the main stage.

The Library works like a mini file browser. You can use it to find and use symbols, create new symbols, or delete symbols you no longer need.

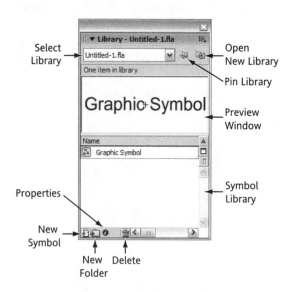

An alternative way to convert an object to a symbol is to use the Library as a shortcut and drag an object into it from the stage. Let's give this a try.

14. On the main Timeline, use the Rectangle tool in Object Drawing mode to draw a square anywhere on the stage.

15. Using the Selection tool, click the square to select the Drawing Object you just created.

16. Drag the square to the lower part of the Library. A small rectangle (or a plus sign, depending on your system) appears at the bottom of your cursor, suggesting that you want to add something to the Library:

When you release the mouse button to confirm, a familiar dialog box appears:

Yes, it's the Convert to Symbol dialog box again.

17. Name your symbol Square Symbol, click the center-left square of the Registration matrix, and give the symbol a Graphic behavior.

Notice that your new symbol has been added to the Library, and you can see a preview of the symbol in the preview pane. The preview also shows the square to the right of the registration point.

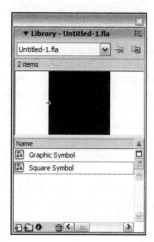

The ability to drag an object into the Library to convert it into a symbol is another one of Flash's shortcuts. There's no standard way to create a symbol—just use the way that best suits your way of working. The useful thing about this particular approach is that you can choose where in the Library you want to put the new symbol by dropping it into a specific folder. You'll look at how to create folders in the Library in a moment.

Before moving on to the next part of this chapter, let's take a quick look at manually adjusting the registration point of a symbol.

18. Double-click your new Square Symbol in the Library so that Flash displays Edit Symbols mode. Select the square with the Selection tool.

19. Choose the Window ➤ Info menu option to bring up the Info panel:

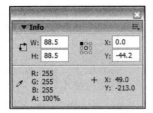

The X and Y boxes on the right are the coordinates that determine the position of the registration point.

20. Enter a value of 14 in the Y box and press ENTER. You'll notice that the registration point is now closer to the top of the square. The registration point is always fixed, so rather than move the registration point, entering a new value into the Info panel actually moves the square relative to the registration point.

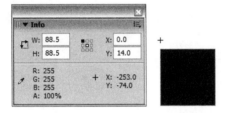

The Info panel provides you with greater flexibility when positioning your graphics in relation to the registration point.

You might be wondering why you have these various options for positioning the registration point of your symbols. Well, if you wanted to make a loading progress bar, you would set the registration point to the center left point, and if you were animating a flower growing from the ground, you would set the registration point to the bottom center of the flower symbol. When you scale a symbol within a tween, the default point the scale works from is the registration point, so it makes sense to make the registration point line up with what you want the symbol to do.

Registration points other than the center point are commonly used in ActionScript scenarios such as building a preloader bar. You'll see how they can have a beneficial effect when animating content a little later in the book.

It's very important to note that the registration point of a symbol (the cross) is very different from the circle (the center point), even though they start off in the same place by default.

The registration point defines the true origin of the symbol—it's "where the symbol is," and the position of the registration point gets exported to the final SWF. The registration point is the same for all instances of a given symbol. If you change the registration point of one instance, the registration point for all instances will also change. When you come to use ActionScript, it's worth remembering that ActionScript uses the registration point, not the center point, to decide where something is on the stage.

The center point is there as a helper during authoring, and it doesn't exist in the final SWF. The center point is the point that many authoring tools (such as the Transform tool) take as their center when you use the authoring tools or motion tweens (which you'll look at in Chapter 6), but it has no relevance in the final SWF. The center point can be different per instance, and this makes it useful when you're using the tools on a per-instance basis.

The differences between the registration point and the center point confuse even longtime users of Flash on occasion and can particularly confuse ActionScript programmers if they're looking at the center point and assuming it's the registration point.

If all this sounds far too confusing, there's a very simple piece of advice that will always make it much clearer: if you ever need to make the registration point and center point occupy different places on a symbol to make the use of a toolbar tool easier, always move the center point back so that it's in the same place as the registration point when you're done. You can move the center point by selecting your instance with the Transform tool and dragging the center point. That way, the registration point and the center point will always be the same, and your worries and confusion melt away!

Let's now go back to the Library window and see what else you can do with it.

Working with the Library

The New Folder button allows you to create folders in your Library as a means of organizing your symbols.

1. In the Library window, click the New Folder button (second from the left at the bottom of the window). A new folder appears in your Library with its name highlighted:

2. Type Circle Folder as the new folder's name and press *ENTER*. Flash automatically sorts the contents of the Library into alphabetical order, so your new folder will jump above the Graphic Symbol.

> *Alphabetical order is great for most things, but sometimes you want the folders to be listed at the top of the Library, followed by symbols (as on many operating systems). An easy way to do this is to put a space in front of all folder names, so "my folder" becomes " my folder".*

3. Click your Graphic Symbol in the Library and drag it onto the Circle Folder icon. As you'd expect from a file browser program, the Graphic Symbol is now located inside the new folder.

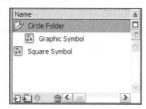

You can tell it's inside the folder by the level of indentation.

4. Double-click the Circle Folder icon to close the folder and hide your symbol. Double-click the Circle Folder icon again to reopen the folder. Double-clicking the name of the folder now will allow you to rename it; if you do this by mistake, just press *ENTER* to leave it as it is.

5. With the folder open, click the Graphic Symbol to highlight it and then click the Properties button in the Library:

This will open the Symbol Properties dialog box, from which you can rename your symbol or change its behavior—that is, its *type*:

6. Click Cancel to close the dialog box without making any changes.

7. Click the Square Symbol to select it. Next, click the Delete button (the trash can icon) in the Library.

Unlike delete operations in other applications (including previous versions of Flash), the current version of Flash does not put up a "Are you sure you want to delete stuff?" confirmation window. The reason for this is that deletions from the Library can be undone with Edit ➤ Undo or *CTRL+Z*.

8. Select the Graphic Symbol and drag it out of the folder so that the Graphic Symbol icon is at the same level of indentation as the Circle Folder icon, and then delete the folder:

It can be difficult to achieve this when there is only one folder in the Library for some versions of Flash, but an easy way to move a symbol outside a folder is to drop it on the Name bar (as just shown).

You'll now be back where you started with just the single original Graphic Symbol in the Library. Next, let's put an *instance* of this symbol on your stage.

9. Click the blue arrow above the Timeline to get out of edit mode and back to the main stage.

10. To get an instance of your symbol onto the stage, drag the name of your symbol out of the Library and release it on the stage. You can also drag the image thumbnail from the top of the Library panel. Don't worry about placing it too precisely—you can always move the symbol around again later.

You now have a single instance of your symbol on the stage.

11. To illustrate how easy it is to reuse symbols, drag another couple of instances of the Graphic Symbol and put them anywhere you like on the stage.

Graphic⊕Symbol

Graphic Symbol

Graphic Symbol

That's a lot easier than making each component separately every time, isn't it? Notice that you've selected all three instances on the stage, and each one displays a little cross, indicating that it's a symbol.

Perhaps the best thing of all here is that even though you now have three images on the stage, they still take up the space of only one picture in the final SWF file. This is because the instances of the symbol on the stage are really just coordinates that tell Flash where to put a copy of the content of the master symbol stored in the Library.

Now you have your instances of the symbol on the stage. What if you decide that you want to change the symbol in the Library that they're based on?

Modifying symbols

When you change the symbol defined and stored in your Library, all the instances of that symbol on your stage will change as well.

Modifying a symbol in the Library

1. Select the Graphic Symbol in the Library, and then double-click its picture in the preview pane. This will open Edit Symbols mode.

2. Select the symbol on the Edit Symbols stage, and then select the Text tool from the Tools panel. In the Properties panel, choose a text color that's obviously different from the original color.

3. Click the Scene 1 tab below the Timeline to return to the main stage. Here you'll notice that all the instances of your graphic symbol have changed to the same color as the master in the Library.

Being able to change all instances of a symbol at once like this is clearly a very powerful feature that makes it easy to redesign and amend significant parts of your movie without having to edit each and every symbol throughout the movie. You can just change the symbol in the Library that the individual instances are based on. However, sometimes you want to change just one instance . . .

Modifying an instance on the stage

1. Select one of your instances on the stage, and then select the Free Transform tool from the toolbar. Your symbol will change to show the Free Transform tool's handles.

Graphic Symbol

Graphic Symbol

Graphic⊕Symbol

2. Roll over the center point (the cursor will show an "o" below the pointer when you're over it), and move the center point so that it's over the "G" in Graphic.

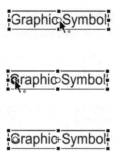

3. Rotate the instance by hovering near the top-right corner of it until you see the rotate cursor as shown, and then rotate the instance by about 30 degrees. Notice that the symbol rotates from the center point at the "G."

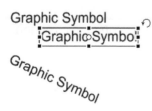

4. Rotate one of the other instances in the same way, but this time don't move the center point first. Notice that the instance rotates from a different center point.

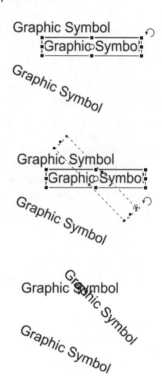

5. Using the Selection tool, select another one of the instances. Using the Properties panel's Color drop-down, select Brightness and change the amount to 75%.

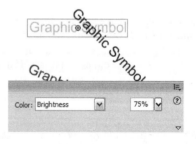

Although you have three instances of the same symbol, each instance is now different in some way—they have different positions and orientations, and one even has a different color!

This technique is rather similar to the way three automobiles can be exactly the same make and model, but each has a different mileage and is a different color. Each car is fundamentally the same as the others, but it's also customized in a number of minor ways. Although these individual differences are small, they can add up to a big difference in appearance—for example, a heavily customized version of the car might even look like a totally new model.

6. Double-click any of the instances to edit it in place. Change the text as you like. Notice that the other instances change to reflect the new text, although they also still reflect the per-instance changes you've made.

Working with multiple Libraries

Often, you'll have more than one Flash document open. Each document will have its own Library. In this section, you'll examine the features of the Library panel that can help you manage this situation.

Working with two Libraries

Before you begin this exercise, close all open FLAs, saving any you wish to keep.

1. Open a new Flash document with File ➤ New. Immediately save this document with File ➤ Save and call the file doc1.

2. Open another new Flash file and follow the same process, calling the second document doc2. You'll have two tabs at the top of your Timeline, one for each file, and you can switch between the two documents by clicking the tabs.

3. In doc1, create a square. Make it a graphic symbol called square by selecting it and pressing *F8*.

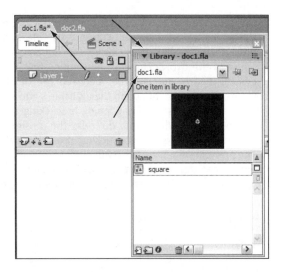

Notice that there are two places on the Library panel telling you that the Library being shown is the one for doc1. This makes three places in all (the tab above the Timeline, the title bar, and the drop-down in the Library panel) telling you that you're working on doc1.

4. Click the tab for doc2. In this document, create a circle, and make it a graphic symbol as you did in step 3. This time, call the symbol circle.

5. Notice that when you clicked the tab for doc2, the Library panel automatically changed its title and drop-down to show the Library for doc2. Click between the two documents, and notice that the Library follows your switches between the documents, updating its titles and the available symbols. You can stop this from happening by clicking the pushpin icon. When you do this, the pushpin changes so it looks as if it's sticking into the panel. The pushpin "pins" the Library in place so that it no longer changes when you change documents. If you now switch between tabs, the Library will not follow your document switches.

Unpin the Library panel. The panel will now follow document changes again.

6. While you're in doc2, use the drop-down on the Library panel to select doc1. You're now in doc1, but looking at doc2's Library.

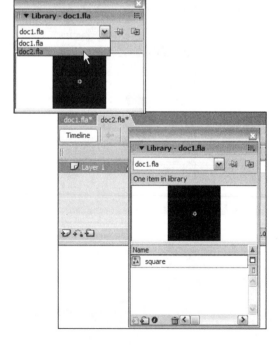

Drag square from the Library onto the stage. You've added a symbol from doc1's Library and placed it on the stage of doc2.

7. To the left of the pushpin icon is the New Library Panel icon. Click this icon.

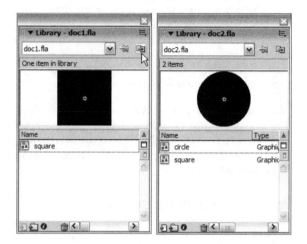

Another Library window appears and shows the current document's Library (doc2). Notice that doc2's Library now contains both the circle and square symbols.

8. As you now have a Library open per document, you might as well pin both panels. Click the pushpin icon for both panels, making sure that you're showing the two different Libraries.

9. Double-click the square symbol in either Library, and then edit it in some way. Notice that the same symbol in the other Library doesn't change. Once you copy a symbol between files by dragging and dropping between multiple Libraries, you're creating a copy between documents, not a linked instance.

You could be forgiven in thinking that multiple Libraries are very confusing, despite their versatility and configurability. I think they can be a blessing in disguise, and I recommend that you do the following:

- If you have only one Library panel open, unpin it. This way, your one open Library will always change to reflect the current document.

■ Keep multiple Library windows open only as long as you need them (i.e., because you want to copy symbols between open documents). If you no longer need to have multiple Library panels open (i.e., you've finished your copying), close the Library panels until you only have one left, and then unpin and leave open the one remaining Library panel. This brings you nicely back to the first bullet point, which is the preferred way of leaving the Library panel.

Let's now experiment with the second, slightly more complex type of symbol: the button symbol.

Button symbols

Buttons are essential features of any interactive website, and they're the key to any good menu or site navigation interface. Why? Because you're used to clicking buttons and having them do things for you—it's almost an unconscious action. Using buttons is such an obvious thing that you're often unaware you're doing it when you're interacting with a website or software application. However, if you ever go to a site whose navigation architecture doesn't provide you with buttons, you'll quickly become aware of just how vital they are.

It's amazingly easy to create buttons in Flash and include them in your movies, and they're one of the components that take Flash from being a great animation package to being a web application development tool. Flash buttons are important because they take you into the world of true interactivity, where your site visitors can control their experience. Whether it's jumping from movie to movie or kicking off a series of complex actions, buttons can be the way in. In Flash, button symbols embody the behaviors that open up the interactive world.

To get you started, you'll build a simple button and go through the button's basic features and capabilities. Later in the book, you'll do even more interesting and important things with buttons.

Creating a button symbol

Let's create that button symbol. First, you need a shape to convert to a symbol.

1. In a new Flash document, select the Oval tool in Object Drawing mode and draw a circle with a stroke and fill of your choice. To adjust the properties of the circle, select it with the Selection tool and go to the Properties panel. You'll see the circle's dimensions in the W and H boxes in the bottom half of the Properties panel. If you can't see the bottom half of the Properties panel, click the arrow on the bottom-right corner of the Properties panel to extend it. I've made my circle 120 pixels across to create a big, hefty button:

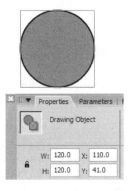

2. Select the circle and change it into a symbol, either by using the Modify ➤ Convert to Symbol menu option or by pressing the *F8* shortcut.

3. In the Convert to Symbol dialog box, choose the Button behavior type. Name your button Button Symbol, give it a central registration point, and click OK.

You should notice two things: the new symbol appears in your Library and, if you bring up the Properties panel, the symbol's name is displayed next to an icon with a pointing finger over a rectangle—this is the icon for a button symbol.

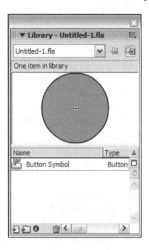

4. Double-click the instance of Button Symbol on the stage to open Edit Symbols mode again.

> Editing a symbol by double-clicking its instance on the stage sends Flash into Edit in Place mode. This mode is particularly useful for changing a symbol when you need to view it in relation to other symbols on the stage.

5. You may have noticed that your Timeline has changed:

Whenever you create or edit a button symbol, you'll see this *button-specific* style of Timeline. This Timeline is visible only in Edit Symbols mode, and every button symbol has this same kind of special internal Timeline. This Timeline controls how the button will behave when you interact with it.

Every button Timeline has only four frames, each of which controls a different aspect of the button's behavior. The names above the four frames—Up, Over, Down, and Hit—refer to the four possible conditions that a button can be in. These conditions are called **button states**. Unlike normal Timelines, a button Timeline will only ever use the four frames shown. Although you're allowed to add new frames after the fourth frame (Hit), the button symbol will never use them, so it's a bit of a wasted exercise! (You can, of course, add additional layers to a button's Timeline.)

Button states

The states of a button are defined in the four frames of the button's Timeline, as described in the following list. Each frame describes what the button will look like and what it will do when the button is in that state.

- **Up**: This is how the button looks in its static state when it's in the movie interface waiting for a user to interact with it.

- **Over**: This is what the button will look like when the user runs his mouse over it.

- **Down**: This is what the button will look like when the user clicks it.

- **Hit**: This is a special state that you can't see in your finished movie. The Hit state is the part of the button that is clickable. Think of it as a target for the mouse—hitting this target will make the button work. Make sure that whatever part of the button you want people to be able to click is defined in the Hit state. It doesn't have to be pretty, as users will never actually see the Hit state graphic, but it's important to clearly define the Hit state.

Let's see how these states work by defining them for your circular button symbol.

Making your button work

At the moment, your button is just a single-state, lifeless circle that might as well be a static graphic symbol. What your button needs is that extra something that makes a button a button: interactivity. You'll define this interactivity in the four frames of the button's Timeline.

Notice that only one of the frames on the button's Timeline is actually a *keyframe* (i.e., the first frame, which represents the button's Up state). The other three frames are currently blank:

This is because Flash assumes that you want to display the circle you drew when the button is in its Up state. You can edit this keyframe and change the image that's displayed if you want to.

To create the other three states for the button, you first need to convert the three blank frames in the Timeline into keyframes. Remember, a keyframe is what defines a significant change to a piece of Flash content. By defining these keyframes and their content, you're telling Flash how you want your button to behave.

1. Click each of the three blank frames individually in the button's Timeline and press *F6* to insert a keyframe. You now have a full Timeline:

2. Click the Over state in the Timeline. Click the circle on the stage.

3. Select a fill color from the Properties panel (or from the Tools panel) that's different from the original button symbol color. The color of your button automatically changes to reflect your new choice.

4. Select the Down state keyframe in the Timeline and select the circle on the stage. Change the circle's fill color to another color in the same way. Leave the Hit state as it is for now.

5. Test your movie by using the Control ➤ Test Movie menu option or by pressing *CTRL+ENTER* (*CMD+ENTER* on the Mac). This opens a new window that displays what your finished movie will look like when it's rendered in the web browser.

6. Move your mouse over the button and it changes to the color you defined for the Over state.

7. Click the button. While you hold the mouse button down, the button displays the color defined in the Down state keyframe.

You've just created your first button and taken your first steps toward interactivity. It was pretty easy, wasn't it? But remember, what you're learning here about button states is the basic foundation on which you can build an infinitely complex universe of interactivity.

8. Close the Test Movie window to display Edit in Place mode.

At the moment, you haven't defined a Hit state for your button; Flash is currently using the image from the Up keyframe to define the Hit state (because you copied the Up state to the Over, Down, and Hit states in step 1). Let's be more explicit.

9. Click the Hit state keyframe on the Timeline and use the Rectangle tool to draw a big rectangle (any color you like) around your button.

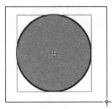

10. Open the Test Movie window again. This time, even though everything looks the same, when you run the mouse over your button you'll see it change color before you get to the actual button itself.

This is because you defined the Hit state (which is invisible to the user) as a larger area than the (visible) button. You may be wondering why you would ever want to do this. Normally you wouldn't, but there is one case where this technique is incredibly useful—when you want to use an irregular button shape that contains gaps, as you'll see in the next exercise.

11. Either by undoing your previous operations or by deleting the rectangle and drawing a circle, replace your rectangular hit area with the previous circular one.

Making buttons from irregular shapes

1. Select each keyframe of your button symbol in turn. For each circle, select the Modify ➤ Break Apart menu option to break the Drawing Object into a fill and stroke. With the Selection tool, click the fill to select it and press *DELETE*. You should now be left with a button that consists of a hollow circle.

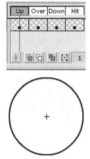

2. Test the movie again. This time when you move your mouse over the button, nothing will happen. It may flicker on and off when you go over the stroke, and this gives you a clue to what is happening. The Hit state of the button is defined as the stroke only, so the area within the button is *not* clickable. This makes your hollow button very user-unfriendly—nobody would be able to use it! This is where the Hit state comes in handy.

3. Go back to Edit Symbols mode and click the Hit state keyframe. Using the Paint Bucket tool, fill the stroke with a color of your choice.

4. Test your movie again. As your mouse moves over the button, the button will work because there is now a solid hit area inside the button, which means that the whole of the inner area of the button is defined as the hit area.

Previous versions of Flash required that you use a solid hit area for text fields, because in those versions, only the actual letters of the text would be clickable if you used the text field as the hit area. In Flash 8, the text field box is the hit area, so you're OK. However, it may be a good idea to always use a solid rectangle for your button hit area if you're using text as the Up, Over, *and* Down *states, if only because you may need to make your site backward compatible with previous versions of Flash. Clients are notorious for telling you that you can design a site for the current version of the Flash Player, but then deciding against it because the site failed to work on the boss's five-year-old desktop, and he wants answers!*

5. Close the Test Movie window, and then click the Scene 1 tab to return to the main stage.

There's an easy way to see and edit all the symbols in your movie. There are two buttons above the Timeline on the right:

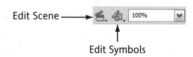

If you click the Edit Symbol button, a drop-down menu will appear with a list of all the symbols available to you in your movie's Library:

The list will show Library folders as submenus. For example, if you were to place all your symbols in three Library folders called animation stuff, content, and interface stuff, your list would contain three submenus, each corresponding to one of the folders:

When you click one of the named symbols, Edit Symbols mode for that symbol opens. Try it with the symbols in the current Library (or quickly make some up in a new FLA and see). You can go back to the main stage by either clicking the Scene 1 tab as you've done before or clicking the Edit Scene button and then selecting Scene 1 from the menu that pops up.

If you look at the Properties panel when you're in Edit Symbols mode, you'll see options to add sound and script to your creations on the right. You'll look at this later in the book.

Next, though, let's examine the third type of symbol in Flash: the movie clip symbol. You'll use movie clips more and more as you progress through the book.

Movie clip symbols

The movie clip symbol is the third and final member of the Flash symbols set. Movie clip symbols—usually referred to as **movie clips** or simply **clips**—are vitally important components in Flash movies. The simplest explanation of movie clips is that they are a movie within a movie. You can use them to create entirely self-contained pieces of action that you want to run independently of the rest of the things on the main Timeline. Movie clips can have multiple layers just like the main Timeline, and they can contain many graphic, animation, and sound components. An example of a typical movie clip would be a clip that encapsulated a logo with some background music. You can have the music playing and the logo fading in and out repeatedly throughout your whole main movie while other action changes around it.

> *Like the button symbol, the movie clip symbol and the graphic symbol have their own internal Timelines. However, a movie clip symbol's or graphic symbol's Timeline isn't limited to the four standard frames. As you progress through this book, you'll find that these other two symbols are extremely useful for creating complex animations. The movie clip symbol really comes into its own when you add ActionScript, because you can control a movie clip's Timeline with code, and this allows you to create animation that changes depending on what the user does.*

Movie clips can be very complicated, containing all manner of actions and animations. In this section, I'll just introduce the basics of what movie clips are and how to use them.

Creating a movie clip symbol

1. You need an uncluttered stage, so close the current Flash document and create a new one.

2. On the main stage, use the Rectangle tool in Object Drawing mode and draw a square (any color you like). Select the square and convert it to a symbol. Make sure the symbol's behavior is set to Movie clip and its registration point is at the center. Name the new symbol Square Clip.

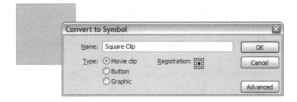

3. Double-click the square with the Selection tool to open *Edit Symbols* mode.

Notice the Timeline inside your new movie clip. This Timeline works like the one above the stage in the main movie. The difference is that your movie clip symbol's Timeline applies only to what happens inside the symbol itself. Any action and animation you create using this Timeline will be encapsulated inside this movie clip. Anything you can do in your main movie, you can do inside a movie clip. That means you can create completely self-contained units of movie content that you can add to your main movie by dragging the movie clip symbol onto the main stage. Let's make a quick shape tween as an example.

4. Still inside your new movie clip, click frame 20 and press *F6* to insert a keyframe.

5. Click outside the square in frame 20 to deselect it, and use the Selection tool to pull in the sides and make an irregular shape:

Now that you have two keyframes with distinct content in them, let's animate the shape tween.

6. Click frame 1 and go to the Properties panel. Select Shape from the Tween drop-down menu to create a shape tween between the two keyframes (just as you did with your mushroom movie in Chapter 1).

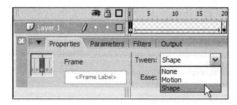

7. Click the Scene 1 icon above the Timeline to get back to the main stage.

8. Open your Library if it's not already displayed. It contains your Square Clip. The blue sunburst next

to the symbol's name is the icon that identifies movie clip symbols.

9. Click the icon for the Square Clip. There are two controls at the top right of the preview pane:

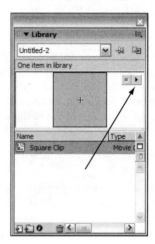

10. These two controls, which may remind you of the Play and Pause buttons on a DVD or CD player, are used to preview your movie clip inside the Library window. (These controls are also available when you select a button symbol in the Library.) If you click the Play button, your movie clip will play in the preview pane. You can use the Stop control to halt playback.

11. Drag a couple of copies of your Square Clip from the Library onto the stage.

12. Press *ENTER* to preview your movie. Nothing happens. This is because movie clips aren't rendered in preview mode.

If you want to see your movie clips play, you have to use the Control ➤ Test Movie (*CTRL+ENTER*) menu option. Alternatively, you can publish your movie by pressing *F12*. If you do this, you'll see your animations. Movie clips can do much more than this, but you'll have to wait until you read the later chapters to find out just how powerful they really are.

13. Save your movie as `movieclip.fla`.

14. Close the `movieclip.fla` movie.

It's probably worth mentioning here that graphic symbols have similar functionality to movie clips. The main difference is that movie clips can be scripted (i.e., they can be controlled via ActionScript), whereas graphic symbols cannot. The file sizes of graphic symbols are slightly smaller than those of movie clips, so if you want just a symbol with a simple tween, it's probably worth using a graphic symbol.

Another good thing about graphic symbols is that their tween animations *are* shown if you press ENTER or drag the playhead around the main Timeline (a technique known as **scrubbing** in animator circles). Many animators who use ActionScript-free tween-based animation throughout their presentations swear by graphic symbols over movie clips. See the animations of Adam Phillips (www.biteycastle.com) for several examples from an animator who swears by graphic symbols because of their ease of use for nonscripted animation.

Movie clips and the main Timeline

When you drag an instance of a movie clip symbol onto your stage, you bring with it all the action you've added to the movie clip's Timeline. When Flash finds the instance of the symbol in a keyframe on the main Timeline, it digs down into the symbol and plays the content that it finds encapsulated in the symbol's internal Timeline. Simultaneously, Flash continues along the main movie's Timeline, rendering any content that it finds there. In this context, you can think of movie clips as separate loops that start and then run their course while the main movie's playhead continues along the main Timeline. Your movie clip is still integrated with the main movie, though—it shares the host movie's frame rate and background color, for example.

Another way of thinking about movie clips is that they're the "children" of the main movie. The main "parent" Timeline plays in sequence, and when it comes across a movie clip symbol in a keyframe, it spawns a movie clip. After Flash has "given life" to the movie clip, that movie clip has an independent life of its own while the main Timeline continues separately.

Imagine a movie where you create a static background layer (a gradient) that lasts for 50 frames:

When you test your movie, you see the static image displayed for 50 frames, and then the movie loops and starts again. Now suppose that you create a keyframe at frame 10 and drag a morphing square movie clip from your Library into it. Next, you could add a morphing circle movie clip in a new keyframe at frame 25:

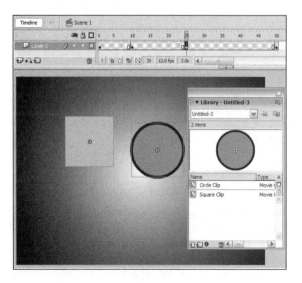

When you test your movie, you'll find that the static background will appear for a few frames, and when the playhead hits the keyframe at frame 10, the morphing square movie clip is triggered. The main movie playhead will continue along the main Timeline until it encounters the morphing circle at frame 25, at which point it will start that movie clip before continuing to display the static background until frame 50—the end of the movie. It's very important to remember that launching these movie clips doesn't pause or stop the playback of the main Timeline; all three playback elements (the main Timeline, plus the two internal movie clip Timelines) play simultaneously.

Morphing Square Movie Clip in Frame 10

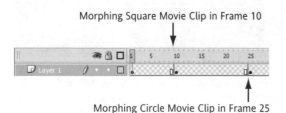

Morphing Circle Movie Clip in Frame 25

A movie clip has a mind of its own; that is, its behavior is embedded in its internal Timeline. However, the parent Timeline can have the authority to tell the child movie clip what to do. It can use ActionScript commands to tell the movie clip to stop, start, change position, and so on. You'll see this in practice after you've learned some ActionScript.

So far, you've dealt exclusively with symbols in the Library that are attached to the specific movie that you've been working on. But you can also reuse symbols from other movies' Libraries.

Sharing symbols

An extremely useful feature in Flash is the ability to import symbols from other movies' Libraries. This is particularly useful for projects in which you might be working on a number of Flash movies at the same time and want to share the symbols from one movie to the next. You might also consider creating a Library that stores commonly used symbols for a number of Flash movies.

One other benefit of sharing symbols is that you can also share fonts. If you're working on a Flash presentation with someone who has fonts that you don't have, you can share your partner's font symbols.

Let's start by seeing how to share symbols, and then you'll move on to learn how to share fonts.

Using symbols from other movies

1. Select File ➤ Close All to close all the other Flash documents that are currently open. When you're prompted to save the various documents, save whichever ones you want. Closing all the other documents will help you focus a little more in this section.

2. Create a new Flash document from the startup screen's Create New ➤ Flash Document option or the File ➤ New menu option followed by Flash Document.

3. Open the new movie's Library window. As you might expect, it's currently an empty Library:

4. Make sure you don't still have movieclip.fla open; close it if you do. Go to the File menu and choose the Import ➤ Open External Library option.

5. In the resulting dialog box, navigate to the folder where you stored your movieclip.fla file and select it.

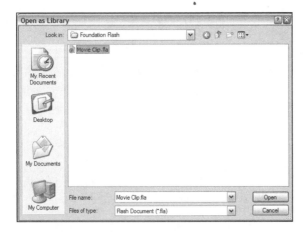

6. Click the Open button, and a new Library window containing the symbols in the `movieclip.fla` file will appear.

You now have the symbol from the first movie you made available to use in your new movie, in much the same way that you were able to drag symbols from multiple Libraries earlier. Notice this time, though, that the Library window is grayed out and has no drop-down menu at the top. It's also missing the pushpin and Open New Library icons. This is because the FLA corresponding to this Library isn't open.

You can transfer the Square Clip symbol into the current FLA by dragging it onto the stage or into the Library for the current FLA (much like you did with multiple Libraries). When you do either, the symbol will

now appear in the current FLA's Library. This means that you can build up a collection of common symbols and share them between different movies—another labor-saving device from Flash! Flash also includes a feature you can use to share Libraries across networks and even over the Web, but coverage of this feature is beyond the scope of this book.

Sharing fonts over Flash movies

Font symbols allow users to share fonts through different Flash files. They're very useful when working with other people (such as a client) who might have a set of fonts different from the set you have. Let's see how to share and retrieve fonts.

1. Open a new Flash document.

2. Open the Library (Window ➤ Library) and select New Font from the Library options drop-down menu.

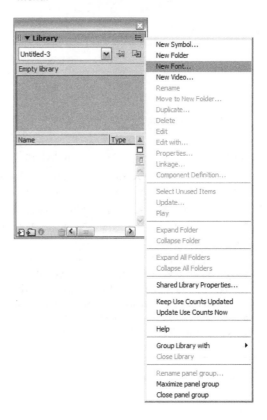

3. In the dialog box that appears, enter Midnight Train in the Name field and select Georgia (or a font of your choice if you don't have Georgia) from the Font drop-down. Click OK.

A font symbol will appear in your Library:

4. Save the movie as font_share.fla and close it.

5. Open a new Flash document (yes, another!) and select File ➤ Import ➤ Open External Library.

6. Select the font_share.fla file. After you confirm this, the Library of the font_share.fla file will open.

7. Drag the Midnight Train font symbol onto the stage. When you drop the symbol, you'll see no change to the stage. The font dubbed Midnight Train will now be available on the Font drop-down menu, suffixed with an asterisk. You can see this by selecting the Text tool and looking at the Font drop-down.

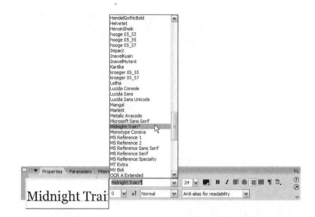

This new font can now be used just like any other font.

8. After you're done with this file, close it.

> *You have to select a* Name *field that is different from the font name (i.e., you should not make the* Name *field* Georgia *in step 2 of this exercise). If you make the name in the* Name *field the same as the font name, Flash will accept the name, but the font symbol will most likely not work!*

Finally in this chapter, let's work on your case study project and implement some of the concepts just discussed.

Case study

In this chapter's case study segment, you'll create symbols for your project. You'll make your button into a symbol, and then you'll start to build up your site's navigation using multiple copies of that symbol, demonstrating the reusability and therefore the power of symbols.

Creating symbols

1. Open the case study movie you worked on at the end of the previous chapter.

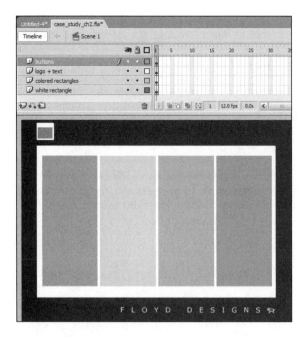

At this point, your interface objects should be sitting on their separate layers. You need to convert some of your objects into symbols.

2. Select the shape in the top-left corner (you need to select both the red square and the white square behind it) and select Modify ➤ Convert to Symbol. In the dialog box that appears, name the symbol generic button, and give it a center registration point and a Button behavior.

3. Double-click the button on the stage to edit it. This will allow you to edit the symbol within the context of the rest of the document.

You might notice that the other elements of the stage are washed out; this is to help you to concentrate on your active symbol alone. This mode of editing symbols is called Edit in Place.

4. Select the Over state and insert a keyframe (Insert ➤ Timeline ➤ Keyframe or *F6*).

5. On the Over state, use the Paint Bucket tool to change the red square to green.

6. Still in the Over state, use the Line tool to draw a white line from the bottom of the shape up to the large white rectangle. Use the Properties panel to set a stroke thickness of 3.

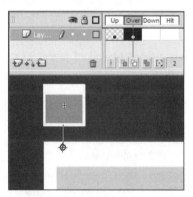

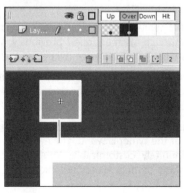

7. Return to the main stage and drag three copies of the generic button symbol onto the stage. Place these next to the first button.

8. Test the movie using Control ➤ Test Movie. Hover the mouse pointer over the buttons to see the red change to green and the added white line.

9. Select the name/company text and your representative icon using the Selection tool and convert them to a single graphic symbol called logo.

Remember, to select more than one symbol or item, hold down the SHIFT key when making subsequent selections.

---

10. Save your Flash document and close it.

Summary

In this chapter, you took a preliminary look at the nature, creation, and storage of symbols in Flash. You learned that

- Symbols are self-contained pieces of movie content that you can create once and then use many times in your movies.

- An instance is a copy of a symbol on the stage.

- Symbols are stored in the Library, and you can organize the Library and use it to share symbols between different movies.

- Symbols have their own internal Timeline, which allows them to work independently from the main movie's Timeline.

- Graphic symbols are typically used for still graphics, although, as mentioned previously, some animators prefer them over movie clips.

- Button symbols have a standard four-frame internal Timeline. This Timeline includes the different button states.

- Movie clip symbols are the multitalented superstars of the symbols world. Their internal Timelines are infinitely customizable. You can embed the same kind of multilayered graphics and sound content in movie clip symbols that you can on the movie's main Timeline. It's also possible to have graphic and button symbols as well as other movie clips within a movie clip symbol.

There are lots of premade buttons and other symbols already stored in Flash. You can access them via the Window ➤ Common Libraries menu option. Open some examples and check out their construction in Edit Symbols mode.

You'll see much more about symbols and their uses later in this book. In the next chapter, you'll examine the features that Flash gives you to help manage and arrange multiple pieces of content on the stage.

Chapter 4

MANAGING CONTENT

What we'll cover in this chapter:

- Assembling and placing content precisely on the (three-dimensional) Flash stage
- Grouping objects for consistency and convenience
- Using grids, rulers, guides, and alignment tools to place objects exactly where you want them
- Transforming objects with control and confidence
- Stacking multiple objects inside a layer
- Splitting content with Distribute to Layers
- Managing layers with folders
- Tracking your actions with the History panel

In this chapter, you'll examine the tools and facilities that Macromedia Flash gives you for aligning and arranging objects on the stage. In doing so, you'll be working on the stage in *three dimensions*: width, height, and depth.

When you create movies that have only a couple of visual components, arrangement and alignment aren't really issues, but if you build larger-scale movies or if you want to make your movies look more elegant, you need to ensure that the components in your movie are effectively and harmoniously set up. Additionally, when your movies begin growing in size and complexity, you need ways to group content elements together so that they're easier to maintain and amend. Flash provides you with plenty of tools for these tasks, and getting a handle on these tools will save you a lot of pain and frustration.

Let's begin by seeing how Flash can ease the burden of moving elements around and editing them while maintaining proportions and relative positions.

Grouped objects

You've already seen that grouping objects or creating Drawing Objects can help prevent you from cutting objects in half or picking up just the fill. Although grouped objects and Drawing Objects are similar in many ways, grouped objects have one big advantage over Drawing Objects: a Drawing Object can contain only raw shapes (strokes and fills), whereas a grouped object can contain *anything*.

In the following exercises, you'll look more closely at grouping objects and the benefits it brings. You can think of grouping as an easy way to organize and manipulate multiple objects.

Grouping multiple objects

1. Open a new Flash document by choosing File ➤ New and selecting Flash Document.

2. Using the Rectangle tool in Object Drawing mode, draw a square shape anywhere on your stage. Then draw a smaller circle on a nearby part of the stage with the Oval tool.

3. Use the Selection tool to drag a box (or, to use the proper term, a **marquee**) around both objects to select them, and then group them using the Modify ➤ Group menu option (CTRL+G on Windows; CMD+G on the Mac). Now when you move one of the objects, the other will move with it, staying in exactly the same position relative to the other object.

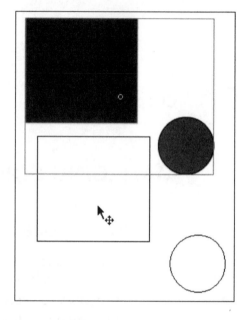

This is clearly a useful feature when you're dealing with large numbers of objects and you don't want to move them around individually by hand, and it will help you maintain the design and look of your movie when you're amending it.

You can group lines, fills, buttons, graphics, movie clips, and text—pretty much anything you can put on the movie stage. A sure way to tell whether an object is part of a group is that a thin colored highlighting line appears around the outer edges of grouped objects. You can change your default highlight color using the Edit ➤ Preferences menu option (Flash Professional ➤ Preferences on the Mac) and amending the Highlight color option on the General page.

It's also extremely easy to ungroup objects in Flash.

4. Click your grouped shapes with the Selection tool to select them, and use the Modify ➤ Ungroup menu option (*Shift+Ctrl+G* on Windows; *Shift+Cmd+G* on the Mac). They will be returned to two distinct Drawing Objects.

5. Use the Line tool and unselect Object Drawing mode. Draw a triangle on your stage, and fill it with color.

6. Drag a box around all three of your objects with the Selection tool and group them together.

It would be a laborious process if every time you wanted to edit a specific line or fill within a group, you had to ungroup it, edit it, and then group it again. Flash gets around this by having an **Edit Group** mode, which you'll learn how to use in the next exercise. This mode is used to add, subtract, or change elements in groups.

Editing a group of objects

1. To enter Edit Group mode, simply double-click your group or select the group on the stage, and use the Edit ➤ Edit Selected menu option.

When you're in Edit Group mode, notice that something has changed below your Timeline. In the same place where the symbol name is displayed in Edit Symbols mode, it now says Group with an icon next to it similar to that of a graphic symbol.

This is Flash's visual cue to you that you're currently editing a group of objects. Another visual cue is that when you're in Edit Group mode, as with Edit in Place mode when you're editing symbols, all the objects on the stage apart from the group you're editing will be dimmed and inaccessible.

2. In Edit Group mode, change the shape of your rectangle using the Selection tool and move it to somewhere else on the stage.

Note that groups don't have a Timeline, even though when you're in Edit Group mode, they may look like they do (because the Timeline is still shown). The Timeline you see is the Timeline the group is on, not the group's own Timeline.

3. Return to the main stage by using the same method as you would from Edit Symbols mode: click the Scene 1 button or the Back button to the left of the Scene icon, or simply double-click on an empty area of the stage with the Selection tool.

Back on the main stage, everything is still grouped together and moves as one object, but your triangle shape is now happily sitting in its new position in the group.

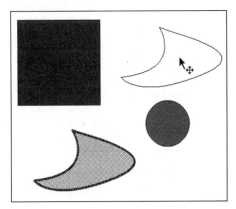

99

4. Select your group with the Selection tool and select Edit ➤ Duplicate. You'll now have two versions of the group on the stage. Move the copy so that it's no longer over the top of the original, and then double-click the copy to edit it. Change the circle in some noticeable way, and then return to the main stage. Notice that only the copy has changed. A copy of a group isn't an instance, and the changes you make to a shape in one group won't always alter contents in other groups. Further, because groups aren't instances, every time you duplicate a group, you're creating a totally new group, and this will use up more memory than if you copied a symbol.

5. Delete the copy by selecting it and pressing the *DELETE* key on your keyboard.

6. Save your file as `group.fla` and then close it. You'll use it later in this chapter.

There's no limit to the number of groups you can have in Flash. In fact, you can have symbols within groups, groups within groups, and even groups within symbols within groups—the possibilities are endless. It's usually best to avoid nested groups, though—if you require multiple group levels, you're usually better off creating symbols than groups. This is because symbols are more manageable—you have more panels for keeping track of symbols (particularly the Library), and you have more control of symbols than you do groups when you come to use ActionScript.

Symbols within symbols

Nested symbols are easily manageable from within the Flash interface.

1. Open a new Flash document by selecting File ➤ New, and select Flash Document on the resulting screen. Select the Line tool and deselect Object Drawing mode. Set the stroke width to 4 in the Properties panel. Draw a rough sketch of the body of a car on the stage.

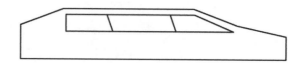

2. Fill the body of your car using the Paint Bucket tool, selecting your favorite color from the Color palette in the Properties panel. If your car doesn't seem to want to fill with color, you may need to zoom in to the corners and make sure there are no gaps. Alternatively, you can click the Gap Size icon in the Paint Bucket options and set it to Close Large Gaps.

3. Drag out a box around the car with the Selection tool and select Modify ➤ Convert to Symbol (or press *F8*) to make the car graphic a symbol. Name the new symbol car, select Movie Clip as its behavior, and give it a central registration point.

4. Double-click the car symbol in the Library to enter Edit Symbols mode. Select the car again by using the Selection tool, as you did in the last step. Select the Modify ➤ Combine Objects ➤ Union menu option to make the shapes inside the movie clip a Drawing Object.

You might be wondering why it wouldn't be better to group the car than to make it a Drawing Object. A Drawing Object is better when you want to work only with raw shapes (i.e., fills and strokes), because the fills and strokes remain directly editable. In a group, you'd have to use Edit in Place mode to edit the fills and strokes.

When you look at your beautiful automobile, you might notice something key missing from it, something vital to making that baby move—your car has no wheels! Time to put it right.

5. While still in the car movie clip, rename the current existing layer car and lock it to prevent any changes. This will keep your car from getting scratched while you do other things to it.

6. Create a new layer by clicking the Insert Layer button.

7. Double-click the new layer name and rename it wheels, because that's what your car needs more than a flame paint job right now. If this layer isn't the topmost layer already, drag-drop it so that it is.

8. On the wheels layer, use the Circle tool with Object Drawing selected to draw a circle near the rear of the car—holding down the *SHIFT* key will keep it in proportion.

9. When you're happy with your circle, select and make it into a symbol with the Modify ➤ Convert to Symbol menu option (or press *F8*).

10. Make it a graphic symbol with the name static wheel and a central registration point.

At this point, your car is a little more able, but it's still more suited to being towed to an auto shop than speeding down the highway. Let's give this baby a much-needed helping hand.

11. Go to your Library (if it's not open, open it using Window ➤ Library) and drag an instance of the static wheel symbol onto the stage. Use the Selection tool to select the new wheel and position it at the front of the car, finally making it stable.

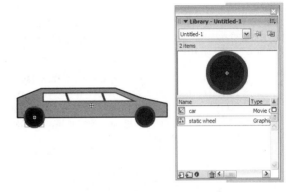

Now, if you were to animate your wheels, you'd have no idea if they were rotating or not. Let's give them something to show a little rotation.

12. Double-click either of the wheels to edit the static wheel symbol.

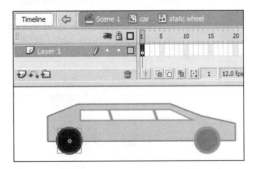

Remember, when you double-click any symbol within another symbol, you're taken to the Edit Symbols mode—inside the previous symbol. You can tell you've gone one level deeper by looking at the icons above the Timeline.

101

To return to the previous symbol, click the symbol name to the left of the one you're currently in, use the Back button, or double-click an empty area on the stage (this includes any ghosted-out area because ghosted areas aren't in the *current* Timeline). This can be a bit confusing at times, but as long as you keep an eye on the icons above the Timeline, you should be able to work out where you are. If in doubt, return to the main stage and work your way through your nested symbols to reach the one you want.

13. In the static wheel edit mode, create a new layer above the current one and select it so you can work on it. Use the Line tool in Object Drawing mode to draw a contrasting horizontal line across the center of the wheel.

Since the other wheel is an instance of the wheel you're currently editing, you'll see it update to show the same line across it. This is one reason why you made your wheels into symbols and not groups.

The line will be used to show the wheels of the car in motion. The next bit may seem a little tricky at first, but will be explained fully in a later chapter—so bear with it for now.

14. Click the Back button to return to the car-editing mode.

15. Select the rear wheel and choose the Modify ➤ Convert to Symbol menu option (or press F8). Name it animated wheel, with movie clip behavior and a central registration point.

This will place your original static wheel, which is already a graphic symbol, within the Timeline of a movie clip called animated wheel. You've nested the static wheel graphic symbol within the animated wheel movie clip symbol. Within this movie clip you'll animate the wheel a little.

16. Double-click the animated wheel on the stage to edit it. The bar above the Timeline will look like the following:

Finally, let's animate your wheel.

17. Click Frame 20 of the Timeline and press *F6* to insert a keyframe.

This time you'll use motion tweening to make the wheel rotate a little (there will be more on motion tweening in Chapter 6).

18. Click Frame 1 and make sure that the Properties tab on the Properties panel is visible (use the Window ➤ Properties ➤ Properties menu option if it's hidden, or use *CTRL/CMD+F3*). In the Properties panel, select Motion from the Tween drop-down menu.

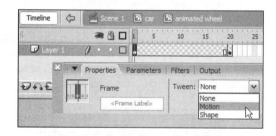

The frames in the Timeline should have turned a light blue color and there should be an arrow extending from Frame 1 to Frame 20.

19. In the Properties panel again, select CW from the Rotate drop-down menu. (If you can't see the Rotate drop-down menu, click the white triangle in the lower-right corner of the Properties panel.)

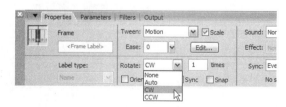

20. In the box to the right of the Rotate drop-down menu (its called the Rotation count), type 3.

This will set the wheel to rotate 3 times in a clockwise direction over the designated 20 frames. (Remember, I'll explain motion tweens in detail a little later in the book).

21. Test the movie with the Control ➤ Test Movie menu option.

If all went well, the left wheel should be turning—the car is almost moving! To make the other wheel move, you need to replace the static wheel graphic symbol with the animated wheel movie clip.

22. Click the Back button to enter the car movie clip's editing mode.

23. Click the front wheel. You could just delete the static version of the wheel and then drag the rotating version from the Library, but that would mean you'd have to place the new wheel in exactly the same position. Instead, you can swap the two wheels directly. To swap the wheels, click the Swap button on the Properties panel (the wheel must be selected for this button to show up).

24. The Swap Symbol window will appear. Click animated wheel and then OK. The symbols have been swapped—but you also need to change the symbol behavior in the Properties panel.

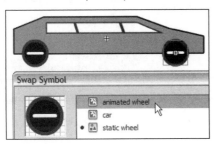

25. With the wheel still selected, change the instance behavior (the leftmost drop-down menu) from Graphic to Movie Clip. When you do this, the icon immediately to the left of the drop-down menu changes from a graphic icon to a movie clip icon.

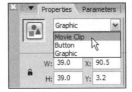

Although the process of swapping symbols may seem longer-winded than simply deleting the old symbol and adding the new one in its place from the Library, swapping is a far quicker process in practice, especially when you need to maintain stage position between the original and the swap.

If you now test the movie with Control ➤ Test Movie, you'll see that both wheels are turning in the same direction, at the same speed. Your car is driving on a treadmill and it's going nowhere fast.

One thing you might notice is that the wheels seem to suddenly stop every now and again (actually, they do it every 20 frames). This is because the start and stop positions of the wheels are the same. Put another way, you have two frames in your animation that are the same (Frame 1 and Frame 20), and you therefore don't have a seamless animation loop. At Frame 20 you have the wheel in the following position:

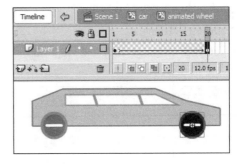

103

For a seamless animation, Frame 20 should actually look like Frame 19, as in the following figure:

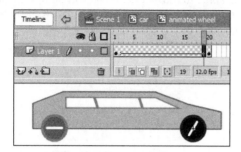

Creating seamless animation loops

1. Double-click either wheel in the car symbol to edit it in place.

2. Select Frame 19 on the Timeline and press *F6* or right/*CMD*-click on the frame, and select Insert Keyframe from the context menu that appears.

3. Right/*CMD*-click on Frame 20 and select Remove Frames from the context menu. Your animation now only goes from Frame 1 to Frame 19.

4. To get back to the full 20-frame animation, drag Frame 19 to Frame 20.

5. If you click on Frame 20, you'll see a warning icon in the Properties panel.

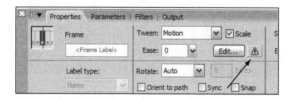

This is because Frame 20 is now a start keyframe as well as an end keyframe. At the end of Step 2, it was the end keyframe of the tween between Frames 1 and 19, and it was also the start keyframe of the (admittedly very short) tween between Frames 19 and 20. Now that what used to be Frame 20 is gone, the second tween is broken.

6. To fix this, select Frame 20. In the Property inspector, change the Tween drop-down selection to None.

7. Save the movie as car.fla and close it for now. You'll give your car traveling independence in Chapter 6.

Although this animation looks fairly basic, it shows that simple tweening combined with nested movie clips is the backbone of animation in Flash. If you're a little put off by the rough-and-ready graphics, try the same exercise again using your nippy little two-seater.

The starting point is in the file car_start.fla. This consists of two Drawing Objects—one for the bodywork and one for the wheel.

The finished animation can be found in the file car_finished.fla.

Now that you know how to create and manage groups and symbols, how can you get them lined up neatly and evenly on the stage? You could always do it by eye of course, but Flash gives you a couple of quicker and more precise methods. You'll start with something you might have come across already: Snap Align.

Snap Align

One of the great features of Flash is the Snap Align option. Snap Align works by snapping objects to the edges of other objects.

When Snap Align is switched on (View ➤ Snapping ➤ Snap Align) and one object is being moved into the vicinity of another, Flash will snap the moved object to the edges of the static shape and will indicate this with a dotted line. One benefit of this is the ability to ensure that objects don't overlap on the stage. A quick example will help show how this works in practice.

In the following screenshot, a rectangle is dragged just above a square. When it's near enough to the square, a dotted line appears, and snaps the rectangle to the square's top edge.

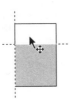

If the rectangle is dragged a little more to the left, Snap Align kicks in again and shows a dotted line indicating alignment with the left edge of the square.

So far so good. The next screenshot shows the same thing, except the rectangle is diagonal to the square.

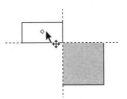

Snap Align also works in a few other ways, as illustrated in the following descriptions and screenshots.

It can snap objects at a distance from other shapes.

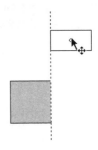

It can snap other (nonrectangular) shapes.

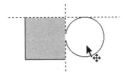

It can snap objects parallel to other objects (at a 10-pixel offset).

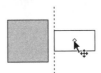

When more than one shape is involved, Snap Align will check all the available edges for a match.

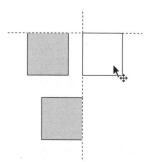

Creating an emerald using Snap Align

Let's use Snap Align to make an emerald shape from a number of small shapes.

1. Open a new Flash document.

2. Draw a square with the Rectangle tool in Object Drawing mode and give it a black stroke and any fill color. (In this example, I've used red.)

3. Select the square using the Selection tool and create four copies of the square using Edit ➤ Copy followed by Edit ➤ Paste In Center. Alternatively, you can use Edit ➤ Duplicate (*CTRL+D*).

4. Move the copied squares so that all five are now spaced apart on the stage.

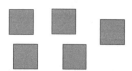

5. Select one of the squares using the Selection tool and drag it to roughly the center of the stage. This will be your center square.

6. Click and drag on one of the other squares and position it above the center square until both the vertical and horizontal Snap Align lines appear.

7. Position the other three squares at the other three sides of the center square. Make sure each time that both the vertical and horizontal Snap Align lines appear. The last maneuver should look like the following image:

Now that you have a cross shape, all you need to add are 45-degree angled corners. To do this, you need to create a triangle for copying and rotating to angle off each corner. To make that triangle, you need to work with a square.

8. Use the Selection tool to click and select an existing square.

9. Select Edit ➤ Duplicate or *CTRL+D* to copy the square.

> You can also drag a square and copy it at the same time by holding down the ALT key. This is a very useful shortcut and worth remembering because it works with everything on the stage.

10. Using the Selection tool, position the new square away from the others so that it can be modified separately.

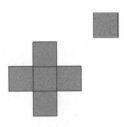

11. Select the Subselection tool.

Use it to click on the stroke of the square. When you're over the stroke, a little point will appear below your mouse pointer. Now if you click, you'll enter into Subselection mode, which enables you to edit the raw points that make up Flash's strokes and fill areas.

> Some other applications call this mode "Point Editing mode."

When you click, Flash will display the four points that make up the square (one at each corner).

You may find that the points are difficult to see. You can change the color of the points by changing the layer color of the current layer (double-click the colored square to the left of the layer title in the Timeline if you need to change it—I recommend always changing the layer color to a color that contrasts strongly with the stage background color (called the Outline Color in the Layer Properties dialog box that appears when you double-click) when you're about to do Subselection editing.

12. Click the upper-right vector point. After you select it, the vector point will appear solid, as in the following screenshot:

13. Press *DELETE* or *BACKSPACE* to remove the point, and voila, a perfect right-angle triangle!

Note that you should avoid holding down the *DELETE* key for too long. If you do this, Flash will delete the point as well as the whole square, because it begins deleting very quickly after the first deletion occurs.

14. Click with the Selection tool to select the triangle Drawing Object just created. Then copy and paste (or duplicate) the triangle three times.

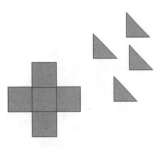

15. Drag one of the triangles to the upper-right corner of the cross. As before, make sure that both vertical and horizontal Snap Align lines appear.

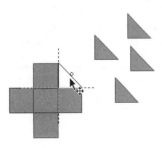

The remaining three triangles must be rotated or flipped to fit the remaining corner plots.

16. Select a triangle and choose Modify ➤ Transform ➤ Rotate 90° CW. Alternatively, type 90° into the Rotate text field of the Transform panel (Window ➤ Transform).

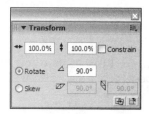

17. Select the next triangle and choose Modify ➤ Transform ➤ Rotate 90° CCW, or type -90 (minus 90) into the Rotate text field of the Transform panel.

18. Select the last triangle and choose Modify ➤ Transform ➤ Flip Horizontal, followed by Modify ➤ Transform ➤ Flip Vertical. You can also use the Transform panel and enter an angle of 180 degrees.

19. Drag the modified triangles into their respective slots, remembering to use the Snap Align option to correctly position them.

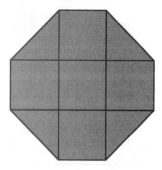

To improve on that dull, flat look, you'll need to add a little depth, which you'll do by using a gradient.

20. Select all the shapes by drawing a box around them with the Selection tool.

21. Click the Fill Color selector in the Properties panel and select the green gradient along the bottom.

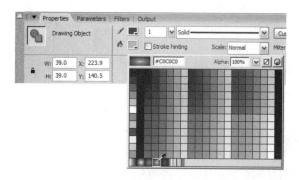

After your eyes have adjusted to it, you have an enchanting emerald.

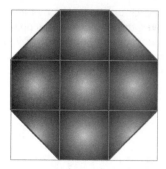

22. Save this Flash document as emerald.fla and close it. You'll improve it in a later chapter.

As you can see in this exercise, the Snap Align option is extremely useful for placing objects in line with each other using their edges.

Now that you've seen how to align objects and shapes relative to each other, I'll show you how to work with Flash's grids and rulers for finer placement from the start.

The grid

By default, the **grid** in Flash gives you a background of fine-lined squares that you can use to guide the placement and alignment of objects.

Using the grid

1. Open the group.fla file you were working on earlier.

2. Switch off the Snap Align option with View ➤ Snapping ➤ Snap Align. This will make it easier to work with the grid.

3. To access the grid in Flash, use the View ➤ Grid ➤ Show Grid menu option. The stage now has a series of grid lines across it.

4. Turn on Flash's grid-snapping feature by clicking View ➤ Snapping ➤ Snap to Grid.

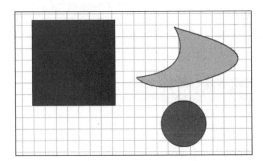

5. With the Selection tool, select the group by clicking the upper-left corner of the square, and drag it around—the whole group will snap to a grid line when it gets near one.

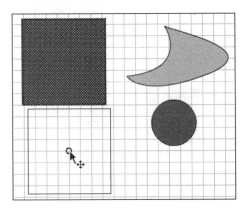

If you miss a corner point within the group when you click and drag, the group won't snap to the grid. Alternatively, you can also snap to a grid using the center point of the group. It can be deceptively difficult to find either the corner or the center—the only solution is to try and try again.

When you click an object and drag it using Snap to Grid, a small black ring appears next to the cursor. This is called the **snapping ring**. When you drag an object close to a grid line, the ring will jump to the grid line and become larger and darker.

The snapping ring snaps to any grid line, but is easiest to snap to the grid at an intersection (where vertical and horizontal grid lines meet).

Experiment with moving your group around the stage with snapping turned on and off, and see the different effects. Also, try zooming in and moving the group again. Notice that it gets easier to position things precisely the more zoomed in you are. The trade off for this is that when zoomed in, you won't be able to see your whole image. The best solution is to experiment until you find a happy medium—which will of course be different for each movie you work on. Usually, the best bet is to move your object to roughly where you want it, then zoom in and fine tune the position.

When you're aligning a shape, you won't always want to do so by dragging it at its center. As mentioned, Flash caters for this by allowing you to drag the shapes by their corners as well. When you drag shapes by their corners, a similar snapping ring appears.

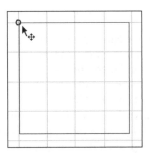

These are the default behaviors of the grid. Flash also gives you the ability to customize the grid and its settings to suit your needs.

109

1. Open the Grid dialog box by using the View ➤ Grid ➤ Edit Grid menu option.

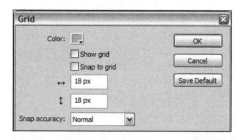

From here, you can change the spacing and the color of your grid lines.

It can be useful to change the grid color if the current grid lines are merging into the color of your movie background, or if you just prefer another color aesthetically. The units of measurement will be the same movie-wide values that you set in the Properties panel and Document Properties dialog box.

The Snap accuracy option allows you to alter how close the snapping ring has to be to something before it will snap to it. So, if you find those lines are just too sticky, you can set it to Must be close. On the other hand, if you want to be seriously snap happy (sorry), you can set it to Always Snap and never feel those middle-of-nowhere blues again. Again, you can experiment with these settings at different levels of zoom.

The option Save Default is the same as Make Default in the Document Properties box—using this will apply these values to all the Flash movies you create.

2. When you're finished, close the dialog box by clicking OK. To turn off the grid, go to the View ➤ Grid ➤ Show Grid menu option again—there will be a check mark next to the Show Grid option, indicating that it's currently turned on.

3. Click the Show Grid option and the check mark will disappear along with the grid lines. Try moving your group around. Even though the grid is no longer visible, your square will still snap to it if the Snap to Grid option is on. To stop this, you have to go into the View ➤ Snapping menu again and click the Snap to Grid option.

As you might expect, the grid isn't shown in your final movie. If you want to see a grid effect in your finished movie, you have to draw one yourself. This is easily accomplished by drawing over the grid in the authoring environment on the back layer using the Line tool with snapping turned on for precision.

Flash has yet more ways of making drawing and alignment easier. Among these are rulers and guides.

Rulers and guides

Guides are an extremely useful feature of Flash, and when used in conjunction with Flash's rulers, they give you a powerful, customizable, and easy-to-use set of alignment tools. Let's see them in action.

1. Use the View ➤ Rulers menu option to display Flash's rulers. As soon as you do this, a pair of vertically and horizontally oriented rulers appear around the stage.

Zero point

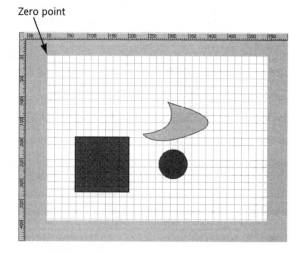

These rulers are marked out in the units currently defined in the Document Properties dialog box. The **zero point** for your rulers (from which everything is measured) is always at the upper-left-hand corner of your stage.

2. Using the Hand tool (it's in the View section of the toolbar), move the stage around and notice how the zero point moves with it.

Rulers aren't just handy for alignment—they're also useful for seeing how big your object is and how all the changes you make are affecting it.

3. Grab your group with the Selection tool and move it around the stage, keeping an eye on your rulers as you do so. Two black lines on each ruler shift position as your shape moves. These lines indicate the dimensions and position of your shape on the stage.

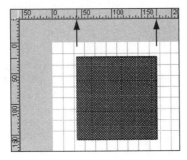

These lines mark the shape at its widest point, so if you have a big irregular shape, Flash puts an invisible bounding box around it and uses the edges of the box for reference.

Another feature of rulers that you might have seen before is the ability to use them to line up your **guides**. Guides are reference lines that help you with shape alignment. The great thing about guides is that you can put guides wherever you like (unlike grids and rulers, which are in a fixed position), and you can add as many as you like. This means that no matter where an object is or what shape it is, you can always use a guide to help you line it up precisely with another shape.

4. Click anywhere on the ruler at the top of the stage and, still holding the mouse button, drag a horizontal guide down onto the stage. (In the following screenshots, the grid has been turned off so you can see the guides more clearly.)

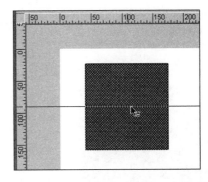

5. Release the mouse button anywhere on the stage to fix the guide at that point. The color of the guide defaults to a rather lurid (yet extremely visible) green, but it can be altered via the View ➤ Guides ➤ Edit Guides menu option. To get a vertical guide, drag a line from the left-hand ruler in the same way.

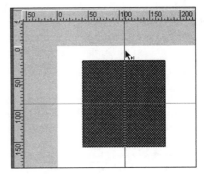

A guide's position isn't set in stone. If you move your mouse over a guide while using the Selection tool, the cursor will change to indicate that you can pick up the guide and move it elsewhere—you can even drag it right off the stage and get rid of it altogether.

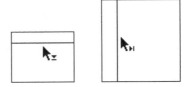

6. Click your horizontal guide to pick it up, drag it to the bottom of your square, and release it to anchor it there.

Just as you can snap shapes to the grid, you can snap objects to guides.

7. Make sure that the snapping functionality is active by going to the View ➤ Snapping menu and ensuring that the Snap to Guides option is turned on.

8. Click a corner of the square and drag it to the guide line until it snaps to it.

To get rid of your guide line, drag it all the way back onto the top ruler and release it. Dropping it anywhere on the ruler will do.

If you have a number of guides on the stage and you want to get rid of them all at once, you can use the Clear All button from the View ➤ Guides ➤ Edit Guides menu option. Using this option allows you to undo their removal by clicking the Cancel button. Alternatively, you can use the View ➤ Guides ➤ Clear Guides menu option, but be careful, because this option is final and can't be undone.

The Lock Guides option in the Edit Guides dialog box will fix all current guides in place, meaning that you won't be able to move them after dropping them in place. This is useful when you're working with a lot of guides for precise placement purposes, and you don't want to pick them up by accident when you're moving other objects around. This may seem a little awkward at first, but with more practice you'll find these guides to be very useful in arranging your work on the stage.

As your movies become more complex, multilayered, and sophisticated, you'll find guides increasingly useful, particularly because they're visible through all the layers of a movie. But as with a lot of things, Flash offers more than one way to align objects.

Alignment

In Flash, the **Align** panel acts as a hub for a number of alignment features. The Align panel allows you to quickly line up, center, and otherwise tidy up the relative positioning of your stage content with a few quick clicks.

Align panel

With the Align panel, you can fine tune the position of multiple objects on the stage by aligning them, spacing them evenly, and even sizing them to ensure they all have exactly the same dimensions.

You access these features via the Window ➤ Align menu option, or (in Windows) by clicking the Align button on the main toolbar.

Clicking the align button (the one on the far right) opens the Align panel.

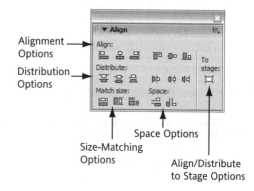

In this panel, you can see all the different alignment options. By default, the 17 options that take up the bulk of the panel work on the objects you've selected on the stage, aligning them in relation to each other. If you turn the To stage modifier on and then use the alignment buttons, the selected objects will be aligned relative to the stage.

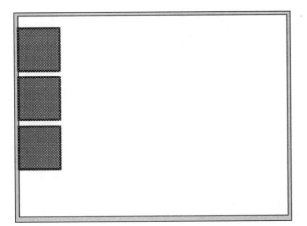

Make sure the To stage modifier is unselected before moving on.

The key to using each of the options is to look at the thin black line on each button and its position relative to the objects shown on the button. This line indicates how the objects will be aligned. For example, look at the first group of alignment buttons at the upper-left of the panel.

In the first button, the black line is to the left of the objects, which means that the objects will all be aligned along their left edges. The next button aligns your objects by their centers, and the third button aligns them along their right edges.

As you'd expect, if you hold the cursor over any of the buttons, a tool tip will help you check out their basic functions.

The best way to learn to use the Align panel is with practice and application. Next, you'll look at examples of the buttons in each of the categories.

Aligning objects

Let's start by aligning objects in relation to each other with the basic alignment buttons. Make sure the To stage modifier is turned off.

The Align options consist of two sets of three buttons: one set for aligning horizontally, the other for aligning vertically.

Horizontal Alignment →  ← Vertical Alignment

1. In a new Flash document, draw three new Drawing Objects: a square, a circle, and a triangle. Make the objects different sizes, similar to the ones shown in the following screenshot.

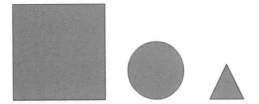

Remember, to make a triangle in Flash, you can create a square and then use the Subselection tool to delete one point; then move the remaining three to form your triangle.

An arguably easier way to create a triangle is to use the PolyStar tool (recall that it's under the Rectangle tool—click and hold on the Rectangle tool to access the PolyStar). Select the PolyStar tool and then click the Options *button in the Properties panel. In the Tool Settings panel that appears, set the* Style *to* polygon *and the* Number of Sides *to* 3 *(you can leave* Star point size *as it is, because it's only relevant for star shapes). You'll now be able to create triangles with a couple of clicks, in much the same way as you can create ovals and rectangles. Using the PolyStar tool really comes into its own when you want to draw lots of triangles.*

When aligning objects, Flash puts a box around the object or group, marking its boundaries, and then uses this box to align by. You'll see this highlighted box for a grouped object, Drawing Object, or symbol when you select it. Flash uses the center of this box as the center of the object or group. For most regular objects (such

113

as squares, circles, and triangles), this gives good results. For irregular shapes, however, this can be a bit confusing, because we humans tend to credit two-dimensional objects with real-world characteristics—we give them weight and volume, for example. In contrast, your cold-hearted computer sees these objects as just a collection of pixels on the screen. For example, the center of the following Drawing Object, marked by a cross, is probably not where you'd expect it to be.

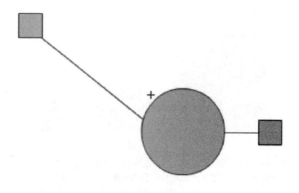

To understand why Flash puts the center point there, look at the same object with the bounding box around it.

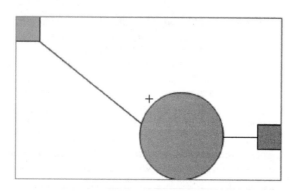

Now you can clearly see that the cross is in the center of the box, which Flash treats as the center of the whole object.

2. Arrange all three of your Drawing Objects on the stage on a rough, unevenly spaced diagonal.

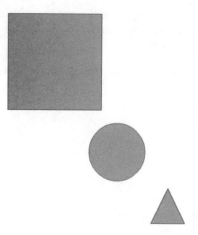

3. Select all the Drawing Objects by dragging a box around them with the Selection tool (or press *CTRL+A*).

4. Click the Align left edge button (located at the upper-left of the Align panel), and your objects will immediately reposition themselves by aligning with the left edge of the leftmost object—in this case, the square.

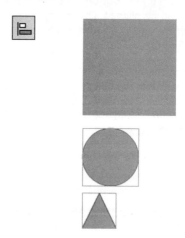

If you had selected the Align right edge button, they would have lined up along the right edge of the triangle.

The Distribute options ensure that there's an equal distance between the respective edges of the objects.

5. Arrange your shapes back into the diagonal, select all three again, and click the Distribute left edge button. Your objects will rearrange themselves in the following manner:

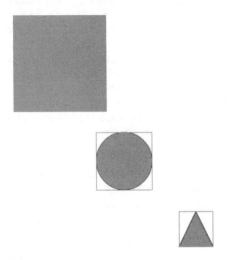

6. To clearly see the effect that this has, turn on the rulers (View ➤ Rulers) and then drag guides out to each of the left edges of the objects.

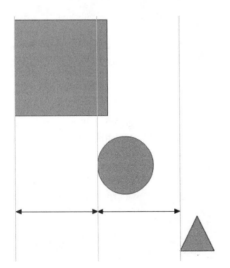

Now you can clearly see that Flash spaced the objects with equal distances between each of their left edges.

7. Remove your guides, either by dragging them individually off the stage or by choosing the View ➤ Guides ➤ Clear Guides menu option.

8. Turn your attention back to the Align panel and click the Match width button (at the bottom-left of the Align panel). Your circle and triangle suddenly grow in size.

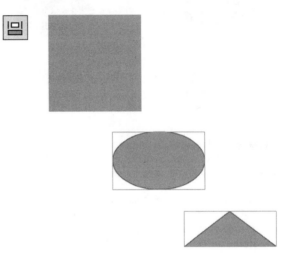

The Match size option works by making all your selected objects the size of the largest one in the selection. So, by clicking the Match width button, you made all your objects the same width as your square. To ensure that all objects on your stage have exactly the same dimensions, click the Match width and height button, and in the blink of an eye Flash will do the job for you. This may come in handy if you're drawing buttons and you want each button to be a different shape, but the same size in relation to the others.

The two Space options at the bottom-right of the Align panel ensure that the gaps between objects are the same size. This means, for example, that you can precisely arrange a set of buttons so that they look just right. Compare the left-hand set of buttons with the evenly spaced selection on the right.

Although in this case the differences in spacing are subtle, an accumulation of unevenly spaced objects in your movies can quickly make things look rough and sketchy.

9. Back in your movie, click the Space evenly vertically button. This is another option for which using guides can help to clarify exactly what Flash has done.

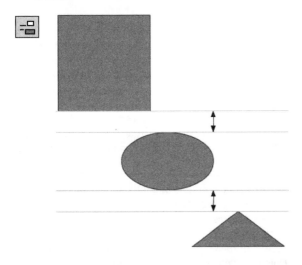

You can clearly see that the spacing between each of the objects is now the same.

The final option remaining on the Align panel is the To stage button on the right side.

This is a global switch that affects all the other options on the Align panel. As you've already seen, Flash has so far aligned all the objects to one object—for example, the largest object for matching size, the leftmost object for aligning to the left, and so on. When To stage is turned on, Flash uses the stage to align the objects instead, so aligning to the left will align the objects to the left of the stage, and matching size will match the objects to the full size of the stage. You can use the To stage option to size an imported graphic image to match the dimensions of the stage—for example, if you wanted to use the image as a background layer.

10. Clear all your guides away, and then click the To stage button to highlight it.

11. With all your shapes still selected, click the Match width button. All your objects are resized horizontally to mirror the width of the stage.

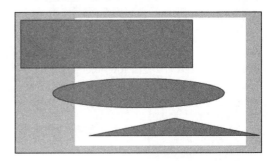

12. You can see that they're all exactly the same width as the stage by clicking the Align horizontal center button. This will align your 3 shapes perfectly to the horizontal center of the stage.

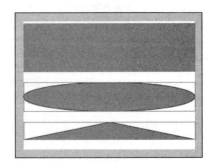

As you've seen in this series of examples, the alignment buttons can drastically affect the way that your objects appear on the stage. You can also see how much easier it can be to use these tools to do the job rather than attempting to align and match everything by eye.

Now let's take a look at how to control objects in Flash in another dimension through depth arrangement and layers.

Stacking order

In Chapter 1 you learned about layers and how they function in a background/foreground relationship. In that chapter's example, when your mushroom was growing behind the moon, you simply pulled the moon layer underneath the mushroom layer and presto, the mushroom grew in correct perspective. A similar effect occurs within individual layers, too: Flash's default behavior is to give objects that are on the same layer a front-to-back order—this is called the **stacking order**.

Only symbols, Drawing Objects, or grouped objects can be stacked in Flash. All other objects—such as hand-drawn shapes (i.e., shapes you draw with Object Drawing mode off)—will fall to the lowest possible level of the layer. You can see this effect when you hand draw two or more shapes on the stage. If, for example, you draw a rectangle and a circle on the stage (with Object Drawing off), they'll both occupy the same plane.

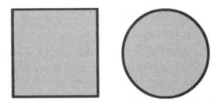

If you drag the circle onto the rectangle and then click away somewhere on the stage, Flash assumes that you want to merge these shapes on this plane.

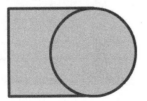

The overlapping areas of these shapes share the same piece of stage real estate. If you click the arc of the circle inside the shape and delete it, the two shapes become a single, fused entity, with all the lines and fills at the back of the layer.

Drawn shapes merge together because their component lines and fills are trying to occupy the same space at the back of the layer.

Unlike hand-drawn objects, however, symbols, Drawing Objects, and groups can be moved backward and forward in relation to the back of the layer. To facilitate this, Flash assigns each new group or symbol that's added to a particular layer a stack position that determines how far up from the back it sits. Flash assigns these positions based on the order in which the symbols or groups are added to the stage. This means that every time you create a new symbol or group, it's placed in front of the ones that were already there.

Let's look at this principle in action.

> **Shuffling a deck of cards**

1. Start a new Flash document and set the movie background color to a warm, casino-style green.
2. Double-click the Rectangle tool, set the Corner Radius modifier to 15, and select Object Drawing mode. You want to create round-edged rectangles that will represent playing cards.
3. In the Properties panel, set the stroke width to 2, the stroke color to black, and the fill color to white.

4. Draw a playing card–shaped rectangle on the stage.

5. Select the Drawing Object and convert it into a graphic symbol with a central registration point. Name the symbol Card Base.

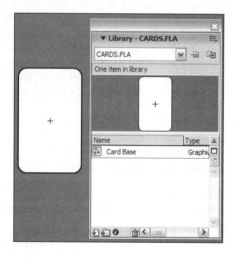

You now have a blank card symbol that you can use for all the cards that you'll show on the stage.

Now you'll create four cards on the stage—the Jack, Queen, King, and Ace. Each card will use the same Card Base symbol as its background, but each will have a different letter on top of that background to indicate its seniority—J, Q, K, or A. You can easily do this by adding separate text boxes on top of each instance of the Card Base symbol.

6. Select the Text tool and choose an appropriate font and color from the Properties panel.

7. Click the middle of your card—this will help you judge what size the font should be.

Make sure you don't go into Edit Symbols mode on the Card Base instance. All you want to do is create a text box that will float above the symbol instance.

8. In the Properties panel, use the font size slider to set the font size to something that will look good on your card.

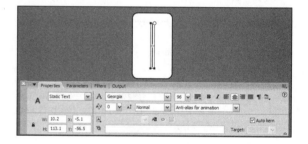

9. Type a capital J for Jack and use the Align panel to center your text on the card.

The simplest way to achieve this centering is by selecting the symbol instance and the text box by dragging a box around them with the Selection tool, and then clicking both the Align vertical center and Align horizontal center buttons on the Align panel.

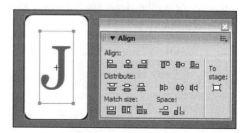

10. Make sure you have both the card and the text selected, and convert them into a symbol by pressing *F8*. Give it the name Jack, a graphic symbol behavior, and a center registration point. Your card and its unique text identifier are now tied together in one symbol.

11. Use the same process to drag three more instances of the Card Base symbol onto your stage. Add the letters Q, K, and A to these three cards, *in that order*. Align the text over each card and then convert all the cards into appropriately named graphic symbols as you did with the Jack card.

When you've finished, you should have four cards on your stage that look like the following:

12. Drag each of your cards to the left so they overlap each other.

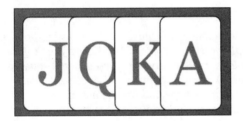

Notice that the Jack, which you created first, is at the bottom of the stack, and the Ace, which you created last, is at the top. The Queen and King are in the correct sequence, too, so the stacking order is currently J, Q, K, A. Flash has faithfully created a stacking order for the cards based on the sequence you created them in.

You can change the stacking order of these cards by using the options available through the Modify ➤ Arrange menu option.

13. Click your King card to select it, and use the Bring to Front option from the Modify ➤ Arrange menu. Your King will now jump to the top of the stack, so that the stacking order (from back to front) is changed to J, Q, A, K.

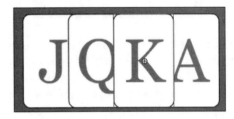

14. Click the Jack and use the Modify ➤ Arrange ➤ Bring Forward menu option.

The Bring Forward option pulls the selected object up one level in the stacking order, so the Jack will immediately be brought forward one space and jump in front of the Queen.

15. To test the Jack's position in relation to the other cards, pick it up and drag it between the King and the Queen. You should see that the Jack is now in front of the Queen.

16. Drag the Jack between the King and the Ace.

You'll notice it's behind both of them. As expected, from bottom to top, the order is now Q, J, A, K.

17. Click the Ace and use the Modify ➤ Arrange ➤ Send Backward menu option. The Ace is moved backward one level, jumping behind the Jack.

18. Drag the Ace up next to the Jack, between the Queen and the King. The Ace is now in front of the Queen but behind the King, and the order is now Q, A, J, K.

19. Click the King and use the Modify ➤ Arrange ➤ Send to Back menu option. This will send the King all the way to the bottom of the stack.

The final order is K, Q, A, J.

20. Save the file as `cards.fla` and leave it open.

This exercise illustrates that you can manipulate the stacking order of symbols or groups to a very fine degree, which can be of real help when you're putting together complicated objects and pieces of content.

> *Continuously selecting a card and using the menu options can become a drudge very quickly, but there's another way of getting to the Arrange submenu: you can right/CMD-click on the object you want to arrange and use the arrange options that appear in the Arrange submenu of the context menu that appears.*

There will be times when you're building something on your stage and you'll find that one component disappears behind another one. If you have a grasp of stacking order, you'll understand why it disappeared and how to get it back. However, there's another way to make the card shuffling a little easier.

Distribute to Layers option

For those of you who found arranging the royal part of the deck a little too much like hard work (even with the nifty context menu speed-up), there's Flash's Distribute to Layers option. Distribute to Layers is incredibly useful for putting order in chaotic situations.

Distribute to Layers takes all the selected objects—symbols, grouped objects, or primitives (simple graphics drawn on your stage that haven't been converted to a symbol or grouped with other graphics)—and calculates associations between them before creating and placing them on as many different layers as required.

Distribute to Layers works differently for different types of selected objects:

- If the selected items are symbols, grouped objects, or text boxes, each individual element is placed on its own individual layer.

- If the selected items are primitives or Drawing Objects, Flash will try to make associations at the geographic location of items. If two or more are touching or in close vicinity, they are treated as one object and placed together on the same layer.

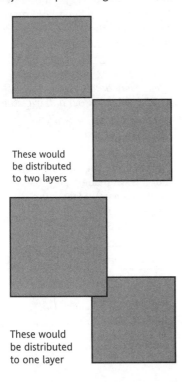

These would
be distributed
to two layers

These would
be distributed
to one layer

- The rule is: if the items are touching, they're hitched forever!

- If the selected items are symbols, the layers they're distributed to are given the symbols' instance names (or symbol names if the instance doesn't or can't have an instance name). This makes Distribute to Layers very useful for cleaning up messes you've made.

Let's give it a try with your deck of cards.

Distributing your deck of cards to layers

1. Open up your `cards.fla` file (if necessary).

2. Select all the cards with the Selection tool and choose the Modify ➤ Timeline ➤ Distribute to Layers menu option.

Each card is placed on its own layer, and each layer is given the same name as the symbol that resides on that layer. There's also an extra layer that has no content; it's just a blank keyframe. This is the layer that all your symbols were taken from. Let's remove this superfluous layer before proceeding.

3. Select the blank layer in the Timeline. Click the Delete Layer icon (the trash can) below the Timeline.

The unused layer is deleted, leaving you with just your card layers.

The final order of your cards in the last exercise was K, Q, A, J, with the king at the bottom. It's easy to change their order by dragging and moving the layers up and down in the Timeline. Let's put them in their correct order with the Ace at the top where it belongs.

4. Click the layers and drag them so that they're in the order shown in the following figure.

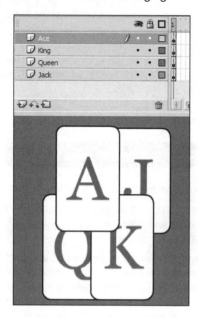

Your cards are now in the correct order—J, Q, K, A.

5. Save the movie as `cards2.fla` and leave it open.

Now that you've seen how Flash can save you a few headaches by organizing your content for you, let's see how it can ease the pain a little more with layer folders.

Layer folders

As you've seen, layers are an excellent means of controlling your content. Flash has a way to organize your content even more efficiently—you can use **layer folders** to bundle together similar layers. A layer folder works just like any folder on your hard drive; it enables you to maintain some kind of control over the chaos of your files.

Let's create a layer folder to place the King and Queen together in their honeymoon suite—away from the prying eyes of the Jack and the Ace—while maintaining the physical depths of all the cards.

1. Select the King layer and click the Insert Layer Folder button.

Flash creates the layer folder above the King layer and names it Folder. Flash automatically suffixes each layer folder name with an incremental digit as each folder is added (Folder 1, Folder 2, Folder 3, etc.). It's worth noting that Flash suffixes layers in the same way.

2. Double-click the layer folder name in the Timeline, type in Honeymoon Suite, and press *ENTER*.

So far, you have a new layer folder with no content in it. You can tell this because the arrow to the left of the layer folder icon is pointing down, meaning that it's open. You can toggle the folder open and closed by clicking the arrow.

Let's give your royal couple some peace and put the King and Queen layers in the Honeymoon Suite folder.

3. Make sure the Honeymoon Suite folder is open, and click the King layer. Then hold down the *SHIFT* key while selecting the Queen layer. Both layers should now be selected.

> To select layers that aren't sequential, hold down the *CTRL* key (*CMD* on the Mac) and click the nonsequential layers.

4. Drag the layers up to the Honeymoon Suite folder. As you do this, a shaded gray bar with a small notch on it appears. Make sure this notch is indented (the folder icon will also be highlighted) and release the mouse button.

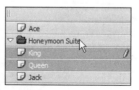

If you placed the King and Queen layers in the Honeymoon Suite folder correctly, your list of layers will look like the following:

The King and Queen layers are in the Honeymoon Suite layer, which you can identify because they're indented. To further prove that they're in the folder, click the arrow to the left to close the folder—now they have some peace and quiet!

With the two layers inside the folder, any actions performed on the folder will also apply to its contents. This applies to locking/unlocking, showing/hiding, moving, and deleting the folder.

Flash gives you three ways of operating in the third (depth) dimension: layers, the stacking order within layers, and layer folders. With experience, you'll develop your own strategies for combining these options, but one rule of thumb is that if you're going to have lots of separate overlapping objects, it's usually best to have them on different layers and keep these controlled in layer folders. The stacking order is particularly useful when you're constructing individual objects and groups that will always be kept together and that you want to assign to a layer using the Distribute to Layers command.

Believe it or not, it's time to introduce a fourth dimension. Here's a history lesson.

History panel

The History panel records all user actions in Flash. At its most basic level, the History panel is a glorified undo list, storing and listing every action—whether it's drawing with the Pencil tool, making a selection with the Selection tool, or changing a primitive into a symbol. Using the History panel is beneficial because it provides you with better control over elements within the Flash environment. If you make an error while creating content, the History panel allows you to quickly backtrack through the actions and revert to a point before the mistake.

The History panel also has some advanced features, which I'll cover in Chapter 9.

The History panel is accessible by choosing the Window ➤ Other Panels ➤ History menu option or CTRL+F10 (CMD+F10 on the Mac). When it's open, it looks like the following:

If you've been working in a Flash document for any length of time, chances are your panel is nearly as full as this one. By default, Flash stores 100 actions, but this can be reduced or increased in Flash Preferences under the General heading of the Preferences window (Edit ➤ Preferences). Undo levels tend to take a lot of system memory, so I wouldn't recommend making this figure much larger unless your computer has lots of memory to spare (something that's becoming more likely in these days of cheap memory). If you have 1GB or more of memory in your computer, feel free to make it more than 100.

You can also select between Document-level Undo or Object-level Undo in the Undo drop-down list. Document-level Undo makes Flash maintain an undo list for the whole document, whereas Object-level Undo makes Flash keep a separate undo list for each object. The difference between the two is that Document-level Undo will undo the things you did in the order you did them, but Object-level Undo will only undo the things you did to *the current Timeline*.

Although Object-level Undo may seem better on the face of it, experience shows that the time you'll most want to undo is when you test an FLA file and it suddenly stops working—it's then usually a case of pressing undo a few times to try to clear what's causing the problem. The problem with Object-level Undo is that you may never clear the problem unless you're on the Timeline where the error was introduced. Also, Document-level Undo is something that you may be more familiar with from other applications, so it's usually the best one to use. As such, it's the setting used in the following examples.

One of the important functions of the History panel is its ability to step back through your actions so you can review them. This is useful in the event you need to undo a significant amount of actions and your fingers become sore from holding down the *CTRL/CMD+Z* keys. With the History panel, you can quickly review any actions you've taken. Let's see how it works in a short exercise.

Using the History panel

1. Open a new Flash document.
2. Open the History panel (if it isn't already open) with Window ➤ Other Panels ➤ History.
3. Select the Text tool and type Flash 4 on the stage.
4. In a new text field below the first one, type Flash MX.
5. Type Flash MX 2004 in a third text field below the previous two. This should leave you with three text fields and three versions of Flash.

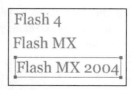

6. Look at the contents of the History panel.

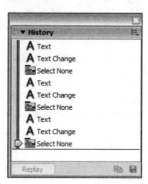

It's not telling you much, is it? It shows you that you did something with three text fields, but it doesn't really tell you what. Lucky for you, Macromedia includes an option to show you specifics. Let's switch it on.

7. Click the History panel menu, located at the top-right of the panel, and select View ➤ Arguments in Panel.

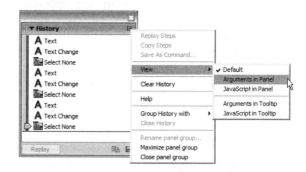

Now the History panel is a little more user-friendly and shows you detail like the position and size of the text boxes, as well as the actual text that you entered (shown as Text Change).

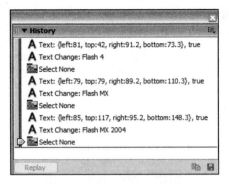

8. Now that you can see some detail, you can see how the History panel really works. Slowly drag the gray arrow on the left up four notches and watch the text on the stage disappear as you do it.

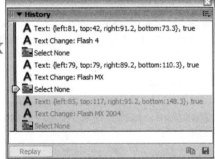

As you move the arrow up, Flash runs backward through the chronological order of actions or events and gives you a snapshot of the stage before the subsequent (now grayed) actions were taken. In the screenshot just shown, the arrow is positioned just before the third text field is added, so Flash shows you only the first two text fields.

9. Drag the arrow back down to the bottom, and the text field reappears. In essence, what you've just done is a number of undos and some redos, the equivalent of six key presses in all. The History panel makes the task significantly easier.

I have to let you in on a little secret I've been keeping from you. The chronological order of Flash releases is incorrect because Flash 5 came after Flash 4 but before Flash MX. Obviously, there are a number of ways to rectify this, but I'll show you how to do it using the History panel.

10. Drag the arrow indicator in the panel up to the third action, or until only the Flash 4 text is visible.

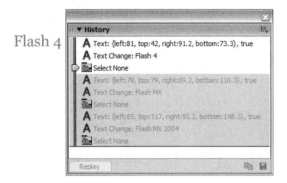

11. Select the Text tool and type Flash 5 below the Flash 4 text. If you look at the History panel now, you'll see that something very strange has happened—history has been changed!

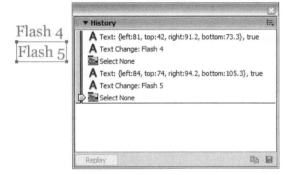

The History panel in Flash works in the same way as time travel: when history is changed, it has a drastic effect. For example, if the Terminator could have worked as Flash does and removed John Connor from the past, there would be no resistance to the evil machines in the future.

By going back through the History actions and adding new text, everything that originally followed is removed. A word of caution—after you do this, there's no way of retrieving any of the lost steps or their content. At this point, not even the Undo command can help you.

This means that you have to add the remaining releases of Flash again.

125

12. Use the Text tool to add two new text fields containing Flash MX and Flash MX 2004 (yes, I know Flash 8 is the latest release, but bear with me!)

13. Select Clear History from the History panel options.

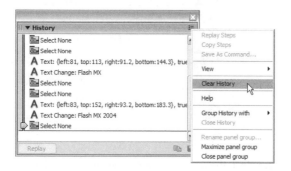

This, unsurprisingly, removes all the actions from the History panel and leaves you with no history and nothing to undo. Drastic? Yes, but Flash requires a confirmation before it completes the deletion.

The History panel is a welcome addition to Flash because of the time saved by using it. To get the most out of it, I recommend that you use it as configured in this book, because this allows you to have an overview of your actions without having to laboriously examine every step.

Even though you've only scratched the surface of the History panel here, in Chapter 9 you'll see how it can be used to help automate content creation and modification, making repetitive tasks a cinch for all users. For now though, let's return to your case study.

Case study

You'll now begin to organize your content into a more manageable form, based on what you've learned so far in this chapter.

Organizing your content

In their current condition, none of the case study elements is neatly arranged or lined up. Let's tidy them up, starting with the big white rectangle.

1. Open the case study movie.

2. Open the Align panel with Window ➤ Align, and switch on the To stage modifier.

3. Select the white rectangle with the Selection tool and click the Align horizontal center and Align vertical center buttons in the Align panel. You're doing this to place the white rectangle in the dead center of the stage.

The white rectangle is now centered. Now on to the colored rectangles.

4. Position the two outer rectangles roughly near the edges of the white rectangle.

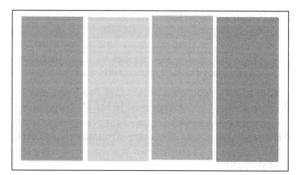

5. Select all the colored squares and click the Align vertical center button in the Align panel. This will position them all at the same vertical position, as well as vertically center them in relation to the stage.

6. With the rectangles still selected, unselect the To stage modifier in the Align panel, and click the Space evenly horizontally button.

This will even out the space between the rectangles. Your rectangles are now in line with each other.

7. Copy the rectangles using Edit ➤ Copy and insert a new layer above the colored rectangles layer and call it content. Lock the colored rectangles layer because you won't need to edit it again.

8. Select the content layer and choose Edit ➤ Paste in Place or press *SHIFT+CTRL+V*.

9. Select the newly pasted rectangles and choose Modify ➤ Convert to Symbol or press *F8*. Give the new symbol the name Content, and then select a movie clip behavior and ensure that it has a central registration point.

The reason you have two copies of the rectangles will become apparent in a later chapter. Before you move on to the buttons, let's finish the white rectangle.

10. Use the Selection tool to select the white rectangle and its stroke, and choose Modify ➤ Convert to Symbol or press *F8*. Make it a graphic symbol with a central registration point and name it white rectangle.

Aligning the buttons and logo

1. Use the Selection tool to move the buttons out of the way, off stage and to the right. This will make it easier to position them with the Snap Align feature.

2. Make sure that Snap Align and Snap to Objects are selected on the View ➤ Snapping menu. These will allow your buttons to snap to the edges of the white rectangle.

3. Select the left button and drag it down to the top-left corner of the white rectangle. Drag it until two Snap Align lines appear, one along the left edge and one underneath the button.

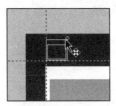

You'll notice that there's a gap between the button and the white rectangle. This is because Flash will Snap Align objects to a spot 10 pixels away from other objects, as well as to other objects right next to them.

4. After both Snap Align lines become visible, release the button.

5. Drag the next button down and position it to the right of the first button. When the two Snap Align lines appear, release the button.

As you might have guessed, you've positioned this button at a 10-pixel offset from the last one.

6. Repeat this process for the last two buttons. When you're done, the buttons should be positioned in excellent regimented fashion.

7. Select the logo and text on their layer and drag it slightly away from its original position.

8. Drag it back to its original position at the bottom right of the white rectangle. As with the buttons, after you see two Snap Align lines, release the button.

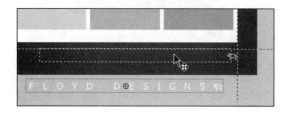

Now that your current assets are all neat and tidy, it's time to add some more.

Adding text to the buttons

1. Select the buttons layer and add a new layer called buttons text. This will position the buttons text layer above the previously selected one.

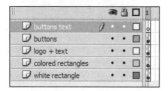

2. Select the Text tool, and click the buttons text layer. Set the font and other options as shown in the following screenshot. (You may have to click on the stage for the Properties panel to change, because the Timeline may have focus.)

3. Use the Text tool to type the words Web, Print, About, and Email anywhere on the stage. You'll reposition them in a moment.

4. Select the Web text field and drag it to the top of the left button. Because Snap to Objects is selected, the text field will snap to the top-center of the button.

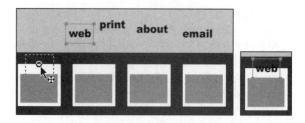

5. Repeat the same action for each of the text fields, so that the buttons read Web, Print, About, and Email, from left to right.

6. Select all the text fields and use the down arrow key to move the fields down pixel by pixel. Four little jogs should be about enough.

When the Selection tool is selected, pressing the arrow keys shifts selected objects 1 pixel in any given direction. To move objects larger distances, hold down the Shift key. The amount you move when you hold down this key depends on the zoom, and is 10 pixels at 100% zoom.

Managing your layers

The last thing to do in this chapter is organize your layers into layer folders. You'll do this logically by asset type.

1. Select the buttons text layer and insert a layer folder. Name this layer folder button assets.

2. Drag the buttons text and buttons layers into the button assets folder, ensuring that you keep the buttons text layer at the top.

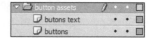

3. Create a new layer folder called background assets, and drag the layers logo + text, colored rectangles, and white rectangle into it. Remember to hold down the *CTRL* key to make multiple nonsequential selections.

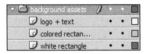

4. Place the background assets folder at the bottom of the layer stack. Your layers should now look like the following:

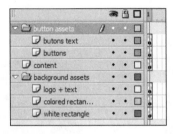

Not only is this nice and tidy, but it will also make future modifications, by you or other Flashers, a whole lot easier.

5. Save and close your case study file.

Summary

In this chapter, I've introduced you to the integral Flash facilities that help you arrange, align, and nest objects. These features are intimately linked with the ability to arrange content in space on the Flash stage in the three dimensions of width, height, and depth.

You saw that

- You can group objects together to maintain their relative proportions and still have access to them for editing.

- You can nest groups within groups, symbols within groups, and so on, giving you the ability to create hierarchies of precisely arranged, related objects.

- You can use Flash's grids, rulers, and guides to draw with a steady hand and sure eye.

- You can precisely place and transform objects by using Flash's Align panel and the Transform menu/panel.

- You can manipulate symbols and grouped objects, which have an implicit stacking order.

- You can better manage and arrange your content as well as nest your layers by using Layer folders.

You were also introduced to the all-seeing History panel, which

- Stores a set number of user actions within the Flash authoring environment.

- Allows you to easily review your previous actions and change one or more if necessary.

In the next chapter, you're going to drill down inside some objects and see how to use color to enrich content and effects.

129

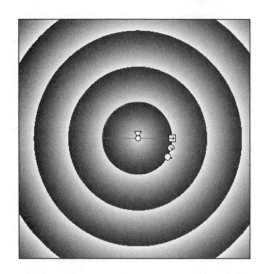

Chapter 5

WORKING WITH COLOR AND IMAGES

What we'll cover in this chapter:

- How Flash renders color
- How to create and save custom colors
- How gradients work, and how to use them effectively as fills on drawn objects
- How to manipulate object fills
- How to import and use bitmaps and other file formats

In this chapter, you'll see how Flash allows you to customize the objects you create by fine-tuning their colors and fill styles. You'll see how Flash handles color, and how you can ensure that the color features are optimized. Additionally, you'll take a quick look at how to import bitmaps and manipulate them in Flash. This is a long chapter with a lot of examples, but stick with it. By the end, you'll handle the color features with confidence and understanding.

Colors, fills, and gradients are the extra paprika on the already tongue-tingling dish that is Flash. If you've used any of the many graphics programs that are available today, you'll be instantly at home with Flash's color-creation methods. If, on the other hand, you're new to the world of swatches and radial gradients, don't worry. By the end of this chapter you'll be whistling R-G-B as easy as 1-2-3, while using the Alpha slider to open new windows into your movies.

It's never going to be entirely satisfactory to discuss colors in a book printed in black and white, but with a little bit of imagination, and by working through the exercises with Flash open in front of you, you'll get through without any problems.

Let's begin by talking about computerized color in general terms.

Color primer

Color on a computer monitor, like on a TV, is rendered using a mixture of three discrete components of colored light: red, green, and blue—hence RGB. When you're working with paint on a white canvas, you know that you need to add colored paint to make the picture. And you've probably also discovered that if you add red, blue, and green paint together in the right quantities and mix them up, you end up with a murky black.

When you're dealing with colored light rather than colored paint, however, the opposite is true. With light, if there's no color present—everything is black—and if you add all the colors together at the right strength, you get white light.

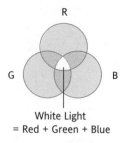

White Light
= Red + Green + Blue

The three color elements can be combined in an infinite variety of mixtures and strengths: blue light on its own will give you a blue screen, but if you add a little green to that blue, you'll see the color change.

Each unique color that a computer monitor displays is composed of different proportions of red, green, and blue. These unique colors can be described numerically by values that specify the amount of red (R), green (G), and blue (B) that you want to display. These values determine the color on the screen. On a computer, these numbers are expressed in base 16, otherwise known as hexadecimal (or hex for short).

In base 10, which you use every day for counting, your numbers fall into familiar columns: one column is the number of single units (1s), the next column is the number of tens of units (10s), the next column is the number of hundreds of units (100s), and so on.

100s	10s	1s	Base 10
4	7	9	= 479

In hex, a different model applies. The right column still expresses the number of 1s, but the next column expresses the number of 16s there are in the number.

256s	16s	1s	Base 16 (Hex)
0	1	F	= 31

Because the second column from the right starts at 16, the units in the columns go up to 15, but they still must be expressed as a single digit. This is achieved by using letters in addition to numbers. In the 1s column, you count from 0 to 9 just like in normal base 10, but the numbers 10 through 15 are expressed with the letters

A through F. So in hex, A is equal to 10, B is 11, and so on, all the way up to F, which is 15. After that, the 1s column returns to 0, and the 16s column increases to 1. Thus, the figure 10 in hex means "1 in the 16s column and 0 in the 1s column."

Back to your colors. Each unique color is the result of combining the three base colors, and each unique color has a six-digit identifier. In this six-digit number, there are two digits for each of the base colors. The first two digits describe the amount of red present, the next two describe the green, and the last two describe the blue. This means that black—the absence of any color of light—is expressed as 000000. That's 00 (hex) of red, 00 of green, and 00 of blue.

	Red	Green	Blue
Black =	00	00	00

The opposite of this is white, which is a mix of all the colors at full strength—so pure white in hex is FFFFFF.

The largest number that can be expressed in two digits in hex is FF, which means (15 × 16) + (15 × 1), making a total of 255. So a color whose number is FF0000 would be 255 parts red, 0 parts green, and 0 parts blue—which means that only red would be displayed on the screen. Play around with the hex values of each base color component in a six-digit identifier to create different colors. The different combinations possible with this hex numbering system give you access to a range of over 16 million colors. Enough, I'm sure you'll agree, for you to find one that you like (even if you can't find a shirt that matches it).

Right now, you're probably thinking "This chapter is supposed to be about color, but all I've had so far is a math lesson!" Hopefully though, this brief explanation will help you to understand how Flash sees color, and from there, how you can best get the effect you want.

Let's take this knowledge and see how it's implemented in Flash. A good place to start is with custom colors. That's where you create your own mixtures of the base colors that you can use and save.

Custom colors

Bored with seeing the same colors everywhere you look? Want to make your whites whiter than white? Then you need the **Color Mixer** panel.

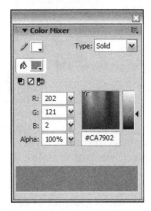

This is where you can get Flash to mix exactly the color you're looking for. The Color Mixer panel is partnered with the Color Swatches panel, which is used for choosing default palette or custom-made colors.

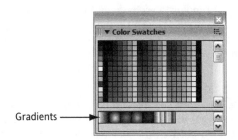

Gradients

The Color Swatches panel will get larger if you click-drag any of its edges. This is a big advantage the Color Swatches panel has over the similar-looking pop-up Color palette that appears when you click the fill and stroke colors in the Properties panel and toolbar. The Color Swatches panel is particularly useful when you want to see large samples of your colors, as in the screenshot that follows.

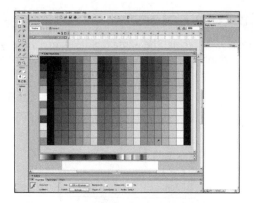

On the Color Mixer panel, you can enter the precise RGB values that you want your strokes and fills to have, and then apply these colors to the objects in your movies. The Color Swatches panel shows you all the colors you have available. (A swatch is the name given to a single color, and a group of swatches together is called a palette.)

The colors shown in the top part of the Color Swatches panel make up the 216 web-safe colors—this is the default palette used by Flash. These web-safe colors are guaranteed to work on any computer using any browser running anywhere in the world, so if you always want your work to render perfectly on any old or superseded browser exactly as you designed it, these are the colors to use.

The web-safe palette dates from the time when many users had computers capable of showing only a limited palette of colors, typically 256. Very few such computers still exist (and if they can only show 256 colors, then there's a good chance they can't show Flash), so in most cases you can ignore the web-safe palette when working in Flash.

It's also worth noting that even if you did stick to the web-safe palette, your colors would cease to be web-safe as soon as you added a gradient, given that gradients use many colors to form their blends. Also, if you added anything with an alpha value less than 100%, you wouldn't be displaying web-safe colors.

So if you're determined to stick to web-safe colors, be aware of the limitations you'll face.

If you're not sure about using a particular custom color you've created, the best thing to do is test your movies and web pages in as many different browsers as you think is necessary. Ultimately, there's a trade-off between how certain you want to be that your page looks tip-top to everyone, and the time and effort it takes to test everything. For most people, testing their movies and sites on up-to-date versions of Internet Explorer and Netscape (or Mozilla) is the norm.

Here's an exercise to take you through the process of creating your own custom colors.

Creating custom colors with the Color Mixer panel

1. Open the Color Mixer panel and the Color Swatches panel from the Window menu.

In the Color Mixer panel, you'll see the familiar Stroke and Fill Color boxes in the same layout as you find in the Property inspector and Tools panel.

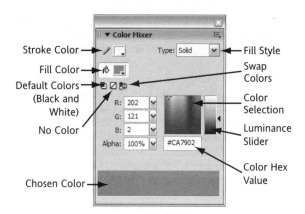

On the right side, there are four input boxes: three with which you can change the RGB value combinations for the current color (using values of 0 through 255 for each base color), and one with which you can set the **alpha** value. Alpha is essentially another word for transparency: 100% alpha is solid opaque color, 0% is fully transparent, and anything between gives an intermediate degree of transparency. Alpha is commonly used to make objects fade in and out of movies and to create windows in objects so that you can see through them. How to use alpha in your movies will be more fully explored in the next chapter, in which you'll look at animation in more detail.

The final tools on the Color Mixer panel are the color selector and luminance slider bars at the bottom-right. The color selector is a quick, visual way to choose a color. Click anywhere on the bar, and that color will automatically be selected. The luminance slider lets you fine-tune that selection. Drag the arrow up and down until you get the shade that you want.

2. Click the square next to the bucket icon in the Fill Color box. The current Color palette appears.

Color Window   Luminance Slider

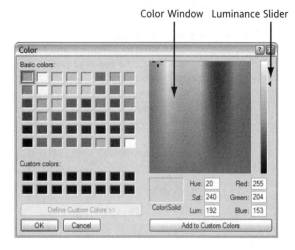

Hex Edit Box
Alpha Value
No Color
Preview Box
Color Picker
Basic Colors
Color Palette

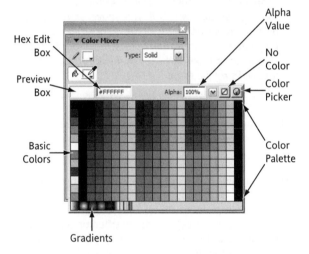

Gradients

On the top row of the color selection box (above all the available colors, and to the right of the preview box showing the currently selected color) there's a box showing the hex value of that color.

#FFFFFF

It can be extremely useful to know the hex value. With this information, you can match the color of your Flash movie to that of the host web page and vice-versa, because web page colors are also defined in hex.

3. Click the Color Picker button—it's at the top right of the Color palette and has a rainbow-hued circle on it. The Color dialog box opens so you can create a custom color.

This is where all your alchemical color mixing takes place. On the left side of the dialog box is a set of basic, solid colors that you can use as starting points. Your attention, though, is no doubt already drawn to that lush, color-drenched pane on the right, which looks like a piece of blotting paper used to mop up a rainbow. This pane contains all the colors that you can use in your movies.

The Mac's color picker, shown in the following graphic, is very different from the PC version, but it works almost exactly the same way.

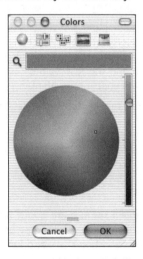

In the Mac-only Color Wheel mode, a color picker takes the place of the color-drenched pane in the Windows dialog box. If you want to adjust the RGB values of your color, simply click the Color Sliders icon from the options at the top and select RGB Sliders from the drop-down menu.

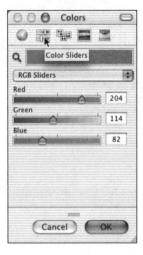

The color-picking options available to the Mac user are more sophisticated than those on the PC, and they're beyond the scope of this chapter. What the Mac doesn't have, however, is the ability to create multiple custom colors in one visit to the picker—you'll have to mix your new colors one at a time.

4. Click the color pane and drag the mouse pointer around. Everything seems to change at once; the colors in the luminance slider shift like a tie-dyed chameleon and the RGB values rush frantically to keep up with your mouse pointer.

5. Release your mouse button and let the chameleon take a rest.

It's time to explain some more about those numbers. To the left of the RGB values are three boxes indicating the hue (Hue), saturation (Sat), and luminance (Lum). Note that on the Mac, luminance is termed *brightness* (and the three color values are thus referred to by the acronym HSB).

These three terms are another way to describe color. The hue is the actual color, and it's a relative of the RGB settings, but with a smaller range.

6. If you drag your mouse pointer carefully in a horizontal line across the color window, only the hue setting changes.

7. If you move the mouse vertically up and down the window, only the saturation setting changes.

> On the Mac, hue is determined by the angle you select on the color wheel, whereas saturation changes as you move nearer or farther away from the hub of the wheel. If you move your mouse pointer along the radius of the color wheel toward the center, the saturation will increase from 0% at the center to 100% at the perimeter, but the hue setting will stay the same.

The saturation determines the amount of the color. A pastel peach color has low saturation, and a vivid red has a lot of saturation.

The final value is the luminance (or brightness). This is the amount of light in the color. So far, you've chosen your original pigment (hue), and you've mixed it into your white base to get the depth of color (saturation). Now you paint it onto a big sheet of glass. You place a light behind the glass—this light determines the luminance. If you use a small, dim light, the color will be a dark, gloomy shade, but if you position a huge arc light behind the glass, the color will become so painfully bright that there will be only a negligible difference between it and white. The luminance value is controlled with the slider bar on the right side of the Color dialog box.

It's worth mentioning that in Flash you can use the HSB color model as your default color value display instead of RGB. If you go to the Color Mixer panel and click the menu icon on the right side of its title bar, a menu appears giving you the option to switch to HSB. For this chapter, though, stick with RGB.

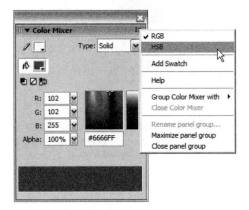

8. Choose a color from the vast spectrum available in the color window.

9. Look in the color preview box to ensure that you have the color you want. You may think this is obvious, but it's very easy to choose a color from the color window and leave the luminance set to 0, which will make everything come out black!

10. Click the Add to Custom Colors button at the bottom of the dialog box.

On the Mac, after you choose the color you want in the selected color box, click OK to return to the Color Mixer.

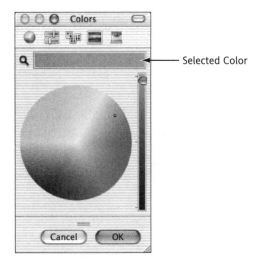

Selected Color

Mac users can go on to the next section—the next load of stuff is for PC users only.

Your color now appears as a swatch in one of the Custom colors boxes on the far left. These boxes serve as a temporary storage area for your swatches. Next time you want to use your swatch, you can come back to this dialog box and it will be there waiting for you.

Beware though, the next time you open the Color dialog box. If you select a color from the spectrum and add it to your custom colors, Flash will automatically overwrite the color in the top-left of your Custom color boxes.

By default, Flash will always save your color into this first box, even if it's currently filled with another color. The only way to specify which box your new color goes into is to click the specific Custom color box you want to use, select your color from the spectrum, and then add the color to the box.

11. Click OK to close the Color dialog box.

Notice that your custom color is currently selected in the Fill Color box of the Color Mixer panel. If you were now to use the Oval tool to draw a circle, it would be filled with your beautiful custom color. Go on, try it . . . you know you want to.

> *It's important to remember one thing when creating custom colors: Flash doesn't automatically save them permanently for you. If you close Flash and reopen it again, all your carefully constructed colors will be gone from the* Custom color *boxes.*

So the question arises—just how the heck do you make your custom colors persist?

Persistent custom colors

Saving custom colors in Flash is unfortunately quite a long-winded process. After you've created your color and defined it as a swatch in a Custom color box, you must then add it to the main Color palette, and finally save it as a color set. Let's see exactly how.

Saving custom colors permanently

1. Make sure the Color Mixer panel is open. Also make sure that the swatch you want to add is displayed as the currently selected fill or stroke color. This means you need to ensure your chosen Custom color box is selected when you close the Color dialog box after choosing your color from the spectrum.

2. Click the menu in the top right of the Color Mixer panel, and have another look at the resulting drop-down menu.

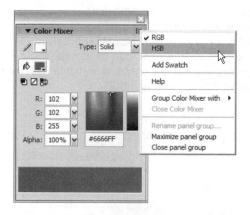

As you already know, the menu contains two options for displaying color values—RGB and HSB—and an option for adding a swatch to a palette.

3. Select the Add Swatch option.

When you open up your Color palette on the Color Mixer panel or in the Tools panel, you'll see your new swatch in a fresh row at the bottom of the palette.

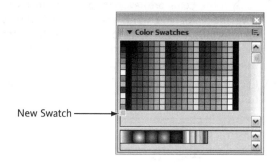

New Swatch

You can now easily select your new color from this palette. Note that you may have to either scroll down or make the Color palette bigger if your palette is shown in a small panel.

After you've added all your new swatches to the bottom of the palette, you still need to save it so it will be available to you in the future.

4. In the Color Swatches panel, click the small icon in the top-right corner to access the drop-down menu options.

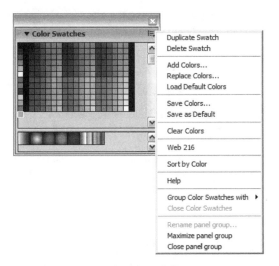

This menu contains all the commands for dealing with swatches and palettes. For the moment, let's just focus on a couple of these options: Save Colors and Add Colors.

5. Choose the Save Colors option, which will open up the Export Color Swatch dialog box. This dialog box will allow you to save your current colors in a permanent file—a color set—that Flash can access in the future.

Flash's default location for these files is in the Color Sets folder, deep within your user settings folder. The exact location of this folder on your machine is typically C:/Documents and Settings/ <Username>/ Local Settings/Application Data/ Macromedia/ Flash 8/en/Configuration/ Color Sets on the PC, and <Hard Drive>/Users/ <Username>/ Library/ Application Support/ Macromedia/Flash 8/Configuration/ Color Sets on the Mac.

6. Navigate to the location where you'd like to keep your swatches, give your color set a name, and then click Save. Your swatches are now saved in a Flash Color Set (CLR) file.

The files that are already in this folder are the ready-made palettes that come with Flash, each one designed to cater to a specific set of requirements. Note that Flash's default behavior is to open the standard color set whenever it restarts.

If you want to access your custom color set again, open the drop-down menu from the Color Swatches panel and click the Add Colors button. This will open the Import Color Swatch dialog box, where you can select the specific color set you want to use to enrich your palette. Then you can use the slider button on the right edge of the Color Swatches panel to scroll through the newly available colors.

There are many ways of creating and describing color, and a detailed analysis of them is beyond the scope of this book. If you're interested in learning more, there are plenty of resources just waiting to be discovered, ranging from the Internet to your local library. The best thing you can do is experiment and see how the different values affect the final color. It's up to you to decide which method you prefer, but remember that your color will be rendered in Flash and on the Web as an RGB value.

Before moving on, though, it's perhaps worth noting another way to save a palette that doesn't use the panels at all—a way many designers (myself included) create and save color schemes for site design. Traditional oil painters tend to create their colors on a real palette, which is usually a piece of wood or a plate. By leaving daubs of color using the Brush tool, you can do the same thing. By placing your colors outside the stage area and on a guide layer (right/CMD-click on a layer title in the Timeline and select Guide from the context menu that appears), you ensure that the colors don't get exported to the final SWF, but you can choose the colors using the color picker.

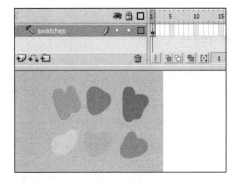

Another big advantage of creating and saving your colors offscreen is that you can make your swatches as big as you like, and you can also move the colors around so that you can get a better idea of how they contrast/complement each other.

In the following image, I wanted to know how two of my proposed colors would appear if I used one as the background and the other as the main foreground color, so I just experimented by laying one color over the other.

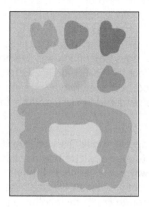

Just like using real paints, drawing freehand swatches can be a much more intuitive process, and can be a lot quicker than messing about with saved palettes. If you don't want to keep the colors in the work area, you can of course also save your swatches as symbols. Simply select all your swatches and press *F8*.

Your next step is to look at color and gradients.

Gradient color

Custom colors are great, but no matter how much work you put in picking and choosing your color values, you still end up with a single flat color. This is where gradients come in. **Gradients** are distinct color features you can apply to your objects' fills.

A gradient consists of a smooth change from one color to another. In Flash, gradients can be simple and pure, with a starting color and an end color, or they can be more complex, with up to 16 different colors. In complex gradients, intermediate colors create distinct "steps" in the gradient, giving the effect of a richer and more complicated spectrum.

Simple Gradient:

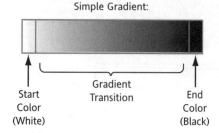

Complex Gradient:

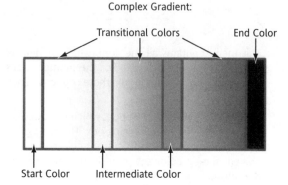

These different types of gradients allow for some pretty spectacular effects, especially when you tween transitions from gradient to gradient. For now though, you'll start with the basics.

This next screenshot shows a simple gradient, which runs from white to black.

This is an example of a **linear gradient**, so named because the gradient runs in a straight line from the first color (white, on the left) to the second color (black, on the right). With linear gradients, you define the start and end colors (and any intermediate ones, if you want a more complex effect), and Flash works out the intermediate colors between them. Flash has a number of predefined linear gradients in its palette, but you can also mix your own, as you'll see shortly.

The other type of gradient is a radial gradient.

Radial gradients have their starting color at the center and their ending color at the outside—the gradient radiates out from the center to the edge. Flash has some standard radial gradients, but once again, you have infinite customization options at your fingertips.

The choice of which gradient to use for a given task is entirely up to your personal taste. There's no right or wrong gradient type; just use the one you think looks the best for what you're trying to do.

Gradients are really just smooth transitions of color between two (or more) distinct colors. If you've ever tried to create a gradient on paper with colored pencils or paint, you know how difficult it can be to get the effect right. Thankfully, Flash gives you a little studio and palette where you can create, preview, and amend gradients to your heart's content.

Making the gradient

To work with gradients, you need to use the Color Mixer panel.

Creating and modifying gradients

1. If the Color Mixer panel isn't open, open it from the Window options menu. You probably already noticed the boxes at the bottom of the Color Swatches panel that don't look like the other solid colors.

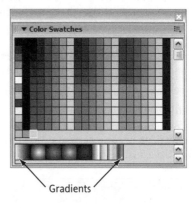

Gradients

These are Flash's predefined gradients. There are five basic (two-color) gradients and two more complicated ones.

2. Open the Color Swatches panel to open the palette. From there, click the black-and-white linear gradient at the bottom-left.

Notice that as you select the gradient, the Color Mixer panel automatically changes to reflect this choice.

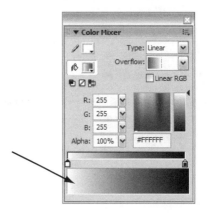

You've chosen the gradient style that you want to use—a simple, linear, black-and-white one. You can now either use this as the fill on a new or existing object, or you can customize it, as you're going to do here.

First, let's ensure that you don't overwrite the default linear gradient.

3. Select Add Swatch from the Color Mixer panel's drop-down menu. (Note that this is the *Color Mixer*, not the *Color Swatches* panel! Its sometimes easy to get confused as many workflows cross the two panels.) This will add a new gradient at the right end of the list on the Color Swatches panel.

You now have your very own gradient to tinker with.

4. Click the new gradient's box at the bottom of the Color Swatches panel to ensure that this is the one you're working on. The currently selected gradient box will have a white outline.

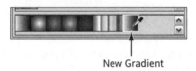

New Gradient

Because you selected a linear gradient, you can see the linear gradient controls in the Color Mixer panel.

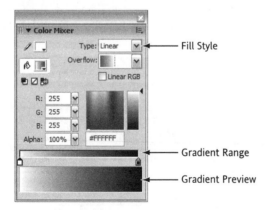

Fill Style

Gradient Range

Gradient Preview

The most important of these controls is the long thin bar across the lower third of the panel. The bar has a white color marker hanging from its left side and a black color marker hanging from its right. This bar shows the **range** of your gradient— that is, its start and end points.

5. Click the white color marker and drag it to the middle of the bar.

The gradient in the preview window on the bottom-left should now be half bleached-out with only a smudge of black creeping in on the right side.

Your selections tell Flash to start the gradient at the white color marker and use the black color marker as the end point. Notice also that the gradient box in the Color Swatches panel has also changed to reflect your alteration.

6. Click the black color marker and drag it all the way to the left side where the white color marker used to be.

Your gradient is now reversed: it consists of a small black stripe on the left with a large white mass to its right.

Now you can start adding to the basic gradient to make it a little more interesting. To do this, you have to add some intermediate color stages to the range bar.

7. Place your mouse pointer below the gradient range bar, just to the right of your current white color marker. When a plus sign appears next to your mouse pointer (indicating that you can add to the current selection), click to place another color marker.

Because you clicked underneath a white part of the gradient, the new color marker will inherit that color. If you had clicked in a black area, you would have gotten a black color marker. A new color marker will always take on the color directly above it in the gradient range bar. If you ever need to delete a paint bucket, simply click-drag it diagonally downwards.

Dragging straight down almost always works, but there's a "feature" whereby if you ever manage to drag a color marker directly downward (without any sideways movement), Flash doesn't remove the color marker. Thus, it's easier to drag slightly diagonally.

8. Click the same way under the gray gradient between the black and white markers.

Again, your new color marker will be filled with the same gray as the color directly above it. Notice that the currently selected color marker has a black pointer at the top and that the body of each color marker indicates what color that marker represents. Furthermore, the slider to the right of the color window shows you the color that's in the current color marker.

You can now change the color content of your color markers and customize the gradient further.

9. Click the color window (the box that looks like it has a rainbow in it) and move the slider to the right of it to select a new color—say, a pure blue. As you change the color, the gradient will change to reflect its new Technicolor glory.

Warning: when you're mixing a gradient, you may be tempted to use the Color Swatches panel or the fill/stroke colors at the top of the Color Mixer to pick the color (you used to be able to select a color the latter way in Flash MX 2004 and previous versions, but not in Flash 8). Don't do it. If you do, Flash will think you want to use a solid color instead of a gradient and it will take you out of the gradient selection in the Color Mixer.

If you actually want to select an existing color from the current palette as a gradient color rather than switch to a solid color, you have to click-hold on a color marker for a second (or double click). When you release, the palette will appear.

10. Click the color marker on the far right and, using the color window at the top right again, change its color to red.

11. Your gradient should now flow from black (on the left) to a very thin, white bar in the middle that rapidly fades into red on the right.

Now that you've created your gradient, how do you use it? Easy. It's now your selected fill for any objects you draw, and if you click the Paint Bucket tool you can use it to fill existing objects.

12. Draw a square with the Rectangle Tool, and you should see something much like the following figure, but in glowing color.

Radial gradients are created the same way.

13. Go back to the Color Mixer panel and select Radial from the Fill Style drop-down menu.

Note that Flash retained the colors you defined on the gradient range bar, but now they're mapped to a radial gradient with what was the left color (black) in the center of the gradient and the right color (red) on the outside.

14. Draw another square next to the first one.

From this, you can clearly see the relationship between linear and radial gradients. They're both based on a spread of colors you define on the range bar, and the way this range is displayed depends on the left-to-right sequence of those colors. You can alter the way the gradients appear by shifting the relative positions of the color markers on the range bar.

15. To save your gradient permanently, use the same technique you used in the previous exercise. Open the menu by clicking the top-right icon on the Color Mixer panel, add the new swatch, and save (or overwrite) your customized color set using the menu option from the Color Swatches panel. Make sure you don't overwrite any of Flash's default color sets.

16. If your gradients get messed up (as sometimes happens while you're experimenting), you can always revert to your saved color set (using the Add Color option from the Color Swatches panel menu), or reload Flash's default colors, as shown in the following screenshot:

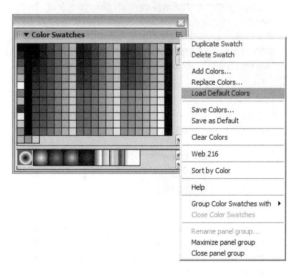

Now that you have an initial understanding of gradients, let's have a look at how they can be used to create light effects in your movies.

Using light and shade with gradients

By combining simple gradients with drawn shapes, it's easy to create convincing light effects that simulate shadow, shade, and light sources. In reality, of course, you can't build true 3D light-sourced objects (you need other packages to create those), but you *can* fabricate an adequate enough illusion to fool the eye. These effects can add real interest and depth to your movies.

Let's explore this by constructing a shaded sphere.

Using gradients to create a shaded sphere

1. Open a new Flash document.

2. Select the Oval tool and use Object Drawing mode. Select the green radial gradient from the bottom of the Color Swatches panel.

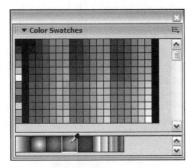

Because you want the sphere to look like a realistic 3D object, you need to remove the stroke line from around the edge.

3. Click the Stroke button in the Tools panel, and then click the No Color button, either at the top of the palette or in the Tools panel.

Now you're ready to draw your circle.

4. Use the Oval tool with the *SHIFT* key held down to keep it perfectly symmetrical. You should now have a black sphere with a green center.

To bring the sphere to life, you need to adjust the position of the green center light.

5. Reposition the center of the fill—the point from which the gradient radiates—using your Paint Bucket tool. Imagine that the tip of the bucket is your light source, and click the top-left side of your circle to readjust this source. You'll end up with a sphere similar to the following:

> Make sure that you have the Lock Fill *option dese-lected when you use the Paint Bucket in this way. If your Paint Bucket seems to be creating solid fills, you probably need to deselect the* Lock Fill *icon.*

And that's it—your very own 3D sphere just waiting to be moved around on the stage and morphed into something else. With this basic technique, it's easy to make more complicated shapes with multiple gradients. Maybe a festive egg . . .

or a metal cube made from two skewed rectangles . . .

145

This method can also be used to improve your emerald from the last chapter.

Removing the strokes also improves the 3D effect. Just in case you aren't sure of the improvement, here's a good old before and after:

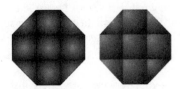

> *Warning: as with custom colors, custom gradients aren't permanently saved when Flash is closed. To save them, you must go through the same process as you did for custom colors. First add the gradient to the palette by selecting* Add Swatch *from the Color Mixer panel drop-down menu. Then click the* Save Colors *command from the drop-down menu on the Color Swatches panel.*

You've seen how to make a basic shape look three-dimensional with a standard gradient. Flash also has features that let you finesse the gradient effects you apply to your objects.

Applying gradients to objects and modifying them

It's all well and good being able to make a perfect linear gradient for your shape, but what if your shape itself isn't perfectly linear? For example, a linear gradient looks fine on a square, but on a skewed parallelogram, the standard gradient doesn't really enhance the impression of a real object with the light falling on it.

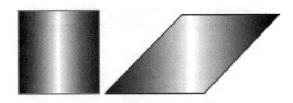

Luckily, Flash provides ways of changing your gradient to suit your shape.

The simplest and least painstaking way of applying the gradient in a non-standard way is achieved with the Paint Bucket tool.

If you draw a filled rectangle on the stage after selecting a linear gradient for the fill, you get a dandy-looking gradient.

The only problem is that all your rectangles drawn with the basic gradient as a fill will look the same. However, you can change this. If you select the Paint Bucket tool with the standard linear gradient as the fill, and then click and drag the mouse pointer to apply the fill to the shape, you can simulate light coming from a different direction.

Changing the angle of your drag will alter the starting point from which the gradient flows. This method is one of trial and error—it also depends on the snapping options you've selected—experiment and see the effects you can get with different gradient types.

You won't be surprised that Flash also has more precise methods of manipulating gradients—with the Fill Transform tool from the Tools panel.

This tool is your key to modifying gradients professionally. In the next exercise, you'll find out how to fit a gradient to a skewed parallelogram and see the methods you can use to alter gradients in a controlled manner after they're on the stage.

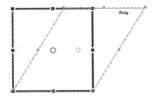

Scaling and rotating linear gradients

First, create your parallelogram.

1. Use the Rectangle tool with Object Drawing mode turned off to draw a square with a black stroke and no fill. Skew your square using the Free Transform tool from the Tools panel. Recall that to skew a shape, you need to hover over one of the lines of the transform square until it turns into two arrows pointing in opposite directions.

2. Fill the shape with a linear gradient. The example uses a custom gradient consisting of two black color markers at each end of the gradient range bar, and a white one in the middle.

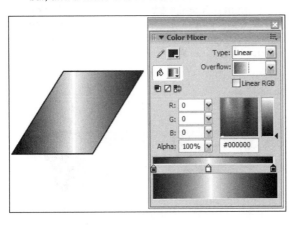

The effect you're trying to achieve with this shape is to make it look like a length of metal pipe. Right now, it looks more like a sheet of metal than a tube. Let's see if you can model it better.

> *If you had drawn the rectangle as a Drawing Object, the fill would have skewed with the outline. However, its worth knowing how to rotate the gradient manually as well, because there are many situations in which you'll want to edit the gradient separately from the shape it's filling.*

3. Select the Gradient Transform tool from the Tools panel.

   Your mouse pointer changes to an arrow with a gradient-filled rectangle next to it as soon as you mouse over the gradient. This indicates that you'll be in Transform Fill mode if you click.

4. Click the gradient that's filling your skewed shape, and two blue lines will appear around your shape. A circle will appear in the center, and a square and a circle will appear on the right side.

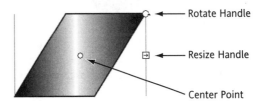

147

These are the handles used to move and transform your gradient; you can think of them as the Scale and Rotate commands rolled into one. When you position your mouse pointer over the center point, it changes into a four-headed arrow. It becomes a two-headed arrow when positioned over the Resize handle, and it becomes curved arrows around a circle when positioned over the Rotate handle, as shown in the following image:

Each of these handles controls a different aspect of the gradient that's filling the parallelogram.

5. Click the center point and drag it to the left side. Release the mouse button to center the gradient around the new point. Notice that the lines at either side of your shape move as well. These bounding lines act as a quick guide to the position, size, and angle of your gradient.

6. Drag the Rotate handle down until the gradient is on a similar slant to the sides of your skewed square.

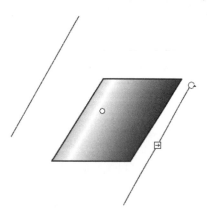

The gradient looks a little too big now, and to your eye it may seem to be bleaching the shape a bit. You can get around this by squeezing the gradient to fit into the shape better.

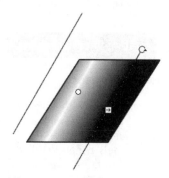

7. Click the Resize handle and move it in until you achieve your desired effect—a strip of metal pipe in low light.

And there you have it, a gradient that you've fit perfectly into your skewed parallelogram.

From here, the sky is the limit and it's only a matter of time before you start building all manner of objects, such as a metallic ice-cream cone, or maybe a cone of metallic fries.

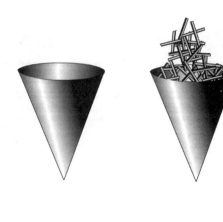

Perhaps they're not that useful in web design, but chrome or faux-3D effects are always useful in user interface design because they lift the 2D screen toward a more realistic 3D feel. You only have to look at your operating system's windows to see how used to gradients you've likely become (and how you've likely stopped noticing them). See if you can spot all the gradients in the screenshot from a Windows XP window below (there are 12).

Radial gradients are also amenable to your creative sleight of hand.

Modifying a radial gradient

When dealing with a radial gradient, there four parameters for transforming the fill, as opposed to the linear gradient's three. The majority of them are the same, but their implementations can appear very different.

1. Open a new Flash document and draw a circle with Object Drawing mode on. Give the circle any fill color and no stroke.

2. Select the first radial gradient in the list and fill the circle in the top corner using the Paint Bucket tool.

3. Duplicate the circle (Edit ➤ Duplicate) and move the copy away from the original.

4. Select the copy and use the Transform panel (Window ➤ Transform) to change its size to 70% of the original. Before typing 70% into either of the top two text fields, make sure that the Constrain option is selected. This will force the transformation to stick to its true circle ratio and prevent distortion.

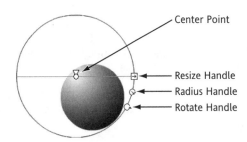

5. Select the Fill Transform tool and click the copy of the (now smaller) circle.

The circle around the radial gradient is the equivalent of the two bounding lines that were on either side of the linear gradient. This marks the shape and the limits of your gradient.

6. Click the center point and drag it around to experiment. You'll notice that the epicenter of the gradient shifts according to the location of this point. (Note that the epicenter was previously located in the top-left because of the fill orientation on the original circle.)

149

7. Drag the center point to the bottom-right corner. So far you have two spheres that aren't talking to each other.

8. Use the Arrow tool to select both circles (or use *CTRL+A* to select all—assuming you have nothing else on the stage).

9. Open the Align panel (Window ➤ Align).

10. Make sure the To stage modifier is switched off, and then center the smaller circle over the larger one using the Align panel.

Can you guess what it is yet? Yes, it's a 3D button. Let's add a little highlighting to the top-left of the inner circle to make it more recognizable.

11. Add a new layer called highlight and draw a very small oval shape on it. This oval will suggest the highlighting.

12. Rotate the oval to –50 degrees using either the Free Transform tool or the Transform panel.

13. Make sure that Snap Align is switched on for the next step (View ➤ Snapping ➤ Snap Align).

14. Drag the oval to the top-left of the inner circle and position it when the two Snap Align lines appear. Then release the mouse button.

The way the snapping occurs depends on how you've got your snapping preferences set. You can play around with these via the View ➤ Snapping ➤ Edit Snap Align menu option.

At this point you should have a neat roller ball–style button with depth, created by using gradients. If you're happy with this, save the movie before you proceed.

Before you move on to the next section, let's experiment with the remaining radial gradient modifiers.

15. With the Fill Transform tool selected, click the inner circle. The modifier points will appear.

16. Click the Resize handle (the circle next to the square) and drag it around. The size of the gradient will be increased or decreased uniformly. After you release the mouse button, the new gradient size will be rendered.

Now it's time for the Rotate handle. Let's illustrate its function with a different object.

17. On a new layer, draw a square with no outline and choose a radial gradient fill. Create it away from the button—hide those other layers, if you like.

18. Select the Fill Transform tool and click the fill. Use the Rotate handle to rotate the fill to your heart's content. But nothing is happening!

Yes, that's right, nothing is changing because you're rotating a circle, and as you know, no matter how much you spin a circle, it always remains the same. The secret is to change the shape of your gradient first, so it's no longer a perfect circle.

19. Click the Resize handle and drag it in toward the center of the shape.

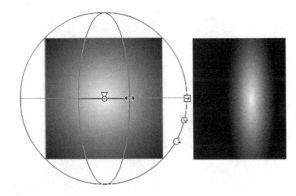

Your gradient is now elliptical.

20. Use the Rotate handle to turn the gradient 45 degrees to the right.

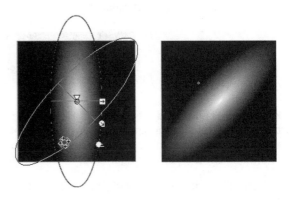

That's better! And better still, that's all for Fill Transform modifiers.

You've now used all the gradient tools except one. So far you've only been able to give gradients to individual shapes and then modify those, but imagine what you could do if you could apply your gradient evenly to a number of objects spread out over the entire stage? That's just what the Lock Fill option lets you do.

Overflowing fills

When you resize a gradient fill, there's a good chance you may make the gradient smaller than the object it's filling. You can make Flash do one of three things when this occurs.

Overflowing fills

1. With Object Drawing turned off, create a long filled rectangle using the leftmost gradient in the color picker.

151

2. Deselect the rectangle by clicking on a blank area of the stage with the Selection tool. Then select the Gradient Fill tool and click the rectangle. Resize the fill so that it's much shorter than the rectangle.

By default, Flash extends the gradient. Flash extends the leftmost color in the gradient (white) to the left edge of the rectangle, and extends the rightmost color in the gradient (black) to the right edge.

You can change this behavior with the Overflow drop-down menu in the Color Mixer panel.

The three overflow options are Extend, Reflect, and Repeat.

3. With the rectangle still selected with the Gradient Tool, select Reflect (the second choice) from the Overflow drop-down menu.

The overflowing area of the rectangle is now filled with repeating versions of the gradient. Every other repeat is mirrored (or *reflected*) so that there's a continuous and smooth graduation.

4. Select the Repeat option. This time the gradients aren't mirrored, so you get obvious disjoints when each gradient copy starts.

The changes in final pattern are even more noticeable when you're using radial gradients, as shown in the following three screenshots:

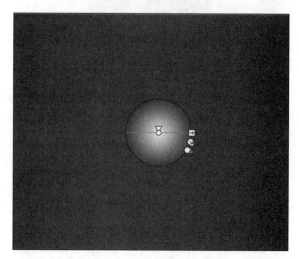

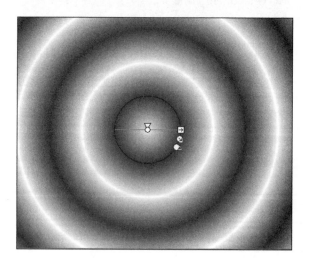

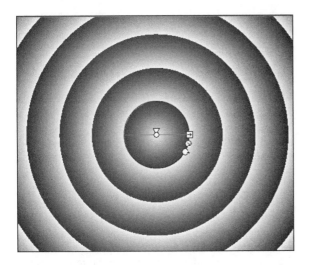

Locking fills

By locking a fill, you can make a gradient span across multiple shapes. That is, you can get the effect of a series of cutout shapes that reveal a common underlying background, almost as if you were opening up little windows to reveal a picture behind them.

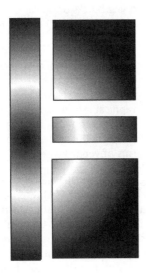

Here's how to use the Lock Fill feature.

Locking a fill

1. Select a gradient from the Color Swatches panel. The book shows the black-and-white linear gradient for clarity, but feel free to experiment with something a little more adventurous.

2. Use the Rectangle tool from the Tools panel to draw a long, thin rectangle with a gray stroke across the stage from left to right.

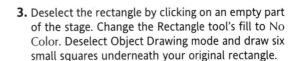

3. Deselect the rectangle by clicking on an empty part of the stage. Change the Rectangle tool's fill to No Color. Deselect Object Drawing mode and draw six small squares underneath your original rectangle.

4. Select the Dropper tool, and then click your big gradient-filled rectangle. This tells Flash to use this particular gradient (and its orientation on the page) as a fill for other objects.

5. Select the Fill tool. Flash automatically changes the mouse pointer to a paint bucket with a small padlock next to it (the sign for—you guessed it—a locked fill).

6. Click each of the squares to fill them with the gradient.

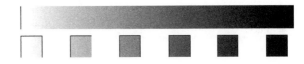

See how the gradient stretches across the six squares as though they were a continuation of the fill in the big rectangle? Flash is intelligent enough to work out the continuation of the gradient beyond the original shape and map it onto the new shapes. This can be a very powerful way to achieve symmetry across your gradients.

153

To unlock these fills, with the Paint Bucket tool selected, click the Lock Fill icon in the Options area of the Tools panel.

This will unlock the fill, and you can now color your squares with any fill you like.

We've spent all our time so far looking at ways to draw images directly in Flash, but it's also possible to create images in external programs and import them into Flash.

Bitmaps

Working with vectors is all well and good, but it has some significant limitations from a creative point of view. Don't get me wrong, I think vectors are great, but they aren't much help if you want to make a website for a photographer or someone who needs to show photographic images.

Well, despair not, because Flash has a number of import solutions, from bitmap to vector file formats. Flash also has the ability to import the ubiquitous PDF file format. In this section, you'll look at the different import options at your disposal with your copy of Flash, and what you can do with the files you've imported when they're on your stage.

As a stand-alone application, Flash can import many major image types, including

- Adobe Illustrator
- FreeHand
- GIF
- JPEG
- PNG
- PDF
- EPS

If you have QuickTime 4 or later installed (download it for free from www.apple.com/quicktime), you can also import the following formats:

- Photoshop (PSD)
- PICT
- TIF

Let's start with probably the most common image type, the bitmap.

Using bitmap images in Flash

A **bitmap** image (otherwise known as a **raster** image) is a generic name for an image that's defined by individual pixels. Typical bitmap formats include JPEG, BMP, GIF, and TIF. The difference between the formats is the particular way each one stores the image data. Bitmaps are generally used for complicated images like photographs or paintings, in which every pixel can make a difference in the finished picture. The problem with bitmaps is that the image file has to describe each pixel that the image is composed of, which often results in a large file, in turn meaning long download times. (Some "lossy" bitmap formats, such as JPEG, can compress images by describing blocks of similar color rather than every pixel, but they do so at the expense of picture quality.)

A **vector** file, on the other hand, describes an image in terms of mathematical expressions—such as the start and end points of a line. This allows vector files to compress a lot of graphical information into a small space. Mathematical line description is great for simple shapes, but it's more difficult to try to describe the Mona Lisa in terms of vectors.

The first thing to remember when you're considering using bitmaps in Flash is that Flash was not designed as a bitmap program. To get the best performance in your movies, it's always preferable to create everything inside Flash using the drawing tools provided, or using vector graphics imported from other software applications. Flash can optimize a vector graphics file to ensure that it's as small (and therefore, as quick to download) as possible. Although it's possible to create a flipbook-style movie by using a sequence of imported bitmaps, this will create such a huge file and take so long to download that most people will have moved on to the next site before the first couple of frames of your movie have loaded.

There will be times when you've created a nice logo in a paint program, and you may be tempted to just pull it into Flash and animate it. Although you can do this, in the long run you're better off doing it from scratch in Flash. It may not look exactly the same, but the benefits of smaller size and higher speed will probably outweigh the small graphical differences. The first rule of thumb when using bitmaps is to think carefully about the trade-off between file size and the graphical benefits that bitmaps will bring to your movie.

Here are a few more rules of thumb—use bitmaps when

- You need photos or lifelike images.
- You need screenshots.
- You need pictures of drawings or artwork.

For anything else, draw it inside Flash or another vector program.

The big downside of vectors is that they can require a lot of processing power to draw quickly. For example, when Flash draws an animated circle, it has to calculate the curvature of the circle on every frame. If Flash could just display a bitmap of a circle, it would in some cases be much faster. Flash 8 gives you the best of both worlds with a new feature called bitmap caching—you can make Flash handle vectors internally as bitmaps, and this can speed up your animations considerably. More on this cool feature in Chapter 6.

You've considered all the pros and cons, you've tried your best to draw your picture in Flash, but you've come to the decision that you're just going to have to import a bitmap image into Flash. So how do you do it?

Working with bitmaps

1. Open a new Flash document, and click the File ➤ Import ➤ Import to Stage menu option to open the Import dialog box.

2. Navigate to a BMP, JPEG, PNG, or GIF file image on your computer (or download the example used here (swirl.bmp) from this book's download section on www.friendsofed.com).

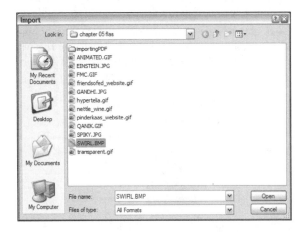

3. Open the file, and your file will be imported into Flash and placed both on the stage as an object and in the Library.

> Warning: Flash uses the original image stored in the Library as a reference point, so deleting it can cause problems with your Flash movie. Even if you break the image apart and convert it to a graphic symbol, it will still be inexorably linked to the original bitmap.

After you've imported the image into Flash, there are a couple of methods you can use to modify it.

4. Right-click (or *CTRL*-click on the Mac) the bitmap symbol in the bottom pane of the Library. This will open a context-sensitive menu with a list of commands that can affect your image.

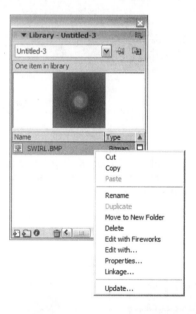

You're mainly concerned with the Edit with commands. The first of these (Edit with Fireworks in this example) opens the default image-editing program that your computer has associated with that file type. The second Edit with command opens a dialog box from which you can choose a program to edit your image. Both of these commands open the bitmap within the selected editing program. When you've finished editing the bitmap, save it and close the program to return to Flash, and

you'll find that the image in the Library will have been updated to reflect any changes you've made.

The second method of altering bitmaps is to modify them within Flash itself. At the moment, the bitmap on the stage is an instance of the symbol in your Library.

5. Double-click the instance on the stage. You might expect Edit Bitmaps mode to open, but instead, nothing happens.

To alter a bitmap inside Flash, you first have to break it apart.

6. Click the Modify ➤ Break Apart menu option.

Your bitmap image is now a shape with no outline, and it's filled with the image from the Library. This shape can be modified as any other shape can be in Flash: you can draw on it, cut bits out of it, and scale or rotate it.

7. Click the Lasso tool. It has three options at the bottom of the Tools panel.

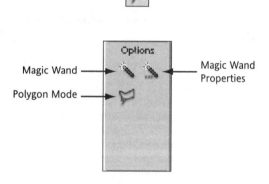

The two important options in the bitmap-editing context are the **Magic Wand** and the **Magic Wand Properties**. The Magic Wand is used to select a specific color in the image. For example, if you have a picture of a sky with clouds and you want to select the sky but not the clouds, you would use the Magic Wand tool. With this tool, you can select the blue areas and ignore the gray-and-white clouds.

8. Select the Magic Wand option. If you've down-loaded the `swirl.bmp` file from the friends of ED website (www.friendsofed.com), click the top-left corner of your image. If you're working with one of your own images, click an area comprised of mostly one color. A small section of the image is selected.

Selected Area →

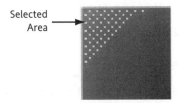

This is because Flash has selected only the sections of the image whose pixels are a very close color match to the original pixel you clicked.

9. Click the Magic Wand Properties option, and a dialog box will appear.

From here, you can alter the settings for the Magic Wand tool.

The Threshold box defines the amount of deviance from the clicked-on color allowed when Flash determines the matching pixels to include in its selection. Imagine a bitmap image of a cloudy sky. If your sky ranges from a deep blue to lighter gray-blue, using just the Magic Wand with its default settings would select only a small piece of the sky. A setting of 10 would allow Flash to select the 10 nearest shades of blue to the one you clicked as well. If you put a larger number into this box, Flash would select a greater portion of the sky.

10. Type 20 into the Threshold box and click OK.

11. Click off the stage to deselect the corner of the image, and click again with the Magic Wand in the same place on the image as you did before.

You can see that Flash selected a much greater part of the image. If you were to increase the threshold number again, Flash would select an even bigger portion.

The other option in the Magic Wand Settings dialog box is Smoothing. This controls the degree to which Flash will smooth the boundaries of the selection.

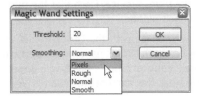

The Pixels setting means Flash won't smooth the boundaries at all; only a very tight range of color will be selected. The other granularity options range all the way up to Smooth, which does as its name suggests—smoothes out the differences between bordering colors.

If you're trying to select a very specific area of color, you should set this to Pixels with a low Threshold (1 or 2). If you're trying to select a large area with variable color, set Smoothing to Smooth and choose a high Threshold figure.

You've already played with solid and gradient fills in objects; you can also fill objects using bitmap images. Using bitmaps to fill shapes in your movies can give some very interesting results. You should always bear in mind that whenever bitmaps are involved, though, a larger file size is sure to follow if you import large bitmaps.

157

1. Working with the same imported bitmap image as before, use the Subselection tool to distort the sides of the shape, increasing it's size.

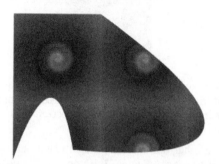

Your image is tiled in the background of the altered shape. Whenever you draw a shape bigger than the bitmap image, Flash tiles the bitmap to fill the shape's outline.

2. Click your shape with the Dropper tool. In the Fill Color box in the Tools panel or Property inspector, a small copy of your image will appear, which means that the current fill color is your bitmap image.

3. To better demonstrate the selected bitmap fill, draw a simple rectangle (with Object Drawing off) on the stage next to the original shape.

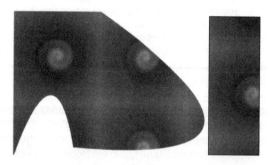

The new shape is also filled with the bitmap, continuing the tiling that appeared when you stretched your original shape. This is because the bitmap image is a locked fill on the stage.

Another useful way to manipulate bitmaps in Flash is to use the Trace Bitmap command.

Tracing bitmaps

Tracing a bitmap converts it from a bitmap image into a series of vectors. Although this sounds like a good thing because it gives your bitmap detail with vector scalability, the results can sometimes be problematic. You should experiment with this feature and judge its usefulness for yourself. Let's walk through an example of bitmap tracing.

Tracing bitmaps

1. Delete the contents of your stage and then drag another two instances of your bitmap image from the Library and onto the clear stage.

2. Select the first bitmap instance and click the Modify ➤ Bitmap ➤ Trace Bitmap command. You'll see the following dialog box:

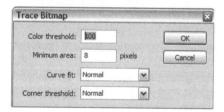

The settings are as follows:

- Color threshold: This works on the same principle as the Threshold setting in the Magic Wand Properties box. A higher number in this field means more colors are considered a match, so your final (traced) image will break down into fewer vector shapes.

- Minimum area: This defines the minimum size (in pixels) that a shape's area can be. The more detailed you want your final image to be, the smaller you should make this number. Keep in mind that a smaller shape area means more shapes, which means bigger file sizes.

- Curve fit: This is similar to Smoothing in the Magic Wand Properties box. Setting this to Pixels ensures that the resulting traced curves will stay faithful to the original bitmap, whereas setting it to Very Smooth will round out the curves in its selection. The smoother a line is, the fewer vectors Flash will need to define it, which will keep the file size smaller.

- Corner threshold: This performs the same task as Curve fit, but instead specifies how far a line can bend before Flash breaks it into two lines with an angular corner. The fewer corners in an image, the smaller the file size.

3. Leave the defaults shown in the previous screenshot, and click OK. Flash converts the first bitmap instance into a group of vectors using the default settings. The result looks like the following:

You can see that this isn't particularly faithful to the original bitmap. Let's try and trace an image that's a little closer to the original.

4. Click your second bitmap instance, and open the Trace Bitmap dialog box (Modify ➤ Bitmap ➤ Trace Bitmap) again.

5. This time, set the values to 10, 2, Pixels, and Many Corners, respectively, and click OK.

I think you'll agree that this looks virtually identical to the original bitmap. Unfortunately, the price you pay for this accuracy is an enormous file. You'll see just how big this file is when you optimize it in the next exercise.

Optimizing bitmaps

Optimizing bitmaps minimizes the number of corners in an image and smoothes out the lines to give a smaller but less precise picture. You can optimize any shape that you've drawn, but the feature is particularly useful when dealing with traced bitmaps.

Optimizing a traced bitmap

1. Select your first image with the Arrow tool (you'll have to draw a selection box around it) and use the Modify ➤ Shape ➤ Optimize menu option to open the Optimize Curves dialog box.

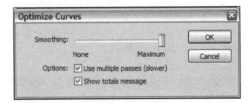

2. Change the settings to those shown in the previous screenshot by dragging the Smoothing bar all the way to the right and checking the Use multiple passes option. This ensures that Flash will optimize the curves as much as possible and create the smallest file it can.

3. Click OK.

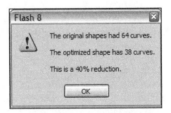

A report window appears, showing the number of curves Flash was able to optimize.

If you look at your image on the stage now, you'll see that it's a lot spikier than it was before because Flash converted all the pixelated smoothness into vector precision. By keeping the Smoothing slider at a lower setting, you keep the image more faithful to the original, but at the expense of optimization.

159

4. Do the same thing with your second (more accurately traced) image, using the same settings as before.

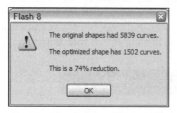

Clearly, tracing bitmaps accurately can leave you with a huge number of curves, which all add up in the final file size. While the first image had only 64 curves, the second had 5839 before optimization and 1531 curves after. The final image though, isn't too shabby a reproduction of the original, and at a considerably smaller size.

The original bitmap image is on the left, the highly optimized vector image is in the middle, and the accurately traced and optimized vector image is on the right. Again, you're on the horns of that old size vs. quality dilemma—and only you can make the ultimate decision about whether those extra kilobytes are worth it.

> *The Trace Bitmap tool won't always give the best results, and it can leave you with very large files. It's sometimes more useful to import the bitmap onto one layer, lock it, physically trace it using the Pencil tool on another layer, and then delete the original when you're finished.*

You'll now focus on another type of bitmap image—the GIF file—and see how Flash treats these when it imports them.

GIF files

The **GIF** (Graphics Interchange Format) file is one of the most commonly used image types on the Internet. What makes GIFs so special is not only that they can be compressed to produce relatively small images, but they can also include animations and single color transparency. When you import a GIF into Flash, you can retain these attributes.

Let's see how, starting with transparency.

Understanding transparent GIFs

GIF transparency isn't as powerful as Flash's alpha setting. With alpha, you can have a range of partial transparencies from completely opaque to totally transparent; whereas with a GIF, the transparency can only be on or off. However, reusing transparent GIFs in Flash can still be useful .

Using transparent GIFs

1. Open a new Flash document.

2. In the File ➤ Import menu, navigate your way to any transparent GIF on your computer, or use the downloadable `transparent.gif` file from this book's page on www.friendsofed.com. You should have a red square on your screen with a hole in the middle.

The hole in the middle is the transparent area of the GIF.

3. Draw a line across the image using the Paintbrush tool. The line should pass behind the image, but should be visible through the hole.

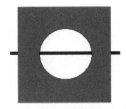

Move the GIF around on the stage. Wherever you put it, you should still be able to see the line through the hole.

Remember that there's not actually a gap in the image such as you'd get if you drew a vector rectangle with Flash's Rectangle tool, and then used the Oval tool to cut a vector circle out of the middle. The hole in the GIF is more akin to a window—it's still a solid image, but it's completely transparent.

> *Flash also supports transparent PNG files. PNGs are often useful because of the PNG-24 format, which has considerably better image quality than the GIF, and also retains transparency. We'll cover PNG import later in this chapter. PNG files are useful as an import format for your images because they're lossless—the compression algorithm used by PNG-24 doesn't alter your image in the same way JPEGs do. Although GIFs are also lossless, they have a far smaller palette (256 colors), so they aren't as suitable as PNG-24 for many images.*

4. To test this, click the part of the line that you can see through the window. If there were a gap there, you'd expect to be able to select the line, but instead, you see the entire GIF image, which you selected.

Next you'll look at animated GIFs.

Understanding animated GIFs

An animated GIF is a collection of static images that play one after another at a specified speed. You can import these into Flash and incorporate them into the main Timeline or into a movie clip's Timeline.

Using animated GIFs

1. Start a new Flash document, and use the File ➤ Import ➤ Import to Stage command to locate an animated GIF and bring it into Flash. Again, I've provided a file on the friends of ED website for you called animated.gif.

2. When you bring an animated GIF into Flash, you'll notice that your Timeline changes.

Flash creates a new keyframe for each frame in your animated GIF, and the number of normal frames between each keyframe depends on the delay specified in the GIF. For example, your original GIF has six frames and a delay of 1/2 second between each frame. This gives you a total running time of 3 seconds ($6 \times 1/2 = 3$).

In Flash, each keyframe is followed by five keyframe-dependent frames, so each of the GIF frames is displayed for six Flash frames. The movie plays at the default 12 frames per second, so each set of six frames will take half a second to display.

Each keyframe reproduces a GIF frame as a bitmap within that frame.

3. Open your Library.

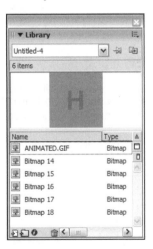

There are six bitmap images, one for each frame of the GIF. The first one is named after the file name of the GIF, and the five subsequent images are named Bitmap followed by a number. If you're going to use animated GIFs in Flash, it's helpful for your reference to create a folder in your Library for the GIFs and store all its frames in that folder.

You can create a similar effect by importing a sequence of images into Flash. If you have a number of images in the same directory named slide1.gif, slide2.gif, slide3.gif, *and so on, and you import the first one, Flash will prompt you to import the rest as a sequence of images.*

Also, if you want to import an animated GIF into Flash but don't want Flash to add the GIF animation to the Timeline, select File ➤ Import ➤ Import to Library. *If you do this, Flash imports the sequential GIF images to the Library only.*

If you click Yes, *Flash imports your sequence of images as keyframes, one after another in a straight line.*

JPEG files

The **JPEG** image format is best suited for photographic images. If you have a photo from a digital camera that you want to bring into Flash, it's probably already in JPEG format.

JPEGs are imported in the same way as GIF images, but they need to be optimized a little differently. JPEG images can greatly inflate the file sizes of your Flash movies if you aren't careful.

Let's bring a JPEG into Flash and see how to deal with it.

Importing and optimizing a JPEG in Flash

1. Open a new Flash document and choose the File ➤ Import ➤ Import to Stage menu option.

2. Locate a JPEG on your hard drive, or use the downloadable spiky.jpg from the friends of ED website. Click Open to import it.

3. After the JPEG image is placed on your stage and in your Library, test the movie with Control ➤ Test Movie.

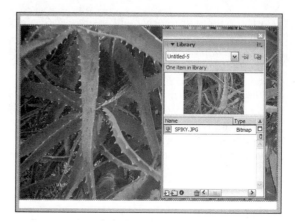

The image looks pretty good, but your Flash movie has a large file size. Flash has compressed the image a little, but not nearly enough.

Let's take a look at the compression settings.

4. Select the File ➤ Publish Settings menu and then click the Flash tab.

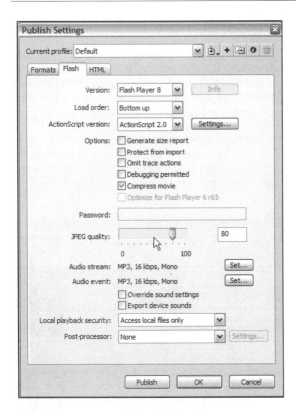

This tab contains the JPEG quality slider, which sets the default compression for JPEG images in your Flash movie (usually 80). Rather than change this setting and affect any future imported images automatically, override this default image quality setting and instead edit the quality of each JPEG individually through the Library, as follows:

5. Double-click the image icon (not the name) in the Library to display its properties.

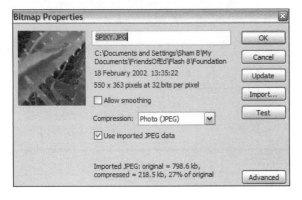

Notice the preview of your image in the top-left corner.

The Allow smoothing option gives Flash control over whether the compression is smoothed out. Sometimes JPEG compression can leave harsh edges or blocky sections. Smoothing eliminates this but increases your image size a little. In most cases, it's better to leave this on, but it's always worth checking your image with and without it to see how much of a difference it makes.

> *Using Smoothing is usually a bad idea if you'll be animating your image, because it can slow Flash down. If an image is moving, most users won't be able to notice the difference in any case.*

The Compression setting allows you to choose the type of compression applied to the image. There are two options—Photo (JPEG) and Lossless (PNG/GIF). Luckily, Flash shows the most appropriate format in parentheses after the file type.

Let's take a look at the last setting and try to shave some kilobytes off your image.

6. Uncheck the Use imported JPEG data box. This will enable the Quality box, which has a default compression quality setting in it. Type 10 into this box and click the Test button.

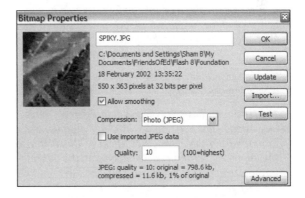

If you look closely at the image in the preview window, you'll see that it looks pretty granular. Place your mouse pointer over the preview window, and when it turns into a hand, drag to see other parts of the image.

163

The JPEG quality information, directly below the Quality field, shows the amount of compression applied, the size of the original image, the compressed image size, and the size of the compressed image as a percentage of the original.

Although the figures look healthy, the image certainly doesn't.

7. Type 30 into the Quality field and click Test again.

The image looks a lot better this time, and the file size is still pretty low. To be sure of the final quality of any image, it's always a good idea to test your movie with Control ➤ Test Movie and assess each image individually. There's no right and wrong when it comes to JPEG compression. The choices you make will depend a lot on the JPEG image itself, the context in which you're using it, and the file size restrictions for the whole Flash movie.

For example, if you're creating a portfolio website for a photographer, you would want to retain as much image quality as possible—a lot of compression just wouldn't show the images as the photographer intended.

If you import a bitmap image in another format into Flash, say a TIF or PICT file, you can still apply JPEG compression to it by opening the image's properties from the Library—JPEG compression isn't limited to imported JPEGs. Better still, if you import a bitmap with alpha channel information in it, you can export the image with JPEG compression and keep the alpha information in the final image even though JPEG doesn't support alpha channels.

You can also apply lossless (PNG/GIF) compression to any imported image.

The reason all this is possible is that Flash converts any image that you import into an intermediate format within the FLA. A side effect of this is that the import file format has no bearing on the output formats available to you when you come to publish the SWF.

You'll now look at importing files from other Macromedia products and get a glimpse of the extended integration between them.

Fireworks files

One of the great things about Flash is its integration with other Macromedia Studio suite products like Fireworks and FreeHand. (We'll cover FreeHand in a moment.) You can import images created in Fireworks and maintain the vector elements in their original form.

The Fireworks native format, PNG, is extremely useful because of its image quality, which is far superior to the GIF format. As an added bonus over GIFs, PNG files also support multiple varied degrees of transparency or opacity.

The following screenshot displays a single Fireworks PNG file (spiky.png) with opacities ranging from 20 to 100%:

Importing Fireworks files is a very simple process. From the File ➤ Import ➤ Import to Stage (or Import to Library) menu, select PNG file. You'll then be prompted with a dialog box.

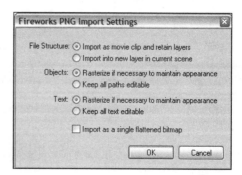

When importing your file, it's wise to retain the original Fireworks file in the best possible format to allow further manipulation in Flash. Here's a run-down of the options available to you:

- File Structure: Select Import as movie clip and retain layers so Flash will place all the Fireworks content in one movie clip and retain the original layer format. Flash creates a new folder in the Library called Fireworks Objects and places a generically titled movie clip in it. Flash will place all Fireworks imports within this folder.

- Objects: Select Rasterize if necessary to maintain appearance when you want to keep the import true to the original file. Select Keep all paths editable to keep all objects editable within Flash.

- Text: Select the Rasterize option wherever possible. Use the Keep all text editable option in situations in which your text is rasterized in Flash and you want to keep it as a vector object.

If the objects and text options don't give you a satisfactory result the first time around, try using the other option. Sometimes a little trial and error is required.

> *Adobe Photoshop and Adobe Photoshop Elements also support the PNG and PNG-24 file formats, and you can import PNGs created from either of these applications into Flash.*

Before you move on, though, it's worth mentioning that although Flash can import bitmaps, it can't always export them back into another application once they've been imported—so make sure you keep the original bitmaps handy.

Enough about bitmaps already! Now let's look at some of the vector import options available in Flash.

Importing vector images into Flash

Vectors are beneficial for many different reasons—from providing infinite scalability to helping you maintain the all-important small file sizes. Remember, the smaller the file size of a website, the more visitors will stick around to appreciate it.

You don't have to create all your vector illustrations in Flash; you can import vector graphics as well. You can import virtually every significant vector format into Flash, from Adobe Illustrator native files to Windows Metafiles. In Flash, you can also import PDF files, which are comprised mainly of vector text and bitmap images.

In this section, you'll look at a few of the vector import options. You'll start with Macromedia's illustration heavyweight, FreeHand.

Importing FreeHand files into Flash

FreeHand is a vector illustration application that was initially used for print, but has quickly become the tool of choice for many serious Flash vector or web designers. Simply put, FreeHand's illustration tools are far more powerful than those in Flash. Many Flash creations start as a FreeHand (or Adobe Illustrator) page and are imported into Flash later for animating or incorporating into a website.

Importing FreeHand files into Flash is easy. Use File ➤ Import ➤ Import to Stage (or Import to Library) and select FreeHand from the Files of Type drop-down menu. After you've selected a file, the following dialog box appears:

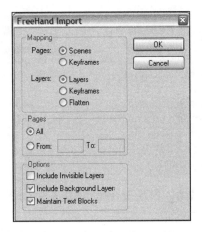

As you can see, you have more options when importing FreeHand files than you did with Fireworks files. Due to its print industry origins, FreeHand organizes documents into multiple pages. These pages can be imported into Flash as separate scenes with one page in each scene, or it can import them into their own individual keyframes.

You can also tell Flash how you want the layers of FreeHand to be imported. If you want to keep everything exactly as you had it in FreeHand, just keep the Layers radio button checked. Alternatively, you can make Flash flatten out the FreeHand file, but none of your text or artwork will be editable, just like with Fireworks.

In the FreeHand Import dialog box, you can specify which (consecutive) pages of the FreeHand file you want to import. You also have a few extra options for importing layers that were hidden in FreeHand, as well as your background layer. You can also make sure that any text is imported as text, and is therefore still editable.

I recommend that you keep the default settings here because that will ensure that all your artwork is editable after it's imported (unless it wasn't vector artwork to begin with).

> *Although FreeHand has better vector tools than Flash, it's worth pointing out that FreeHand (and Adobe Illustrator) are mostly used for print-based work rather than the more optimized graphics required for web use. Whenever you import vector images from outside Flash, your first task should always be to optimize them for the Web using the* Modify ➤ Shape *submenu options.*

Importing PDF documents into Flash

PDF documents are the cornerstone of the print industry and have fast become the de facto standard for eBooks and sharable documents. The beauty of PDFs is their cross-platform compatibility, small file sizes, and excellent quality text. PDFs truly maintain the fonts and layout from the machine that produced them.

PDFs are comprised of a combination of vectors and bitmaps. Generally, all PDF text is vector based, whereas images are a combination of vectors and bitmaps. The use of vector text is especially notable because this allows the text to be editable after it's imported into Flash.

Let's see how to import a PDF.

Importing a PDF

You're going to use a tiny PDF portion of Chapter 2 of the MX 2004 version of this book to import into Flash. The file, chapter2.pdf, is available for download in the Chapter 5 files on the friends of ED website, but you can use any PDF for this exercise. One with two or more pages and bitmaps is preferable.

1. Open a new Flash document.

2. Select File ➤ Import ➤ Import to Stage and locate the chapter2.pdf file, or any PDF on your system. The following dialog box appears:

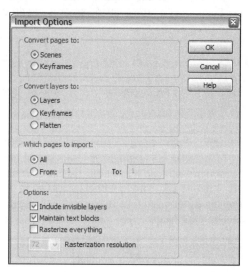

As with the previous import dialog boxes, this presents a series of import options. Like FreeHand, PDF files contain a number of pages. The first option, Convert pages to, specifies how pages should be presented. Even though this defaults to Scenes, in most cases I recommend using the Keyframes setting.

The Convert layers to and Which pages to import options are fairly rudimentary; the default settings are adequate for most situations. The set of Options at the bottom of the dialog box are a little more significant. The first, Include invisible layers, tells Flash to import any visible and hidden layers, and in most cases this is preferable.

The Maintain text blocks option specifies whether the imported text will be editable. You'll usually keep the default selection because it allows you to edit the text and text fields. The last option, Rasterize everything, is a no-no. If this is switched on, all the PDF pages will be imported as bitmap images, which not only increases your file size, but also prevents you from editing the content. The one reason for using this option will become apparent in a moment.

3. Set the options as shown in the following screen-shot, and click OK to import.

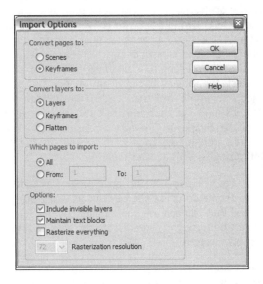

4. After a little processing, you're likely to get the following error message:

This is Flash warning you that some of the fonts in the PDF file aren't on your system. Don't panic; this is quite common.

There are two options. The one you choose depends on how close you want the text to be to the original. The easiest option is Use Default, which will render the text in one of Flash's default fonts—serif, sans serif, or typewriter (more on these later in the chapter). If you select this option, Flash determines the best font from the three for each typeface in the document. Even though this might sound lazy, remember that you can always edit the text fields later and apply fonts at that stage.

The second option is Choose Substitute, which allows you to choose a replacement font for the PDF document, as shown in the screenshot that follows:

In this particular case, one of the missing fonts is a Times New Roman family font, which can easily be replaced with another font from the same family. In scenarios in which you have 10 or so missing fonts, you might not be so keen to replace them all, so go with the Use Default option.

5. In the Missing Fonts dialog box, select Use Default.

After a little while, the content will be on the stage, the Timeline will have a number of keyframes, and the Library will contain the bitmaps and other content from the PDF.

167

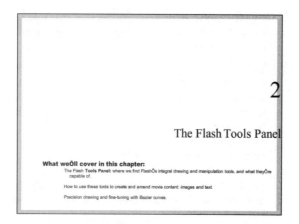

If you're wondering why your content is running into the work area, it's simply because the PDF document is physically bigger than the stage. In most cases, it's usually a good idea to increase the stage size before importing the document.

6. Click the header text field that reads The Flash Tools Panel (if you're using a different PDF, just click any text) and open the Property inspector. As you can see, the text here is fully modifiable.

7. Click the second keyframe in the Timeline and click the image of the Tools panel.

As with the text, this image can be transformed, moved, and modified in any way. Flash has even made it into a symbol for you.

You should now be aware of the possibilities of importing PDF documents. The result of the exercise is available as the file pdf_import.fla from the code download for this book.

Macintosh users will especially benefit from the PDF import in Flash because of the excellent built-in support for PDFs in Mac OS X.

You can use the built-in Save As *PDF option from the Print dialog box, which allows you to create PDFs from any application, as well as the PDF screen grab (CMD+SHIFT+3 or CMD+SHIFT+4). Any of these Mac-created PDF files can then be imported into Flash.*

Now it's time for more vectors.

Vector clip art

Clip art has a wonderful history in print art, presentations, and web pages, so it should come as no surprise that it can be used in Flash as well. The greatest thing about clip art is that, unlike bitmaps, most of it is already in vector format and it can be easily imported and used in Flash.

The easiest file type for Flash to import is a WMF (Windows Metafile) file, which can be imported through the File ➤ Import ➤ Import to Stage (or Import to Library) menu. Because they're already vectors, they're easily manipulated after import.

WMFs are usually imported as groups, so when you want to edit them, you can either edit each group separately or highlight the whole group and use the Modify ➤ Ungroup option to convert them into lines and fills. There are sometimes lines and fills hidden behind others in clip art files, which can increase the file size. To prevent this, ungroup the whole image, deselect the object to let Flash merge the visible objects together, and then discard the hidden ones. Also, it's always a good idea to optimize clip art with Modify ➤ Shapes ➤ Optimize because clip art is made for print and isn't designed to be compact for the Web. Optimizing ensures a lower file size.

Don't be afraid to use clip art in your Flash movies. Some people don't like the way clip art looks, but keep in mind that you can use it as a building block for your own art because you can edit it to the look and feel of your own website.

Images aren't the only visual elements that Flash can handle. It can also use your system fonts and some modification tools to give your movies that extra personal zing.

Fonts and typefaces

It comes as a surprise to some people just how much of a difference a font can make. Fonts are so much more than just "clothes" for words. They can define a website—and a bad choice of font can easily put people off from viewing your movie or staying at your site. Building a font collection is a relatively easy task because the Internet holds many free font repositories, and there are hundreds of font collections on CDs that can be found lurking in computer store bargain bins.

> *Warning: you might not realize that fonts, like images, are usually copyrighted. If you find a font you like and want to use on your site or in your movies, check the copyright on the font and get the permission, or buy a license to use the font. If that seems like too much of a hassle, use system fonts that you know are copyright free, or create your own—although this latter option isn't as simple as it seems.*

One of the advantages of Flash is that it's not as fussy as HTML when it comes to fonts. Although HTML supports the standard fonts—Arial, Times New Roman, and Courier (and a few others)—if you use a more exotic font in HTML, it will be replaced with one of the standard types. It's possible to embed a font in an HTML document, but this is often problematic because Macs and PCs differ with regard to the embedded fonts they use; also, embedding fonts makes your files slower to download.

There are two ways to get over these obstacles in Flash. The first way is to convert the font to a graphic symbol, although this means that the text part of the object can no longer be edited or selected. The other method is to embed the font within the movie. Flash automatically includes embeddable fonts in your movies when you publish them from the FLA file.

Flash also works with TrueType, Open Type, PostScript Type 1, bitmap (Macintosh), and device fonts.

Working with device fonts

Of the five font types just mentioned, the first four are embedded into Flash movies, which bulks up SWF file sizes. The fifth type, **device fonts**, aren't embedded, so the file sizes are much smaller. When you use a device font, Flash searches the computer that your movie is being played on for a suitable font, and then uses that font to display your text.

As mentioned earlier, Flash uses three device fonts—you can identify a device font in your font list because its name starts with _ (an underscore).

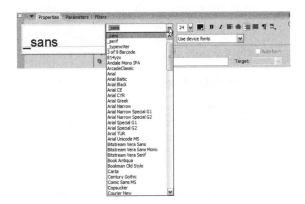

The standard device fonts are as follows:

- _sans, which appears similar to Arial or Helvetica
- _serif, which appears similar to Times New Roman
- _typewriter, which appears similar to Courier

Note that these fonts aren't part of the Flash installation—the actual fonts used are the closest ones Flash finds on your computer.

Be sure to either select the font from your font list when you first use it, or select Use device fonts from the Font Rendering Method drop-down menu, as shown in the following screenshot:

When you use device fonts, there are a couple of issues that you need to consider:

- Flash can't treat device fonts as graphics, so you'll usually have difficulty if you animate anything with device fonts in it. In particular, if you try to tween anything containing device fonts, you may see the text disappear.

- Flash will pick the closest fonts corresponding to the specified device fonts when the SWF is played back by the user, but those fonts may be slightly different to the ones you use, because the user's machine will most likely not have exactly the same fonts installed. This means that the text may end up being slightly bigger or smaller for the user. Don't use device fonts if you need the text to be exactly the same on your machine and the user's.

Working with text

In Flash, you have many of the same commands at your disposal as in a word processing program. Most of the text options in the Property inspector were covered earlier, but there are a few more.

You can change text to any solid color and it will remain editable, but if you want to create more complicated effects, the text must be broken apart and converted to graphics. This will increase file size—but you can give your text some pretty interesting effects.

FLASH

In this case, the text has been broken apart twice to convert it into raw shapes, and then filled with a bitmap fill.

You'll see some more advanced use of text later in the book when you learn how to use text fields for user input and interaction.

Finally, let's work on your case study exercise.

Case study

In the last chapter, you set up your buttons and aligned your elements. Now you're going to import some images for your web portfolio and add a gradient to highlight your company name.

Adding a gradient to the website

The purpose of this gradient is to highlight the company logo and name. You'll do this with a custom gradient.

1. Open your saved case study document.

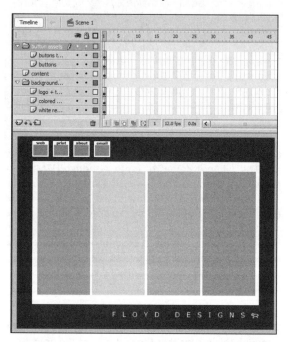

2. Open the Color Mixer panel (Window ➤ Color Mixer) and select Linear from the Fill Style drop-down menu.

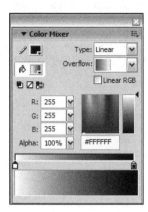

3. Click below the current gradient to add a new color.

4. Change the color of the first marker on the left to the current background color (#003366). The easiest way to do this is to enter 003366 directly into the Hex entry box (it's next to the Alpha slider). Do the same with the last marker. You're doing this because the gradient will consist of two colors, with a different color in the center.

5. Click the middle marker and select a lighter blue (#0033FF).

6. Move the markers nearer to the left edge so they look like the following screenshot:

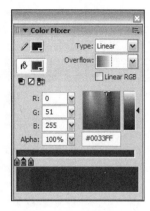

7. Select Add Swatch from the Color Mixer menu at the top right of the panel. Now you can apply it.

8. Insert a new layer called gradient and place it at the very bottom of all the layers.

9. On the new layer, draw a rectangle (using Object Drawing mode) roughly the same size as the stage, with your new linear gradient fill, and no stroke.

10. Use the Align tool (with the To stage option switched on, and using the Match width and height modifier) to ensure that the rectangle is as big as the stage. Then click Align left edge and Align top edge so that the rectangle covers the stage exactly.

For the next step, you need lots of room, so minimize both the top and bottom docking areas. You may also want to lock all other layers except gradient (so that you can edit the rectangle only).

11. Select the Fill Transform tool and click the new rectangle.

12. Use the Rotate handle of the Fill Transform tool to rotate the gradient 90 degrees counterclockwise.

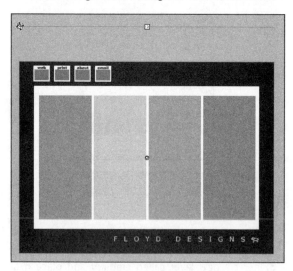

At the moment, you can't see the fill, so you'll have to use the Resize handle to bring the gradient stripe onto the stage.

13. Drag the Resize handle down to the top of the stage and release it.

14. Pull it down a little more until the stripe covers the text and doesn't affect your white rectangle.

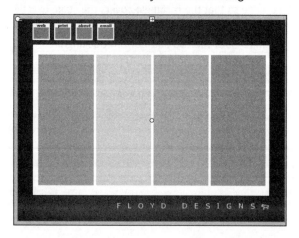

15. Lock the layer to ensure that it doesn't get accidentally changed later. This gradient has lifted your logo off the page significantly. You can now bring the two docking areas back.

Importing images

The last step is to import a few images for your web and print portfolio pages.

1. Select File ➤ Import ➤ Import to Library and download the following files from the friends of ED website:

- fmc.gif
- friendsofed_website.gif
- hypertelia.gif
- nettle_wine.gif
- pinderkaas_website.gif
- qanik.gif
- gandhi.jpg
- einstein.jpg

Don't forget that you can CTRL-click or SHIFT-click to make multiple selections in Windows.

2. Click OK to import the files.

3. Create a new Library folder called imported images and place all the images in it.

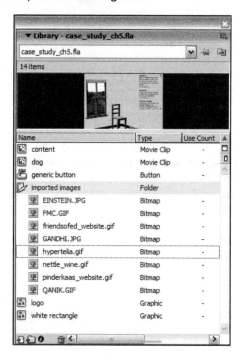

This will keep your Library a little tidier, and make maintenance a cinch.

4. Save your case study file and close it.

You'll be returning to this case study at the end of the next chapter.

Summary

In this chapter, you examined some general Flash features, all of which are targeted at helping you make the objects in your movies more effective.

You saw that

- You can use the palette of web-safe colors that render properly in any browser in the known universe.

- You can create your own custom colors and have great control over their constituent colors.

- You can use hex values to match and amend colors.

- You can use gradients to bring flat objects to life, and you can create, modify, and save your own customized gradients and color sets.

- You have infinite potential to manipulate gradient fills after you've applied them to an object.

- You can import, trace, and optimize bitmap images for use in your movies—but there can be a file size penalty you should be aware of.

- You can import PDFs and files from other Macromedia products easily, and doing so allows you to keep the imported assets editable within Flash.

In the next chapter, you're going to focus on animation through motion tweening.

Chapter 6

MOTION TWEENING

What we'll cover in this chapter:

- Using motion tweening to move objects around in your movies and animate them convincingly
- Scaling, rotating, fading, and changing objects' colors as they move
- Making objects appear to accelerate and decelerate using easing values and easing graphs
- Using onion skinning to view multiple frames simultaneously for making convincing animations
- Creating motion paths for your moving objects to follow
- Optimizing your animations using redraw regions and bitmap caching

The first five chapters immersed you in a number of aspects of Macromedia Flash: its basic layout, its tools, and how it uses symbols and color. You're now going to start combining these different elements in some more sophisticated ways, which will give you plenty of opportunity to test things out, and to practice, practice, practice. This is an important chapter—as well as learning about motion tweens, you'll apply a substantial amount of what you've learned so far in your case study exercise—you'll see the case study take further shape and begin to come to life.

Now you're going to return to the subject of animation, which was touched upon briefly in early chapters when you encountered an animatronics mushroom and a static yet moving car.

Animation revisited

As you no doubt recall, Flash animation is based on the simple principle of representing change over time. When Flash creates a tween animation, it creates the frames between two significant moments of action, which are themselves defined by the contents of keyframes. The replayed sequence of *keyframe, in-between frames, keyframe* is the essence of a Flash animation.

There are two different types of animation that you'll use as a beginner in Flash: the shape tween you used to make your mushroom grow, and the motion tween. A **shape tween** is a morphing operation; you transform an original shape into a different shape by changing the positions of the points of the shape.

Shape Tween

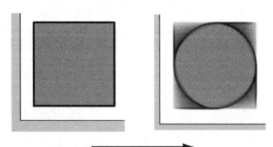

Square morphs into circle over time

A motion tween works by changing **properties**. Properties include things like height, width, and position.

Motion Tween

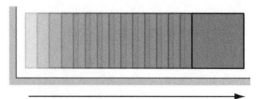

Square migrates across the stage over time

So which of the two types of tween would you use for any given animation?

A shape tween would be used if you wanted to animate something like a square changing into a circle, as in the first figure. To create this animation, Flash would need to change the points of the square so that it became a circle. Other, more typical uses of shape tweens include the following:

- Animating the mouth of a character who's speaking
- Morphing a circular sun into a crescent moon to show the passage of time
- Showing the movement of a sailboat's sails as they move in the wind

A motion tween would be used if you wanted a square to move from the left of the stage to the right—as in the second figure—or if you wanted it to fade in and out.

To create this animation, Flash leaves the points on the square as they are, but moves the whole shape. Other more typical uses of motion tweens include the following:

- Animating a car that moves from left to right across a screen
- Making a company logo fade in on a web page
- Making a boat shrink in size as it sails off toward the horizon

Motion tweens

The simplest motion tween you can create is one that moves an object around on the stage from point A to point B. Motion tweens will only work for symbols or grouped shapes. Here's an example.

Creating movement with motion tweening

Motion tweens tends to produce smaller file sizes, and they tend to be easier to produce. If you have a choice between using either shape or motion tweens, it's generally better to go for motion tweens, and use shape tweens as sparingly as you can. Having said that, shape tweens give the experienced animator more control—they allow you to make the subtle animated changes that add emotion and expression to characters, such as changes in facial expression during speech, or subtle body movements during walking.

In this chapter, you're going to focus on motion tweens, and in the next chapter, you'll look at shape tweening in more detail.

There are other ways to create animation in Flash once you've become more proficient.

One way is through frame-by-frame animation. This is used when the animation is too complex for Flash to create tween frames—a good example being a rotating 3D logo. In this case, you would have to draw each frame by hand (or use a third-party tool such as Swift 3D to do it for you).

The second way is to use ActionScript to control your animation. When using ActionScript, Flash uses your code to specify where animated content should move per frame. This form of animation is the same sort of thing you see in video games—the animation is driven by code. One of the big advantages of code-driven animation is that it can be interactive—the code can base the animation on user interaction. friends of ED has a really great book on this subject: ActionScript Animation: Making things Move! by Keith Peters (friends of ED, 2005). Check it out if you want to explore this more, but be warned that it does contain some quite advanced ActionScript techniques.

1. In a new Flash document, draw a square using Object Drawing mode. Select the square and convert it into a graphic symbol with the name square and a central registration point.

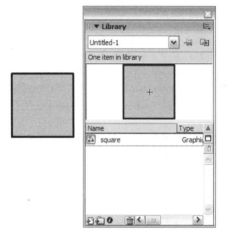

Flash also allows you to create motion tweens with Drawing Objects or groups. Tweens that use Drawing Objects don't allow several types of tween (such as color or alpha fades), and they're also less efficient (for reasons I'll discuss shortly), so its best to stick to the good habit of applying tweens only to symbols.

2. In the Timeline, insert a keyframe at frame 30 (Insert ➤ Timeline ➤ Keyframe or *F6*).

3. In the new keyframe (click frame 30 in the Timeline if it's not currently selected), move the square symbol to the far right side of the stage.

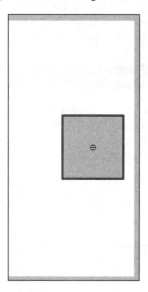

4. Click any frame between 1 and 29 in the Timeline.

5. Open the Properties panel using the Window ➤ Properties ➤ Properties menu option, or by pressing *CTRL+F3* (*CMD+F3* on the Mac), and select Motion from the Tween drop-down menu.

Notice that Flash has drawn an arrow-headed line from frame 1 to frame 29 and colored in the frames. The arrow indicates the length of the tween from frame 1 to frame 29. The tweened frames are colored blue to indicate a motion tween.

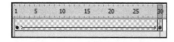

If you see a dotted line instead of the arrow, it means that there's a motion tween between the frames, but it's not executing properly.

This indicates that there's something wrong with the events in the Timeline, and Flash can't construct the tween successfully. In this example, you would need to check that the squares on both keyframes are instances of square.

6. Test the movie and watch the object move from left to right.

This gives you your first tween, but it's not a very good one—it's not very smooth. To make your animation smoother, you need to show more frames per second.

7. Click once on the keyframe at frame 30 to highlight it. Then click-drag it to frame 60. Your tween now runs from frame 1 to frame 60. Select Modify ➤ Document and double the frame rate from 12 to 24. Test the movie.

This time you should see an animation that's twice as smooth. This occurs because you're showing twice as many frames at double the frame rate. The animation still runs for the same amount of time, it just appears smoother.

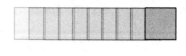

You may now be tempted to increase the tween to frame 120, and then double the frame rate again to 48fps. Although this may seem like a good idea on the face of it, its worth noting that the frame rate isn't how fast Flash will run, it's merely how fast Flash will try to run. If you make the frame rate too high or make the tween too complex, the animation will run slowly (and there's nothing more amateurish than a sluggish animation). As a rule of thumb, increase the frame rate to no more than 24 to 30fps.

As I've already mentioned, you could have created your tween using Drawing Objects or groups. It makes sense to use symbols in your tweens. If you use anything other than symbols, Flash will store an additional version of your tweened content for each keyframe. For your simple tween containing two keyframes, this will immediately double the file size associated with the tween, because you would end up with two identical squares.

For a Timeline full of tweens, this difference may come to a few 100K more! For more complex graphics you should turn your graphics into graphic or movie clip symbols before using them in tweens. In fact, it's a good idea to *always* make anything you want to use in a motion tween into a graphic or movie clip symbol before you start adding your tweens—a good habit learned early is one less bad habit to unlearn later!

The last section discussed how to optimize your animations for file size. Later in the chapter, when bitmap caching is discussed, you'll look at how you can optimize your tweens for speed. Before that, though, we need to delve further into motion tweens, because so far we've barely touched on their power.

You might want the objects in your animations to do more than just move from A to B. You might even think that this plain vanilla motion tween looks kind of wooden and mechanical. By using some of the more sophisticated features of motion tweening, you can make your objects change size, spin around, move in complex patterns, and move more convincingly. Let's look at these features now.

Scaling objects in motion tweens

The first thing you're going to do is scale your object—that is, change its size—as it moves across the stage. Scaling an object using a motion tween isn't the same as the shape tweening, or morphing, you did in the first chapter when you made your mushroom grow. In a scaled shape tween, the shape itself remains the same: only its size changes.

Tweening simultaneous motion and scaling

1. Make the frame rate 12fps again. Click-drag the second keyframe back to frame 30. Delete all the frames after frame 30 by selecting them and pressing *Shift+F5*. In the movie you've been working on, click frame 1 on the Timeline.

2. If it's not already displayed on the screen, open the Properties panel.

   Notice that the Tween drop-down menu's Scale field is already checked.

   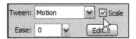

   This is checked by default and there's no reason to uncheck it. **Tween scaling** allows you to change the size of your object over the duration of your animation. With tween scaling turned off in your current movie, the square would remain at its original size for 29 frames, and then suddenly jump to its new size in frame 30. This would look very abrupt, and it isn't the effect you want here.

   You know that the tween scaling option is turned on, so let's scale your tweened square so that it will make use of the default tween scaling feature.

3. Go back to the stage and, while still in frame 1, ensure that the square is selected.

4. Select the Free Transform tool and click the Scale button in the Tools panel options.

The selected object now has a box around it with eight scaling selection handles.

5. Grab the lower-right corner handle and use it to scale the object down to about half of its original size. To keep the square's proportions, hold down the *SHIFT* key as you scale.

6. Click frame 30 on the Timeline, in which the motion-tweened square is located on the right side of the stage. This time, scale the square up by about 50%, using the bottom-left handle to do the scaling. Again, you can use the *SHIFT* key to maintain proportions.

7. Test the movie, and you'll see the square gradually grow larger from frame 1 to 30 as it passes across the stage.

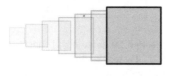

8. To see exactly what the tween Scale option does for your animation, go back to frame 1 and turn it off in the Properties panel by unchecking the box. Now retest the movie and notice the migrating square's sudden change in size when the playhead hits frame 30. With the tween scaling option turned on, Flash is doing all the hard work of "connecting the dots" of the animation, creating a relatively smooth and gradual motion and growth effect.

Motion tweening also allows you to spin objects around as they move on their paths. Again, this is fairly straightforward. Here's how.

Adding motion and rotation

1. Back in frame 1, turn tween scaling on in the Properties panel.

2. Click the arrow next to the Rotate box and look at the resulting menu.

You can rotate an object clockwise or counterclockwise, use Auto, or have no rotation at all. The value in the (currently grayed-out) box to the right of the Rotate menu controls how many times, if any, an object will rotate in the selected direction. The value to the right will remain grayed out unless you select either clockwise (CW) or counterclockwise (CCW) rotation.

You'll see that you currently have no rotation selected—let's change that.

3. Click frame 1 in the Timeline and then select CW in the Rotate drop-down menu. Leave the number of times to be rotated at 1.

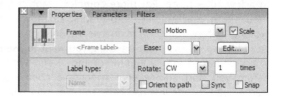

4. Test the movie again, and you'll see the object rotate 360 degrees clockwise during its movement across the stage.

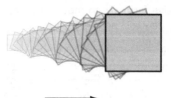

This is OK for a start, but you can also customize the rotation to achieve a more interesting effect.

For instance, you can change the center point around which the square rotates.

5. In the keyframe at frame 1, select the square instance, and then choose the Free Transform tool. As usual, you'll see a white dot in the center of the square. This is the center point.

This shows you the position of the currently defined center point of the shape. This is the point that Flash will use as the center of rotation, and by default, Flash will always position the center point in the middle of the object. This applies both to symbols and grouped shapes.

Click the center circle and drag it to a different position on the square. Do the same for the square at frame 30, and try to put the center point at the same relative position. If you don't have the center point in the same position, you'll see a disjointed animation between the last two frames of the animation, because the center point will suddenly switch position between frame 29 and 30.

6. Play the movie again, and notice the difference in the movement. This time, the square rotates in an elliptical arc as it spins. This is because the axis of rotation has changed to one that is no longer symmetrical (i.e., it's no longer at the center of the square).

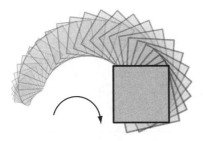

Experiment with placing the center point in different locations, and see the effect this has on your square's style.

The ability to rotate objects around different center points helps you to imbue your objects with character and individuality—essentially, with characteristics that mimic how things move in the real world. This is one of the secrets of really convincing animation. Flash has other features to help you here as well. One of them is easing.

Easing

If you need another way to add a touch of real-world physics to your Flash animations, you can use the easing feature on motion tweens to make an object move more naturally. **Easing** is essentially a way of controlling the apparent acceleration and deceleration of a motion-tweened object.

If you look just above the Rotation field in the Properties panel, you'll see another field called Ease.

Easing is set to 0 by default. On this setting, motion-tweened objects move at a constant speed—as they have in the motion tweens you've created so far. By entering a figure in the Ease box, you can make your tweened objects start slowly and accelerate (easing in), or start quickly and decelerate (easing out).

Easing runs on a scale of –100 to 0 for easing in and from 0 to 100 for easing out. The number represents the amount of easing that's applied to the tween. The further away from 0 you get, the more pronounced the easing becomes.

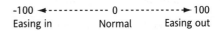

To illustrate how easing can be used effectively, you're going to create an animation of a bouncing ball.

181

Easing a bouncing ball

First, you need a ball.

1. Open a new Flash document. Rename its default layer standard ball.

2. Using the Oval tool with Object Drawing mode off and a suitable radial gradient fill, create a stroke-less sphere on the standard ball layer, and then convert it to a graphic symbol called bad ball.

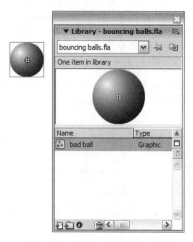

3. Place this ball at the top-left of your stage.

4. Add keyframes at frames 10 and 20.

5. Click keyframe 10 and move the ball to the bottom of the stage. (Remember that by holding SHIFT you can ensure that the ball will drop in a straight line.) If you click keyframe 20, you'll see the ball is still at the top of the stage. You now have three positions for the ball:

   ■ The top of the drop (frame 1)

   ■ The bottom of the drop (frame 10)

   ■ The top of the bounce (frame 20)

   The next step is to animate the bounce.

6. Add a motion tween between frames 1 and 10, and then another between frames 10 and 20. These two tweens animate the fall and the bounce of the ball, respectively.

You can select both sections by clicking the Timeline between frames 1 and 10, holding down the SHIFT key, and then clicking the Timeline between frames 10 and 20. With both sets of frames selected, you can add both motion tweens at once using the Tween drop-down menu in the Properties panel.

Whichever way you add the two motion tweens, your Timeline should now look like the following:

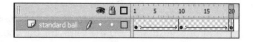

7. Test your movie.

If you want your tween to become a seamless loop, make the content of frame 20 look like the content of frame 19. This issue is discussed in greater detail in Chapter 4.

You can see that the ball drops and bounces—but the movement is too uniform to really resemble a bouncing ball, isn't it? The ball moves at a constant speed, and doesn't reflect real motion at all. You can see this in the image that follows, which traces the path the ball takes on its downward journey. Notice that the ball moves in a very linear way.

Let's add another ball to your animation and try and make it act more realistically, as if it's under the influence of gravity.

8. Lock the standard ball layer. Add a new layer to your movie and rename it eased ball.

9. Create a new graphic symbol on this new layer, consisting of another sphere that's a different color from the last one, but about the same size. Call this symbol good ball.

10. On the new eased ball layer, repeat the steps you took with the bad ball: click keyframe 1, place your new ball at the top of the stage next to the original ball, create keyframes at frames 10 and 20, move the new ball to the bottom of the stage at keyframe 10, and then add two motion tweens to make it bounce.

11. Test your movie and verify that both balls drop and bounce in identical fashion.

Now you can add some easing to the second ball.

12. Make sure you're working on the eased ball layer, select keyframe 1, and use the Ease box on the Properties panel to set the easing to -100 (that's negative 100). You can do this with the slider or by typing in the value. This easing value will only apply to the first motion tween on the Timeline.

Remember, this is the most extreme easing-in value: the ball will start slowly and accelerate as it approaches frame 10—the bottom of the stage position. This will make the ball appear to accelerate as it falls to the bottom of the stage.

13. At keyframe 10, set the easing-out value to 100—the maximum. This will make the ball accelerate out of the bounce, and slow down as it reaches the top of the bounce.

14. Test your movie.

The good ball now looks more like a real ball—speeding up as it falls (easing in) and slowing down as it rises (easing out). This is a good way to mimic the effects of gravity on animated objects—you need to think about how the object would behave in the real world, and add the appropriate easing to the motion tween.

In the following picture, you can see the differences between the two balls. The bad ball (left) moves downward in its unconvincing linear motion, whereas the good ball (right) starts off moving slowly and gets faster. The good ball looks more realistic because it's showing the effects of gravity—it's accelerating. The good ball starts at zero speed and gets faster the closer it gets to the ground—much like a real ball would.

Remember: ease in (-) to speed up and ease out (+) to slow down.

It's also important to note that, with conventional easing, you can only specify easing values once on any single motion tween. To make an object speed up *and* slow down by using easing, as in the previous example, two motion tweens are needed. Each motion tween has its own easing setting, so for every change of speed you want your object to have, you must create a separate motion tween. However, you can have an object that speeds up and slows down numerous times within a single tween if you use custom easing. More on this in a moment.

Another thing to keep in mind when practicing your animations is that if you want two or more objects to move simultaneously, they have to be on separate layers. For example, you can't have two circles in layer 1 with one moving from top to bottom and the other moving from bottom to top. To achieve this, each circle must be in its own layer with its own separate motion tween. Two objects can move on the same layer provided that each has its own tween at separate points on the Timeline.

Adding easing values to keyframes is a little hit-and-miss. Wouldn't it be better if you could view easing graphically? Well, now you can, with a new Flash 8 feature called custom easing. The next few steps show this in action.

15. Lock the eased ball layer and add a third layer called graphically eased ball. Create a third ball symbol as you've done previously. Make the ball into a graphic symbol called graph ball. Add tweening to the new ball such that it does the same as the standard ball.

16. Select the keyframe at frame 1 of the layer graphically eased ball. This time, press the Edit button next to the Ease slider.

You'll see the Custom Ease In/Ease Out window appear. Make sure the Use one setting for all properties check box is checked. The Custom Ease In/Ease Out window consists of a graph with frames on the x-axis and tweening amount along the y-axis. You might remember distance-time graphs from math class. Well, that's exactly what this graph is when you use a motion tween to control position (as you're doing with the ball). The Frames axis is a measure of time (because frames control how long the animation takes). The Tween axis represents how far through the tween the animation is; and when your tween is controlling

position, the Tween axis is synonymous with percentage of distance an object has traveled toward its destination.

When the ball drops from frame 1 toward frame 10, you want it to travel slowly at first and get faster with time. On a distance-time graph, speed is proportional to gradient, so what you need is a curve that starts off shallow (low initial speed) and gets steeper toward the end (high end speed).

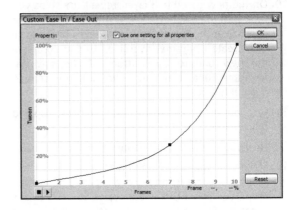

When the ball moves from frame 10 to 20, you want the opposite curve, because this time you want the ball to start off fast and get slower toward the end.

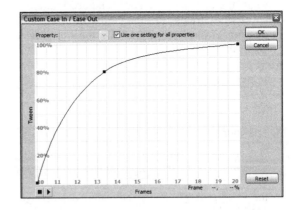

Having said all that, it's much easier to just experiment with the graph until you have the easing you want—so let's move on and do it. Note that you can test out the animation-in-progress at any time by clicking the Play button on the Custom Ease In/Ease Out window, located at the bottom-left corner of the window.

17. For frame 1, you want a *start slow, get faster* graph. Click the point at the bottom-left of the graph. You'll see a line appear with a small circle at the end of it. Click-drag the small circle to change the angle of the line so that it's almost parallel with the horizontal (x) axis.

18. Do the same with the top-right point, but this time make the line almost parallel with the vertical (y) axis.

19. Click the middle of the curve. A new point will appear with a circle on either side of the point. Fine-tweak the position of the point to get a curve similar to the one in the first preceding graph. Click OK.

20. Click frame 10 of the graphically eased ball layer. Repeat the process of steps 17 through 19, except this time create the inverse curve, as you now want a *start fast, get slower* curve.

If you test the movie now, you'll find all three balls move up and down, with the leftmost one being the least realistic, and the rightmost being the most realistic.

The custom easing feature allows you to create much more advanced tweens than any other method. You can create more complex curves by adding more points. For example, the following curve will allow you to have two bounces per tween—something that would be impossible using numerical tweens (and, as an aside, would be impossible to do in one tween in previous versions of Flash, which don't have custom easing).

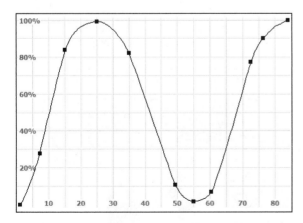

For those of you wondering about the Use one setting for all properties *button that you checked in step 16, don't worry—you'll look at unchecking this later in the chapter.*

If you compare the motion of your graphically eased ball (the rightmost ball in the following figure), you can see that it has a much more pronounced acceleration. Because using the graph allows you to tweak the easing much more finely than a single number would, you have a greater degree of control, and can therefore produce animations that are much closer to what you want to happen.

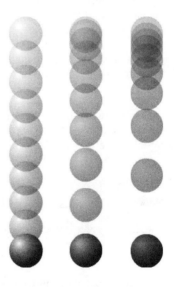

Next, you're going to look at some editing options that can help you when you're creating tweens.

Options for editing your animations

When you want to make minor corrections to your animations or get a sense of the flow and direction of the animated frames, it can be a great help to view more than one frame at once. Flash's Onion Skin tool allows you to do just this. You can edit more than one frame at a time as well.

Using onion skins

Using onion skins allows you to work as though you're drawing each frame on a sheet of tracing paper and piling one on top of another as you work. The term "onion skin" comes from the days when traditional cell-based animators tested animations by drawing outlines on consecutive pieces of transparent paper. Being able to see the outlines of the previous drawing through the semi-transparent paper meant that they could better gauge changes of position, acceleration, and so on over time.

In Flash, however, instead of shuffling through a pile of paper sheets, you need only click a couple of buttons in the bottom-left corner of your Timeline.

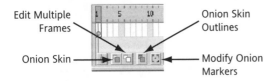

You may never have used these buttons before, but they'll prove to be very useful as your Flash career develops.

So how are onion skins used? Let's go back to your animation of the three bouncing balls. If you unlock all the currently locked layers and then click the Onion Skin button (as shown in the following figure), the transitional world of the motion tween starts to reveal itself.

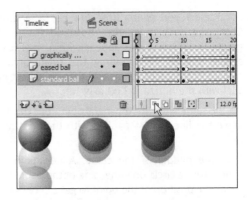

There are a couple of things to notice here.

First, because the playhead is on frame 1, you see both balls in all their glory, clearly defined at the top of the drop. You can also see a ghostly image of each of the balls at subsequent stages of the drop. Note that the appearance of each ball is slightly different in the ghosted frames—this is because two have different amounts of easing and the other one has no easing.

The second thing to notice is the change on the Timeline—two little markers have appeared, spanning frames 1 to 3.

These onion markers define the number of frames that will be ghosted-in around the frame that the playhead is currently on.

If you click the right-hand marker and drag it to frame 20, you'll get a preview of all the movie's frames.

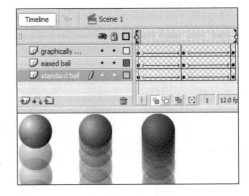

By clicking and dragging the markers, you can alter the range of onion-skinned frames.

If you find that the density of ghosted frames in the onion-skinned view makes it harder to see what's happening on the stage, you can instead view only the ghosted outlines of the animated frames. You can access this feature by clicking the Onion Skin Outlines button, as shown in the following figure.

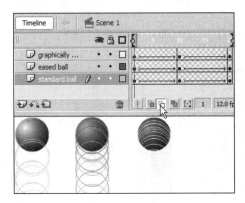

A cluster of tightly packed frames appears at the top of the drop, and only a few appear at the bottom of the bounce; you now have an unobstructed view of the ball. To see things even more clearly, turn off the Onion Skin Outlines option, and switch the Onion Skin option back on. Click frame 20 and drag the end-position version of the rightmost ball (remember this is the ball on the graphically eased ball layer) to the right.

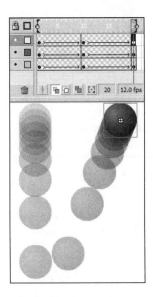

Now you can see the uninterrupted flight of the ball without the down-and-up paths superimposed on each other. Note also that Flash has automatically recalculated and rerendered all the in-between frames. If you test the movie now, you'll see that moving the end-position image results in a new flight path. Onion skinning is an excellent way to see the effect of your amendments to the finished movie.

Let's consider those clusters of frames again. The density of frames shown by the onion skinning is greater at the start of the drop and bounce than at the bottom. This is because when you apply the easing option, Flash uses a tighter time-clustering of frames to simulate slow motion, and a looser clustering to represent high speed. This can be a little counterintuitive until you realize that the apparent speed of an object is determined by a combination of the number of frames and the frame rate. The more frames it takes for an object to move, the slower the apparent motion will be on the screen. When your brain sees only a few images within a fixed time frame, it fills in the blanks and figures that the object must be moving fast. If your brain gets the chance to register more images (frames) in that fixed time frame, it assumes it's because it's seeing a lot of intermediate images.

Let's get an overview of the other onion-skinning options.

The Modify Onion Markers button allows you to alter the way your markers and onion skins appear on the Timeline and the stage.

If you want the markers to always be shown on the Timeline (even when you aren't using onion skins), select Always Show Markers from the Modify Onion Markers menu.

The Anchor Onion option, when checked, prevents your markers from moving as you move the playhead. This means that you see only the frames that are within the markers as you move the playhead. If this option isn't checked and you move the playhead along the Timeline, the markers move with the playhead to show you the onion skins in the section you're viewing.

Selecting the Onion 2, Onion 5, or Onion All options from the menu moves the markers to show varying numbers of onion-skinned frames. For example, selecting Onion 2 will show the current frame plus two onion-skinned frames on either side.

You can have onion skinning enabled as you drag the playhead around the Timeline. When you do this, you may find that complex animations start to appear sluggish. This is because onion skinning forces Flash to draw multiple objects on the stage. To prevent Flash from applying onion skinning to particular layers, lock those layers. This not only speeds up screen redraw, but it also allows you to unclutter the stage and concentrate on particular parts of the animation.

It's important to note that the onion skin effect doesn't export with your movie and is never seen by the end user. If you want to create an onion skin effect for the user, you have to manually create it frame by frame (sorry about that).

Onion skinning allows you to view multiple frames simultaneously; let's see how to edit multiple frames.

Editing multiple frames

Being able to edit several frames at once can be extremely useful—provided that you're careful!

Suppose you decide that everything in your bouncing ball animation needs to be moved to the right to accommodate another graphical element on the left of the stage. Thanks to the Edit Multiple Frames feature, you can do this in one step, rather than having to alter every single frame.

In your bouncing balls movie, click the Edit Multiple Frames button.

Now adjust your onion skin markers so that all the frames in your animation are selected.

Make sure none of the objects on the stage is selected, and use the Edit ➤ Select All menu option, or press CTRL+A (CMD+A on the Mac) to select everything on the stage.

All balls, at all keyframes of their movement, are selected. You can see this is the case by looking either at the Timeline (all keyframes are highlighted) or the stage (all ball positions corresponding to the keyframes are selected).

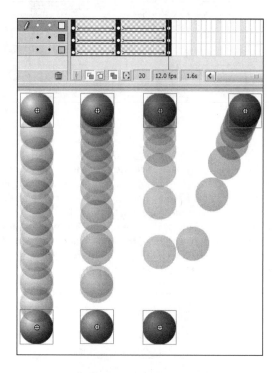

Note that if you had chosen the Edit ➤ Select All menu option without having first chosen Edit Multiple Frames, only the objects in the current keyframe would have been selected. Using Edit Multiple Frames, you pick up everything within the bounds of the onion markers.

Now you can drag all the selected content across the stage to its new position.

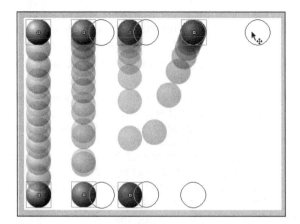

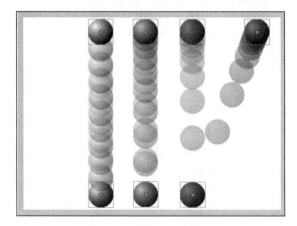

This option can be a real time saver because you don't have to worry about precisely repositioning everything frame by frame—another great example of how Flash can do your work for you.

Motion tweening isn't limited to controlling the movement of objects. It can also make them fade in, fade out, and change color. Let's see how.

Motion tween effects

There are two ways you can make an object slowly disappear and reappear in the motion-tweening context: changing an object's alpha value, or changing its tint. Alpha, as I've mentioned before, is really transparency, and tint is part of an object's color characteristics.

These two attributes possesses different qualities, and it's up to you to decide which one to use when. Let's work through examples of both of them, starting with alpha—and then you can decide for yourself.

Fading with alpha

1. In a new Flash document, create a new graphic symbol—a simple filled square is used here. It doesn't matter if you choose to use Object Drawing or not, but make sure your movie's background color is set to white.

2. Place the graphic symbol on the stage (at the center) in the default keyframe at frame 1, and then insert new keyframes at frame 15 and frame 30. Change the name of the layer to alpha.

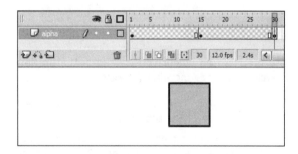

3. Click frame 15, select the symbol, and open the Color drop-down menu in the Properties panel.

Hidden in this drop-down menu are the various effects that you can apply to your symbol.

4. Select Alpha from the drop-down menu, and then set the alpha slider to 0%. This setting will render the symbol totally transparent in the keyframe at frame 15.

5. Add two motion tweens from frames 1 to 15, and from frames 15 to 30, respectively.

When you test your movie you'll see the object fade in and out as you gradually increase and decrease the square's level of transparency. When you get to frame 15, at which the transparency is 100% (invisible), you can see through the square completely. The tween from frames 15 to 30 fades the square back in, gradually obscuring the movie background again.

Now you'll achieve the same end result again using the tint approach.

Fading with tint

Use the Flash document you created in the previous exercise and retain the white background.

1. Lock the alpha layer and then insert a new layer. Select the new layer and rename it tint.

2. Place a second instance of your graphic symbol on the stage at frame 1 in the new layer. Place the symbol above and inline with the previous one. Insert keyframes at frame 15 and frame 30, as before. Note that if you place the new instance on the alpha layer, you'll break the original tween (Flash will show a dotted line instead of a solid line).

3. At keyframe 15, select the new symbol and open the Color drop-down menu in the Properties panel.

4. This time, select Tint from the drop-down menu.

Unlike the alpha effect, the tint effect has a percentage value and RGB values. With tint, you effectively place an opaque layer of color on top of the object's existing color (rather like adding a wash of color over a painting to tint it). The parameters of the tint effect control the color used and its opacity.

5. Set the tint's opacity value to 100% and choose white from the Tint Color box.

When you choose white, the RGB values are all set to 255, indicating that all the constituent colors of white are present at full strength. Each of the three R, G, and B boxes has its own slider, which lets you control the amount of each base color in the tint color. If you prefer to use hex values to select your colors, open the palette and type in the appropriate value in the hex field.

By setting your values to 100% and white, you're telling Flash to place an overlay of completely opaque pure white on the symbol.

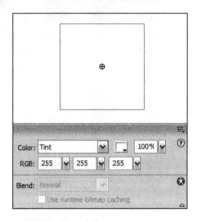

6. Add motion tweens from frames 1 to 15 and frames 15 to 30.

7. Play the movie.

Again, you'll see the object fade in and out just as before, but this time the mechanism underlying the effect is different. The alpha effect literally makes the object disappear by decreasing its opacity and making it transparent, whereas the tint effect changes the color of the object itself. The great thing about alpha fades is that you don't have to ensure that the color of your object changes to match the background—the background color shows through naturally. However, the trade-off is that this process is more CPU-intensive—it's harder for computers to process, and it's a bit slower. Using tint is a little more involved because you need to alter the color settings, which can be complicated if you have multi-colored objects and backgrounds. Let's look at the differences between the two.

8. Lock the tint layer. Add a new layer and call it background. Place the background layer below the other two.

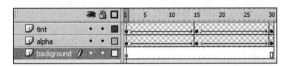

9. Using the Text tool, add two static text fields away from the symbols, both containing the text background text. Move each of these text fields onto the two symbols and release them. They will appear below the symbols as shown in the following figure. Test the movie.

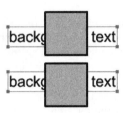

You'll see that the text shows through the alpha fade, but not through the tint fade.

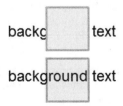

10. Using Modify ➤ Document, change the stage color to a bright red, and then test the movie. You'll see that the alpha fade still works as before, but the tint fade now looks different—you can now see what a tint really is: a change of color, rather than a fade.

Using alpha is the easy way to fade, but tint is important in that it allows you to change the colors of your objects during your animation.

Although the alpha fade may seem to be the better effect of the two, Flash has to draw everything at least twice when performing alpha fades—it has to draw the fading object and anything that shows through it. In a tint fade, Flash only has to show the tinted symbol; this means that a tint fade will usually be twice as fast, and this is especially important when you're tweening complex shapes.

Color change animations

Let's look at how to change the color of an object during a motion tween.

Changing object color mid-tween

In this example, you'll move an object across the stage and change its color as it moves.

1. In a new Flash document, create some text to apply the color effect to (check in the Properties panel that you're typing Static Text). You can use any font, but a large blocky sans serif font best illustrates the effect (the book uses 48-point Arial Black). Use black for the text color, and set the Font rendering method drop-down menu choice to Anti-alias for animation.

Setting the font-rendering method to Anti-alias for animation gives less anti-aliasing than Anti-alias for readability, but results in faster tweens. You would typically use Anti-alias for readability on text that will remain in the same place and won't be animated.

When tweening text, you shouldn't use _sans, _serif, or _typewriter as your font. These are the system fonts and they're not designed to be animated—they may disappear partway through a tween if you scale or rotate them. Also, make sure that the Font rendering method drop-down menu (in the Properties panel) isn't set to Use device fonts.

The reason for this is that Flash doesn't store the shape data for system fonts, and therefore treats them as graphics (i.e., Flash doesn't have enough information to be able to scale or rotate their shape outlines). The upside of system fonts is that they can be rendered quickly and stored within an SWF file using very little file space, so you should use them when you want fast, efficient text—but don't use them if you want to animate the text in any way.

2. Select the text and convert it into a graphic symbol. Although both symbols (movie clips, buttons, and graphics) and grouped objects/Drawing Objects can be motion tweened, only symbols can have color tweens attached to them (another good reason to always use symbols in motion tweens).

3. Place the symbol on the stage at frame 1 (if it isn't already there) and create three more keyframes at frames 10, 20, and 30.

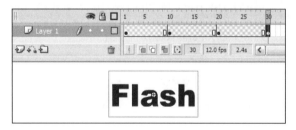

4. At keyframe 10, select the symbol and open the Color drop-down menu in the Properties panel.

5. Select Tint from the Color drop-down menu and change the tint amount to 100%. Then use the color selection palette to change the color to red.

6. Repeat this procedure at keyframe 20, but select green as the tint; and again at keyframe 30, this time selecting blue as the color. Now your text should be red at keyframe 10, green at keyframe 20, and blue at keyframe 30. If you test the movie now, you'll see it changes color in jumps.

7. Add three motion tweens to the Timeline between frames 1 and 10, 10 and 20, and 20 and 30.

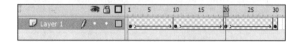

8. Now if you test your movie, you should see your text undergo a chameleon-like color change.

Experiment with clicking each of the keyframes in succession and dragging each particular instance to a different position on the stage. (Doing this with onion skinning turned on will give you some groovy psychedelic effects.) If you do this and then play the movie, you'll see that the tint (and alpha) effects can be combined with actual motion around the stage.

There's something else of real significance here: although you had only one instance of the graphic symbol containing your text on the stage, you were able to change its color in three different keyframes, using the Tint option on the Color drop-down menu. What's more, you were able to drag each of the different colored versions of the text around on the stage independently. You can do this because each different colored version of the text in each different keyframe is effectively treated as a separate instance of the graphic symbol. That is, all the instances have the original symbol as their base, but each instance has properties you can change independently of the underlying symbol.

You've already seen how you can change the tint and alpha of an individual instance, but you can also scale, skew, and rotate instances—all without affecting the underlying symbol. However, if you edit the underlying symbol in Edit Symbols mode, these changes will ripple through to all the instances (although any instance properties you've set—tint, alpha, etc.—will be retained).

Instance 1 | Instance 2 | Instance 3 | Instance 4

Underlying symbol + tint (red) | Underlying symbol + tint (green) + scale | Underlying symbol + tint (blue) + skew | Underlying symbol + alpha

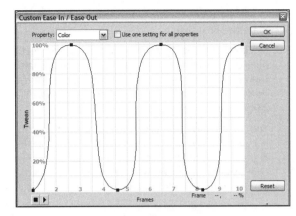

This facility gives you a tremendous amount of flexibility and power in the way that you use symbols. Furthermore, if you've taken my advice and moved the positions of the text as well as changing the color at keyframes 10, 20, and 30, you can also experiment with using two sets of easing—one for the color change and one for the motion change.

For example, rather than making the text change gracefully from black to red between frames 1 and 10, you can make your text flash between black and red by doing the following:

1. Select the keyframe at frame 1. Press the Edit button on the Properties panel to bring up the Custom Ease In/Ease Out window.

2. Uncheck the Use one setting for all properties check box. The Property drop-down menu will now become active. Select it and choose Color.

By creating an easing graph like the one that follows, you'll create some pulsating text—it will flicker between red and black.

You can now make your objects grow, shrink, spin around, speed up, slow down, disappear, and change color. You can also vary the rate that a tween occurs via easing, and fine-tune the easing to create complex easing graphs using custom easing.

In all such cases, though, your objects are still moving in straight lines. You can, however, get them to move in complex patterns like curves, loops, and zigzags as well. To add these features to your animation, you need to learn to use motion guides.

Motion guides

A **motion guide** is a path you draw for an object to follow during a motion tween. The motion guide is invisible outside of the authoring environment, and it sits on a special layer underneath the object you're tweening. Let's create a motion guide and see how it works.

Using motion guides

In this exercise, you'll animate the boat you created in Chapter 2 and add a flying fish animated on a motion guide.

1. Check that the snap feature is on by selecting the View ➤ Snapping ➤ Snap to Objects menu option and making sure that the option is checked. You want your drawn object to snap crisply to an underlying motion guide.

193

2. Open the `boat.fla` file from Chapter 2. Let's animate the boat first.

3. Select all the boat graphics (including the text), hide or lock all the other layers if necessary, and use *F8* or Modify ➤ Convert to Symbol to turn the boat into a graphic symbol called boat. Give it a central registration point.

You might have noticed that your boat symbol instance is on. This is because the text layer was the highest layer in the order of the boat's selected components. Because the layer name text is a little counterintuitive, let's rename it.

4. Double-click the text layer name and rename it boat instance. Delete the layers at the bottom that are now empty, and then move the waves layer to the top.

5. On the boat instance layer, insert keyframes at frames 10 and 20, and then extend all the other layers up to frame 30 by selecting frame 30 in each layer in turn and pressing *F5*.

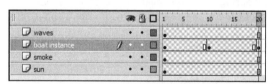

6. On frame 10 of the boat instance layer, move the boat down the stage about 10 pixels. You can do this by tapping the down arrow key 10 times.

7. Use the Tween drop-down menu in the Properties panel to set a motion tween from frames 1 through 10 and 11 through 20.

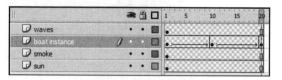

8. Test the movie and you should see the boat gently sway on the water. Pretty idyllic, but something is missing—the waves need motion.

9. Select the waves and convert them to a graphic symbol called waves with a central registration point. (You can select the waves quickly by selecting frame 1 of the waves layer).

10. As with the boat instance layer, insert keyframes on frames 10 and 20.

11. On frame 10, shift the waves about 10 pixels to the left. This will create a gentle lapping movement.

12. Insert motion tweening between frames 1 and 10, and 11 and 20, as before.

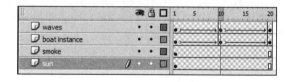

13. Use Insert ➤ New Symbol to create a new graphic symbol called fish.

14. In the new symbol, draw a small fish.

15. Once you're happy with your little fishy, return to the main stage and create a new layer called fishy above the boat instance layer and beneath the waves layer.

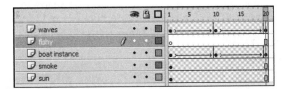

16. Drag a copy of the fish symbol onto the fishy layer.

17. Lock the boat instance and the waves layers to prevent them from accidentally being modified.

18. Click the waves layer's Show Outline button to allow you to easily work behind it.

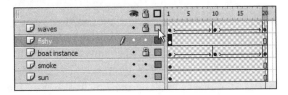

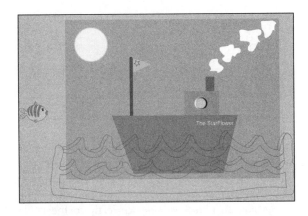

Now you're ready to animate the fish.

19. Select the fish and position it at the left side of the stage beneath the wave.

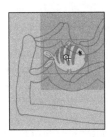

20. Insert a keyframe on frame 20 of the fishy layer.

21. On the second keyframe, place the fish at the right side of the stage.

22. Add a motion tween between the two keyframes. If you now run the movie, you'll notice that the fish is currently hidden beneath the waves. But you're going to make it jump—this is where the motion guide comes in.

23. Select the fishy layer and use the Insert ➤ Timeline ➤ Motion Guide menu option to create a guide layer. Alternatively, you can click the Add Motion Guide button below the layers.

The motion guide layer will automatically appear above the current layer, and it will inherit the name of the layer that it's a guide for, prefixing this with the word Guide and a tiny icon of a bouncing ball—the signifier for a guide layer.

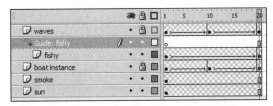

195

It's on the motion guide layer that you'll draw the motion path that you want your object to follow. A motion path is simply a drawn line.

24. Click the guide layer to select it, and then use the Pencil tool (with Object Drawing mode turned off) to draw the path that you want your object to follow. Draw the path at the location on the stage where the action will take place—you can always move it later if you want.

The motion path itself can be any length or shape you like: up, down, side to side, a zigzag, a curve, a loop—just so long as it's a continuous line with no gaps. You don't have to use the Pencil tool—the Line tool, Pen tool, and Brush tool will work; and even unfilled rectangles and circles can act as motion guide shapes. The important thing is that you have a line on the guide layer.

The motion path must be a raw shape, otherwise it won't work. You must therefore have Object Drawing mode turned off when you create your motion guide, and you should avoid grouping the motion guide or turning it into a symbol or Drawing Object at any later time.

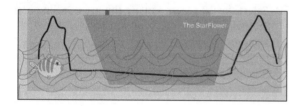

The screenshot uses a black stroke at a thickness of 3 so you can see the guide clearly. Remember, you don't need to worry about the color of the path because it won't be displayed in the final movie. Also, you can treat the line just like any other object: once you've selected it on the guide layer, you can resize it, trim it, skew it, and so forth.

Now for the exciting part: making the object travel along the motion guide. To do this, you need to snap the object to the start and end points of the motion path—that's why you've got two keyframes: one for where the guided motion tween will start, and one at the end of the action.

25. Lock the guide (Guide: fishy) layer so that you don't accidentally click the guide line.

26. On the first keyframe on the fishy layer, select the fish (click on the fish's center point) and move it to the start of the guide line. Once it snaps to it, release it. This is why you ensured that View ➤ Snapping ➤ Snap to Objects was switched on.

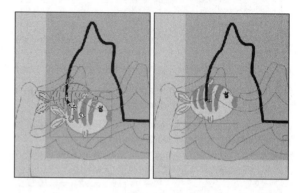

27. On frame 20, the second keyframe, pick up the fish and snap it to the end of the line.

28. Drag the playhead along the Timeline to view the motion.

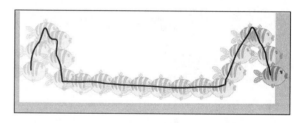

Finally, select Control ➤ Test Movie to watch your flying fish attack! The book's version is downloadable as boat_animated.fla.

29. Although motion guides are fairly simple to create, getting an object to snap correctly to the guide takes time to get used to—failing to get the object to snap properly is a common problem. In this example, clicking on the center point of the fish helps out a lot, but occasionally it can take a few attempts to get it just right—so practice and don't get discouraged.

> *The motion guide layer must be the same length as the Timeline for the object being guided.*

Keep in mind that if the animation is 30 frames long, the guide layer's Timeline has to be 30 frames long too. In this exercise, you inserted a keyframe at frame 30 on the object layer and then added the motion guide layer. Flash automatically added 30 frames to the guide layer to match the fishy layer that the guide layer was spawned from. Flash is intelligent enough to look at the contents of the layer and work out where to put the keyframes in the guide layer—provided that you decide how long the actual animation will take and mark its boundaries first.

Adding keyframes to a layer after creating a motion guide will alter the length of the animation. For example, if you create a new movie and draw an object on the stage in the default keyframe at frame 1, and then immediately add a motion guide layer, the guide layer will only be one frame long. If you then added a keyframe at frame 30 on the object layer, that layer would now be 30 frames long but the motion guide would remain one frame long. The resulting problem is that the motion guide itself won't exist after frame 1.

You can get around this problem by adding frames to the guide layer, but it's much easier to plan things out, create the animation layer, and then let Flash create an appropriate guide layer when you ask it to.

> *Motion path effects can produce some really wild results, especially when combined with the other effects discussed earlier in the chapter. Once you've got the basic idea down, experiment with different color combinations, Timeline lengths, and motion paths. The possibilities are endless.*

Before you move on, you can use your animation to see what Flash actually does when it draws your animation frames. Knowing this allows you to create animations that are optimized for fast animation.

When Flash runs through the Timeline, it doesn't draw every frame in its entirety. Instead, it only redraws the parts of the stage that it thinks have changed. These areas of change are called redraw regions. For fast and efficient animation, it's a good idea to review these redraw regions to confirm that the overall animation is running efficiently.

This particular animation isn't all that taxing to the Flash player, so you won't get much out of looking for efficiencies. The animation is, however, simple enough for you to learn the principles of creating complex animations that won't cause the Flash player to slow down.

Viewing redraw regions and using bitmap caching

1. Using the animation you just created (or use our version, boat_animated.fla), test the movie. While you're testing the movie, right-click on the stage and select Show Redraw Regions.

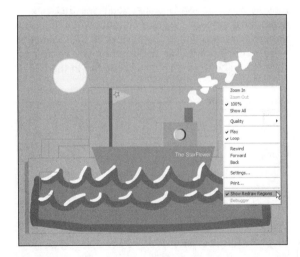

You'll see a number of rectangular red outlines appear. These are the redraw regions, which change as the animation progresses, showing what has actually been updated on the screen during the movie. The bigger the redraw regions you see, the more work Flash is doing per frame.

197

If you're looking to minimize the redraw regions to speed up the animation, there are a couple of things that reviewing the redraw regions will show you.

The redraw region that encloses the ship extends to the top of the flagpole, but a lot of this redraw region actually contains blue sky. You could reduce this region considerably by shortening the height of the flag, thus reducing the amount of blue sky that's unnecessarily redrawn.

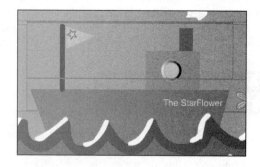

If you stop the boat and waves from moving and then look at what the fish is doing, you'll see that Flash is generating unnecessary redraw regions when the fish is underwater and hidden from view. If this animation were running slowly, one optimization you could consider would be to stop animating the fish in the underwater frames.

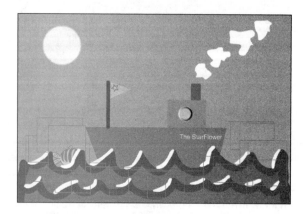

More redraw regions are generated when lots of things are moving at the same time. One thing you could do in your animation is alternate between the ship bobbing up and down and the sea moving left to right, such that only one of the two animations occurs at any one time. Although it might seem like this could degrade your animation, most users wouldn't even notice the difference, if it were done carefully.

A second way to optimize your animations is to use bitmap caching. When you do this, Flash attempts to render movie clips as bitmaps whenever it can. To understand why this can be beneficial, consider the following image:

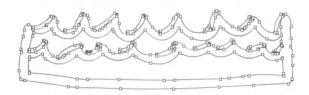

This shows what Flash has to draw every time it has to render the redraw region that contains the waves. As you can see, the waves contain lots of points. This means that there are lots of curves as well, and Flash has to recalculate each line between the points and create the related fills. For an animation running at 12fps, it has to redraw all the points/fills 12 times per second. As you can imagine, that's a lot of calculations.

Although vector-based graphics have many advantages (sharper edges, small file sizes, etc.), they can require a large amount of computing power to draw, particularly when they contain lots of points to be redrawn in every frame.

When you're using bitmap caching, Flash looks at the redraw regions—if it finds elements like your waves (in which the render region moves around but the stuff inside the render region doesn't actually change), it converts them into bitmaps.

After conversion into a bitmap, Flash no longer has to recalculate the points that make up the waves, but instead simply moves the bitmap. This process can significantly reduce Flash's workload. Let's see how you can make Flash treat your waves as a bitmap.

The redraw overhead can become particularly large if you use gradients as a fill. Although gradients look cool, Flash has to work through lots of calculation to get all that beautiful color blending right (and may have to do it each and every frame).

2. Select the waves in frame 1 of your boat animation. (You may have to unselect the Show Layer as Outlines icon on the waves layer's title bar.)

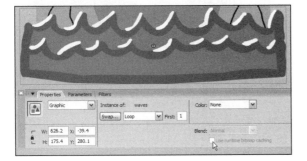

The Use runtime bitmap caching check box will appear in the Properties panel as shown in the following screenshot. There's a problem though—it's currently grayed out. This is because bitmap caching can only be applied to movie clips. First, you need to make this wave's instance behave as a movie clip.

3. In the Properties panel, change the Instance Behavior drop-down menu choice (on the far left) from Graphic to Movie Clip. When you do this, the Use runtime bitmap caching check box becomes selectable. Check this check box.

4. Repeat steps 2 and 3 for the wave keyframes at frames 10 and 20.

5. Test the Movie.

Um . . . there's no difference!

That's the way it should be—Flash needs to do less to redraw the render region associated with the waves, but you don't see any difference in the animation. However, you would start to see a difference if you had continued to refine the animation. For example, if you added a few seagulls flying across the screen, a port in the distance, and other ships in the distance, then the animation might start to slow down unless you made use of bitmap caching.

Note that bitmap caching doesn't work well for some movie clips. In Chapter 4, you looked at creating a car with rotating wheels. If you revisit that animation, you'll see that the wheels are constantly changing.

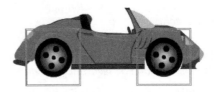

Bitmap caching isn't suitable for the wheels because the graphics within the render region are constantly changing due to the rotation. If you were to define bitmap caching for the wheels, Flash wouldn't do anything untoward—it would still try to optimize the wheels by rendering them as bitmaps, but since no opportunities to optimize via bitmaps would occur, no speed efficiency would be gained.

Keep in mind that bitmap caching is handled automatically—you just have to check the Use runtime bitmap caching check box, and Flash will decide the best way to draw each render region per frame. When Flash decides to redraw a render region as a bitmap, there will be no perceptible difference in the end animation—it will look like the animation is still using vector graphics throughout. Thus, bitmap caching can give the advantages of vector crispness and small file size while at the same time giving the speed advantage of using bitmaps.

Creating tween animations can be a long and laborious process, so you shouldn't make it even harder by attempting to optimize absolutely everything. Most animations will run just fine without optimization. Optimization becomes important when you start creating complex animations that visibly slow the Flash player down.

Despite this, there are a few general rules to bear in mind when creating Flash animation:

- *When designing your symbols, consider the fact that Flash only uses rectangular redraw regions. A symbol that creates a large rectangle with very few pixels that actually change (such as a long diagonal line) makes inefficient use of its redraw region.*

- *Consider the fact that small graphics will create small redraw regions.*

- *Avoid creating animations for anything that can't be viewed (such as your submerged fish). You know it can't be seen, but Flash doesn't.*

- *Consider using bitmap caching for any complex vector shapes.*

- *Always use bitmap caching for filter effects. (Filter effects will be touched on briefly in a moment.)*

Bitmap caching will become particularly important when you look at advanced animation in Chapter 9. In particular, Flash allows you to apply the same sort of advanced effects to interactive animations that graphic applications such as Photoshop allow you to apply to static images. Such effects include drop shadows, filtering/colorization, and advanced per-pixel graphic effects.

Unlike Photoshop, however, Flash allows you to add these effects within interactive animations, and even in real time. To give you an example, recall your car from Chapter 4, shown in the following image:

In this version, a runtime bevel has been added to the car's bodywork, giving it a nice faux-3D effect. Not only can you add a bevel, but you can change the amount of bevel as your animation progresses. You could use this to alter the apparent lighting on your car's body as it passes a streetlight. Although Flash doesn't support 3D objects, the creative designer can come up with some pretty cool tricks that can fake 3D effects.

The bevel filter is a subtle effect—if you can't see it in the image, look at the file car_finished_bevelfilter.fla.

Runtime filters and effects are very cool features because they allow you to significantly enhance your graphics. However, unless you use bitmap caching for effects like the one you see on the car, the redraw time can go up considerably. This is particularly apparent when you apply multiple filters to moving objects or create advanced effects such as real-time bitmap stretching ("goo" effects), real-time texturing, and plasma or particle effects.

Case study

Now that you have your basic interface, you're going to add a little motion to spruce up the website when it first appears. You'll do this with a couple of simple motion tweens.

Animating an intro

The animation will be performed in the Content movie clip that you created in Chapter 4. The Content movie clip will contain all your website pages and, as you'll discover here, an intro sequence. The intro sequence will consist of a number of motion-tweening text assets and a bouncing dog. The intro sequence will be played as soon as the viewer enters your website.

1. Open your saved case study file from the previous chapter.

2. Locate the Content movie clip on the center of the main stage—it's on the Content layer and contains the four colored rectangles—and double-click it to enter Edit in Place mode. Editing it this way will allow you to work while the rest of the site is still visible.

As always, you know you're in Edit in Place mode because the rest of the screen is washed out.

3. Rename the current layer animated rectangles. As mentioned in previous chapters, it's always good practice to name your layers so they're easy to edit later.

4. Insert two new layers called welcome to text and floyd designs text above the colored rectangles layer. These layers will house some simple text-based motion tweens.

5. On the welcome to text layer, use the Text tool to type welcome to. Leave two spaces between the words. (These extra spaces will allow you to position the text over the white lines between the rectangles.) Use 24-point Arial. Don't worry about the text field's position—you'll move it in a moment.

6. Ensure that Snap Align is on (View ➤ Snapping ➤ Snap Align) and drag the welcome to text to the top-left corner of the left rectangle. When it snaps to the top corner, release it.

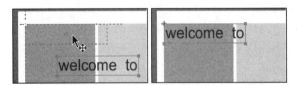

7. With the text still selected, hold down *SHIFT* and press the down arrow key to move the text down 10 pixels (assuming you're at 100% zoom). Use the left and right arrow keys to position the text horizontally so that the gap between the words is over the white line (pressing an arrow key will move the text one pixel in the arrow direction).

8. Set the text to the color of the orange rectangle. The best way to do this is to click away from the text (so that the text field is completed), and then click on the text field with the Selection tool to select it. Next, click the color selector in the Properties panel, and then click the orange rectangle.

When you do this, the mouse pointer changes to the pipette mouse pointer, which you should recognize from the Dropper tool. Selecting a color this way is a nice shortcut and it saves you from having to use the Dropper tool directly.

201

9. Make sure only the text is selected, and select Modify ➤ Convert to Symbol. Give it a graphic symbol behavior, the name welcome to text, and a central registration point.

10. Select the layer floyd designs text.

11. On this layer, add a static text field with the text Floyd Designs inside it (this time use only a single space between the words), in 28-point Arial, and set its color to the light green of the second rectangle.

12. Position it at the bottom-right corner, 5 pixels from the bottom of the colored rectangles. As with the welcome to text, ensure that the gap in the words is over the white line between the two rectangles.

13. Select the Floyd Designs text and convert it to a graphic symbol called floyd designs text.

The interface should now look like the following image:

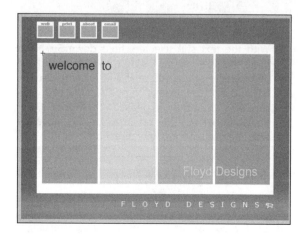

Now it's time to animate the text. Here's what's going to happen: first, the welcome to text will tween in from off-stage left to its current position. Once it's in position, the Floyd Designs text will alpha tween in from an alpha of 0 to 100%.

14. Insert a keyframe on frame 15 of the welcome to text layer.

15. Return to the keyframe on frame 1 and move the welcome to symbol off-stage left. This will be the starting position of the text. Its ending position is already set at frame 15.

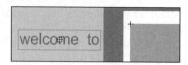

16. Select a frame between 1 and 14 and select Motion from the Tween drop-down menu in the Properties panel.

17. Extend the frames on the animated rectangles layer to frame 15 using F5.

18. Test the movie to see the motion. It's all right, but it needs something—a little alpha tweening action.

19. On the first keyframe, select the off-stage symbol instance and select Alpha from the Color drop-down menu in the Properties panel.

20. Change the alpha value to 0% using the slider or by typing it into the text field to the right. This will make the starting instance completely transparent.

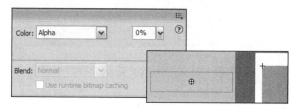

21. The welcome to tween is now complete. Now it's time to tween the Floyd Designs text.

22. Click to select the keyframe on frame 1 of the floyd designs text layer. A rectangle will be added to the mouse pointer, indicating that you can move this keyframe.

23. Drag the keyframe to frame 15 in the Timeline. This means that the tween, as the director has ordered, will take place once the welcome to text is in place.

24. Insert a keyframe at frame 30 of the floyd designs text layer using the *F6* key.

25. Return to the first keyframe (at frame 15) and select the floyd designs text instance.

26. In the Properties panel, select Alpha from the drop-down menu and set the value to 0%.

27. Click any frame from 15 to 29 and set a motion tween using the Properties panel.

28. Before you test it, use *F5* to insert additional frames on the other two layers so that all layers up to frame 30 are all populated. Then test it using Control ➤ Test Movie.

So far, so good, except it's looping insanely. Don't worry about that, you'll fix it in a later chapter.

Animating with a motion guide

In this section, you're going to animate your little mascot, Floyd. He's going to scamper across the screen before settling above the Floyd Designs logo.

1. While still in the Content movie clip, insert a new layer above the others called dog tween.

2. Drag an instance of the dog movie clip to the bottom-left of the stage. Use the Free Transform tool to scale it until it's about the same height as the Floyd Designs text.

3. Select the keyframe on the new dog tween layer and drag it to frame 25. This animation will take place just before the end of the Floyd Designs tweening.

4. You want your dog, Floyd, to run from left to right, but at the moment, he's pointing to the left. To fix this, select the dog symbol, and then bring up the Transform panel. Uncheck the Constrain check box, and enter -100 in the Width text-entry box. Floyd will now be pointing to the right.

5. You could also do with this instance of the dog looking a little different from the white dog on the main logo. With the dog still selected, select Brightness in the Color drop-down menu on the Properties panel, and set the brightness to -100. Your dog will now be shown with a black outline.

6. Insert a new keyframe at frame 65. This gives your dog a full 40 frames to sprint across the stage.

7. On keyframe 65, drag the instance of the dog to the bottom-right of the far right colored triangle.

8. Insert a motion tween between frames 25 and 64. This will make your dog travel in a straight line from one point to the next. Now for the guide.

9. Select the dog tween layer and click the Add Motion Guide button below the Timeline.

10. On frame 1 of the guide layer, use the Pencil tool (with Object Drawing turned off) to draw a squiggly line from the bottom-left to just above the Floyd Designs text. Give Floyd the dog a little jump just before he reaches the text.

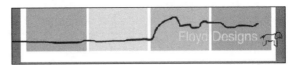

As before, a thick dark stroke has been used here to make it easy for you to see.

11. Ensure that View ➤ Snapping ➤ Snap to Objects is on, and snap the dog to the end of the line on both keyframes. You may want to lock all other layers when you do this to make sure you select only the dog.

12. Extend the frames on all the other layers to frame 65 using *F5*, and run the movie. If Floyd runs in a straight line, he isn't snapped properly. If necessary, go back and retry—when it's correct, you'll add the final touch.

Motion tween scaling for effect

Now you're going to scale some text and create an alpha fade for a dramatic effect.

1. Still inside the Content movie clip, insert a new layer at the top called floyd designs grow.

2. Select the floyd designs text instance on frame 30 of the layer of the same name, and copy it (Edit ➤ Copy or *CTRL+C*).

3. Insert a blank keyframe (*F7*) on frame 65 of the floyd designs grow layer.

4. Use Edit ➤ Paste in Place (or *CTRL+SHIFT+V*) to paste a copy of the Floyd Designs text in exactly the same spot. You won't see the stage change much (because you've pasted another version of the Floyd Designs text over the original one), but you'll see the keyframe turn from hollow to solid, signifying that text has been added to this keyframe.

5. Insert a keyframe (*F6*) on frame 75 of the same layer.

6. On this keyframe, select the text instance and open the Transform panel (Window ➤ Design Panels ➤ Transform or *CTRL+T*). You may want to lock all other layers to make sure you select only the text in the current layer.

7. In this panel, ensure that Constrain is checked, and type 150% into either of the boxes at the top.

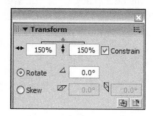

This will scale your instance to 150 percent of its original size.

8. With the instance still selected, change the alpha value to 0% using the Color drop-down menu in the Properties panel. The text will now grow and disappear at the same time.

9. Select any frame from 65 to 74 and set a motion tween.

10. Extend all the frames on the other layers to frame 75 using *F5*.

Your Timeline and stage should look like the following:

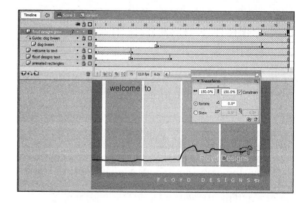

Run the animation to see the overall effect. So far, you've got a nice little intro for your website, but you'll go to town on it in Chapter 9 when you get into advanced animation effects.

11. Save your case study movie and close it. You'll find the current version of the case study, case_study_ch6.fla, in the downloadable files for this book.

Summary

You've traveled quite a distance in this chapter, passing through the varied landscape of motion tweening.

In this chapter, you saw that

- You can use motion tweening to move objects around the stage, and you can use motion paths to guide the objects and onion skins to see multiple frames in the animation.

- You can alter objects as they move, and you can fade them into the background, change their tint and scale, and rotate them.

- You can simulate acceleration and deceleration for more convincing animation using easing and custom easing.

- You can optimize your animations for performance using redraw regions and bitmap caching.

In the next chapter, you're going to have some fun with motion tweening's sibling: shape tweening.

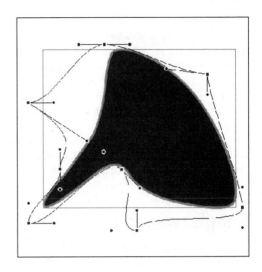

Chapter 7

SHAPE TWEENING

What we'll cover in this chapter:

- Using shape tweening to morph shapes into something new, rich, and strange
- Morphing text into shapes and vice versa
- Using shape hints to overwrite Flash's default shape tweening behavior

Now that you've seen what motion tweening can do and you understand the power of Macromedia Flash as an animation workhorse, it's time to climb to the next rung on the ladder. So far, you can move a shape around the stage, but it is still the same shape at the end of the animation, even if you can change things like scaling, color, and position. By the close of this chapter, you'll be able to start the race with a tortoise and finish it with a hare, though Darwinians might not be too happy with what happens in between.

Shape tweens

Shape tweening is similar in concept to its motion tween counterpart, and using it is just as easy. The results, however, are often more impressive.

The basic idea is that at point A in time you have one object, and at a later point B you have another object. Between the two points, you have a gradual shape-shifting transformation from object A to object B. Like this, for example:

You already encountered shape tweening in the first chapter when you made a mushroom grow, and in this chapter you expand and add detail to that knowledge, fleshing out the whys and hows of shape tweening.

How shape tweens work

Shape tweens work just like motion tweens in the sense that you provide a starting point in one keyframe and an ending point in another, and Flash fills the intervening frames. And like motion tweens, it's advisable to have only one shape tween at any time on a layer—this way, you get more predictable results and less mayhem on the stage. Of course, if you want to shape tween multiple objects into one object at the same time, the objects will have to be on the same layer. It's really a question of necessity: If you need your tweens to interact with one another, they have to be on the same layer, but if they don't interact, keep them on separate layers.

The most important thing to remember when creating shape tweens is that unlike motion tweens, shape tweens must involve shapes or drawing objects and not groups or symbols. For a shape tween to work, the basic attributes—the stroke and fill—must be able to change so that it can morph the original shape into something else. The simplest way to ensure that all the elements you want to shape tween are "shape tween-able" is to select all the objects and use the Modify ➤ Break Apart menu option to ensure they're broken down into their constituent elements.

Let's play.

Squaring the circle

First, you set up a basic shape tween and then play with it to understand the finer points of tweening. The simplest objects in Flash are squares and circles, so you use these in your first example.

1. Create a new Flash document, and draw a circle with Object Drawing mode turned off and a black line and fill in frame 1.

2. Click frame 15, and press *F6* to insert a keyframe. You now have 15 frames full of nothing but a circle.

3. In the keyframe at frame 15, draw a large, filled square (again with Object Drawing mode off, and a black line and fill) over the top of the circle.

4. If you want to position the square more "squarely" over the circle once you've drawn it, don't forget you can always turn on the Onion Skinning and View layer as outlines options in the Layer Properties dialog box. You can bring up the Layer Properties dialog box by right-clicking (*CTRL*-clicking on Mac) the layer name in the timeline and selecting Properties from the context-sensitive menu.

Now you have your beginning and end keyframes, so all you need to do is tell Flash to morph from one shape to the other over time by putting a shape tween between the two keyframes.

5. Click the timeline anywhere between the two keyframes, open the Properties panel, and select Shape from the Tween drop-down menu:

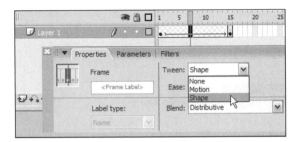

6. Select the Selection tool, and then click a blank part of the timeline to deselect your other frames. You can see that the frames are colored pale green and have a solid arrow on them.

7. If you click the Onion Skin Outlines button just below the timeline and arrange the onion skin markers to encompass all 15 frames, you'll see a rather beautiful rendering of the shape tween:

All this indicates that you've got a functional shape tween on your hands.

8. Select Control ➤ Test Movie to preview the movie. The circle transforms smoothly into a square. It's as easy as that.

At the moment, the animation loops back to the beginning when the playhead hits frame 15, meaning that your smoothly morphed square suddenly jumps back to being a circle again in a fraction of a second. Ugly. To correct this, you need to create some extra frames that will facilitate the smooth return of the square back to

the circular starting image—this will make the animation loop much smoother.

9. Close the movie preview window and deselect the Onion Skin Outlines button for now.

10. Click frame 1; your circle should automatically be selected for you. Then choose Edit ➤ Copy (*CTRL+C* on Mac), and click frame 30.

11. Press *F7* to insert a blank keyframe. It's important that it's blank because you don't want this frame to inherit the image of the square from the previous keyframe.

12. Use Edit ➤ Paste in Place to put the copied circle in exactly the same place in frame 30 as it is in frame 1.

13. Click between frames 15 and 30 on the timeline to select them, and use the Properties panel to create a shape tween:

Now when you select Control ➤ Test Movie to preview your movie, you'll see a smooth transition from circle to square and back to a circle again. It's strangely mesmerizing to just sit and watch this simple shape beating out its regular morphing rhythm, but if you're going to get any further you'll just have to close that preview window and return to the Flash interface.

14. Click the keyframe in frame 15, and drag your square a little way off to the side. Preview your movie, and you'll see the circle move as it tweens into the square, and then move back as it returns to being a circle.

But if you can get motion effects on a shape using a *shape* tween, what's the point of a *motion* tween? The simple answer is computing power—it takes more power to perform a shape tween than it does to perform a motion tween. Running a lot of shape tweens will noticeably slow down the computer, but the same number of motion tweens will run a lot smoother. Don't forget that you can have only one type of tween in the same frame on the same layer; you can't combine them. It's a question of judgment—use motion tweens whenever you're just *moving* an object, and use shape tweens whenever you want an object to change in some way as it moves.

Table 7-1 explains when to use each type of tween.

Table 7-1. Comparing tweens

Use shape tweens to	Use motion tweens to
Tween shapes into different shapes	Move groups or symbols without altering them
Tween the gradient fills of objects	Tween the color, size, angle, or transparency of objects
	Make a motion guide or custom easing available. Note that you can use shape tweens to change shape, color, or position at the same time as you change the shape or gradient fill of the shape.

Now that you have the basics of shape tweening under your belt, let's get a little more sophisticated. First you'll use the Free Transform tool to modify your shapes, and then you'll create some text-based tweens.

While working through the last example, you may have noticed that the Edit *button is not present when you click on a shape keyframe. This means that you cannot use custom easing for a shape tween, so that's one more difference between shape and motion tweens to consider.*

Irregular shapes

The Free Transform tool is essential for creating organic amorphous shape tweens. In this exercise, you tween a regular shape into an irregular one.

Here you'll use two more advanced modifiers of the Free Transform tool. In this exercise, we will be using the Distort and Envelope tools:

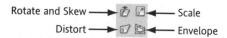

Rotate and Skew ——➤ 　　 ◀—— Scale
Distort ——➤ 　　 ◀—— Envelope

Squaring the circle

This animation will start with a regular circle, and transmogrify into something that's really quite indescribable (in a good way, of course).

1. Open a new Flash document.
2. Change the frame rate of the movie to 30 fps in the Document Properties dialog box (Modify ➤ Document).
3. Ensure that the Properties panel is open (Window ➤ Properties ➤ Properties) and then select the Oval tool.
4. In the Oval tool options in the Properties panel, select a black fill color and a red stroke color.
5. Set the stroke thickness to 4:

This will allow you to see the outline tween clearly as well as the fill.

6. Use the Oval tool to draw a fairly big circle on your screen (you don't have to use Object Drawing mode in this case, but we have).
7. Insert a keyframe on frame 20 of the timeline using *F6*.
8. With the circle still selected, click the Free Transform tool, and choose the Distort modifier.

9. Drag the square points around the shape and change the overall shape of the circle.

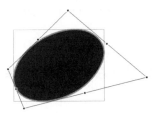

10. Click any frame between 1 and 19 and select Shape from the Tween drop-down menu in the Properties panel.

11. Test the movie to view your first morph. Pretty cool, huh? Well, it does get better.

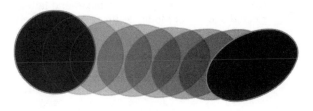

12. Insert a keyframe at frame 40.

13. Use the Envelope modifier on the shape on frame 40 to create a new version of the shape. Don't try to mimic our shape; just go with the flow and experiment:

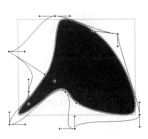

14. Select a keyframe between 20 and 39, and select Shape from the Tween drop-down menu. Test your movie.

It's a Flash protoplasm!

The animations might show your fantastic manipulations, but it doesn't quite create a breathing organism. To make this happen, you need to make the animation loop.

15. Select all the frames and choose Edit ➤ Timeline ➤ Copy Frames.

16. Insert a blank keyframe using *F7* on frame 41.

17. Paste the frames into the new keyframe using Edit ➤ Timeline ➤ Paste Frames.

18. Select all the frames from 41 to 80 (the easiest way to do this is click-drag-release frames 41 to 81—this will highlight frames 41–80), and select Modify ➤ Timeline ➤ Reverse Frames. This will alter the direction of the animation, creating a loop of animation.

19. Test the movie using *CTRL+ENTER*. Your shape has an organic breathing motion. Using the Free Transform modifiers is essential for morphs and globular animation through shape tweens. The key to using these modifiers confidently is plenty of experimentation.

After that quick blast of amoeba-creation, let's look at a more common use for shape tweening text.

211

Common tweening text effects

In the following exercises, you tween pieces of text so they are transformed into different pieces of text, and then you morph shapes into text.

The main thing to bear in mind when working with text is that to be able to tween it, you must first break it apart to convert it into a graphic. This means that you can no longer edit it as if it were a text field, so ensure that the text is *exactly* how you want it to be before you break it apart.

First, the text-to-text tween.

Text-to-text tweening

This animation starts with one word and uses shape tweening to change it into a different word.

1. Create a new Flash document, and in frame 1, use the Text tool in conjunction with the Properties panel to write a big chunky This is my first, on the left side of the stage:

This is my first

We used Arial Black at 35 point.

2. Select frame 30 and create a new keyframe (*F6*).

3. Still on frame 30, highlight the text with the Text tool, delete the text (but not the text field it is in), and then type text 2 text tween... into the text field and move it to the right side of the stage:

text 2 text tween...

4. Use the Selection tool to select the text field that that you just created (*don't* select the text by dragging while still inside the box), and use the Modify ➤ Break Apart menu option to break the text into separate letters:

text 2 text tween...

Flash breaks the original text field into several smaller text fields—not exactly how you need it to be. It's worth remembering that Flash does this because it can be very useful for creating interesting text effects. Each letter is contained in its own text field, so each letter can be changed or moved individually.

5. Make sure you have all the text boxes and letters selected and select Modify ➤ Break Apart again to break them into graphics.

text 2 text tween...

The text is no longer editable text but has been broken apart to raw fills. You can see this is the case by deselecting the broken-up text and dragging at the perimeter of one of the letters with the Selection tool. If you try this, be sure to undo it to get back to the broken text . . . or alternatively, you can just take our word for it and move quickly on to the next step!

6. Break apart the text in frame 1 in the same way you just did to the text in frame 30, remembering to break the text apart twice.

7. Click between the two keyframes on the timeline, and use the Properties panel to create a shape tween.

8. Preview your movie to see the first words morph into the second while moving across the stage.

This is my first

ᵀᵒ⁴Ⲭ ᵇˢ♏ᵞ♥⁹ᵖₛᴝ

text 2 text tween...

We said earlier that shape tweens would only work on shapes that have been reduced to their constituent lines and fills. If you've already created a symbol for your movie and you want to animate it, you can, providing that you first break it apart. Let's see how this works.

Shape-to-text tweening

In this example, we will show how to make five squares morph into the word Flash.

1. Open a new movie and draw a strokeless black square on the stage—make the square about three quarters of an inch (2 cm/60 pixels) across. If you want to be precise, you can enter the width and height values into the Properties panel to get exactly 60. Although shape tweens will work perfectly well with Drawing Objects, it is usually better to draw your shapes with Object Drawing mode turned off. Flash will turn all the Drawing Objects into raw strokes and fills internally anyway, and if we use raw shapes throughout, we are less likely to be surprised by the way Flash sometimes turns our Drawing Objects into shapes.

If you want to tween two or more overlapping shapes that were created as Drawing Objects, you may see Flash do odd things (because it doesn't seem to know what to do with the area of overlap). There are two ways to get around this.

The first is to put each Drawing Object on its own layer and tween them as separate shape tweens.

Another way that sometimes (but not always) works is to avoid the use of Object Drawing mode. When you do this, the areas of overlap are "cut away," so Flash doesn't have to worry about them.

Way back in Chapter 1, we created a growing mushroom animation. You may have wondered then why we did not make the stalk touch the top of the mushroom. Well, now you have the answer—we wanted to keep the animation simple and use only one tween and one layer. The best way to do that was to specify a stalk with a gap at the top.

If you were to go back and put the two ovals of the mushroom on separate layers, then tween the mushroom via two tweens (one on each layer), you would find that you could now make the stalk and top of the mushroom overlap.

2. Convert your square to a graphic symbol called Square by selecting the square and pressing F8.

3. Drag four more instances of your square from the Library to make a total of five—one for each letter in the name of the world's greatest piece of software.

4. Align the squares neatly using Snap Align (which you switch on by selecting View ➤ Snapping ➤ Snap Align) or the Align panel (Window ➤ Design Panels ➤ Align). Either way, make sure that the squares are a small distance apart.

5. Use the Modify ➤ Break Apart menu option to convert your squares into their component fills.

6. Insert a keyframe in frame 20. This keyframe will inherit the broken-apart squares from the first keyframe.

Now you want to create the letters that spell out the word Flash—one letter to fit in each square.

There are two ways to fit the letters over the squares. The most precise way is to type the word as it is, break the one text field apart into five smaller text fields, position each individual text field correctly, and then break them all apart again. Phew. Another method is to write the word as one piece of text, and then modify its size and spacing to fit over the squares. Because you're using a simple tween, you can get away with using the second method. If you were designing a more complicated tween, it would probably be better to treat each letter individually.

7. Use the Text tool to write Flash on the stage. Choose a text color that contrasts nicely with black.

8. Select the text field with the Selection tool and move it so that it's over the squares on the left side:

9. Use the Selection tool to select the text field again, and then use the Letter Spacing slider in the Properties panel to adjust the text spacing so that the letters are positioned over the black boxes. The Character Spacing slider is directly below the Font menu (the one on the left containing 40 in this screenshot):

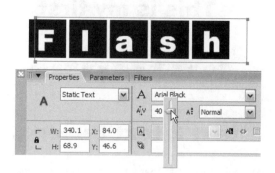

Don't worry about getting things too precise: just so long as the letters are roughly in the right place, things will be OK.

10. Click away from the text field to deselect it.

11. Still on frame 20, click each of the black boxes behind the letters and delete them:

12. This will leave you with just the word Flash on the stage.

13. Now that the boxes are out of the way and you can see clearly, highlight the text and change its color to black.

You're finished working with the text *as text* now, and it's time to break it up.

14. Select the text with the Selection tool and use the Modify ➤ Break Apart menu option twice to convert it to a graphic. If you don't perform this action twice, your text will still be in text fields.

15. Everything is ready for tweening, so click between the keyframes on the timeline and use the Properties panel to add a shape tween. Your tween should now work perfectly when you preview your movie.

If some of the animations look a little odd to you—like the way that the A square transforms into the A—don't worry; you'll learn ways to tweak these little gremlins later in the chapter.

First, though, you look at ways of making your shape-tweened animations more enjoyable for your viewers. For the most control here, you really need to use some of the ActionScript that we don't cover until later in the book, but here are a few simple methods you can use right away.

Natural-looking tweens

Whether you move a morphing object across the stage or keep it stationary as it changes from shape to shape, there's one slight drawback to using only two keyframes: the object immediately begins to tween in frame 1. This can be a problem. For instance, with a text tween, the user usually needs to see what the text says before it starts to change into the next word or shape.

In our previous example, the text was whole only in the final keyframe, which means that it was perfectly readable for only 1/12 of a second—not long enough for

the average person to read. The way to change this is to add a "buffer zone" of frames that contain the tween-free text to the beginning or end of the tween. The static images in these frames will mean that Flash appears to pause over the static text.

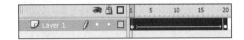

In the same example from the previous exercise, you make one small change before adding the buffer zone—you make it go backward.

1. Click the layer name in the timeline to highlight everything that's on that layer:

2. Use the Modify ➤ Timeline ➤ Reverse Frames menu option to reverse the order of the selected frames. Your movie starts with the word Flash, and then tweens into the five squares. We've done this to make the changes that you're about to apply stand out more clearly.

3. Select all the frames again, but this time drag them across the timeline until the last frame is in frame 30, and then release them:

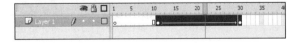

Notice that as you drag, a little rectangle is added to the mouse pointer indicating that you are dealing with a selection of frames. There will be ten empty frames at the beginning of your movie. Your animation will start at frame 11 and run through to frame 30:

4. Click the first keyframe of your movie (now in frame 11). Select all the text that's in it using the Selection tool.

5. Copy the text to your computer's clipboard by using Edit ➤ Copy (CTRL/CMD+C).

6. Click frame 1, and use the Edit ➤ Paste in Place menu option to paste your text into the frame in the exact position as it was in frame 11.

7. Preview your movie. The text will stay on screen for about a second, and then tween into the five squares. It's now easier to read the text before it starts to change into the shapes. Obviously, if you had more text, you'd want to have a longer buffer zone to allow people more time to read it.

Note that you can copy most things into your computer's clipboard using CTRL/CMD+C, except Flash frames in the timeline. To copy frames, you have to use the frame-specific options in Edit ➤ Timeline. You can also use CTRL/CMD+ALT+C and CTRL/CMD+ALT+V.

Now that we have covered different shape tweens, let's spice things up a bit by looking at changing color while tweening.

Tweens with color

You've already used the Tint feature in motion tweens, and now you will add color to your shape tweens. In the previous chapter, you made text fade through different colors by using the Tint effect, and in the following example you expand your Flash text animation to include color.

Coloring your shape tweens

1. Still using the movie from the last example, click the layer name again to select all the movie's frames.

2. Drag them so that the final frame is now at frame 50.

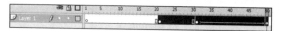

3. Click your first keyframe (now in frame 21) to select all the text, and Edit ➤ Copy it to the clipboard.

4. Click frame 1 of your movie, and use Edit ➤ Paste in Place to put the copied text on the stage:

5. Move the playhead to frame 10 and use *F7* to insert a blank keyframe. Then paste your text in place on this keyframe in the same way you did for frame 1.

You now have your basic structure set up and are ready to tween. The only thing left to add now is color.

6. Click back in frame 1, select the text shapes on the stage, and change the color in your fill color box to red. The text on your stage will change to reflect this.

7. Do the same for the keyframes in frames 10 and 21, but use the colors green and blue, respectively.

8. Create shape tweens between all the keyframes to make your timeline a lean, green tweening machine:

9. Preview your movie to see your text waltz through the spectrum before settling for black and tweening into the five squares.

10. As an added touch to show the power of Flash, click frame 50 to select your squares and change the fill color to yellow. When you preview your movie now, you see the final animation changing shape and color at the same time.

Shape tweening color has a couple of features that motion tweening color cannot do easily. First, you can give each letter in the word Flash a different color, and the shape tween will tween all five letters correctly. Motion tweening would require a separate tween per layer to do the same thing.

Second, shape tweening can tween between gradient fills. You can try this in your movie, although gradients really only show up if you use large letters.

As noted previously, you can't use custom tweens with shape tweening, and so there is no Edit button next to the Ease value.

So how do you get even tighter control? With shape tween modifiers, of course!

Shape tween modifiers

As with many other elements in Flash's expansive toolkit, shape morphing has modifiers and helpers that you can use to tweak your tween. The place to look, as always, is the Properties panel, in the Ease and Blend fields:

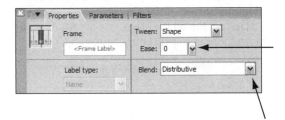

In shape tweens, easing acts exactly the same way as it does with motion tweens—it controls Flash's ability to speed up and slow down the action at the beginning or end of your animations. Here's a quick reminder on the effects of easing:

- Easing in to a value of –100 makes the shape tween start slowly and accelerate as it progresses to the end of the tween.
- Easing out to a value of 100 makes the shape tween start quickly and slow down as it progresses to the end of the tween.

Unlike motion tweens, shape tweens also offer the option of playing around with the sharpness of lines in your tween—the values for this are set in the Blend drop-down menu.

- A Distributive shape tween creates an animation where the intermediate stages of the tween are smooth and irregular with no straight lines.
- An Angular shape tween creates an animation where the intermediate stages of the tween preserve corners and straight lines.

An Angular blend is used to shape tween shapes that have straight lines and corners, but if the shape has no corners, Flash will revert to a Distributive blend.

Now that you know how to create and work with basic shape tweens, you'll get those promised tweaking methods that'll bring them a bit closer to perfection.

One of the best enhancers available to you is the shape hints feature.

Shape hints

Shape hints are used with shape tweening to give you a higher degree of control in the morphing process. To apply shape hints, you must select a frame that has shape tweening already set on it. If it doesn't have shape tweening attached, Flash won't allow you to add hints.

When you create a shape tween, Flash automatically takes the "easiest" route to turn one shape into another, but that route doesn't always give the precise visual effect you're after. This is where shape hints come in. You can step in and override Flash's default tweening and finesse things to your taste. Shape hints can be a little complicated to implement in a complex movie, and they can give some spectacularly strange results when they go wrong, but with practice you can get a beautiful tween every time.

There's one other factor to note: shape hints demand a lot more processing power than straightforward tweening. If you can get away with not using them, it's best to avoid them rather than risk your movie slowing down when running on less powerful computers. If you really have to use shape hints, it's better to use them sparingly.

Shape hints work by highlighting particular points on a shape, and telling Flash explicitly where those points should move to on a subsequent frame after a motion tween. Suppose you created a movie that had a square in frame 1 and a triangle in the same location in frame 15, and you wanted to shape one tween into the other:

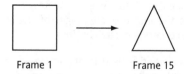

| Frame 1 | Frame 15 |

If you get Flash to make the tween, it does something slightly counterintuitive: instead of pulling the top-left and top-right corners of the square into the middle to form the point of the triangle, it twists the square through some weird contortions to perform the tween—as shown in this sequence:

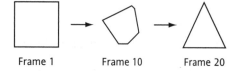

Frame 1   Frame 10   Frame 20

Using shape hints, you can force Flash to pull the two top corners of the square into the center, giving you a slightly more intuitive tween:

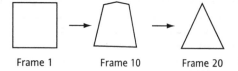

Frame 1   Frame 10   Frame 20

You mark the specific points that you want to "steer" in your initial shape, and you mark where you want them to end up in your final shape:

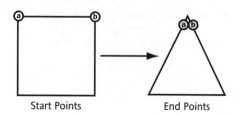

Start Points   End Points

Each hint is represented by a different letter so you know which matches up with which. The only drawback to this is that you can have a maximum of only 26 shape hints, but that should be plenty. If you need more, you should consider splitting your animation up onto different layers because it is probably too complicated anyway. Let's see this in action.

Using shape hints to control your tween

1. Start a Flash document, and with Object Drawing mode turned off, draw a big yellow rectangle with a black outline on the stage. Use proportions similar to those of our rectangle here:

2. Use the Line tool (Object Drawing mode off again, and throughout this exercise) to draw two lines forming a triangle on one side of the image, and then fill it with the same yellow color:

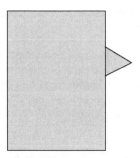

3. Select the part of the line that acts as the base of the triangle where it meets the rectangle, and delete it, leaving a shape like this:

4. Draw a small blue circle with no stroke inside the rectangle on the right side, just above the triangle:

This is the eye of your (admittedly basic) face.

5. Click frame 30 and press *F6* to insert a keyframe.

You're going to make an animation of the face turning from looking to the right to looking to the left, with the face looking straight at you in the middle of the tween. The first thing you need to do is make the image in the final frame look in the opposite direction.

6. In the new keyframe at frame 30, use the Modify ➤ Transform ➤ Flip Horizontal menu option to turn it around.

7. Insert a shape tween between the two keyframes and preview your movie in all its glory.

Of course, because this exercise is about fixing tweens that go wrong, you probably guessed something like this was going to happen. So now you have to go about fixing the tween.

8. Click the first keyframe, and use the Modify ➤ Shape ➤ Add Shape Hint menu option. A little red circle with an "a" in it will appear like a beauty spot in the middle of the face:

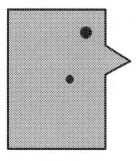

This is the first of your shape hints. Note that it's red at the moment.

Shape hints appear by default in the center of the shape that you are tweening. Remember that the center of the shape is defined by the invisible bounding box around it, and is not always where you might think it should be.

9. It's easier to work with shape hints with snapping turned on, so make sure Snap to Objects is checked in the View ➤ Snapping menu.

10. Click the shape hint and drag it to the top-left corner of the head:

It's still red.

Shape hints work best if you start with the top-left point and then work counterclockwise around the shape. They can produce some beautiful but unexpected results if you get them in the wrong order.

11. Click the keyframe in frame 30, and you'll find a corresponding "a" shape hint (also red) there. Because you added a shape hint to the start image, Flash assumed that you want one for the end image too. Attach the shape hint in frame 30 to the top-right corner of the face.

Notice that when you click away from the shape, the shape hint turns green. This indicates that it's properly attached to the shape and that its corresponding shape hint in the first frame is also attached properly. If you click back on the first frame, you'll see that it turns yellow. This green-yellow signal means that shape hint "a" is locked on and ready to fire.

> Shape hints can be a little quirky, and you may find one that seems to refuse to turn green. When this happens, sometimes the best course of action is simply to start again by undoing a few times, then positioning the shape hint again.

12. If you preview your movie now, you'll find that it still doesn't look natural. A few more shape hints will sort this out, so go back to your first keyframe and add another three shape hints.

If you ever find that Add Shape Hint is not available in the menu, go back to your keyframe and make sure everything on it is selected. Shape hints can only be added when the object that you're tweening is selected. If you ever lose sight of your shape hints,

make sure that the View ➤ Show Shape Hints menu option is checked.

When you add those three shape hints in succession, they're all added one on top of the other on the stage. This may seem a bit confusing at first, but you'll soon get used to it. The top hint will be "d" because that is the fourth one you created.

13. Drag the three new shape hints out to the other three corners of the rectangle, working counterclockwise from the first point:

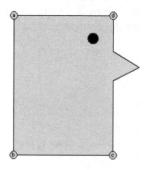

14. Go to your end keyframe and drag the hints out from their little cluster in the center, but this time, reverse the relative left/right positions of the shape hints. The shape hint that corresponds to the chin of the face in the first frame should still be on the chin in the last frame, but it is on the other side of the stage because the face is turned around. Your finished shape should look like this in the last frame:

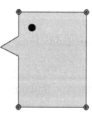

15. Preview your movie, and the face should look as if it is turning from right to left. It's still not quite right, though, because the eye seems to float through an out-of-body experience before returning to normality in the last frame. Guess what? Time for some more shape hints.

16. Go back to the first frame and add another couple of shape hints. Place the hints on either side of the eye:

17. Go to the last frame and place the hints in the same relative (but horizontally flipped) positions on the final face:

18. If everything worked correctly, your face should turn more naturally when you preview your movie. If you want the eye to blink as the tween flows, just add another couple of hints to the eye, one at the top and one at the bottom, the same in both keyframes. The face should now flip perfectly and wink at you cheekily.

To remove shape hints, simply drag them off the stage, just as you would to get rid of a guide. You can also right-click on a hint and select Remove Hint from the context-sensitive menu that appears. Dragging the hint off the stage in any frame will affect both frames that contain the hints. The alternative method is to delete all the hints at once and start again. This can be achieved via the Modify ➤ Shape ➤ Remove All Hints menu option.

Shape hints can be confusing at first, but it's important to be aware of what they are, what they can do, and how you can use them to add more control to a shape tween. If you're dealing with a complex shape tween and no number of shape hints seems to help, you may want to try adding a "staging post" frame for your animation halfway through, and include a keyframe containing an image of what the animation should look like at midpoint. You can then add two tweens, one on either side, to link the three keyframes. This makes it a little easier for Flash to follow and should give better results. This is more time consuming, but it may wind up being easier than letting Flash decide how the tween will work, as well as save you the hassle of adding and positioning multiple shape hints.

Here are some other ways to make shape tweens more successful and less likely to turn into a mess mid-tween:

- Use Modify ➤ Shape ➤ Optimize to reduce the amount of shape data that Flash has to work with—the less Flash has to do, the less it has to do wrong!

- Remove all the strokes and/or reduce the number of separate solid areas.

- Make the start and end shapes similar. By *similar* we mean that they should contain roughly the same number of points and curves, as well as the same number of perimeters. The number of perimeters is particularly important. It is better to shape tween an "O" shape into another "O" shape rather than try to tween it into a "C" shape, for example. The "O" has two perimeters (an inner one and an outer one) while the "C" has one that goes all around it, so Flash will create a confused mess of shapes mid-tween, because it doesn't know what to do with the extra perimeter.

- Split complex shapes into several layers and create a number of simple shape tweens rather than attempt one big, complex one.

Case study

In this section, you'll use shape tweens to add transitions for your case study website's pages.

Making the rectangles shape tween

Until now, the colored rectangles in your site interface have done little but glare back at you as you worked on the case study. In this section, though, you will make each of them grow individually to cover the content area. The premise is that when a visitor clicks a page, a rectangle grows to fill the screen, and the content for that page is displayed in the newly revealed area.

Let's begin.

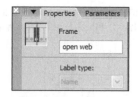

1. Open your saved case study document.

2. Double-click the Content movie clip instance to enter Edit in Place mode for that symbol.

First things first, let's tidy up your scruffy-looking layers!

3. Click to select the top layer and insert a new layer folder called intro.

4. Select all the layers except animated rectangles by clicking the top one and Shift-clicking the bottom one:

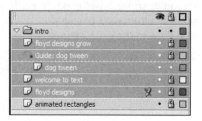

5. Drag all the selected layers into the intro layer folder and close it by clicking the small triangle to the left of it. Lock and hide the folder. Unlock the layer animated rectangles if it isn't unlocked already.

6. Click the animated rectangles layer and insert a new layer called frame labels. This will be used to store frame label references to the activity you are about to create.

7. On frame 76 of the frame labels layer, insert a blank keyframe using F7.

8. Open the Properties panel (Window ➤ Properties) and click the new blank keyframe.

9. In the Frame label input field of the Properties panel, enter open web.

The reason you enter this as a frame label is quite simple. As we briefly explained earlier, each page will have a transition—a shape tween—when it is clicked. During this tween, the colored rectangle that corresponds to the page in question will grow so that it covers the screen. The labels we are adding at the moment will be used later to signpost the start and end of each of the tweens.

10. Click frame 76 of the animated rectangles layer and press F6 to insert a new keyframe. This will create a new keyframe with a copy of all the original colored shapes:

As you might have guessed, you don't need all the rectangles. Each transition consists of a single rectangle growing to fill the screen, and therefore, you need only one for each shape tween. Easy.

Uh. Hold on a minute . . . If only one shape is growing, what happens to the other rectangles? Is the shape growing over the white rectangle alone?

Fear not, you've already taken a precaution for this in an earlier chapter! Remember the copy of the rectangles you left on the main stage? It is perfectly aligned to these shapes, so when each individual shape grows here, the rest of the shapes appear to stay as they are. This will—and you'll have to believe us for the moment—create the illusion of a rectangle growing and squashing the others.

Before you delete the other rectangles, you need to measure all the rectangles' combined width. This will make sense in a moment!

11. Select all the colored rectangles and make a note of their width in the Properties panel. Write this down—you'll need it a number of times:

The width will be the combined width of all the rectangles, including the spaces between them.

12. On the keyframe on frame 76 of the animated rectangles layer, select the three rectangles on the right and delete them, leaving only the far-left lawn-green rectangle:

13. Now it's time to create the shape tween. Insert a new keyframe on frame 91 of the animated rectangles layer.

14. On this keyframe, select the rectangle and set its width to the value you previously noted (or copied) using the Properties panel. The easiest way to do this is to click the padlock next to the W and H fields to the right of the Properties panel so that the W and H fields are no longer connected by a line, and then enter your remembered value in the W field. Alternatively, if you wish, you can use the Info panel instead (Window ➤ Info).

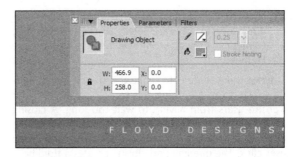

15. Select the rectangle and center it both vertically and horizontally using the Align panel.

16. Once you have the rectangle covering all the colored ones on the main stage, click a frame between 76 and 90 and set a shape tween using the Properties panel.

17. Drag the playhead over the frames to view the open shape tween:

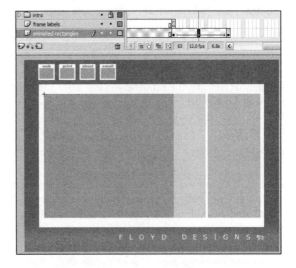

18. Next you'll create the close tween. Do this by copying the existing tween and reversing it. Insert a blank keyframe on frame 92 of the frame labels layer and add the frame label close web.

19. Select all the tween frames from 76 to 91 on the animated rectangles layer and select Edit ➤ Timeline ➤ Copy Frames.

20. Insert a blank keyframe at frame 92 of the same layer, select it, and choose the Edit ➤ Timeline ➤ Paste Frames menu option.

21. Now, to reverse the direction of the frames to produce the close tween, select all the newly added frames and select Modify ➤ Timeline ➤ Reverse Frames.

The last thing to do is to make the closing tween a little shorter. You are doing this to prevent any of your website users from having to wait too long. A closing tween looks far more professional than only having opening tweens and an immediate snap-back on each user click. The opening and closing creates a fluidity.

22. Click to select the last keyframe on the animated rectangles layer, and drag it back to frame 100. This will make it just over half the length of the opening tween.

23. After you do this, you'll notice that you have some dotted frames after the keyframe. Select these and delete them with Edit ➤ Timeline ➤ Remove Frames or *SHIFT* + *F5*.

You now have two transitions for your first page.

24. Select Control ➤ Test Movie. The intro sequence runs, then your opening sequence plays, followed by your closing sequence.

In the final website, the timeline will halt after the intro and wait for the user to click the buttons, but for now, this will have to do until you know how to program the interactions.

Let's animate the other pages.

25. Insert a blank keyframe on frame 101 of the frame labels layer. Label it open print. This will be the start of your second set of transitions, for the print page.

26. Insert a blank keyframe on frame 101 of the animated rectangles layer. You now need to copy the second rectangle from one of the previous frames.

27. Click the animated rectangles layer before frame 76 and select the second rectangle from the left. Select Edit ➤ Copy to copy it.

28. Return to the blank keyframe on the animated rectangles layer—frame 101—and use Edit ➤ Paste in Place to paste the copied rectangle in the same position. Now you should be on familiar ground.

29. Insert a keyframe on frame 116 of the animated rectangles layer—15 frames on from the last one.

30. On the new keyframe, as before, make the rectangle cover all four of the rectangles visible from the main stage by using your previous width reading. Once you have it scaled, center it.

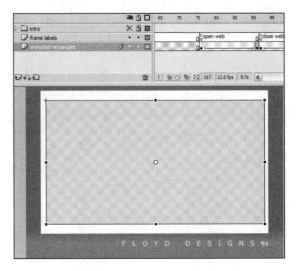

31. Select a frame between the two keyframes and set a shape tween in the Properties panel.

That completes your second "open" tween; now for the closing motion.

32. Insert a blank keyframe on frame 117 of the frame labels layer and label it close print.

33. Select frames 101–116 of the animated rectangles layer, and copy them with Edit ➤ Timeline ➤ Copy Frames.

34. Insert a blank keyframe using *F7* on the same layer.

35. Paste the frames on this keyframe using Edit ➤ Timeline ➤ Paste Frames.

36. Select all the frames and reverse them using Modify ➤ Timeline ➤ Reverse Frames.

37. Select the keyframe on frame 132, and move it to frame 124 to shorten the closing tween.

38. Remove the excess frames (from frame 125 on) by selecting them and choosing Edit ➤ Timeline ➤ Remove Frames (or *SHIFT+F5*).

39. Test the movie to watch the two sequences. It's certainly starting to come together! Now all that remains to do is to add the final two transitions for the remaining rectangles. Here are the steps for each rectangle.

Open sequence

1. Insert a new blank keyframe on the frame labels layer (on the frame following the last keyframe) and name it (use open about the first time, and open email the second time).

2. Copy the original rectangle from a frame before 75 on the animated rectangles layer and paste it to a new keyframe on the same layer.

3. Insert a keyframe 15 frames later and resize its width to the value you wrote down earlier.

4. Set a tween between the two keyframes.

Close sequence

1. Copy the frame sequence, and paste it to a new keyframe following it.

2. Insert a blank keyframe on the frame labels layer (parallel to the last keyframe on the animated rectangles layer) and label the first one close about, and the second one close email.

3. Reverse the pasted frame sequence and shorten it to run for eight frames.

If you follow these steps twice, you should have a timeline something like this (give or take a few frames!):

Once you are done, test the movie, and you might get the feeling that you are being given a psychedelic sliding doors demonstration. Groovy!

Summary

In this chapter, you took a gentle stroll around the world of shape tweening, thereby adding another tool to your increasingly powerful armory.

In the case study, you added the lion's share of your website's animation. In later chapters, you will control these opening and closing tweens with ActionScript, triggered by button-based interaction.

You saw that

- Shape tweening complements motion tweening. It enables you to morph shapes into other shapes, morph shapes into text, and more.

- Shape tweens operate on lines and fills rather than the grouped shapes and symbols that motion tweens act upon.

- Shape tweening can be combined with color changes and movement.

- Shape hints give you a fine degree of control over the way a shape tween will work.

In the next chapter, you're going to look at a technique that can add engaging visual effects to your Flash movies, especially when used in conjunction with shape and motion tweens—masking.

Chapter 8

MASKS AND MASKING

What we'll cover in this chapter:

- Masking is a powerful feature that allows you to selectively show and hide content. You can create a mask and apply it to a layer so that only content underneath the mask is visible. You'll explore the basic principles of masking and see a range of different examples and applications.

This chapter introduces masks in Flash. Masks are used to selectively show and hide content in a Flash movie. Using masks, you can create great effects in your movies: illusions of depth, movement, illumination, and more—as you'll see in this chapter.

I think you'll find masks indispensable once you grasp the techniques for using them. Some Flash designers don't seem to embrace the usefulness of masks, possibly because the effects you can create with them are more at home in animation than standard website design. But once you've seen the results that masks can help you achieve, I think you may well be a convert.

What is a mask?

Very early in this book, I showed you how layers can be used to simulate depth. If you're animating a character—let's call her Jane Doe—walking across the stage and behind a house, you put the house on a layer at the front of the movie, and Jane on a layer behind the house.

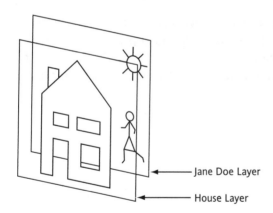

Jane Doe Layer

House Layer

As Jane walks across the area occupied by the house symbol, Flash knows that you want the house to stay in front because of the layer order you assigned. This gives the appearance that Jane is walking behind the house and creates a sense of depth in the animation.

Suppose you want to show Jane walking around *inside* the house? That's more difficult, isn't it? You want Jane to be visible when she's behind a transparent part of the house front—the windows—and invisible when she's behind an opaque object such as a solid wall.

In Flash, to make part of the front layer opaque and part of it transparent, you need a mask.

When you create a mask, it's as if you lay a piece of paper over the animation and block it all out. You then cut a hole in the paper and reveal a section of what's underneath. In Jane's case, you need to create a piece of paper shaped like a house, and then cut holes in the paper where the windows and door should be.

Once you've cut out the holes, you can place the mask in front of the background animation of Jane walking across the stage. You can then either move the mask around so that different sections of your animation are revealed, or make the objects in the animation pass across the holes, appearing and disappearing as they do.

That's the basic principle of masking in Flash—you just use electronic layers to create your masks rather than paper and scissors.

When would you need to use a mask in Flash? Here are a few examples:

- When you want to show text scrolling from left to right across a TV screen. You only want the text to be visible when it's behind the area corresponding to the screen.

- When you want to zoom in on an area on a picture and keep the viewable area inside a constant-sized window. As the picture is magnified, you want to show only the zoomed area of the picture and hide all other areas.

- When you want to simulate text being typed on the screen so it appears letter by letter, from left to right.

None of these effects can be created using layers alone. In each case, you want to hide *part* of your object, and that's exactly what a mask will do.

With the house example discussed previously, you might be thinking "Hey, wait a minute! You wouldn't need to go to the trouble of using masks if you just created a house graphic with holes in it!" And you would be absolutely correct.

Masking only really comes into its own when the mask itself is *animated*. Masking allows you to create an "animated hole" or "animated cutout" that can be tweened or otherwise animated independently from the main graphics. When used this way, masks can be used to create the following:

- *Cutouts that can be selectively turned on and off*: Suppose your house is part of an animation in which the windows are initially dark because the lights are all off. Once Jane walks in and turns the lights on, you're able to see her in the house. By using a mask that only becomes active when the lights go on, you can simulate this effect.

- *Cutouts that move*: Imagine that you're Jane, and you're in the house looking for the light switch. If you're lucky enough to have a vehicle key with a built-in torch, you could use that to help you out. When you switch the torch on, you would only be able to see stuff within the torch beam. This would be rather like a moving-circle cutout—another mask—except this time the circle moves as you swing the torch around. Animated cutouts are very useful in animation. They allow you to selectively reveal things, thus allowing things to appear slowly over time, or to appear via a cool masked transition, in which the object is revealed in an eye-catching way rather than merely appearing.

- *Cutouts that change shape*: If you animated Jane closing her curtains, the cutout area representing the area of the window that you can see through would change shape as more and more became hidden. The obvious way to do this would be to animate the curtains closing. Another way would be to animate the part of the window that you can still see through via a mask—that is, rather than animate the closing curtains, you could animate the closing gap in the window. Sometimes, animating the latter is easier than animating the former—especially if you need to do this for several windows and the curtains are all different colors (and therefore require a different animation for each color). Animating the gap can be easier because it's the same animation for each window, and it's independent of curtain color.

■ *Cutouts that are invisible*: When you're creating symbols, you often only want parts of the symbol to be visible, but you also want to hide whatever's hiding the symbol. Um, I think we need an example to clarify. Suppose you're creating a racing game—you have an animation of a race car driver and you want to place the driver in the car. By masking out everything below the driver's shoulders, you can put him above the car, and he'll appear to be sitting in it.

If you tried to do the same thing by hiding the lower part of the driver with a visible shape, whatever you used to hide him would foul the side of the car, and your end result would look less than seamless. Although this might seem like a pretty obscure example, this issue actually turns up time and time again when you try to create common user interface elements such as scrollable windows or drop-down menus—if you need to hide an object with something, you often need to hide the "something" as well. A mask does this perfectly—it hides parts of a masked object *and also hides itself*.

To illustrate masking, let's create an animation based on the first example: text scrolling across a TV screen. You'll find the completed FLA of this example in the download section of the friends of ED website as maskTV.fla.

Putting on your mask

First, you need your TV set.

1. In a new Flash Document, rename the default layer TV.

2. In the default keyframe at frame 1, create your TV by drawing a shape that looks something like this:

3. Create the TV any way you like, but create it with Object Drawing unselected (i.e., Merge Drawing mode).

The (slightly retro) TV in this example was made by drawing the basic shape with black lines of thickness 3. The straight lines were bent using the Selection tool to give the impression that the TV is a freehand drawing, and the antenna and some chunky control knobs were added. If you want, you can use the Pen tool and the Subselect tool to create a Bezier-finessed masterpiece—it's really up to you. (Just make sure you end up with a TV that has a screen!)

A tip for drawing things in the cartoon style used here is to draw with thick black outlines (stroke-hinted lines with a thickness of 3 pixels were used here to create sharp lines), like Warner Brothers did in the psychedelic Sixties.

230

4. Use the Paint Bucket tool to fill your drawing with color.

In your movie, you want your text to appear only on the TV's screen, so you need to create a mask that will show the text only when its position corresponds to an area inside the boundaries of the screen.

5. Add two new layers above the existing TV layer—Broadcast and Mask.

Mask will be your mask layer, and Broadcast will contain all the objects—the text—that you want to show on the TV screen. The order of the layers *must* be TV, Broadcast, and Mask, from bottom to top.

Now for the clever part. Remember that the Mask layer is the piece of paper that you'll use to hide and reveal the underlying Broadcast layer. You're going to cut a hole in your paper that's the same shape as the screen of your TV, so that whatever you put on the Broadcast layer will only be visible when it's inside the TV screen.

6. Select the filled-screen area of the TV—not the stroke. (You haven't made the TV into a symbol yet, and you didn't create it as a Drawing Object—this is so you can select the screen on its own easily.)

7. Copy the screen part into the clipboard with Edit ➤ Copy.

The next thing to do is use this screen shape to create the masked area on the Mask layer.

8. Select the Mask layer and paste the screen in place with Edit ➤ Paste in Place.

9. Hide all the layers except the Mask layer, and you should just see the pasted screen as shown here:

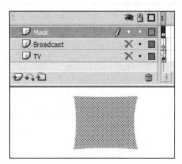

It's a good idea to make your mask areas a striking color so that you can easily differentiate them from other movie content. Using a color that you would rarely use in your movie designs is a good way to help you make that differentiation. Let's choose a bright pink.

10. Select the Paint Bucket tool and fill the screen shape on the Mask layer with a bright pink.

> *There's one oddity of Flash masks—they're the inverse of real-life masks. The virtual Flash version of the house mask discussed earlier has cut-out areas, such as the windows and door. In the current example, you want your virtual card to be in the gap area only—that is, the screen.*

Although it might seem counterintuitive for a mask to be a solid filled color, trust me. Flash isn't constrained by the same laws of physics that stop light from passing freely through a piece of paper. So long as Flash knows the shape of the mask, you can make it any color you like—Flash just ignores the color and sees only the shape.

When this TV screen–shaped mask is being used, you'll be able to see anything on the underlying layer that falls behind the pink area, and nothing that's in the areas outside the mask.

11. Lock the Mask layer so that you don't select anything on it by accident, and unhide the TV and Broadcast layers.

12. On the TV layer, select the whole TV (you can do this easily by pressing *Ctrl+A* to select everything that isn't locked) and convert it into a new graphic symbol called TV Symbol.

13. Lock the TV layer and unlock the Mask layer.

14. Select the screen-shaped mask on the Mask layer and convert it into a graphic symbol. Name it Screen Mask.

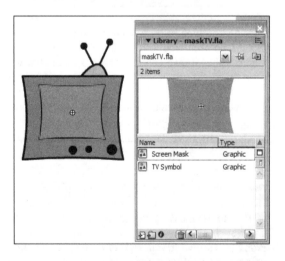

When you're working with masks on one layer, it's always a good idea to lock the layer containing the masked objects so that you can't inadvertently select both objects at once.

Now you're going to tell Flash that you want your floating TV screen shape to act as a mask.

15. With the Mask layer selected, choose the Modify ➤ Timeline ➤ Layer Properties menu option and click the Mask radio button in the Layer Properties window.

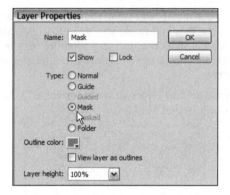

16. Leave all the other values as the defaults, and click OK.

You've now converted the Mask layer so that it will act as a mask. Now, all Flash sees on this layer is the screen shape that you want to use as the mask.

Notice that the Mask layer's appearance has changed in the Timeline.

The little checkered oval at the left identifies this layer as a mask layer.

Now you have to tell Flash which layer you want the mask to be applied to.

17. Select the Broadcast layer and choose the Modify ➤ Timeline ➤ Layer Properties menu option. This time, select the Masked radio button to designate the Broadcast layer as the one that you want the TV screen shape to mask.

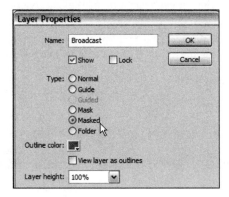

18. Click OK.

Again, there's been a change with your layers in the Timeline.

Note that the Broadcast layer now has an indented icon that looks like a folded sheet of paper, indicating that this layer has a mask applied to it.

19. Unlock the TV layer.

The checkered oval icon on the Mask layer tells you that you've created a mask. The indented checkered icon on the Broadcast layer tells you that this is the layer to which you've applied your mask. The Broadcast layer is the one that the screen shape on the Mask layer will apply to, hiding part of it from view.

> *It's vital to note that the layer, or layers, that you want to be partially hidden must be placed below the mask you've created.*

You won't see the effects of the Mask layer yet because the Broadcast layer currently has nothing in it. Let's put a message on the TV.

The first thing you need to do is increase the length of your movie to give you enough time to read the text that will shimmy across the TV screen.

20. Increase the movie length so that it lasts for 100 frames. To do this, click frame 100 in the Mask layer, and before you release the mouse button, drag the mouse pointer down to select all three layers. When you release the mouse button, press *F5* to create 100 frames in each layer.

If you ever want to see more frames in the Timeline (as you can see in the previous screenshot), you can click the Frame View button at the top-right of the Timeline. Clicking the button brings up the menu shown in the following screenshot. If you click Small, Flash will compress the frames that are displayed horizontally, and you'll see a greater number of frames in the Timeline.

21. Now for the content: in frame 1 of the Broadcast layer, use the Text tool to add the text stay tuned to this channel... to the right of the TV, and level with the center of the TV screen. This example uses a black, 26-point Comic Sans font, but you can choose any font except the system fonts (_sans, _serif, and _typewriter). This is because Flash needs to treat the text as a graphic, which it can't do with system fonts.

22. Convert the text into a graphic symbol called Text.

Now you'll make the text move across the screen.

23. In the Broadcast layer, add a keyframe at frame 100. With the new keyframe selected, move the text to the left of the TV to establish its end position after it has scrolled across the screen.

Hint: you need to keep the text at the same horizontal position, and the best way to do this is press the *SHIFT* key as you drag the text with the mouse.

24. Click any frame in the middle of your Timeline. Then use the Property inspector to add a motion tween between frames 1 and 100 of the Broadcast layer.

25. The last thing to do to make your mask work is lock both the Mask layer and the Broadcast layer.

Flash will only show the effects of a mask in the authoring environment when all the affected layers are locked. If you want your masks to work in this way, always lock all affected layers. The mask will work in the final SWF file whether or not you lock them.

26. You can see the masking in action by scrubbing the playhead across the Timeline (click-drag the playhead back and forth along the Timeline). Press *F12* to preview your movie in a browser. You can also select Test Movie (*CTRL+ENTER* or Control ➤ Test Movie). Or even live it up a little and try both.

When you test your movie, you should see the TV with the scrolling text appear on the screen only where the mask is. With a little extra work, this would make a good loading page for someone's website.

You see how this can be a very powerful technique. The TV screen is a totally non-uniform shape, as is the rest of the TV. Simply by defining the area you want to display using a mask, you're able to achieve the complex effect you want with very little effort. The sequence of steps needs to be maintained, but after a little more practice and experimentation, you'll be turning out masked movies of your own.

Notice that this effect would be difficult using just a television graphic with a hole where the screen should be. Using masks rather than holes also leads to much better effects than static holes. If you go to www.futuremedia.org.uk *and navigate to* future-media ➤ burnmedia ➤ monster, *you'll see a TV effect that's based closely on the simple example above, except that there's also a fade-in effect, in which the televisions change from line drawings to solid televisions. This effect is created via—you guessed it—masking!*

The Futuremedia site is the book project for the book Foundation ActionScript for Flash (Flash MX 2004 and Flash 8 revisions), and you can download the source files from www.friendsofed.com.

Remember that when you create a mask, you have to specify the layer or layers that you want it to act upon. Only the sections of these layers that lie under the cut-out shape(s) you draw on the mask layer will be visible in the finished movie.

Another thing to be aware of is that all the mask effects that you create can be embedded inside movie clips and reused in all sorts of different ways. You can build great little animated masking effects, embed them in movie clips, and then use multiple copies of those movie clips to get all sorts of impressive action on the stage.

OK, you've created a mask and tweened some text across it to good effect. Let's see how to animate the mask and how to mask several layers at once.

Animated masks and masking multiple layers

You can also use masks and keep the background stationary while the mask itself is animated, selectively hiding and revealing different parts of your animation. You're going to learn how to do this now. You'll also see how one mask can be used to cover and reveal several layers at once.

Moving the mask

1. Create a new Flash Document.
2. Change the movie's background color to black using the Property inspector or by selecting Modify ➤ Document.
3. Using the Text tool, add the large bold white text shown in the following screenshot (remembering not to use any of the system fonts) in the center of the stage, and rename the layer Text.

4. Add a new layer and name it Spotlight. In this layer, draw a filled white circle that's a little bigger than the height of the text.
5. Convert the circle into a graphic symbol and name it Spot.

6. Make your animation 50 frames long in both layers by clicking, dragging, and pressing *F5* in the same way that you did in the last exercise.
7. Add a keyframe (*F6*) in frame 50 of the Spotlight layer. Your Timeline should now look like this:

8. With the new keyframe selected, move your Spot symbol to the far end of the text, after the u, and create a motion tween between the two keyframes.

   The circle will now move over the text when you play your movie. Here's a preview of its motion with Onion Skin Outlines turned on.

9. Turn the Spotlight layer into a mask layer as you did earlier, via the Modify ➤ Timeline ➤ Layer Properties menu option. Select the Mask radio button from the Layer Properties window for the Spotlight layer, and select the Masked radio button when you repeat the process for the Text layer.
10. Lock both the layers and test the movie—the layers in your Timeline should look like this:

235

There's a problem with the movie at the moment: you see the text revealed by the round shape of the spotlight as it travels along, but the circular shape of the spotlight doesn't really come across. That's because the background is totally black—a real spotlight would illuminate the background as well as the text. Let's remedy that.

What you need to do is make the spotlight illuminate the background slightly. To do this, you'll draw a gray area behind the text on a new layer. This will be lit up in contrast to the text as the spot passes across it.

You must do this exactly as described; otherwise the Spotlight layer won't act as a mask to the new layer.

11. Select the Text layer and add a new layer. Name your new layer Gray.

You want your Gray layer to be behind the text, so you must move it to the bottom of the stack of layers.

12. With Gray still selected, drag the layer to the bottom, under Text. Your Timeline should look like this:

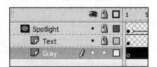

Notice that both the layers Gray and Text have the indented icons next to them, signifying that both will be masked by Spotlight. Flash has automatically made your Gray layer a masked layer because of its adjacency to the mask layer when you created it.

13. Select Gray and draw a medium-gray rectangle that covers the whole area that the circle will travel over. Unlock the Text layer to help you decipher exactly where your rectangle needs to go and how big it should be.

14. Lock all the layers again and test the movie.

You'll now see what looks like an illuminated spotlight move from left to right, lighting up the darkness to reveal your text. The following screenshot shows a graduated interpretation of the spotlight moving across the text in the movie you just created.

What's actually happening is that your circular "window" is moving across white text on a gray background—but the effect is quite striking. How about adding more keyframes to the mask layer and more motion tweens, creating a sweeping searchlight effect that moves up and down as well as from side to side? (The Custom Easing graphs will come in handy here.) Or maybe a motion path that sweeps out in a spiral? Or a spotlight that starts small and grows bigger as the animation continues? Or . . .

We've only touched on the power of animated masks. The number of effects that you can create with these features in Flash is limited only by your imagination. So practice, practice, practice.

One of the coolest ways to use masks is to make the mask an animation. The mask can be a tweened object, or it can be a movie clip with a nested tween inside it.

As a general rule, if you can't think how a Flash effect was created, it was probably created using masking of some sort. For example, check out the page-turning effect at www.iparigrafika.hu/pageflip—it's something that you might spend ages working out, and you would never suspect it uses masking, but the whole effect actually relies on it!

If you want to see some spoilsport spill the beans on the trick (warning, it uses fairly advanced ActionScript), try Googling "page turn Sham Bhangal."

Now let's look at some more text/mask combinations.

Using masks with text

Masks can be used particularly well with text. Text can act as the mask itself, as you'll see later, and masks can simulate the effect of words appearing on the screen as if they were being typed. This is achieved by another method of animating the mask: instead of moving the mask around the stage, you can scale it to make it grow—revealing more of the layer beneath it as it does so. Let's see how.

Simulating typed text

1. In a new Flash document, rename the default layer Text, and add a new layer above it called Mask.

2. You now need to turn your layers into mask and masked layers. Now that you're getting good at masking, here's a quick alternative to the Modify ➤ Timeline ➤ Layer Properties menu option method used in your last two exercises. You can save some time by right-clicking (CTRL-clicking on Mac) the Mask layer and selecting Mask. Much easier!

3. With the Mask layer selected, right-click that layer and select Mask from the context-sensitive menu that pops up. Mask becomes a mask layer, and Text automatically becomes a masked layer. Note that both layers are locked.

4. Unlock both layers by clicking the topmost lock icon so that you can add some content to them.

5. Change the movie's background color to a hue of your choice, and then add some text in the Text layer.

The ghostly font of 1974...

This example uses a pale green on a dark green background—just in case there are any of you out there who are nostalgic for the days of corporate dumb terminals.

6. You want to make the text look as if it's being typed in letter by letter. In the Mask layer, create a long white rectangle that completely covers the text, and then convert it into a graphic symbol with a center-left registration point. Call the new symbol Mask.

You've given this shape a center-left registration point because you're going to make the text gradually appear by scaling the white rectangle—a little like a preloader bar. If you scale the rectangle with the registration point in the center, both ends are going to get shorter or longer because scaling is done relevant to the registration point.

At this point, ensure the rectangle is positioned correctly, covering your text. Make any adjustments to its position until the text is fully obscured by it.

7. Make the movie 50 frames long in both layers and then add a keyframe to the Mask layer at frame 50.

8. In frame 1 of the Mask layer, shorten the mask using the Free Transform tool and drag the right side of the rectangle to the left so that it's too short to cover any of the text.

The ghostly font of 1974...

9. Click any of the frames between 1 and 50 and add a motion tween with the Properties panel. This will create an animated mask that slowly reveals more and more text as it gets bigger. Remember that only the text that's covered by the mask will show up in the final movie—the growing rectangle is like a cut-out window on paper gradually being torn open to reveal what's underneath.

10. Lock both layers and test your movie. Your text will gradually appear as the mask rectangle scales up and out to the right.

Don't worry that the mask will show only parts of letters—the transition is usually too fast for the viewer to see that it isn't actually typing a word at a time, but revealing the words bit by bit. If it starts to look too obvious when you test the movie, simply shorten the motion tween by 10 frames or so by choosing the Edit ➤ Timeline ➤ Remove Frames menu option—making sure that the playhead isn't on a keyframe. Alternatively, if you really want to emphasize words as they're created, rather than using a constant wipe, add some extra keyframes along your Timeline, stop the motion tween for the desired time, and then pick up the tween again.

Now for another mean text-related masking technique.

A text-shaped mask

One of the easiest ways to create an instant mask is to use text as the mask. When using text in this way, it's a good idea to use a simple, heavy, bold, closely-spaced font. Using this kind of font will mean that a larger proportion of the image behind your mask is shown. For this reason, Impact or Arial Black are good choices, as is the Haettenschweiler font shown here:

Haettenschweiler

Let's use this meaty-looking font as a mask in a practical example.

Masking with text

For this effect, you'll create a color gradient and mask it using a piece of text.

1. Open a new Flash document and rename the default layer text.

2. Create a static text field in the center of the stage using a bold, thick font, similar in length to the following:

spectrum

The book uses a black, 65-point Haettenschweiler. If you don't have that font, try Arial Black, which is a more common thick font.

3. Create a new layer and call it gradient. In this new layer, create a filled gradient that's taller and considerably wider than the text—like this:

The book's example uses the last gradient to the right for the fill color, selected from the bottom of the Color Picker palette.

4. Make sure that the gradient layer is underneath the text layer by dragging it in the Timeline.

5. You want use a motion tween on the rectangle, so convert it into a graphic symbol with a central registration point and name it Rectangle.

6. Make text into a mask layer and gradient into the layer that's being masked. Remember, the quick way to do this is by right-clicking the mask layer and selecting Mask from the context-sensitive menu.

7. Unlock both layers. Make your animation 50 frames long by clicking, dragging, and pressing *F5* in the now familiar way.

8. At frame 50 in the gradient layer, add a keyframe. Move the Rectangle graphic symbol in this frame to the left.

9. Select any frame between 1 and 50 on the gradient layer and add a motion tween using the Property inspector.

10. Lock both layers and test your movie. You'll see the text cycle through several colors as the gradient moves past it.

![spectrum]

There's an additional cool modification you can make to this effect, and that's to add a border to the text. This will improve the effect because, as it stands, the lighter colors in the spectrum can make the outline of the text difficult to see on some screens.

11. Select the text layer and create a new layer above it. Call the new layer text outline.

12. Unlock the text layer and then copy the text to the text outline layer using the Edit ➤ Copy and Edit ➤ Paste in Place menu options.

13. With the text field on the text outline layer still selected, break the text apart twice with the Modify ➤ Break Apart menu option. Hide the other layers.

14. Select the Ink Bottle tool and change the stroke color to black in the Tools panel.

15. Click all the outlines in the text. To do this for the word spectrum, you'll also have to click the interior outlines inside the p and the e. You might want to zoom in to get a better view while you're using the Ink Bottle tool.

> In Flash 8, there's a cool new shortcut for this: after breaking the text apart, use Modify ➤ Combine Objects ➤ Union *to turn the text into a Drawing Object. Then use the Tools panel color wells to set the fill to no fill and the stroke to black. With Drawing Objects, you don't have to use the Ink Bottle!*

16. With the inner text still selected—*SHIFT*-click each letter to reselect it if it has become unselected—press *DELETE* or go to Edit ➤ Clear to delete the filled areas of each letter so you leave only the outline.

17. Test your movie. You'll see the color of your text change again, but this time with a more clearly defined outline.

Notice that the text outline layer doesn't need to be locked for the mask effect to be seen, as it's not masking anything or being masked.

A really cool variant of this is to use a bitmap instead of a gradient. In a similar way to the computer typing you simulated earlier, you can use a bitmap to gradually fill your mask and reveal your text. Here's how.

Filling your text with an image

You're now going to use a bitmap image called skyline.bmp to slowly fill a text mask. This image is included in the downloadable files from the friends of ED website—or you can use any image of your own choice, of course.

1. Set up a new Flash document. Rename the default layer Image and add a second layer called Text just above it.

2. Make Text into the mask layer and Image into the masked layer.

3. Unlock the layers by clicking the top lock icon, and in the Text layer, create a text field containing the word or words that you want to make appear, in the center of the stage.

4. Bring skyline.bmp (or your own image) onto the Image layer by selecting the layer and using the File ➤ Import ➤ Import to Library menu option to navigate to the image in the dialog box. Pull the bitmap from the Library onto the Image layer. (You don't need to position it just yet, so drag it anywhere on the stage.)

5. Convert the imported image to a graphic symbol called Skyline Object and give it a center registration point.

6. Scale Skyline Object so that it's about the same height as your text, and place it on the stage so that its right edge is nearly at the left edge of your text.

7. Make your animation 50 frames long (both layers) and insert a keyframe at frame 50 on the Image layer.

8. With the new keyframe still selected, move Skyline Object so that it's behind the text. Then click anywhere on the Image layer between frames 1 and 50 and assign a motion tween from the Property inspector.

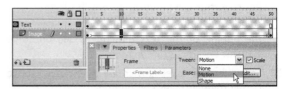

9. Lock both layers and test your movie. Here's a simulation of the effect you'll see:

Because your bitmap is moving, you can get away with quite a low resolution, so the download time can be surprisingly quick. Be aware that an effect like this, combined with a large bitmap, can become quite slow on older computers if your text fills the screen. Try applying text outlines to this example like you did in the previous one.

You can now create a layer that's a mask and apply this mask to layers that are labeled as masked. This is yet another powerful feature that you and your imagination can implement in conjunction with other techniques such as tweening, animated fades, and so on.

OK, that's it for the basic masking techniques. I think you'll agree that you can create some scintillating effects with them. The best way to learn more from here is to experiment and let your imagination run wild.

Later in the book you'll look at how to use movie clips as masks, using a little bit of ActionScript to create some interaction on them.

Case study

In this section, you're going to begin creating some content for your pages, specifically the web page. The web portfolio page, in case you hadn't already guessed, will feature screenshots and text information on some websites that you've previously created.

1. Open your saved case study Flash file.

2. Locate and double-click the Content movie clip instance on the stage to edit it in place.

3. Within the Content symbol, insert a new layer called pages, and place it above the frame labels and animated rectangles layers. This is to make sure that the content appears above the rectangles so you can see it!

4. Insert a blank keyframe on frame 91 of the pages layer.

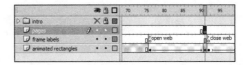

You've positioned a frame here to house the web page content. Its actual position is at the very end of the open web shape tween, meaning that your animation will have finished, and the rectangle will be fully grown.

5. Before you proceed, lock all the other layers except the pages layer to make sure that you don't accidentally alter any of them.

6. Select the Text tool, set the font to 12-point Arial, and set the color to a dark blue (#003399). Type the following (or similar) and center it with the Align panel:

Floyd Designs specialize in Flash websites

with a twist.

Please click on any of the links to the left

for example screenshots and further info.

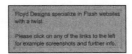

7. Use the Selection tool to select the text field, and convert it into a symbol with *F8* or Modify ➤ Convert to Symbol. Make it a movie clip symbol with a central registration point and give it the name web content.

8. Double-click the new web content movie clip instance on the stage to edit it in place.

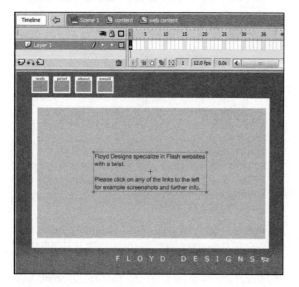

9. Rename the existing layer web examples and add three more layers below it, called invisible buttons, buttons text, and thumbnails.

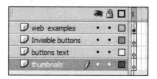

10. Switch on the rulers using View ➤ Rulers. This will enable you to position your elements a little more neatly.

11. Click the left ruler and drag a guide from it to the 250-pixel mark just left of the registration point. Then release it.

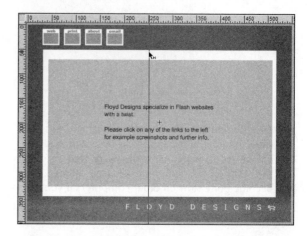

12. Lock the guide in place by clicking View ➤ Guides ➤ Lock Guides to prevent the guide from being moved.

13. Switch on Snap to Guides if it isn't already on by selecting View ➤ Snapping ➤ Snap to Guides.

14. Use the Selection tool to drag the text so that the text's left-hand edge is exactly on the guide.

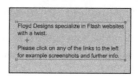

15. Center the text vertically using the Align panel.

16. Insert a blank keyframe on frame 2 of the web examples layer (*F7*).

17. Open the Library (Window ➤ Library or *CTRL+L*) and drag a copy of the friendsofed_website.gif image out of it. Position the image in the top-right corner of the green rectangle, so that its left edge snaps to the guide.

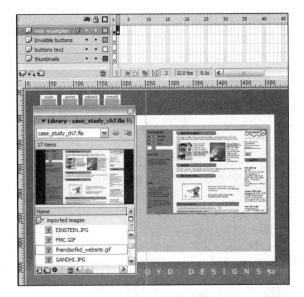

18. Select the text tool and type the following text anywhere on the stage, including the line breaks as shown. Use the same font, size, and color as you did earlier (12-point Arial, #003399).

friends of ed

A website created for the multimedia book

publishing company using HTML, Flash and

ASP technologies.

19. Drag the text field below the image and snap its left edge to the guide.

20. For a little emphasis on the website name, select the text friends of ed and change it to bold in the Property inspector.

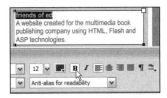

21. Add five more keyframes on this layer (*F6*)—one for each of the examples.

You're going to save a little arrangement time by swapping the bitmaps and simply editing the text field as required.

22. Select the keyframe on frame 3 and click the image to bring up its Property inspector information.

23. In the Property inspector, click the Swap button. This will allow you to replace this image with another from the Library.

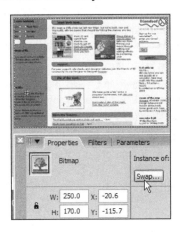

243

Once you've done this, you'll see the following window:

24. Select pinderkaas_website.gif and click OK.

The image on the stage is now replaced with the chosen image. Easy peasy, eh? No aligning, dragging, or hassle, just an easy action. Editing the text isn't as easy, but it's nothing to panic about either.

25. Select the Selection tool and double-click the text field. Then select all the text in the text field and delete it.

26. Enter the following text as shown (remembering to change the title to bold):

pinderkaas

A website created for the book Flash Math Creativity. Created using Flash, HTML, and CGI.

Okay, that's two examples done pretty quickly. Rather than go through all the steps again for the others, just repeat these steps for keyframes 4 to 7.

27. Click next keyframe.

28. Select the image and swap it using the Property inspector (follow the order of nettle_wine.gif, qanik.gif, hypertelia.gif, and fmc.gif).

29. Highlight all the text and delete it.

30. Replace each with a blurb. Here are the blurbs in order:

Frame 4:

nettlewine

Record label website. Created in HTML and PHP.

Frame 5:

qanik

Nostalgia site. Created in HTML and Flash.

Frame 6:

hypertelia

Creative site made with 3D, Flash, and PHP.

Frame 7:

flash math creativity

Friends of ED mini-site. Created using Flash and HTML.

31. Select the title in the text field and make it bold.

When you're done making the amendments, proceed with the next steps.

Creating the navigation elements

In this section, you're going to create buttons that will guide your viewers through the example pages.

1. Select the keyframe on frame 1 of the buttons text layer and select the Text tool.

2. Click on the left side of the guide and type the following:

friends of ed

pinderkaas

nettlewine

qanik

hypertelia

flash math creativity

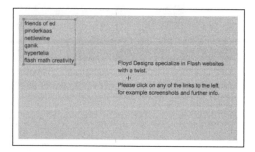

3. Extend the frames on this layer to frame 7 using *F5*.

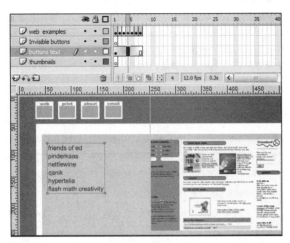

4. Ensure Snap Align is on using View ➤ Snapping ➤ Snap Align.

5. Pick up the text field you just created and drag it so that its top edge snap aligns to the top of the image to its right.

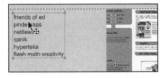

Now you're going to create some invisible buttons to put over these text fields. Hold on a minute, did I just say invisible buttons? I sure did!

Creating invisible buttons is one of the classic Flash tricks, having carved its place into Flash history way back in Flash 4. The purpose of an invisible button is to allow user clicks without requiring a physical presence on the stage. In this instance, an invisible button will be placed over each website name so you still see the website name, but not the button covering it.

Creating an invisible button is quite simple. In fact, you already have the ability to do it. Once I show you how it's done, you might kick yourself.

6. Extend the frames on the invisible buttons layer to frame 7 using *F5*.

7. Click the keyframe on frame 1 of the invisible buttons layer and select the Rectangle tool.

8. Draw a long, thin rectangle, with any fill color and no stroke, to cover the last line of the text flash math creativity.

9. Select the rectangle and press *F8* to convert it into a symbol with the following details:

10. Double-click the newly created symbol instance to edit it in place.

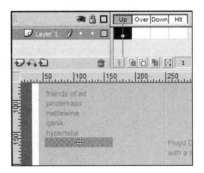

11. Here's the magic bit that will send the rectangle to the Bermuda triangle. Drag the keyframe from the Up state to the Hit state.

Et voila! That's it! You now have an invisible button.

12. Go back one level to the web content symbol Timeline, and you'll notice that the rectangle has been replaced by a pale blue aura. This is your invisible button.

13. Create five duplicates of the invisible button and position them roughly over the text titles. Align them horizontally using Snap Align.

14. Select the top and bottom invisible buttons separately, and center them vertically over their respective texts, as neatly as possible.

15. Select all the invisible buttons and use the Align panel's Space evenly vertically option. Make sure they don't overlap each other (you can scale them a little if they do). This will align them vertically and neatly.

16. Save your case study movie and close it.

Okay, that's it for this rather lengthy case study section. In the next installment, you'll add some of that interactivity I promised you.

Summary

You've seen that masks in Flash can help achieve a range of pretty snazzy effects. You can make masks as simple or complex as you want, and you can encapsulate masking functionality inside movie clip symbols.

You saw that

- A mask is created on a special mask layer.
- A mask layer is applied to a masked layer (or layers).
- The mask layer and all the layers it's applied to must be locked for the mask effect to be displayed.
- A mask can be static or animated.
- A mask can be useful for hiding and revealing selected parts of an animation, achieving a sense of depth, and animating bitmap images as if they were vectors.

In the next chapter, you're going to examine advanced animation and commands, as well the filter, a new feature of Flash.

Chapter 9

ADVANCED ANIMATION, EFFECTS, AND COMMANDS

What we'll cover in this chapter:

- Adding cool automated tween-driven effects with timeline effects and filters
- Recording and reusing your workflow with commands
- Using interactivity—the fundamentals of interaction, events, and event handlers in Flash
- Adding Flash filter and blend effects
- Creating interactive Flash sites with behaviors

In this chapter, you're going on an adventure. The purpose of this expedition is to advance your Flash skills even further. Until now you've been steadily trekking up the hill, and by the end of this chapter, you'll have reached a point where you can hoist your flag.

After this chapter you'll be a different kind of Flash user: a power user! Not only will you be able to automate the creation process using commands, but you will also be able to create interactive websites. On the way up the hill, you'll look at Flash's power user methods of making complex animations and timeline, filter, and blend effects.

Get your hiking boots on, and let's start trekking!

Timeline effects

Timeline effects are for Flash users who want to create cool Flash animation transitions without spending too much time with the laborious tweening such animations usually entail. To those of us in the know—that's you and me—timeline effects are basically automated motion tweens and graphic effects. The main benefit of timeline effects is the time gained from using them.

Imagine a situation in which you want some text to grow on the screen. Given your current knowledge, you would probably use a couple of keyframes, the Transform panel, and a motion tween. The same result with timeline effects is only a couple of clicks away because the process has been automated.

Each timeline effect has a preview window where different parameters are set. The number of parameters depends on the depth and type of the effect. Here is a preview of the Blur effect:

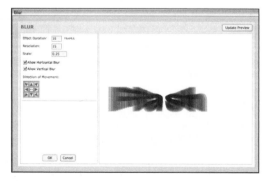

The default list of effects is separated into three categories, each with its own effects. The list includes

- Assistants
  - Copy to Grid
  - Distributed Duplicate
- Effects
  - Blur
  - Drop Shadow
  - Expand
  - Explode
- Transform/Transition
  - Transform
  - Transition

You'll look at these a little later in this chapter.

In case you didn't already know, timeline effects are very easy to use. You apply them by simply selecting an object on the stage and choosing the desired effect from the Insert ➤ Timeline Effects submenus.

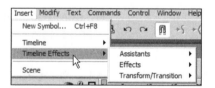

Once an effect is selected, the Preview window appears, showing the parameters for the effect. Finally, once these parameters are set and confirmed, Flash will render the effect. Let's give it a shot.

Timeline effects are a good way of creating quick and simple effects for use in situations where you want to create an eye-catching transition or other animation. They have one or two downsides, the main one being that, as of Flash 8, the program now supports a similar but more advanced and more compelling set of effects called **filters***, and these are much more versatile.*

We will look at filters after looking at timeline effects, and let you decide!

Using timeline effects

In this exercise, you're going to create some movie-style titles using timeline effects.

1. Open a new blank Flash document.

2. Select the Text tool, and type Flash (or whatever you want) into a static text field (you must use static text; otherwise the effect may not work). We've used Arial Black at 26 points, anti-aliased for animation. Center the text field horizontally and vertically on the stage using the Align panel.

3. Insert a keyframe at frame 10 of the existing layer by clicking frame 10 and pressing *F6*. The reason you've done this is to give your viewers a chance to read the text before you apply a timeline effect that will render it virtually illegible.

4. Select the text on frame 10 if it isn't already selected, and select Insert ➤ Timeline Effects ➤ Effects ➤ Blur. You'll now see the preview and parameters window for the Blur effect.

As you can see, Flash has automatically created a preview on the right of your text blurring. This current preview is rendered according to the parameters on the left.

Note that the Preview pane distorts the actual size of your timeline effects. Animations in the preview pane are scaled down or up so that the whole effect can be shown, so effects on the stage might be larger or smaller than you expected.

The current parameters for this effect are in the left of this window. Changing the values of these parameters will alter the appearance of the effect.

Let's briefly look at the parameters for the Blur effect:

- **Effect Duration**: This specifies the frame length of the timeline effect animation. After a little more investigation into timeline effects, you'll see that this is a common parameter for all the animation-based effects.

- **Resolution**: This specifies the quality of this particular effect. From an animation point of view, this denotes the number of copies of the text that are used to create the effect. A higher figure here will create a smoother and more seamless effect, but it will most likely demand more power from the computer processor. In most cases, however, the default value is adequate.

- **Scale**: This represents the scaling value for the overall blur. The default setting of 0.25 makes the text blur to a quarter of the size of the original.

- **Allow Horizontal/Vertical Blur**: These settings specify the directions of blurring. The default, with both boxes checked, makes the object blur in both directions.

- **Direction of Movement**: This is the direction of the blurring and is specified from a matrix grid. As default, the object will scale from the center outward. The options available here are dependent on the previous selection.

5. Change the Effect Duration value to 20 and the Direction of Movement to North-West.

6. Click the Update Preview button in the top right of the window.

> *Note that the Preview pane does not update automatically. After making changes to the parameters, you have to click the* Update Preview *button for the new animation to be shown in the preview.*
>
> *Also worth noting is that you should not press the* ENTER *key after entering values in the text entry requesters. Pressing the* ENTER *key is the same as clicking the* OK *button at the bottom of the window—Flash will assume you are done changing the parameters!*

After a little while, the effect preview in the right pane will be updated. Both the direction of the blur movement and the length of the effect change (but you are pretty unlikely to notice the latter!). Whenever you make any changes to the parameters in this window—whatever the effect—you have to click this button to update the preview. Although the absence of a live update might seem peculiar, you'll soon get used to it.

We've chosen 20 frames as the duration here to nicely round up the length of the Flash text (including the timeline effect) on the screen to 30 frames (giving us a last frame of frame 29). However, you don't want to text to blur in this direction in the final effect. (We only did this to show you how the Preview pane works!)

7. Set the Direction of Movement back to the center selection and click Update Preview.

8. Click OK to render the effect. After a little computation, you'll be returned to the main stage, where you might notice a few key things:

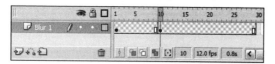

First, the frames have been extended beyond the second keyframe—a full 19 frames as you specified in the parameters. Second, the name of the layer has changed to that of your chosen effect, suffixed with a number. Last, the text has been changed into an instance of a symbol called Blur n (where n is a number). This symbol represents the effect you just created. If you open the Library (Window ➤ Library or *CTRL/CMD+L*) you'll notice a few new symbols have been created.

Blur 1 is the symbol that features the effect, and the Effects folder contains elements required by this effect and others. In the event that you want to change the content of your timeline effect—for example, the actual text in the current example—you will most likely find the necessary modifiable symbols in this folder. You'll see how this is done a little later.

If you have chosen to undo the Blur effect or had to make more than one attempt at it, your symbol might be called Blur 2, Blur 3, and so on.

If you attempt to edit a timeline effect symbol like Blur 1 or if you attempt to edit the timeline frames it occupies, you'll be greeted with a slap on the wrist and a warning:

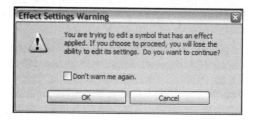

9. If you click OK, the timeline effect will no longer be modifiable (you'll see all about modifying effects in a moment). Unless you really want to edit the symbol, click Cancel.

10. Insert a new layer with a new keyframe on frame 30.

11. Use the Text tool to type Sham Bhangal or some text of your choice. Center the text using the Align panel:

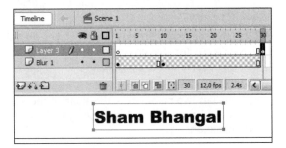

12. On the same layer, add a new keyframe at frame 40. This is where our second transition will start, giving the user 10 frames to read your name. With the text selected, choose Insert ➤ Timeline Effects ➤ Transform/Transition ➤ Transition. As before, the Effects window will appear:

This time we've selected the Transition effect. As you can see, this effect is like a video wipe.

Most of the parameters for this effect should already be familiar to you by now, with the exception of the Direction parameters:

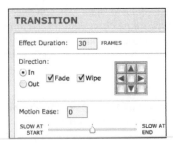

- **Effect Duration**: This option specifies the number of frames the effect will last for.

- **In/Out**: This option specifies whether the selected object wipes in or out. If you want an object to appear, use In. If you want an object to disappear, use Out. By default, this is set to In.

- **Fade**: This option makes the object alpha out or in.

- **Wipe**: This specifies whether or not the wipe effect is used. If this is disabled and the Fade option is enabled, the transition becomes a simple alpha tween. If this is enabled and the Fade option is disabled, the transition becomes a wipe only. If both Fade and Wipe are selected, the transition will include both a fade and wipe occurring simultaneously. If Fade and Wipe are both deselected, you end up with no transition.

- **Wipe Direction**: This sets the direction of the wipe. A right-pointing wipe, for instance, makes the object appear left to right, and makes it look like our text is being written . . .

Sha

Sham Bh

- **Motion Ease**: This specifies the easing amount (we have looked at easing in Chapter 6—recall that it specifies the acceleration of the animation). You can change the easing between -100 and +100 by either entering a new number directly into the Motion Ease text entry field, or by moving the slider along the scale.

13. Change the Direction to Out and click the down-pointing arrow in the grid. Then ensure that Fade and Wipe are checked.

14. Set the Effect Duration to 30 frames. Leave the other options as they are and click OK to render the effect.

15. As before, you'll notice the layer name has changed and the Library has a few more symbols. Let's finish your titles with one last effect.

16. Insert a new layer and place a keyframe at frame 70.

17. Use the text tool to type Kristian Besley (or whatever you like).

18. Insert a new keyframe at frame 80. You're doing this for the same reason you did earlier—you will start the transition at frame 70 because you want people to be able to read the name between frames 70 and 80 before it transmogrifies!

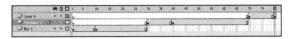

19. Select the text on frame 80 and select Insert ➤ Timeline Effects ➤ Effects ➤ Explode. As you'd expect, you get the Effects window.

You might have noticed that there are quite a few parameters here! There isn't anything too complicated, but there is a lot of it to go through. Let's take a look at some of the important elements:

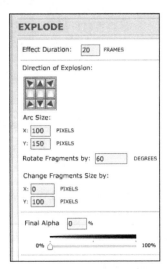

- **Arc Size (x and y)**: This represents the arc in which the fragments move. At their defaults of 100 and 150 (x and y, respectively), the fragments move up more than across. Experiment with these values significantly to see the different effects you can get.

- **Rotate Fragments by**: This parameter controls how much the fragments rotate over the course of the motion. The fragments will rotate incrementally to this set value over the whole of the animation sequence.

- **Change Fragments Size by**: This specifies the full size increase (or the final size) of each fragment over the course of the animation.

- **Final Alpha**: The final opacity of the fragments. As with the last two parameters, the alpha of the fragments will be steadily reduced over the course of the animation.

20. Set the Effect duration to 10 frames and change the Final Alpha to 50%. Leave the other options as they are. Click Update Preview and then click OK.

21. Test the movie using Control ➤ Test Movie. Pretty neat huh?

Unfortunately, you've intentionally put some mistakes in on the last effect (no cussing!), so you're going to have to rectify them. How do you do this? Simple.

22. Select the symbol on frame 80 and click the Edit button from the Effect section of the Property inspector. Alternatively, select Modify ➤ Timeline Effects ➤ Edit Effect:

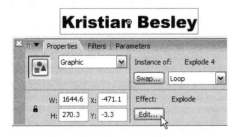

To remove a timeline effect, you can select the effect symbol instance (such as Explode 10 in the screenshot) and choose Modify ➤ Timeline Effects ➤ Remove Effect or right-click it and select Timeline Effects ➤ Remove Effect from the context-sensitive menu.

In either case, this will remove the effect and return your object to its original form.

The familiar Effects window will now appear, allowing you to make the relevant changes to the effect.

23. Change the duration to 20 and the final alpha to 0%. Then click OK and test the movie again.

That's better! But it's still not quite cinematic enough, is it? Well, you can't give the viewer popcorn, but you can certainly get the colors right. As you are probably aware, the typical cinema titles scheme is white text on a black background.

Let's change the color of the text inside the effect to white. There are two ways to do this, and you're going to use both of them.

24. Open the Library and open the Effects Folder by double-clicking it.

25. Locate your equivalents of the Sham Bhangal and Flash text symbols. In our Library these are effectSymbol and Symbol 1, respectively.

26. Double-click the first of them to enter edit mode and change the text color to white using the Property inspector.

27. Do the same for the next one, changing it to white as well.

That's two out of three. The last one isn't so easy, and if you open up the EffectExplode folder, you'll see why:

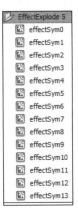

True to its name, the Explode effect has broken your text into many tiny fragments, and changing the color of the text in each of these would be a long, tedious job. Luckily, you can change its color in one fell swoop, via the symbol instance on the stage.

28. Select the symbol instance on frame 80, and use the Color drop-down of the Properties panel to set a white tint to 100%:

29. Select the Kristian Besley text on frame 70 and change its color to white using the Properties panel. This text is not a symbol (because it is not actually part of a timeline effect, so Flash has left it as a text field), so change it to white by clicking the text color picker. Do the same for the Flash text on frame 1.

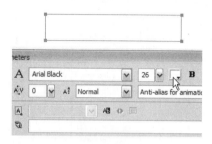

30. Select Modify ➤ Document and change the background color to black. Test the movie and view your sophisticated titles created with almost zero effort:

It's not as easy as that in Hollywood!

As you've seen in this exercise, timeline effects can be used to create complex animations without the hard work normally involved in creating such intricacies. Even though some of the effects are almost as easily achieved with keyframes, effects like Blur and Explode would take a great deal of time and effort to finesse, and even then they wouldn't be as easy to modify as the built-in timeline effects.

Other kinds of timeline effects

In the previous exercise you saw a few key timeline effects, so let's run through the others before you move on. Even though you won't be using them practically here, we recommend that you experiment with them to see what . . . ahem . . . effects you can create. As you'll become aware as you experiment, the most convenient thing about timeline effects is the ability to change their parameters at will.

Let's look at the remaining timeline effects category. All these subcategories are located under the Insert ➤ Timeline Effects menu option.

Assistants

The Assistants effects are in place to help you with repetitive graphic tasks. The first of these, Copy to Grid, takes the selected object and creates a grid of copies using it. A single selected circle, for example, creates a grid of four using the default settings:

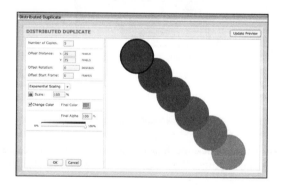

The second assistant, Distributed Duplicate, takes the object and duplicates it a given number of times. The parameters allow you to alter an almost infinite number of the duplicates' attributes, from color to rotation:

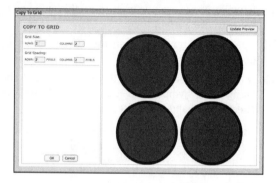

Effects

The Effects category concerns animation effects. The two effects that you've not seen are Drop Shadow and Expand.

The Drop Shadow effect allows you to instantly apply a drop shadow to any object:

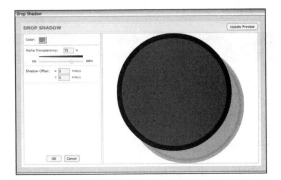

The parameters allow you to change the color and alpha of the shadow, as well as its offset position from the shadowed object.

> We will see later that you can create much better drop shadows using filters.

The Expand effect is used to make shapes grow and move at the same time. One of the significant bonuses of using this (other than the Transform effect, which you'll see in a moment) is the two-way animation it creates, allowing shapes to grow and contract. This effect only works on groups or symbol instances.

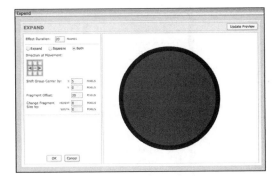

Transform/transition

The Transform effect is the most noteworthy of all the timeline effects simply because the motion that it produces is an important part of most Flashers' day-to-day Flash work. The parameters here range from scaling, to positioning, to coloring, and so on. In fact, anything that can be done on a two-keyframe motion tween is performed here in one simple package:

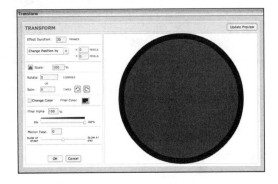

As you've seen in this section, timeline effects can save you a considerable amount of time. The chances are that you won't have a use for all of the timeline effects, but you'll find yourself returning to some key effects again and again. That said, if you have the time to put in some tweening graft, go ahead and do it because one of the limitations of timeline effects is the inability to carry on your motion sequences beyond the sequence of specified frames.

As we mentioned at the outset of our discussion of timeline effects, there is a better way of creating some of the effects we have looked at so far. Timeline effects are really just a series of automated processes. They make life easier for you, but don't really give you anything that you could not do yourself using tweening.

Another Flash system called Filters *does* give you something new. If you have used an image-editing program such as Photoshop, you will know that a filter in digital art is a series of instructions that manipulate the pixels in an image to create something new. Flash filters are much the same in that they allow you to vary a graphic by applying a per-pixel transformation on it. Flash filters differ in one major respect to image editing programs, though: they allow you to add the effects in real time so that you can create animations from the filter effects!

Some of you might be wondering how bitmap-based per-pixel filters can be made to handle the vector content (fills and strokes) that Flash uses. Flash converts areas containing vectors into bitmaps as part of the process of applying filters, but does this in a way that is transparent to you. Thus, you get the best of both worlds without having to lift a finger! Flash gives you the sharp edges and low file sizes associated with vectors at the same time as the per-pixel effects that bitmap-based transitions allow. Cool!

Let's continue your expedition of effects with this exciting new Flash feature!

Filters

Filters are only available in the Flash Professional edition of Flash.

Filter effects can be found by selecting the Filters tab on the Properties panel or by selecting the Window Properties ➤ Filters menu option. Filters are best understood by simply getting stuck in and trying them out, so let's roll up our sleeves and get stuck in right away . . .

Using filters to add transitions

Rather like timeline effects, filters can be used to create animated transitions. We used the Blur timeline effect earlier, and now we will see how to create the same transition using filters. As we will see, filters can give a much better effect because they are applied on a per-pixel basis.

1. Open a new Flash document. Select Modify ➤ Document to open the Document properties window. Make the background black and set the frame rate to 24 fps.

2. In the center of the stage, add some white text of your choice. Make the text fairly large (we used 26-point Arial) and use the Anti-alias for animation aliasing option.

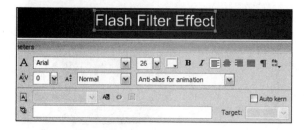

3. With the text on the stage still selected, click the Filters tab on the Properties panel. You will see a box to the left containing <None>.

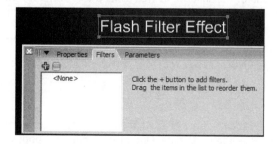

This tells you that you have no filters applied at the moment. Click the + icon at the top left of this box to begin adding a filter. A drop-down will appear. From this drop-down, select Blur.

Some of you will be a little underwhelmed by the available filter choices when compared to timeline effects. Don't be! The cool thing about filters is that you can apply several to the same movie clip, and in doing so, you can create a number of new and different effects.

Note that you select the text to apply a filter effect and not the keyframe it is on. This is the opposite of timeline effects, which are attached to keyframes. From what you already know about instances, you will probably realize that attaching the effect to the text is the more efficient, because you are modifying the text rather than creating a new symbol that contains the effect. Timeline effects work by creating new symbols per effect, and this can create relatively large files if you use a lot of effects.

4. The text Blur will appear in the box, showing you now have a Blur filter applied, and you should see the text looking a little blurred to prove the filter is working.

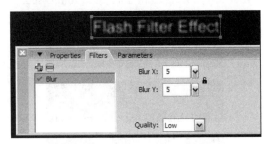

5. Insert a keyframe at frame 20 and then select the text on that keyframe. This instance will also have the Blur filter applied to it (since the keyframe at frame 20 is just a copy of frame 1). We want to remove the filter effect on this frame. You can do this in several ways, including

- Deleting the filter from the filter list completely by selecting the blur and pressing the - icon at the top.

- Setting the Blur X and Blur Y values to 0, giving a blur with zero effect.

Click the little green checkmark in front of Blur. It will turn into a red cross, signifying the filter effect is disabled.

Only the second one will work for our animation because anything you want to animate between two keyframes has to be present on both keyframes. Select the Blur X and Blur Y values and set them both to 0. You now have a filter effect on frame 20 with zero strength.

6. We currently have a low filter value at the keyframe at frame 1. To create an effect where the text goes from invisible and slowly comes into focus, we need to add much more of a blur effect. Select the instance on frame 1 and get back to the Filters tab on the Properties panel. (Note: If you don't see the Blur filter listed, it's probably because you don't have the text selected.)

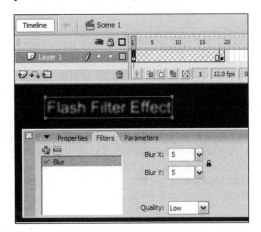

We want a lot more blur than we currently see here, so set the Blur X and Blur Y values a lot higher. Set them both to 100.

> Using the sliders associated with the values will get you to 100, but typing directly into the text entry boxes allows you to enter up to 255. This is something to remember when you want to create really far-out effects—direct entry allows you to overdrive the effect with values between 101 and 255.

7. Select any frame between frames 1 and 20 and add a motion tween.

8. Select frame 60 and press *F5* to add some frames at the end of the effect (i.e., to allow the user to actually see the text!).

If you now test the movie, you will see the text fading in via what looks like a fairly realistic blur effect. It looks rather as if you are viewing the text through a camera that is focusing in on the text from an initially totally unfocused state.

However, the tween isn't very smooth. It seems to flicker a little, and this is because we have left the default quality low. When tweening filters, it's often necessary to select the highest filter quality; otherwise you will see flickering or other discontinuities.

9. To fix the flickering, select the text on frame 1. (You may have some difficulty finding your text because it is blurred to nothingness . . . pressing *CTRL/CMD+A* or temporarily showing your layer as outlines will help you find it. Alternatively, you can just click wildly on the stage for a bit!) Once the instance is selected, set the Quality drop-down to High. Repeat for the instance on frame 20.

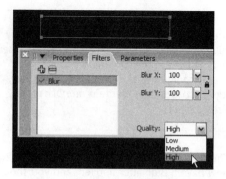

You should now have a smooth text transition, with your text moving from unfocused to focused.

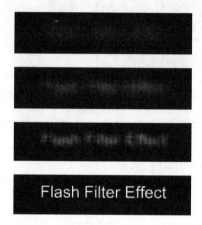

Even better, if you look at your Library, you will see that there are no instances there. Flash doesn't create masses of symbols as in timeline effects, meaning that there is less for the end user to download when your effect is on the web.

Filters are not just for tween transitions, though—far from it! You can use filters to make stuff look a lot more interesting. By adding more than one filter to text, you can create some way-out effects, as we will see next.

Neon text

In this example, we will create some glowing text by using more than one filter.

1. Create a new Flash document with a black stage and a 24 fps frame rate as per last time.

2. Select the Text tool and create some white static text on the stage. We have used 26-point Arial. As we will not be animating this text, select Anti-alias for readability.

3. With the text selected, go to the Filters tab of the Properties panel, and use the + icon to select a glow filter. Give the filter a high strength value (we have used 380%) and a medium quality. Using the color picker to the right of the blur values, select a green color. Your text will now start to glow with an unearthly green tinge . . . rather like a neon effect.

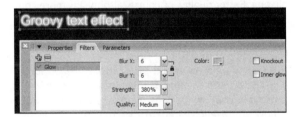

4. We could do with making our effect jump out a little more, and to do this we will give it a drop shadow. Click the + icon again, this time selecting the Drop Shadow filter. Notice that there are now two filters in the list.

5. You can't currently see the drop shadow because a black shadow on a black stage is a little inconspicuous. Change the shadow color by using the color picker, selecting a yellow. Change the quality to Medium and the distance setting to 7.

Groovy!

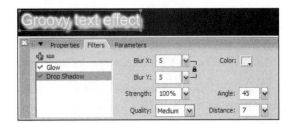

Filters can be used extensively with text to create some quick effects, and doing so is a good way to learn the ins and outs of filters. Here are some we produced earlier:

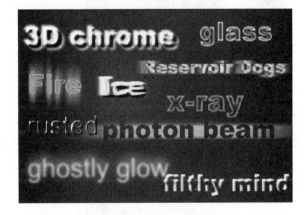

Most of the above text effects have been applied to the same font: Arial Black. Notice that these effects make this font look like several different fonts—a useful feature when you are on the Web, because actually using several fonts could add several hundred kilobytes to your final site if you let it! Why do it when you can fake it?

If you want to have a look at how we created them (or want to see them in their full Technicolor glory), have a look at `filteredText.fla` in the code download.

If you don't have Arial Black installed, open `filteredText2.fla`. *This version uses* _sans *only. The final SWF from this FLA comes in at an amazingly low 670 bytes, much smaller than if you had to create the same text effects using bitmaps (which was the usual way in previous versions of Flash).*

These are not just static text effects of course—you can tween the filters, so you could tween our fire effect into the ice effect . . . or have a look at our attempt (`fire2ice_tween.fla`).

OK, so you've seen some cool filter effects; how would you go about making your own? Easy—sit down for an hour and play with the controls. All you really need to know is what each control does in isolation—and we are about to spill the beans on that one in a moment.

When looking at the filters, you will see some general controls. Let's take a look.

The Blur X and Blur Y controls allow you to blur the text in the x and y directions. If you click the padlock so that the two values are connected, you can keep them equal. This effect is useful for creating glows and shadows—and of course blurs.

Strength controls the amount of the effect, and usually changes the brightness of the effect. It is useful for controlling the brightness of glows, the darkness of shadows, or the amount of beveling.

Quality controls just that: the quality of the effect. Higher quality results in better transitions and greater aliasing. Better quality, of course, also means more computation, which can be an issue on slower computers.

When using filter effects, it is always a good idea to use bitmap caching as much as you can, as well as keep your animations modest, especially if you have a low-end minimum spec that the client has specified.

Angle controls the angle of the effect. It controls the direction of drop shadows.

Distance controls the offset between the effect and the original. This value specifies the distance of the drop shadows from the original text, and is typically used in conjunction with the angle.

The Knockout, Inner shadow, and Hide object checkboxes control how the effect interacts with the original.

Although these three effects can be a little more difficult to get the hang of than the others, they can completely change your effect. If we apply a drop shadow filter to some text using the following settings:

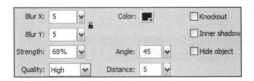

we end up with an effect like this:

Flash filters

Note that none of our checkboxes is checked.

Checking Knockout forces Flash to remove (or "knock out") all pixels of the original text shape, leaving you with just the shadow:

Checking Inner shadow forces Flash to apply the shadow to the inside of the text rather than the outside. You won't see the effect of this change unless you make the shadow a different color from the text. Creating inner shadows is a good way of "eating into" your original text to create weathering effects. If you also hide your original text (we explain how to do this a couple of paragraphs down), you are left with the inner shadow only, and this is a good way of creating text that looks like glass or other semitransparent materials.

The effect here is created using a strong white inner shadow (make the shadow color the same as the stage color [white], check Inner shadow, and ramp Strength to 1000%):

Flash filters

Using Knockout and Inner shadow **together is a good** way of creating effects where your text looks as if it is embossed onto the stage or cut out from it. The following effect was created in this way:

Here, the text looks as if it has been stamped into the stage.

The Hide object checkbox allows you to hide the original text. Note this is not the same as Knockout (where the text and everything underneath it is simply ignored), because Hide object still draws whatever was under the text. If you use Hide object in a drop shadow, you will see just the shadow, but not the text that is creating the drop shadow:

As you can see, there are many varied effects to be created with the available filters . . . but a word of warning:

When text effects first became available in the graphic design world (via Adobe Photoshop and its advanced layering techniques), everyone started using them, and they quickly became a cliché through overuse.

We expect exactly the same thing to occur in web design now that you can create a multitude of text effects easily with Flash. The main reason we have spent so long with text effects is not because text effects are a design essential, but because they are an easy route to come to grips with how filters work.

More usefully, filters can be used to make simple symbols into more complex graphics quickly and easily. By applying filter effects to simple buttons and movie clips, you can create complex-looking designs using only basic graphics. The advantages of doing this are low file size associated with the simple graphics, and the reduction in time it takes to create simple filtered graphics rather than creating complex graphics by hand.

So, now we have got some experience with filters by creating cool (but soon to become cheesy) text effects, let's move on into the world of real web design and have a look at how we can integrate more subtle filter effects into our designs.

Creating a menu in 120 seconds

Have a look at the file `fileMenu.fla`. It was literally created in two minutes. This speed of production occurred because we used filters on very simple shapes (actually, we used only a filled circle and one stroke). All the shadows and 3D effects are created using filtering, thus saving us a lot of work (and, incidentally, it also saves massively on bandwidth of the final SWF).

If you test the movie and roll over or click any of the buttons, you will see that rolling over a button makes the button glow slightly, telling you that the button is a clickable area; if you click the button, it "presses down" in a way that suggests that it is a real physical object.

This menu is the sort of thing that you would use in your first self-promotional site as a designer. Getting a quick site up with a resume, portfolio, and contact email is the best way to break into the world of Flash design.

The menu is actually quite similar to one used by the author on his first site . . . except that his took significantly longer than 2 minutes using the tools available then (Flash 3 and Photoshop for the drop shadows)!

Since you have to read the instructions from this book, it will probably take you longer than two minutes, but I guarantee that it will take significantly less than the time I took to create an almost identical menu using the tools available in Flash 3 when creating my first portfolio site.

Um . . . Well, OK . . . it took me well over an hour all those years ago. Ouch!

1. Open a new Flash document.

2. On the stage, create a 30×30-pixel circle with a white fill and a black, 1-pixel stroke.

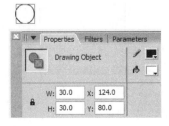

You can create this quickly (if you are going for the 120 seconds!) by selecting the Oval tool, then ALT-clicking on the stage and entering 30 for both the height and width in the Oval Settings window that appears.

3. With this circle selected, press *F8* to make it a symbol. Make it a movie clip called button circle.

4. Create a new symbol with the Insert ➤ New Symbol menu option. Name it 3D circle button, and make it a button.

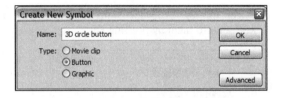

5. You will now be in edit mode for the button symbol you just created. With frame 1 of the button's timeline selected, add an instance of button circle, aligning it to the center of the button stage.

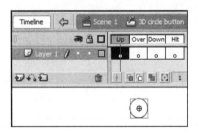

6. Now comes the cool part. Add a bevel filter to the button circle. Make sure the bevel has these settings: Blur X and Blur Y: 5, Strength: 60%; Quality: High; Shadow: black; Highlight: white; Angle: 45, Distance: 5; Knockout and Inner shadow deselected.

265

7. Next, add a drop shadow with these settings: Blur X and Blur Y: 6; Strength: 50%; Quality: High; Color: black; Angle: 45, Distance: 5; and none of the checkboxes selected.

8. Select frames 2, 3, and 4 in turn and add a keyframe to them by pressing *F6*.

9. Select frame 2 (the Over state of the button), and then select the circle in that keyframe. Add a glow, giving it the following parameters: Blur X/Blur Y: 5, Strength: 85%, Quality: High; Color: 00FFFF; Knockout and Inner glow deselected.

10. Our glow is below the drop shadow, and this is making it less bright. To fix this, drag the glow filter up and drop it between the drop shadow and bevel.

Our button's Up and Over states are now completed; we're halfway there! Well . . . actually, much more than halfway there, because the next two states are simple!

11. To create the Down state, select the down keyframe and then select the circle instance in it. To make the circle look as if it is being pressed down, we need to reverse the bevel. This is because if you press something in so that its shape changes from convex (sticking out) to concave (sticking in), the direction of the shadow changes. To do this with our bevel filter, simply change the distance value to -2. Add the glow filter to this instance as you did in the Over state, remembering to move this filter up so that it is between the bevel and drop shadow.

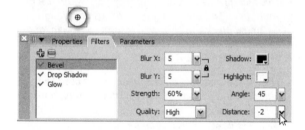

12. Finally, we can delete all the filters from the Hit state, as it will never be seen. To do this, simply select each filter in turn and click the - icon.

Our button is now complete.

13. Go to the main stage. Delete anything that is still on the stage. Call the current layer line and on it draw out a black, 1-pixel-thick curved line as shown, placing it near the top-left corner of the stage.

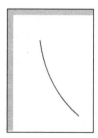

Note that the easiest way to create this curve is to draw out a straight line using the Line tool. Then, select the Selection tool, and click-drag on the center point of the line to drag it into a curve.

14. Create a new layer called menu.

15. On this new layer, drag four instances of the 3D circle button. Note that the button appears without any filters applied in the Library preview panel, but it gains its filter effects as soon as you drag instances of the button onto the stage.

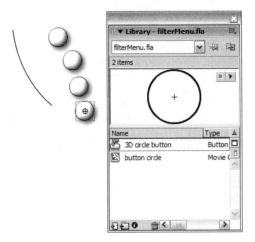

16. Drag the buttons over the line so that they look like connected circles. If you have created your buttons with central registration points (as we have), you should find that you can easily make the buttons snap right onto the line using the snap options.

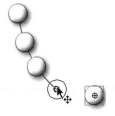

17. Finally, all that remains is to add the text next to the buttons. We added a simple drop shadow to our text, but nothing too strong . . .

We have ended up with a professional-looking menu. Our buttons have a realistic click animation, and we have used our filter effects in context, rather than going for over-the-top effects with high wow ratings but low longevity.

As a final note, before we move on from filters, it's worth mentioning that filter effects can significantly slow the Flash Player down unless you optimize wherever possible. Don't worry, though; the optimization is as easy as remembering to click a checkbox.

Every time you use filter effects, it's a good idea to select whatever you applied the filter to and check Use runtime bitmap caching. This ensures that Flash will use bitmap optimizations whenever it can. You can do this whenever you apply a filter to an instance (button or movie clip). Although you can also apply filters to text fields, you cannot make Flash use bitmap caching on them, so it's a good idea to always turn your text-with-filter-effects into movie clips if you are likely to have lots going on and performance may become an issue.

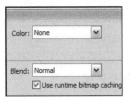

Flash 8 has another trick up its sleeve when it comes to creating per-pixel effects: blend modes.

Blend modes

Those of you who have experience in Photoshop or Fireworks will recognize the filters as similar to those available in Photoshop.

Photoshop and Fireworks also have blend modes. A blend in these applications is a per-pixel, filter-like effect that is able to alter all the pixels in an object by comparing each pixel in the object with whatever is underneath it. The blend affects the Photoshop/Fireworks layer it is applied to and anything under it.

Flash now allows you to do exactly the same sort of things with movie clips. Blending is something that doesn't seem like a big or useful feature, but as any Photoshop/Fireworks user will tell you, it is crucial to modern digital art!

Blending and layering are routinely used together in all digital art. Blending allows you to composite separate bitmaps together to create seamless compositions. Along with filters (which Flash also supports), blending can be used to color-correct or enhance images.

Flash supports all three of the major tools in digital art (layering, blending, and filtering) and it supports them all for vectors, bitmaps, and video, and it supports the animation of all three in real time. This means that Flash now offers a major increase in creative possibilities to the content creator looking to explore web motion graphics as an artistic medium.

*There's even more, though: once you get through your Flash foundation, you will soon realize that these effects can be applied through code, and that multiplies the artistic possibilities to no end, because each effect can be **interactive**.*

Blending is most noticeable when you are adding bitmaps somewhere along the line—either as a static bitmap or as a video. (They also work well with complex vectors, such as vectors with gradient fills.)

This is because blends work by looking at the pixels of one object and using the color values to manipulate another object in some way. This works well when there is a lot of variation at the pixel level, and this occurs most often with bitmap images.

Blend modes allow you to

- Add interesting texturing effects to movie clips. For example, you can "dirty up" a clean vector by blending a bitmap with it. This allows you to create cool grain and "grunge" effects, or just make your clean vector shapes look a little more interesting, weathered, or organic.

- Create runtime color corrections. When you import assets, some of them may be a little too washed out or too deep for your color scheme. Using blending allows you to color-correct them. This is particularly useful when you receive assets from a client where they don't quite fit in with the design color scheme, but you can't easily redo them (such as video).

- Create transitions. Blends can be animated, and this lets you create some really spectacular transition effects.

- Simulate 8-bit masking. We have already created 1-bit masks with Flash masking. Using blend modes allows you to simulate 8-bit masking, or "masking with alphas."

- Simulate video with bitmaps. One of the sneakiest uses of blend modes is in making still images look as if they are video transitions. An animated blend applied to a photograph can make the photograph look as if it is part of a video sequence, allowing you to get away with having far less bandwidth-heavy video than you actually have!

If you import your assets from Fireworks, many of the Fireworks blend modes will be preserved and converted to Flash blend modes. This also works for filters!

Using blends

Applying blends is actually much easier than applying filters. This is because blends do not require any parameters. All you have to remember is that you can only apply blends to movie clips.

1. Open a new Flash document and import a bitmap onto the stage (File ➤ Import ➤ Import to Stage). It is best if the image contains lots of colors and contrasts, and is around the same size as the Flash stage (550✕400 pixels). If you can't find such an image, use our example file (a file with the image already imported), image01.fla.

2. Lock the layer the image is on and rename it to image.

3. Create a new layer called blend clip.

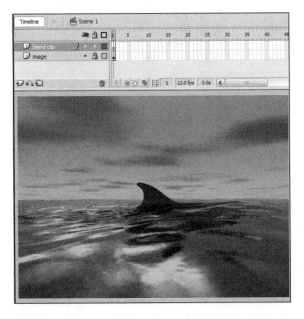

4. On the blend clip layer, create a large rectangle using Object Drawing mode. Use the rightmost gradient fill in the color picker. This fill looks like the color spectrum of sunlight (or for the nonphysicists among us, it contains all the colors of the rainbow). Select no stroke. Draw out a rectangle across the middle third of your image.

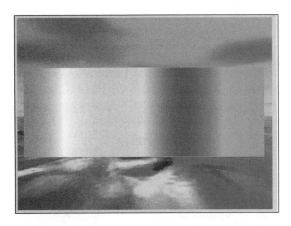

5. Unselect the rectangle you just drew by clicking outside the rectangle with the Selection tool. Using the grayscale gradient (the leftmost gradient in the color picker), draw another rectangle below the color one. Feel free to refer to our work-in-progress file, image02.fla.

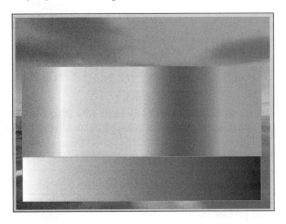

6. Select both rectangles and press *F8* to make them both a symbol. Make them a movie clip called blend.

The movie clip we have just created contains many of the available colors (top rectangle) and tones (bottom rectangle), and since blending is a color-based process, we are well set up to see how bending different colors and tones will affect the underlying image.

7. Time to add a blend mode! With the rectangle selected, open the Blend drop-down list in the Properties panel.

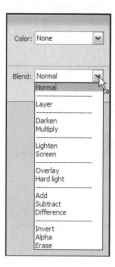

8. Select Multiply. You will now be able to see through the movie clip. The colors and tones of the movie clip seem to be colorizing the underlying image. The effect is rather like what you would see if you viewed the image through a semitransparent and colored candy wrapper!

The Multiply blend mode takes the pixels on the bitmap and multiplies their values with the pixels directly underneath. This results in the pixels in the underlying image becoming darker and moving toward the colors in the movie clip . . . which is a technical way of saying "it looks like you are viewing the image through a candy wrapper that is colored like the movie clip."

9. Select the Blend drop-down list again, and this time select Screen. The movie clip now looks as if light is shining through the wrapper and hitting the bitmap. As the light passes through the movie clip, it is colorized by it, and this color is projected onto the bitmap. If this sounds a little difficult to imagine, think of a slide projector projecting a photo of the movie clip onto a wall that has the bitmap on it as a poster.

10. Try each of the color blend modes: Darken, Multiply, Lighten, Screen, Overlay, Hard Light, Add, Subtract, Difference, and Invert in turn.

So, what is the usefulness of each of the blend modes?

Well, blend modes are best investigated by playing around with them for a while, but we can offer a few pointers.

Multiply and Darken are useful for superimposing the dark parts of one image onto another. In this image, I have superimposed three images of an arm onto the image from the previous exercise. The three arm images (left to right) have the Normal (no blend), Multiply, and Darken blend modes applied.

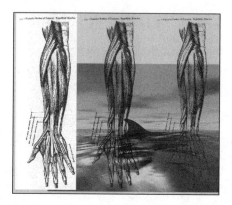

The Screen, Overlay, and Hard Light blend modes are useful when you want to texturize an image (or video) with another image. In the shot that follows, there are four instances of an image of a rocky surface placed over our original image. The blend modes (left to right) are Normal, Screen, Overlay, and Hard Light. Notice that the last three blends apply the same rock texture in different ways, getting darker as you move toward the right. Such blending is useful for aging a bitmap or applying various film grain effects to clean video. Adding film grain effects to a video is also a good way to hide any artifacts you would otherwise see in the video due to compression issues (we will look at video compression issues in Chapter 12).

The Add and Subtract blend modes can be used as 8-bit masks if you blend images with large light or dark areas (dark areas become transparent or semitransparent in the blends).

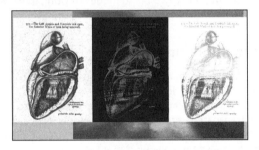

Blending can be used to add textures to vectors if you want to give them a worn, dirty, or more real-world look—which is useful when you want to lose the "made out of bright plastic" look that vectors usually give and go for a more realistic look. In the image that follows, two vector circles have a bitmap texture over their left side, and this bitmap has an Add blend applied. Notice how the blend imparts the bitmap texture on the vectors, giving them a very nonvector appearance.

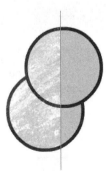

We have only touched on the abilities that bend modes bring to Flash. The folks at http://conclaveobscurum.ru/ and http://oculart.com/ will have a field day with this stuff . . . and so will you if you have experience with Photoshop or Fireworks layer blending!

Nested blend modes

There are three other blend modes that we have not touched on: Layer, Alpha, and Erase. These are very useful when you have nested blend modes. Although they can be difficult to understand, they are the *really* cool ones to play around with once you have understood the basic ones. We've created a few example files to get you started on these three additional blend modes.

Layer blending

Layer blending changes the default way Flash layers are rendered to the way they are done in other applications. Layer blending is a useful mode to use when you are importing content from a layer-based image application (such as Photoshop or Fireworks) and you want the blended content to look the same in Flash. Layer blending is particularly important when you have nested blends.

OK, I know, you're confused . . . a quick example should sort that out right away. Have a look at the example file image03.fla.

If you look in the Library, you will see that there is a graphic symbol called circle. This is a simple filled circle with a thick stroke.

Now look at the symbol overlapping circles. This is a movie clip containing two circle symbols. The two circles overlap.

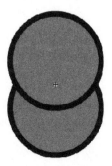

271

There is a problem with nested overlapping symbols in Flash; they tend to render in a nonintuitive way (when compared to other applications), and this can cause problems when you import content from other applications into Flash.

If you look at image03.fla, you will see that we have dragged an instance of overlapping circles onto the left side of the stage. We have then applied an alpha effect to it (using the Color drop-down list on the Properties panel) and this reveals the problem:

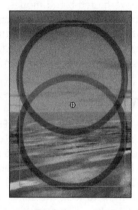

Flash has made **both** circles semitransparent, and you can see **both** circles in the overlapping area.

There is another version of the overlapping circles instance to the right of the stage, and this one has the same alpha effect applied, but also has the Layer blend mode applied. The nested circles inside this movie clip show an alpha, but the overlapping area does not show through.

Layer blending is thus important when you want to maintain a sense of depth between layers where underlying layers would otherwise show through.

Layer blending is also important because it must be used for the other two blend modes to work, as we will see next.

Alpha blending

The Alpha blend mode allows you to add an alpha mask to your movie clips. This lets you selectively hide parts of a movie clip, and also allows your mask to have semitransparent areas. Because blending can also be animated, alpha blending is a cool way to add high-quality transitions to your content.

Open file image04.fla. You will see that our movie clip now has a section cut out of it. The cutout region is a rectangle with the text "alpha" in it. Further, this text is blurred at the edges:

You are probably a bit underwhelmed by this, given that some of you will know that you can already do the same thing by importing a PNG-24 image with an alpha channel. If you zoom in on the stage, however, you will see this:

The pixels of the bitmap start to pixelate (because the image is . . . uh . . . made of pixels), but the faded parts around our text do not become pixelated. This is because the faded areas are **vector based**, and they are computed at runtime (like all good vectors are). This means that we can zoom into our mask and not lose any quality.

If you double-click the masked movie clip, blend, you will see that there is some text in the movie clip alphaText. This is our alpha mask. You will have difficulty seeing this movie clip because it is invisible, but you should be able to locate it by locking the layer content and pressing *CTRL/CMD+A* to select everything on the remaining layer, mask. Once you have found it, double-click alphaText to see what is inside.

You will see a text field with a blur filter applied to it. We have taken some standard text and applied a blur filter to it, and this blur effect has been picked up by the Alpha blend!

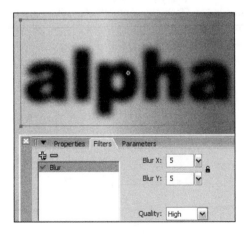

Digital artists will see that this is a very useful feature of blends and filters: they are **cumulative**. A filter applied to an object will be fed into any blend, which is then applied to the filtered object.

So how did we do this? For an Alpha blend to work, you have to place a movie clip (the mask clip) into the movie clip you want to mask (the masked clip). The mask clip should have its blend mode set to Alpha, and the masked clip must have its blend mode set to Layer. You will see that this is exactly what we have in the example file image04.fla.

It is very important to remember to set the masked clip's blend mode to Layer. If you don't do this, the Alpha blend inside the masked clip will stop working.

> *Alpha masks are used often in digital photo-manip-ulation to make separate images that are laid over each other to appear as if they are part of the same image. A masked edge with an Alpha blend (also called a feathered edge) blends the join between two images using a gradual blend rather than an abrupt join. Using an Alpha mask clip with a blur applied to it allows you to do the same thing in Flash.*

Erase blends

The final blend mode, Erase, is simply the reverse of Alpha. Changing an Alpha mask clip to an Erase blend clip inverts the mask.

You can see this done to our example image in image05.fla in the code download.

We have only touched on the power of filters and blends and their ability to create some truly expressive animated web art, not least because we could write a whole book on it!

For those of you who want to know more about blends and filters, you may find it worthwhile to learn a little about Photoshop first. Many of the techniques used in Photoshop are now relevant to Flash.

Photoshop is also very important for web design in general, so if you want to be a well-rounded web designer rather than a Flash designer, you will have to learn Photoshop at some point anyway.

Commands can be much more complex than the examples we explore in this book. If you want to consider the possibilities in greater depth, have a look at the Extending Flash book in the Help panel (press F1) or take a look at Extending Flash MX 2004 (friends of ED, ISBN: 1590593049). Although this book is for Flash MX 2004 (a.k.a. Flash 7) rather than Flash 8, JSFL has not changed between the two versions, so the book is still up to date.

With the JSFL (JavaScript Flash) language, you can do everything from customizing the authoring environment a little to speed up your workflow, to creating your own tools in the toolbar!

The next couple of advanced features are not graphic in nature, but are things that will enhance your workflow or allow you to add something very cool—interactivity—to your designs. They may not be as whiz-bang as the stuff we have just looked at, but they are very useful for getting your sites done on time . . . and time is money!

Automated commands

If you've ever used actions in Photoshop or macros in Microsoft Office packages, you'll know how you really can't live without them. For those of you not fortunate enough to have used them, it's time for another history lesson.

In a nutshell, commands in Flash are simply automated actions that can be played back. The benefit of using them is that boring tasks can be repeated with a single click. Commands are most easily created from History panel steps and are run from the Commands menu:

Creating a library of commands will allow you to save considerable time by automating tasks that you perform regularly. Once you are aware of what commands can do, you'll no doubt look to optimize your working practices by automating those little-but-time-consuming jobs. But before you tackle one of those jobs, here's a reminder of the amazing keeper of time, the History panel.

Reacquainting yourself with the History panel

If you've forgotten the function of the History panel, your memory obviously isn't as good as its memory is. In short, the History panel stores your movements and actions in the Flash environment. Any time you draw a square, move something, or make a new symbol, the History panel records it:

The History panel was originally discussed in Chapter 4. If you need a refresher, don't hesitate to turn back the pages, but don't panic too much because you'll revisit most of its functions in a moment.

If you accidentally perform some activity, fear not! Just select Clear History *from the History panel menu. Clearing the history in this way only clears the history in the History panel—it isn't an "undo everything I did on the stage" kinda thing!*

Now that you recall the purpose and function of the History panel, how can it help you? The History panel is central to recording commands, so you'll have to use it if you want to create commands. This is because Flash, unlike Photoshop or Office packages, doesn't have the ability to record your actions "live." However, the History panel is just as good—if not better.

Once you've recorded a number of actions, you need to convert them into a command. Commands are created by highlighting or selecting a number of History panel entries and clicking the Disk icon in the bottom left of the panel:

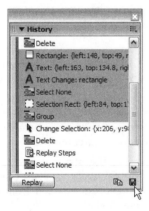

The command is then given a name and is added to the Commands menu. Let's give it a go.

Creating your first command

1. Create a new Flash document and open the History panel. At this point, be careful not to click or do anything unnecessarily. (You don't want to fill the History panel with unwanted actions!)

2. Open the History panel, if necessary, using Window ➤ Other Panels ➤ History. Then select View ➤ Arguments in Panel from the History panels menu. This will provide you with more detail in the panel.

3. With Object Drawing mode selected, use the Oval tool to draw a simple circle in the top left of the stage. Don't worry too much about the colors:

4. Click the circle to select it.

5. Use Edit ➤ Copy to copy the circle and Edit ➤ Paste in Place to paste the duplicate in the same location as the original. It will be selected by default.

Hold down *SHIFT* and use the *ARROW* keys to move the circle to the right, out of reach of the original.

So far you have two rather dull-looking circles on the stage. Nothing exciting, but you have some dynamite History entries to work with! In our screenshot, the last three entries are the ones that we're going to make into a command. Why? Let's explain.

The rather drab command that you're going to make will perform one simple function: it will copy whatever is selected (in this case a circle) and paste and position the copy over and to the right of the original. Now let's look at the three actions:

- Copy: This represents the copy you made of the selected object. Within the context of the command, this will copy whatever the user has selected. Remember that the only prerequisite of this command is to have something selected.

- Paste: true: This shows the Paste in Place that you performed. Within the command this will paste whatever is on the clipboard—conveniently what you have just copied—onto the stage. The word true specifies a Paste in Place.

- Move: {x:110, y:0}: This action is a record of the movement of the circle 110 pixels to the right. The coordinate details stored here—x and y—are offsets from the original position of the circle. These are not to be confused with (absolute) x and y screen coordinates. Each time this particular action is run, the newly pasted object will be positioned 110 pixels across from its original position.

Before you cast your command in stone, you can give it a trial run.

6. Highlight the three required actions in the History panel:

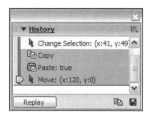

7. Ensure that the second circle is still selected. Click the Replay button at the bottom of the History panel. Once this is done, you should have another circle on stage, positioned across from the previous one:

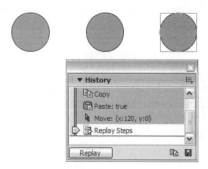

Success! Click Replay again to create another . . . Hurrah! It works. Finally, to save you from having to work in the History panel forever, you can attach the actions to a command.

8. With the three actions still selected, click the Save selected items as command (the Disk icon) at the bottom left of the panel.

In the dialog box that opens, give the new command a name. We've called ours copy paste move!:

Now open the Commands menu to view the newly added command. This allows you to run this command from within Flash at any time in any Flash document, and with any object.

Pretty fancy, huh? Before you go on, let's quickly look at the other options on this menu:

- Manage Saved Commands: This is where you can rename or delete any saved commands. Pretty useful for removing commands that you are only likely to use once.

- Get More Commands: Selecting this option will display a Macromedia web page where you can download various prebuilt commands.

- Run Command: This allows you to run commands saved as external JavaScript Flash (.jsfl) files. These might have been downloaded from the previous menu option—Get More Commands.

Now to check that your command works:

9. Select the Rectangle tool and draw a small shape anywhere on the stage.

10. Select the shape and choose the newly created command from the Commands menu. As before, a copy of the selected shape is positioned to the right of the original.

Your command is functional. Before you revel in the glory, there is something important you should know.

11. Clear the contents of the History panel by selecting Clear History from its menu.

12. Use the Pencil tool to draw a single squiggle of any description on the stage. If you now look in the History panel you'll notice a red x below the Pencil icon alongside the lone entry. True to symbolic form, the evil red x is informing you of something bad!

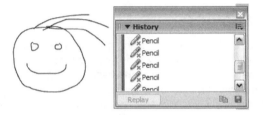

In fact, it indicates that this History entry cannot be replayed or added as part of a command. If this sounds disappointing, don't worry. The majority of actions that cannot be reused aren't the type of things that you'd want to re-create—you would not want to create a command that creates one particular squiggle, but you would want to create a command that added a drop shadow and bevel to any object to create instant button-like shapes. To put it another way, you don't normally want to make commands that draw specific shapes, but you would want to create more general commands that edit something specific that is already drawn on the stage. To discover what actions can and cannot be used, leave the History panel open while you work and look for the red x.

Creating a reusable command

As we've already pointed out, one of the great things about creating commands is their reusability. Common actions are easily converted into commands and reused again and again. Even as you worked through this book, you have no doubt come across a number of recurring actions, which you could have condensed into reusable commands.

Reusable commands can be a major time-saver if they are created correctly. For instance, in the last exercise you made a conscious decision to require a selection

from the user. This decision is key because that command could be applied to any object on the stage.

> *When creating commands, it is always a good idea to draw a basic shape or symbol. If you are editing a symbol, return to the main stage. Then select your shape/symbol and clear the history. Then, perform the actions that you want to form the command, and save all the commands in the History panel when you have reached the end point.*

In a situation where you aim to create a reusable command, assume the user (even if that is just you!) has made a selection of whatever the command will be applied to, and will run the command from there.

In the following image, you can see our attempt at creating a general beveled button shape. We created a circle, converted it to a movie clip, and then added a bevel and drop shadow filter to it. Once we recorded our actions, we tried running them on another oval movie clip, and then a rectangle. You can see our results to the left of the History panel. Notice the exact commands we have selected—only the ones that add the filters, but not the ones that create the shape or turn the shape into a movie clip. This is the hallmark of a general command that will be useful to you: only save the actions that affect something that is already on the stage and selected.

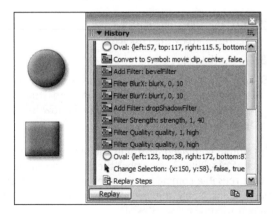

Let's see this in practice.

Creating a "center to stage" command

In this exercise, you're going to create a simple command to automate one of the most common actions that you've used throughout the book—centering. Without any knowledge of commands, centering horizontally and vertically requires at least two actions, assuming you have the Align panel open and the To Stage modifier on.

You're now going to make these actions one click away.

1. Open a new Flash document.
2. Use the Rectangle tool in Drawing Object mode to draw a square with any fill and stroke color.
3. Select the square and open the Align panel (Window ➤ Design Panels ➤ Align, or *CTRL/CMD+K*).
4. In the Align panel, switch on the To Stage modifier.
5. Click the Align horizontal center and Align vertical center buttons. This will center the square on the stage.
6. In the History panel, select the last two actions:

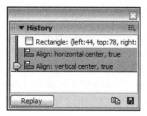

7. Click the Save selected steps as command button (represented by the Disk icon).
8. Give it the name center to stage.
9. Move the rectangle away from the center, and with it selected, choose the new command from the Commands menu. The rectangle will now be centered on stage.

This simple command illustrates the ability (within the limits of possibility—remember the dreaded red x!) to create reusable commands. Even though this last command is incredibly minimal, the time you'll save by using it will make it worthwhile.

If this isn't impressive enough, remember that any commands you create in Flash, including this one, will be stored permanently on the Commands menu for any future Flash sessions. Commands library, here you come.

You've still got a ways to go in this chapter, so grab a coffee, change the CD, and get ready to proceed. If you thought commands and timeline effects were good, you ain't seen nothing yet.

Behaviors

You're now going to start moving away from the predictable world of tweens and "animation on rails," toward something new—**interactive control of the timeline**. Instead of allowing the timeline to run sequentially, you will add features that allow the user to change its flow so that it can skip frames, start, or stop. That's a very powerful feature because it allows you to create navigation and interactive animation.

Behaviors work by automatically adding code instructions to your symbols, using Flash's scripting language, ActionScript.

Behaviors create code that the developer will most likely never look at. They create code that is written in a format that is not conducive to update or enhancement. (It's actually written in an older dialect of ActionScript that was all the rage way back in Flash 5.) If you want to learn modern ActionScript, we strongly recommend you don't look at the code generated by behaviors—at least, not until you feel competent enough in ActionScript to explore alternative coding styles. You will be writing the modern dialect of ActionScript in Chapter 10.

Although behaviors are simple drag-and-drop procedures, you do need to know the principles behind how they (and ActionScript in general) work. You will take a slight detour to learn about what interactivity actually is, and how it is implemented. You will also look at when you can (and can't) attach a behavior, an issue that can be confusing at first.

Interactivity

Interactivity in the world of Flash means that when your content is running in the user's browser, it responds to something that the user does or reacts to a predefined set of conditions. For example:

- Branching out of the movie's linear playback and playing a different movie clip when the user clicks a button or when the playhead hits a particular frame.

- Saving the user's name and e-mail address, which they've typed into a couple of text boxes.

- Confirming the user's order when they've added things to their shopping cart in a Flash e-commerce site.

- Playing different songs on a Flash jukebox.

- Dragging around pieces of a puzzle in a Flash jigsaw.

- Creating a game where the graphics move around in an intelligent fashion, reacting (but not being controlled by) the user's interaction. A good example of this might be a Space Invaders–type game.

All these examples rely on Flash's ability to respond to **events**.

An event is simply something that happens as a result of something that is an input to Flash. When you create an interactive movie, you plan the things that can happen, build an interface (buttons, text-entry boxes, etc.) that will allow the user to make those events happen, and create the ActionScript that will handle those events.

In most Flash content, the user is not the only thing that can generate events. Flash can also get data from a server, and respond to events such as "a JPEG image has just loaded into the Flash player."

Flash itself can also generate events (one is generated at the start of every frame by Flash itself, and this event—onEnterFrame—is perhaps the most used event in Flash animation).

In high-end Flash programming, there is always a need for sections of code to respond to each other, and a custom form of event handling (called Listener events) can be used by the ActionScript programmer to define a reliable and simple way for event-like messages to be broadcast between code sections.

So, don't be fooled into thinking that the only thing that can generate events is user interaction. As you advance in your understanding of Flash, you will see that there are many things going on underneath the Flash bonnet!

Events and event handlers

In order for interaction to take place, you need to have an event and an event handler. For example, when you visit a friend, you walk along the street until you reach his or her building. When the "reaching the building" event takes place, the "I've reached the building" event handler in your brain responds by turning your steps toward their door. Something of significance—an event—has occurred, and a piece of processing has been carried out to handle it.

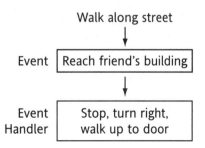

279

Now you push the doorbell or intercom button to let your friend know you've arrived. Your friend will then come to the door, look out of the window to see who's there, or grunt down the intercom.

Pressing that button is another event, and this time your friend responded to it—he handled it in that he did something when the buzzer sounded. From here you and your friend can discuss what you're going to do with your day—your extended interaction with your friend starts with the push of a button. If your friend had been out or hadn't answered the door, your "he's not home, I'll go to the mall" event handler would have kicked in. In the real world, events and event handling are complex—infinite, even. In Flash, you can control the environment, so in your interactive movies you can plan for an anticipated range of events and handle them all.

And that, more or less, is interaction.

Let's examine one of the primary and most intuitive of tools that Flash gives you for interaction with the user—the button.

Buttons as interactive elements

In an interactive Flash movie, an event is triggered by clicking the mouse button or dragging the pointer over something on the screen—typically a button. The event handler here will be a set of instructions that is attached to the button. These instructions tell Flash exactly what you want it to do when the user clicks that button and triggers the click event. These instructions can be created using behaviors, which are ready-made code sections for the most common interactivity building blocks. Although you don't need to create any code to use them, you do need to know the concept of the event-event handler pair because you have to specify (but not write) them.

It's important to realize the following two important points when using behaviors (or for that matter, raw ActionScript, covered in Chapter 10).

Symbols on their own do not create interactivity

A button on its own does not produce interaction. A button placed in a movie has its default states—Up, Over, Down, and Hit—but it won't actually do anything interesting unless you explicitly tell it to. You've already seen that you can add keyframes to the button's internal timeline and change its display in each state, which makes the button more interesting to look at. But the button is still essentially dumb—all it can do at the moment is detect events such as when it's rolled over or clicked. To boost the button's intelligence, you have to attach a behavior to one or more of its states: the ActionScript element, created for you behind the scenes by the behavior, creates the interaction:

Basic button
Cursor changes to hand cursor when user rolls over the graphic

Full Button
As Basic button, plus the graphic changes between the Up, Over, and Down States

Scripted button
As Full button, plus a script runs when the user either rolls over or clicks the button

Use ActionScript to display previous image

Use ActionScript to take user to new page or movie

When you've attached the behavior to your button, the button waits for the user to interact with it.

In some programming languages—BASIC, for example—once your program starts, the program code is always running. In Flash, your program—the ActionScript (which is what behaviors end up as)—is attached to a button and will only run when the button detects a particular **interaction** carried out by the user. As your knowledge of Flash increases, you'll see why this is a much better way of creating user interfaces. One of the main features of advanced Flash sites is their use of buttons to start off lots of simple little sequences that, together, form a complex, fully animated, and interactive user experience.

As you progress in the next couple of chapters, you'll see that a button in Flash can be much more than just a switch. In addition to detecting simple things like mouse clicks to provide navigation, the button can be used to launch whole avalanches of actions in motion.

Movie clips and buttons only behave on a timeline

You can only attach behaviors to instances of symbols on a timeline. You should not attempt to attach a behavior to a symbol in the Library. You can, however, attach a behavior to a symbol that is on the timeline of a symbol in the Library.

Why? Because the Library is simply a store; nothing in it is active and capable of doing much of anything until you place it on a keyframe. This is one of those things that is simple for experienced Flash users, but it totally confuses the beginner, so let's go through it slowly with an analogy.

Before you buy a CD player, it is kept in a stock room somewhere. It will most likely have a bit of plastic or a retaining screw somewhere in it that prevents the laser head inside it from moving or the spindle turning. This is to protect it from bumps and knocks during transit. The upshot of all this is that you can't play anything on it while it is set up for storage. Once you buy it and remove the packaging and all the protective bits of plastic, you can start to use (or interact) with it. The same applies to symbols in the Library; they are not ready to be used when they are in the Library because something needs to be done to them first. This process is simpler than unpacking a CD; in the virtual world of Flash you simply drag the symbol onto the stage. This is the equivalent of unpacking the CD player and plugging it into a power supply. All the software connections are created to make the symbol work (a process called **instantiation**). That's the point when a symbol is ready to work with behaviors.

> Note that you can't attach behaviors or code to a graphic symbol. If you need to, make it into a movie clip first.

If you buy a car with a CD player, the situation is different. When the manufacturer built the car, someone had to test the CD player, so even though the vehicle may be in storage, the CD player will still be set up to work. The CD player is **embedded**; it is part of a larger product, and for that larger product to be built, the CD player has to be working when the product leaves the factory and goes into storage. A button inside a movie clip works in exactly the same way. The only thing that changes is the terminology. In this case, the button is **nested** (rather than embedded), but it works via attached behaviors for much the same reasons as the embedded CD player—it has already been wired to work inside its larger parent, even though the parent is in storage within the Library.

To further extend the analogy, the car factory also has a storeroom of CD players that haven't yet been fitted into a car. They will be in the same state as the CD players in the first example—they are not embedded so you can't use them yet—they are still in storage. In the Flash world, an embedded button can have a behavior attached to it, but the version of the same button that is not embedded (and in the Library) cannot, again for the same reasons as the car CD player—it's only wired up to work (or instantiated) when it's inside the parent.

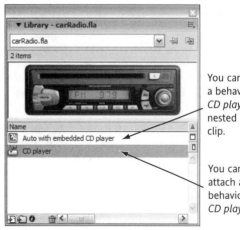

You can attach a behavior to *CD player* nested in this clip.

You cannot attach a behavior to *CD player*.

OK, that's all the theory. Let's start with a simple example—an FLA containing some interaction via buttons and behaviors.

Creating a simple button

To create an interactive element in your movie, you need a button on the stage waiting to be clicked giving you an event—and some ActionScript attached to it to handle the event and tell Flash what to do.

Before you look at attaching behaviors that respond to mouse clicks, let's make sure you're getting the most out of your buttons by creating a simple button and slowly developing its abilities.

1. Create a new Flash document and rename the default layer buttons.

2. Go to View ➤ Grid ➤ Show Grid and then View ➤ Snapping ➤ Snap to Grid, and ensure that both are checked—this will help you position your symbols on the stage more accurately.

3. Create a new graphic symbol (*Ctrl/Cmd+F8* or you can click the New Symbol icon at the bottom left of the Library, or you can select Insert ➤ New Symbol) and name it circle. Make it a red circle with a black outline.

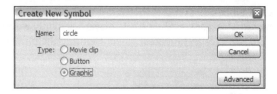

4. We want to make the circle central. Those of you who still have the Commands ➤ center to stage command (that we created a few pages back) are in for an easy ride—simply select this command.

The rest of you who deleted it get their comeuppance—you have to do it the hard way. Open the Align panel (Window ➤ Align). Click the To stage button in the Align panel. With your circle symbol selected inside the button symbol, click both the Align horizontal center button and the Align vertical center button:

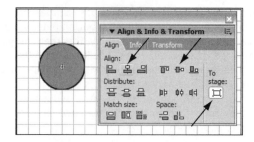

Don't put your new symbol on the stage just yet.

The reason you've created a graphic symbol before making it into a button is that you'll be using the circle many times within the button itself. By making the circle a symbol beforehand, you're allowing Flash to reuse the circle symbol, thus saving time and space.

5. Create another symbol (using any of the routes described in step 3), creating a new button symbol called button. Click OK.

Inside the button symbol, you'll see a blank stage with the button icon at the top. The timeline contains the four button symbol states: Up, Over, Down, and Hit.

Remember the definitions of the four states of the button symbol:

- The **Up** state is how it looks in its original size and position.

- **Over** is how it will look when the user's mouse passes over it.

- **Down** is how it will look when it's clicked.

- **Hit** contains filled spaces that denote the areas the user must be over to click the button.

6. With the playhead at the Up state, click the circle graphic symbol icon in the Library and drag an instance of it onto the stage inside the button:

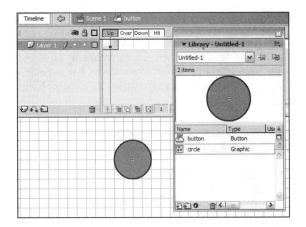

You're going to need to know the exact position of your symbol in the Up state—this is so that you can make the different visual renderings of the button's other states consistent. To do this, you'll use the Align panel again (or that rather useful center to stage command!) to place it in the exact center of the stage.

7. Using either the Align panel or the center to stage command, align the circle so that it is central within the button (exactly as we did in step 4).

Only the Up frame of the button's timeline currently has a keyframe in it. To start bringing the other states to life, you need to add keyframes.

8. Add a keyframe (using *F6*) to each of the other three states. You have now put an instance of the graphic symbol circle into each state of your button symbol:

In the finished movie, you want to make this button get bigger when a visitor's mouse pointer rolls over it, and get smaller when it's clicked. You can do this by scaling the instance in each of the button's state keyframes. You're going to scale each one by a specific amount.

9. Display the Transform panel using Window ➤ Transform (or simply use the tabs if you still have the Align panel open) and select the Over state in the button timeline.

The Transform panel is useful for adding precise rotation, skewing, and scaling to symbols and shapes.

10. With the circle graphic selected, make sure that the Constrain box in the Transform panel is checked—this ensures the proportions of the circle are maintained—then type 120 in either the horizontal or vertical scale fields and press the *ENTER* key to apply the scaling.

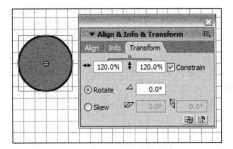

11. Make sure that the center position of the button stays in exactly the same place as in the Up state; otherwise the button will appear to move slightly when animated. You might need to drag the scaled version back to the central position—or you can use the Align panel or the command again.

Also, don't make the Over state much bigger than the Hit state. You'll see why when you test the button: the parts of the Over state that are outside the Hit state won't respond to the mouse.

12. Select the Down state and scale the circle instance down to 80%.

Although it's not vital in this exercise, it's a good idea to make the Hit area a solid-black object to avoid missing unfilled holes that, as explained earlier, could result in the button working erratically.

13. To do this, select the keyframe in the Hit state and then click the circle on the stage. From the Color drop-down menu in the Properties panel, select Brightness and move the slider to -100%:

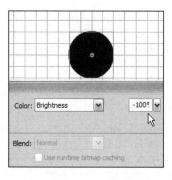

You can confirm that the Hit state circle has the same location and size as the Up state instance either by looking at all four states simultaneously using the Onion Skin tool or by checking that the x and y values in the Properties panel match for each state.

14. Click the Scene 1 text toward the top left of the timeline to return to the main timeline and put an instance of the button symbol at the center of the stage by dragging it out of the Library. Make sure you drag the button symbol and not the circle graphic, because the two symbols look the same!

15. Test the movie. You'll notice that when the mouse rolls over your button, the mouse pointer changes from an arrow to a hand icon and the button gets bigger. When you click and hold the mouse button, the button graphic gets smaller:

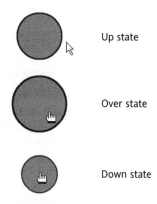

Up state

Over state

Down state

That's the basic button defined. Time to accelerate its evolution into a more intelligent species of button.

Creating animated buttons

Flash allows you to define a movie as one of the button states. This feature allows you to create buttons that have complete animations within them. Let's create a simple animation and add it to the Over state of your button.

Putting a movie into a button

1. Double-click the button symbol in the Library to edit it. Select the Over and Down states of the button from the previous exercise in turn, and press the Reset icon (at the far-right bottom corner) in the Transform panel (or use Modify ➤ Transform ➤ Remove Transform). This will return both states' circle instances back to the same size as the Up state.

Now you'll create a simple movie that'll play when the user activates the button.

2. In the Library window, click the New Symbol button and create a new movie clip symbol called circleMovie.

3. In frame 1 of the new movie clip, place an instance of the circle symbol at the center of the stage—use the Align panel (or your center to stage command) to correctly center this horizontally and vertically.

4. Add a keyframe at frame 10 and then use the Transform panel to reduce the size of the frame 10 circle instance to 40%.

5. Add a motion tween between frames 1 and 10. If you turn on onion skinning between frames 1 and 10, you should see the button make the vaguely psychedelic pattern shown in the following screenshot—simulating the way your button will shrink when its Over state is activated:

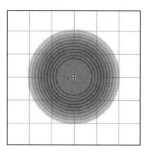

Once you've finished looking at the groovy pattern, click the Onion Skin Mode button again to turn it off.

You're now going to put your animated circleMovie symbol into the Over state of your button symbol—replacing the instance of the graphic symbol circle that's currently there.

6. To edit the button symbol, double-click its icon in the Library, and then select the Over state.

7. Select the circle symbol instance in the Over state and use the Properties panel's swap button to swap it for an instance of circleMovie.

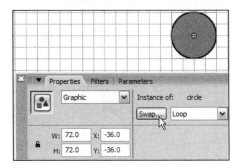

When you click this button, the Swap Symbol window will appear. Double-click the symbol circleMovie and the swap is done.

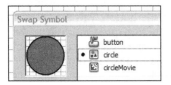

Although the symbols are swapped, you also need to change the behavior. To do this, change the instance behavior from Graphic to Movie Clip via the Properties panel.

You could have also simply deleted circle and added circleMovie in its place, but this way, you learn about swapping symbols as well!

8. Test the movie with Control ➤ Test Movie.

9. Notice that when your mouse pointer goes over the button, you see a looping animation of a smoothly receding button.

Although the animation you chose here is not really that impressive, remember that you can have any number of animated effects embedded in a movie clip inside the button. Just make sure that the first frame of the animation is the same size as the rest of the button states—from there, your Over state button image could morph into a mushroom, a dog, a flying fish—anything you like. Also, note that you should never animate the button's Hit state.

Although you now have a button with visual feedback, the button is still silent. Real buttons tend to click or squeak or ring. Let's add a sound.

Although Flash will allow you to add a movie clip for any button state, the Over and (occasionally) the Up states are the only ones you should consider doing it for. The Down state doesn't last long enough for anything to happen (it exists only for the time between the mouse click and release), and the Hit state represents the button's hit area, and you don't need to animate it—unless you want to confuse everyone by having a changing and invisible hit area!

Creating buttons that talk

The first thing you need is a sound file. You can use any kind of sound file you have on your computer, or you can download one from the Internet. It's beyond the scope of this chapter to specify the ins and outs of sound issues (we look at sound in Chapter 12), so instead let's simply use an appropriate sound.

Making your button buzz

The first thing to do is to get the sound into your movie's Library.

1. Download the file blip.wav (or search for a suitable sound on your hard drive—your operating system will most likely have a few button sounds). To import it into Flash, select File ➤ Import ➤ Import to Library. In the Import to Library window (shown as follows), select All Sound formats in the File of Type drop-down menu at the bottom, and then browse to your sound file.

2. Your Library window should now look something like this:

Ideally, you would now edit the sound to optimize it, but you'll leave all that until Chapter 12. Right now, what you need to do is attach the sound to the button.

3. Double-click the button symbol in the Library to go into Edit Symbols mode.

4. Create a new layer called sound—this layer will be used to hold the sound your button will make.

5. Add a blank keyframe to each of the button states using *F7*.

6. Select the Down state on the sound layer.

This is the button state that usually has a sound—putting your sound here will make the button sound off when it is clicked.

7. In the Property inspector, click the Sound drop-down menu—this will show you all the currently available sounds. Unimpressively, only the one you just imported will be there. (Also ensure that the Sync drop-down is set to Event.)

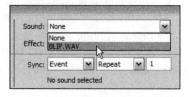

8. Select your sound from the drop-down.

Look closely at the Down keyframe after you've done this. There's a tiny blue wave shown on the keyframe to signify that a sound has been attached there:

9. Test the movie. Hear your sound when you click the button? Yes? Then you're done!

10. Save your movie.

When you add sound to a button's Down state in the way that you've done here, you're adding sound to *all* instances of the button. This is a major advantage for adding sound to a previously silent website. If your website uses many instances of a single button symbol, you only need to add sound once for *all* your buttons to have sound.

The features of behaviors

Earlier, we likened clicking a Flash button to what happens when you ring someone's doorbell. Having a Flash button all by itself is like ringing the doorbell at a house where nobody's home, or where the wiring's been disconnected. The button you've just created looks pretty enough, but beyond the default state-related animations and sound that you've just explored, it doesn't trigger anything when you click it. It doesn't really handle the click event. When a user clicks a button, the sound or embedded animation that plays isn't what you're really concerned with—you're interested in where that button's going to take you, or what it's going to make happen. You need to wire up the button.

We also talked about the fact that behaviors can only be added to symbols once they are on a timeline (via our discussion about CD players). We called this process **instantiation**, and the copy created on the timeline is called an **instance**.

If you get into a discussion with someone about the technical ins and outs of Flash, the word instance will crop up an awful lot because almost everything of consequence in a working site or application is one.

By attaching a behavior to a button instance, you can make your buttons take you somewhere.

To start demonstrating the features of behaviors, you're going to create a simple movie in which Flash asks the user to pick one of two options, and then responds differently for each response. This implies a logical branching in your movie rather than a straightforward linear playback. You'll present the user with two colored buttons and the user will click one of them, causing Flash to go to one of two possible places. This ability to branch and make alternative choices is an important principle in creating interactive movies.

Before you can attach a behavior and make an interactive movie, you need to create a basic front-end for the user to interact with. This will contain buttons that access the different places the user can go. You're going to set these up now.

Creating a basic front-end

1. Continue working with the button movie from the previous exercise. If you have not completed the previous exercise, you can start with our file, basicButton.fla.

2. Drag another instance of your button symbol from the Library out onto the main stage—make sure you drag in the button symbol and *not* the graphic symbol or the movie clip (as we mentioned previously, this is easy to do because they all look the same!).

3. Position the two button instances so they're next to each other in the center of the stage.

4. With one of your button instances highlighted, select Tint from the Color drop-down menu in the Property inspector, and make the button blue using the color palette to the right of the Color drop-down menu.

5. You've just altered the properties of this specific instance of the button symbol: the underlying symbol has remained the same. Remember that each individual instance has a range of properties that you can change via the Property inspector.

6. Repeat this Tint change for the other button, but make this one pink.

7. Create a new layer called text and use a static text box in which to type pick your favorite color above the two buttons.

Your stage should look like this:

Here, you've used the same button symbol twice, but made them look different by changing the color of each instance. This is a timesaving (and file size reducing!) trick used by many Flash web designers to help workflow when creating sites that have many different buttons on them. They just create one master button and then change the appearance of each instance. Remember, you can use filters and blends as well as color tinting (if you have Flash Professional, that is).

Now you need to set up two areas of your site that Flash will go to when each button is clicked—one area for the pink button, and one for the blue button. You're going to put these areas in a separate layer called content. At the moment, your content will just be simple text messages, but it could be anything up to and including completely new pages within a Flash website.

8. Create a new layer, and call it content, and put it above the two existing layers.

9. Extend all layers up to frame 30 by selecting frame 30 in each layer and pressing *F5*. Your timeline should now look like this:

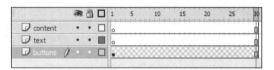

10. In the content layer, add keyframes at frame 10 and 20.

11. Lock all layers except content. In frame 10 add the text message you clicked pink! as shown in the following graphic:

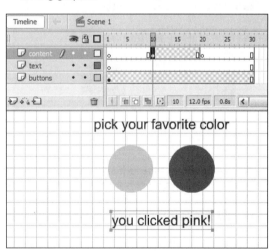

In frame 20, do the same, except change the text to read you clicked blue!.

12. You now need a layer that will signal your jump points via labels. Add a new layer called actions as shown in the next screenshot, and add keyframes at frames 10 and 20. So that you don't inadvertently move your graphics around, lock all layers except actions.

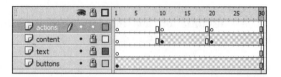

You named the new layer actions *and not* behaviors *because a behavior is prewritten ActionScript. When you add the behaviors, all you are really doing is adding code—you may not be writing it yet, but you will by next chapter.*

When the user clicks any of the buttons, you want Flash to jump to particular points in the timeline—specifically, the two keyframes you just added at frame 10 and 20, both of which will have content specific to the pink or blue choice.

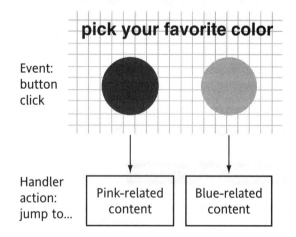

You'll now label these two keyframes so that they're properly signposted—which means that you can then use behaviors to jump straight to them.

13. Select frame 10 in the actions layer. Go to the Property inspector and type pink in the Frame field:

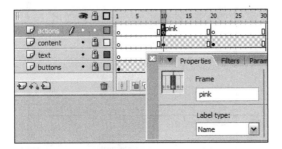

What you've done here is attach a label to frame 10 of the actions layer. This is a pointer or flag for the frame, and with it in place, you can use a behavior to jump directly to this frame from anywhere else in the movie or an event of your choosing. That's a pretty powerful thing to be able to do—bypass the linear tyranny of the timeline and jump around inside the movie.

> *You can also jump to a frame number, but the frame numbering will change every time you add a frame, so it isn't recommended—although it used to be the only way to do it in very early versions of Flash, and it took ages to create long animations because of it!*

Notice that Flash has added a little flag in the timeline and is displaying the label name next to it.

You can use this label as a reference point for the pink button–related content that you want the user to be able to display.

Now you need to label the blue keyframe in the same way.

14. Click frame 20 in the same layer and add a new keyframe. In the Property inspector use the Frame field again to label the new keyframe blue:

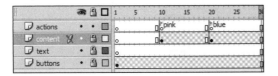

You've created two separate messages, each of which lives on its own separately labeled section of the timeline. You can use those labels as reference points that you can jump straight to using behaviors.

Attaching behaviors to frames and buttons

You now have a simple front-end for the user to interact with and two alternate locations to move to from the two buttons. However, when you play the movie at the moment, the playhead will zip through the movie in a resolutely linear fashion: the frames will still play out as in a normal linear animation. You need to shout "STOP!" at frame 1 so that the front-end hangs around and gives the user time to ponder the alternatives and make their choice.

To do this you add a behavior to a frame in the timeline, telling the movie to halt at a particular point. This will give the user all the time in the world to choose a button. To react to a button click, you attach a behavior **to** each button. Once you've added your behaviors, you'll have a fully working interactive movie.

To summarize:

- You can add behaviors **to a frame** so that the associated ActionScript is triggered when the playhead reaches that frame. In this case, you will add something at frame 1 to tell Flash to stop at frame 1.

- You can attach a behavior **to a button** so that the ActionScript is only triggered when the user clicks the button. Here, the user triggers the event and the ActionScript handles it via the behavior code you will attach to the buttons.

> *Flash treats everything that happens as an event. Not only are nonperiodic occurrences (such as the user clicking a button) events, but so are sequential or periodic occurrences, such as entering a new frame—an event is generated on every new frame. This means that although attaching to a frame and attaching to a button may seem like two different techniques, they are actually exactly the same; you are attaching a behavior to the thing that creates the event.*

Adding behaviors to a frame

1. Select frame 1 in the actions layer. Display the Behaviors panel if it isn't already open (Window ➤ Behaviors). Notice that the text at the top of the panel reminds you that you will attach your behavior to frame 1 of the layer actions.

2. Using the plus sign (+), select Movieclip ➤ Goto and Stop at frame or label.

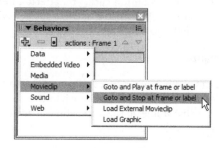

You will see the window shown in the following screenshot. The defaults are what you want (stop this timeline at frame 1), so you don't have to do anything other than make sure you are seeing what we say should be there.

Also worth noting is the little a that appears above frame 1 when you click OK. This signifies that code (or actions) have been added to the frame.

If you test the movie now, you will see that the timeline doesn't play through anymore—it simply stops at the first frame, which is exactly what you want.

You used a behavior to achieve your first objective of keeping the buttons visible—and static—so that the viewer can choose their favorite color via the buttons.

What Flash needs to know next is where you want to take the users when they click one of those buttons. To do this, you're going to attach some ActionScript to each button. These pieces of ActionScript will hook up each button to its dedicated piece of content—you can use the labels to tell Flash and your behaviors where to go. But Flash also needs to know **when** to move to a new frame.

Remember the events and event handlers that set off your "visit a friend" interaction earlier in this chapter? You want your interaction in this movie to start with the user doing something with their mouse pointer on or near your button. What you're trying to detect here is called a **button event**. You can ask Flash to detect one or more types of button event. The most common ones are as follows:

- A **Press** event occurs when the user clicks the button. You may think that this would be the event of choice to ask Flash to detect, but it actually causes Flash to race off and start doing new things as soon as the button is clicked. This doesn't leave any time for the user to see the button working—for instance, running the nice animation that you've built into the button.

- A **Release** event is when the user releases the mouse button after a press, and it's what you use in many situations because it allows you to see the button in its Down state.

If you think back to any sites you have visited recently, you will notice that many interface buttons you interact with don't detect a press, but instead act on an entire **click**, *a.k.a. a press-release.*

To detect a click, you only need to detect the second event (the release) because a press always precedes a release.

- A **Release Outside** event occurs when the user presses a button and then drags the mouse away from the button without releasing the mouse button. The event is triggered when the mouse button is finally released. Why would you use this event? If your buttons are very small, the user could inadvertently drag the mouse pointer outside the button area before they release it. In this situation, you could ask Flash to detect either Release or Release Outside.

- The **Roll Over** and **Roll Out** events are used to detect whether the mouse pointer is over a certain area. Buttons set up to detect only these two events don't usually look like buttons at all. For example, if you had a bitmap picture of the world and you wanted a bit of text at the bottom of the map to change to reflect which country the mouse pointer was over, you would add a lot of country-shaped buttons. Think of buttons asked to detect Roll Over and Roll Out events as "mouse position sensors" rather than true buttons, and this class of button event will start to make more sense.

Note that in real life, the only event of consequence is "clicking the button." In the world of computers, things are much more tightly defined, and even in something simple like hitting a button, there are more events than you might have expected. This shouldn't put you off, though, because in most cases, you only need one event—the Release event. You will only need the other ones once you start making all those cool and wacky interfaces that Flash is so famous for.

Adding a behavior to a button

1. You want to work with the buttons, so lock everything except the buttons layer. Click the pink button to select it. The Behaviors panel will change to show that you are about to attach a behavior to a button:

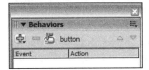

2. Click the plus sign (+) and select Movieclip ➤ Goto and Stop at frame or label. In the window that appears, change the bottom text entry box from 1 to pink as shown here:

Note that the behavior for a button is called "Movieclip" instead of "Movieclips and Buttons." Obviously, space is a premium in drop-down menus!

The Behavior panel will now change to reflect what you just attached. The left column describes the event and the right column displays what the event handler will do. To change either, simply click them (although they are all set up as you want them by default):

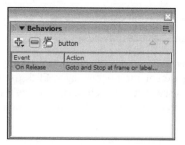

If you test the movie now, you will see that the pink button works. Clicking it will send the timeline to the frame you labeled pink, and the content for that frame (the you clicked pink! text) will be shown:

pick your favorite color

you clicked pink!

3. All you now need to do to complete your example is to add the same behavior to the blue button. Repeat steps 1 and 2, but this time click the blue button and enter the label blue.

Now your buttons are functional and can be used to allow the user to hop from place to place at will. That's interactivity!

Case study

In the last case study, you began creating your web portfolio page. In this section you'll finish this page, and make it fully functional.

1. Open your saved case study document from the previous chapter.

2. Open the Properties panel (if necessary), and click the content movie clip instance on the main time-line.

3. Type content_mc in the Instance Name text field in the Property inspector:

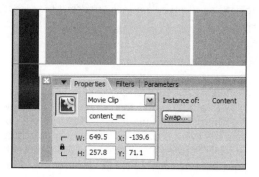

Giving it an instance name will allow you to control it with behaviors and ActionScript. You'll cover instance names in detail in the next chapter.

4. Double-click the content movie clip instance to enter Edit in Place mode.

5. Within the content movie clip, move the playhead to frame 91 and click the web content instance on the stage. Note that if you are unsure whether you have clicked on the right thing, you can see the name of the current thing you have clicked on (if it is a symbol) in the Properties panel—you should see the text Instance of: web content in the Properties panel, as per the image that follows.

6. Type web_mc into the Instance Name text field in the Property inspector:

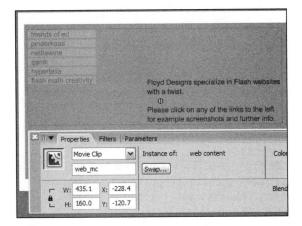

7. Double-click the web content symbol instance to edit it. You're now going to attach some behaviors to the buttons here to make them work. Before that, though, you need to stop the playhead on the first frame here.

8. Insert a new layer above all the others and rename it actions.

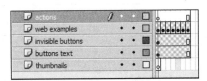

9. Select the first keyframe on the actions layer, and open the Behaviors panel (Window ➤ Behaviors).

10. Click the plus sign (+) in the Behaviors panel and select Movieclip ➤ Goto and Stop at frame or label.

11. In the dialog box that appears, select web_mc from within content_mc using the tree diagram (this will most likely be already selected, as this is the movie clip you are editing at the moment). This is the movie clip your behavior will stop.

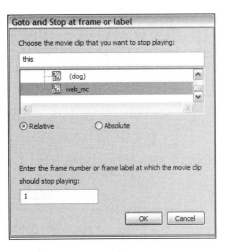

12. Click OK. That's your playhead halting done. Now on to the buttons.

Adding behaviors to the buttons

1. Select the invisible button covering the friends of ed text. The corresponding content for this button is on frame 2, so you need to send the playhead there with a behavior.

2. Click the plus sign (+) in the Behaviors panel, and select Movieclip ➤ Goto and Stop at frame or label.

3. In the dialog box that appears, make sure the top text field reads this and that web_mc is selected in the tree (they should all be this way by default). Change the bottom text field to read 2:

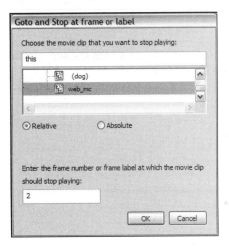

4. This refers to frame 2 within this movie clip time-line. Click OK to confirm this action, and the Behavior panel will change accordingly.

Now it's time to do the same for the rest of the buttons.

5. Click the invisible button covering the text pinderkaas.

6. Click the Add Behavior button (represented by a plus sign) in the Behavior panel. Select Movieclip ➤ Goto and Stop at frame or label.

7. In the dialog box, ensure the top field reads this, and the frame field is set to 3.

8. Repeat this process for the remaining buttons. Use the following details:

- nettle wine—frame 4
- qanik—frame 5
- hypertelia—frame 6
- flash math creativity—frame 7

Once you are done adding behaviors to all the buttons, you can give it a test. One useful way to test an individual piece of content alone, in this case a movie clip, is to use the Control ➤ Test Scene menu selection. This will preview the current scene (or timeline) that you are in. You can tell this (as usual) using the scene navigator above the timeline.

9. Select Control ➤ Test Scene to preview the movie.

Um . . . who turned out the lights? You will see nothing except a blue background! Where has the text gone? Well, the text is there, but it just happens to be the same color as the background so you can't see it. Let's switch the light on for a minute.

10. Close the preview and open the document proper-ties (Modify ➤ Document).

11. Change the background color to white and then click OK.

12. Preview the scene again using Control ➤ Test Scene:

hypertelia
Creative site created in 3D, Flash and PHP.

This time you can see the text, and better still, you can press the buttons to change the website preview on the right side. Before you change the background color back, there are a few more buttons to create. These new buttons will be thumbnails of the actual screen-shots, arranged in a diagonal row.

13. Close the preview movie.

14. Select the blank keyframe on the thumbnails layer and drag a copy of the `friendsofed_website.gif` image from the Library anywhere onto the stage. Lock all layers except thumbnails:

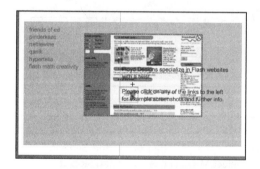

15. Open the Transform panel (*CTRL/CMD+T* or Window ➤ Transform) and select the image.

16. Ensure that Constrain is ticked, and type 30% into either of the top two text fields. Then press ENTER to render it:

17. Ensure that Snap Align is switched on (View ➤ Snapping ➤ Snap Align), and move the image so that it snaps with the button text field and the main text to its right.

18. When the image is in place, release it.

19. Select the image and duplicate it with Edit ➤ Duplicate or CTRL/CMD+D. This will place a duplicate down and to the right of the original. It will also instantly select the duplicate:

20. Select Edit ➤ Duplicate or press CTRL/CMD+D again. This will duplicate the duplicate, producing a duplicate of the duplicate down and to the right of the first duplicate!

21. Create duplicates in the same way until you have six images in all:

Flash has done you a great favor here because it has created a pretty pattern all on its own. (OK, you helped it out a little bit, but give it some credit please.) You're going to keep the images positioned as they are; all you need to do is to swap them with the required images.

22. Select the second image from the top and select Swap in the Property inspector.

23. In the dialog box that appears, select pinderkaas_website.gif.

24. Exchange the other images in the same way, in this order from top to bottom:

- nettle_wine.gif
- qanik.gif
- hypertelia.gif
- fmc.gif

It should then look like this:

Now you need to add interactivity to these images; at the moment, however, they are raw images. As you are already aware, to attach behaviors or ActionScript to objects, they have to be a button or movie clip symbol. You could convert them all by hand, but Flash can do this for you another way.

25. Select the top-left image and click the Add Behavior button (represented by the plus sign) in the Behavior panel. Choose Movieclip ➤ Goto and Stop at frame or label.

Immediately, Flash will see the error of your ways, and convert the selected object into a symbol (called Symbol 1 (or Symbol followed by another number).

26. As usual, the Behaviors panel will appear:

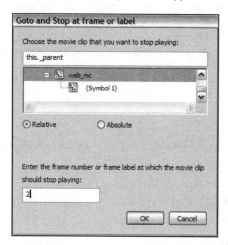

Symbol 1 here is the generic instance and symbol name that Flash has given your selected object. It's not particularly intuitive for future modifications, but you can live with it here. If it really annoys you (and it should!), you can go back and change the symbol names in the Library when you have finished this chapter.

27. Click OK to add the behavior. Now you need to do the same with the other images, linking to their corresponding frames.

28. Select the other images in the row, and repeat the process just outlined, each time selecting web_mc, and specifying frames 3–7 as necessary. Remember each time to select the web_mc instance so the top text field reads this._parent. Here's the keyframe list:

- Frame 3: Pinderkaas
- Frame 4: nettlewine
- Frame 5: qanik
- Frame 6: hypertelia
- Frame 7: flash math creativity

29. Extend the frames on the thumbnails layer to frame 7 by pressing the *F5* key.

30. Select Control ➤ Test Scene to test the thumbnail buttons. Now your viewers have two forms of navigation.

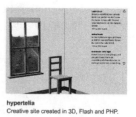

hypertelia
Creative site created in 3D, Flash and PHP.

Now that you can see that it works, you can change the background color back to its original setting.

31. Select Modify ➤ Document and change the background color back to dark blue (#003366).

Letting the users know where they are

In this section, you're going to label each page to let users know which page they are currently viewing.

1. From your current position within the web content movie clip, step back to the Content movie clip.

The next part is simple but a little fiddly, so here's a quick heads-up of what the timeline will look like when you are done:

2. Click frame 92 of the pages layer and insert a blank keyframe by pressing the *F7* key. You've done this to prevent the web page from appearing on the timeline where it shouldn't (i.e., it should only appear on the "Web" page—the page you see when you click the Web button at the top left).

3. Click frame 91 of the pages layer and select the Text tool. Lock all layers except the layer pages.

4. Type FLOYD DESIGNS :: WEB in 15-point bold Verdana anywhere on the stage. Set the color as #003366.

5. With Snap Align still turned on, position the text field in the white area above the top right of the green rectangle. When it snaps vertically and horizontally to the green rectangle, release it:

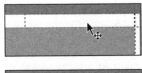

6. Copy the text field using Edit ➤ Copy or CTRL/CMD+C.

7. Insert a blank keyframe (*F7*) on frame 116 of the pages layer.

8. Select Edit ➤ Paste to place a copy of the last text field on the stage.

9. Double-click the text field and change it to read FLOYD DESIGNS :: PRINT.

10. Drag the text field using the Selection tool to snap in the top-right corner as you did with the last one.

11. Click frame 117 of the pages layer and insert a blank keyframe to prevent the print page from appearing elsewhere in the movie. If you didn't do this, the print page would still be shown during the closing animation.

12. Insert a blank keyframe on frame 140 and paste another copy of the text. This time change it to read FLOYD DESIGNS :: ABOUT and position it in the top-right corner.

13. Insert a blank keyframe on frame 141 to stop the about page from running on for too long.

14. Insert a blank keyframe on frame 165, paste the text, and change it to FLOYD DESIGNS :: EMAIL.

15. Position it as before, and insert a blank keyframe on frame 166 to clear it.

That's it. Before you finish this chapter, there is one tiny thing left to do—add some sound!

Adding sound to the buttons

1. In the interests of safety, save the case study in its current state.

2. Double-click the symbol generic button in the Library to edit it. This is how it looks at the moment:

3. Click the Down state frame, and press *F5* to extend the previous state onto it.

4. Insert a new layer and name it sound:

5. Insert a blank keyframe on the Down state of the sound layer (*F6*). You're going to trigger a sound to play when the button has been clicked.

6. Select File ➤ Import ➤ Import to Library to search for a sound to import.

7. Select a suitable sound, or use our file, `blip.wav`.

8. Select the keyframe on the Down state of the sound layer, and choose the BLIP.WAV sound from the Sound drop-down in the Properties panel.

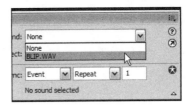

Your button will now have a sound attached to its Down state:

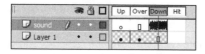

9. Test the movie using Control ➤ Test Movie (or *CTRL/CMD+ENTER*) and click any of the buttons at the top left of the screen. Even though they don't actually control your navigation yet, the length of the sound will just about cover the opening shape tween of each page. Nice!

10. Finally! Save the case study file.

In the next chapter, you'll use ActionScript to pull things together so that you can interact using the main buttons.

Reader's voice: Hey! Hey! Hey! What about all those cool filter effects and stuff we looked at? Can we add them now? They will make this site look **much** *better . . .*

Our answer: Well, first, they are only available to Flash Professional users, and we don't want to add them just yet because they will make the site look different for the non-pro users. There is a bigger reason, though—too much eye candy added early on in a design can hide bad design. It's far better to add effects when you have a solid design in front of you, because then the effects make a good design look better, rather than making a poor design look passable. Thus, we add effects when we have all the basic stuff—the user interface, symbol placement, and animations—working correctly.

Summary

In this chapter, we introduced the important concept of interactivity, and you started to see how Flash implements this using behaviors.

This was an important chapter because the simple examples that you've seen here will be a foundation that you can build on, both in the next chapter specifically and in the rest of the book more generally, because they establish the core idea of interactivity and the way it's implemented via events and event handlers.

You saw that

- Timeline effects allow you to quickly create professional animations, the parameters of which can be customized and modified at any time.

- Frequently used sequences of actions within Flash can be saved as commands. These actions are selected from the History panel.

- Some History panel entries, denoted with a red x, cannot be saved as part of a command.

- Interactivity is about bringing the Flash movie to life and giving the user an interesting and satisfying experience.

- The principles of events and event handlers are at the heart of interactivity. Events—like a user clicking a button—happen, and you create actions or behavior that will respond and cope with these events.

- A powerful way of adding interaction in Flash is by using buttons. Buttons can have media—such as animation, sound, and movie clips—embedded in their default states, and they can be made even more intelligent by attaching ActionScript to the button events that buttons can detect.

- ActionScript is the string that ties together all the components of a Flash movie or website. In this chapter, you didn't write the code, but more importantly, you learned a lot about the principles that underpin ActionScript.

- Behaviors can be attached to frames in the timeline, or to buttons and movie clip instances—that is, buttons and movie clips that are on a timeline.

- You can use behaviors to jump to specific areas inside your movies, and this stops your movies from being fixed animations on rails, and turns them into interactive content, where the user decides where they want to go and what they want to see.

In the next chapter, you'll explore the next stage in your journey toward Flash ActionScript. You will no longer use behaviors—you will write ActionScript directly. Sounds daunting, but you have already seen most of the theory, so don't worry!

Chapter 10

ACTIONS AND INTERACTIONS

What we'll cover in this chapter:

- Introducing ActionScript, the programming language that makes Macromedia Flash so powerful
- Understanding syntax
- Looking at the ActionScript environment and how to write scripts in Flash (and how not to)
- Creating interactive Flash sites with buttons and your own handwritten ActionScript

This chapter moves you a significant way along in your Flash journey. You're coming to the crest of a hill, and a whole new vista of Flash possibilities is going to open up. There, bathed in sunlight, is the land of **ActionScript**. In the previous chapter, you looked at behaviors, which are self-contained ActionScript building blocks that prevent you from getting your hands dirty with writing code yourselves. That's fine for basic sites, but to understand Flash properly (and to use all its advanced features effectively), you have to know at least basic ActionScript.

One thing we should say right at the beginning is that ActionScript is not for everyone. If, after dipping your toes into its waters for a while, you find it confusing and bewildering, that's fine. You may decide to use behaviors instead for now, and revisit ActionScript again later. Not knowing ActionScript well is not the same as not knowing Flash well: Flash is a very flexible tool and there are always at least two ways to do everything—so do it the way that feels right for you.

ActionScript vs. behaviors

In Chapter 9, we likened clicking a Flash button to what happens when you ring someone's doorbell. Having a Flash button all by itself is like ringing the doorbell at a house where nobody's home or where the wiring's been disconnected.

There are two ways to add wiring to a doorbell. One is to go out and buy a doorbell off the shelf. All you need to do is attach it to a wall, connect the wires, and plug it in. You don't have to do much else other than tighten a few wire terminals and drill a couple of holes in the wall. That's a cool way of doing it because all the electronics that control the chime are encased in the box, and you don't have to worry about it. That's also the problem, though—you **don't get an understanding of how it works**. You can't fix it if it breaks, and more importantly, you can't upgrade it if you want it to, for example, control the back door chime as well as the front.

The harder way around is to learn enough about electronics to design your own doorbell. Once you do that, you realize that there wasn't that much in the box anyway! It's only a little circuit that drives a buzzer, with

the doorbell completing the circuit. Furthermore, when you look at the "off the shelf" doorbell, you might start to notice little oddities, like the transformer in there that is configured for U.S. voltage levels of 110V, or the 240V you see in some other countries, such as England. There may even be some sort of selector switch at the front of the box that allows you to choose between the *Mission Impossible* theme tune, *Boys of Summer*, or *Jingle Bells*, so the bell plays your chosen tune whenever someone presses the button. The point is, if you design your own doorbell, you don't need to mess with these extra features; you simply design what you want, making the whole thing simpler. And Flash is the same:

- You can use a drag-and-drop behavior. It's fast and efficient, but at the expense of reducing your understanding of the problem, and it offers a solution that addresses problems that may not be part of your particular task. It's also a "one size fits all" solution—and how many times have you bought a one-size-fits-all shirt and thought "Mmm, fits perfectly, almost as if it was tailor-made for me?" Me neither.

- You can write your own code. It's a harder route, but it opens up a much wider vista than just creating button scripts. You can write other things that you can't use behaviors for, such as Flash games, advanced interfaces that no one else has even thought about (let alone wrote a behavior for), and so on. You can also create custom code that is exactly suited to your needs and fits the problem perfectly. A cool side effect of writing your own code is that you can extend it later, so over time, your website will evolve from a simple button menu affair to one of those oh-so-fancy Flash sites where the whole thing is so integrated, you can't even **see** the buttons, never mind attach a behavior to them.

> *Another cool side effect of knowing ActionScript is that there is currently a big commercial demand for it, and a lot of jobs require ActionScript. If your aim is to become a commercial Flash web designer, then knowing ActionScript will open many doors.*

Don't worry if scripting puts you off. ActionScript is arguably one of the easier web scripting languages to learn if you are a designer for a number of reasons:

- **It is a visual language.** ActionScript is most often used to create animation or interactivity, so the end result is visual.

- **There is only one "latest version" of it.** Some web scripting languages (such as JavaScript or PHP) have a number of different dialects, and some lines of code do slightly different things depending on which browser you are using. ActionScript is much less variable, and this makes it easier to pick up.

- **It is integrated into the Flash authoring tool.** You don't need to move away from the familiar Flash authoring environment to use ActionScript, and this makes it very easy to integrate into what you already know about Flash.

- **It has a beginners "script assist" mode.** Most programming languages have to be typed directly into a text editor. With ActionScript, you can do the same (and most long-term ActionScripters end up entering their lines that way), but as a beginner you can use the Script Assist mode. In this mode, Flash holds your hand much more, and assists you in writing your code.

- **It can be as difficult as you want it to be.** Where you end up with ActionScript is up to you. There is no "high end" or "low end" with ActionScript—if it creates the Flash content you need to create, then everything is good! ActionScript can be simple 5-to-20-line scripts that control buttons and time-lines within a single SWF. You can also write 1,000-to-5,000-line web applications in Flash, and to write such code, you would most likely need to learn a particular type of ActionScript called class-based ActionScript.

To start demonstrating ActionScript's features, you're going to revisit the example you created back in Chapter 9, but this time you will not be using behaviors—you'll write the darn thing yourself.

Don't worry because we will be taking this all slowly. We have already used behaviors, and we'll start writing our own code by using the Script Assist mode in this chapter. We will move on to try direct typing later in the book.

Before you can add some ActionScript, you need to see what ActionScript actually **is**.

Scripts, programs, and code—it's all Geek/Greek to me

That's what a lot of you are thinking so far, right? You have questions like "I thought code was written to create something called a computer program, so what's this 'script' thing?" and "Why am I programming inside a visual animation application?"

Programming and scripting

When you write a totally new stand-alone application (such as Flash itself, Microsoft Word, or Doom 3), you write in languages such as C++. This is a complex endeavor, requiring teams of highly skilled programmers.

When you just want to add some customizations to Microsoft Word for yourself, create a new level for Doom, or add a bit of intelligence to a web page, you don't need to create applications; you just need to tell the current application what to do. That is what a **scripting language** does. ActionScript is a scripting language—it tells the Flash Player what to do, and it requires the Flash Player to be present before it will work. Rather than a program or application, a scripting language is used to create, um . . . scripts. These are one or more short sections of code that tell the main application what to do. In Flash, you attach scripts to keyframes.

You can attach scripts to other things, such as directly to a button or movie clip, but a modern ActionScript coding style avoids this. As a beginner, attaching scripts to keyframes alone will give you the good habits needed to become an advanced ActionScripter much quicker, and also has the cool side effect of making your learning curve much simpler. Better all round!

Programming languages and scripting languages are not the same thing:

- Programming languages are meant for heavy-duty projects like creating Photoshop from scratch. They require around a zillion years at college to learn, and most people don't bother trying because life is short enough as it is.

- Scripting languages are designed to create much simpler and shorter bits of code that specify how an application should run. Because they are designed to create simpler stuff than application building languages, you don't need that zillion years in college to understand them.

That's a real relief to the typical beginner Flash designer, who's likely thinking "Whuh? Programming? I'm a graphic/web designer—there must be some mistake!" In fact, scripting languages are designed on the premise that the people using them will not be trained programmers at all. Phew!

Scripting and animation

The stuff you've done so far in Flash has been cool, but (apart from behaviors) has been defined at authoring time. When you create a tween animation, it will do exactly the same thing every time you run it. Well, folks just loved all those wacky Flash animations and spent hours watching them five years ago, but nowadays the novelty has lessened, and folks want to interact. They want animations that do things differently every time and provide things like challenging entertainment or efficient user interfaces. They want to be able to play a Flash version of Asteroids online, they want to book a hotel room using an interactive Flash interface, or they want an e-learning application that not only teaches how to learn Microsoft Office, but also emulates it.

ActionScript-based content can do all this, and has become more and more important in the last few years. Tweening, although still a big part of Flash, is becoming less frequently used.

Understanding scripting

Rather than go straight into animation, you will rework the navigation example you looked at in Chapter 9, this time without behaviors—you will write the code yourselves. Before you do that, though, you need to get deeper into ActionScript and cover a number of important concepts:

- ActionScript syntax
- The Flash scripting environment

Syntax

Syntax is something that is common to all languages, not just computer languages.

> *Syntax refers to the way you structure words into sentences. It doesn't refer to what the words mean, but only to the structures that they are placed into form-readable text or intelligible conversation.*

In spoken English, you have a wide and varied syntax, full of special clauses and more than one way to say the same thing. There are very good reasons for all this variability and redundancy:

- The different ways of saying the same thing add to the **expressiveness** of English; you can add emphasis or a personal style to what you say or write.

- The redundancy in the spoken word means that you can understand what someone means even if you don't understand every word. You can usually understand what others are saying even if they use a different dialect or speak with an unfamiliar accent because the redundancy means you only have to pick up **most** of what was said.

The big difference between human syntax and computer syntax is that computers don't expect unfamiliar dialects or accents; computer language syntaxes are typically simple but very precise. This precision can seem totally alien to us; you don't usually expect someone to fail to understand you just because you don't speak or write in exactly the same accent as them—but that's the way computer languages work!

Luckily, ActionScript has very few syntax rules. In fact, it has only three that you need to think about when writing basic scripts:

Rule 1: End each line with a semicolon

Each line of script ends with a ";"—the following are both permissible:

```
line;
line;
line;

line; line; line;
```

If you press *ENTER* at the end of each line, Flash will be able to guess where all the semicolons need to go, so this is also OK (although you should get into the habit of putting the semicolons in—it fosters good practice that will pay dividends when you get onto more advanced scripting):

```
line
line
line
```

The following, however, **is not** OK because Flash has no way of knowing where a new line starts:

```
line line line
```

Rule 2: The object, method, and argument

In English, you very often have three main types of word in most sentences: a noun (person, place, or thing); a verb (action); and an adjective or adverb (description).

Put together, you have sentences like "John runs quickly."

Flash is the same, except the syntax is **much** more precise, and also much simpler. Instead of a noun, you have an **instance** (also called an **object**); instead of a verb you have a **method**; and instead of an adjective/adverb, you have an **argument**. Each means something similar to your noun-verb-adjective in English syntax.

Computers are precise, so you can't use subjective terms like **quickly**. You and I have some idea of what quickly means, and the range of values that would be understood as quick movement if John was a toddler, an Olympic runner, or if he were running through waist-high molasses. Trouble is, a computer doesn't have the same subjective worldview we do because it doesn't know anything about our world. Instead, it understands only nonsubjective or numerical terms—called **arguments** (and also called **parameters** in some quarters)—such as "John runs at 5 miles an hour." The 5 isn't subjective; it's a value that needs nothing else to describe it—it's precise, and that makes it an argument that Flash can work with.

The argument is always enclosed in brackets after the method, and the object and action are always separated by a dot (.). In ActionScript, this sentence would become *John.run(5)*.

Note that in some cases, the `object.method(argument)` structure is actually a single line of ActionScript, so from rule 1, you could say the following if the fact that John is running at 5 mph is all you wanted to say: *John.run(5);*.

> *Some of you may have noticed that the computer version of your line has changed in its implication somewhat. "John runs quickly" is **descriptive**, whereas `John.run(5);` seems more like a **directive**. The computer version looks like you are telling John to do something, rather than describing what he is doing. This is not a mistranslation; it is a window into what code actually is—a set of **instructions** or **commands** that tell the computer what it should be doing. You will even sometimes catch programmers referring to code as instructions or commands because that is what code really is.*

The `object.method(argument)` form is not always written out in full, because some of its parts can be **implied**. For example, there is an ActionScript command called `stop()`. This has no object and no arguments. It still uses them, though (the `stop()` command means "stop the current timeline on the current frame," so the implied object is the current timeline, and the implied argument is the current frame); they are just not written in the line for brevity (for a stop, the object and argument is always the same, hence there is no need to write it).

However, even if you don't need the object or the arguments, it is still a good idea to consider what object and argument Flash will actually end up using, if only because one of the biggest reasons ActionScript code runs but doesn't do what you want it to (called a "runtime error") is when you are incorrectly assuming the missing object and/or argument. More on this later.

Rule 3: The code block

In the same way that English sentences can form paragraphs, ActionScript lines can form a **block**. A block encloses a number of lines, and begins with an opening curly bracket, also known as a brace ({) and ends with a closing curly bracket (}).

```
{
  line;
  line;
  line;
}
```

A code block is much like a paragraph in that both contain a section of lines that are related in some way. In normal language, a paragraph contains sentences that are related to the same subject or theme. A paragraph is really a line that has grown too long—if you have so much to say that it doesn't fit in a single line, you make that line into a paragraph of lines.

Code blocks are similar. A block of code can be a way of creating a "line that is so long it now needs to be a paragraph." This type of block is called a function, and it is the most often used block in Flash.

As we mentioned earlier, code is directive; it tells Flash what to do. So there is another reason a block is important in Flash. A block can be used to tell Flash how to run the lines or what task the block represents.

Here's an example of each type in pseudo-code (i.e., plain text that is not real code, but is formatted in the correct syntax):

```
Do this ten times {
  line;
  line;
  line;
}
```

A **loop block** lets Flash know that the lines within the block need to be repeated a number of times. This is a "how to run the lines block"—rather than run the lines within the block once, the lines need to be repeated a number of times.

Loops are very useful in coding, because most things you get computers to do are repetitive or number-crunching tasks that require the same set of instructions to be repeated many times.

A block is also used in event handlers; the start of the block denotes which event you are looking at, and the block contents are the event handler.

```
When you see a click{
  Do these lines;
  Do these lines;
  Do these lines;
}
```

This is a "what the task represents" block. It tells Flash that this block is an event handler for a click, and the lines within the block should be run each time a click is detected.

> There is one more, final rule. This final rule (which you will look at later) has to do with building **expressions**. If you understand 4 = 3 + 1 then you're already a lot closer to understanding expressions than you might think!

And that's it! These are the core rules you need to know to write basic scripts. There are also a few other rules that, although not specific to ActionScript, are part of good ActionScript style.

Camel case

When you name anything in ActionScript, it's common practice to use camel case. ActionScript doesn't like spaces (and when it does, they are there for your benefit—Flash actually removes them internally before running each line), so you have problems when you want to use an instance called John Doe instead of simply John. The way to get round this is to use camel case—John Doe becomes johnDoe, New Masters of Flash becomes newMastersOfFlash, and camel case becomes camelCase. The rule for creating camel case instance names is to start with lower case, and add an uppercase letter at the start of each new word.

> It's called camel case because of the humps you create by adding capitals in the middle of a string of lowercase letters.

Indenting

If you look at Rule 3, you will notice that the script lines within a code block are indented. This makes reading a script much simpler because it's easy to see which lines are in a block and which are outside it. Indenting is such a good idea that Flash adds it automatically to your scripts as you write, as you will see later.

Use code blocks often

Written language looks better and is more readable (or "scans better" as editors seem to call it) if it is written using paragraphs. Once you get into paragraphs, you will find that it also makes writing as well as reading easier, because it adds **structure** to your text. Your writing will be split into paragraphs where each new change or concept has its own paragraph. This makes what you were thinking about as you were writing easier to follow, because the structure puts each of your lines into a definite **context**.

Code is the same; it is easier to understand code if you split your code into separate blocks, each of which performs a specific task. When you read your code back, most of your lines of code will now have a context—"this line of code is part of this task." Like a well-edited book, your code will then "scan better."

> The "Use code blocks often" rule is an interesting one, because the actual implementation of this rule can totally change the look and feel of your code.
>
> When you are starting out, you will probably separate your code into blocks only when you have to (using such blocks as loops and event handlers). This style of coding is useful for **small scripts** (10–20 lines) because it is easy to write and requires very little planning.
>
> Later on, you may realize that using blocks to structure your code into functional blocks (where you split your code into larger tasks or "functions") makes sense. This gives your code a high-level structure that is based around what it is doing, and this type of code is often called **structured code**.
>
> Finally, when you are building very large Flash applications, you will start to use very formalized code blocks, where you divide your code into general "templates" for tasks that you know your code will need to perform often. This third way of writing is called **class-based programming** (because class is another way of saying template). It is useful for managing projects that would otherwise require long scripts because it can be used to separate your long script into many simpler, smaller scripts.
>
> Learning ActionScript is a great way of getting into programming, because ActionScript is one of the few languages that allows you to not only write code in any of the three styles, but also mix and match the styles within a single FLA!

Those are the basic syntax rules. What about actually entering code into Flash?

The Flash scripting environment

To create basic scripts in Flash, you use two panels: the **Actions** panel and the **Properties** panel. If you are using the vanilla panel settings (select Window ➤ Workspace Layout ➤ Default if you want to get back to them), the two panels appear in the lower-middle docking area, as shown in the following graphic:

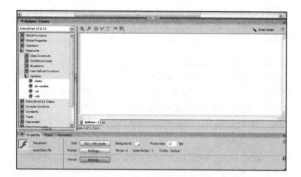

The Actions panel is used to enter scripts (from the default setup, you will have to open it to see it in its full glory). The big blank pane to the right of the panel is the text entry area for your scripting.

The Properties panel is used to add the link between ActionScript and the graphical interface: the **instance name**. This is the "John" in the example we talked about earlier.

First, a bit of setup. Scripts can get rather long and contain lots of lines, so it's a good idea to number them. To do this, select the Actions panel's drop-down menu (via the little pop-up menu at the top right of the panel) and make sure Line Numbers is checked.

Let's enter some code. You'll redo the button example from the previous chapter, this time writing it all yourselves—with a little help from flash via Script Assist.

Writing your first script

You now know enough to do away with behaviors and write the code yourself, so that is exactly what you will do!

You'll start with the button symbols you created in the previous chapter. You will find `scriptStart.fla`, the FLA to start this exercise, in the code download for this chapter. It is the same as the example in Chapter 9, minus the behaviors.

If you have grown attached your own version of the FLA, all you need to do is remove all the behaviors so you can replace them with your own code. To do this:

1. Select frame 1 in the layer actions (the keyframe with an a). In the Behaviors panel (Window ➤ Behaviors), select the one behavior that you see (it will have a Goto and Stop at frame or label action) by clicking its Action column. Click the minus (–) icon at the top left to delete it.

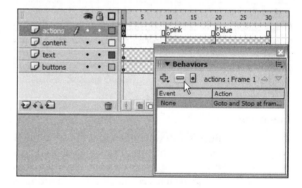

2. Select each button in turn, and in the Behaviors panel, select the behavior and delete it with the minus icon as before.

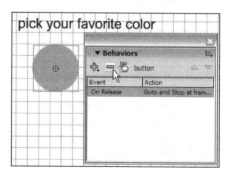

For the more lazy/cautious, you can also look at the completed FLA for this exercise, `scriptCompleted.fla`.

If you test the movie as it stands, the timeline doesn't stop, and you will see the text below the buttons change between you clicked pink, you clicked blue!, and no text. You first need to halt the timeline on frame 1.

Adding your own scripts using Script Assist

1. Select frame 1 in the actions layer, then click the Script Assist button (in the top-right corner of the Actions panel).

The top of the Actions panel will now change to show the Script Assist area. This will change as you create your script, providing help in creating your lines. At the moment, it isn't doing much (because neither are we), but it will soon spring into life (because we will)!

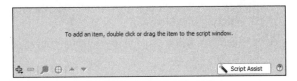

The top-left pane in the Actions panel contains a set of icons that look like little books with arrows on the front. The first book is labeled Global Functions. Click this book icon to open the book. You will now see the book icon change to an open book, and a list of more books will appear below it. Click the one labeled Timeline Control.

You should have opened a path of books that looks like this (expand the panel to get a better view if you need to):

2. Inside the open Timeline Control book you'll see a list of circled arrows. These are ActionScript actions.

3. You're in the right ballpark; all you have to do is find the action that will do what you want—stop a timeline. It doesn't take much guesswork—you want to use the stop method (they are listed alphabetically). Double-click it. You will see the following appear in the right pane:

This is your full action. How do we know this? Because the Script Assist area is not asking us to do anything!

309

> *"Actions" are a simplified form of the more general* `object.method(argument)`. *You don't need to specify the object with actions (in this case, the timeline you want to stop) because Flash assumes you want to stop the timeline the code is attached to. This makes actions easier to work with.*

4. Finally, according to the rules discussed earlier, you'll probably be thinking about adding an argument at this point. However, you don't need to tell Flash how to stop ("stop" is precise enough as it is; you want Flash to stop now and do nothing). You don't therefore need an argument, so the line is complete.

> *We don't need to enter an argument, because "stop" doesn't need one, in much the same way that the sentence "John stops running" could be written as* `John.stop()`.
>
> *Notice that we write* `stop()` *rather than* `stop`. *We add the* () *around the argument even when there is no argument. What is really happening here is that we are* **actually specifying an argument, but that argument is nothing**. *The* `object.method(argument)` *syntax is always used internally by Flash even when some of it is not needed.*
>
> *It's worth noting that when we say a method doesn't need arguments, we are really just saying "Flash knows what it needs to do by implication, so we don't need to provide the arguments." All methods need arguments; it's just that sometimes we don't have to provide them explicitly. We still provide them in some way—for example, we add the* `stop()` *action to the timeline we want to stop, rather than add that timeline as an argument.*

Congratulations! You've just entered your first line of ActionScript. Some of you are thinking "Whoa! All that work just to type **that!?** I could have entered that by hand!" Well, exactly! As you learn ActionScript, you will realize that although there are many objects, methods, and arguments, 90 percent of your code will consist of about 5–10 percent of the available ActionScript, and you will very soon know them all by heart. When you do, you will be writing `stop();` as fast as you can type it, probably about a second slower than you just read it now!

If you test the movie now, you will see that the timeline stops at frame 1. Next stop, the buttons.

Getting back to the noun-verb-adjective analogy, you know that it is John who is running in the sentence "John runs quickly" because you see his name. You do not yet have names for your two buttons, and you need these before you can add the instance part of your syntax. The first thing you need to do is give your two buttons instance names.

5. Select the pink button. In the Properties panel, you will see the following:

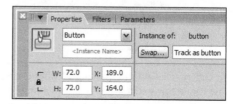

6. The text entry box currently with <Instance Name> in it is where you specify the name of the instance you want to attach your code to. Change the instance name by clicking anywhere inside the box and entering pinkButton.

7. Do the same for the blue button, calling it blueButton.

> *ActionScript 2.0, which is what you are writing, is case sensitive. This means that* pinkButton *is not the same as* pinkbutton *or* Pinkbutton. *This has two implications:*
>
> - You have to type instance names exactly, or Flash will get it wrong by assuming you mean another name.
> - You can have buttons called pinkbutton and pinkButton, and Flash will recognize them as two different buttons. Although you can do this, it is a recipe for confusion, and we strongly recommend that you use only distinct camel case instance names throughout your ActionScript.

Now that you have instance names, ActionScript can start referring to them, and you can create the code for the event-event handler pair for them.

8. You now need to add an onRelease event for each button. Using the book and arrow icons in the left pane, go to ActionScript 2.0 Classes ➤ Movie ➤ Button ➤ Event Handlers ➤ onRelease and double-click it.

You will see the following lines appear as lines 2 and 3:

```
not_set_yet.onRelease = function() {
};
```

This defines a (currently empty) event handler block for a button onRelease event. An onRelease event occurs in much the same way as our button release behaviors worked—when the user releases the button, the onRelease event handler will run. The onRelease event handler will be whatever we place between the { on line 2 and the } on line 3.

9. At the moment, Flash doesn't know which button we want to define this event handler for.

Continue the line by clicking in the object field. Enter pinkButton in this field, making sure that you enter this name exactly. When you have entered this instance name, your code will look like this:

```
stop();
pinkButton.onRelease = function() {
};
```

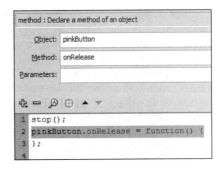

If you are not confident with your typing skills, you can get Flash to enter pinkButton for you. The little target icon will become available when you click inside the Object field (you may have to press the BACKSPACE key for this to happen). Click this icon.

This brings up the Insert Target Path window. Select pinkButton from the tree at the top, and make sure the Relative radio button is selected.

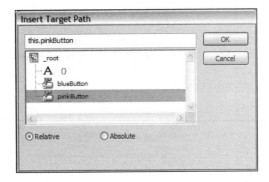

If you choose this route, the code will look like this:

```
stop();
this.pinkButton.onRelease = function() {
};
```

This adds this.pinkButton instead of pinkButton. For our code, these two instance names are equivalent (we will see what this means later).

You just added a code block that defines a button onRelease event. The start of line 1 defines the instance you are defining your event for, pinkButton, and the event (which is really just a special type of method) is onRelease. At the end of line 1, you have an opening curly bracket to define the start of the code block that will be the event handler, and line 3 is the closing curly bracket that ends the block. Your text cursor is at line 2—Flash is waiting for you to enter the event handler code in the block it has just created.

10. Make sure line 2 of your code is highlighted (click it if it is not). Using the books again, go to Global functions ➤ Timeline Control, and double-click goto. You code will now look like this:

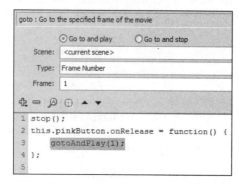

Select the Go to and stop radio button at the top of the Script Assist area. Using the Type drop-down, select Frame Label. Select the Frame drop-down and select pink.

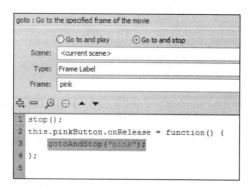

We have now completed the code to

■ Stop the main timeline (line 1)
■ Add an event handler for pinkButton (lines 2–4).

Script assist mode always displays syntax errors (or missing parts of a line) in red, so if there is no red in your script, you can now test it.

You should see that clicking the pink button works, but clicking the blue one does nothing. We still need to add the event handler for the blue button. We *could* add the handler for the blue button in the same way we added the pink button's handler, but there is an easier way: we can jump out of Script Assist and copy and paste the code we already have:

11. Click the Script Assist button to exit Script Assist mode.

12. Highlight lines 2 through 4 and press CTRL/CMD+C to copy the lines to the clipboard. Place the cursor on line 5 (if you don't have a line 5, place the cursor at the end of line 4 and press ENTER). Press CTRL/CMD+V to paste the copied lines.

```
1 stop();
2 this.pinkButton.onRelease = function() {
3     gotoAndStop("pink");
4 };
5 this.pinkButton.onRelease = function() {
6     gotoAndStop("pink");
7 };
8
```

13. We now have two identical event handlers. To start customizing the second copy so that it becomes the handler for the blue button, jump back into Script Assist mode by clicking the Script Assist icon. You may be more comfortable with typing the code directly, in which case you can elect to stick with direct typing.

14. To change line 5, select this line, then replace pinkButton with blueButton.

15. To change line 6, select the Frame drop-down and select blue.

That's the full script. Test the movie and you should see the same things happen as you saw in Chapter 9. If you don't, the following tips may help:

- Check that the instance names that show up in the Properties Panel when you select each button are **exactly** the same as the ones you use in the code: pinkButton and blueButton.
- The two frame labels are pink and blue.
- The code is exactly the same as the listing just shown.
- Compare your FLA with our finished one, scriptCompleted.fla.

What have you gained by writing your own script instead of using behaviors? Well, you gained a number of very cool features:

- You have all your code in one place—frame 1 of the main timeline. Behaviors are spread all over the place, and it is **very** easy to forget where they are in a large FLA. This way, you have a single script, which you can find easily, and even print out if you need to.
- The code is much shorter and more compact than the behavior code because you made it do **exactly** what you need and no more.
- You can customize or extend it later.

Actually, you're going to customize/extend it right now.

Linking your movie to a URL

In this exercise, you're going to use ActionScript to redirect the user to a web page with a specific URL, depending on which button they click. You're going to do this by adding more ActionScript.

Using ActionScript to jump to a URL

You're going to create two very simple drawings of a girl and a boy to display underneath the stereotypically color-gendered content in the goto keyframes (pink for a girl and blue for a boy, like your buttons). You're then going to put an **invisible button** behind each drawing and use ActionScript to link the drawing to a web page when it's clicked.

> *The completed FLA for this part of the chapter is* scriptURL.fla *if you get stuck.*

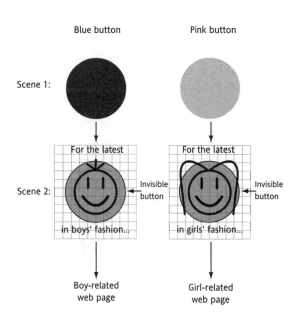

1. Continue using the same button-based movie you used in the previous exercise.

2. Create two new graphic symbols called girl and boy, and in each one, draw an image of a girl and a boy, respectively.

   Leave it to your own ingenuity and good taste to create your own boy and girl drawings, but make sure you include a line of text that'll entice the user to click the invisible buttons that you'll add soon:

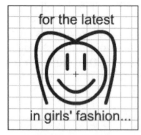 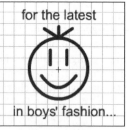

3. Lock all other layers except content. In the content layer select the keyframe pink. Drag an instance of girl out of the Library and position it under the you clicked pink! text. Do the same for the keyframe blue using the boy graphic symbol.

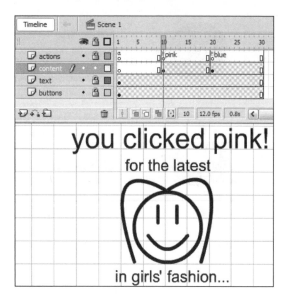

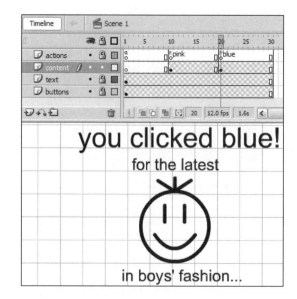

4. Add a new layer called url buttons as shown. Lock all layers except url buttons. Add new keyframes at frames 10 and 20 in this layer.

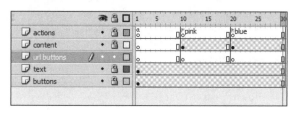

5. Select frame 10 in the url buttons layer, click your button symbol in the Library, and drag it onto the stage behind the girl symbol.

6. Scale the button so that it completely surrounds girl. You should have something like this:

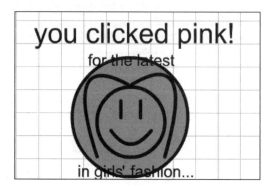

Now you want to take users to a new web page when they click the button behind girl.

The ActionScript you attach to this button will tell Flash to go to the web page specified when the user clicks and releases the mouse over this button. You do this using the getURL action.

7. Before you can control the new button, you need to give your new button an instance name. Select it, and in the Properties panel, give it the name girlLink:

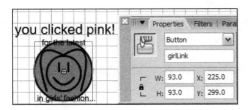

8. Repeat steps 5, 6, and 7, to add a button called boyLink on frame 20 of the url buttons layer:

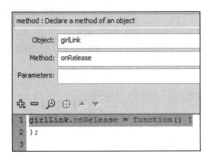

9. Select frame 10 in the actions layer (the one labeled pink). You may have to unlock this layer first. You will add your event handler for the girlLink button here. In the right pane of the Actions panel, select ActionScript 2.0 Classes ➤ Movie ➤ Button ➤ Event Handlers and double-click onRelease. Select the Object field in the Script Assist area and enter girlLink.

method : Declare a method of an object	
Object:	girlLink
Method:	onRelease
Parameters:	

```
1 girlLink.onRelease = function() {
2 };
3
```

10. You now need to add something within the event handler block you have just created. Select the Global functions ➤ Browser/Network book and double-click the getURL action. This action makes the browser open a new URL. Click the URL field and in it, add any URL that takes your fancy, such as http://www.friendsofed.com—or a URL of your choice—it can even point to a file on your own machine if you like:

Notice that you've added the whole URL here, including the http:// bit, making the address an **absolute** one. It's always a good idea to do this in Flash; otherwise the command may have strange effects on certain servers.

> *Why not add your script to that already on frame 1? Well, you can only define a script for an instance name if that instance name currently exists. As soon as Flash sees an instance name in a script, it will look on the current frame. If it doesn't find it, it will not be able to do anything with the associated script lines because there is nothing to control with them. You can only define scripts for an instance name for your button when that button is actually on the timeline, and the first frame you can do this for our* girlLink *instance is frame 10.*

11. Select the keyframe labeled blue in the actions layer and repeat the process to create an event handler for boyLink, going to another URL of your choice.

```
1 boyLink.onRelease = function() {
2 getURL("http://www.futuremedia.org.uk");
3 };
4
```

315

You can test the movie now, and will find that when you click the boy and girl images, a new page will appear (assuming you are online or go online when requested to do so by your browser) corresponding to your URLs.

12. The red buttons behind the boy and girl icons are not really needed for your graphic design, so you can make them disappear (while still maintaining their button functionality) by making them *transparent*. To do this, select each of the two buttons on the pink and blue labeled keyframes, on the url buttons layer. Select the Color drop-down menu on the Properties panel and select Alpha. In the slider that appears to the right of the drop-down menu, change the value to 0%. The buttons will now be invisible, but they will continue to work, giving the impression that the boy/girl icons are the buttons. Sneaky, huh?

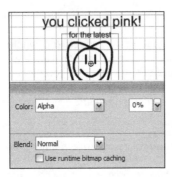

There is a slight problem, though—now you can't see the buttons either! To fix this, click the Show Layer as Outlines *icon for the* url buttons *layer.*

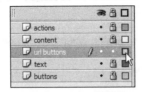

In this chapter, you learned how to give Flash instructions to jump to new parts of your movie when it detects the user clicking a button. More importantly, you created event-driven scripting yourselves, without using behaviors. There's probably more unanswered questions going through your mind about ActionScript, but you're already realizing its power. Some of you will want more of the same—don't worry, there's **much** more!

Case study

In this section, you're going to create a simple email page, and move toward finalizing your navigation.

Creating your email and contact page

1. Open your saved case study document.

2. Select the content symbol instance on the main stage and double-click to edit it in place:

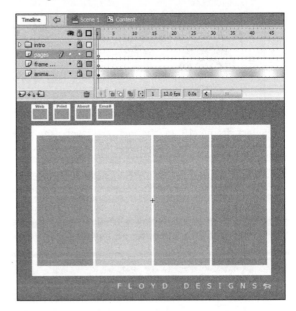

3. Scroll the timeline to frame 165. This is where your email page is located:

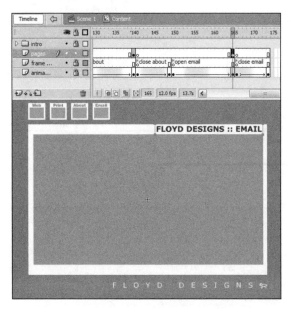

4. Lock all the layers except the pages layer, and select the keyframe on frame 165.

5. Select the Text tool. Set the color to #003366 and the font to Arial, 15 point, bold.

6. Use the Text tool to type the following as seen:

Here at Floyd Designs,

we welcome your comments,

queries or praise!

7. Select the text field and open the Align panel (*CTRL/CMD*+*K*). Click the To Stage icon.

8. Center the text field vertically with Align vertical center, and align it to the left of the center point using Align left edge:

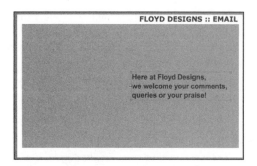

9. With the text field selected, select Modify ➤ Convert to Symbol (or press *F8*). Give it the name email content, a movie clip behavior, a center-left registration point, and then click OK.

10. Select the new instance on the stage and give it an instance name of email_mc.

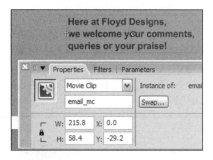

11. Double-click the new instance to enter Edit in Place mode.

12. Within the email content movie clip, select the Text tool and type an @ symbol in the top-left corner of the green rectangle area. Do this in 20-point Arial bold, in white.

13. Select the @ text field and select Insert ➤ Timeline Effects ➤ Effects ➤ Drop Shadow.

> *If you are using Flash Professional, you may want to consider using a drop shadow filter instead of the drop shadow timeline effect.*

14. In the Drop Shadow settings, change both the x and y Shadow Offset values to 2. Click Update Preview to view the new effect:

One significant thing you might have spotted is that your white character is rendered invisible due to the white background; this is one of the flaws of timeline effects.

15. Click OK to render the timeline effect. This creates a new layer called Drop Shadow followed by a number. Lock this layer:

16. Back on the stage, select the Text tool and set the Properties panel as seen here (Arial, 15 point, color #003366, anti-alias for readability):

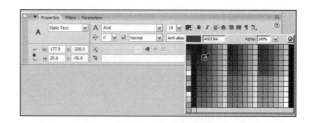

17. Select the Layer 1 layer and type floyd@floyd-designs.inc (or your own email address) below the @ text field.

18. Position the text field in line horizontally with the @ symbol (switch on Snap Align if necessary or use the Align panel), and a little below it:

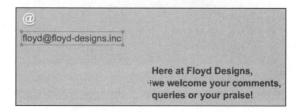

You'll modify this text a little later by turning it into a button and attaching appropriate ActionScript to it. Before that, instead of the page name, you're going to put a postal address.

19. Zoom in to about 400 percent and use the Rectangle and Line tools to draw an envelope:

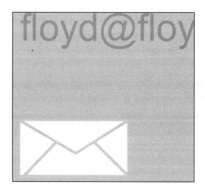

20. Select the envelope and group it (*CTRL/CMD+G*). Zoom back out to 100 percent.

21. Use the Text tool with its current settings to type the following:

Floyd Designs,

Floyd Tower,

Main Avenue,

Floydsville,

94710

22. Align the text field to the envelope above it, leaving a little vertical gap. Your cosmetically complete email page looks like this:

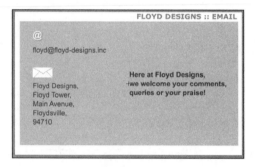

Now, as promised, you're going to put in an email link.

Creating a mailto link

Even though you might not be aware of the term **mailto**, you will no doubt have used a countless number of them. A mailto is a hyperlink that opens up the user's default email application and creates a new email message to the given email address.

The following ActionScript opens your default mail application (if it's not already open):

```
myButton.onRelease = function () {
  getURL ➡
    ("mailto:webmaster@friendsofed.com");
}
```

It then creates a new blank email to the friends of ED webmaster (don't all do this at once!):

Because of Flash's security features, this code will not work if you try it with Test movie. *View the movie in a browser with* File ➤ Publish Preview ➤ HTML *(or press F12 if you have the default settings).*

You're going to do a very similar thing in your case study website by creating a button with a mailto link to the given address.

1. Use the Selection tool to select the floyd@floyd-designs.inc text and press *F8* to convert it into a symbol. Call it mailto button, with a button behavior and a central registration point.

2. With the new button instance still selected, give it an instance name of mailButton in the Properties panel.

3. Double-click the button instance on the stage to edit it in place.

4. Insert a new keyframe on the Over state by pressing *F6*.

319

5. Select the text field on the Over keyframe, and change its color to white:

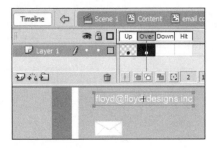

6. Insert a keyframe on the Hit state, and draw a rectangle to cover all the text. Select Modify ➤ Arrange ➤ Send Backward to put the rectangle behind the text.

Adding a solid shape as your hit state was something you had to do in previous versions of Flash; otherwise the button would only be selectable if the user clicked on the text (and not the text background). Thus, if the user clicked on the inside of an "o", nothing would happen! This is no longer the case in the current version of Flash, but it is still a good idea to add a solid background, if only to make sure that your site is as backward compatible with Flash MX2004 and previous versions of Flash as possible.

Click the Back button in the top left to return to the email content timeline:

Contrary to what we said earlier in the chapter, you're going to use behaviors just one more time. The reason for this is speed—you have a lot to get through in this chapter!

7. Select the button instance and open the Behaviors panel (Window ➤ Behaviors).

8. Click the Add Behavior button (represented by the plus sign) in the Behaviors panel, and select Web ➤ Go to Web Page:

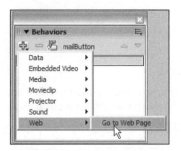

9. In the dialog box that appears, set the details as follows and click OK:

Once you are done, you've finished with your email page. Nice and simple, but functional. Once the case study is done, you can spruce the pages up to your own taste. For now, though, you're going to use some ActionScript to program your navigation.

Coding your navigation

You actually did all the hard work creating your opening and closing pages a very long time ago, and until now they've just opened and closed continually because of a lack of halts in the timeline. In this section, you're going to make the website navigation functional, if not complete.

1. Click the Back button above the timeline to return to the Content movie clip timeline.

2. Insert a new layer above all the others called actions.

3. On the actions layer, insert a blank keyframe (using *F7*) on frame 75. This corresponds with the end of the intro sequence.

4. Insert a blank keyframe on each frame where a shape tween ends. You'll start off with frame 91:

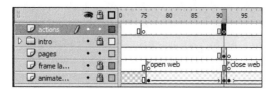

5. To try and help you further here, here are the frame numbers in your case study file (yours might be slightly different):

91, 100, 116, 124, 140, 149, 165, and 174

Place a blank keyframe on each one.

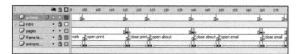

6. Select the keyframe on frame 75 of the actions layer.

7. Open the Actions panel if it isn't already in view. Make sure you are in Script Assist mode, and if you are not, click the Script Assist button. In the top-left pane, find Global Functions ➤ Timeline Control ➤ stop and double-click it.

This will add a stop() action to the keyframe at frame 75.

This will cause the movie to stop after the intro animation has played.

8. Come out of Script Assist mode by clicking the Script Assist button.

Select the stop() line of ActionScript and copy it (*Ctrl/Cmd*+C). You're doing this because you are going to add this code to all of the previously added keyframes.

9. Click all the blank keyframes on the actions layer (as listed), click in the Actions panel each time, and paste the copied code (*Ctrl/Cmd*+V).

When you are done, all the keyframes should have a little a above them. For now, you're done with this timeline.

10. Return to the main timeline using the Back button. Lock all layers except buttons. You will find this layer in the button assets layer folder.

11. Select the Web button on the top left of the stage, and give it an instance name of webButton in the Properties panel. Do the same for the others, giving them instance names of printButton, aboutButton, and emailButton, respectively.

12. Insert a new layer called actions, and place it above all the others.

13. Select the keyframe on the actions layer and open the Actions panel. Enter Script Assist mode by clicking the Script Assist button.

14. In the left pane, open the books ActionScript 2.0 classes ➤ Movie ➤ Button ➤ Event Handlers.

15. Double-click onRelease from within the Events book. As before, you'll see this:

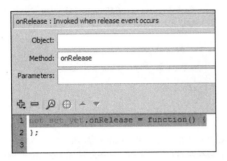

16. Select line 2. Double-click onRelease again, so that your code now looks like this:

```
1 not_set_yet.onRelease = function() {
2 };
3 not_set_yet.onRelease = function() {
4 };
```

Repeat this process twice, so that you end up with four event handler blocks:

```
1 not_set_yet.onRelease = function()
2 };
3 not_set_yet.onRelease = function()
4 };
5 not_set_yet.onRelease = function()
6 };
7 not_set_yet.onRelease = function()
8 };
```

17. Click line 1 to select it. In the Object field, enter the text webButton to change the very first not_seen_yet to read webButton:

```
Object: webButton
Method: onRelease
Parameters:

1 webButton.onRelease = function() {
2 };
3 not_set_yet.onRelease = function() {
4 };
5 not_set_yet.onRelease = function() {
6 };
7 not_set_yet.onRelease = function() {
8 };
```

18. Do the same for lines 3, 5, and 7, entering the names printButton, aboutButton, and emailButton. Remember that the case **and** spelling must match.

```
Object: emailButton
Method: onRelease
Parameters:

1 webButton.onRelease = function() {
2 };
3 printButton.onRelease = function() {
4 };
5 aboutButton.onRelease = function() {
6 };
7 emailButton.onRelease = function() {
8 };
9
```

We need to make our buttons control the timeline our pages are on, so we need to add a gotoAndStop() as the handler code for each of our buttons. Unfortunately, the timeline we need to control with the gotoAndStop() is not the current timeline, so we cannot use actions.

We actually need to control the content_mc movie clip, and to do this we have to use something we looked at in the start of this chapter—the full object.method (argument) form of gotoAndPlay. Let's see how this works:

19. Select line 1 of your script. Open the ActionScript 2.0 Classes ➤ Movie ➤ Movieclip ➤ Methods books in the left-hand pane of the Actions panel.

20. Double-click the gotoAndPlay entry. This will add a new line at line 2 as shown here:

```
webButton.onRelease = function() {
    not_set_yet.gotoAndPlay();
};
printButton.onRelease = function() {
};
aboutButton.onRelease = function() {
};
emailButton.onRelease = function() {
};
```

```
1  webButton.onRelease = function() {
2      not set yet.gotoAndPlay();
3  };
4  printButton.onRelease = function() {
5  };
6  aboutButton.onRelease = function() {
7  };
8  emailButton.onRelease = function() {
9  };
10
```

We have the method (gotoAndPlay) defined, but the object and argument are not yet defined.

21. Type content_mc in the Object field. Uncheck the Expression checkbox and enter open web in the Frame input field.

OK, we know you've been dying to. . . test it with Control ➤ Test Movie. Click the Web button and you'll be directed, opening tween and all, to the respective page. One thing to note here is that frequent clicks of the button will ruin the effect due to the same opening animation being played over and over—for the moment at least (you'll sort this out in the next chapter).

Right now, though, you've got to add code for the other buttons. The quickest way to do this is to copy and paste line 2.

22. Exit Script Assist mode. Place the text entry cursor at the ends of lines 4, 6, and 8, then press the *ENTER* key. This gives you a blank line in each of the remaining three event handlers.

```
1  webButton.onRelease = function() {
2      content_mc.gotoAndPlay("open web")
3  };
4  printButton.onRelease = function() {
5
6  };
7  aboutButton.onRelease = function() {
8
9  };
10 emailButton.onRelease = function() {
11
12 };
13
```

Select line 2 and press *CTRL*/*CMD*+C to copy it to the clipboard.

```
1  webButton.onRelease = function() {
2      content_mc.gotoAndPlay("open web");
3  };
```

Paste this line into lines 5, 8, and 11.

```
1  webButton.onRelease = function() {
2      content_mc.gotoAndPlay("open web");
3  };
4  printButton.onRelease = function() {
5      content_mc.gotoAndPlay("open web");
6  };
7  aboutButton.onRelease = function() {
8      content_mc.gotoAndPlay("open web");
9  };
10 emailButton.onRelease = function() {
11     content_mc.gotoAndPlay("open web");
12 };
13
```

23. We need to change the three lines we have just added as follows:

323

Select line 5. Change the Parameters field from open web to open print.

Select line 8 and change open web to open about.

Select line 11 and change open web to open email.

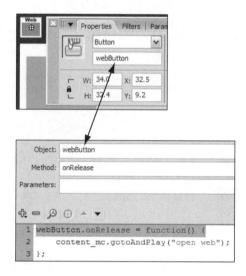

Your script should now look like this:

```
webButton.onRelease = function() {
    content_mc.gotoAndPlay("open web");
};
printButton.onRelease = function() {
    content_mc.gotoAndPlay("open print");
};
aboutButton.onRelease = function() {
    content_mc.gotoAndPlay("open about");
};
emailButton.onRelease = function() {
    content_mc.gotoAndPlay("open email");
};
```

24. Test the movie again to see if all the links work. If they don't, check that the instance names that you see if you click each of the buttons match the instance names you have used in the script, and that the frame labels also match:

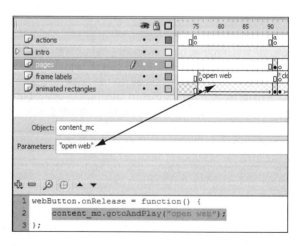

If any of the buttons still don't seem to be working properly, check that

- You are using the correct instance name for the content clip, content_mc in both the Properties panel (click on the content clip and look at the instance name in the Properties panel), and in the script.
- You have quote marks (" ") around the frame labels in the gotoAndPlay() methods.
- If all else fails, have a look at our version of the file, case_study_ch10.fla.

If all has gone well, you should start to see the navigation coming together.

> If the animations seem a little jerky to you, you can increase the frame rate to 25 or 30 fps via Modify ➤ Document.

There are no closing animations as of yet, but that will come in the next chapter when you have learned about variables.

Summary

In this chapter, we introduced the important concept of scripting your own interactivity, and you started to see how Flash implements this using ActionScript. This was an important chapter because the simple applications of ActionScripting you've seen here will be a foundation that you can build on, both in the next chapter specifically and in the rest of the book in general.

You saw that

- Interactivity is about bringing the Flash movie to life, and giving the user an interesting and satisfying experience.
- At the heart of interactivity are the principles of scripting events and event handlers, and their relationship to instance names and scope. When things—events like a user clicking a button—happen, Flash looks for a code block that is denoted as to be run when that event occurs, and the event handler is executed.

- A powerful way of adding interaction to Flash is by using buttons. Buttons can have behaviors such as animation, sound, and movie clips embedded in their default states, and they can be made even more intelligent by attaching ActionScript to the mouse events that buttons can detect.
- ActionScript creates the event handler and links it to the event. It is a scripting language for Flash, which means it is used to control the Flash Player.
- ActionScript should only be attached to frames in the timeline if you want to maintain a good scripting style.
- You can use ActionScript to jump to specific areas inside your movies, and you can even jump to specified web pages and sites.

In the next chapter, you'll explore ActionScript in more depth and see more ways that it can work for you.

```
 1  webButton.onRelease = function() {
 2      content_mc.gotoAndPlay("open web")
 3  };
 4
 5  printButton.onRelease = function() {
 6      content_mc.gotoAndPlay("open print
 7  };
 8
 9  aboutButton.onRelease = function() {
10      content_mc.gotoAndPlay("open about
11  };
12
13  emailButton.onRelease = function() {
14      content_mc.gotoAndPlay("open email
15  };
16
```

Chapter 11

INTELLIGENT ACTIONS

What we'll cover in this chapter:

- ActionScript
- Increasing interaction
- Giving instructions to specific objects (or instances) on the stage
- Variables and conditional statements
- Storing values for later use within scripts
- Allowing Flash to make choices about what to do

In the previous chapter, you used ActionScript to make a multisection interactive Flash movie that allowed the user to navigate through various routes. You may be a beginner, but you have already aced behaviors and are now going it alone by creating your own code, something you will continue to do in this chapter.

ActionScript can be used to do much more, including supercharging frames and buttons so they are much more talented than their ordinary cousins. This is at the heart of why Flash is a much richer and more flexible environment for web page production than HTML—and is the reason Flash can be used to produce sites that are more interactive and dynamic in the way they allow the user to move around. Some Flash sites even seem to think for themselves.

This chapter will show you how to start giving your Flash sites these qualities. In the previous chapter, you simply controlled the main timeline, but you can get much more out of Flash if you use ActionScript to control symbols. You can make Flash throw movie clips around the screen in a dynamic, organic way, based on how the user is interacting via buttons or the mouse position, or something else more complicated, such as a fiendish plan you've coded in ActionScript for Flash to follow without any external interaction. You will also explore more thoroughly a few of the concepts we introduced in Chapter 10, particularly **dot notation** and the importance of **instances**. If you are a little fazed by the last chapter, don't worry too much; we will revisit all the important concepts because they are so crucial to your understanding of ActionScript.

As with the previous chapters on ActionScript, you may find this chapter a little daunting at first, particularly because ActionScripting may be intimidating to those of you coming from a Photoshop/graphic design background. Bear in mind that ActionScript is one of the easiest scripting languages to learn, and a good way to gain knowledge of programming in general.

The power of ActionScript

In the previous chapter, you saw that ActionScript is *event driven*. This means that the actions you told Flash to perform are carried out only when an event you specified takes place—when the mouse pointer does

something specific or when a frame containing some ActionScript is encountered on the timeline. This makes ActionScript easy to write. For example, once you've created a working button, all you have to do is add an ActionScript to it that tells Flash what the button should do. There's no long, obscure program to write—you just decide what you want Flash to do, generate the appropriate bit of ActionScript, and then move on.

Whenever I think of Flash scripts, I have this irrational mental image of a little superhero with a letter "A" on his chest. Made up of normal Flash frames, he has come to you from the planet Interactivity to free you from the clutches of his archenemy, a secret organization known only by the initials HTML.

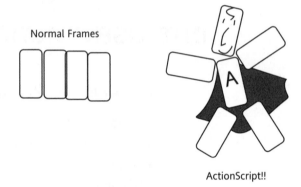

Normal Frames

ActionScript!!

Ridding the world of boring, static web pages wherever they may exist, with powers that give one command the abilities of 100 lines of JavaScript . . . Is it a bird? Is it a plane? No . . . It's ActionScript!

Shucks! Now he's embarrassing me!

ActionScript is fundamentally much more dynamic than, for example, a button rollover or a linear animated movie. With ActionScript, you can control just about every attribute of just about everything on the stage. Surreal as it sounds, ActionScript enables individual elements of your movie to talk to each other. A button symbol can tell a movie symbol, "When instance X of me is clicked, you start playing from frame Y." Buttons no longer just control navigation as in plain old HTML; **they also control other instances**, such as movies and graphics. When controlling each other, instances need to be able to access each other, and they do this by forging paths to each other. The system used to form such paths is known as **dot notation**.

Defining instances for dot notation

With dot notation, you can make one instance in your animation—a button, for example—tell another instance what to do. Before we can demonstrate this concept, you need to create a couple of symbols so that one can tell the other what to do.

Let's create a little face . . . something you can tell to be happy or sad, depending on your mood.

> *Make sure you save the movie you work on throughout this chapter; you'll be enhancing its capabilities with ActionScript as you progress through the book.*
>
> *You can find the finished movie,* smilerMovie.fla, *on our website, in the code download for this chapter. This file has all the ActionScript you will be developing in this chapter already attached to it. If you want a version with just the graphics in it (so you can add the ActionScript yourself), use* smilerMovie_start.fla. *If you also want to fast-track this exercise to the point where we start adding the code, open* smilerMovie_start.fla *and skip to step 24.*

1. In a fresh Flash document, create a new movie clip symbol (Insert ➤ New Symbol) called smiler.

2. Inside smiler, create two new layers. From the bottom up, rename your three layers face, eyes, and smile. These layers are to hold the separate parts that will make up your face graphic.

3. Place a yellow circle about 200 pixels high by 200 pixels wide, with a black stroke 8 point thick, in the center of the stage on the face layer:

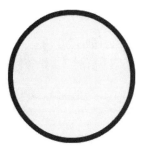

> *Note that you can create a circle to an exact size by selecting the Oval tool and Alt-clicking on the stage. When you do this, a window will appear requesting a height and width setting.*
>
> *You can of course just create a circle and then alter the height and width in the Properties panel.*
>
> *If you have the* center to stage *command (that we created earlier) still in the* Commands *menu, you can then use that to center the circle.*

4. In the eyes layer, use two lines with the same stroke width as your circle to add two eyes:

5. Select the smile layer and add a horizontal line where the mouth should be:

We know what you're thinking: your face should be smiling.

6. Make all the layers 15 frames long and add a keyframe in the smile layer at frame 15:

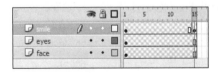

Now you'll animate the mouth so that it goes from a smile to a frown, passing through all the intermediate expressions in between. To do this, you'll set up a shape tween from frame 1 (smiling) to frame 15 (frowning). For the next part to work, you must not have the mouth selected (if you have, simply click a blank part of the stage).

7. Choose the Selection tool and go to frame 1 of the smile layer. Put the pointer on the midpoint of the mouth until the pointer displays the curve attachment and drag the center of the mouth down to make your face smile:

You may find working on the smile easier by locking the smile *and* face *layers.*

Hmm . . . Not quite as enigmatic as the Mona Lisa, but if you're happy with it, we're happy.

8. Add a new layer called actions. Using the Properties panel, add a label happy to frame 1 of this layer.

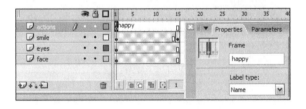

Select frame 1 on the smile layer and select Shape from the Tween drop-down menu.

A light green shape tween will now extend from frame 1 to frame 15.

You'll notice that you have nothing else on the smile layer. This is a requirement in **all** tween animation, as you'll remember from earlier in this book. You'll confuse Flash if you have more than one item in the layer, and your tween won't work. Also, note that the smile object is just a drawn shape and **not** a symbol—if it were, this would also prevent the shape tween from working.

9. Select frame 15 of the smile layer. Your face here is in its expressionless, neutral position. By using the pointer in the same way as before, make the face frown. Select the frowning line and move it downward slightly. Hold down the Shift key when you move the frown to keep the frown in the same horizontal position as you move it down vertically.

10. Add a new keyframe on frame 15 of the actions layer. Use the Properties panel to add a label called sad to the keyframe at frame 15. (You won't see this label on the timeline because there's not enough space to show it, but you will see a little flag in the frame to show that it's been labeled):

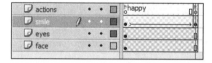

11. You can see the motion that smiler will perform by selecting it in the Library window and clicking the Play button, using the Onion Skin tool to see all the frames at once, or dragging your playhead through the timeline:

You also want to label the neutral facial expression. The exact position of this will depend on how you drew the mouth, but it should be somewhere near the middle of the movie.

12. Drag the playhead up and down the timeline until it is on the frame where the smile is closest to the straight horizontal line you drew originally.

13. Insert a keyframe at this frame on the actions layer. Use the Properties panel to label it neutral:

Each of these labels corresponds to a different expression: you want to be able to select the expression you want to see. To do this, you need a button to click.

14. Using Insert ➤ New Symbol, create a new graphic symbol and call it rectangle. This symbol will form the basis of your button.

15. Inside the graphic symbol, draw a yellow rectangle:

You're going to put text over the top of your button eventually, so make sure the body of your rectangle is big enough for some text. We made ours 140 pixels wide by 50 pixels high.

16. Again using Insert ➤ New Symbol, create a button symbol called rectangle button.

17. Inside the button symbol, drag an instance of the rectangle symbol onto the stage. Open the Info panel (Window ➤ Info), and click the center dot in the 3✕3 matrix so it looks like this:

This will make the panel measure positions from the center of the button.

18. Enter 0 in both the X: and Y: boxes. This centers the rectangle exactly at the center of the button stage:

> As we mentioned before, it's important that the graphics in a button's states all line up. For that reason, it's a good idea to always center buttons. Then, if a button ever starts to look wobbly when it's used in your final movie, you'll know all you have to do to correct the problem is set its position in all states to X:0.0; Y:0.0 with the Info panel.

19. Add keyframes to the Over state and the Hit state.

We suggested earlier in the book that it was a good idea to make the shape in the Hit state a distinctive color. Here, however, because you know that the square is solid, you don't need to change the shape in the Hit state from yellow to a distinctive black by adjusting the brightness, but you may want to do so for good practice.

You'll let the users know they're over the button's "click" area by making the button a lighter shade when it's in the Over state.

20. Select the Over state in the timeline, and then select the rectangle. Choose the Brightness option from the Properties panel's Color drop-down menu and set it to 40% using the slider:

21. Go back to the main stage in Scene 1 and add two new layers. Rename your three layers, from the bottom up, face, buttons, and text:

22. Select the face layer and drag an instance of smiler onto the stage from the Library. Then, in the buttons layer, add two instances of the rectangle button symbol. Your stage should look like this one:

> If you find that you made your graphics too big to fit them all on the stage, use the Free Transform tool to scale them down a little.

Now to give the user some hints about which buttons they might want to click.

23. In the text layer, use the Text tool and the Properties panel to add the words better and worse on top of the buttons as shown. Then at the top of the stage, type How do you feel?.

You can test the movie now if you like. When you go over the buttons, they should become lighter, and the face will continuously change from happy to sad, but nothing will happen when you click either button.

24. Save your Flash document for safekeeping. Our version of the file up to this point is available as `smilerMovie_start.fla`.

The next step is to use the buttons to control what mood `smiler` is in, but before you begin adding the ActionScript, let's look at how **dot notation** works in theory.

Dot notation

It may not sound very exciting, but dot notation has incredible possibilities for your Flash movies.

Dot notation in Flash and ActionScript is a way of expressing a **path** through a movie. It gives you a way of targeting a particular object and telling it what to do, irrespective of its position in the movie's structure. If you want to direct a particular piece of ActionScript at a specific movie clip, or if you want to tell an instance of a square symbol to change its alpha value to 10, you can do that by specifying that object's location using dot notation.

A typical line of dot notation ActionScript would look like this:

```
square._x = 100
```

This line would move the square instance to an x (horizontal) position of 100 on the stage. Notice the dot before the _x? Perhaps this is what gives dot notation its name!

> *You may recognize this as something you already used in the previous chapter. You used ActionScript lines like* `instanceName.gotoAndStop();` *and* `instanceName.onRelease=function()` *earlier, although we didn't let on what it was called.*

Dot notation enables you to reference any instance within the Flash movie, but for this chapter, we'll stick to one location for all your instances. We'll look at how to reference different locations in the movie using paths later in the book.

Dot notation only works on individual, **named instances** of a symbol. Let's briefly refresh your memory about what an instance is and why you use them. We also want to make sure you are clear on the difference between an instance name that appears in the Properties panel and the symbol name that appears in the Library.

> *As your knowledge of ActionScript increases, you will realize that dot notation can be used to access much more than just instances. It can also be used to access just about anything in Flash. Dot notation can be used as a way of defining paths between timelines (which is how we are using it here), but it can also be used to navigate within other hierarchies, many of which may be unfamiliar to you at the moment. The most important other hierarchy that dot notation allows you to navigate within is the class structure.*
>
> *As your experience of ActionScript increases, you will also begin to realize that Flash treats everything as an instance (or "object"), and this means that you can access almost anything that the Flash Player is capable of accessing through dot notation.*

The original "master" symbol that sits in the Library is the **template**, and any instances of it that you put on the stage will be replicas of this master symbol. Whereas the version in the Library is the original, think of the instance on the stage as a clone, permanently linked to its master. An instance will **always** look and behave like its original, and when the original changes, **all** its instances will change as well. This characteristic is what differentiates an **instance** from a **copy**: If you simply draw a square on the stage, copy and paste it next to the original, and then go back to the original and change it, the copy would not be affected in any way because a copy has no link to its original.

When you create new symbols, you give each a symbol name that appears in the Library. In the FLA you are building at the moment, you used the names rectangle, rectangle button, and smiler. The symbol names are just descriptive labels that are attached to each symbol in the library so you know what each one is; Flash doesn't use them at all. Note that the symbol name can have spaces.

In the previous chapter, you also used the instance names pinkButton and blueButton. The instance names are used by Flash. Unlike symbol names, instance names have very definite rules defined by Flash (or more correctly, *ActionScript*—the rules for defining instance names are part of ActionScript's rules for naming things):

- They must be typed the same way every time you use them (including case), and it's a good idea to stick to camel case.

- They can't include spaces.

The instance names are unique to each movie clip or button you put on stage, and if you don't give a name to a particular symbol, you cannot control it via ActionScript because Flash won't know which name to reference it with.

You can see the link between originals and instances for yourself by altering the rectangle symbol you created in the last exercise.

Symbol templates and instances

1. If you haven't done so already, save your FLA. In the Library window, double-click the rectangle button symbol to go into Edit Symbols mode (you may want to lock the text layer while you do this so that you don't inadvertently select the text above the rectangle). Double-click the rectangle you see (this time, you are clicking on the rectangle symbol). The top of the timeline should now look like this:

2. Select the yellow rectangle with the Selection tool. Use the Free Transform tool to stretch it at the top and the bottom.

3. Click Scene 1 at the top of the timeline to go back to the main stage and notice that both instances of rectangle have mimicked the change made to their Library-housed template:

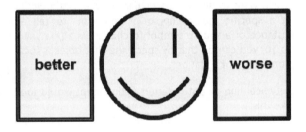

4. If you test the movie, you will see that all button states (Up, Over, Down, and Hit) have now changed—the buttons still do the same thing; it's just that they now use the bigger rectangle. Exit the current FLA (don't save the changes) and reload the file you saved in step 1.

The rectangle symbol you put in each state of the rectangle button symbol changed and, consequently, the instances of rectangle button on the stage changed as well. The changes you made to the original symbol rippled through to all the instances associated with it. This is a big advantage for editing and changing your website—Flash can just follow the link to each instance of the original and make the necessary changes.

When you change a symbol, you alter its **primitive attributes**. Primitive attributes are things that all instances share in common, and they do not change between instances. This means that if you change a primitive attribute, all instances will reflect the change.

You can also make changes at a per-instance level:

5. With the newly loaded FLA, select one of the buttons on the stage by clicking it, and then scale it. You will see that this time only one of the buttons changes:

6. Press *CTRL+Z* (undo) to make both buttons the same size again.

An instance has **properties**, and these are what you have just changed. There are two cool things about properties as opposed to primitive attributes:

- Each instance has its own set of properties, which are created as soon as you drop a symbol onto the stage. There are a number of properties, such as the ones that control the position of your two button instances (and that is why you can place them at different positions on the stage). There are also other properties that control the scale of the buttons; you changed these for the left button.

- ActionScript can control the properties of each instance, **as long as it has some way of identifying the instance**. As we discussed previously, that identification property is the instance name.

Let's see how this can work.

7. Select each button in turn (make sure that you do not select the text instead—lock the text layer again if you need to). Using the Properties panel, give the left and right buttons the instance names leftButton and rightButton:

8. You can now control the properties of your two buttons via ActionScript. To do this, first add a new layer above the others called actions:

9. Select frame 1 of the new layer and open the Actions panel. We will not be using Script Assist for this line of code, so make sure the Script Assist button is deselected. Enter the following line of code by typing it directly into the Actions panel. Check your spelling after (noting the capital B in leftButton), and make sure _yscale appears blue (if it's not blue, you spelled it incorrectly).

```
leftButton._yscale = 200;
```

Although we could have entered this line of code using Script Assist, direct typing has a number of advantages, the most important one being that Script Assist is really there as an aid to writing ActionScript that you are unfamiliar with. If you need to enter a fairly easy line of code, or one that you are familiar with, you will do it quicker via direct typing.

335

Most users will alternate between Script Assist and direct typing when entering code—using Script Assist when they are unsure, and entering the rest of their code using direct typing.

We will be using a lot of direct typing in this chapter to give you a taste of the process, but feel free to dive back into Script Assist if you feel the urge!

10. If you test the FLA now, you will see that your line of code has scaled the left button. This time, you didn't do the scaling; **ActionScript did it for you!**

This might seem like a fairly boring example, but consider this—what if you scaled every frame by a small amount or moved the button a little every frame. In both cases you would end up with animation created by ActionScript, something called scripted animation. The really cool thing about doing it this way is that your ActionScript can think before it animates; things move around as if they have a brain, rather than sticking to fixed tween railroad tracks. This is the basis of interactivity in Flash.

This is a fairly fundamental concept in Flash, so let's have a closer look at how you did it.

Our line still kind of looks like the `instance.method(argument);` syntax, but now you have something else. You have

```
instance.property = value;
```

You can change the instance's property by equating it to a new *value*. In this line of code

- You can access properties as well as methods via dot notation: dot notation is a general "glue" used in ActionScript to form lines by adding stuff separated by the dots.

- You can **equate** one thing to another by using the equal sign (=) much as you do in math. This type of line is called an **expression**; it expresses something that has to be done by Flash. In this example, it expresses that the scaling of leftButton is 200%. This is a **literal value**. This is a value that never changes—you will scale by 200% every time.

There are lots of other properties you can play with before moving on. Here are a few you might want to try:

```
leftButton._rotation = 90;
leftButton._alpha = 50;
leftButton._x = 200;
```

You can even try all four lines at the same time. See if you can guess what will happen before you test it!

Dot notation has at least two forms: one to access methods, and one to access properties. It can also be used in expressions to change properties, which is the basis for scripted animation.

Phew! That's a lot to take in. Let's expand the idea a little by taking control of the smiler instance.

Changing properties with dot notation

1. Select Smiler on the stage and open the Properties panel. Give it an instance name of smilerFace.

At the moment, smilerFace plays continuously during your movie, but you want it to stay on the neutral expression until one of the buttons is clicked.

To do this, you're going to control the smilerFace instance's _currentframe property. This is a number that signifies which frame in the timeline the movie clip is on, starting with 1. Rather than changing it directly as you did previously, you will use an old friend: the gotoAndStop method.

Using methods such as gotoAndStop hides the fact that you are still really only changing properties. Methods work by changing properties as well, but the advantage of using them is that you don't have to worry about the underlying properties. Because they have been written for us, there are lots of features that make them easier than accessing properties directly. For example, gotoAndStop gives you additional features that you can use instead of raw frame numbers, such as frame labels. Hiding the properties of an instance by controlling it using methods is called abstraction.

2. Select frame 1 of the actions layer and delete the code that you added earlier. If you are in Script Assist mode, you can delete a line by clicking the "-" icon at the bottom left of the Script Assist area. If you are not in Script Assist mode, you can delete the lines by highlighting them and pressing the ENTER, BACKSPACE, or DELETE keys.

Before you begin your coding, let's take a closer look at some of the buttons above the text box in the right pane of the Actions panel to see what they do and what benefit you can gain from them (buttons described from left to right):

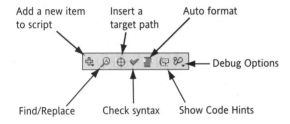

- **Add a new item to script**: Opens a list of all the ActionScript commands available for adding to your script. You can select a command from this menu and it will appear in the script, similar to the left pane you used in the previous chapter.

- **Find/Replace**: Allows you to find a piece of text within the active script pane. Also allows you to replace the found text with a new text string.

- **Insert a target path**: Locates instances in your Flash movie. You'll look at this in more detail in a moment.

- **Check syntax**: Checks the validity of your code. If Flash locates a syntax error, it will print the errors in the Output panel, detailing the location and reason for the error(s). As you learn ActionScript, you'll begin to see the Output panel more and more—don't worry—this is normal for anyone learning ActionScript (and even the masters from time to time!).

- **Auto format**: Formats your ActionScript to look neat, tidy, and correctly indented.

- **Show Code Hint**: Makes the direct typing mode a lot easier! Code hints appear to suggest the correct arguments required for ActionScript methods. Hints will appear whenever you type the open parenthesis to begin the arguments section of an instance.*method*(arguments) structure:

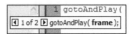

You can hide the code hints by right-clicking the Show Code Hint button, but for now we recommend that you leave this on until you are fully familiar with ActionScript.

- **Debug Options**: Debugging is the process of checking your ActionScript and removing any glitches contained in it. The Debug Options icon displays a debug options menu.

Now that you've looked at all the buttons in the Actions panel, let's give one of them a try.

3. Make sure that you have frame 1 of the actions layer selected, and that you deleted all scripts from the right code pane. Also make sure that you are not in Script Assist mode. Then click the Insert Target Path icon.

This reveals all potential targets in the movie that you can control. You can control everything with an instance name beside it:

In this case, you see that _root, smilerFace, leftButton, and rightButton are the only things available. The A() represents the text on the text, which you are not concerned with at the moment.

4. Click smilerFace to select it, and leave the rest of the window unchanged. Then click OK.

The Actions panel now contains the dot path this.smilerFace.

We know what the smilerFace part of this path is, but what about the this part? The this is most relevant to code blocks that are event handlers. Because our code is not part of an event handler, we don't actually need the this, so we can do without it. Therefore, delete this. (this, and the period that follows it).

> Flash will always add the this part of a path whenever you use its automated scripting features (such as Insert Target Path). Flash doesn't know whether your code is part of an event handler or not, and always adds this just to be sure. However, when you don't need it, this can make your code confusing, so it is a good idea to delete it.
>
> The use of this is tied into a programming concept called **scope**. We will look at scope in Chapter 15.

5. You've now pointed Flash at the correct target. Including this is only relevant in a code block. Because you are not in a code block, remove the this and the dot that follows it to leave you with just smilerFace.

What you want Flash to do is make the smile movie start on its neutral, expressionless face. You labeled that frame neutral, so that will be your argument in gotoAndStop().

Let's tell Flash exactly where to go . . .

6. Type a dot after smilerFace in the Actions panel:

7. Type gotoAndStop(into the right-hand pane after the dot you just entered.

As soon as you type the open parenthesis, Flash thinks you will add an argument in a moment, so it displays a hint:

If you can't see the hint, click the Show Code Hint icon in the Actions panel. Flash shows you the correct syntax for the gotoAndStop command. You already have the first two elements in place; the field that is required is shown in bold text: frame.

8. Complete this line of ActionScript by typing "neutral");.

> As you have probably noticed by now, the code is color coded. The smilerFace part will be black, the gotoAndStop will be blue, and the neutral will be green.
>
> Flash prints all keywords (properties, methods, or actions that Flash recognizes) as blue and text between quotations (called "strings"—something we will look at later in this chapter) in green. Everything else is black.
>
> You can often use color coding to your advantage.
>
> For example, if we had chosen the instance name face instead of smilerFace, we would have seen face show up in blue, telling us that ActionScript already has something called face (it is actually to do with fonts—face is a property that defines the font face). Using instance names that become blue is a bad thing (your code will look confusing to other designers, and you may even confuse Flash, breaking your code). If an instance name you have chosen is anything other than black, it is a good idea to go back and choose another instance name.

If your gotoAndStop *does not appear as blue, it is because you have misspelled it and Flash doesn't recognize it. You need to type this exactly (the capitalization as well as the spelling needs to be correct). It is easy to type* gotoandStop *or* goto and stop *when you are starting out, so look at the color of every keyword to make sure it is blue.*

All the colors can be configured by selecting Edit ➤ Preferences *and clicking the* ActionScript *category.*

Also, if you failed to add a closing parenthesis to the neutral *part, you would see the* "); *at the end of the line (and any text you add in line 2) show up as green. This would tell you that you are missing a* " *somewhere.*

Make sure your code looks OK and has no errors by clicking the Auto format and Check syntax buttons in turn.

Once you have corrected any errors, you can test the movie. You will see that your face has stopped animating and is paused on the neutral frame:

How do you feel?

We now need to add some code to define your button events. The only difference is that you will be controlling the smilerFace timeline instead of the main timeline.

9. Because it is customary to place event handlers before other code, place the cursor at the start of line 1 and press *Enter* on your keyboard a few times to create some space. We will also be doing

something else in a moment—typing our instance names—and this also needs to be done before the line we have so far:

First, we need to type our instance names. Typing is a way of telling the Actions panel what each instance name actually is. After typing, the Actions panel will know that smilerFace is a movie clip, and leftButton and rightButton are buttons. The cool thing about the Actions panel knowing this is that it will be able to help us even more—so much so that direct typing will become almost as easy as Script Assist!

10. Using direct typing, add the following lines as lines 1–3:

```
var leftButton:Button;
var rightButton:Button;
var smilerFace:MovieClip;
```

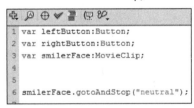

If you now add the following on the next available free line:

```
smilerFace.
```

. . . as soon as you enter the . you will see a drop-down menu appear:

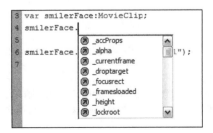

339

This drop-down is the autocomplete feature. Now that Flash knows that smilerFace is a movie clip instance, it can list many of the things that you may want to enter following smilerFace. For example, if we wanted to enter gotoAndStop(), we could save typing it by selecting it from the autocomplete. You can scroll the autocomplete via the scrollbar, but this takes your hand away from the keyboard, so you may instead want to use the arrow keys.

If you even want to avoid using the arrow keys as much as possible, you can type the first few letters of what you want to enter (e.g., enter go to start typing in gotoAndStop) and the autocomplete will go to the nearest keyword, gotoAndPlay. Pressing the DOWN arrow once will then take you to gotoAndStop.

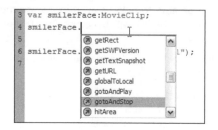

Press ENTER to accept the gotoAndStop. Flash doesn't stop helping you there either, because it will then start showing you code hints:

So, using autocomplete and code hints gives you loads of help when you are typing code directly—almost as much help as Script Assist if you use both features, and remember that direct typing has the advantage of being a much faster script entry option than Script Assist! Oh, and remember that you can also use Insert Target Path, so you may be using direct typing, but you can probably get away with actually typing almost nothing!

Delete the line you just added at line 4.

Now you need to add ActionScript to the buttons. leftButton will make the face happier, and rightButton will make it sadder. To do this, you have to move one frame to the left or to the right in the smilerFace timeline. Here's a reminder of what the smilerFace timeline looks like:

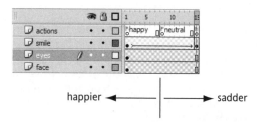

Don't go to your smiler timeline to check, because you need to add the code we will be adding to the timeline you are currently on—the main timeline. Don't move a muscle from where you are!

11. Let's wire the buttons next. You will recall from the last chapter that the basic code block to define a button click-release event handler is

```
instanceName.onRelease = function(){
}
```

What you want to do is create such a block for each of the two buttons.

12. Type this code directly or use the left pane (as you did last chapter). You can also use the Insert Target Path icon to make life easier. Either way, make sure you end up with this:

```
leftButton.onRelease = function() {

};

rightButton.onRelease = function() {

};

smilerFace.gotoAndStop("neutral");
```

```
1  var leftButton:Button;
2  var rightButton:Button;
3  var smilerFace:MovieClip;
4
5  leftButton.onRelease = function() {
6
7  };
8
9  rightButton.onRelease = function() {
10
11  };
12
13  smilerFace.gotoAndStop("neutral");
14
```

You've added the basic event handler blocks; now all you have to do is put some code in them to define the event-handler code.

You want to create an ActionScript that tells Flash to make the face smile when leftButton is clicked, and make the face frown when rightButton is clicked. More accurately, the ActionScript will instruct Flash that when it detects a user clicking and releasing her mouse button over one of the two buttons, the face will jump to the happy or sad label on the timeline.

13. Now that you've used ActionScript for a while (and also because you know how to get Flash to help you write your code), you can probably create these commands a little more confidently. Add the lines highlighted here as lines 2 and 6:

```
leftButton.onRelease = function() {
    smilerFace.gotoAndStop("happy");
};
```

```
rightButton.onRelease = function() {
    smilerFace.gotoAndStop("sad");
};
```

```
smilerFace.gotoAndStop("neutral");
```

```
1  var leftButton:Button;
2  var rightButton:Button;
3  var smilerFace:MovieClip;
4
5  leftButton.onRelease = function() {
6      smilerFace.gotoAndStop("happy");
7  };
8
9  rightButton.onRelease = function() {
10     smilerFace.gotoAndStop("sad");
11 };
12
13 smilerFace.gotoAndStop("neutral");
14
```

14. Click the Check syntax and Auto format buttons to check and format the code, and then test the movie.

You should see the face go from euphoria to abject sadness, all at the click of a button.

If you don't see this, then you can check your FLA against our work in progress file, smilerMovie01.fla.

There is at least one question to answer here: Why is this any different from the pinkButton and blueButton stuff last chapter?

This chapter's exercise is fundamentally different because you are controlling a timeline **other than the main one**. This is the key to creating great sites and impressive interactive content with Flash. The inter-relationships and control of timelines is what makes Flash designers stay up at night thinking "If I scaled that embedded timeline, but at the same time rotated the one it is in. . . . Wow! It moves in a receding spiral!"

You now know how to use **dot notation** to control instances and enable bits of your animation to boss each other around. But you can also give Flash the power to make decisions for itself by using two more of ActionScript's special powers: **variables** and **conditional structures**.

Teaching your movie to think for itself

Using ActionScript to help Flash make structured decisions enables you to build very advanced Flash interfaces. This feature allows Flash to move beyond being merely a graphical interface for web pages and enter the domain of full-fledged web applications and games. By adding ActionScript to a Flash web page, you can do more than just make it interactive—you can give it a brain.

At the moment you only see the frames of the smiler movie that you labeled: happy, neutral, and sad. It would be nice if you could see all the intermediate frames and expressions as well.

Currently, clicking the better button displays the best expression and clicking the worse button displays the worst expression. You want to be able to click the better button to make the movie go one frame nearer to the happy label, or frame 1, and show you a **slightly** happier expression. Similarly, when you click the worse button, you want the movie to go one frame nearer the sad label at frame 15, and show you a **slightly** sadder expression. You want to give smiler a more nuanced range of expressions rather than just the two extremes.

Essentially, what you want to do is go to the previous frame when the better button is clicked, and to the next frame when the worse button is clicked.

To do this, you need an ActionScript that tells Flash to make smilerFace move back one frame when the better button is clicked and move forward one frame when the worse button is clicked.

But—and it's a big **but**—what happens when you reach the first or last frame of the movie?

If the better button is clicked when smilerFace is at frame 1, or if the worse button is clicked when face is at frame 15, the actions you told Flash to carry out will be impossible and your instructions won't make any sense.

We need Flash to be able to decide what action it should take in these circumstances—whether it should move to another frame or stay where it is. To be able to do this, Flash must know what frame it's currently at. You can tell Flash where it's at by using **variables**.

Variables

A variable is a named container in which you store **values** or data that you want to use again and again while a program—or Flash movie—is running. A variable is essentially a bit of computer memory to which you give a name. You store information in this memory location, and when you give Flash the name of the variable, it knows where to find the information you stored.

There are two types of values in Flash you need to look at—**literals** and **expressions**. A variable can be used to store either.

A **literal** is a value that doesn't change; that is, whenever you run a line of code containing a literal value, the literal value will always be the same. A literal value will be something like a name, an address, or the color of your eyes. It's a value that you want to read as a fixed thing.

If you wanted to tell Flash your eyes were blue, you would define this variable like so:

    eyeColor = "blue";

The quotation marks ("") around the value denotes that it is a piece of text, or in programming terms, a **string**. It won't change until you change your eye color. Although your eyes could be any color at all, Flash will deduce that now they're blue, and they'll always be blue—until you tell Flash otherwise.

You could also tell Flash how many eyes you have:

    numberOfEyes = 2;

In this case, you are telling Flash you have two eyes.

An **expression** is different from a literal value. Its value is not fixed; its value can change, and if you run your line of code twice, the value may be different between the two occasions.

For example, look at the following statement:

    Number of dollars in my pocket + ➡
    number of dollars in my pay check

This is an expression: it has two component parts, each of which needs to be evaluated and added together before a final figure can be calculated. If we worked through this expression last year and again today, we would get two different results, even though we used the same expression.

To tell Flash that the number of dollars in your pocket is 10, write

    dollars = 10;

The "10" here is a literal value. It will always be 10. Most things start off as literal values when you set their first value (or in programming terms **initialize** them). It's what happens to the values next that makes them interesting.

Having given Flash this information, you can now forget how much money you have and get Flash to keep track of your accounts. If you were to find a dollar on the floor and put it in your pocket, you could tell Flash that you now have one more dollar than you had before. You would write this:

    dollars = dollars + 1;

Flash would then make the value of dollars equal to 11. If you found another dollar under the sofa, you would use the same expression again to give you 12.

By contrast, running: numberOfEyes = 2; more than once still yields 2 eyes, which is why the value is a literal. You will never get a value other than one on the left of your face and one on the right of your face.

> *Note that the line dollars = dollars + 1 is not an equation (although it looks a bit like one). In an equation, the equals sign means just that—the left side of the equals sign must be numerically equal to the right side. This is obviously not the case here, because if "dollars" was 10, then 10 = 11 just doesn't make sense.*
>
> *An equation is a **mathematical rule**, but programming is not about rules—it is about instructions (recall that code is instructive—it tells the computer what to do). Thus, the equals sign means something slightly different in programming—it is an **assignment**.*
>
> *An assignment means "make the left side of the assignment whatever you see on the right side." This is an instruction to the computer that tells it how to work out what the current value of a variable will be. Thus, the line*
>
> ```
>     dollars = dollars + 1;
> ```
>
> *means "find out the new value of dollars, and add 1 to the value you already have for dollars."*

You can apply this knowledge to your movie and get Flash to keep track of what frame of smilerFace you're on. You can create a variable, call it smilerFrame, and store the current frame number inside this variable. Once Flash looks at this variable and knows which frame you're starting from, it can add or subtract one frame from this variable each time a button is clicked. The value of smilerFrame will change using an expression that essentially says

```
    smilerFrame = smilerFrame + 1
```

or

```
    smilerFrame = smilerFrame - 1
```

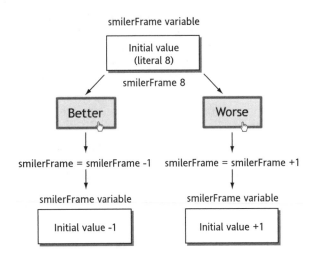

These expressions will create the new value of smilerFrame and store it in the variable. Let's put this into practice.

Using variables

Your first step is to find the frame number that corresponds to the neutral expression of smiler. You can then store this value in the smilerFrame variable and use it as the starting point for the frame-by-frame movement from happy to sad.

Earlier, you attached ActionScript to the first frame of the movie, which told Flash that at the start of the movie, face should be on the frame labeled neutral. This is the frame number that you'll use as the initial value for your smilerFrame variable.

1. Double-click the movie symbol icon of smiler in the Library to go into Edit Symbols mode.

2. Move the playhead to the frame containing the neutral label. You'll be able to see exactly what frame this is by looking in the frame-counter pane at the bottom of the timeline:

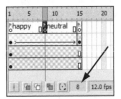

343

In our example, neutral is on frame 8, but in your movie it could be different depending on how you drew the mouth. You can now make your smilerFrame variable equal to 8 (or whatever the value is in your movie) by making Flash do all the thinking for you.

3. On the main timeline, click frame 1 on the actions layer.

4. You should now see your script again. Place the cursor at the end of the script and enter the following line:

```
var smilerFrame = smilerFace._currentframe;
```

Press the Auto format icon to get rid of any blank lines. Your code should now look like this:

```
1  var leftButton:Button;
2  var rightButton:Button;
3  var smilerFace:MovieClip;
4  leftButton.onRelease = function() {
5      smilerFace.gotoAndStop("happy");
6  };
7  rightButton.onRelease = function() {
8      smilerFace.gotoAndStop("sad");
9  };
10 smilerFace.gotoAndStop("neutral");
11 var smilerFrame = smilerFace._currentframe;
12
```

The var keyword is used to tell Flash to create (or initialize) a new variable. It is used the first time you use a variable. ActionScript is a pretty tolerant language, and it won't mind too much if you don't use var, but if nothing else, the inclusion of var makes your code easier to read—it denotes where in your code each variable is initialized.

The use of var *is important when you get into more complex ActionScript (particularly when you get into using functions and also later when you may start writing your own classes). Getting into the habit of using* var *is therefore good practice for later.*

Your new line of code sets the smilerFrame variable to its initial value at the center of the happy/sad continuum as soon as the movie starts. It also directs the movie to the middle of the smiler instance's timeline, pausing the movie there with a neutral facial expression and waiting for the user's input.

Now you need to change the ActionScript instructions that are attached to each of the buttons. Instead of telling face to go all the way to the happy or sad label of the smiler movie clip as soon as they're clicked, you want them to tell smilerFace to move forward or back **one frame at a time**.

When you found a dollar, the new value of the money in your pocket became **dollars** + 1. Similarly, when a button is clicked and the timeline moves one frame forward or one frame back, you want to *update* the value of smilerFrame as either

```
smilerFrame = smilerFrame + 1;
```

or

```
smilerFrame = smilerFrame - 1;
```

You'll still be using the gotoAndStop action to make smilerFace move up and down the timeline, but you'll now tell it to go to the previous frame or the next frame. Fortunately, Flash has built-in facilities to help you do this.

However, you still have the problem of what Flash will do when you get to either end of the timeline and it can't physically *go* to the previous or next frame. How do you stop Flash going off the end of the movie?

You use a **conditional statement**.

Conditional statements

A conditional statement allows your Flash movie to make choices on which code block it decides to run, based on the situation it finds itself in. This means you can tell Flash to follow the instructions you've given it only if certain conditions apply. Helpfully, **if** is the name of the action you'll use to insert a conditional statement in your button.

If, in the dollars example, your pockets were only big enough to hold a hundred dollars, you'd add a conditional statement in your instructions to Flash. That statement would tell Flash that every time you find a dollar, put it in your pocket only if dollars (the variable) is less than 100. If dollars already equaled 100, Flash would know to ignore the rest of the instruction.

Let's define the conditions that must apply in your smilerFace movie for Flash to follow your instructions.

When the better button is clicked, you want it to tell smilerFace to go to the previous frame of smilerFace if—and only if—smilerFace is not *currently* on frame 1. If smilerFace is currently on frame 1, the smilerFrame variable will equal 1. If smilerFace is *not* on frame 1, smilerFrame will be greater than 1.

Flash will go to the previous frame if you're at a frame greater than 1 (smilerFrame > 1). If smilerFrame equals 1, the movie will not move when the better button is clicked.

Let's add this instruction and conditional statement to the better button.

Updating the button with sexier ActionScript

We now need to change the code in the event handlers to use the smilerFrame variable.

1. Highlight line 5 of your code.

```
4 leftButton.onRelease = function() {
5     smilerFace.gotoAndStop("happy");
6 };
```

2. Press the *DELETE* key. This will leave you with the following:

```
4 leftButton.onRelease = function() {
5     |
6 };
```

Before you tell smilerFace to go to the previous frame of smiler when it's clicked, you need to add your conditional statement. Remember, you only want your instructions carried out if smilerFrame > 1.

3. Type the following:

```
if (smilerFrame > 1) {
```

Be careful to get the spelling of smilerFrame exactly right; otherwise Flash will think you're talking about something else. In particular, make sure you stick to the camel case (uppercase at the start of every new word, lowercase everywhere else with no spaces).

As you typed the if command you probably noticed the code hint tooltip. Remember that this is Flash's way of helping you fill in the argument for the if, in this case a **condition**.

You now have to tell Flash that if smilerFrame *is* greater than 1, it should decrease that value by 1 in preparation for the next time the button is clicked: you have to update the value of smilerFrame to reflect the fact that the playhead has moved up one frame. By tracking the value of smilerFrame in the same way as it would with your dollars, Flash will always know where smilerFace is on the smiler timeline.

4. Press the *ENTER* key to place the cursor on a new line:

```
4 leftButton.onRelease = function() {
5     if (smilerFrame > 1){
6         |
7 };
```

Notice that the cursor has been indented because you are writing the code block associated with "yes, smilerFrame is greater than 1."

5. Type the following and then press *ENTER* to place the cursor on a new line:

```
smilerFrame = smilerFrame -1;
```

You now need to tell Flash to move the playhead along the timeline.

6. Enter the following new line:

```
smilerFace.prevFrame();
```

Your code for the better button is almost complete. Like any event handler, an if statement must be closed with a curly bracket. Let's place one.

7. Type a closing curly brace (}) on the new line. It will immediately realign itself to be in line with the if statement.

8. Click the Auto format button above the right pane to clean up your code.

```
1  var leftButton:Button;
2  var rightButton:Button;
3  var smilerFace:MovieClip;
4  leftButton.onRelease = function() {
5      if (smilerFrame>1) {
6          smilerFrame = smilerFrame-1;
7          smilerFace.prevFrame();
8      }
9  };
10 rightButton.onRelease = function() {
11     smilerFace.gotoAndStop("sad");
12 };
13 smilerFace.gotoAndStop("neutral");
14 var smilerFrame = smilerFace._currentframe;
15
```

Your leftButton event handler should now look like this:

```
leftButton.onRelease = function() {
  if (smilerFrame>1) {
    smilerFrame = smilerFrame-1;
    smilerFace.prevFrame();
  }
};
```

The better button is now ready to use.

9. Test the movie. You'll see that face will get happier each time the better button is clicked, whereas it will go straight to its sad expression when you click the worse button. (Clicking the worse button may also stop the better button from working because it doesn't use smilerFrame yet.)

Notice that although your code has an error in it (i.e., the fact that clicking the worse *button stops the* better *button working is an error), Flash doesn't tell you about the error if you click the* Check *syntax icon. The* Check syntax *icon does just that—it checks whether the code is using correct syntax. A bit of text like this is syntactically correct:*

"All trees are covered in bark. Bark is created by dogs when they open their mouths and make a noise. It is then collected and glued onto trees at night by a special process involving pixies and a fertile imagination."

But it is not actually true. Code can be syntactically correct, but can still do something wrong, and syntax checks will not fix this for you.

Now you need to make the worse button fully functional. You need to repeat the same sequence of steps as you did for the better button, but with some significant changes to your conditional statement and to the instructions.

10. In the same way you added the new event handler code for leftButton, add the following code for rightButton, taking care to note the differences (which appear in bold so you don't miss them):

```
rightButton.onRelease = function() {
  if (smilerFrame<smilerFace._totalframes)
  {
      smilerFrame = smilerFrame+1;
      smilerFace.nextFrame();
  }
};
```

The _totalframes property holds the number of frames in a movie clip timeline. For smilerFrame's timeline, it will be equal to 15. We could, therefore, just as easily use

```
if (smilerFrame<15 {
```

except that we would then have to change the 15 every time we changed the number of frames in the smilerFace movie clip. If we use _totalframes, Flash would update the value as the length of the timeline changed, and it would do it automatically, so we don't have to worry about it any more.

11. When you are happy with the result, click the Auto format icon so all the extra spaces are removed, giving you the final listing:

```
var leftButton:Button;
var rightButton:Button;
var smilerFace:MovieClip;
leftButton.onRelease = function() {
    if (smilerFrame>1) {
        smilerFrame = smilerFrame-1;
        smilerFace.prevFrame();
    }
};
rightButton.onRelease = function() {
    if (smilerFrame<smilerFace._➥
            totalframes){
            smilerFrame = smilerFrame+1;
            smilerFace.nextFrame();
    }
};
smilerFace.gotoAndStop("neutral");
var smilerFrame = smilerFace._currentframe;
```

Notice that the `if` code is now double-indented. This is because it is a nested code block; the `if` block is within an event handler block.

12. Test the movie again. Now both the buttons will make the mouth move incrementally. You'll see smilerFace change its expression smoothly from happy to neutral to sad and back again as the buttons are clicked.

13. Save the movie.

There has been a lot to take in, but this chapter has covered fundamental concepts for creating top-quality Flash sites.

Understanding what instances are and how dot notation can be used to control them will enable you to give your sites a far greater degree of interaction for the user to enjoy and marvel at. In addition to navigating the site, your users will be able to do things like start or stop movies and affect the appearance and behavior of movie elements. You can do a whole lot more with **dot notation**, and the basic skills you've gained here will provide a solid footing for learning fancier stuff later in your Flash career. Indeed, you have two more advanced chapters on ActionScript later in the book, so we hope that this whets your appetite.

You've also been introduced to the use of variables and conditional statements. These are the features that give Flash the ability to think for itself. When used together, they give Flash some fairly powerful decision-making abilities.

Finally, you have some understanding of instances, properties, methods, and abstraction.

We've had a lot of queries in previous editions of the book, asking us how to make the face change without having to repeatedly click the buttons, how to add text that changes to reflect what the face is doing, and so on. If the answer intrigues you, have a look at `smiler_enhanced.fla`, found in the code download. Many of the concepts used in the code for this file are discussed later in the book, so you might want to revisit it later.

Case study

In this case study, you're going to add more ActionScript to enhance your navigation.

1. Open your saved case study document.

2. Select frame 1 of the actions layer, and open the Actions panel using *F9*. Here is how you left it in the previous chapter:

```
1  webButton.onRelease = function() {
2      content_mc.gotoAndPlay("open web");
3  };
4
5  printButton.onRelease = function() {
6      content_mc.gotoAndPlay("open print");
7  };
8
9  aboutButton.onRelease = function() {
10     content_mc.gotoAndPlay("open about");
11 };
12
13 emailButton.onRelease = function() {
14     content_mc.gotoAndPlay("open email");
15 };
16
```

Now you're going to use variables to store information about which rectangle should open and which one should close. By doing this, you can play each closing sequence before the next opening one. Your sequence looks (or loops) like this:

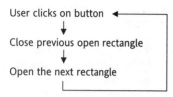

Let's break this down into ActionScript reasoning:

- The user clicks a button, and you store their selection (this is actually a frame label) in a variable.

- The closing sequence plays.

- Once the closing sequence has ended, the value saved from the user's click is retrieved, and the playhead is sent to this retrieved frame label.

- Once the opening sequence has ended, the playhead is halted with a stop frame.

The previous diagram and reasoning is all well and good, but you've actually skipped one key bit of information: Which came first, the chicken or the egg? OK, it's not quite as mind-boggling as that, but it is a pretty important factor in your portfolio site.

The steps assume that you already have a sequence to close before your opening one, but in fact, you don't. If you were to dry run this sequence for the first time, you'd quickly realize that there is no closing sequence to run, and you'd be waiting forever—well, maybe.

Given this, the first time a user clicks a button in the movie, you show her an opening sequence. Every time after that, you show her a closing sequence first, followed by an opening sequence:

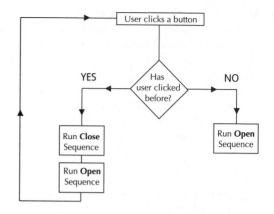

From a Flash ActionScript point of view, you can use a single variable to check whether the user has clicked anything. You'll see how in a moment.

3. Select all the code on line 2 of your code and delete it. It sounds drastic, but it isn't:

```
1  webButton.onRelease = function() {
2
3  };
4  printButton.onRelease = function() {
```

4. Type the following code carefully as the new event handler code for webButton, in between the curly brackets as seen here. Then click the Auto format icon to tidy up your code:

```
webButton.onRelease = function() {
  toOpen = "open web";
    if (userHasClicked == true) {
      content_mc.play();
    } else {
      content_mc.gotoAndPlay(toOpen);
      userHasClicked = true;
  }
};
```

```
1  webButton.onRelease = function() {
2      toOpen = "open web";
3      if (userHasClicked == true) {
4          content_mc.play();
5      } else {
6          content_mc.gotoAndPlay(toOpen);
7          userHasClicked = true;
8      }
9  };
```

In this code, note the following:

- On line 2 you create a variable called toOpen to store, predictably, the frame label of the chosen open sequence.

- Line 3 uses a conditional statement to check if the variable userHasClicked is true. This variable is used to check if this is the first click. (A little later you will initialize it as false.) In this conditional, you are checking if this is anything but the first click. If this condition is met, you set the playhead moving with a simple play method on line 4.

- The conditions (userHasClicked == true) and (userHasClicked) are the same thing. If userHasClicked is true, then the two expressions become (true == true) and (true) respectively, which both equal true. If userHasClicked is false, then the expressions become (false == true) and (false). Both of these are false. Thus, our line if (userHasClicked == true) { can also be written as if (userHasClicked) {. We have used the longer version because it is easier to follow.

- The code on lines 6–7 is run in the event that this is the first click because userHasClicked is set to false. The code on line 6 sends the playhead in the content movie clip to the frame label value stored on line 2. The line 7 code changes the value of userHasClicked to true, meaning that any subsequent clicks will run the closing animation before the opening one.

Don't worry too much about understanding absolutely everything about this code just yet. We will revisit many of the concepts a bit more in Chapters 15 and 16.

This chunk of code is almost the same for each button, so you'll do all the buttons now.

5. Select the code from lines 2 through 8 and copy it using CTRL/CMD+C.

6. Highlight the handler code for the printButton onRelease event on line 11.

```
9  };
10 printButton.onRelease = function() {
11     content_mc.gotoAndPlay("open print");
12 };
```

7. Paste the previously copied code using CTRL/CMD+V. Click the Auto format button again to tidy up your code.

8. Change the value of the toOpen variable to open print:

```
10 printButton.onRelease = function() {
11     toOpen = "open print";
12     if (userHasClicked == true) {
```

9. Select the handler code within the aboutButton curly brackets, and paste lines 2 and 8 of the code over it.

10. Change the toOpen variable to open about.

11. Paste the code over the existing emailButton code, and change toOpen to open email.

12. Before you move on, add the following to the end of the code:

```
var userHasClicked = false;
var toOpen = "";
```

349

The code for the buttons is finished for this chapter.

```
1  webButton.onRelease = function() {
2      toOpen = "open web";
3      if (userHasClicked == true) {
4          content_mc.play();
5      } else {
6          content_mc.gotoAndPlay(toOpen);
7          userHasClicked = true;
8      }
9  };
10 printButton.onRelease = function() {
11     toOpen = "open print";
12     if (userHasClicked == true) {
13         content_mc.play();
14     } else {
15         content_mc.gotoAndPlay(toOpen);
16         userHasClicked = true;
17     }
18 };
19 aboutButton.onRelease = function() {
20     toOpen = "open about";
21     if (userHasClicked == true) {
22         content_mc.play();
23     } else {
24         content_mc.gotoAndPlay(toOpen);
25         userHasClicked = true;
26     }
27 };
28 emailButton.onRelease = function() {
29     toOpen = "open email";
30     if (userHasClicked == true) {
31         content_mc.play();
32     } else {
33         content_mc.gotoAndPlay(toOpen);
34         userHasClicked = true;
35     }
36 };
37 var userHasClicked = false;
38 var toOpen = "";
```

To make the code functional, you now have to add some code to the various frames in the content movie clip.

Adding frame code

1. Double-click the content movie clip instance on the stage to edit it in place.

2. Scroll along the timeline to frame 100.

3. Click frame 100 of the actions layer and look in the Actions panel. At the moment, it has a stop frame that you added last chapter:

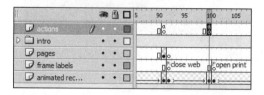

4. Delete the stop code and click the Insert Target Path icon. We want the current timeline to go to the label currently held in variable toOpen. Our variable is on the main timeline, so to access toOpen, we have to define a path to it. In the Insert Target Path window, select _root, and make sure the Relative radio button is selected. Click OK.

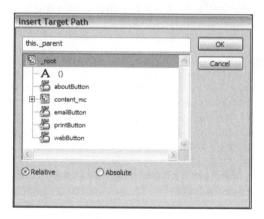

Following our general rule that if it isn't in a code block, you don't need the this, so delete it. Your code so far looks like this:

We want to access the variable toOpen, so add that to the end of your path:

We want to go to the frame label stored in variable toOpen, and to do this, we use _parent.toOpen as an argument for a gotoAndPlay. Change your code as shown.

```
1  gotoAndPlay(_parent.toOpen);
```

Your line should read

gotoAndPlay(_parent.toOpen);

Note that we use a dot path to our variable in much the same way as we would do if toOpen was a movie clip. Everything in Flash is on a timeline (or to use the correct terminology, "is scoped to a timeline"), and for ActionScript to find anything, you have to specify its dot path and name. If the code you are writing happens to be on the same timeline as what you are trying to access, you can omit the path, because Flash will assume the current timeline if you don't give it a path.

The reason that you have added this code in this particular place is clearer by looking at the timeline.

Frame 100 is the last frame of the web closing sequence, and therefore, once the closing animation has played, this line of code instructs the timeline to move on to the selected opening sequence stored as toOpen.

What we have here is a way of giving the interface a **memory**. When you click a button, Flash makes a note of which page you want to go next by storing a keyframe label value in toOpen.

5. Select this line of code and copy it.

6. Select frame 124 and replace the existing code with that on the clipboard.

7. Repeat this for frames 149 and 174.

When the playhead hits any of these frames, it reads your code and redirects the playhead to the relevant play sequence.

8. Save your case study document.

9. Test the movie and try any of the buttons out. Pretty impressive so far, but there is one significant bug that you'll sort out in the next chapter.

Too lazy to find out, eh? Click any button twice in a row and see if anything strikes you as unusual.

Summary

This chapter has built further on the ActionScripting foundation you established in the previous chapter. You've taken an important step toward being able to create well-integrated, intelligent, and responsive movies using ActionScript.

You saw that

- **Labels** provide reference points for you to jump to using ActionScript.

- You can name specific instances of movie clip symbols on the stage using the Properties panel. Naming an instance—instantiating it—means that you can use that name in scripts and manipulate that instance using ActionScript commands.

- You can use actions to point at particular instances on the stage and pass them instructions about how they should behave.

- The goto action is used to jump to an individual frame number or label within a movie clip's timeline.

- You can add intelligence and decision making to your movies using variables and conditional statements:

  - **Variables** are memory locations where you can store values and information for later (re)use.

  - **Conditional statements** let Flash decide what action to take, depending on the conditions it finds.

If you want to do serious, industrial-strength work with Flash, you need to learn ActionScript. You'll be returning to explore ActionScript in much more detail later in the book.

In the next chapter—**sound and video!**

351

Chapter 12

MULTIMEDIA: SOUND AND VIDEO

What we'll cover in this chapter:

- Creating or acquiring sounds and music to use in your movies
- Exploring the types of sound and video that Flash can handle, and the best ways to get sound into and out of Flash
- Manipulating sound and video inside Flash once you've got it there
- Examining the particular issues related to sound implementation in Flash, such as potential pitfalls and strange effects
- Examining Flash video issues, including when it's best to compress imported videos

This chapter will show you how to use sound and video to enhance your Flash movies. You've already attached sound to a button in a previous chapter, but here you'll be opening up the world of Flash multimedia and climbing right inside.

Non-Flash multimedia websites have always separated the sound and video content from the rest of the site. For example, embedding a video into a separate, stand-alone application was the norm with standard HTML websites. With Flash, multimedia elements such as sound and video can be integrated to be consistent with a website's overall look and feel.

The key to getting multimedia onto the Web without compromising loading times is **optimization**—so we'll go through all the things you'll need to consider when you're finally ready to export your movie. You'll look at sound and video elements separately, and consider the implications of each when you add them to your movies.

In this chapter, you'll construct a soundtrack that will play alongside your website's visual content. In this example, you'll separate the soundtrack and the visual content to minimize download time. By doing this, the website will load first, allowing people to begin navigating while the soundtrack loads in the background and starts playing when it's ready. There's another advantage to keeping the sound and visual components apart: if you want to change or replace your soundtrack, it's much easier to do if the soundtrack is separated from the rest of the content.

Before you look at sound in the first section, I recommend that you download the set of sounds from the friends of ED website (www.friendsofed.com) to get the most out of the examples in this chapter.

Plug in those speakers and let's rumble.

Sound on the Web

Sound on the Web used to be problematic, and then a little thing called MP3 came along and blew everything else out of the water. Before the advent of MP3, there were really only two options for the web designer: MIDI and sampled sound files.

MIDI (Musical Instrument Digital Interface) is a format that's understood by all digital musical instruments, all music cards, and most sound cards.

For most sound formats, the sound file contains a digital representation of the actual sounds, with the corollary that a higher quality representation of the sound implies a larger file. The advantage of MIDI is that it doesn't hold representations of the sounds themselves—it holds the instructions for how to play them on a specific instrument. This means that MIDI files are very small and compact compared to other formats. It's a bit like raster versus vector graphics: a MIDI file is similar to a vector in that it's an instruction to do something, not a direct representation of the thing (the sound). MIDI can also be embedded in simple HTML.

A MIDI sound card contains a bank of instruments that the MIDI file instructs the card to play at certain times, volumes, pitches, and so on. This can be a problem because only the instruments embedded in the card can be played. New instruments can sometimes be added to the card, but this means a loss of standardization because you can't guarantee that everyone will have the correct instrument, resulting in another instrument being substituted for it.

The problems with MIDI are that it's not a universal standard, and that the final sound output depends on the quality of your MIDI-compatible synthesizer or music card. More importantly, MIDI is a music language only: it can't be used to create vocal sounds or non-musical effects such as a door slamming.

The other pre-MP3 option was to have sampled data in the various sound formats of the time—WAVs, SNDs, and AIFFs. These were big and bulky and tended to be a major headache during download. Waiting an extra 30 seconds for a voice to say "Hi there," on a homepage didn't really cut the mustard! Additionally, not all sound formats were understood by both PC and Mac platforms, causing further bugs and uncertainties.

Then along came MP3. MP3 is a sound format that compresses sounds intelligently via several different filters to give a much smaller file size for a given quality than any other sound compression system (with the exception of MIDI, which as previously explained, is really an electronic music language for instruments). MP3 is now *the* standard for music files on the Web, in the same way that Flash is the standard for high-impact, highly interactive websites. It therefore comes as no surprise that Flash supports MP3.

> *Although the MP3 format has without a doubt revolutionized audio on the Internet, you shouldn't forget about the speedy take-up of broadband as another major factor. The widespread availability of broadband has allowed video and sound to become major players on the Web. If the UK is anything to go by (the number of broadband users has recently exceeded those with dial-up), then the days of the dial-up modem are all but gone in many parts of the world.*

Flash and MP3

When using Flash and MP3, once the music is embedded into Flash, it can be heard on the Web—but it can't be copied in the same way that regular MP3 data can be downloaded.

Although MP3 simplifies the sound export options available from Flash considerably, there's still the problem of getting the sound into Flash in the first place. In this section, you'll experiment with different ways of doing this.

Without further ado, let's start honing your Flash multimedia skills by using sound. Creating and manipulating sound is probably something novel to many new Flash users, so there are some separate tutorials in this chapter. Let's begin, logically enough, with how to create or source the sounds you want to use.

Creating sound

The first issue when getting sound into Flash is acquiring your sound files. There are generally only two options:

- Get them from a sound library CD or a website offering public domain sounds.
- Create the sound samples yourself.

There are a lot of sites out there that rip off their sounds from obscure dance or hip-hop records. The implications of this may not be too serious when you're starting out, but when you create sites commercially, a revelation that you're using material in violation of copyright can be both costly and embarrassing. The easy and safe option is to get your sounds and loops from a royalty-free website, such as

- www.partnersinrhyme.com
- www.shockwave-sound.com
- http://echovibes.com
- www.flash-sounds.com
- www.musicbakery.com
- www.opuzz.com

Now I'll briefly illustrate a typical route for *creating* sounds for Flash.

There are two main types of sound you'll want to capture: incidental sounds and music. Incidental sounds are things like doors slamming or cows mooing, which can easily be recorded with just a microphone, a handy cow, and the free sound-recording software that comes with your computer (such as Sound Recorder on the PC or Garageband for the Mac). You could record music in the same way, but the results would be huge files with poor quality. The best way to get high quality music onto a computer is to create it yourself.

One of the techniques that you'll learn later in this chapter is how to create a full sound score, optimized for the Web. One of the best ways to utilize sound on the Internet is by creating a **sound loop**. This means that you start and stop with exactly the same noise, so you can repeat the sound endlessly and smoothly without any obvious breaks in it. The advantage of this is that you only need to download one small file that can carry on playing for a long time. Because music loops are one of the hardest sounds to create *well*, we'll work through the thought process that goes into them before moving onto the creation itself.

To create music professionally, you would use a sequencing program along with a battery of expensive synthesizers and instruments—however, you can obtain simple (and relatively cheap) entry-level sequencers from the Web (try googling "sequencer," and you'll find many options). Instead of using expensive physical instruments, you can use the sequencer to control your sound card's *built-in* instruments via MIDI. The real advantage of this method is that all current sound cards support playback of sampled sound (as well as sound capture via a microphone). If you have a decent sound card, you probably have a full synthesizer and sampler sitting in a slot in your computer right now. The sound quality of internal sound cards won't be a problem because you'll be compressing the sounds extensively for web transport, and in the end there won't be much difference between cards. Once you've created your musical masterpiece, it's necessary to **export** it from your sequencer as audio.

This chapter's accompanying sound files were created by importing the sequencer/synthesizer output into Sound Forge—a popular sound-editing program made by Sony. A cheaper, cut-down version is available at 44 KHz and 16-bit, which is the equivalent of CD quality. Using Sound Forge, you can also **normalize** the sounds. Normalization takes the loudest sound in the sample and increases/decreases the overall volume based on this level, setting it as the highest point in the possible range of sounds in your movie. This ensures that there's a much greater range available for the quieter sounds in your file, thus avoiding excessively loud quantization noise (hissing) during the sampling process. If you don't have any really quiet sounds in your file, this isn't really necessary.

After this Sound Forge–based processing, the sounds in this chapter were passed through a package called ACID (from the same makers as Sound Forge) to create a seamless loop, and then saved to the computer. If you're using a Mac, use Garageband to edit your sounds and create your loops. The most common formats for saving in are WAV files (PC) or AIFF files (Mac). This chapter uses WAVs as the default file format for sounds—but if you're using a Mac, just substitute this for AIFFs—all the processes remain the same.

The files are now ready for importing into Flash.

To allow you to use the individual sounds, I've included them with the files in the download section of the friends of ED website. The sound files have been kept at CD quality throughout the sound capture process, for the following two reasons:

- The maximum (best) sound quality that Flash can export is limited by the sound quality at which your file is imported. The better your input, the more flexibility you have with the output. There's always the chance that you may want to use better quality sounds, as Internet transmission speeds creep up and more people have faster connections. By keeping the files at CD quality, you're never in danger of having to rerecord samples.

- You may want to create screen savers or other non-web applications, and these will be able to use CD quality sound because bandwidth won't be an issue. In this case, you wouldn't have to rerecord the sounds because they would already be at the highest quality.

Of course, you may not have CD-quality *output* available, but as a general rule, try to keep your sounds at the highest quality your setup can manage—you may just save yourself from major hassle later on.

Importing and exporting sound with Flash

In the last section, I gave a brief overview of how to get audio onto your computer so that it's ready for importing into Flash. You'll now look at how to get it into Flash, and how to optimize it for export onto the Internet.

To import a sound, all you have to do is use the File ➤ Import menu.

Flash can import a number of sound formats: WAV, AIFF, and MP3 are probably the most popular. If you've created your own sounds, it's strongly recommended that you keep them as full-quality WAV files and not MP3s, because MP3 is what's called a **lossy** format. This means that to get the largest amount of compression, the computer intelligently discards sounds that it thinks you won't hear. The problem with this is that there's a drop in quality, and once the sound information is discarded, it's lost forever. Although you may not be able to hear the differences, you'll see them in programs like Sound Forge and ACID, and you may start to have trouble synchronizing the lower quality sounds as precisely. This is because the waveforms have started to blur, making accurately locating the sound's start and stop positions much more difficult. This is much the same effect as when you use low quality JPEG images, and the image colors and edges start to look washed out and blocky.

> *Although I won't be covering it in this book, it might be useful for you to know that Flash can dynamically load MP3 files with ActionScript. This is done using the* loadSound *method of the* Sound *class, which is covered in Foundation ActionScript for Flash 8, to be published by friends of ED in February of 2006.*

Let's get your fingers busy and work with some real sounds.

> *If you haven't already visited the friends of ED site and downloaded the sound files that accompany this section, do so now. Go to* www.friendsofed.com, *navigate to the book's download page, and download the relevant sound files. Both CD-quality and Flash-optimized (and therefore smaller) versions of the files are included.*

Bringing sound into the mix

1. Open a new Flash document and save it away as soundtrack.fla.
2. Use the File ➤ Import ➤ Import to Library command to open the Import dialog box, and select All Sound Formats from the drop-down menu.

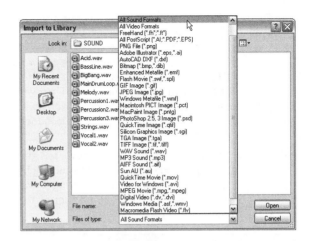

3. From here, navigate to where you saved your downloaded sound files, open them all, and add them to your Library (you can do multiple selections in the PC dialog box using *Shift*-click or *Ctrl*-click, or simply select all files in a folder by pressing *Ctrl+A*).

Once the sounds are imported (which may take a while on slower machines, and you may see a progress bar as Flash imports the files), they'll appear in your Library.

The preview window will show a waveform representation of the selected sound. If you see two separate waveforms, the sound was imported in stereo. If you click the Play button in the preview window, Flash will play one loop of your *original* sound. It's important to remember that Flash will play the sound as it was when you imported it, ignoring any compression you may have added inside Flash since the original import.

4. Display the Sound Properties window for the MainDrumLoop sound either by double-clicking its speaker icon in the Library, or by selecting it and pressing the Properties icon at the bottom of the Library window.

![Sound Properties dialog window showing MainDrumLoop.wav file information and export settings]

This window displays the basic information for the selected sound file, including how the sound will be exported in the final movie. The form Flash will export the sound in is dependent on your selection in the Compression drop-down menu.

5. Click the Test button, and your sound will play in its original state. If you leave this set to Default, Flash will take the settings from your Publish Settings window's Flash tab (this window is covered fully in Chapter 14). At the moment, the default compression settings are MP3 at 16 Kbps (kilobytes per second), but you won't hear this difference until your movie is published.

6. In the Compression drop-down menu of the Sound Properties window, change the setting to MP3.

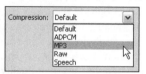

This will open up another list of options.

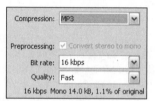

Note the text at the bottom of the window. This text tells you how big your file is and how much it has been compressed. For example, the original file was 1236.4K. Using MP3 compression, you got the size down to 14K, an amazing 1.1% of the original file size.

7. Click Test now to hear the compressed sound. Notice that it doesn't sound quite the same as your original sound.

You can juggle the file size against the quality by playing with the MP3 settings until you reach a happy medium. The Bit rate is another way of expressing the sampling rate of the sound—it's found by multiplying the sampling rate (in Hz) by the number of bits per sample. The Quality defines the conversion algorithm used. Leaving it at Fast means that Flash will convert to MP3 quickly at the expense of quality. Setting it to Best will give you the best conversion quality, but Flash will take slightly longer. This setting has no effect on file size, it's just an anachronism from the days when computers took ages to compress sound—if you have a modern computer, it will probably do the conversion in a blink of an eye no matter what setting you use, so go for Best.

8. When you've tweaked your sound to what you consider to be the best balance (this chapter uses 48Kbps for the sound quality and relative file size), click OK to confirm the settings. If you decide later that your sounds are taking up too much room, you can always go back and change the settings to give a smaller size.

9. Tweak the rest of the sounds to give the best results for you. You'll use these optimized sounds later.

10. Save the Flash document.

> *Sounds can be a major part of the download for the final movie. If you're using sounds, it's recommended that you don't simply accept the default sound settings or set the export options globally. Play around with the settings for each sound individually, and choose the most appropriate setting for each one by considering the sound quality you hear and offsetting this against the relative importance of the sound. Be fairly brutal with this because sound files may make your final website unviewable if they're large and uncompressed.*

In particular, you might consider the following:

- Making button-click sound files as small as the compression allows: the sounds will be a lot deeper and a bit muffled—but hey, what's the difference between one momentary click sound and another?

- Making less prominent sounds lower quality: if you have a big thumping bass line and percussion up front, do you really need all those background effects to be high quality?

- Understanding when to use stereo: the human ear is very poor at sensing the direction of deep sounds, so stereo isn't really necessary for things like thumping bass lines. MP3 takes this into account during its compression, but other methods may not.

I'll end this section with a discussion of the different sound-compression methods (called **codecs**, which stands for **co**mpression/**dec**ompression) available. In practice, the only way to be sure you've used the best

settings is to keep tweaking and testing until you're happy with the audible result.

ADPCM exists mainly for compatibility with Flash 3. It can sometimes give good results for short sounds such as button clicks, but for longer sounds or musical samples, it's best to stick with MP3. As always, the only way to be certain is to try them all and pick the one that's best for you.

MP3 is the compression codec of choice for the Internet in general. You'll find that it gives the best sound for the smallest file size. It works by splitting the sound up into frequency bands and then applying numerous filters and tricks, based on which sounds the human ear would hear. This weeds out redundant information before recompiling the sound.

If you have a definite maximum file size, work your way down the Bit rate menu until the desired file size is reached. MP3 also allows you to select stereo when going above 16Kbps, but because of the way MP3 compression works, this won't always make a huge difference. Often on a stereo track, most of the sounds in one channel are mirrored in the other: part of the MP3 compression cycle is to compare the two channels and delete all the mirrored information from one and just mark the differences in the other channel. When the track is played back, one channel plays in stereo until it comes across a marked difference, and it plays that difference in the other channel. With this method, the size of the track is almost halved while still remaining true to the original. MP3 then performs a number of other more complicated routines to get the track size down even further.

Raw has no compression routine, and as its name suggests, it exports raw digitized sound. You can reduce the file size by specifying a lower quality, but your final file size will generally be much higher than using any of the other methods. You would only use this method if you were running the final movie from a hard drive in applications, such as Flash screen savers. The raw format does have the advantage that it's the fastest way to play sounds. When using something like MP3, a certain amount of the Flash Player's time can be spent decompressing the sound, so if size isn't an issue but speed is, you might be better off choosing this.

Speech is a form of compression that's best, predictably, when used on recorded voice tracks. Because voices record at a lower frequency than most sounds—including music, for example—this allows you to use a lower sample rate—5 KHz or 11 KHz are acceptable. Try this when you have a voice track for your Flash movies. Flash uses the Speech codec when it's performing real-time compression (via the microphone object), and its selling point is speed rather than compression, so you may find that even for raw speech, MP3 is better.

In all the options just listed, it's important to note that putting the sound-sampling settings higher than the original imported sound won't produce better quality sound (it can actually create worse quality in some cases).

Also worth noting is that it's a common mistake when optimizing sounds to compare the optimized sound against the original. If you simply listen to the sound in its own right, you tend to go for lower compression rates, which is more realistic—web listeners won't be comparing the sounds against the original either.

Using sound in Flash

You saw how to attach sound to a button state in Chapter 10. Attaching sound to a Timeline is almost identical in nature, but there are additional sound features Flash offers that I've not yet touched on. Let's repair that state of affairs right now.

Attaching sounds to the Timeline

This is as easy as it sounds: you create a keyframe and attach a sound to it. There are, however, several options that can be selected to make full use of the sound and extra optimization facilities offered by Flash. Although the number of drop-down menus may seem a little daunting, it all fits together in a fluid movement when you're actually adding the sound. The best way to illustrate this is to try it.

Attaching sounds to the Timeline

1. Continuing with the last exercise, change the name of the soundtrack.fla movie's default layer to percussion 1. Then insert a keyframe in frame 5. You should now have the following basic setup:

2. Open the Properties panel if it's not already open. From here you can attach your sound and add effects and different timings to it. If the keyframe in frame 5 isn't already highlighted, click it. Open the Sound drop-down menu from the Properties panel—all the sounds in your Library will appear in a list.

3. To attach a sound to your keyframe, select it from this list—scroll down the list and click Percussion1.wav. Once you've selected your sound, a little waveform appears in the keyframe. Right now it just looks like a straight line because you can only see a small fragment of it.

4. To rectify this, add frames by pressing *F5* at frame 90 so that you can see the end of the waveform just poking into frame 89.

5. Test your movie. You should hear a short pause, and then the sound will begin playing at frame 5.

6. Click your sound in the Timeline (the keyframe at frame 5) and return to the Properties panel. The next thing to look at is the Effect drop-down menu.

This option allows you to add audio effects via a volume envelope. The envelope allows you to see and control the volume in different parts of the sound.

7. For an example of this, select Fade left to right from the Effect drop-down menu, and then click Edit (next to the menu) to display the Edit Envelope window.

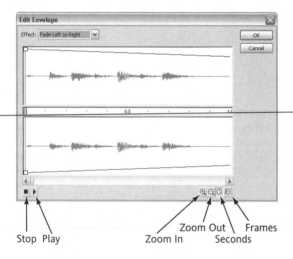

Once the Edit Envelope window appears, use the Zoom buttons on the bottom-right until you can see the full waveform.

Stereo sounds are split into two channels, one for the left speaker and one for the right. This window contains two panes—the top pane shows the waveforms for the left audio channel, and the bottom pane shows the waveforms for the right channel. You'll always see two channels, even if the sound you're editing is mono—the one channel will just be repeated twice. The scale between the two panes represents time, which can be measured in seconds or frames. You can toggle between the scales with the two buttons on the bottom-right.

You can test your sound at any time by using the Play button.

Superimposed on top of the waveforms are a couple of lines with little white squares at their ends. These lines depict the volume envelope, and they can be used to control the volume of your sound. The top of the pane represents 100% volume, and the bottom is silence. Because you selected Fade Left to Right, the top pane (the left channel) will have a diagonal line running from the top at the beginning of the sound to the bottom at the end, whereas the bottom pane will show the opposite. This means the sound in the left speaker will start at full volume and drop to nothing, and the sound in the right speaker will start at nothing and rise to full volume, giving the effect of the sound panning from one side to the other.

8. Press the Play button to hear the effect.

9. The squares on the lines are control points, much like on Bezier curves, and they can be dragged to change the shape of the envelope—try it now.

10. Drag the control points higher and lower, and use the Play button to preview your changes. You can add up to eight control points by clicking anywhere on either the top or bottom pane. When you add a point in one pane, Flash adds an identical point in the other. You can easily make some pretty strange sound effects by playing with these settings.

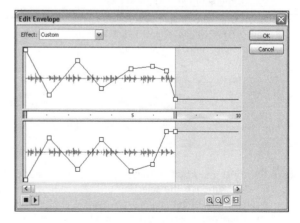

11. To get an idea of some basic effects, run through the Effect drop-down list at the top of the window, and notice how the envelope changes to reflect your selection.

Always play your sounds after you make an alteration to ensure you're achieving the effect you want. As with most things, the best way to appreciate how it works is to play with it and learn by listening to the effects you make. Notice that you can still zoom in and out using the magnifying glass icons while you're editing the envelope—this allows you to be more precise with the timing of the control points.

12. Select None from the Effect drop-down list to cancel all effects you've added to the sound, and then click OK to close the dialog window.

You want no effect because you want the sound to play just like the original (no fade or pan effects)—but feel free to come back later and experiment.

As you may have already begun to realize, the volume envelope can be very powerful when creating sound effects. For example, the sound of an approaching car can easily be simulated by importing a basic engine noise, and using the envelope controls to make it slowly increase in volume. The same engine noise could also be used to simulate the car moving from left to right across the screen by using the Fade Left to Right effect. Through clever use of the envelope controls, you could even incorporate both of these effects into the same sound. Many more complicated effects are possible with these controls, but they're beyond the scope of this book. For now, just knowing these basics will stand you in good stead.

13. Open the Sync drop-down menu in the Properties panel. This will give you a list of four options—Event, Start, Stop, and Stream.

The most important of these options are Event and Stream. Although the selection of these Sync types will have little effect on your movie while you're testing it in Flash, they have a profound effect on how Flash loads the sounds during Internet playback.

14. Leave this selection set to Event.

15. Save the Flash document once again.

Sounds in Flash take precedence over animations and videos, and follow their own separate "lifetimes." For example, imagine you have an animation that's 10 seconds long, and a sound that also lasts for 10 seconds. You could tell Flash to start them both at the same time and expect them both to finish at the same time. In reality, though, if someone runs your movie on a slow computer, your sounds can easily get out of sync, especially if you're streaming sounds (sending the file down bit by bit as it plays). If you run the 10-second animation/sound example on a slow computer, it might get halfway through the sound and animation without a problem, but then have to pause the animation as it waits to load the next part of the sound arriving down the wire. If it were the other way and the animation was the problem, Flash would try to skip frames to allow the sound to play smoothly.

- The Event option tells Flash to treat the sound the same way it treats movie symbols. It will only load one version of the sound into its Library when the movie is first played, and will reuse the sound if it has to play it more than once. Event sounds aren't played until the whole sound has been loaded, and they aren't locked to the Timeline. If you have an event sound that lasts 10 seconds, but the user's computer is too slow to maintain the frame rate, the sound may not end on the frame you would have expected. The problem with this is that your movie may take longer to begin playing because Flash is loading all of the sounds before it starts.

- Stream tells Flash to start loading the sound directly from the Internet as a constant sound stream. Flash starts playing the sound as soon as it has approximately 5 seconds of the sound loaded. If you repeat the same sound several times, Flash will reload the sound each time because it's not kept in the computer's memory. When you have several sounds all streaming at the same time and stopping at the same time, Flash will mix them all together when it creates the SWF file for Internet playback, and will stream back only one channel. Additionally, Flash will lock the sound to the Timeline. This means that if the sound gets ahead or behind of the main Timeline, Flash will stop or skip frames to make sure the sound stops at the right instant. This can cause choppy animations as Flash tries to keep the frame rate up with the sound, but it does ensure your animation keeps in sync with your soundtrack.

A good analogy for event vs. streaming sounds is the difference between owning a song on CD (event sound), and listening to it on the radio (streaming sound). To own it, you first have to go out and buy it, but after that you can play it as often as you like, and pause it if you want to do something else for a while. If you listen to it on the radio, you can listen to it once all the way through every time it's played—but if you want to do something else for a moment, you can't pause it, and if you turn the radio off, you have to wait for the song to be broadcast again before you can hear it again. The good thing about the CD is flexibility, but you have a larger initial outlay (you have to buy it). The good thing about the radio is that you don't have any initial outlay, but you lose flexibility in its use.

Having said all that, the choice between Event and Stream is usually easy. If the sound is relatively short and will be played more than once or looped, select Event. If your sound is a long, non-repeating, introductory tune that has to start playing immediately, select Stream. It's usually more economical to build tailored sounds from scratch that can be easily looped if they need to be. In this case, you'll rarely have to use the Stream option, and will therefore save your sounds from having to be reloaded when you want to reuse them.

The Start option is almost identical to Event except that it won't allow more than one version of the same sound to play at the same time. The Start option prevents the second sound from starting up, and will leave the previous sound to finish playing. For example, if you have a long sound attached to a button and you don't use the Start option, it will replay every time the button is pressed—and rather than stopping the first sound if the button is pressed again, Flash will just start playing the new sound on top of the original one, turning your carefully constructed sounds into a mess! The Start option allows you to avoid such undesirable situations.

The Stop option does just what it says—it stops the sound attached to the keyframe and all other versions of the same sound file that are already playing.

On the second drop-down menu in the Properties panel are the options Repeat and Loop, both of which deal with the number of times the sound is played.

Selecting the Repeat option will allow you to specify the number of times the sound will play. Setting this to 1 or 0 will make the sound play once only, without repetition. Selecting the Loop option here will cause the sound to play over and over forever—certainly longer than anyone is likely to listen to it! With either option, when you have a repeating sound, the volume envelope will extend across all of the loops, allowing you to apply fades and effects across the whole sound, not just each individual segment. This is useful for repetitive sounds like car engines and helicopter whirrs.

Now let's examine some of the quirks of sound in Flash.

Flash sound issues

There are a fair number of unexpected things that can happen when you're using sound in Flash. These surprises have put off many otherwise competent Flash web designers from dabbling much further than adding sound to the odd button click in Flash. It's important that you're aware of these from the beginning so that you won't have too much trouble with them later.

These unexpected results have been with Flash for a number of revisions, and look set to stay, so don't treat the methods listed below as workarounds for the current version, but rather as the way you have to do it every time in Flash.

- The Flash Player sometimes gets its synchronization wrong when all the sounds start on the first frame of your movie or the first frame of any scene. For this reason, it's a good idea to start all sounds at about frame 5. It's also worth noting that if you have a sound on a gotoAndPlay action in a movie with a long Timeline and high frame rate, it's a good idea to put the sound a few frames after the destination frame.

- From time to time, Event-synchronized sounds may not last as long as they should, or may not sound as if they start on the same frame, even though they're set to do so on the Timeline. There's a little trick that you can use to correct this: In addition to starting your sounds at frame 5, try adding a new layer with a one-frame sound in frame 4 and setting it to Stream. This is called a "kicker" layer, because it seems to kick the Flash Player into action and make it behave like it should. Use a small sound and remember to set its volume envelope to nothing, so you won't hear anything when it plays. You'll need to do this for every new scene you have that contains any Event sounds attached to a Timeline that are supposed to start at the same instant. Alternatively, you can create a very short sound sample specifically for use as the kicker in all your projects. A potential danger with this technique is that if you have a movie with very intense animation, the streamed kicker will force frames to be skipped, including the possibility of skipping other code and sound keyframes.

- Event sounds are only synchronized to the Timeline when they're started. If, for some reason, the computer fails to keep up with the frame rate, your carefully triggered sounds can start to play too late, leaving gaps and—worse—becoming unsynchronized. There are three ways around this:

- When you're ready to publish your movie (more on this in the Publishing chapter, Chapter 14), set your movie playback to Auto High. If you've set your movie quality to High, Flash will try to maintain the picture quality of your animations at a maximum and won't be too bothered about maintaining a constant frame rate. This may result in your sounds being triggered too late because the Timeline itself is "getting behind." You can lower the quality to Auto High from the HTML tab of the File ➤ Publish Settings menu. This tells Flash to maintain a

high quality until it's in danger of becoming too slow, at which point Flash will drop the picture quality to keep up. Flash can therefore compensate intelligently.

- Drop the movie frame rate.

- Use advanced ActionScript. Rather than attaching your sounds to frames, you can create a code-based sequencer that uses the Sound.onSoundComplete() method. Unfortunately, this process is a little beyond the scope of this book, but it's covered in *Foundation ActionScript for Flash 8* (to be published in February of 2006).

- Whether you're producing a professional website or one for personal use, it's still best to test it out on a minimum spec computer. Although this used to be a major issue, it's becoming increasingly less so as the average computer becomes faster. The other option is to forget the issue completely unless someone reports a problem, which is less likely to happen as time goes on, but it still can stop that person from ever returning to your site.

Now that you know about how to acquire or create sound loops and avoid some of the pitfalls associated with sound, it's time to do something a bit more useful than attaching the odd click to a button or a few low quality sound effects to the Timeline.

Integrating sound

In this section, you'll create a full soundtrack. There are few websites that actually have such a thing, possibly because of all the problems that have been encountered with Flash's Event sound type, so you're now beginning to walk a trail less trodden, one that many before you have been afraid to follow. You may be a beginner, but that's no excuse for being afraid. Enjoy.

Creating a movie soundtrack

A feature of Flash that I've not talked about yet is the loadMovie action. This action allows Flash to run more than one movie at the same time. One of these movies could be your website's visual content, and the other one could be the soundtrack.

In this chapter, you'll create a soundtrack movie, and I'll show you how to add it to a website movie when I talk about publishing in Chapter 14. Your soundtrack won't be a traditional Flash movie because it will have a blank stage—the Timeline in the soundtrack movie will control sound only. Don't be put off by this; it will all begin to blend together when you get to the Publishing chapter. For now, let's paste together the loops you imported earlier and make a polished soundtrack.

In your soundtrack.fla Flash document, you should already have a full, optimized Library, and one layer containing a percussion sound.

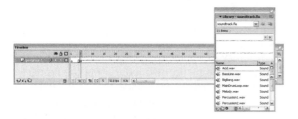

These sounds have been specially selected to allow the creation of a number of different compositions, or in the more modern parlance, they allow different remixes of the same tune. You can bring certain elements to the fore or delete others to give completely different styles. For example, you can use strings and melodies for an ambient sound, or focus on percussion for a more insistent sound.

As you saw earlier, the sounds were created for looping and reuse, so you'll use event syncing throughout. Taking into account the problems that can occur with Event sounds, the first thing you must do is add a kicker.

1. Create a new layer and name it kicker.
2. Insert a keyframe in frame 4 of the kicker layer, and then attach the BassLine.wav sound (although you can use any sound) to the keyframe.
3. In the Properties panel, set the Sync drop-down menu option to Stream.

4. Insert a blank keyframe in frame 5 of the kicker layer. Because you set the sound to Stream, you want to make sure that the sound plays for only one frame before stopping.
5. Click back to frame 4, and then click the Edit button in the Properties panel to open the Edit Envelope window for the BassLine sound. Drag the control points to the bottom to set the volume to zero for both channels, and then click OK to close the window.

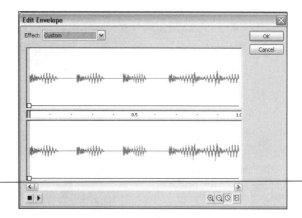

There's no need to change the Loop/Repeat option in the Properties panel because you want your sound to play only once.

6. Because it's imperative to know where in the Timeline you are at all times (you'll have to count beats and frames to sync everything up just right), you'll add a comments layer to hold labels. Add a new layer above your kicker layer, and name it comments.

The layer will automatically match the length of your longest layer—in this case, the percussion 1 layer. If it needs to be any longer at any stage, you can always lengthen it. You could also make this layer a guide layer so that it doesn't get exported into the final movie, but because it contains nothing but labels, it won't make much difference.

7. Insert a keyframe in frame 4 of the comments layer, above your kicker sound. Use the Frame field on the left of the Properties panel to put a comment in this keyframe that reads //Kicker and Percussion 1. Don't worry if the label is too long for the text field. The labels on this layer will let you quickly see what's happening, and when, in your soundtrack.

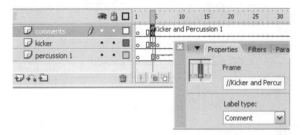

Adding two forward slashes (//) in front of a frame label makes it a comment—Flash won't include it in the final SWF, and it exists only for your benefit in the FLA.

---

8. Make sure that your percussion sound is set to be an Event sound that doesn't repeat. Unless otherwise stated, this will be the setting for all the other sounds, too. Don't forget!

As a safety check, let's make sure that this sample looks how you expect it to. In Sony's ACID program, the samples were 7 seconds long each. The movie is playing at 12 fps (frames per second), which for 7 seconds equates to 84 frames. The sample starts at frame 5 and ends at 89, which seems about right.

The percussion sound is two bars long, and so are all of the other samples. You're writing a dance track, so the pattern you must follow is to create four bars before inserting a change. This is the standard pattern for all dance and most pop music, so it's one to remember. This means that you need another two bars before you can have a new pattern, so you must repeat this pattern once more.

9. Insert a keyframe in frame 89 of the percussion 1 layer, and attach another Percussion1.wav sound using the Sound drop-down menu in the Properties panel.

10. Play your sound through to make sure there are no glitches in it. Insert frames as you did before, until you can see the whole sound wave on the Timeline—this will allow you to easily sync other sounds to the end of it. If your sounds are a little out of sync, try moving their starting keyframe forward or backward until you find where they sound best.

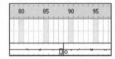

You may be wondering why you didn't just repeat the first sample for two loops using the Properties panel. You could have done that, but remember that Event sounds are only synchronized to the Timeline when they're started. The longer the event sound lasts before you attach a new version to the Timeline, the more chance there is of your sound getting slightly out of sync with the Timeline.

Next, you'll add a new loop, Percussion2.wav, which is a slightly fuller rhythm with more bass.

11. Add a new layer called percussion 2 to put the sound in, and move this layer to the bottom of the list. This means that your layer order follows the order of the samples in the soundtrack. If you need to see all your layers at once, click the bottom of the Timeline and drag it down until they're all in view.

12. Add a keyframe in this layer at the frame immediately after the first percussion loop finishes, and attach the Percussion2.wav sound to it.

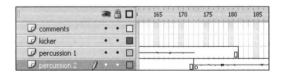

> *If you're having trouble finding the ends of the sounds, you can set the frames to a longer size by clicking the icon at the top-right of the Timeline panel and selecting* Large *from the drop-down menu.*

13. Add a keyframe to your comments layer above where you started the new sound, and label it //Percussion 2. You can also extend the Timeline a few frames after the keyframe so that you can see the full comment text, as shown in the following graphic:

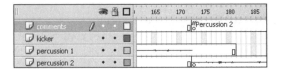

This label reminds you that you're now in the second set of four bars, and that you're using the second percussion sample. Documentation of music files is pretty much a necessity. You may recognize all the individual waveforms now—but in six months, when you want to spruce up your website and decide on a celebratory remix, it may take you some time to find where each new sound comes in on the composition.

14. In accordance with the four bar rule, repeat the Percussion2.wav sound at the frame after it ends, in the same way as you did for Percussion1.wav. (In the book's example, this is at frame 257).

> *The four bar rule is there for the main loops that shape your composition, but you can have sounds that start and finish before and after a four bar interval. Some samples do this in the final file,* soundtrack.fla.

15. Next, you'll add two sounds that will start at the same time in the third set of four bars. Prepare the Timeline by adding two new layers to the bottom, calling them percussion 3 and big bang.

Extend your Timeline until you see the end of the last sound (if you haven't already). Insert your new sounds in their respective layers immediately after the end of the second Percussion2.wav sound. In the book's example, this occurs at frame 341.

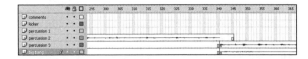

16. Update your comments layer to include the new sounds.

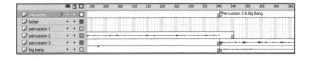

17. Preview your movie to hear your soundtrack. Now that you have more than one sound playing at the same time, one sound will start to overshadow the other. This can be corrected by messing with the relative volume of each track to make for a more pleasing composition.

18. You want to bring the BigBang.wav sound to the fore, so open up the Edit Envelope window for the Percussion3.wav sound, and lower its volume by dragging the control points down a bit. Then return to your movie and play it again. If the volume needs to be adjusted again, go back and drag the points a little lower. Repeat this until you're happy with the results.

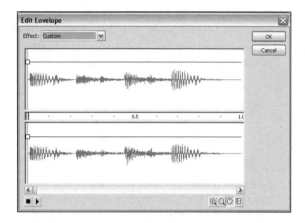

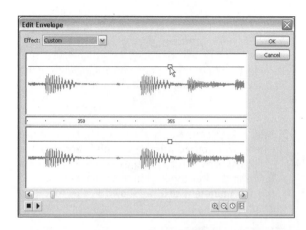

You can also easily bring the volume back up to 100% after the BigBang.wav effect has played. By doing this, you can insert another Percussion3.wav track afterward at full volume without producing a noticeable jump in the sound.

19. Look on your Timeline, and note which frame the BigBang.wav sound finishes in (it will be around frame 355).

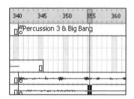

20. Go back into the Edit Envelope window for Percussion3.wav and change the timer to Frames (click the button next to Help and you'll see the frame numbers of your movie appear in the Edit Envelope window).

21. Move along the sound until you come to the frame you noted as the BigBang.wav sound's endpoint (around frame 355), and put in another control point.

22. Move about 10 frames forward to give a gradual volume increase, put in another control point at 100% in both panes, and press OK.

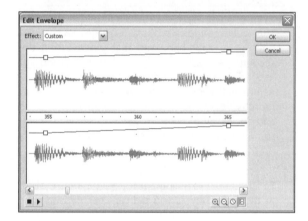

23. Play back your soundtrack. It should play smoothly all the way through, and you probably won't even notice the change in volume at the end.

To sum up, the process for adding new sounds is as follows:

1. Create a new layer and name it after the sound.

2. Insert a keyframe in the new layer where you want the sound to start.

3. Attach the sound to the keyframe using the Properties panel.

4. Add a label to your comments layer so you can track what's happening.

5. Add frames to the layer until you can see the end of the waveform.

6. Play the soundtrack and decide if you want to make any volume or synchronization changes.

7. Make any changes you need, and play the sound again to make sure you're happy with it.

8. Either add another copy of the sound afterward, or start a new sound on its own layer.

24. Use the other sounds you've been provided with—or ones you've created yourself—and put them together to create your own complete soundtrack. Don't worry if it ends up quite long; that's what the soundtrack is for—to provide a backdrop while the visitor is at your site.

At the end of the soundtrack, you're going to put in a loop so that a section of it will carry on playing forever.

25. Add a label in your comments layer at the end of your last sound and call it End loop.

26. At (or around) the End loop frame, add sounds as you did before. Note that in the book's example, the sounds no longer start at the same frame—the longer your Timeline, the more likely this becomes.

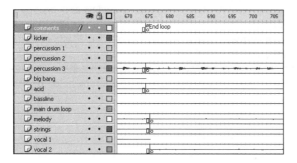

27. Using the Sound section of the Properties panel, set all the sounds in your final loop to play forever. To do this, select the keyframe(s) below the End loop comment and select Loop in the Properties panel.

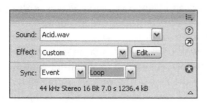

Because the sounds start at around the same time, they're synchronized to each other and won't fall out of time with one another. They may fall out of time with the Timeline, but that doesn't really matter anymore because no new sounds will be started that need to be synchronized to any particular event.

28. The final thing to do is to put a Stop action in the End loop keyframe in the comments layer. If you want to have a number of separate soundtracks, say, for different sections of your movie, you could keep them all as different scenes in your main soundtrack movie and call them when required. By putting a Stop action in here, you're making sure that Flash won't start playing them when it gets to the end of your first soundtrack. Just select Stop from the Sync drop-down menu in the Properties panel.

That's it; your musical masterpiece is finished. Now just crank up the volume, press Play, kick back, and enjoy—until you get sick of it and turn it off.

When the Output window appears during the movie preview with the text SWF contains multiple copies of a sound item, *don't panic! This is Flash's way of telling you that the movie features instances of a sound or group of sounds set to different* Sync *settings* (Start/Event *or* Stream)*, meaning that it will need to load them more than once. A sound set to* Stream *(in this movie, your kicker sound) loads, plays, and is removed from memory, meaning that future uses of it in the movie, whether streamed or not, will have to be loaded from scratch. Sounds using* Start *or* Event *will be loaded from the Library, so they only need to be loaded once by the Flash movie.*

29. Save your movie.

And that's more or less all there is to the basics of putting music in Flash. Simply add or subtract sounds every four bars and you're on your way. The only thing I haven't talked about sound-wise is how to integrate something like this into a website. The problem with sound files is that they can be some of the largest things in your site, so it's a good idea to load them only when you're sure the user wants to listen to them. Let's see how to do that.

369

Assuming you have created a soundtrack called soundtrack.fla using the steps just outlined, make sure that you have a file called soundtrack.swf in the same folder. (You'll have this if you've tested the soundtrack at least once.)

> *Although* soundtrack.fla *is on the download page for this chapter, it's a little on the large side (around 13MB). To carry out the next exercise, you need only a folder with* soundtrack.swf *in it, which is a much more reasonable 200K.*

Integrating the soundtrack into a website

1. Create a new FLA, and save it in the same folder as soundtrack.swf. Call this new file soundLoader.fla.

2. In soundLoader.fla, add two layers and rename the three layers you now have actions, text, and buttons (from top to bottom).

3. On the stage, create two buttons and give them instance names of sound_btn and noSound_btn.

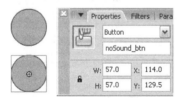

4. In the text layer, next to sound_btn, add a static text field with the words sound on in it. Add another text field with the words sound off in it next to noSound_btn.

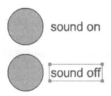

5. Add the following script on frame 1 of the actions layer:

```
sound_btn.onRelease = function() {
  loadMovieNum("soundtrack.swf", 100);
};
noSound_btn.onRelease = function() {
  unloadMovieNum(100);
};
```

A Flash presentation can consist of **levels**. Flash SWF files can be arranged in a stack (much like layers), and this occurs at runtime. The lowest level is called _level0, and the next is _level1, all the way up to approximately _level16000. The advantage of using levels is that you can allow users to decide whether they want to load them, which can save a lot of downloading.

In the book's example, the soundtrack.swf file is loaded into level 100 if the user presses the top button, and unloaded again when the user presses the bottom button. Simple, easy, just the way it should be!

Well-designed sounds that can be seamlessly looped are gold dust to the Flash designer because they make the production of optimized soundtracks to go with your website just a matter of dragging and dropping sounds onto the Timeline. Also, an understanding of how and how not to lay down sound in Flash will prevent you from falling into the traps that befall many Flash beginners. The use of sound in Flash for soundtracks and incidental effects will hopefully help lift your website designs above their mute contemporaries.

Next, let's have a look at how you can enhance your Flash movies using video.

Video on the Web

Until Flash started doing video, it was primarily served on the Web through three players—QuickTime, RealPlayer, and Windows Media Player. Although each format was sufficient for serving video, the most common problem with them was their lack of integration within a web page. The standard fare for website video with these players was an ugly pop-up window appearing unlike the rest of the website and ruining the overall gestalt. If you added the various compatibility and platform issues—the broken plug-in symbol was common, missing codecs even more so—the case for the three prime players wasn't as convincing as it should have been. There had to be another way . . .

Then a company called Macromedia decided to turn their little vector animation plug-in, called Flash, into one that dealt with video too. Simply put, Macromedia saw a huge gap in the market and decided to pounce on it. With Flash's rapidly increasing takeup (a reputed 98% of the world's computers currently have the plug-in installed), they decided to take on the three video moguls.

And it worked. Flash is now among the most popular video players on the Web and it's still on the rise, as more and more companies decide to serve their video content using Flash. If this wasn't enough, Flash answers the problems that the standard video plug-ins had with ease.

- Compatibility: the Flash plug-in is available for the three major operating systems (Windows, Mac, and Linux) and a growing variety of mobile phones and PDAs.
- Website integration: Flash videos sit anywhere they want to in your movies and they can be shaped, colored, masked, scripted, and so on.

Flash uses either the Sorenson Spark or On2 VP6 codec to embed video into Flash movies. Why are there two? The fact that there are two codecs is a sign of Macromedia's further ambition to overtake the other video players on the Web. When video was introduced in Flash MX, Macromedia got Sorenson on board to include their codec, but with this current release of Flash, Macromedia has chosen a better-quality, newer codec to ensure better competition with high-quality video formats like Real and Windows Media.

When a video is inserted into Flash, it's encoded into either chosen codec format and is then available from the Library like any other media.

Let's talk about how to make video content before I get on to importing and working with it in Flash.

Creating video

If you have a Mac or are using Windows XP, you already have your own resources for generating video content. Since the Classic (pre–OS X) days, Macs have come with a free version of iMovie, and more recently, Movie Maker was bundled with all copies of Windows XP, meaning that there's an increasingly large pool of computer owners with the resources to carry out non-linear video editing on their machines.

Non-linear video editing means that your video is on a storyboard that you can edit any part of. Traditional linear video editing dictated that you had to start at the beginning and work your way through the video. If you got to the end and wanted to go back to edit a few frames near the beginning, the likelihood was that you would destroy anything after those frames.

Digital video (DV) cameras now regularly come with desktop editing software. This was made a lot easier by Apple and Sony's recommendation and development of the FireWire interface (also known as iLink on Sony products), along with powerful yet affordable software like Apple's Final Cut Express and Adobe Premiere. This means that creating movies with excellent picture quality at home is possible, and that's somewhat of a revolution. The revolution, which has taken Hollywood by storm, allows anyone to shoot and edit their own features without the expense of reels of film and edit time.

The uses of these technologies aren't exclusive to the amateur filmmaker. Many Hollywood productions have embraced the DV format, including director Mike Figgis in the film *Time Code* and George Lucas in some evil vs. good movie set in a galaxy far, far away. The miniDV format (usually associated with smaller handheld cameras) has found a home in documentaries, such as *Super Size Me*, and music videos. If all this talk of DV and FireWire doesn't apply to you though, don't worry—there are still many options available.

- Windows users: If you don't have a system with a FireWire port, there are many cheap capture cards available that work with analog and DV cameras. Most of these come with some basic editing software to get you going and will enable you to export in a format suitable for importing into Flash. Alternatively, you can buy a cheap FireWire expansion card and join the DV revolution!

- Mac users: If you're reading this, you most likely have built-in FireWire capability and a copy of iMovie. If you have a DV camera too, what's stopping you? You can get the latest version of iMovie free from the Apple website.

- Digital Camera users: If your budget is too tight for a DV camera but you have a digital stills camera with video functionality, this footage can also be used in Flash. Although the frame rate and quality will be considerably lower, you can produce some cool effects.

With all import options considered, you'll benefit greatly if your footage is shot on a DV camera using miniDV format tapes. The ability to shoot high-quality videos is increasing as the price of DV cameras drops and higher quality cameras are released onto the market.

As a cheap investment, FireWire is also worth considering. It's fast enough to comfortably import video, and also allows the application to take control of DV cameras for reviewing rushes—removing the need to fiddle with the tiny play, rewind, and stop buttons on the camera.

Flash-friendly formats

Making video suitable for use in Flash is easy. Most (if not all) video-editing applications will enable you to export your footage to a suitable format, such as MOV or AVI files. In all cases, try to export the content with little compression and at a reasonable size, because Flash will take care of any scaling or compression on import. Just for the record, the following is a list of all the footage formats that Flash can import on both platforms:

- By default on Mac and Windows, Flash can import FLV (Flash Video) format files.

- If QuickTime 7 (or higher) is installed on Mac or Windows, Flash can handle AVI, DV, MPG, MPEG, and MOV files.

- If DirectX 9 (or higher) is installed on Windows, Flash can handle AVI, MPG, MPEG, WMV, and ASF files.

There are occasions when Flash has issues with importing sound with video clips. To save yourself any problems, it's best to keep your footage saved in its original format wherever possible. That way, you can export the footage in a suitable format so that Flash can import the sound with the clip.

Before you begin, make sure you have some video clips handy, or have downloaded the video files that are available on the friends of ED website.

Using video with Flash

Now that you know which formats you need, let's import a video clip into Flash.

Importing video

In this exercise, you're going to import a video in the quickest way possible. The video, REDCAR.MOV, is available for download from the friends of ED website. This video was shot in New York on a DV camera.

1. Open a new Flash document and save it as redcar_video.fla.

2. Use File ➤ Import ➤ Import to Stage to open the Import dialog box, and select All Video Formats from the drop-down menu.

3. Navigate to where you saved the download files and select REDCAR.MOV, or locate another clip from your hard disk. Select the clip you want to import and click Open.

4. The Import Video wizard appears. On the first page of the wizard, the file name of the selected file is displayed. Unless you want to change your video selection here, click Next to proceed.

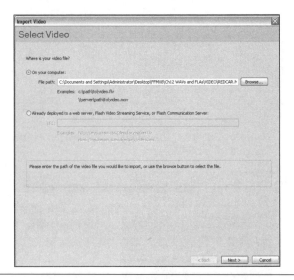

5. On the next page, Deployment, is a number of options for how the file will be presented. Select Embed video in SWF and play in timeline here, and click Next.

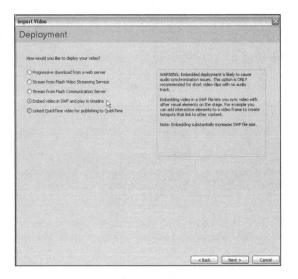

I'll talk a little about the other options here later in the chapter.

6. The next page of the wizard appears, Embedding, asking a multitude of things. Select the same options as shown in the following screenshot, and click Next to proceed.

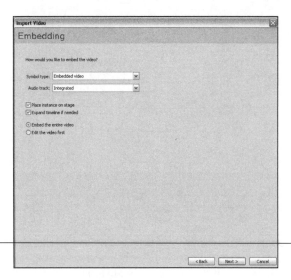

You're instructing Flash to do the following things:

- Insert the video as a raw video.
- Keep the audio and video together.
- Place a copy of the video on the stage.
- Insert the entire unedited video.

As mentioned, in this exercise, you'll concentrate on importing a video at the most basic level. You'll look at the editing options available to you in a moment.

7. On the final screen of the wizard, Encoding, select Flash 7 – Modem Quality (40kbps) from the drop-down menu at the top of the window. This selection is a preset created with modem users in mind, so the compression will be pretty severe.

8. Once you're done, click Next. You'll now see the Finish Video Import dialog box, with a brief list of the selections you made.

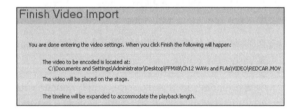

9. Click Finish to finally import the video.

You should now see a progress bar—note that the import might take a while, depending on the file size of the clip you imported and the speed of your machine.

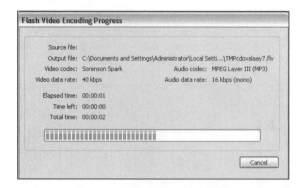

Once this is done, the video will be placed on the stage and in the Library.

10. Drag the playhead along the top of the Timeline. You'll see that the content of the movie changes according to where you are in the Timeline.

11. Test the movie with Control ➤ Test Movie. It's worth comparing your compressed movie's file size to the original uncompressed MOV file. You can preview file sizes with the Bandwidth Profiler, which you'll have a more detailed look at in the next chapter.

12. With the test movie still open, select View ➤ Bandwidth Profiler.

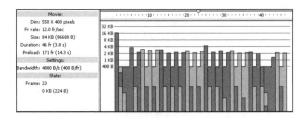

If you look at the left pane of the top part of the screen, you'll see that the file size, shown under the Movie category, is listed as 84K. The size of the original MOV file is around 1100K, so this is an incredible savings, but the loss of quality is considerable.

Later on you'll learn a little bit about how to find a happy medium—good quality with a smaller file size—through optimizing.

Right now, though, you're going to have a little fun.

Treating a video clip like any other Flash symbol

If you think being able to import video into Flash is enough, you don't know the half of it. One of the real cool aspects of using video in Flash is that when a video is embedded in a symbol, it can be used like any other symbol instance. Let's quickly see what you can do with it to make your videos a little more fun.

1. Make sure that the Flash document from the last exercise, `redcar_video.fla`, is open. Select Modify ➤ Document and change the stage width to 640 pixels and the height to 240. The reason for this will be apparent in a moment.

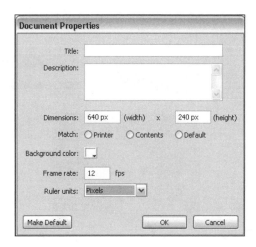

2. Select the embedded video on the stage and convert it into a movie clip symbol using Modify ➤ Convert to Symbol or *F8*.

3. Give it the name video_mc and a central registration point. Then click OK.

You'll then be prompted as shown in the following screenshot.

Flash is offering to save you a little time here by expanding the Timeline within the movie clip to display the whole length of the video clip—how considerate!

4. Click Yes to allow Flash to expand the Timeline.

375

5. Now double-click the newly created movie clip to view its contents.

Yes, you're right, it doesn't look that much different to what you had already. Except that this time the video is within a movie clip instance and you can do things to it.

6. Return to the main Timeline and remove all the frames, leaving only the keyframe (make sure you do this in the main Timeline, and not inside the movie clip—otherwise you'll lose all but one frame of your movie).

Now that the video is extended within the movie clip, you don't need the excess frames here. As with other movie clips, the video will run through with only one keyframe. It will also loop infinitely unless you tell it not to. OK, now for a little fun.

7. Select the video movie clip on stage and duplicate it using *CTRL+D*.

8. Select one of the movie clip instances and flip it using Modify ➤ Transform ➤ Flip Horizontal.

9. With the flipped instance selected, open the Align panel (*CTRL+K* or *CMD+K* on the Mac) and use Align right edge with Align/Distribute to Stage switched on.

Use Align vertical center to center the instance vertically. You can probably guess why you resized the stage now—it's to accommodate two instances of the video perfectly.

10. Ensure that Snap Align is on (View ➤ Snapping ➤ Snap Align), and position the other instance alongside the flipped one. Ensure that it snaps vertically and horizontally, and then let it go.

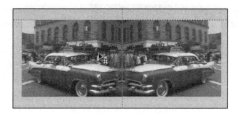

11. Now test the movie using Control ➤ Test Movie. Stop! They're going to crash . . . Ahem.

As you can see here, you've created a very simple mirrored effect with only a little effort. You can create some truly remarkable effects using a little flipping and some masking. Now for a little coloring.

12. Select the flipped movie clip on the right and open the Properties panel (Window ➤ Properties).

13. Choose Advanced from the Color drop-down menu in the Properties panel.

14. Click the Settings button and set the colors as shown in the following screenshot to modify the colors of the movie clip.

15. Test the movie to witness the effect.

In this exercise, you've just scratched the surface when it comes to being creative with video in Flash. Flash video can also make use of blend modes, masking, and any other effects that can be applied to a movie clip. These simple effects will hopefully inspire you to play with Flash video in a highly visual manner, and they help to emphasize why video in Flash is more flexible than content served in the three other major video players, Windows Media Player, RealPlayer and QuickTime.

Now that you've had a little taste of video creativity, it's time to enter the cutting room.

Editing video clips in Flash

As well as changing video appearance, Flash can be used to edit video clips. Even though the editing abilities in Flash don't compare to Premiere, Final Cut, or even iMovie, their presence alone means that your workflow can be greatly enhanced, and it makes video even more accessible to all Flashers.

Let's get in the zone.

Editing a clip

In this exercise, you're going to clean up a single clip with a little editing. The clip used here was shot on a digital stills camera using the built-in movie capture at 10 fps. It was imported via USB from the camera's memory card. See, everyone *can* do video.

1. Open a new Flash document.

2. Select Modify ➤ Document and change the frame rate to 10 fps. This will allow you to match the Flash document frame rate with that of the video.

3. Select File ➤ Import ➤ Import to Stage. Locate and select bella_the_cat.mov (or any other video file you want to edit) and click Open.

4. On the first wizard screen, click Next to proceed, unless you want to change the file for import.

5. On the next screen, Deployment, select Embed video in SWF and play in timeline.

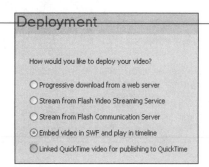

As before, you've opted to embed the video within the SWF file. The reason you're choosing this option is because it allows you to edit the video here in Flash. The other option that would be of interest to you is Progressive download from a web server (Flash Professional only).

This option works differently because it pulls (or loads, to be exact) the video content in from an external source, as opposed to placing the video within the Flash SWF. With this option, the video is loaded in from elsewhere on the server (or local machine), much like an image is loaded into a HTML webpage. The benefits of using this method over the embedded method are numerous, and include the following:

- The audio and video will remain synchronized.

- The overall combined file size (the SWF and the external video) will be smaller.

- The video content will be contained in a Flash component with basic navigation controls.

- The video content will stream.

So, in reality, this method is preferable over the embedded method that you're using, but it's available in Flash Professional only, and it doesn't allow you to edit the video—which is what you're going to do now.

6. Click Next to continue to the next screen.

7. On the Embedding screen, you'll see the following selections:

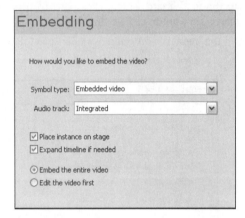

Symbol type relates to how the video is treated upon import. Previously, you selected Embedded video, which placed the video on the main Timeline. The other options, Movie clip and Graphic, would place the video within a symbol. Select Movie clip from this drop-down menu.

The Audio track drop-down menu provides two options: Separate and Integrated. The default selection, Integrated, forces the sound to be imported with the video. The Separate option splits the sound from the video and places them both as individual entities in the Library.

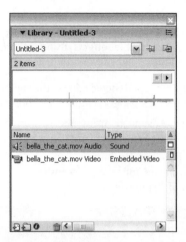

The soundtrack on this particular clip is little more than white noise (there are some finger clicks and cat-attention-grabbing tactics, but nothing that you really want to keep), so select Separate, and disregard the sound.

Ensure that Place instance on stage is unchecked and Expand timeline if needed is checked (both options are self-explanatory). Last, select the Edit the video first radio button to allow you to chop and change the video clip.

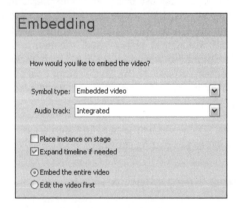

8. Once you've made these selections, click Next to proceed.

9. On the next screen, Split Video (where all the editing is done), you'll see Bella—sideways!

Clip Library   Preview Pane

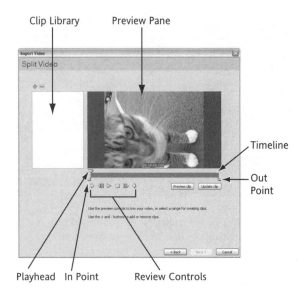

Timeline

Out Point

Playhead   In Point   Review Controls

To make things a little interesting, the video was filmed in portrait format. Of course, this isn't a problem for Flash—remember that you can treat video clips just like any other movie clip, so you can correct this later.

10. Press the Play button (the right-pointing arrow) to view the clip.

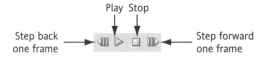

Play Stop

Step back one frame → ◁III ▷ ☐ III▷ ← Step forward one frame

You'll notice that the clip consists of two shots, one filmed up-close and one shot from above.

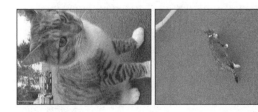

Unfortunately, the transition from the first shot to the second is far from seamless. With a little editing, though, you can trick the eye into making it look like one feline movement, shot with two cameras. The most logical way to do this is to

match the prowling motion from the first clip with the second. In plain English, this means you have to trim a little off the end of the first shot, and some off the start of the second shot.

11. Experiment with dragging the playhead around. This allows you to review the clip in the same way as Flash's Timeline playhead.

12. Using the playhead, locate the frame in which Bella is in full stride before turning her head. For those of you without the patience required for frame-level detail work, drag the playhead so the timer shows 00:00:09.631.

For precision frame-by-frame placement, use the Step forward/back one frame buttons, or the left and right arrow keys on the keyboard.

13. Once you have the correct frame location, click the Set out point to current position button.

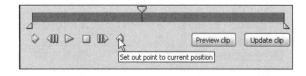

This will move the "out point" (represented by the little triangle on the right below the Timeline) to the same position as the playhead. The area shown in blue is your specified clip area. When you "make the cut" and create the clip, the area in blue will be converted into a discrete clip.

379

14. Before you use the scalpel, click the Preview clip button to view the current state of your clip-to-be. If you aren't happy with the selection, click the out point—it will turn blue to show it's selected (note also that the playhead turns gray to show that it's deselected)—and move it to where you think it should be by dragging it, using the Step forward/back one frame buttons, or using the arrow keys.

15. Once you're satisfied with the clip, click the + button at the top-left of the window.

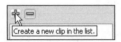

This will take the selection and make a new clip with it. The new clip is added to the pane on the left. This area is where all the created clips are stored.

The currently selected frames have been rendered as a new clip and given the same name as the original clip. You're not going to be working with many clips, so there's no need to rename it here. However, clips can be renamed by double-clicking them.

Now that you have the start clip, it's time to make the second and final clip, using a different selection.

16. Drag the out point all the way to the end of the Timeline. This represents the end of your second clip.

17. Locate the frame in the second shot in which Bella is in full stride, and move the in point to it. Again, I'll save you the frustration by telling you the frame location—00:00:14.885. Remember to use the left and right arrows for greater precision.

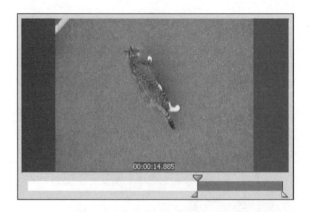

18. Once you've set both the in and out points, view the clip using the Preview clip button. If all is good, render the selection as a clip using the + button again. This clip is now appended to the end of the clip list.

> To reedit any created clips, click them in the list. When you do this, the in and out points of the chosen clip will reappear. Move these as necessary and then click Update clip to render it again.

You now have two individual clips ready for import. You'll combine them once they're imported.

19. Click the Next button. In case you haven't noticed, you're done editing! However, you always have the option of returning to the Editing screen by clicking the Back button.

The next screen, Encoding, covers compression, physical size, and cropping.

The first thing you see here—besides Bella staring at you—is a drop-down menu with a number of compression presets. The presets here come in two distinct types: various bandwidth presets for Flash 7 and Flash 8. What's the difference? Well, the new adoption of the On2 VP6 codec in Flash 8 means that only users with the Flash 8 plug-in will be able to view video encoded with this codec. Videos encoded with the Sorenson Spark codec will run on older versions of the Flash plug-in (back to 6). Logically, if you want a wider audience for your video, it's advised that you use the Sorenson Spark codec. However, if you want vastly superior quality at a smaller file size, you should opt for the On2 VP6 codec. As a secondary (or primary, depending on which way you look at it) concern, you should consider your audience's bandwidth capabilities.

Right now, you're going to ditch these presets and look at the options in detail.

Compressing video in Flash

In this exercise, you'll see how to create a custom setting and learn about the different compression options available.

1. On the Encoding page, click the Show Advanced Settings button. This will open up a number of options on the Encoding tab, as shown in the following screenshot:

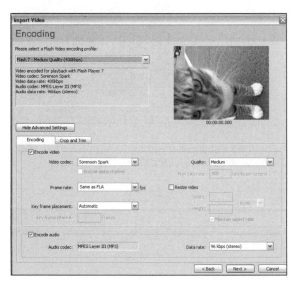

There are a number of modifiable options, so let's run through them starting with the Encode video section.

Video codec: This specifies the codec to encode the video with. As mentioned a little while back, only use the On2 VP6 codec if your audience has the Flash 8 player installed—otherwise use the Sorenson Spark codec. If possible, use the On2 VP6 codec due to its considerably higher image quality and comparatively smaller file size. Using the On2 VP6 codec will also allow you to use an alpha channel for transparent video content.

Frame rate: This specifies the actual number of frames displayed per second. The higher the frame rate, the better looking the video. Typically, NTSC (used in the US, as well as other countries) runs at 30 fps, while PAL (Europe) runs at 25 fps. The options here allow you to synchronize to the Flash document frame rate, the original video rate, or an alternative custom numerical value. If a frame rate higher than the Flash document rate is specified, Flash will cap the video rate.

Note that when synchronizing your video to the Flash document frame rate, if the frame rate of your Flash movie is slower than the video clip, some frames are lost on import. This will also reduce the file size as frames are spaced out to replace those that have been removed. If you've synchronized your clip, and choose later to change the frame rate of your Flash movie, you'll need to reimport the clip. (You can get some wacky effects by experimenting with this option.)

Key frame placement: This is used to control the frequency of complete frames, or keyframes, in the clip. The number you choose determines the number of frames before the next keyframe. In between keyframes, only the parts of the image that change are stored, meaning that the file size is smaller. If this is set to a low number, such as 1, a complete frame is stored for each frame of the clip, resulting in a larger file size, but this enables the movie to run much better on slower machines. Note that unless you have a particular preference here, leave this set to Automatic.

Quality: This is the required quality of the clip after importing and applying compression. If you set this to Low, the compression will be high but the image quality will be very poor. The more compression you apply to the clip, the smaller it will become—at a sacrifice to the image quality. It's best to try changing these settings for different clips because you might find that some clips will look better than others following the same amount of compression. The project you're working on might also be restricted by file size, so you need to take that into account too.

Specifying a custom value here allows you to give a maximum data rate in kilobytes per second. This value specifies the approximate required download speed in Kbps. The amount of compression applied to the clip is based on this setting. For instance, if the intended audience includes 56Kbps modem users, a value below 56Kbps is required. Typically, a lower value is required for connection speeds and fluctuations to be taken into consideration. The higher this value, the less compression is applied and the greater the quality of the clip.

Resize video: This setting allows you to modify the physical size (in pixels) or dimensions (in percent) of the clip. Unchecking Maintain Aspect Ratio will distort the clip, so beware!

Note—for an idea of file size guidelines for different bandwidths, use the following common pixel sizes:

- Modem users: 240 × 180
- ISDN users: 320 × 240
- Broadband users: 480 × 360.

The Encode audio section has one option, Data Rate. All audio is encoded in MP3 format—however, this setting specifies the quality of the audio (see Quality in the preceding section for information on data rates). 128Kbps is typically CD quality.

2. Set the compression settings for the clip as shown in the following graphic:

What have you changed here? You chose medium quality, selected the On2 VP6 codec, and unchecked Encode audio. You haven't changed that much, but now you can see what everything means!

3. Click on the Crop and Trim tab. The crop settings let you mask off unwanted areas of the movie using the four directional sliders. The masked-off areas are then removed from the imported video. A wide-screen movie (ignoring your movie's current orientation) might look like the right-hand image that follows.

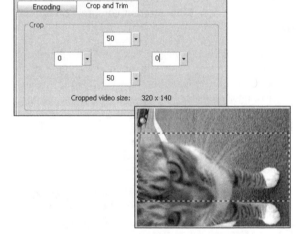

In this example, top and bottom sliders are used to mask off the unwanted areas.

4. Reset all the crop markings to 0 and click Next to proceed.

The next screen shows a summary of your actions.

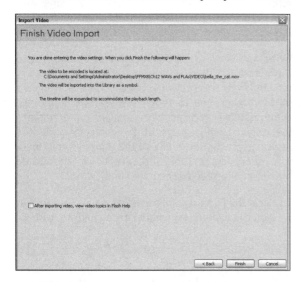

5. Click Finish to import the video. As before, you'll now see an import progress bar, followed by another for the second clip. Once they're done, the videos and movie clips can be seen in the Library (an instance won't be put on the stage because you told it not to).

The next step is to combine the clips to act as one. This is made easier because you can add the second video clip (listed as bella_the_cat.mov 1 Video in the Library) to the end of the movie clip that contains the first video (bella_the_cat.mov).

6. Before talking about all these videos and movie clips gets confusing, rename the bella_the_cat.mov movie clip full video mc. Change the name of bella_the_cat.mov 1 Video to part 2 video.

7. Double-click full video mc to edit it. You'll see that the Timeline is already extended because you told Flash to do it in the Import Video wizard. Now, if you add the second part of the video after the length of the first clip, you should have a seamless video. Note also that the video is positioned with the registration point to the top-left.

8. Insert a blank keyframe on frame 117, just following the video.

9. Drag a copy of part 2 video from the Library onto the stage. You'll immediately get a prompt to extend the Timeline to show all the frames of the video. As before, click Yes to allow Flash to tease out the frames.

10. Use the Align panel or the Info panel to position the video at the top-left. The full video mc movie clip is now complete.

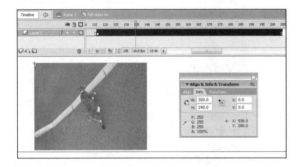

11. Return to the main Timeline and drag a copy of full video mc from the Library onto the stage.

12. Test the movie, using Control ➤ Test Movie to view the whole video. Select View ➤ Bandwidth Profiler to see how big the SWF is.

The size is just under 900K, compared to the original of 3470K. This is a significant savings due to the compression settings, but note that virtually none of the quality is lost (the original would have been compressed on the digital stills camera). Given these conservative settings, you might be able to squeeze more kilobytes out of this movie with only a little loss of quality.

As mentioned previously, different videos will all compress differently in Flash, and it's best to experiment with each one individually to establish compression settings that best suit the clip you're working with (although Flash's preset options are a good guideline to start from).

Video with lots of motion doesn't compress well in Flash because there's little to reproduce and carry forward from the previous frame. Videos that have a similar background to reproduce on each frame will compress well, such as a newsreader, for example—the only changing parts of the image will be the newsreader's motion, while all the things around them will remain static (unless they're doing an outside broadcast at a speedway competition).

13. Save the Flash document as cat_video.fla so that you can experiment with it later should you wish to.

> *Once a video is encoded and embedded in the Flash Timeline, it can be recompressed. To recompress a video, double-click the embedded video in the Library to view its properties, and click* Update *to view the encoding settings.*

Again, you've only just scratched the surface when it comes to using video in Flash. As with other aspects of Flash, video comes alive when you start using ActionScript to manipulate it. Combined with the effects you can achieve by simply adjusting color settings, using the Free Transform tool, using blend modes with video, or adding masks, you can easily achieve great-looking results.

The best thing you can do now is experiment, but don't forget about the rest of the book—there's lots more for you to learn that can help enhance what you've already discovered so far!

Case study

In this section, you're going to create a nice and simple "about" page, using a little video to spruce it up.

1. Open your case study movie.

2. Double-click the Content movie clip instance on the stage to enter Edit in Place mode for it.

3. Move the playhead along to frame 140 in the Timeline.

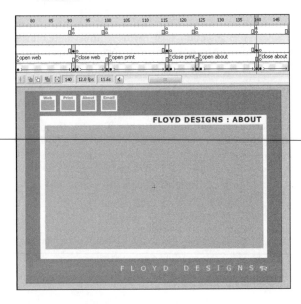

This is the location of the "about" page.

4. Select the keyframe on the pages layer. This is where you'll add your "about" content.

5. Use the Text tool to type the following text in dark blue (#003366),15-point Arial.

Floyd Designs is a multimedia company based in Floydsville.

We create websites, CD-Roms, kiosks, and web applications using Macromedia Flash.

To join your list of satisfied clients, get in touch with us via the email page.

6. Center the text field using the Align panel.

7. With the text field still selected, press F8 to convert it into a movie clip symbol. Call it about content and give it a center registration point.

8. Double-click the about content instance on the stage to edit it in place.

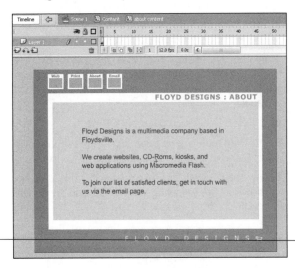

9. Rename the existing layer text and move the text field near to the left edge. Hold down the SHIFT key to ensure that its vertical position doesn't change.

You're doing this to create space on the right edge for your videos. Videos? Well, yes and no. You're going to use one video three times.

385

Importing and placing the videos

Because of the usual traumas of videos bumping up file size drastically, you're going to use a nice small compressed video a few times to create a nice visual effect.

1. Within the about content movie clip's Timeline, insert a new layer called video 1.

2. Select the keyframe on the new layer and choose File ➤ Import ➤ Import to Stage.

3. In the file dialog box that opens, locate the REDCAR.MOV file from earlier in the chapter. Then click OK. Now you'll select the import options as usual.

4. On the Select Video page, click Next.

5. On the Deployment page, select Embed video in SWF and play in timeline. Click Next.

6. On the Embedding page, specify the settings shown in the following screenshot, and then click Next.

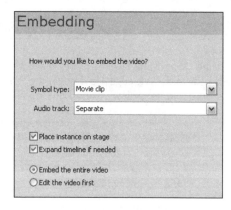

7. On the Encoding page, select Flash 7 – Modem Quality (40kbps) from the drop-down menu.

8. Click the Show Advanced Settings button.

9. Click the Resize video checkbox and specify the following:

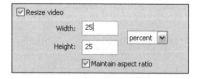

10. Last, uncheck the Encode audio checkbox, and click Next.

11. On the next screen, click Finish.

12. You'll now see a mini-copy of the video that you saw earlier on the stage.

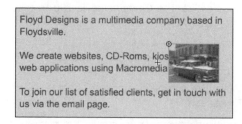

13. Use the Selection tool to move the video movie clip to the top right of the orange rectangle.

14. Select the video movie clip and copy it (CTRL + C).

15. Insert a new layer called video 2, and insert a blank keyframe on frame 5 of it.

16. Select the keyframe, and press CTRL + V to paste a copy of the video movie clip.

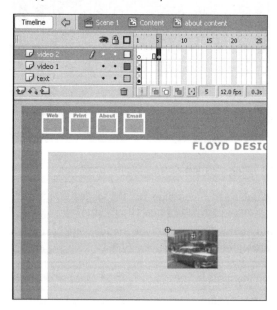

17. Insert another new layer called video 3 and place a keyframe on frame 10.

18. Select the new keyframe and paste a copy of the video.

19. Extend all the frames on each of the layers to frame 15 with *F5*.

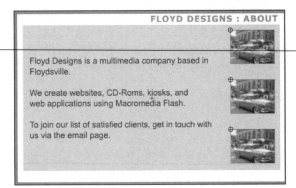

20. Arrange the video movie clips in line along the right side of the orange rectangle, with the video 1 layer instance at the top, the video 2 instance in the middle, and so on. Use the Align panel to make sure they're aligned and that there's even spacing between them.

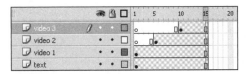

Floyd Designs is a multimedia company based in Floydsville.

We create websites, CD-Roms, kiosks, and web applications using Macromedia Flash.

To join our list of satisfied clients, get in touch with us via the email page.

21. Test the movie with Control ➤ Test Movie. The videos never really get a chance to play right through, do they? As soon as the car is in full flow, it skips back to square 1.

What's actually happening here is what happens to all movie clip Timelines—they loop. The playhead in this instance is running from frame 1 to 15 and back to the start over and over again.

The way to get around this is to stop the playhead on the last frame to prevent the looping. You can do this with your new best friend, ActionScript.

22. Insert a new layer at the top called actions.

23. On the actions layer, insert a new keyframe on frame 15.

24. Select the keyframe, and open the Actions panel (*F9*).

25. Type stop (); in the Actions panel.

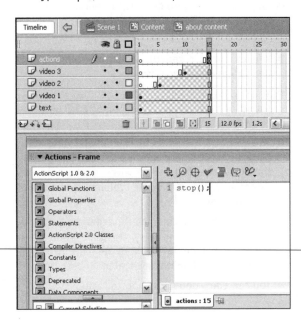

26. Test the movie again and click the about page. This time, your videos are smooth, running at a 5-frame offset. Simple, but effective.

27. Save your case study movie.

Summary

If used well, sound and video can add an extra dimension to your Flash movies and websites. You already knew that you could attach sounds to buttons, and in this chapter you also learned how to incorporate multiple sound elements onto the Flash Timeline.

You saw that

- You can import generic or purpose-built sounds and videos into your Flash movies.

- You can process and optimize the properties for a sound or video once you've imported it into the Flash Library.

- You can attach sounds to keyframes in the main Timeline (or inside a movie clip's Timeline) using the Properties panel, which gives you access to an extensive range of panning, volume, syncing, and looping effects.

- You can create a complete, independent, soundtrack movie that will play alongside your visual movie—you'll see how to integrate these two components in the Publishing chapter.

- You can edit video clips imported into Flash.

- You can specify compression settings for your video in detail.

- You can import video clips as symbols into your Flash Library.

- You can modify video clips instances just like any other symbol instance.

- You can affect the visual appearance of your video clips through your old friend, the Properties panel.

- You can import video clips into your Flash Library and you know how to manage them on the Timeline.

- You can reimport videos to optimize their compression settings in the Import Video Settings window.

I've briefly discussed optimizing movie settings in this chapter—in the next chapter you'll examine this aspect of creating Flash movies in a little more detail.

Chapter 13

OPTIMIZING

What we'll cover in this chapter:

- The nature of the Internet, and how this affects your Flash movie
- How to attract your target audience
- How Flash can transmit content across the Internet effectively using streaming
- How Flash's tools for optimizing your movies download and display on the Internet
- Techniques for designing optimized Flash movies
- Loading content on demand
- Organizing the space on the stage efficiently

Picture the scene: you finish your Flash website and it looks great. Excitedly, you put it up on the server that's hosting your site, replacing that boring old HTML site you've had for years. You're sure to get more visitors as word spreads about the multimedia extravaganza your site has become.

Two days later, you check the number of visitors, anticipating a massive surge. But wait . . . surely not! The number of visitors has actually gone *down*.

There's a very good reason for this, and one that the first-time Flash designer needs to take careful note of. The site may look great when it's running from your hard drive, but once it's up on the Internet, the rules are very different. All those multimedia bells and whistles have made for a bigger and fatter site—and one with a longer download time. The average web surfer has a very short attention span, and while she's waiting for your site to appear, the rest of the Internet is trying to entice her away from your sluggish download and onto *their* web pages.

Once you've discovered all the exciting features that Flash has to offer, the next lesson is always the hard reality of download time. It's something that you must **always** bear in mind when designing Flash sites that'll be accessed over the Net.

Flash and the Internet

Now that we've broken your dream a little, we'll use the rest of this chapter to do what the army does: build you back up and give you some insights into the practicalities and disciplines you're going to need to turn your Flash dreams into reality.

Before you look at how your Flash files behave on the Internet, let's recap what the Internet and World Wide Web are, and revisit some other terms you'll have heard but perhaps never really understood.

The Internet

The Internet's existence was instigated by the US Department of Defense, who needed a fault-tolerant system that provided basic communications services between computers: file transfer, email, remote logon, and remote control of computers—all of which had to work, irrespective of different computer types or operating systems. The solution was designed to be able to take the hits a communications system would get in battlefield use. To achieve this, the system had to be able to carry on even if parts of it were knocked out, and it had to be accessible by a number of different computers (from handheld laptops to big dirty mainframes, and everything in between).

The technology that achieves this, and which makes the Internet work the way it does, is a **transmission protocol**, something that goes by the catchy title of **TCP/IP**. This transmission protocol is the universal "vehicle" that everyone uses on their networks to move data between remote computers. As the slash in TCP/IP suggests, this vehicle comes in two parts.

IP (Internet Protocol) is the tractor that shunts data around across the network, based on a destination address called the **IP address**. The IP number is a unique numeric code used to identify any computer on the Internet. It's a 4-byte value expressed by converting each byte into a decimal number from 0 to 255, and then separating each byte with a period, so an example IP could be 245.239.99.34, or 22.254.0.128. The Internet Protocol is a technology that takes the thing that you want to send—a file, an email, whatever—and encodes it as a series of little data packets that can be sent down the wires that connect up the different IP numbers.

The data that's passed between different IP numbers is directed across the Internet by special communications computers called **routers**. Routers are like switching stations that direct data to its target destination. Each router passes the data that it receives on to the next closest working router to the target address. The routers are arranged to be intelligent enough to pick the fastest available route for the data to take. Because the network is in a constant state of flux, your data might be directed via an infinite number of possible routes—but the router will do its best to pick the optimal route for you.

TCP (Transmission Control Protocol) is the technology that **verifies** that the data got to its destination. IP doesn't care if the packets of data are sent out of order, or even not sent at all. It's up to its big brother TCP to make sure that all the data eventually gets to where its sender intended.

In terms of hardware, the Internet looks like a lot of nodes (or computers) all connected together. Although it may seem rather anarchic and organic, there is actually a broad structure.

Nodes tend to be grouped together in clusters, and these have a large, high-bandwidth transmission point called a **hub** at their centers. Such hubs are sometimes connected together by very large bandwidth links called **backbones**, which connect large population areas or continents.

The World Wide Web

The Internet, therefore, is a network of physical networks across which you can send, receive, and view files using the transport methods of TCP/IP.

The World Wide Web is a more recent development that came about because there was a need to access multimedia files containing music, pictures, and video across the network of machines. The World Wide Web is characterized by a number of different ideas—in particular, the **web page** and the **hyperlink**. A web page is a text file—the HTML (HyperText Markup Language, which is a system of **tags** and **plain text** that defines how a web page should look and behave) documents that you are probably already familiar with. The HTML page may be only text, but it can also contain hyperlinks to other assets (image files and other graphic objects such as the Flash SWF file, or any other file, such as a PDF, downloadable zip file, etc.). These links are essentially web addresses (aka a **URL**—Uniform Resource Locator) that specify where the assets are to be found). When a web **browser**—software that is capable of reading the HTML (such as Firefox or Internet Explorer)—parses the HTML page, it uses these addresses to load the graphic assets, and these files (along with the HTML file's tags and plain text) are parsed to create the final, human-readable web page. There is another kind of link that appears on web pages: the web **link**. When a user clicks a link, the browser looks in the associated web address for another HTML file, and parses it to create a new page. Thus, the user can navigate from page to page by clicking links.

The Web consists of two parts: browsers, which we have already discussed, and **servers**, computers that can host and disseminate HTML files and the related documents.

It's these universally agreed-upon components of the Web, coupled with the expandability and versatility of the underlying TCP/IP and communications hardware, that have made the Internet such a success.

Now when a client asks you what the Internet is, you can tell them. But one of the key things you need to know about before you put your work out on the Net is **bandwidth**.

Bandwidth

Bandwidth denotes how much data will travel along a given path in a given time, or how much information a modem can download and how quickly.

Bandwidth is measured in bits or bytes per second—a bit being the smallest individual morsel of computerized data: a 0 or a 1. The higher the bandwidth, the faster things get to and from your computer. Different types of content demand different amounts of bandwidth to be used effectively—for example, it takes more bandwidth to download a typical animation file in one second than it does to download a static text page in the same time. Because the size of the "pipe" you send the data down to a user's computer is fixed by the capacity of his or her modem, you need to think about the size of your movie and how long it's going to take to get down the pipe and onto the user's screen. Photographs, sound files, and video clips all add to the bandwidth required to quickly download a web page.

Data sent over the Internet will usually get to its destination, but neither the sender nor the receiver knows when this will occur or the route that will be taken. Over time, the average transmission rate becomes fairly constant, but because of the nature of TCP/IP and the way that it parcels data into little packets as they're transmitted, it's unwise to assume a given transmission rate over a short period. Again, there are implications here for the way you design your movies—as you'll see when we discuss streaming later in this chapter.

A full Internet connection is only as fast as the slowest part, meaning that slow computers along the transmission path will tend to drag down the average transmission time across the whole network. Although this "lowest common denominator" factor is not so much of a problem now, it can still rear its ugly head during peak times when the servers—the computers that source web pages—become overloaded.

Suppose a large number of people are trying to access the same web page. The server is just a computer, and can only reply to requests for web pages at a given rate. Thus, some browsers will not receive a reply in time (or at all). When this happens, the browser will assume that the assets or web page it asked for are not actually there at all, and the requested web page will not be displayed, or will be displayed with some assets missing.

> *Some servers (especially the free ones) have very low limits imposed on their bandwidth, and they slow down or stop serving your site when this limit is reached, rather than because they are being overworked. It only takes a few hundred visitors for some of them to stop serving your website—meaning that your site will appear to be down for a short while. You really do get what you pay for when you decide to put a site up on a free—or amazingly cheap—server!*
>
> *Never put a commercial site on a free server if you can help it—they are designed for sites that expect a very low number of visitors, and that can't be your site, now can it?*

These problems show up sometimes as numerous pauses, repeat attempts, and connection losses when trying to connect to popular pages at peak times.

The important thing to remember is that the time it will take your potential viewer to download your Flash site file depends on what's in your file and (within the constraints of the Internet we've just discussed) how quickly their computer can read it. This means that when you make a Flash site you not only have to consider *what* you put in your Flash movie file, but *who* you want to be able to see it. Who is your audience, and what assumptions do you make about their computer equipment?

The end user—your audience

If you're coding your site on a super-fast Mac, what happens if the user has a slow PC? There have been all sorts of discussions about this on the Flash newsgroups for some years, leading to accusations of elitism and/or Flash snobbery on the one hand, to the "take no chances" attitude of some corporate Flash designers on the other.

The following are some general rules to keep in mind before putting your site on the Web:

- No user will wait more than 15 seconds for your site to download if nothing interesting is happening at the same time unless you're a cool enough Flash designer to warrant the wait, or they are viewing a long animation feature. Times have changed, and to be blunt, pointless-but-pretty just doesn't cut the mustard anymore, so even the real guru designers have to live with the 15-second rule these days.

- A cutting-edge, designer Flash website should be viewable using a two-year-old computer's standard hardware configuration.

- A commercial Flash site should be viewable on a standard three-year-old computer.

- The speed of connection you can assume is largely dependent on two things:

  - Whether your target is a business or design audience (assume they have a connection that was "cutting-edge" 18 months ago) or a domestic user (assume the worst!).

  - The relative affluence of your target audience. Although there are always accusations of web elitism, this is a rule that actually works—people who want to buy an expensive car will expect a high-end site to sell it to them. There are very few text-only sites belonging to prestige car manufacturers!

Another very important point to bear in mind when thinking about HTML pages that contain basic web pages and HTML pages that contain Flash content is this: it usually doesn't matter in which order the images and other files that make up a web page load up, as long as they load up. For a web page containing Flash content (or any other similar multimedia), the order is crucially important. If you have a Flash button with a sound attached to it, the sound cannot play unless the sound file is loaded into the browser by the time the user clicks the button.

When you create Flash content, you need to consider the timing of content delivery to the end user in a way that a traditional HTML web page designer never has to consider at all! We will look at one implication of this—streaming—in the following section.

Now that you've absorbed all this techno-jargon, you'll be aware just how easy it is to lose your movie file in the digital jungle that is the Internet/World Wide Web. To ensure your file survives, it's essential to understand the concept of **streaming**, and to consider how to use it when designing Flash movies for the Internet.

Streaming

As we said, the bits of your Flash file that will make your site stand out from the crowd—your movies, sound effects, and so on—are the bits that will take a long time to download. If you have them all at frame 1 of the timeline, your user's modem will be unable to download your movie right away and the user will have to sit and look at nothing until the download is complete. Your visitors will most likely get bored and take their business elsewhere.

However, when streaming is used, your Flash presentation starts playing before all of it has loaded into the user's browser. By starting the Flash page as soon as there is enough information to show **something** rather than waiting until the whole thing has loaded, the user waits much less time before viewing part of the website. This means that you can hold the user's attention while the cast of your all-singing, all-dancing, interactive masterpiece is downloaded.

Well-thought-out Flash sites often have a specific scene at the beginning that loads up immediately, allowing the viewer to watch it as the rest of the movie is downloaded. This type of scene is called a preloader. We'll look at preloaders more thoroughly later in this chapter.

Streaming, as you saw when using sound in your movies, is a very good thing. Although it doesn't make things load faster down the user's pipe, it intelligently organizes what's needed in the movie and when, so that everything is loaded in the best order. Used efficiently, streaming can ensure that everything in your movie is downloaded *before* it's needed on the stage, meaning that the movie will play smoothly without any pauses to wait for an image or a movie clip to appear.

When a user requests a Flash web page across the Internet, Flash has to send the user two things:

- The Flash movie's timeline, including attached ActionScripts and "non-instanced" components (things that aren't stored as symbols) such as text and drawn shapes that haven't been converted into symbols

- The Flash Library, including the sounds, symbols, and bitmaps used in the movie

When Flash sends this data across the Net, it will send the movie timeline *in frame order*. If the movie is split into separate scenes, it will send the scenes in the order they appear in the Scene panel. Flash will also arrange the transmission of Library symbols so that they're sent in the sequence in which they appear in the timeline (and **not** the order they appear in the Library).

You can think of your web-bound movie as having two markers traveling along its timeline. The first one is the **streamer,** which tracks how much of the movie has been downloaded and is ready to play. The second is the **player**—which points to the current frame being played:

Streamer: How much have I downloaded?

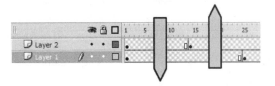

Player: What frame am I on?

For streaming to work, the streamer always has to be in front of the player. If the player catches the streamer, the movie will pause because the next frame of animation has not yet been loaded. To avoid the player constantly playing tag with the streamer and causing a pause every time it catches up, it's a good idea to give the streamer a head start. We call this head start a **streaming buffer**. A streaming buffer operates by starting off the streaming process before the playback starts, giving Flash a chance to download some of the movie onto the user's computer in advance of the playback starting.

> *Streaming is not the only way to deliver multimedia content to the end user. Another common way is to split your site into small chunks—separate SWFs—that are delivered as separate downloads.*
>
> *Doing this ensures that the time the user has to wait for something to happen is reduced, because they only have to wait for part of the site to load each time.*
>
> *This technique will be discussed later in the chapter when we look at loading content on demand.*

To illustrate this, imagine a movie that has a movie clip symbol called A in frames 10 and 30, a graphic symbol B at frame 20, and a drawing on frame 40 that isn't a symbol, like this:

Flash would follow this sequence during streaming:

- Start the **streamer**, sending the timeline data beginning with frame 1. As it sends each frame, Flash also sends all timeline ActionScripts. If the streamer reaches frame 10 before the player, movie clip A will start to load. If, during this

process, the player catches up to the streamer, the movie will pause as it waits for the movie clip to load.

- Once the movie clip A has loaded, the streamer will race toward frame 20, leaving the player plodding along the timeline, playing back the content that's been downloaded so far. Hopefully, the graphic symbol B will have loaded by the time the player reaches frame 20.

- At frame 30, the streamer sees a new instance of the movie clip symbol A that it has used before. It doesn't have to load it again because the information is already in the Library. It just adds the instance name (and any other instance-specific information—such as the instance position, orientation, alpha, etc.—on the timeline) to the movie clip A in the Library and re-creates the instance without having to download it again.

- At frame 40, the streaming marker sees a drawing on the stage that has not been converted to a symbol. The information for this drawing is not in the Library—instead, it's attached to the frame in which it was drawn. The streamer will load the information as part of the frame data, but because the data is not in the Library, the drawing cannot be reused in the same way as in frame 30, and it will have to be loaded again if it is encountered in another keyframe.

The idea of streamers and players may be a little hard to visualize, but Flash has something that lets you see these two markers in action and work out how Internet download times will affect your Flash presentation's delivery to the user's browser. That's what we're going to look at next—the **Bandwidth Profiler**.

The Bandwidth Profiler

The Bandwidth Profiler lets you preview how your movie will behave as it downloads in the real (bandwidth-limited) world.

The first thing to be aware of is that Flash's Bandwidth Profiler assumes **constant** transfer rates. Having read the introduction to what the Internet is, you'll realize that the Bandwidth Profiler graph is a close approximation at best, and a downright fiction at peak traffic times (or if you are using an—ahem—cheap server!).

However, you can use the Profiler to get a good idea of which stages of your movie are going to be problematic for a user to download, even if you can't get *exact* precision for all times.

Using the Bandwidth Profiler

1. Create a new Flash document and make it 20 frames long by clicking the timeline at frame 20, and pressing *F5*:

2. In frame 1, type the following into a static text box: This is a test to see how I can optimize this movie using the Bandwidth Profiler in the center of the stage in 24-point Times New Roman (or a similar font, but not serif):

This is a test to see how I can optimize this movie using the Bandwidth Profiler

3. Convert the text into a graphic symbol with *F8* or by choosing the Insert ➤ Convert to Symbol menu option. Call the symbol text1.

4. At frame 1, under the text you've already placed on the stage, add a new static text box containing this text: Flash will be made to load two pieces of text in different fonts, and we'll use the Bandwidth Profiler to optimize the movie. Use 16-point Arial for this text. Again, you can use a similar font (Helvetica tends to be more popular than Arial on Macs), but make sure you don't use _sans.

5. Make the text a graphic symbol as before, and call it text2. Your stage will look something like this:

This is a test to see how I can optimize this movie using the Bandwidth Profiler

Flash will be made to load two pieces of text in different fonts, and we'll use the Bandwidth Profiler to optimize the movie

6. Save your FLA as bandwidthTest.fla, and then test your movie by pressing *CTRL/CMD+ENTER*.

7. While the movie's playing, go to the View ➤ Bandwidth Profiler menu option or press *CTRL/CMD+B*. A graph will appear:

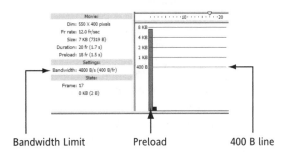

Bandwidth Limit   Preload   400 B line

At the far left of the graph, there's lots of useful-looking information under the headings Movie, Settings, and State. To the right is a little bar graph that tells you how much data is downloaded during each frame. Under Settings, you'll see something like Bandwidth: 4800 B/s (400 B/fr). This tells you the amount of information, in bytes, which can be read per second and per frame. The red line at the 400 B point on the graph also shows this. This is the **Bandwidth Limit**, and it represents the maximum throughput a particular modem can handle.

Your Bandwidth and Bandwidth Limit figures may differ from those shown in the screenshot: there are five different values it can have, as you'll see now.

8. Look in the View ➤ Download Settings submenu:

> 14.4 (1.2 KB/s)
> 28.8 (2.3 KB/s)
> ✔ 56K (4.7 KB/s)
> DSL (32.6 KB/s)
> T1 (131.2 KB/s)
> User Setting 6 (2.3 KB/s)
> User Setting 7 (2.3 KB/s)
> User Setting 8 (2.3 KB/s)
> Customize...

You'll see the options 14.4K, 28.8K, 56K, DSL, and T1 listed on this menu, and one of them will be checked. Do those numbers and acronyms sound familiar? They're modem speeds, and these options represent the download rates that the Bandwidth Profiler can simulate.

9. Our Bandwidth Profiler is currently simulating download using a 56K modem—set yours to the same.

If you look under the Movie heading in the left of the Profiler window, you can see figures of approximately Size 7KB and Preload: 18fr (1.5s, depending on the exact fonts your machine has installed). This tells you that the movie is a 7KB download in total. Because everything appears in frame 1 of your movie, Flash has to preload everything *before* frame 1 can be played. This preload time, the time the user will wait to see the movie, is approximately 1.5 seconds.

Try changing to simulate a 28.8 modem, and if you really want to see how we used to live, try out the 14.4 modem as well. As you can see from the Size and Preload figures at these different settings, some people are going to have to wait longer than others to see this movie. Now that you have a feel for how different modems have different download times, let's see what we can do about it.

> *For multimedia sites, it is difficult to create compelling sites that work well for a user who has anything below a 56K modem. Although you might be forgiven into thinking you will never be asked to test your site for anything below 56K, bear in mind that many mobile devices may be using 56K or lower connections, so the 28.8K and 14.4K modem speeds are not anachronisms from the past just yet!*

If you look toward the top of the Profiler, you can see a little marker that whizzes back and forth while the movie is running. This is the player we described earlier. What a help it would be to see the streamer as well. You can!

10. Select View ➤ Simulate Download. Did you catch that? Let's see it again in slo-mo.

11. Choose the 14.4 modem setting from the View ➤ Download settings submenu and select the View ➤ Simulate Download menu option again (this restarts the download simulation).

Nothing happens for a second or so except some frantic activity going on under the State heading at the bottom left of the Profiler (you may have to increase the height of the Profiler window by dragging the lower edge of it to see the new stuff). Then you'll suddenly see a green band along the top of the Profiler. The data in the frames covered by the green band is what has already been loaded.

The leading edge of this band is the streamer and the distance the green band is ahead of the player is your streaming buffer.

In this movie, you have no streaming buffer at all. The player catches the streamer at frame 1 as it waits for your symbols to load. You need to go back and redesign your movie to allow streaming to take place so you can spare your user that second of waiting. As we're sure you'll appreciate, this wait can be a lot longer for more complex movies—but the method needed to avoid it is the same one we're about to use.

> *Although you may be thinking "I can forget this stuff—I'll be designing high-bandwidth sites for the more discerning clients!" it's worth bearing in mind that bandwidth concerns are always an issue on the Web—as bandwidth goes up, the client will want to use more heavyweight assets, such as sound or video (and now with the current version of Flash, even multilayered video that uses alpha channels!).*
>
> *As a Flash web designer, you will always be trying to fit in more content than a typical user's connection can handle, and there will be download waits even if your spec says you can assume a fast user connection. Being able to design a site around bandwidth bottlenecks is one of the defining features of a good web designer, and this is especially true for Flash web designers.*

12. Close the Test Movie window and go back to the main stage.

13. Delete all the text from frame 1 and add two new blank keyframes at frames 5 and 15:

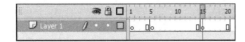

14. With the keyframe at frame 5 selected, drag an instance of the text1 graphic symbol onto the center of the stage. At frame 15, do the same with text2.

15. Test the movie—making sure the Bandwidth Profiler is still running (*CTRL/CMD+B*)—and use the View ➤ Download Settings submenu to set the modem speed to 14.4K.

16. To see the streamer again, go to View ➤ Simulate Download.

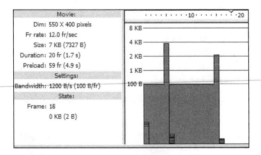

You will see something like this graph to start. The green bar, or streamer, will race ahead to frame 4 almost immediately—even on the 14.4 modem—because these are blank frames. These blank frames are your streaming buffer—the time you have to start streaming before the player starts trying to play back the movie in the user's browser. The player will move along at its usual "one frame every twelfth of a second" pace until it catches the streamer at frame 4, where the streamer has been delayed by the first peak in the data graph.

Frame 4 is the end of the streaming buffer. The player will now have to wait while the extra data that's needed for frame 5 (the text1 symbol) is loaded before it can play that frame.

When you test the movie with Simulate Download turned off, the extended pause at frame 4 is not shown. By using Simulate Download, we're simulating what the movie would look like during transfer and playback across the Internet.

However, you can see that there will be a pause before frame 5 just by using the graph. The first download spike on the graph tells you that the modem can't preload all the data needed before the frame is due to be played.

This is perhaps not surprising for a 14.4 modem because the bandwidth limit allows only 100 bytes per frame to be downloaded.

The spike on the graph also tells you how much you've exceeded the bandwidth limit by, enabling you to judge how long the pause in playback will be.

> *Notice that the profile scale is not linear. This scale, from the 1KB line upward, is an exponential function of 2. Don't worry if you never paid attention in math when you did exponential functions; all it means is that every value on the scale is double the value below it. Flash will create an appropriate scale for whatever amounts of data it needs to display.*

You can see that the data contained in frame 5 is almost 4KB more than can be downloaded in one frame. The modem we're currently simulating takes a second to download 1,200 bytes, so the movie will pause for almost four seconds. To give the modem enough time to download the data for frame 5 we'd need to add over 50 blank frames to the start of your movie—keeping the viewer waiting for playback to start and giving them a very dull first impression of your site.

Even then, your movie will pause once more at the second spike on the graph when text2 is being loaded, and fixing this will require further lengthening of your already protracted movie.

On a 14.4K modem it's still very difficult to avoid pauses due to the very low bandwidth limit. In this case, you will have to accept that even streaming can't solve the problem. You can easily switch to something a little more current by selecting the 56K modem from the View ➤ Download settings submenu.

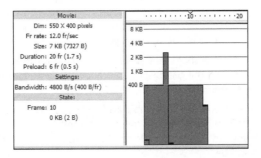

As you can see here, the use of a 56K modem makes the second spike disappear, but you're still stuck with the first one at frame 5 when the data required for text1 again takes you over your bandwidth limit.

17. Go back to the movie and add six more blank frames (*F5*) before the first keyframe:

18. If you test the movie now, you'll get a bandwidth profile something like this:

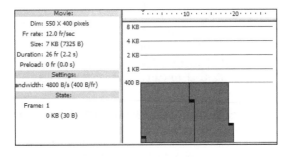

Notice that the bars *never* go above the bandwidth limit. This means that when downloaded by a 56K modem, the movie will run smoothly with no pauses.

How did we know that we had to add six frames? The spike was about 2k (2048 bytes) over the 400B line, and six frames at 400 B/s (6×400 = 2,400 bytes) would remove it.

The streamer will always be ahead of the player because all the data needed for each frame is loaded before it needs to be played—you gave your movie a sufficient streaming buffer.

In short, the movie will look and behave the same whether it is viewed from your hard drive or over the Internet with a 56K modem.

The movie you just created is fairly simplistic, but the theory you applied is the same for much bigger sites. Here's a bandwidth profile for a real commercial site:

There's an initial preload at frame 1, but after that, the site is always inside the bandwidth requirements of a 56K modem. Why did its designer choose a 56K modem? This particular site is for a nightclub. Its designer considered two of the guidelines mentioned earlier: the target audience—in this case 18- to 26-year-olds—and the relative affluence of this audience. Thinking about these factors allowed the designer to reason that the people coming to view the site would have at least a 56K modem at the time the site was going out. The designer reasoned correctly—the hit rate for the nightclub site jumped when this Flash site was used!

If you see a peak on the Bandwidth Profiler for one of your movies and want to know which frame is causing it, click the peak and the movie will go directly to the offending movie frame on the stage. Remember, though, the bar graph is arranged in the order that streaming will take place, and the bar you click will rarely represent the frame that the numbering along the top of the graph (which is the current frame being played) suggests it should. You can see which frame you clicked by looking under State *to the bottom left of the screen.*

As you can see, the Bandwidth Profiler is a vital tool. With it, you can tailor your movie to meet the bandwidth constraints of your target user. With the Simulate Download option activated, you can actually see how bandwidth will affect your movie in real time, and alter things accordingly.

There are some sites that don't use streaming at all. Instead, they load the whole movie in one go. For example, Flash animations that lip-sync to sound don't use streaming because even a slight slowing down of playback would greatly affect the movie, and cause sound to lose sync with the animations. However, the designers judge that their viewers will be prepared to wait for this spectacle.

A lot of unstreamed sites are Flash showcase sites where Flash designers show off to other Flash designers or potential clients. As fledgling Flash users, you're unlikely to be aiming your sites at these people and consequently your audience is unlikely to have the same level of technical equipment to view sites as these people do.

For most web audiences, long waits for websites are a real turnoff. Although the Internet is getting faster all the time, low bandwidths (or rather, "lower bandwidths than you need to put all the cool stuff you want in your site"—a common problem for all web designers!) are still with you for a sizable section of the web audience, so you must learn to overcome them. The Bandwidth Profiler is a powerful weapon to have in your armory in this respect.

You may not be aware of it, but content created for the Flash Player 6, 7, and 8 is compressed by default when published. Vector objects, text, and ActionScripts are all compressed. But be aware—if you are authoring for the Flash Player 5, you'll need to switch this compression off. You can do this by going to File ➤ Publish Settings and deselecting the Compress Movie option on the Flash tab.

The Bandwidth Profiler takes into account any file compression during SWF compilation—the Bandwidth Profiler will assume compressed file sizes if there is a check against Compress Movie in the Publish Settings window (select File ➤ Publish Settings, *then click the* Flash *tab).*

The only reason you might want to turn compression off is when your SWF content is already compressed by other means. This would occur if you have a lot of video in your SWF. Video is already compressed via the video compression routine, so compressing the SWF again gives no real advantage. The disadvantage is that every compression requires a decompression when the user views your content, so you may want to decline the unneeded compression of the SWF.

Optimizing and fine-tuning Flash movies

There are a number of things you can do to make your movies leaner and compact for Internet download. In this section, we'll summarize all the Flash methods that allow you to achieve responsive sites before looking at how to optimize space for content on the stage. First, we'll look at what to consider when planning your site.

Note that there are ways to optimize your movies in other ways, especially for performance and speed (using bitmap caching and optimizing your vectors via point reduction). We looked at these features of Flash earlier in the book.

Structure

Perhaps the most important aspect to get right for a responsive site is a well-defined structure and download flow. You need to sit down and think about which major keyframes the user will see, and in what order, before you jump into Flash and start creating the movie. For example, an MP3 site would probably consist of the following keyframes (each of which would be the start of a new area of the site):

- Preloader
- Intro
- Main
- About
- Downloads
- Links

When visiting the site, the viewer would most likely

- See the preloader, and be taken to the intro keyframe, where the timeline will stop.
- From there, the user would click a button and be sent to the main keyframe.
- Because he or she has come here looking for MP3 files, the user would go straight to downloads.
- Once he or she has set off a music file download, the viewer will probably browse the about section to find out more about the music.
- The viewer will most likely exit from about or via your links section.

This analysis of the way your site will be used dictates that you want the preloader, intro, and main content to be loaded in that order, and this is therefore the order content related to them should be arranged on the timeline. By second-guessing what your audience will do and streaming content in the appropriate order, you'll make your site more responsive for most visitors. In this case, your preference would be to make downloads the next block of content on the timeline, followed by about, and then by links. If you arrange your content in a random order, you have no way of ensuring that it will be loaded in any useful order, and will therefore have to preload the whole site before any of it can be viewed. Although even many professional sites do this, it should be considered bad practice.

In a slightly more subtle vein, the average user in this example will spend little time in the main section because it is just a route to the downloads section. You can design that into the site by making the main content easy for the user's modem to download, thus buying time for the downloads section to be loaded more quickly as well. Structuring your Flash site in this strategic way is the hallmark of a good web designer. It will come with practice, and all designers will always be somewhere on that particular learning curve, struggling with the same problem that you face as a beginner!

Use the right components in your movie

Choosing the correct basic pieces to build up your site with is another area where forethought is required.

It's wise to use symbols wherever possible because symbols possess two very desirable properties that make them bandwidth friendly:

- The attributes of a symbol (size, color, etc.) can be changed for an individual instance via the Properties panel.
- Flash downloads each symbol only once, and bases all instances of the symbol on the single downloaded version in the Library.

This means that instead of building a blue button and a red button separately, you can have a single gray button that Flash will download once but will use to produce two tinted instances. If you don't make an object a symbol, Flash will not store it in the Library after download, and will have to download it again the next time a copy of it appears in the movie.

One part of your site is an exception to this rule: a "starting credits" movie that you want the user to see first. If this is the case, and you make your starting credits a movie clip symbol, Flash will not begin playing it until it has completely loaded. If, however, you created the starting credits as animations that are placed directly on the main timeline of your movie, Flash would begin to play the content as soon as the first frame streams in.

The way you use fonts in your final movie will also affect the download time. If your movie contains text written in a sans serif font such as Helvetica, a serif font such as Times, and a typewriter style font such as Courier, all three font files will need to be downloaded before the movie can be viewed. If, however, you use the generic _sans, _serif, or _typewriter styles to write your text in your original file, the text in the downloaded version will be written using fonts on the user's hard drive that match these styles. No font files will have to be downloaded as part of the Flash file, and the download time will be reduced.

In general, every time you use a new font, Flash will have to download the font shapes you've used. If you're designing a site that contains a lot of text, make sure that you use the same font throughout. Because some fonts look very similar on the screen, you may not notice you're using two different fonts and are inadvertently adding to the download time of your movie. Be wary, also, of using complex fonts:

THIS FONT REALLY FITS IN WITH THE STYLE I AM GOING FOR BUT HOW BIG A DOWNLOAD IS IT?

Before you use such fonts, look to see how big the font files are. They may really look cool, but some complex fonts can take up to 32K just for ten or so characters, leading to unnecessary download delays. Try before you buy!

It's always a good idea to choose simple and clean fonts for your Flash designs, unless there is a compelling reason not to. A good default choice is the Verdana font. Also consider Helvetica/Arial, but bear in mind that they have been used so often in typography since 1980 that they are becoming a bit of a cliché!

Not only does a simple font face such as Verdana download quickly, it also displays more quickly than more complex fonts because Flash has fewer points to draw.

Optimizing elements

It's important to do everything possible to keep the file size of your Flash movie as low as you can. Let's look at the tools Flash provides for lowering the amount of data taken up by the individual elements of a movie.

Reducing the memory used by vector shapes

1. Create a new Flash document and add three blank keyframes to the timeline so that there are four in total:

2. Use the Pencil tool in the Ink mode to draw an abstract shape at frame 1. Make your shape very curvy, like ours:

3. Select your shape and copy it. Then select frame 2 and use the Edit ➤ Paste in Place menu option to copy your shape onto the stage in this frame. Do the same at frames 3 and 4.

4. Select the shape in frame 2 and go to Modify ➤ Shape ➤ Smooth.

5. Select the shape in frame 3 and go to Modify ➤ Shape ➤ Straighten.

6. Select the shape in frame 4 and go to Modify ➤ Shape ➤ Optimize and drag the slider to maximum.

The Smooth option will make your shape more rounded, in the way that shapes drawn with the smoothed Pencil tool appear, and Straighten, as you've no doubt surmised, will make your shape more angular in the way shapes drawn with the straightened Pencil tool appear. These commands can be repeated over and over again to make the shape more rounded or more angular.

The Optimize option will reduce the number of curves that make up the shape. Like the previous two commands, it can be applied multiple times—but only until Flash reaches a point where no more curves can be removed.

403

7. Test your movie, and make sure the Bandwidth Profiler is turned on (View ➤ Bandwidth Profiler) and select View ➤ Frame by Frame Graph.

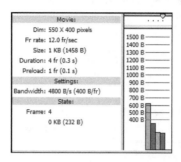

This graph shows you the file size per frame—that is, it doesn't assume streaming. This graph is useful in showing you which frames contain the highest file size.

The graph will be the same shape whichever modem setting you use. It shows you that the modified versions of your shape on frames 2–4 will download more quickly than the original drawing on frame 1. As designers, we must decide how much we're prepared to alter the appearance of our movie components in our quest for a faster download time.

One designing eye also needs to be kept on the size of any sound clips or bitmap images you use because the bigger they are, the longer they'll take to download. You discovered how to optimize bitmaps and sound files earlier in the book—you need to weigh how much they add to the movie's appeal against how long the user has to wait to see them.

Optimizing tricks and tips

Here are a few ideas that'll get you started on the route to efficient and responsive sites.

As we said earlier in the chapter, the key to good design is structuring your site so the elements load in the order they're needed. Make sure you load up all the functional and informative components first, such as the buttons that enable the site to be navigated, and let the eye candy that you put in to show off appear later because not everyone will want to wait for it.

One question that sometimes pops up is how to make Flash load symbols *before* they're needed. You would need to do this if, for example, you wanted a responsive site and were prepared for Flash to pause at the beginning while essential symbols were loaded. This is done using a **preloader**. A preloader is a scene created solely to occupy the user's attention while the symbols your site requires for later use are downloaded. Remember, once they're in the Library, Flash doesn't need to reload them every time they appear.

In order to load the symbols without the user seeing them, you tell Flash they're appearing in the frame that's playing, but place them in the work area **outside** the visible stage. However, you want the viewers to look at something so they don't get bored and lose patience with your downloading site.

What a good preloader needs is a simple animation that plays as the download takes place, and some informative text to let users know they won't have to wait too long. You can see a good example of this at www.2advanced.com/perspectives:

If you don't want to detail specific items that are in the process of being loaded, you could use a loading bar (like the progress bar used here, at http://pdl. warnerbros.com/wbmovies/corpsebride/flashsite/ main.html).

At this site, while the preloader is displayed, an initial Flash animation trailer is being loaded that will play immediately. The trailer introduces the site and simultaneously allows large amounts of content to be loaded to the user's computer in the background.

These two methods, however, can be seen as overkill! If you have to give "percentage loaded" figures as your site is downloading, your download may be too long in the first place! Be warned—while Flash designers expecting a fantastic Flash interactive experiment may be prepared to wait for this content, the average web surfer will leave the site before it is completely loaded.

As always, the decisions whether to use a preloader or how you organize the loading of your site's content should always be determined by the user's hardware and motivation for visiting the site.

Loading multimedia on demand

A great tactic for optimizing your website is to load the content required on demand. Using the loadMovie and loadSound commands from your base Flash file, you can call in another SWF, MP3, or JPEG file. The bonus of doing this is that you only have to call content when the user requires it, meaning that the initial download overhead is much lower.

The loadMovie command works by loading content into a level above the main movie or into a movie clip target. Here's an example of how the ActionScript command would look when loading a SWF file into a movie clip:

```
mymovieclip.loadMovie ("myfile.swf");
```

It's worth mentioning that content loaded with the loadMovie command does not replace any of the content stored in the base SWF.

The MovieClipLoader methods (introduced in Flash MX 2004) are a better bet when you want to load large or many files into a Flash site. MovieClipLoader has a number of events associated with the loading process, and you can define event handler functions that tell Flash what to do when the load is complete. Using the MovieClipLoader class is beyond the scope of this book as it is not a beginner topic. Learning how to use MovieClip.loadMovie is a better option for now, especially when a good understanding of it will help you learn about more versatile ways of loading your content.

Let's try this out to get a better idea of what options it gives you.

Using loadMovie to create a functioning record player

1. Open a new Flash document and save it as record_base.fla.

2. Rename the default layer record player. Create another two layers called blank and actions so that you end up with actions being the top layer, and record player being the lowest.

3. Draw a simple record player on the record player layer. Our attempt is a 1960s retro design (as seen on old instruction manuals), from a bygone era when music decks didn't have integral hard drives.

You're going to give the record player a record to play by loading an external SWF file. Until then, it's a sad and lonely record player.

4. On the blank layer, create a new movie clip symbol (Insert ➤ New Symbol) called blankClip. This movie clip will be used in its current form—totally empty. The reason for this is that you will load the external SWF file into this movie clip.

5. Without editing or adding anything to the movie clip's timeline, click the Back button to return to the main timeline. Drag a copy of the blankClip symbol from the Library and place it on the stage.

405

You'll notice that because the symbol is empty and it is selected, it's represented on the stage by a circle and a cross. If you deselect the movie clip by clicking elsewhere (such as on the record player graphic), it is represented by just an unfilled circle:

6. Place the blankClip at the top left of the stage (0,0) by selecting it and entering the coordinates in the X: and Y: input boxes of the Info panel. Note that the height and width of the movie clip is also 0 (because of course there is nothing in it!). With it still selected, give it an instance name of target via the Properties panel:

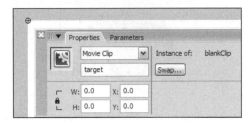

This will be used to load in the external SWF file. Let's add the code to load in your (as yet, uncreated) SWF file.

7. Insert a keyframe (*F6*) on frame 25 of the actions layer. Select frame 25 of your record player layer and extend your frames up to frame 25 by pressing *F5*. Do the same with the blank layer.

8. Select the keyframe back on frame 25 of the actions layer and open the Actions panel (*F9*).

9. Type the following into the Script pane:

```
target.loadMovie("record_on.swf");
stop();
```

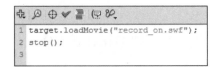

The code here might look similar to the dot notation you looked at in Chapter 11. The target instance of blankClip will load a movie clip over itself. This is much the same as if you swapped blankClip for another movie clip in the Library during author time except that here you are getting Flash to do it for you at *runtime,* and you are asking it to load an *external* file (both of which make for a much more powerful way of doing things). The main timeline is then stopped.

If you test the movie now, nothing will happen—at frame 25 the Output window will open with the following—or similar!—message:

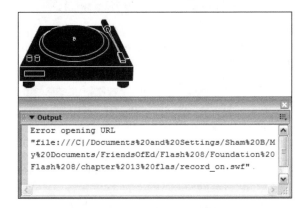

This error occurs because Flash is expecting to find a file—record_on.swf—that is not there. Let's give your record player something to play—a nice tune.

10. Save the current record_base.fla but leave it open.

11. Open a new Flash document and save it as record_on.fla and in the same directory as record_base.fla. If the name sounds familiar, that's because it's the same as you entered in the code earlier.

The first thing you need to do is match the record player from the record_base file with the new file.

12. Return to the record_base document using the Window menu and select the record player graphic by clicking it with the Selection tool.

13. Press *CTRL*/*CMD*+*C* (or select Edit ➤ Copy) to copy the record player to the clipboard.

14. Return to the record_on Flash document and use the Edit ➤ Paste in Place menu option to position it in the same location as in the other movie. Rename the current layer to guide, and make this layer a guide layer (the quickest way to do this is to double-click on the layer title icon to bring up the Layer Properties window, then select the Guide radio button). Finally, lock the layer and make it show outlines only (to do this, click on the colored block to the far right of the layer title).

15. Add a new layer called record. Draw in the rest of the scene, by placing a record on the turntable.

You may find it easiest to construct the record by creating it as a separate symbol first, then sizing it to fit onto the record player.

16. Save the movie in the same location as record_base.fla—this is very important because otherwise the loadMovie command will not work. Use Control ➤ Test Movie to publish the record_on file. When you do this, notice that the record is the only thing that gets exported. The record player is on a guide layer, and is there for your benefit only—it does not exist in the final SWF.

You might not be aware that Test Movie actually produces a SWF file. This is all that you need.

17. Return to the record_base Flash document and use Control ➤ Test Movie again. If all has been done correctly, the record player will be lonely for a short while, and will then be given a lovely record to play. If this hasn't worked, make sure that you gave the blankClip an instance name and that both your files are saved in the same folder—these are the most common places to go wrong.

Your turntable movie is finished. It could do with a little sound and a button to start the record, but now that you know how to load in external SWFs, we'll leave this for you to play and experiment with.

> *If you look at our finished version, you will see that we have added an animation of the record dropping onto the turntable. You could also make the needle arm rotate onto the record, but because we are using a faux 3D, you would either have to have a very good idea of perspective, or know a 3D package such as Electric Rain (eRain)'s Swift3D (www.swift3d.com).*

Loading video files, MP3s, and JPEGs

Now that you've seen how to use the loadMovie command using an external SWF file as an example, it's worth knowing how to work with other file formats so that you are able to call these on demand too.

Video

A typical system for working with video files on popular sites such as www.quicktime.com is to provide the user with a number of different files for their relevant bandwidth. QuickTime in particular has movie trailers for users with 56k, 100k, and 300k bandwidths. The files for the different users have been specifically sized and compressed so that the user gets the best possible experience without the long download time.

This technique can also work for you. By creating a number of different sized SWF files from the same video clip, you can use the loadMovie command to simply load the required file size content on demand.

This means that lower-end users will not have to wait, and higher-end users can view the content in full-blown, luscious quality. Neat, huh?

JPEG and PNG

Flash 8 has support for importing JPEGs, GIFs, and PNGs on the fly, meaning that—as with the video tip—you can load content that specifically caters to the user's bandwidth (and patience!). Image files can be imported directly using the loadMovie command, for example:

```
movieclip.loadMovie ("mypicture.jpg");
```

If you are new to Flash, this will make your work a lot easier!

Flash can load JPEGs into a text field. Text fields can be made to render HTML, and the <img> tag is supported.

Displaying a JPEG file in a text field

1. Find or create a JPEG image, and place it in a folder of your choosing.

2. Create a new FLA and save it in the same folder as the image.

3. On the stage of your FLA, create a dynamic text field big enough to show your image on frame 1 of a new FLA. Name the layer html.

4. Select the text field and give it an instance name (for example, htmlField). Make sure that you click the Render text as HTML icon on the Properties panel (the one that looks like an open and a closed angle bracket together, i.e., <>.) This enables the text field's ability to display HTML formatting.

5. Create a new layer called actions. In frame 1 of this layer, add the following code, replacing myjpg.jpg with your image name. Also, note the different quotation marks you are using—double quotes (") around the whole string and single quotes (') around the image name.

```
htmlField.htmlText = "my image -➡
                    <img src='myjpg.jpg'>";
```

Test the movie. You should see the image appear in the text field as soon as Flash sees the line of code. Loading images (and even other content, such as SWFs) using the <img> tag is cool because the content will act just like true HTML text—it will load only when it needs to be displayed. This is different from traditional Flash sites, which tend to load lots of content that may not be seen at all and can contribute to a larger-than-expected download time.

> *The downside of the implementation of the <img> tag is that it is a little temperamental about where it places text around it, and whether it works at all—placing the caption after the <img> causes the <img> to stop working altogether!*

PNG files have the advantage of using a lossless format—although a PNG reduces file size, it does it by only compressing the file data rather than reducing the amount of uncompressed data present. This means that the compressed and original image look the same. Another advantage of PNG files is that they can contain **alpha channels**.

You can use PNG files in much the same way as we used JPEGs here, but PNGs have a major trick up their sleeve because of their ability to contain alpha channels.

Take a look at the example file pngLoader.fla. If you scrub through the frames (click-drag the playhead up and down the timeline), you will see that we have an animation of an autumnal leaf floating across a blue sky.

Make sure that the file `leaf.png` is in the same folder as `pngLoader.fla`, then test the movie. You will see the leaf waft across the screen as expected, but the second and subsequent times, the leaf is replaced with a *real* autumnal leaf!

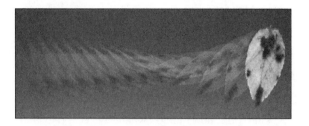

Not only does the replacement leaf look like a real, textured leaf, but it isn't constrained by the normal rectangular bitmap shape—the edges of the leaf are the shape of the leaf itself!

An alpha channel contains alpha information—the amount of visibility per pixel—as well as the color of each pixel, allowing you to make all the background pixels in a bitmap image invisible. By making all the "leaf" pixels have full opacity (black pixels) and all the background pixels have full transparency, we give the impression of cutting the leaf out from its background.

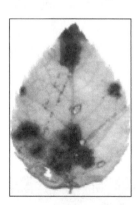 

Alpha channels are not just for creating "masks," though—you don't just have to have pixels that are fully transparent or opaque; you can have pixels in between, allowing you to create feathering and blending effects between bitmaps, and between bitmaps and vectors.

Alpha channels are not just a "pixel mask" that is used to hide pixels; they can also be used as part of an artistic technique. Using alpha channels along with blending modes can be used to composite (blend or merge) images together to create digital collages, and this technique is used often in the world of Adobe Photoshop.

So how does our vector leaf suddenly become a real (bitmap) leaf? Look at the code in the last keyframe of the `actions` layer.

```
leaf.loadMovie("leaf.png");
```

Our leaf instance, `leaf`, has the real leaf image, `leaf.png`, loaded into it, so that when the animation runs a second time, the bitmap leaf has overwritten the vector one.

This is a good principle to know about; you can start an FLA with low-bandwidth content in it (the vector leaf), and slowly replace it with high-bandwidth images (the bitmap leaf) and other content.

However, there is a problem in this switch. The animation is moving so fast that the added quality of using a real leaf is lost. Our vector leaf may be simple, but when it is moving, it looks realistic enough.

When animating content, bear in mind that moving graphics can be much simpler than nonmoving ones. In fact, one trick often used in Flash is to keep things moving, because this makes them look a lot more complicated than they actually are—motion costs a lot less in bandwidth than appearance!

MP3

As with bitmaps, the ability to import MP3 files is also available. This is the basic command format to load a streaming sound (denoted by the true in loadSound). Use the Vocal2.mp3 file from the code download section of Chapter 11 to set this up, saving the FLA with this code in the same folder as the MP3.

```
target = new Sound (this);
target.loadSound ("Vocal2.mp3", true);
```

When using your own MP3s, note that Flash is very picky about loading MP3s, and you should test this before running your code. In most cases, if the authoring environment is happy loading the MP3, the Flash player will be happy during runtime as well. If in doubt, look at the MP3 files you use in Chapter 12—looking at their MP3 file attributes via your MP3 conversion software will give you the clues you need.

Now that you've seen how to load content only when it is required, you have a valuable insight into how many websites are created with multiple SWF movies and loaded content. The code to load a sound (or image) could be placed within a Button script so that it only loads when the user clicks a button that requests the content.

```
myButton.onRelease = function(){
   target = new Sound (this);
   target.loadSound ("Vocal2.mp3", true);
};
```

The procedure to load an event sound is complicated a little by the fact that if you try to play a streaming sound before it is totally loaded, you won't hear anything. The following code fixes this by loading the sound when the button is clicked, but not playing it until the sound is completely loaded, as defined by the onLoad event:

```
myButton.onRelease = function() {
   target = new Sound(this);
   target.loadSound("Vocal2.mp3", false);
   target.onLoad = function() {
     target.start();
   };
};
```

Last-minute checks

Armed with the information in this chapter, you're now able to ensure that your Flash sites will be suitable for exposure on the Web. When you complete authoring a Flash movie, view it with Show Streaming on and ask yourself the following questions:

- Does the movie run smoothly when using the modem my target audience is most likely to have?

- Does it ever pause at inappropriate times because of streaming?

- Is the user made aware that they'll have to wait (and for how long) whenever a preload is required?

- If my site is running slow because of high bandwidth, what can I get rid of—is the tune that plays every time a button is clicked *really* necessary?

- Would it be better to load my content on demand?

- Am I making the most of the space available on the stage—and how can I utilize the space better?

Case study

In this section, you're going to create the print page and display some illustrations. Given what you've learned in this chapter about using loadMovie to load content on demand, you're going to show thumbnail versions of the images which, when clicked, load the full-sized JPEGs.

For this exercise, you will need the image files gandhi.jpg, gandhi_thumbnail.jpg, einstein.jpg, and einstein_thumbnail.jpg from the code download for this book.

Creating a print page and displaying illustrations

1. Open your saved case study document.

2. Double-click the content movie clip instance to edit it in place.

3. Within the content movie clip's timeline, scroll the playhead along to frame 116:

4. Select the keyframe on the pages layer and type the following text in 14-point Arial in color #003366 as shown:

Floyd Designs specializes in cover designs and illustrations. Please click any of the thumbnails above to see example screenshots.

5. Use the Selection tool to move the text field to the bottom-left corner of the green rectangle.

Now to import the thumbnail images!

6. Select File ➤ Import ➤ Import to Library and locate einstein_thumbnail.jpg and gandhi_thumbnail.jpg in the File dialog box, and then import them.

7. Open the Library (*CTRL/CMD+L*) and drag a copy of both newly imported images onto the stage.

8. Position them in the top-left corner and align them neatly:

We used the left half of the screen purposely because the other half will be the display area of the full-sized images. Before you get to the other half, let's finish this one.

9. Drag a copy of the invisible button symbol from the Library onto the stage. You're going to reuse this symbol to make simple buttons for your historical figures. To do this, you need to use the good old Free Transform tool or the Properties panel.

10. Select the invisible button instance and use the Free Transform tool to modify the shape to cover the thumbnails only.

11. With the invisible button instance still selected, press *CTRL/CMD+D* to duplicate it.

12. Position both invisible buttons in the same position as the thumbnail images.

13. Select each button instance in turn and give them instance names of einsteinButton and gandhiButton, respectively:

Before you write any button code, create the target instance for your images to load into. This is done with a blank movie clip instance.

14. Select Insert ➤ New Symbol. In the dialog box that appears, give it the name blank mc and make it a movie clip.

The symbol will be in Edit Symbol mode, which is the usual behavior, but it is not where you want to be at all.

15. Return to the main stage and double-click the content movie clip instance.

16. Scroll to frame 116 and select the keyframe on the pages layer again.

17. Open the Library if it isn't already open, and drag an instance of blank mc onto the stage.

18. Select the blank mc instance and drag it to just below the "F" of Floyd Designs. If you have Snap Align on, it should snap to the same vertical position as the thumbnails and the side of the text field.

19. The last thing to do here is to give it an instance name. Select the blank mc instance and give it the name jpegLoad_mc in the Properties panel.

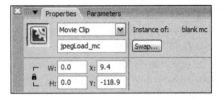

Adding the ActionScript

In this section, we're going to add the required code to the invisible buttons. When either button is clicked, the corresponding full-sized image will be loaded into the blank mc instance.

1. Select frame 116 of the actions layer, and open the Actions panel (*F9*).

2. Add the following code:

```
1 stop();
2 einsteinButton.onRelease = function () {
3     jpegLoad_mc.loadMovie ("einstein.jpg");
4 }
5
```

```
stop();
einsteinButton.onRelease = function () {
    jpegLoad_mc.loadMovie ("einstein.jpg");
}
```

Simple enough, isn't it? When einsteinButton is clicked, the full-sized image is loaded into the specified movie clip instance target. The benefit of doing this, as opposed to how you created the web page, is that the images are loaded on demand only.

3. Copy code lines 2–4 and paste the code into line 5.

4. On line 5 of the code, change einsteinButton to gandhiButton and on line 6, change einstein.jpg to gandhi.jpg. Your code should read as follows:

```
stop();
einsteinButton.onRelease = function() {
    jpegLoad_mc.loadMovie("einstein.jpg");
};
gandhiButton.onRelease = function() {
    jpegLoad_mc.loadMovie("gandhi.jpg");
};
```

Both your buttons are now functional. All you need now are the full-sized images.

5. Place the full-sized images, gandhi.jpg and einstein.jpg, in the same folder as the case study FLA and the SWF.

6. Test the movie and click the Print button, followed by a click on their original images to show the full-sized image:

Easily done, and extremely beneficial for your users. This means that they won't have to wait until the whole website loads before seeing any images. Cool!

7. If Gandhi is scaring you a little too much, save the case study document and close it.

Summary

You've now seen the technicalities of how you make sure your Flash movie gets where you want it to go in the form you intended, and in a manner that's satisfactory for the user.

You saw that

- The **Bandwidth Profiler** lets you see
  - How your movie will play on the Internet.
  - Where any pauses in playback will occur.
- Streaming is used to smoothly download the components of your movie before they are needed on the stage.
- A **preloader** can buy you time to download your entire movie in one go.

In the next chapter, you're going to look at the issues involved in preparing your movie for publishing on the Web.

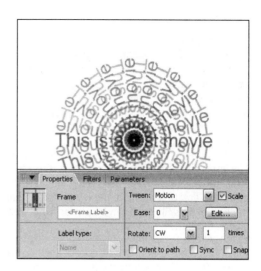

Chapter 14

PUBLISHING

What we'll cover in this chapter:

- The formats available for publishing and when to use them
- How to create the necessary files to get your movie ready for the Internet
- The principles of putting your files on the Internet

You've spent days—weeks, maybe—creating the perfect movie, and you're bursting to show it to the world, but so far only your dog and a few bewildered family members have been able to see it. Relax—the waiting is over—this chapter is here to help you and your movie make the transition from the cozy world of the local hard drive to the hustle and bustle of the Internet. It's time to go public.

The essential process is this: when you're happy with your movie, you use Flash's File ➤ Publish menu option to create a viewable file that you can share with the world. This file can then be put on your website.

When you're preparing your movie for display on the Web, there are a number of output formats you can choose from when you finally publish the movie.

Web formats

One of the things that makes Flash so successful on the Web is its small file size, and this is where publishing comes in. Up until now you've been working only with FLAs—the files in which your movies are created. When you publish your movie, Flash compresses the FLA, removes all the redundant information, and leaves just the instructions for a sleek, streamlined, multimedia presentation. The default output file from the Flash publishing process is a SWF (pronounced "swiff"). Associated with the SWF file is the HTML file. The HTML file has an embedded link to the SWF, plus information on how the browser should display it.

All web content is usually based on an HTML file that is loaded and decoded (or "parsed") by the browser. The parsed information then tells the browser what else it needs to load to build the final web page. Although some browsers can display a SWF without the HTML file, it is always a good idea to include the HTML because it is the standard way of defining any normal web page, and is thus likely to work on all browsers.

Including SWF and HTML, the more common file types and their usual file extensions are

- Flash—`.swf`
- HTML—`.html`
- Animated GIFs—`.gif`
- QuickTime—`.mov`

You can make your files as simple or as complicated as you want. Flash's publishing process means that you simply select the output options you want, and Flash does the rest for you, producing files that can be migrated straight onto your website and put into the public domain.

Let's look at each of the common output formats.

Flash

The full name for the standard Flash file format is **ShockWave for Flash**, hence SWF. The Flash Player is the software that plays the SWF files on the user's browser. The Flash Player is now a standard across the Internet, and you can more or less assume that anyone who wants to watch Flash movies already has the Flash Player installed on his or her machine. In the transition from Flash MX 2004 to Flash 8, however, there's a slight hitch—new movies built in Flash 8 are compatible with only the last version of Flash Player, so anyone with an older version will have to download the new Flash Player 8 to be able to see your movies. There *is* an option to export your movie in older Flash formats when you publish it, but doing this means that the viewer won't be able to see some of the new features available in Flash 8. For most of the things we've covered so far in the book, this won't be a problem, but if you intend use the On2 VP6 video codec, filters, blend modes, or some of the more advanced ActionScript techniques, you'll have to export your movie in the Flash Player 8 format. It's a trade-off: if you want to reach the widest audience, you'll be advised to always put a Flash MX 2004 (Flash 7) or older compatible movie onto the Internet, at least until this new version of Flash has been around for a few more months. However, if you want to show off some of the new Flash 8 features, your viewers will have to use Flash Player 8.

Flash Player 8 is more optimized than Flash Player 7, and it will run content significantly faster than previous versions of the player. In fact, the general rule is that the performance of each version of the Flash Player is greatly increased over its predecessor. This speed increase is usually enough to encourage many web-savvy users to download the new plug-in pretty soon after its release (so take-up of the new player might be quicker than you'd think!).

The Shockwave for Flash format is part of a larger standard called Shockwave. This standard is used in Macromedia's Director software, and it means you can incorporate your Flash movie seamlessly into Director. Director is a general multimedia-authoring tool that is designed to produce multimedia presentations for applications such as CD-ROMs and screensavers, as well as web applications and interactive 3D environments. The main difference between Flash and Director is that Director has been designed for general multimedia, and not just small, size-optimized, web graphics. Director can do many things that Flash is not designed to do, such as use real 3D (using 3D models and cameras) and provide greater synchronization between multimedia streams.

HTML

HTML stands for HyperText Markup Language. HTML is not a language in the same way that ActionScript is—HTML is a **formatting** (or markup) language whereas ActionScript is a **scripting** language. This means that HTML consists of special instructions that tell the browser how to format the text and graphics on a web page. It's these instructions, or *tags*, that are the heart of HTML, and they are also its major weakness. HTML was only designed to present simple text data and static images. At its inception, this was enough, but as the Internet expanded, HTML became more and more old-fashioned and heavy. On the plus side, HTML is an integral, universal feature of the World Wide Web. Its ease of use and total compatibility make it a good choice if you want simple information to be readable by absolutely everyone. One of its main features—links from one page to any other—was a defining feature that led to the current popularity of the Web as a tool for quickly acquiring information. Additionally, of course, you don't need a plug-in or player for HTML to work.

The real problems with HTML start when you try to add multimedia or interactive elements to a web page. Because HTML wasn't designed for this, you have to use JavaScript (the scripting language that ActionScript is based on) on top of HTML, which moves away from 100-percent compatibility with all browsers. There are new versions of HTML and other supporting languages for multimedia and wireless devices in the works, but for the time being at least, there will be much less support for them on the Web than there is for the Flash Player.

As a Flash designer, you have to know a bit about HTML because it's what carries your movie on the Web. To make your movie accessible over the Web, your movie file will be hosted inside an HTML file. Luckily, it's easy to publish your movie embedded in an HTML file, which you can then simply integrate into your website. As you'll see later in this chapter, all you have to do is tell Flash a few simple things about how you want the final movie to behave in the browser window, and Flash will generate the appropriate HTML file. You still may need to do other things with this Flash-generated HTML, however, because parts of your HTML document can perform tasks that Flash can't, like making descriptions and keywords for the web page available to search engines.

Furthermore, most Flash web pages don't just consist of a Flash movie on its own—they're usually made up of many separate elements. Things like hit counters and advertising banners must integrate seamlessly with the Flash portion of your site. In this chapter, you'll look at Flash's HTML publishing controls, but not the HTML site design and creation side of things: that's a whole subject of its own. However, many books and websites are dedicated to HTML if you want a more thorough understanding.

If the idea of writing or editing HTML is unsavory to you, it might comfort you to know about Macromedia's other flagship product, Dreamweaver. Dreamweaver is a WYSIWYG HTML editor—a visual environment for creating HTML pages. In short, you can design your web page freely and Dreamweaver will create all the HTML markup for you.

WYSIWYG, by the way, stands for What You See Is What You Get.

Animated GIFs

Animated GIFs were an early attempt at animated content on the Web. We touched on them briefly when you imported them into Flash in an earlier chapter, but you can also export your Flash movie as a GIF. Why would you want to do this? For the simple reason that you don't need a special plug-in to view them. You can guarantee that everyone who can view images on the Web (and that really is just about everyone) will be able to view your movie. This is the reason why many banner ads are created as animated GIFs—they're universally viewable, and thus reach the maximum number of eyeballs. You can harness this accessibility in your own sites by having a Flash version and an animated GIF/HTML version of your site on the Internet, allowing people to visit either depending on their preferences. It's possible to export some or all of your Flash movie as animated GIFs via the export options, which we'll cover later in this chapter.

QuickTime

QuickTime is Apple's Internet multimedia technology. The advantage of using it rather than Flash is that it can be integrated with QuickTime technologies (such as QTVR); it can be set up to run with QuickTime server-streaming content, and it has a fairly large user base. You can embed a Flash SWF file in QuickTime as a multimedia channel, but only Flash content (including ActionScript) up to Flash 5 is supported. You can also export your Flash presentation as a QuickTime MOV file via the publish options.

So, how do you publish the movie?

Putting on the show

Once you've produced your movie, you have to create the necessary files for people to view it outside the Flash authoring environment. The way this happens is controlled by the settings in the File ➤ Publish Settings window:

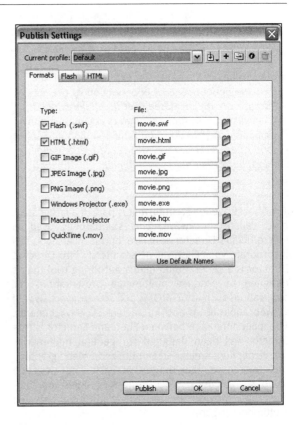

Each of the formats listed earlier is for playing your movie in a different environment, such as the Internet, a QuickTime movie, a stand-alone file that can be run on a computer without the Flash Player installed, or even as a static picture. It's important to realize that the file you've been creating won't be the file that's finally used in any of those applications. The "work in progress" FLA file will be converted to one or more new files that can be read by the target software.

The general method is as follows:

1. Select the way you want to publish your movie via the Publish Settings window.

2. Preview the movie.

3. Once you're happy with your publish settings, publish the movie. The requested files are placed in the same folder as the source FLA file by default, although you can change this by clicking the folder icons and selecting a new location for any of the created files.

4. Upload the published movie onto your server.

Let's walk through the publishing process.

Creating and publishing a basic movie

To start, you'll concentrate on the simplest and easily the most popular option: publishing a Flash movie in a form that can be viewed by anyone who's got a browser with the Flash Player installed. First, you'll create a simple movie to publish.

1. Start a new movie and place a static text box on the stage. In the text box, enter This is a test movie in a big, bold font:

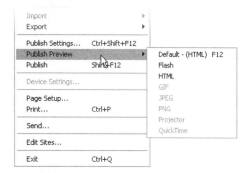

This is a test movie

2. Use the Align panel to make sure your text is in the exact center of the stage. To do this, display the Align panel (Window ➤ Design Panels ➤ Align), click the To stage icon, then click the Align Horizontal Center and Align Vertical Center icons.

3. Press *F8* to convert the text into a graphic symbol called text graphic with a central registration point. To make the registration point central, remember that you have to click the central square in the 3✕3 grid that appears in the Convert to Symbol window.

4. Insert a keyframe at frame 20 of your main timeline.

5. Using the Properties panel, add a motion tween between the keyframes at frame 1 and 20, and set it to rotate clockwise one time:

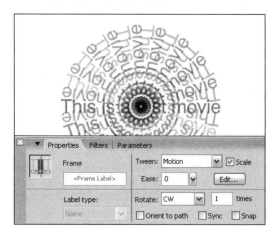

6. Test your movie (*CTRL+ENTER*). It's a simple movie, but it'll be effective for our purposes here.

7. Create a new folder on your desktop, and save your movie in it as movie.fla.

   If you look in your folder, there will be one file in it—the FLA that you just saved. When you publish your movie, Flash will automatically put all its output files in this same folder, so if you're building a big project, it's a good idea to keep everything in a dedicated folder.

8. Go back into Flash and select File ➤ Publish Preview. A submenu will appear listing the publishing options:

   If you haven't altered the default settings, you'll see three options available: Default, Flash, and HTML. When you publish your movie via File ➤ Publish, Flash creates output files in all the formats that are in bold letters on the Publish Preview menu—in this case, SWF and HTML. When you select the options found in File ➤ Publish Preview instead, Flash allows you to view and create the output files one at a time.

9. Select the Flash option: this will take you to the familiar Test Movie screen.

   On this screen, Flash shows you what the movie will look like on its own. It has compiled your source FLA file and produced a SWF file, which is what is played.

419

10. Go back to the Publish Preview menu and select the HTML option. You'll see the same movie, except this time it's being played in your default browser. When you select this option, Flash creates an HTML file and embeds the SWF into it.

11. Look at the folder you stored `movie.fla` in. You'll see that there are now three files in it:

The SWF is the Flash movie file that's playable in the Flash Player. The HTML file (actually, Flash creates a file containing a more recent dialect of HTML, XHTML) is just a text HTML document containing the formatting tags needed to display the page in a browser, plus a link to the SWF (on the thirteenth line of this text):

```
<html xmlns="http://www.w3.org/1999/xhtml" xml:lang="en" lang="en">
<head>
<meta http-equiv="Content-Type" content="text/html; charset=iso-8859-1" />
<title>movie</title>
</head>
<body bgcolor="#ffffff">
<!--url's used in the movie-->
<!--text used in the movie-->
<object classid="clsid:d27cdb6e-ae6d-11cf-96b8-444553540000"
codebase="http://fpdownload.macromedia.com/pub/shockwave/cabs/flash/swflash.cab#version=8,0,0,0" width="550"
height="400" id="movie" align="middle">
<param name="allowScriptAccess" value="sameDomain" />
<param name="movie" value="movie.swf" /><param name="quality" value="high" /><param name="bgcolor" value="#ffffff"/>
<embed src="movie.swf" quality="high" bgcolor="#ffffff" width="550" height="400" name="movie" align="middle"
allowScriptAccess="sameDomain" type="application/x-shockwave-flash"
pluginspage="http://www.macromedia.com/go/getflashplayer" />
</object>
</body>
</html>
```

SWF file link

When this HTML file is previewed in the browser, it will give you this result:

There's a slight problem with the way your movie is shown in the browser. The size is right—its dimensions are the same as we set in the Document Properties dialog box—but it appears in the top-left corner of the screen. You can change all that by giving Flash different publishing settings to work with.

12. Select the File ➤ Publish Settings menu option and display the Publish Settings window again:

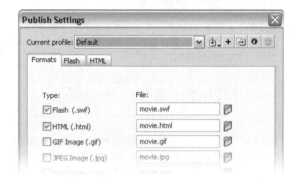

On the Formats tab of the Publish Settings window, you can select the file formats in which your movie will be published. You'll see that at the moment there are checkmarks in the boxes for Flash and HTML—these correspond to the options that were available to you on the Publish Preview menu. At the top of the window are tabs corresponding to these two selected options.

13. Click the GIF Image check box, and a new GIF tab will appear at the top of the window:

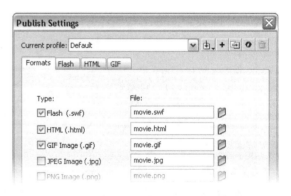

14. Uncheck the box, and the tab disappears. The tabs contain the individual settings for each of the file types that are checked in the Type list.

15. Click the HTML tab to display the following window:

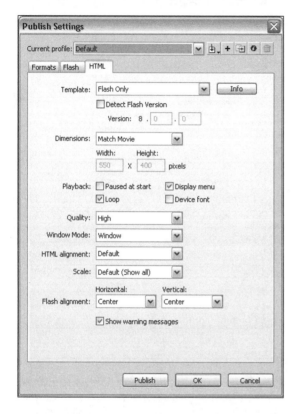

We'll be covering all these options in detail later in the chapter, but for now, let's just get your movie to play how you want it to.

16. You want the movie to take up the *whole* of the screen when it plays, and this is done through the Dimensions drop-down menu:

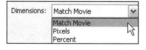

At the moment, Match Movie is selected so your browser will always keep the movie at the size set in the Document Properties window—in this case, the default 550×400 pixels. If you resize your browser window, your Flash movie will stay the same size and will begin to be cut off when the window gets too small:

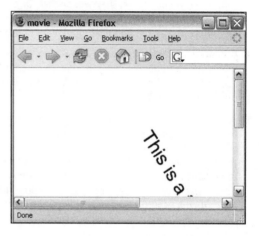

The other problem with defining a stage size in pixels is that if someone is using a different screen resolution than you, the movie will be a different size on his or her screen. If you design your movie to be the perfect size on your 1280×960-pixel monitor and your viewer is viewing it on an 800×600 screen, she won't see quite what you intended. You can stop this from happening by changing the Dimensions setting to Percent. The Percent option refers to the size in the browser window, not the pixel size of the movie, so 100 percent will always fill the entire browser window, no matter what size or resolution it is. Neat.

> *Without wanting to take the wind out of your sails at this point, it is important to point out the disadvantages of scaling your movie larger or smaller than its intended size:*
>
> - *Bitmaps: When bitmap images are shown larger than their intended size, they will distort (or pixelate), reducing their quality significantly. This can often cause JPEG images to look very poor.*
>
> - *Processing power: When a movie with processor-intensive animation or many gradients is scaled up, some slower machines will suffer with playback (movie speed is reduced).*
>
> - *Text: There are a number of issues when it comes to text, but we'll highlight a couple of major issues. First, scaling a movie down can obviously reduce the legibility of text in the movie making it illegible. Second, when a movie is scaled up or down, the layout of dynamic text is changed dramatically, so this might ruin your carefully planned design.*

17. Change the settings to Percent, ensure the Width and Height boxes both read 100, click OK and use File ➤ Publish Preview ➤ HTML to preview your movie again.

These settings are good because you know your movie will always stay central and fill the window.

Which Dimensions option you choose is a matter of preference. If you want your movie to be in an exact area on your web page and remain in the same proportions, choose the Match Movie settings. If you want it to play at a certain percentage of the screen size on any computer at any resolution, choose the Percent setting.

The most common settings used in commercial sites are shown in the following graphic. The SWF does not scale and always stays in the middle of the browser window. Return to the Publish Settings window and change your settings to those shown:

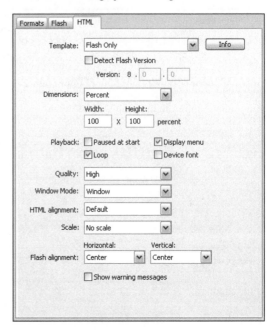

> *You can also save publishing options as templates in XML format, which is very handy. Click the Import/Export Profile icon in the top right of the Publish Settings window, and select Export from the menu that appears.*

> *To import it to a new FLA, use the Import option from the same drop-down menu. You can also save Profiles as part of the current template by clicking the plus sign (+) icon. This saves the current publishing configuration as a new option in the Template drop-down menu.*

18. Go back to the Publish Settings window and click the Formats tab.

Notice that each of the file formats has a box next to it that displays the name of your movie. These boxes show what your movie will be called when you publish it in that format. It's vital to be able to see which file corresponds to which format. If the extensions are not visible on your computer, it can be a problem telling them apart at a glance.

Change the names of your two selected file types to movie_flash.swf and movie_html.html, respectively. Also check GIF Image and JPEG Image and change the filenames to movie_gif.gif and movie_jpg.jpg.

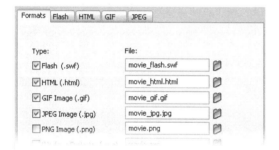

19. Click the Publish button. If you look in the folder where you originally saved your movie, you'll see a whole host of files there now. You added the file type to the name because some operating systems don't show file extensions in many views. For example, as you can see in the following graphic, without the file type added to the name, it would be quite difficult to distinguish between the GIF and JPEG version.

movie   movie   movie_flash   movie_jpg   movie_gif   movie   movie_html

20. Double-click the movie_swf.swf file in your folder, and your movie will play in the stand-alone player (provided you installed the Flash Player when you loaded Flash onto your machine, of course!):

21. Close the player and double-click the movie_html.html file, and your movie will now start playing in your web browser.

> *These two files—the SWF and the HTML files—are all that you need to put your movie on the Internet.*

You could delete your FLA file now and still be able to display your work on the Web. This isn't recommended, though, because if you ever wanted to go back and edit your movie, you'd need the FLA. You should try to keep all your project files in one folder so you can easily find them again if you need to. It's also always a good idea to archive your FLAs onto CD or some other backup media.

Now that you've gone through the process once, let's take a more detailed look at the publishing options and how and why you'd use each one.

The many faces of Flash

Flash can do a lot of things, but it can't do **everything**. For this reason, there are many different publishing options that allow you to do much more with your Flash movie than create a SWF.

1. Open the Publish Settings window, and check *all* the Type boxes. A tab will appear for each type, with the exception of Windows Projector (.exe) and Macintosh Projector.

2. For ease of reference later, change the name of each file to include its format as you did before. The projector files are stand-alone executable files that are used if your movies will be viewed offline, such as screensavers, or if you want to email your movie to a friend who doesn't have the Flash Player. The projector files contain a miniaturized Flash Player inside them so anyone can view your movie. A projector file is also useful when you want to create content for non-web applications (such as on a CD-ROM).

> Note: Windows users will see the extension .hqx alongside the Mac projector type, whereas Mac users will see nothing alongside it. Don't worry about this for now as we'll cover it in more depth later in the chapter.

3. When you've finished, you'll have a screen like this:

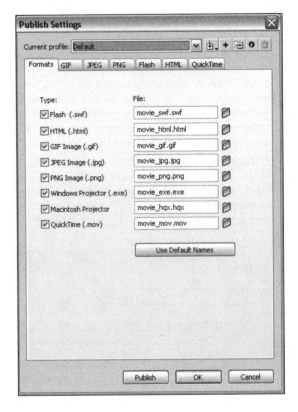

The two most important and most used tabs are Flash and HTML, so let's focus on these two.

> At the time of this writing, QuickTime (currently on version 7) can only handle Flash content up to Flash 5. If you need to publish QuickTime, you will have to export your movie as Flash 5 or lower via the Flash tab of the Publish Settings window.

Flash file publishing options

The Flash tab is where you specify exactly how the SWF file will be created:

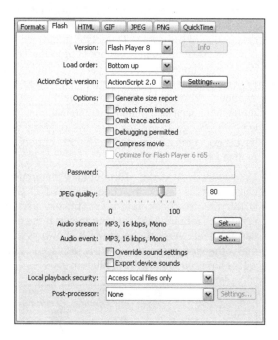

This tab contains the following significant options:

- Version: Use the Version drop-down menu to select the version of the Flash Player for which you want your movie published. It is recommended that you export to an earlier version of the Flash plug-in until the Flash 8 plug-in becomes more commonplace. The only time you should definitely use Flash Player 8 is when you need to include some of Flash 8's extra functionality, such as the advanced ActionScript commands. These commands are highlighted in yellow in the Actions panel when you set the version to lower than Flash Player 8.

- Load Order: This specifies the order in which Flash will load the layers for the first frame of your movie. It can load from the bottom layer up or from the top layer down. This option only has an effect when your movie is viewed over a slow connection, when the failure to load layers that are critical—such as the layer containing the navigation buttons—could result in a degraded user experience. In files that include ActionScript, make

sure that the layer with ActionScript in it is the last to be loaded because the code usually expects everything else to be loaded before it (and may not work if it is not). If you follow this book's convention and always put the ActionScript in the top layer called actions, you should always keep this setting as Bottom up.

- Options: Select from the following options:

  - Generate size report: Creates a text file that tells you about the final SWF file. The file can be useful when you're optimizing your movie because it gives you a frame-by-frame breakdown of the movie's size, and useful information about any symbols, sounds, pictures, and text that are in there. The exact content of this file is a bit beyond the scope of this book, but it's fairly straightforward when you view the file.

  - Protect from import: Stops anyone from importing your SWF file back into Flash and copying all of your hard work. There are applications that allow a malicious user to break this protection, but you are still advised to use it for your final site.

  - Omit Trace actions: Makes Flash ignore any Trace actions you might have included in your movie. Trace actions are commands that allow you to track the value of a variable in your movie and display it in the Output window while the movie is running. This is very helpful for you when you're debugging your movie, but you don't want it popping up when someone else plays your file.

  - Debugging Permitted: Allows you to use the Debugger panel on the final presentation, which can be selected from the Flash Player pop-up menu. This is useful when you're trying to track any bugs in your final movie, but again, it's not something that you want other people to be able to use. It's also possible to protect this option by entering a password in the Password box. This permits only those who know the password to use the debugging options.

- Compress Movie: Although Flash compresses movies somewhat by default, this option allows Flash to further compress the Flash movie when publishing. As mentioned earlier, ActionScript code, video, and text benefit most from this, but vector shapes are also compressed. This option cannot be used for movies intended for use with player versions earlier than Flash Player 6.

- Quality: These are global settings for imported artwork and sounds, and they will only affect the movie components that you did not optimize separately. As you discovered in earlier chapters, it's always best to optimize all aspects of your movie separately because this provides the best compression-to-quality ratio.

HTML file publishing options

The HTML tab specifies how to configure the HTML file that will be published.

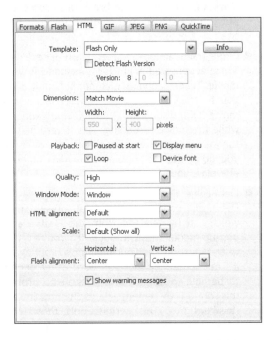

- Template: This specifies the type of HTML file you want the SWF to be embedded into. Each different template includes specific types of HTML tags that allow you to extend the HTML file's functionality. There are more options in Flash Professional than Flash Basic. The Info button will give you a brief description of the selected template, and which file it is. The HTML template files are kept in the Flash 8/en/First Run/HTML folder (or the equivalent folder if you are using an international version) on Windows, or Macromedia Flash 8/First Run/HTML on the Mac, so if you're an HTML/XHTML whiz and want to change them, back up the originals and have a go. In most cases, the Flash Only option will be fine.

- Detect Flash Version: This option determines whether some JavaScript code is placed in your HTML file to check the user's plug-in version against the required one for your movie. If the user has a suitable version, the movie is shown as normal; otherwise some error text is displayed along with a link to the latest Flash plug-in:

- Once the HTML file with the detection code has been produced, you can customize the JavaScript detection code to react differently when the user doesn't have the required plug-in version. For instance, you could show them alternative (older!) Flash content; redirect them to an HTML version of your website; or show them a cool image along with the Flash download link to entice them in. Come on . . . come on . . ..

- Dimensions: As you've already seen, this allows you to change how your movie is displayed on the screen. You can use your movie dimensions, specify another movie size, or scale your movie to a percentage of the user's browser dimensions.

- Playback: Options include the following:

  - Paused at start: Means the user has to tell the movie to play before it will do anything.

  - Display menu: Displays a menu when a user right-clicks (or *CTRL*-clicks on Mac) your movie. This menu allows the user to control the playback of the movie, change the movie quality, and zoom in to see all that lovely vector detail. Switch this off if you don't want your users to have these options. Many commercial sites switch this off so users don't try to switch to low-quality settings or zoom into the graphics to have a close look at how it was all put together.

```
Zoom In
Zoom Out
Show All

Quality              ▶

✓ Play
✓ Loop

Rewind
Forward
Back

Settings…

Print…

Show Redraw Regions
Debugger

About Macromedia Flash Player 8…
```

The contents of this menu can be customized using the ContextMenu *class in ActionScript. Look in* ActionScript 2.0 Classes ➤ Movie ➤ ContextMenu *within the ActionScript reference for information.*

- Loop: Plays your movie continuously if selected, or only once if it's not. This option is overridden by any stop actions you have, and can also be overridden by the user.

- Device font: Replaces any static text in your movie with a system font, which can cut down on file size, although you have less control over which font is used. Flash uses the closest one it finds on the user's machine, but these days it's usually very close as long as you use the generic fonts—_sans, _serif, and _typewriter).

- Quality: This option allows you to set the rendering quality that your movie will play at—the lower the quality setting, the faster it will run on a slower computer. We recommended you set this to Auto High to allow Flash to drop the quality to maintain frame rate and synchronization if it needs to. It's not worth worrying about setting this to a lower quality—if users are having problems with the quality, they can change it themselves at their end.

- Window Mode: These options affect how some advanced Dynamic HTML (DHTML) commands can interact with your movie in certain browsers. Most of the time, you'll want to leave this set to Window.

- HTML alignment: This allows you to specify the position of your movie window inside the browser window. Default will center the movie, and the other options will align it along the desired edge.

- Scale: If you've changed the size of your movie with the Dimensions option earlier, you can use this option to define how your movie is scaled to fit into the browser window.

- Flash alignment: These two options allow you to set the vertical and horizontal alignment of your movie inside its window, and how it will be cropped if it needs to be.

- Show warning messages: When this box is checked, any errors discovered when the HTML file is played—for example, images that aren't where they say they are—are displayed as messages on the browser when the user views your site.

Until you become more familiar with the intricacies of HTML/XHTML coding, you won't need to alter many—if any—of these options. The Dimensions option is the most important thing to be aware of at this stage, and you can experiment with the rest when you become more experienced.

The remaining publishing formats in the Publish Settings window are fairly self-explanatory. We'll give you a brief rundown of them and highlight the most important options.

GIF, JPEG, and PNG

These bitmap export options are of particular interest to the Flash designer because they allow the easy creation of both a Flash **and** an HTML version of your website. All these formats will publish the first frame of your movie as a static image. The exception to this is GIFs, which can also be animated. You can specify an individual frame for Flash to publish by putting #Static as a label on that frame.

GIF seems to be the best option for publishing a static image because its compression routines are well suited to Flash's solid colors. If you use a lot of gradients in your movie, though, these can come out horribly dithered—it's worth checking the Remove gradients box and replacing the gradients with solid colors to achieve a better-quality image.

GIF files also have the option to be animated. When you publish your movie as an animated GIF, Flash saves each frame of your movie as a GIF frame that'll be played through in a flipbook manner to give the appearance of animation. This is best for HTML versions of sites or for doing small animations such as advertising banners that you want to be viewable on all computers.

> *Note that ActionScript is ignored when creating an animated GIF; the timeline will simply run from end to end.*
>
> *Also note that in some versions of Flash 8 we used to test this on, the animation seemed to be messed up when we tried to export an animated GIF using the methods we've already discussed. This problem should be rectified in the final product, but if you get any problems with this, try using File ➤ Export ➤ Export Movie, then choose to save as Animated GIF from the Format drop-down menu. Then choose a filename and save location, and click OK, and your animated GIF should come out fine.*

If the image you're exporting contains a lot of gradients or imported artwork, the best option is to publish it as a JPEG file. As you move the Quality slider to the left, the file size gets smaller but the quality of the image deteriorates—and vice versa.

It's worth playing with this option in conjunction with the Publish Preview option to find the best balance for your image. There's also an option to set the image as a Progressive JPEG. This is a method for loading images on slower computers: the computer will load an interlaced version of the file (for example, every fifth line), and then fill in the image one set of lines at a time.

PNG is the only image format supported by Flash that includes an alpha channel for transparency. Remember that a transparent GIF has pixels that are either fully transparent or fully opaque, but a PNG image can contain degrees of transparency. To use this option, you must have the Bit Depth set to 24-bit with Alpha.

> *A PNG-24 image will be very large and is not really designed for the Web, so don't be tempted to use it as such. Select 8-bit if you want to use the PNG in a web page. The file size should be comparable to (or less than) a GIF.*

QuickTime movies

Publishing your movies in QuickTime format allows you to use them with other QuickTime files.

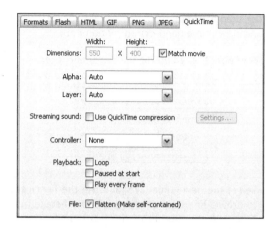

The Flash movie will be published on its own track inside the QuickTime file, which can then be edited from inside QuickTime Pro—a program made by Apple for the creation and editing of QuickTime files. The options control how the Flash track will interact with other tracks inside the movie, and which type of QuickTime controller to use to play the movie. It's a good idea to select the Flatten box because it tells Flash to build all the external files (such as graphics or movies) into the final QuickTime file, allowing it to be played as a stand-alone file on any computer. If this box is not checked, the final file will be smaller, but it will depend on links to the external files. If these files are moved or renamed, the movie won't be displayed correctly.

Projector files

If you ever aim to create Flash movies for CD-ROM or (downloadable) full-screen games, the projector file will come in mighty handy. Besides the alluring option to run Flash movies full screen, projector files also have the benefit of being stand-alone, so you never have to worry about whether the user has the Flash plug-in (or hassles about which version they have if they do). The way a projector file works is by creating an application (aka a program) and placing in it a copy of the Flash plug-in and your Flash movie content. On Windows, a projector file has the .exe extension, while the Mac version has a (usually hidden) .app extension. What's most important is that a double-click of either will launch the projector file like any other software application. Neat-o.

Warning: Creating a Mac projector file on Windows creates an HQX file, which is a compressed archive rather like a zip file. If you intend to distribute a Mac projector file along with your Windows one, you will need to extract the projector file first. Either get a Mac user friend to do this for you or get a copy of Aladdin's StuffIt Expander for Windows.

Just in case you hadn't already noticed, the Projector publish type doesn't have a publish settings tab. In fact, Flash just creates a basic projector file and goes home early for tea and scones. Unfortunately for us, while Flash is putting its slippers on, we'll be stuck in front of the monitor for a little longer making our projector file work how we want it to.

So what exactly do we want our projector file to do? OK, let's imagine that we're working on an addictive Flash game with a friend. (Coincidentally, the game is set to halve productivity in offices all over the world—it's *that* addictive):

"First, we want our users immersed in the game, so we'll make it full-screen."

"Great . . . but if the boss is around they might need to run it in a smaller window."

"Yeah, you've got a point. If they are anything like our eagle-eyed boss, he'll see the game however small it is."

"How about an exit button or a key on the keyboard they can press that quits the projector file automatically?"

"But then you'd lose your score. Hmm . . . How about the game pauses and switches to a spreadsheet, to make it look like you're hard at work on that report that was due in last week?"

The two key-required functions pointed out here are toggle full-screen and quit. Let's make a quick projector file and see how they are achieved.

429

Creating a full-screen projector file

In this exercise, we'll create our first projector file and make it run full-screen.

1. Open the `fullscreen.fla` file from the code download for this chapter. The file contains the fish (who you might remember from earlier in the book), a button, and a blue background. If you don't have this file, create a new movie, save it as `fullscreen.fla`, and draw a fish on the stage.

2. Select the fish in its entirety and convert it into a graphic symbol called fish using the *F8* key. Give it a central registration point.

3. Rename the default layer Sea Scene and position the fish off-stage left and around vertical center. Don't be too fussy as we're going to animate him.

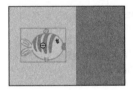

4. Insert a keyframe at frame 50 of the Sea Scene layer and set a motion tween between frames 1 and 50.

5. Select the keyframe at frame 50 and move the fish to off-stage right. This will be his destination point. The fish will swim from left to right, appearing and disappearing from the edges of the stage.

Rather than have him swim in a straight line he'll weave up and down on a hand-drawn motion path.

6. Add a motion guide for the Sea Scene layer.

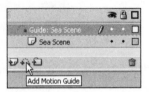

7. Select the new guide layer and use the Pencil tool to draw a line from off-stage left to off-stage right. To create the illusion of the fish looping around, I've started and ended my line around the vertical center of the stage and have made sure that the line goes well off-stage (note: the fish has been hidden in this screenshot):

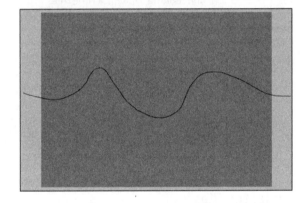

8. Now snap the fish to both ends of the line at keyframes 1 (left side) and 50 (right side). To make sure the fish will snap, ensure that View ➤ Snapping ➤ Snap to Objects is switched on.

Now test the movie to check that the fish moves along the guideline. If he does, we'll proceed to the projector file part! First, we need three buttons on stage to turn full-screen on, turn full-screen off, and quit the application.

9. Create a new layer called buttons, and, if you downloaded this file, drag three copies of the red button symbol from the Library onto the stage. If you created this file from scratch, you can either draw a new button and convert it to a button symbol, or get a premade one from Window ➤ Common Libraries ➤ Buttons.

Arrange the buttons at the bottom of the stage with one button to the right (this will be our quit button):

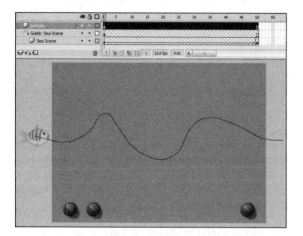

10. Give the buttons instance names (from left to right): max_butt, min_butt, and quit_butt.

11. To help us identify between the max_butt and min_butt buttons, use the Free Transform tool to make the min_butt about 50% smaller:

12. Insert a new layer called actions, and add the following code to frame 1 of the layer:

```
max_butt.onRelease = function() {
    fscommand("fullscreen", true);
};
min_butt.onRelease = function() {
    fscommand("fullscreen", false);
};
quit_butt.onRelease = function() {
    fscommand("quit");
};
```

If this looks like a lot of stuff to type, it might encourage you to know that this is all the code for this movie. The basic premise is that every button has an onRelease event handler, so when they are clicked, the code block will run. Each of these blocks contains an fscommand function.

> fscommand *functions are used by Flash to communicate with applications, including web browsers and the Flash projector.*

If you now preview the movie using Control ➤ Test Movie, you'll notice that the buttons don't do *anything*. This is because the fscommands are specific to Flash projector files. So we need to tell Flash to produce our projector file for us so that we can see the buttons in action.

13. Open the Publish Settings window via File ➤ Publish Settings.

14. Depending on your chosen operating system, check either the Macintosh Projector or Windows Projector option, then click Publish.

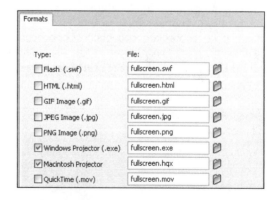

15. Now locate the projector file and double-click to open it.

With the projector file open, if you click on the maximize button, the movie will go full screen:

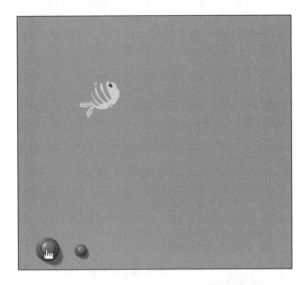

A full-screen aquarium, pretty cool, huh!?! Yeah, it could do with a few more fish I admit . . .

Once you start missing your desktop icons, click on the minimize button. It will then return to normal size. While the movie is normal size, notice that all the commands that we scripted are available: Exit is located on the File menu (Quit Flash Player on the Flash Player menu for Mac) and Full Screen is located on the View menu:

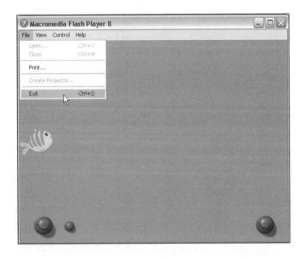

However, in full-screen mode the menus aren't visible, so this is why our buttons come in handy. Don't forget that having games and CD-ROMs running full-screen really does intensify their overall experience.

Now, add a few more fish if you feel like it, and when you're done we'll return to getting your website online.

Uploading your files to the host server

To make your movies available to the viewer, you need to upload them onto your hosting server so that people can access them over the Internet. This task is always fraught with danger the first time you do it, but like riding a bike, after you get it right once, it just seems to come naturally. The options available to you when you upload your files depend on the web hosting company you're using, and it would be impractical to provide you with instructions on how to do it all in detail. We'll cover some of the basic principles here, but always check with your ISP to make sure you know all of its distinctive ins and outs.

The key stages in the process are as follows:

1. Choose your ISP and establish how much space they'll give you for your website and what features they'll support.

2. Find out the specific upload locations and procedures for your ISP.

3. Transfer your movie files up to the host site based on these procedures.

Most modern browsers have upload abilities built into them, so once you have all the information just outlined, it's only a matter of entering the correct address in the browser and dragging files into the browser window to upload them.

The first issue you come across when you're getting your web page up and running is deciding exactly which files you need to upload. The only files that you need are your SWF and HTML files. Remember, the FLA file is just the authoring file; it isn't required once you've published your movie. Also, you don't need to upload any fonts, images, or other external files (unless you are using features that allow external assets) because Flash will embed these into your final SWF movie.

The second issue you'll come across is deciding what to call your HTML file. If the file is going to be a page inside your website, you can call it whatever you like as long as you include a link to that filename from another web page. If, however, your movie is going to be the first page of your website, you'll need to name it according to the protocols of your web server. Typically, the first HTML page of a site is called index.html, but you'll need to check this with your web hosting company. When you type a web address into your browser, you usually just type the URL, for example www.friendsofed.com, and the browser automatically searches for the web page called www.friendsofed.com/index.html. It's just a convention designed to save people from having to type /index.html at the end of every web address. If you did not rename your file, the user would have to know to type www.friendsofed.com/movie_html.html into their browser to get to your movie.

The final hurdle is actually getting the files up onto the server. To perform file transfers to the server, you use a special protocol called FTP, which stands for File Transfer Protocol. You can either use a shareware program to do this (try CuteFTP for Windows or RBrowser for Macintosh), or one of the many site-creation programs, such as Microsoft FrontPage or Macromedia Dreamweaver, which contain built-in features to help you upload your files. As mentioned earlier, though, your browser probably already supports FTP if it is a recent version, so there is now much less need for specialized programs.

From here, you pass beyond the bounds of Flash, and out into the brave new world of the Internet.

Case study

You're almost home free with your case study website. In this chapter, you're going to publish the movie and set up the necessary files on your hard drive that you'll need to upload your website onto the Internet.

1. Open your case study document.

2. With the Flash document open, go to File ➤ Publish Settings to display the Publish Settings window. On the Formats tab, select the Flash and HTML boxes (the entry in the File field may be different than the following screenshot—it'll be whatever you saved your case study movie as):

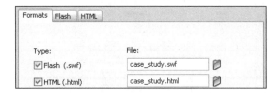

3. On the Flash tab, set the JPEG quality to 80%. This will shear off a bit from the file size, but not so much that it will degrade the quality of the images you imported:

Even though we've taken the easy route here of allowing all our images to be compressed by Flash's default compression, it is always advisable when working commercially (or aiming to ensure quality versus file size) to set the compression rate of each image individually.

4. On the HTML tab, uncheck the Display menu box so that the menu does not appear when users right-click the movie.

5. You want the Flash movie to scale in the user's browser without losing its original proportions. To do this, select Percent from the Dimensions drop-down menu and leave the Scale selection as Default (Show all):

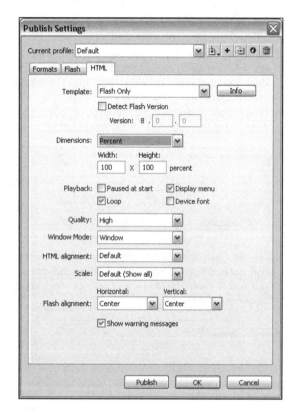

6. That's it! Click the Publish button, click OK, and look in the folder on your hard drive where you've stored the files for this case study:

Open the HTML file to test how your SWF looks in a browser:

7. Save your case study document and close it.

When you upload your website to the Internet, don't forget that you need to include the einstein.jpg and gandhi.jpg files because these are external files that the Flash movie calls on with the loadMovie method.

Summary

In this chapter, we've given a brief survey of the issues related to getting your finished movies ready for viewing up on the Web.

You saw that

- Flash has publishing options that will build all the output files you need to get your movie online.

- The most common publishing option for Flash is to embed a SWF file inside an HTML page.

- Flash will create the HTML file that hosts your movie, and you can tweak the HTML if you like.

- You can adjust the way your movie displays in the user's browser—and other attributes, too—by manipulating the values in the Publish Settings window.

- Projector files are self-contained Flash movies that don't require the Flash plug-in for viewing and can run in full-screen mode.

- Once you've created the viewable files, you need to consult with your web hosting company about getting your files up on your website.

In the next two chapters, we're going to delve deep into the heart of ActionScript to whet your appetite for code.

Chapter 15

INTERMEDIATE ACTIONSCRIPT, PART 1

What we'll cover in this chapter:

- Implementing the first steps of intermediate ActionScripting:
  - Planning larger-scale ActionScripts
  - Performing basic input and output

- Taking ActionScript further:
  - Understanding the logic of a Flash movie's internal structure with relation to dot notation
  - Getting movies to talk to each other using dot notation and code scope in ActionScript
  - Animating objects dynamically with ActionScript and user input

So far, you've gained enough Flash know-how to earn the grade of beginner—you're not a novice anymore, that's for sure. However, the rest of the book is going to take you further and enable you to earn your wings as an intermediate Flash user. The impressive effects on cutting-edge Flash sites will no longer baffle you—after the next two chapters, you'll have insight into the methods that top Flash designers use to create those cool-looking sites.

This is the starting point of your road toward mastering Flash. This chapter and the next will teach you the three main programming techniques you need to get going on your journey. They are

- Intelligently breaking down a problem and forming a structured plan to resolve it

- Treating a movie clip symbol as an *object* and understanding its relationship to the main Timeline and to other movie clips

- Using structured programming

I'll cover the first two points in this chapter, and introduce the basics of the third so you can hit the ground running when you get to Chapter 16.

The rest of this book has a much steeper learning curve than the previous chapters, and assumes you know how to perform basic actions (which were covered in Chapters 9 to 11) without being shown all the steps explicitly. However, I want as many readers as possible to get their wings, so if after reading the relevant section, you feel you haven't mastered one of these skills, go back and practice a little until you get the hang of it. The things I discuss in this chapter will make the difference between a plain vanilla Flash site and one that's packed with interesting and engaging features.

Planning your complex ActionScript: A practical overview

This chapter's author worked in several software-heavy environments before going into multimedia and web design. These were at a different end of the spectrum—industrial display systems and safety-critical computer-control systems at nuclear plants. Working with this intense level of coding teaches two things about effective programming that are applicable to complex ActionScripting—which is really programming by another name.

- You must start by looking at the *problem* and not the solution, and then refine the problem until you have a collection of simpler problems to solve.

- You must treat these individual problems as small, self-contained tasks, and be able to code and test each small solution as you go along to make sure it's working properly. Once the discrete components are tested and working, you can integrate them and test again.

You're going to put these ideas into practice by modifying the Smiler movie you created in Chapter 11.

Some people are very sensitive about their age, so when someone asks, "How old do you think I am?" you need to reply with care. If your guess is close to the correct age, you'll please them. But if you're a long way off in either direction, you're likely to offend, and may need to retreat quickly.

You're going to make your Smiler equally sensitive about its age. Fishing for a compliment, it will invite you to guess its age. If your guess is way wrong, it will put on a big frown, but as your guesses get closer to its actual age, the happier Smiler will get. When you guess exactly right, you'll see Smiler's biggest possible smile.

This is going to involve quite a big change to the existing Smiler code. Following the advice just offered, the first question you need to ask is, "What exactly is the problem I'm trying to address with complex ActionScript?"

Defining a problem

Is guessing Smiler's age the ActionScripting problem? No—that's the *user's* problem. You're creating the code for Flash to respond to the user's guess. Let's think about exactly what you want Flash to do by walking through the user's typical interaction with Smiler—this will help you identify the contours of the problem and the subproblems that it's composed of.

1. You want to define a number that the user doesn't know—Smiler's age—and you want to constantly check this number against the user's guess.

2. You want to detect when the user is wrong and, if so, by how much, and then convert the size of the user's error into an expression on Smiler's face.

3. The more wrong the guess is, the more Smiler will move toward its biggest frown, at the "sad" frame.

4. As the user's guesses get nearer to Smiler's age, the happier it will get—moving toward the "happy" frame. When the user guesses the exact value of Smiler's age, Smiler will put on its biggest smile and the game is finished.

How do you check that you've defined the problem correctly? By thinking it through and ensuring there's nothing else you want your program to do. If necessary, you talk to your client to confirm that you've analyzed the problem correctly.

> At this stage, it's important to think only in terms of what you want Flash to do—now isn't the time to think about exactly how you're going to make Flash do it. You need to keep your mind untainted by solutions until you've got a clear idea of the problem and its subproblems.

You'll find that most problems can be stated in a similar form to the one just described, even if they're very complex. A programmer would call the list of things that ActionScript needs to do a list of requirements. This list doesn't state the solution; it just states *what needs to be done*. Because these are the only requirements you have for the interaction of Smiler and the user, you can be reasonably confident that your list is a general statement of the *whole* problem. A programmer would call these the **high-level requirements**, and would break each requirement down into a list of smaller, more detailed requirements for the program. This list is called a **requirements specification**.

The multi–billion dollar super-computer programs that refuse to work don't usually fail because they've been coded incorrectly. They fail—almost without exception—because the *wrong problem* was defined at the planning stage, so the programming solution that was built based on that definition didn't fulfill the requirements of the actual problem. This can mean that the programmers aren't all working toward the same clearly defined goal. Although all the sections of the program work in isolation, when they're put together, the different chunks can't be integrated properly and nothing works. This emphasizes the importance of planning, and it's why you're not going to jump straight into creating the ActionScript for the new, improved Smiler. Instead, you're going to take things stage by stage, and guarantee that you come up with an effective solution.

Breaking down the Smiler problem

You now need to break down, or decompose, your high-level requirements into more detailed basic requirements. You keep breaking things down in repeated iterations until you have the simplest list possible things that can't be broken down any further.

A first iteration has subpoints of each original point (1.1, 1.2; 2.1, 2.2; etc.) and a second iteration has subpoints of each of these (1.1.1, 1.1.2, 1.1.3, etc.).

Let's work out Smiler's detailed requirements specification, based on the high-level requirement you've already specified.

1. Define a number representing Smiler's age.

2. Acquire a number (let's call it guess) from the user, and check it against age.

3. Compare the difference between age and guess and apply this value to the Smiler movie in order to make it go to a particular frame to indicate how close the guess is.

4. If the difference is zero, make Smiler go to the "happy" label on the Timeline—Smiler's biggest smile—and stop. If the difference is *not* zero, repeat from point 2.

You can now break this down further in your first iteration by asking more questions about the nature of the problem. For example:

- How big a number can age be? Can it be 450? Can it be 6.124569081?

- Can guess be the word "five" or does it have to be the number 5?

- How many frames should Smiler have?

This is what your first iteration might look like:

- 1.1: Define a variable—age—that's between 1 and 99.

- 2.1: Elicit a text entry from the user that's numeric.

- 2.2: Assign this text entry to a variable, guess.

- 3.1: Create a new variable, difference, that's equal to age minus guess.

- 3.2: If difference is a negative number, convert it to a positive number of equal magnitude.

- 3.3: In the Smiler movie clip, go to a frame number that's equal to difference to represent how far out the user's guess is.

- 4.1: If difference is 0, stop. Otherwise repeat from 2.1.

Through refining your problem, you've almost written yourselves a set of instructions to solve it with.

If you put 1.1 to 4.1 in order, you end up with a list of what you need to do to reach a solution to the overall Smiler ActionScripting problem. This powerful technique goes by the name of **top-down design**: you've defined the high-level problem—the top—and then worked down into the problem by splitting up the requirements into their simplest forms. By the end of the process you have a problem that's so well defined that it has become the answer itself—and the path to the final specification is traceable all the way back to the top-level problem you're trying to solve.

*The converse coding style, **bottom-up design**, looks at the problem from the other way around— by starting at the bottom and asking questions such as, "What are the basic building blocks of this problem?" It then builds these blocks as software entities called objects, each of which is based on templates called classes that are used to define what objects are. The first set of classes (called **superclasses**) is then extended to form more precise classes, and thus a more precise solution. This coding system is called object-oriented design. You need to know structured programming to be able to use it well, so that's what you'll concentrate on in your foundation—although, because Flash is itself object-oriented, I've shown you how to follow the object-oriented hierarchy of properties and methods that ActionScript is arranged around.*

The Smiler example is a fairly simple problem, and you probably could have worked out the answer in your head without listing your requirements. However, when you're working on a bigger coding project, you won't have that luxury. The top-down method of planning and problem definition will save a lot of time and brainpower when solving more complex problems, and it will help ensure that you're solving the right problem in the right way.

By giving your problem a defined structure, you're forcing your ActionScript to follow a similar, structured form. You'll write ActionScript that's well thought-out and that addresses each requirement in turn.

For the beginner, thinking of the task in terms of the *problem* rather than the ActionScript has yet another— rather more subtle—advantage. If you think only in terms of the code solution, you'll only ever use the Flash skills you've already got a handle on. However, if you define the problem properly before thinking about the code, you may well hit upon the requirement for tasks you can't yet do. You'll be forced to try new methods to achieve this—instead of repeating the tasks you already know how to do and allowing your Flash programs to become stale. By looking at what you need to solve a problem, rather than what problems you can solve with the skills you already have, you'll constantly improve your skills and upgrade your Flash technique.

You now know what you need to change in the old Smiler to create a new, age-sensitive version. However, before you can solve the problem defined by your requirement specification, there are one or two pieces of Flash know-how you need to acquire. For instance, point two asks you to get the user to guess Smiler's age: so you need to know how to allow the user to input text, and how to get Flash to use that input.

Basic input and output

So far, you've seen that ActionScript allows you to create variables that you can store values in, and that Flash uses these variables in the background without the user being aware of them.

Sometimes, as in the Smiler movie, you want to have these variables visible on the screen so that you (and the user) can see what they are. In Flash, getting and displaying variables—whose values can change, remember—is done with **input text fields** and **dynamic text fields**. Although I touched on using input text fields, most of the text fields you've used up to now have contained **static text**, which, as its name suggests, doesn't do anything but sit in its box (even if the box itself is animated). Before I explain the two new types of text, there's something about the text fields themselves that needs to be explained.

If you just click once on the stage with the Text tool while you have Static Text selected in the Text type drop-down menu on the far left of the Properties panel, you'll create a text field that will extend indefinitely as you type into it. The text field will only move to a new line when you press the ENTER key. This text field, with undefined width, has a circle in the top-right corner.

If, however, you click and drag on the stage with the Text tool and make your text field a wide rectangle, this field will have a width defined by the size of the field you dragged out. The text you type into it will wrap onto the line below when the text reaches the edge of the field. This text field, which has a *defined* width, has a square in the top-right corner.

A text field with an undefined width will become a defined-width text field if you alter the width of it at any time. Additionally, you can revert a defined-width text field to an undefined-width field by placing your cursor over the little square and double-clicking.

Now I'll show you how to use text fields for input and update them dynamically.

Using input text and dynamic text

Let's try an experiment.

1. Create a new movie and use the Text tool to drag out a text field onto the stage. Make it around 150 pixels wide. Change the default layer name to Text.

2. In the Properties panel, use the Text type drop-down menu to change the text from Static Text to Input Text.

3. Notice that the square at the top right of the text box has moved to the bottom right, and that there are new fields visible in the bottom half of the Properties panel.

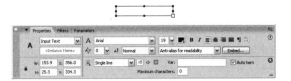

This text field is now enabled as an input field in the finished movie. The additional fields in the bottom section of the Properties panel allow you to control the behavior of that input field.

You'll use these fields to tell Flash that you want to store the user's input in a variable.

4. In the Instance Name field, enter inText. Change the Maximum characters field to 10, set the line type to Single line and click the Show border around text button. Also click the Align left button. Your panel will now look like this:

Selecting the Show border around text option means that the outline of the text field will appear in the movie—this can be very helpful for users, because they don't want to have to search too hard for the text input area.

5. Test the movie.

6. Click inside the text field box and enter some text. You can enter up to 10 characters, the maximum you specified.

You've created a text input area for the user on the stage, and the text typed into it will be used later to set the value of a variable.

You can now also create an output text area that will keep you informed about the current value of the variable.

7. Paste a copy of the text field you just created underneath the original.

8. Working with the new text field, change the text type in the drop-down menu in the Properties panel to Dynamic Text. Also, change the instance name to outText.

9. Deselect the Show border around text button and the Selectable button.

10. Insert a layer above the text layer in the Timeline and name this new layer Button. Add a button-sized circle to the stage in the new layer. With the circle (and any stroke it may have) selected, press *F8* to make it a symbol. Make it a button, and call it input button.

11. With the button still selected, give it an instance name of inButton using the Properties panel.

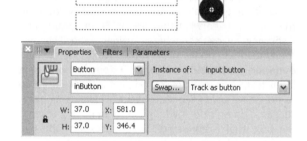

12. You now need to add an event handler for your button. Insert a new layer named Actions above the Button layer.

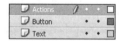

As usual, you'll add some code on this layer.

Cut!

OK, those of you who thought you were going to use Script Assist again, put your hands up. Well, without wanting to disappoint those of you with arms stretched, at this stage you're going to graduate to the next level: typing code *freely*.

By typing the code in this chapter and the remainder of the book, you can take advantage of the significant speed increase involved with this method of entering code. If you're a little daunted by the prospect, Flash's **code hinting** will aid you during your transition.

Code hinting is Flash's way of providing you with a clue as to what information it's expecting you to give it. Once you type something Flash recognizes, it will show you what it needs you to type next. If you use the gotoAndStop method as an example, you can see that Flash is prompting you for a *frame* (shown by Flash in bold).

If Flash needs more than one bit of information, it will highlight the different required elements as you type.

If you ever lose the code hinting tool tip, click the Show code hint button in the Actions panel and it will reappear.

Before you return to your experiment, I have two final ideas to leave you with here:

- If the going gets too tough when typing code, or you encounter something unfamiliar in ActionScript, don't forget that you can use Script Assist to help you out.

- Alternatively, double-clicking (or dragging) a command from the left-hand pane of the ActionScript panel will make it appear in the code along with a few handy pointers.

OK, let's remove those stabilizers and ride on, *freely*.

13. Select frame 1 of the Actions layer and add the following code in the Actions panel:

```
inButton.onRelease = function () {
    outText.text = inText.text;
};
```

14. Test the movie.

    You can enter text in the upper (input) text field, and as soon as you click the button, the value you entered appears in the lower (dynamic) text field. What's happening here? The text property of a text field allows ActionScript to access the text currently in a text field. By equating outText.text to inText.text, you copy whatever you just placed in inText to outText. The top text field is set up to allow user input, and the lower text field is set up to allow display of that input.

    Rather than tell the user what he or she already knows, as you're doing here, you can instead make Flash do something useful to the data you input before it displays it or outputs it for your viewing.

15. Select the lower text field again and change it so that it's an Input Text field. Click the Show border around text button, and enter 10 in the Maximum characters field. In the Properties panel, change the instance name to inText2.

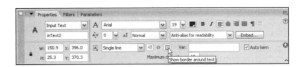

    You're going to get Flash to add the input to inText and inText2 together and display the result in a third text area. You need to define this third text area next.

16. Draw a third text box in the text layer to the right of the button and make it a Dynamic Text field.

17. Make sure the Selectable button is unselected and the Show border around text button remains selected.

18. Give the new text field an instance name of outText.

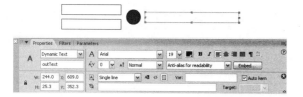

Now you need to let the user do something new—when he or she clicks the button, you want the values in the two text fields on the left to be added and displayed in the right one.

19. Select frame 1 of the Actions layer, and modify the code as shown in the following screenshot:

```
1  inButton.onRelease = function() {
2      outText.text = inText.text + inText2.text;
3  };
```

Remember that the code is case sensitive, so make sure yours look like this example—that is, that all your variable names are in camel case, and the method and action names onRelease, function, and text are all in a dark blue.

20. Test the movie. Enter a number in both of the left fields, and then click the button to see the result of the addition.

Um, you have a problem—the numbers didn't add together in the intended way.

What went wrong? When you enter anything in a text field, Flash assumes that the values you enter are text (or, to use the correct term, **string literals**). When you tell Flash to add the two text values, Flash does a string addition, which is called **concatenation**—that is, an action that puts the second bit of text after the other to make a single string. That's *not* what you want. You want Flash to assume the two inputs are *numbers* and to do an *arithmetic* addition. To do this you use Number(). This will turn your inputs into numbers, and

thus Flash will be forced to do an arithmetic add. I've changed the circular button to a plus sign (+) here to better show what happens to the inputs when the button is clicked.

```
1  inButton.onRelease = function() {
2      outText.text = Number (inText.text) + Number (inText2.text);
3  };
```

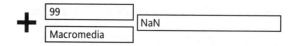

It works! And you can even add decimals.

21. Try typing letters into one or both of the fields and clicking the button. The dynamic text field to the right shows NaN, or "Not a Number."

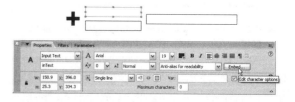

An informal rule in programming states, "If you're taking input from the user, assume that the user is a monkey." This isn't a reference to the monkey with a keyboard whose random typing produced Shakespeare; what I mean is that you have to cater to all the *wrong* inputs as well as the *right* one, and you should write code that expects the wrong answers and can handle them. Your code has to be able to cope if the user types 89g6!trc instead of 896. Let's see how to add an intelligence filter (or should that be stupidity filter?) to an input field.

Select both of the input text fields (hold down the *Shift* key to select more than one) and click the Embed button in the Properties panel to display the Character Embedding window.

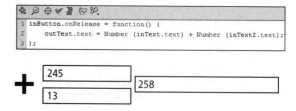

This window lets you specify what can be typed into or displayed in this input or dynamic text field. Flash assumes you want to allow input of *all* the standard English text characters, unless you select any of the options. You'll see the window shown here:

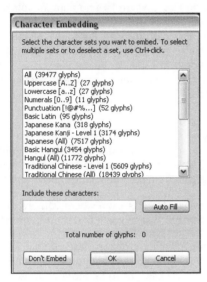

22. Since you want only numbers to be entered in the input fields, select Numerals [0..9] (11 glyphs) from the list. This allows you to enter any number that contains the numerals 0 to 9, plus the decimal point.

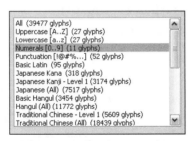

23. The user might also enter a negative number, so you should add that as well. In the Include these characters text entry box, enter a hyphen (-).

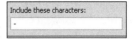

24. Test your movie again. Now you can monkey about all you want—Flash will only allow you to type in text up to 10 characters in length, and it must be integers from 0 to 9, a decimal, or a hyphen.

Of course, it's still possible to add incorrect entries such as 98-9 instead of 98.9 or 9.9.9 instead of 99.9.

ActionScript possesses a math library that contains functions such as sin, cos, tan, and so on, that allow you to develop this simple movie into a working calculator program.

Remember the Smiler specification you were planning before? You've just discovered an important building block that allows you to code it up in Flash. Now that you've got the hang of input and output, getting the user to guess Smiler's age later in the chapter will be no problem at all.

First, though, you need to learn a little more about dot notation and how to use it with paths in ActionScript.

Referencing paths with dot notation

As you discovered earlier, dot notation in ActionScript is a way of expressing the `instance.method(argument)` or `instance.property` code structures, enabling you to build your lines of ActionScript. The thing that hasn't been discussed is that the instance name doesn't just have to be a name, it can also incorporate a **path** into the instance.

> *If this name and path-plus-name stuff seems a little strange, this analogy might help:*
>
> *John lives down my street. If I need to leave him a quick letter or note, I will write it on a piece of paper and deliver it to his house, addressed simply to "John."*
>
> *Jake lives in a different city than me. When I want to send him a letter, I have to put "Jake" plus his full address on the letter because I need to specify which (of many) Jakes I want to receive my letter.*
>
> *This address is just the same as a path. Whether I use a path depends on whether the person I need to communicate with can be identified with just a first name, or whether this person requires a longer address. If you want to reference something on the same Timeline, you don't have to add a path. Otherwise you have to specify the path to the new location. The reason why you got away with not using dot notation so far is because everything you have done up to now involves stuff that's always on the same Timeline.*

Remember the structured planning you went through at the beginning of this chapter? You broke the Smiler problem down into manageable chunks or subproblems. If you now structure your movie correctly, you can address each of your requirements in a separate movie clip. You can then use dot notation to make these movie clips converse with each other and control the movie as a whole.

What does the path consist of? Here's another analogy: on your computer, you have a hard drive with various folders and subfolders—often nested several layers deep. To get to a particular folder, you use Windows Explorer, or you click the drive's icon on the Mac to open the folders you want to look at.

On my computer, the path for the folder of this text file (the one that I'm writing now, which will eventually be made into the book you're reading), is based on its position in the folder hierarchy. The actual path for this file's location is C:\Documents and Settings\Sham B\My Documents\Apress\Flash8\Foundation Flash\ chapter 15\.

This path tells you how to get to this text file starting from the hard drive, C:\, which is the lowest level, or **root level**. (Note the tree-like nature of the way these networks are linked.) What I'm saying here is that to get to the file, I have to go into a folder called Foundation Flash, where I'll find another folder called chapter 15, and if I open that folder, the file I want will be there. This path through the folder hierarchy gives me the entire journey, starting from the lowest level—the hard drive. If I specify the path in this way, starting from the hard drive level, it's referred to as the **total** or **absolute** path.

If I were already at C:\Documents and Settings\Sham B\My Documents\Apress\Flash8\Foundation Flash, I could express the route to the document relative to where I'm starting from—I don't have to go back via the hard drive level. The path from here would be simply chapter 15\.

This is saying, "Starting from where you are, open the folder chapter 15, and you'll find the file you want."

Flash uses a similar structure, except that instead of seeing levels of hard drives and folders, it refers to SWF files and movie clips, or to be more accurate, it refers to their **Timelines** and **subtimelines**.

Consider a Flash movie that has the following:

- A main Timeline (or root Timeline, called _root in Flash) that has one scene—Scene 1.
- A movie clip called Apress on frame 27 of Scene 1.
- A movie clip called FoundationFlash on Apress's Timeline at frame 20.

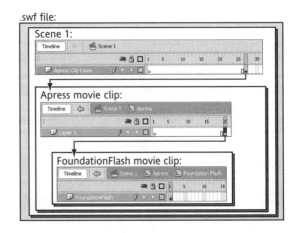

To access an object or frame on FoundationFlash's Timeline, you could use the following absolute path in your ActionScript: _root.Apress.FoundationFlash.

Because the path just shown is an absolute path, starting at the _root and working its way through the nested Timelines, I can safely issue it from anywhere and know that Flash will be able to find its way down the path, to the FoundationFlash *movie clip's Timeline.*

Note that each of the levels in this hierarchy is separated by a dot—hence the term **dot notation**. You can use this notation to specify the path that you want Flash to follow—and you can use it to point to any object, anywhere in the movie.

What if you want to access something in FoundationFlash's Timeline from within the Apress movie clip? You could use the full, absolute path defined earlier, but because you're *almost* where you want to be, you can just give a shorter *relative* path in ActionScript as follows: FoundationFlash.

This path will start from where you are, and look for the next level of the path inside of the Apress movie clip.

Apress movie clip:

FoundationFlash movie clip:

'Foundation Flash'
ActionScript

And there's a special ActionScript command if you want to go *back* a level (e.g., from FoundationFlash back up to the Apress clip): _parent.

Apress movie clip:

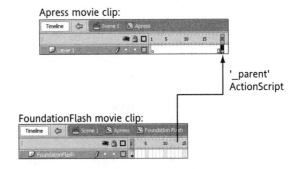

FoundationFlash movie clip:

'_parent'
ActionScript

You can also string these commands together to go back more than one level: _parent._parent.

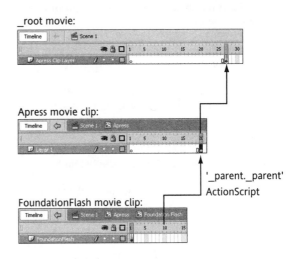

_root movie:

Apress movie clip:

FoundationFlash movie clip:

'_parent._parent'
ActionScript

Going back to your hard drive, you'll notice that you actually have more than just a C: drive. There are also A: and D: drives on most computers.

447

You can navigate to those drives by specifying their paths—such as A:\.

Similarly, you can include **external** movies in the paths you use in ActionScript. To access a separate SWF using dot notation, just replace _root with a reference to the external SWF's level: _level0 for the SWF at level 0, _level1 for the SWF at level 1, all the way up to level 16,000 (which is the maximum number of levels you can have). In fact, 16,000 is the maximum number of symbols you can have in the Library, and 16,000 is the limit for just about everything in Flash.

In terms of the original analogy of your hard drive:

- SWF files—movies—are the equivalent of your separate hard drives.

- A movie's main Timeline is the equivalent of the root path of each hard drive.

- Individual movie clips are the equivalent of folders and subfolders.

On your hard drives, you use paths to access *files*. Flash allows you to access *instances* and *variables*.

To specify a variable at the end of a path, as with other dot notation, just precede it by a period (.). The full path for a variable called userinput in the FoundationFlash movie clip would be _root.Apress.FoundationFlash.userinput or _level0.Apress.FoundationFlash.userinput.

In your Flash movies, you'll find the root level is displayed as level 0.

Many movie clips, many variables

Let's extend this discussion and think more about variables, the way they can be on different Timelines, and how the same variable has to be referred to from different places in different ways.

Let's look at how this works in a brief exercise.

1. Create a new FLA.

2. In the root Timeline (that's the Timeline on the main stage—you're going to be speaking in this new terminology from now on) add three layers: actions, text, and clips.

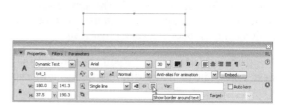

3. Select frame 1 of the text layer and insert a dynamic text field. Using the Properties panel, make the text nonselectable by switching the Selectable button to off, and give it a border by clicking the Show border around text button.

   This text field will display the first of our two values, so give it an instance name of txt_1 (make sure the text font color you've selected is *not* the same as the background color).

4. Now insert the following code on frame 1 of the actions layer:

   ```
   a = 3;
   txt_1.text = a;
   ```

   This code is doing two things. First, on the initial line of code, a variable named a is created that holds the number 3. Then, on the following line, the text property of the text field is set to hold the value of the a variable. OK, if you're thinking, "Why did I do that on two lines when it could have easily been done on one?" Well, there are endless reasons why two lines are better than one, but in this case it's because you want to see how different variables can be stored in different places.

5. Run this movie and you'll see a text box with the number 3 in it—not the most exciting movie you've made in this book. Bear with it, though, because the point this example illustrates will open your eyes to a wealth of exciting possible movies.

6. Back in the main movie, create a new movie clip called Mclip. Add new actions and text layers to it as you did for the root Timeline.

7. Create a similar nonselectable dynamic text field on the text layer, click the Show border around text button, and this time give it an instance name of txt_2.

8. To help you remember that this text field is *inside* Mclip, you're going to label it. Draw a static text field next to the dynamic one and type This is inside Mclip into it (select a different text color from the text in the dynamic text field). Then draw a line between the two text fields to clearly label it.

This is inside Mclip

9. In frame 1 of the Mclip movie clip's actions layer, use the Actions panel to add the following lines:

```
b=10;.
txt_2.text = b;
```

As before, this code is creating a variable before setting txt_2 to the value of b.

10. Go back to the root Timeline. Place an instance of the finished Mclip on the clips layer, and give it the instance name mClip_mc using the Properties panel.

11. Test the movie.

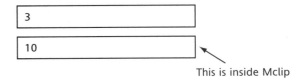

This is inside Mclip

Now you have a variable in the root called a, which is equal to 3, and a variable in the movie clip instance mClip_mc called b, which is equal to 10. Here's the current variable/text field relationship:

Main Timeline: ActionScript

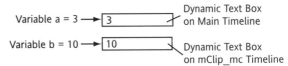

Now you're going to see how it's possible to have a variable name that has more than one value.

12. Inside mClip_mc, change the first line of ActionScript in frame 1 from b=10; to a=10;.

13. In the same place, change the second line of code to this: txt_2.text = a;

You've now set two variables, both called a, to two different values in two different places. The a=10; ActionScript inside mClip_mc is initializing a *new* variable called a, inside mClip_mc. This mClip_mc-specific variable is a *different variable* from the variable a that's being initialized on the main Timeline, _root. You can think of them as the following:

- _root.a
- _root.mClip_mc.a

These are *absolute* references. They will work wherever you are in the Timeline hierarchy, because they start from the lowest level, _root. This is much the same as starting at C:/ when specifying a file path on your hard drive.

449

Main Timeline: ActionScript

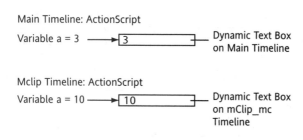

Each variable is associated with the Timeline on which it was initialized.

14. Test the movie to see how Flash implements this.

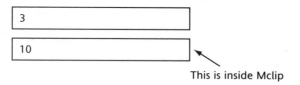

This is inside Mclip

Both text fields will show the same values as they did before. Although both text areas register as a variable, one is showing 10 and the other is showing 3 because the two different variables have different scopes. The a variable spawned from the main Timeline applies to the main Timeline, and the a variable spawned inside mClip_mc applies to the movie clip only.

Another way to think of this is that the absolute path is actually part of the variable name. So you have two different variables, named _root.a *and* _root.mClip_mc.a. *This is how Flash handles the situation internally, and closer to the way Flash actually thinks.*

15. Try running the movie again, but this time select the Control ➤ Debug Movie menu option instead of Control ➤ Test Movie and take a look in the Debugger window.

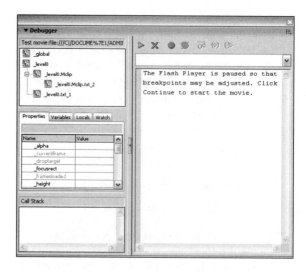

Once again, Flash is showing you the path to each of your movie components: the path for the main stage/Timeline is _level0, and the path to the movie clip is _level0.mClip_mc, showing you that mClip_mc is inside _level0. You can also see that txt_2 is inside mClip_mc, while txt_1 is situated on the main Timeline (_level0).

Treat _level0 *as the same as* _root. *There are one or two subtle differences, but let's not get bogged down by them right now.*

As the icons suggest, the main or root Timeline is just another movie clip: _level0 is represented by the same kind of icon as mClip_mc. This is something worth remembering as you advance further into Flash because all the things you learn to do with movie clips can also be applied to the root movie itself.

16. At the moment, the Debugger is paused. To start the movie and run your ActionScript, click the Continue button (the green arrow).

17. Now, if you click the Variables tab on the left side of the Debugger window, and have one of the paths selected, Flash will display the values you've assigned to your variables.

With _level0.mClip_mc selected, you'll see that the value of a is 10. Then select _level0, and you'll see that here it has a value of 3. (You'll also see a variable that represents the version of the Flash Player that's running. This can be ignored because it doesn't affect your programming.)

You now have two variables: one is called _root.a and the other is called _root.mClip_mc.a. Each variable is defined on a separate Timeline, and exists in only one place. The version of a inside mClip_mc only applies to that movie clip.

The way Flash handles variables per Timeline ("Timeline variables") are exceptionally useful because they allow you to reuse a movie clip. For example, imagine you built a movie clip that controlled a single space invader using the internal, movie clip–specific, variables called invaderPos, invaderDead, and firePhotonTorpedo. If you then put another 10 alien movie clips onto the stage, you would have 10 space invaders with 10 sets of discrete, internal, Timeline variables, all being individually controlled.

Accessing variables from different code scopes

Just as variables have scope, code blocks have their own scope as well. Let's look at this in a little more depth before you try it out.

Recall that scope in code applies to a code block in the same way that the subject of a paragraph should be the first thing that's mentioned. The following is a spoken-language equivalent of scope:

John is a fast runner. Someday he might make the Olympics.

You define the scope of the paragraph (John) so you can later refer to it in general terms such as "him" or "he."

In ActionScript syntax (noting that ActionScript doesn't have "he," but instead uses the much more general term "this"), the same thing would be as follows:

```
John is a fast runner {
   Someday this might make the Olympics;
}
```

John and this are two ways of saying the same thing. Let's look at how you would refer to subjects *other* than John if you wanted to refer to them in a block that was scoping John.

John is a fast runner. Someday he might make the Olympics. Paul is good at swimming, so they better start clearing the mantle for all that gold.

Paul isn't the subject of the paragraph, so you can't use "he" in the same way to represent Paul instead of John.

If you're referring to the person named Paul, who is here with you in the conversation, you just say "Paul." In Flash, this is the same as the subject being on the same Timeline as the code. You don't need to specify where the subject is because by referencing it in this way—it's understood that it's on the same Timeline as the code.

So you would have

> **John** is a fast runner {
>   Someday **this** might make the Olympics;
>   **Paul** is good at swimming;
> }

If the subject weren't on the same Timeline as the code, you would have to specify which subject you mean.

> **John** is a fast runner {
>   Someday **this** might make the Olympics;
>   **Paul** (the one who is in your presence) is good at swimming;
>   **Paul** who lives at number 32 down the road is not into organized sports, but prefers trekking.
> }

So how does that convert to Flash programming? When you write code that's in a code block that can cause the code to have a different scope to code outside the block (i.e., event handlers) you have to take into account *where the code is scoped*.

Add the following code (line 2 onward) to frame 1 of the root Timeline:

```
a = 3;
trace("-from _root-");
trace(this.a);
trace(a);
trace(_root.a);
trace(mClip_mc.a);
trace(this.mClip_mc.a);
trace(_root.mClip_mc.a);
```

The trace() action allows you to ask Flash to show you some of its variable values while you test the movie. You're asking it to tell you the values it sees for code that's not within a code block, so it will look at where the code is: _root. Even if you understand scope completely, you'll be a little surprised at the result.

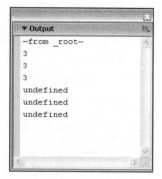

Whether you use this.a, _root.a, or a doesn't matter in this case because you're already at _root, so this becomes _root, and anything with no dot path is taken to be in the code scope, which is _root again.

However, the code can't find the variable a in mClip_mc. The three attempts to read the version of a in mClip_mc all give undefined, which is Flash's way of saying "Either it doesn't exist or it doesn't have a value"—but it *must* have a value because you set it to 10 on the first frame of mClip_mc! The reason it doesn't equal 10 has nothing to do with scope. You may think Flash runs code concurrently, but it doesn't. The code attached to _root is run first, the code in any Timelines on _root runs next, and any code on Timelines nested in those clips is run after that. When this code first runs, there is no variable a in mClip_mc because the code to set it up hasn't run yet! To fix this, follow these steps:

1. Go into mClip_mc and delete the code layer. This deletes the a = 10; code.

2. Add the line myClip_mc.a = 10; as part of the current script, as shown:

```
a = 3
mClip_mc.a = 10;
trace("-from _root-");
trace(this.a);
trace(a);
trace(_root.a);
trace(mClip_mc.a);
trace(this.mClip_mc.a);
trace(_root.mClip_mc.a);
```

This time, you define everything before the trace() actions run, and you see the following:

The three versions of your path to a on the Timeline mClip_mc also all work. Note that adding this.a and a is the same thing if you're already at this (which is always the case for code that's not within a code block). You never have to add this outside of a code block.

Now let's see how a change of code scope will affect this.

3. Change the script as follows:

```
mClip_mc.onEnterFrame = function() {
    trace("-from mClip_mc's event ➡
            handler block-");
    trace(this.a);
    trace(a);
    trace(_root.a);
    trace(this._parent.a);
    trace(_parent.a);
    delete (this.onEnterFrame);
};
a = 3;
mClip_mc.a = 10;
trace("-from _root-");
trace(this.a);
trace(a);
trace(_root.a);
trace(mClip_mc.a);
trace(this.mClip_mc.a);
trace(_root.mClip_mc.a);
```

The scope of the code within the block is changed from _root to mClip_mc in the same way our athletic friend becomes the subject of a paragraph. This time this actually does something because the code scope and where it is are two different things.

```
▼ Output
-from _root-
3
3
3
10
10
10
-from mClip_mc's event handler block-
10
3
3
3
undefined
```

In particular, note the following:

- Using a and this.a allows you to look at the two versions of a on the two different Timelines. Although this is a cool way to quickly access different variables, it's also a quick and easy way to access the *wrong* variable!

- The last pair of dot paths refer to this._parent and _parent. The parent Timeline is the Timeline a movie clip is on, and the first version tries to access mClip_mc's parent, _root. The second dot path attempts to access the root Timeline's parent, but given that _root is the lowest level, it has *no parent*, so you get no value, or undefined.

Before you put this into practice, let's think about the dynamic animation I promised you at the start of the chapter.

Dynamic animation

For dynamic animation to work, you have to be able to target a movie clip and alter some aspects of its appearance or action. To do that, you work with a movie's properties. You can view these properties by looking at the movie in Debug mode.

Viewing a movie clip's properties

1. Open one of your movies—preferably one with a movie clip attached to the main Timeline.

2. Choose the Control ➤ Debug Movie menu option to display the Debugger window with the movie in test mode.

3. Click the Properties tab (about halfway down on the left side of the Debugger window) and extend the size of the Properties pane if necessary.

When you get the Debugger window up, you'll see something like the following image, though you may have to adjust the size of the window. (If the Call Stack is covering it, drag the call stack title bar downward.)

The top-left pane shows you the hierarchy of movie clips in the movie. It also gives you the path for each nested movie clip, starting at the root with the main Timeline, and down to the movie clip inside Scene 1. Note the dot separating the nested clip from the Timeline.

Movie clips have more aspects than just the variables that you define and set. The names and values shown in the bottom pane of the Debugger window when you click the different movie clips are the properties of the movie clip. All movie clips will have this same set of properties, but the values for the properties in an individual movie clip will differ.

Essentially, properties are just like variables except that they relate to a particular aspect of the movie clip, such as its size, rotation, position on the stage, or whether all its frames have streamed in yet. There's one difference between variables and properties that you may already have guessed. If you change a property of your movie clip at any stage, you'll alter its appearance on the screen—it will be animated, because animation is just that: creating change. You're going to do this in a moment with dot notation and event handlers, but first let's try doing it *manually*.

If you go to the Properties tab on the Debugger while the movie is being tested, you can directly see the effects of changing properties.

4. Double-click the box in the table to the right of the _x property. You'll see it turn into a text entry box. Enter the value 10.

_visible	true
_width	38
_x	10
_xmouse	-149
_xscale	100

5. You should see the movie clip suddenly move to somewhere near the left side of the stage (you may have to move the Debugger window to find it). Do this several more times, but add 5 to the value every time, so you enter 15, 20, 25, and 30.

See that? Rather than a sudden change of position, you're changing the _x property by small values, so the change in position is regulated and looks as if the movie clip is *moving* from left to right. This is the basis of ActionScript-based animation. Spend a moment trying to change other properties, but don't change them too far from their original values. (You might make the clip shoot off the edge of the screen and you'll never find it again!) This is by far the best way to get an idea of what properties allow you to do. Notice also the effects of reducing _x (clip moves to the left), increasing _y (clip moves down), and decreasing _y (clip moves up).

The Flash coordinates are based on print conventions rather than math conventions, so the origin is at the top-left corner (the start position of line 1 in a print-based page), and not in the bottom-left. You'll see this if you set both _x and _y to 0—the clip will jump to the top-left corner of the stage. This is of course why the _y property seems to act the wrong way around to anyone with a math background—in a print-based layout, the y-axis points downward.

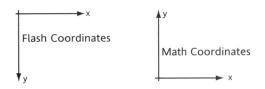

Flash Coordinates

Math Coordinates

Feels like you're a puppet master controlling a mannequin, doesn't it? But you won't be there when folks are looking at your content online, so you can't do it manually then. Instead, you need to have another puppet master that you can leave instructions with about what you want to happen. Your proxy puppet master is Flash, and the instructions are ActionScript.

Creating dynamic animation with dot notation

You can now use your knowledge of levels, variables, and properties to execute a simple example of a new kind of animation and control. You'll create a dynamic animation that responds to user keyboard inputs.

1. Open a new movie, change the background color to black, and make sure that the stage is the default 550 × 400 pixels.

2. Create a new movie clip symbol called spaceship, rename the movie clip symbol's default layer ship, and draw a spaceship that looks like it just emerged from a 1980s video game. Don't make the spacecraft too complicated; you're aiming for a retro feel here. Also, because Flash will be moving your ship around the screen, it will be easier and smoother if the spaceship has a less complex shape. Make sure the center line of the spaceship is also the center of the movie clip (denoted by a little cross).

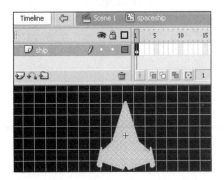

3. In the root Timeline (remember, that's the Timeline on the main stage), rename the existing layer ship and insert a new layer called actions.

4. In the new ship layer, drag an instance of your spaceship movie clip onto the stage. Position it at the bottom of the stage and scale it so that it looks like player one's spacecraft from the Space Invaders arcade game. Using the Properties panel, give the spaceship movie clip the instance name ship_mc (you'll see why you added the _mc to ship_mc in a moment).

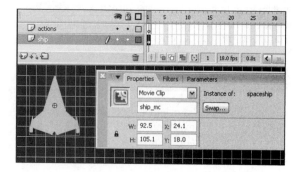

You want to be able to move this spacecraft left and right as it dodges the alien hordes in its epic battle to save the planet. To do this, you need to know two things about this spaceship:

■ Its position

■ How fast it will move

To get this information, all you need to know is the spaceship movie clip's _x property, which is its position on the x-axis of the screen—how far from the right of the screen the spaceship is. The ship is at the extreme left when _x=0, and the extreme right when _x=550. Once you have this value, you can assign it to a variable called shipPos, which you'll use to keep track of where the ship is.

5. In the root Timeline's actions layer, at frame 1, open the Actions panel and type the following:

    shipPos =

6. Click the Insert a target path button (at the top of the Actions panel) and make sure the Relative radio button from the Insert Target Path window is selected.

You'll now see that the paths are shown from _root, giving you an idea of where the ship instance is located from the main Timeline of the movie.

7. Select ship_mc as the target path, and then click OK.

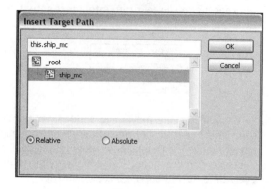

Flash has now added your path for you, and you now see the following:

    shipPos = this.ship_mc

Let's consider why you need this as your path to ship_mc. As mentioned earlier, this is a keyword that's shorthand for the current scope in a code block. When you're outside a code block, you don't need it. Whether or not you keep it is up to you, but let's delete it here.

> Another way to think about this is the file structure analogy: you're already in the folder (Timeline) containing your chosen clip, so you don't need a path.

    shipPos = ship_mc

8. Add a dot after ship_mc. As soon as you do this, you'll see a drop-down menu appear. When you add _mc to the end of any instance name, Flash knows you mean a movie clip, and this means Flash is able to provide you a little help. Long-term users don't tend to use the _mc because it prevents them from using pure camel case, but because you're dipping your foot into longish scripts for the first time in this chapter, you'll use it for now.

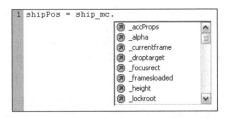

9. Find the _x and select it (you can use the keyboard up and down arrows to scroll—it tends to be faster). Once you've selected it, add a semicolon to end the line. Your ActionScript should now read

```
shipPos = ship_mc._x;
```

If you would like to see the other properties available to manipulate movie clips and other objects, open the ActionScript 2.0 Classes ➤ Movie ➤ MovieClip ➤ Properties book in the Actions panel.

You'll use some of these in the next exercise.

The ActionScript you've added will equate the shipPos variable with the value of the ship movie clip's x (horizontal) position.

You need to assign two more variables: speed, to set how fast your spacecraft will move (in pixels per keypress) and shipDead, which will be either true or false depending on whether your ship is dead.

10. Still in the first frame of the actions layer, add the following ActionScript:

```
shipDead = false;
speed = 5;
```

This sets the value of shipDead to false, and the value of speed to 5, leaving this frame's finished ActionScript looking like this:

```
1  shipPos = ship_mc._x;
2  shipDead = false;
3  speed = 5;
```

11. This is your initialization part of the code, so it's a good idea to label it as such. To do that, add a comment. A comment is any line that starts with two forward slashes (//). Add such a line at the start of the code so far.

```
1  // Initialize
2  shipPos = ship_mc._x;
3  shipDead = false;
4  speed = 5;
```

> *Comments are used to explain what's happening in code in plain English (or plain Spanish, or plain Italian, etc.). As comments are meant for your reference alone, they're disregarded by Flash's compiler. (You might have noticed that the comment line is grayed out—this is Flash's way of emphasizing this.)*
>
> *Even though adding comments might just seem like a few more unnecessary keystrokes, they're invaluable to any programmer because they allow you (and others) to look at your scripts in a few months time and still make sense of what you were doing in your code.*
>
> *Also, if you've done something cool in your code and you want to show off to others, comments allow you to do so!*

Now you'll add the input and movement part. How should you do it? Because it's something you want the ship to respond to every frame, you want to use the MovieClip.onEnterFrame event. This will run every time the playhead enters a new frame interval.

The onEnterFrame *event is one of many event handlers that respond to an internal event. You can create basic interactivity with buttons that respond to user events, but for more advanced stuff, you need also to be able to run code depending on what Flash itself is doing—this is implemented with internal event triggers.*

The onEnterFrame *event is the most used internal event in Flash because it's what you attach code to if you want the code to run every frame. Code that runs every frame can be used to create animation by moving a movie clip a little bit (by varying properties) every frame—the scripted version of what you did earlier in the Debugger.*

Although this event is called onEnterFrame, *it will occur even if you have a stationary playhead. It will occur every frame even if you have a single-frame Timeline and a playhead that doesn't move out of the current frame. In fact, even though its name suggests differently, the* onEnterFrame *event isn't really dependent on frames and Timelines (as we've come to know them in Flash) at all—it's simply relative to the frame rate of the movie.*

12. It's customary to add your event scripts (and, in fact, any code that uses the function block) as the first thing in a listing, so give yourself a little room above the current script by adding a few blank lines before the // Initialize comment.

13. Insert the following lines of code beginning at line 1. When you add the dot at line 1, you'll see the drop-down menu appear again. This time, continue writing as far as .on. You'll see that Flash is constantly looking for the ending that best fits what you've started to write, and by the time it sees .on, it has picked the right bit for you. This feature is called **auto complete**. Once the part you want is highlighted, press the *Tab* or *Enter* key to automatically insert it.

```
1  ship_mc.onEnterFrame = function () {
2
3  }
4  // Initialize
5  shipPos = ship_mc._x;
6  shipDead = false;
7  speed = 5;
```

This is your event handler block, and you'll start inserting your code from the blank line at line 2. Note that you could have used the Insert Target Path window to add the ship_mc part of ship_mc.onEnterFrame if you wanted to.

Also worth noting is that you're now writing within an event block, and the scope has been defined at the start of the block as the movie clip ship. This means that if you want to access any of its properties, you should use this. If you want to access any variables on the main Timeline, you shouldn't use this.

14. The first thing you should do is check that the left and right arrow keys are pressed. To do that, you can use the Key class. This is used to detect keypresses on the keyboard. Add the following code at line 2:

```
if (Key.
```

Make sure you use a capital "K"—all classes in Flash start with an uppercase character—although it can be difficult to make out the difference between "K" and "k." As soon as you hit the period, Flash reveals the auto complete choices again. Either scroll down to or add enough of the text for Flash to find isDown, and then press the *Tab* or *Enter* key to insert it.

```
1  ship_mc.onEnterFrame = function () {
2      if (Key.isDown (
3  }                    Key.isDown( keyCode )
4  // Initialize
5  shipPos = ship_mc._x;
```

This time Flash is showing you a code hint indicating that you need to enter a key code for the key you want to detect as isDown. You want the left arrow key (the keycode for this is Key.LEFT). Start typing it, and you'll see auto complete come to your aid. When you've added this, finish the line with a)) {, so that it looks like this:

```
if (Key.isDown (Key.LEFT)) {
```

Once you've done this, press the *Enter* key to start the next line.

You're now starting a **decision** block. The code in the if will only be executed if the key you specified is down. You want to move ship_mc to the left, and to do that, you have to subtract the variable speed from the currently scoped clip's _x value. To do all this, enter the code as follows:

```
1  ship_mc.onEnterFrame = function () {
2      if (Key.isDown (Key.LEFT)) {
3          this._x = this._x - speed;
4      }
5  }
```

Then click the Check Syntax button and the Auto Format icon to check and tidy up your code. It should look something like this:

```
1  ship_mc.onEnterFrame = function() {
2      if (Key.isDown(Key.LEFT)) {
3          this._x = this._x-speed;
4      }
5  };
6  // Initialize
7  shipPos = ship_mc._x;
8  shipDead = false;
9  speed = 5;
```

You can now test the movie. You should see that you can move the spaceship to the left.

15. Go back to the script, and add another if below the one you already have. This time, you look for a right arrow key and add speed.

```
1  ship_mc.onEnterFrame = function() {
2      if (Key.isDown(Key.LEFT)) {
3          this._x = this._x-speed;
4      }
5      if (Key.isDown(Key.RIGHT)) {
6          this._x = this._x+speed;
7      }
8  };
```

16. Test your movie. You can use the left and right arrow keys to move the spaceship left and right. How cool is that?

> *You can vary the speed value to get a faster ship movement. Set it to around 10 and increase the frame rate to 18 fps. (Double-click the little box that gives the frame rate on the lower edge of the Timeline to reach the Document Properties if you decide to do this.)*

This is a pretty basic movement, but you're using the main principles of dot notation to alter the properties of the spaceship movie clip, and are therefore able to move it at will—its movement isn't fixed, as it would be in a simple motion tween. This kind of dynamic animation is often called **sprite movement**. Furthermore, you're mixing it with scope, using and omitting the this within the event handler to choose between the scope of the event handler (with) and the Timeline the code is on (without). Although the former skill seems to be sexier at the moment, it's the latter that will make you an expert if you work on it.

You haven't finished yet. Next, you're going to simulate the effect of your spaceship being killed by the marauding hordes of alien invaders. You're not going to create the aliens themselves, but your knowledge will soon be sufficient for you to do that. When your ship is destroyed, you want to change the value of the shipdead variable you initialized in the movie's first frame from false to true.

17. In the root Timeline, select the keyframe in the actions layer and open the Actions panel.

18. Add the following lines of code within the onEnterFrame event handler block:

```
if (Key.isDown(Key.SPACE)) {
  shipDead = true;
}
```

After correcting and formatting your script, you'll have the following:

```
1  ship_mc.onEnterFrame = function() {
2      if (Key.isDown(Key.LEFT)) {
3          this._x = this._x-speed;
4      }
5      if (Key.isDown(Key.RIGHT)) {
6          this._x = this._x+speed;
7      }
8      if (Key.isDown(Key.SPACE)) {
9          shipDead = true;
10     }
11 };
```

You've set the movie up for the entire user input. Now you need to make the spaceship display change in response to the spacebar being pressed. You've just attached the code to the spacebar for the sake of this exercise. It's actually intended to simulate the outcome of alien fire hitting your spacecraft.

19. Open the spaceship movie clip and create a new layer called actions. Extend both layers to frame 11. Select frame 11 of the actions layer and add a keyframe. Attach a stop() action on this keyframe.

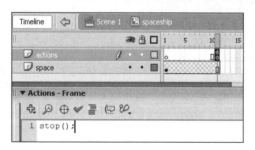

20. On the space layer, place a keyframe at frames 3, 5, 7, 9, and 11.

21. Delete the ship graphic on the keyframes at frames 3, 7, and 11. Your Timeline should now look like the one shown in the following graphic. If you press play on the controller (*ENTER* on the keyboard), you'll see the spaceship flash in a typical "bloop-bloop-blippity-bloop—game over!" retro video game fashion.

22. You now need to add some code to animate to the death sequence when the spacebar is pressed. Go back to the main script on frame 1 of the root Timeline. You should be getting good at this, so go right ahead and change the code as shown:

```
ship_mc.onEnterFrame = function() {
if (Key.isDown(Key.LEFT)) {
    this._x = this._x-speed;
}
if (Key.isDown(Key.RIGHT)) {
    this._x = this._x+speed;
}
if (Key.isDown(Key.SPACE)) {
    shipDead = true;
    this.play();
    delete (this.onEnterFrame);
}
};
// Initialize
ship_mc.stop();
shipPos = ship_mc._x;
shipDead = false;
speed = 10;
```

```
1  ship_mc.onEnterFrame = function() {
2      if (Key.isDown(Key.LEFT)) {
3          this._x = this._x-speed;
4      }
5      if (Key.isDown(Key.RIGHT)) {
6          this._x = this._x+speed;
7      }
8      if (Key.isDown(Key.SPACE)) {
9          shipDead = true;
10         this.play();
11         delete (this.onEnterFrame);
12     }
13 };
14 // Initialize
15 ship_mc.stop();
16 shipPos = ship_mc._x;
17 shipDead = false;
18 speed = 10;
```

So what do the new lines do? Line 15 stops the Timeline of ship_mc, so it will sit at frame 1 until you press the spacebar. When you press the spacebar, the code block containing lines 9, 10, and 11 (of which 10 and 11 are new) will run. Line 10 causes the Timeline you stopped in line 15 to start playing. You also need to stop running the onEnterFrame script, and line 11 does just that by deleting the event handler. This means that the spaceship really is dead—the software "brain" that controls it via the onEnterFrame is effectively destroyed, and all that's left is the exploding ship hull—the flashing graphic that remains on the screen for a short time afterward.

Notice that you changed the speed to 10. This is because the ship didn't seem to be moving fast enough. It also shows an important point—you *could* have set lines 3 and 6 to the following:

```
this._x = this._x-5;
this._x = this._x+5;
```

To do that, however, you would have to find every 5 and change it to 10. That would have required a long script and been an error-prone and difficult task. It's far better to use variables for all your values rather than literal numbers, because then you can change them in one place—the initialization code section.

Some of you might be thinking, "Hang on, though—what does the shipDead variable do? It's set to false when the ship is alive, and as soon as it dies, I set it to true, but shipDead is never used in the script to control my spaceship, and I can't see why it's even needed—what gives?"

Well, that's all true. shipDead *is not* needed by ship_mc itself. In computer graphics, one of the problems is that no graphic can actually "see" another graphic. You can't say, "Hey aliens, when you see the player is dead, you can all go back into formation and sit there gloating for a bit." The alien graphics are blind in that they only know what they're told through variables—they don't see the screen that you see, where it's obvious something has just happened. shipDead is such a variable. It's a signal or "flag" to other movie clips in the game that the player has just died. Other graphics "see" whether the player is still alive or dead through looking at this variable rather than the ship_mc graphic itself. In the next section, you'll learn how to wire this flag to another movie clip that shows the standard "game over" message when the ship dies.

> Although you're still a beginner, in this example, I tried to show you some advanced techniques. The way you kill the spaceship by destroying its event handler is a powerful technique. The way the shipDead *flag is used to signal a game condition to other graphics is also an advanced motion graphics technique. Finally, the way almost all the code for your animation is in one script is the preferred way of writing scripts in Flash 8, and something that has been used by advanced coders since Flash MX. If you've read the previous editions of this book, you'll have noted a change of emphasis regarding the code, and this is for a specific reason: the standard of Flash coding has gone up considerably, and some previously advanced techniques can now be considered at beginner or intermediate level.*

Creating advanced animation communication schemes

Once you've seen how to create code for simple script-based animations, you soon realize the next stage of interactivity is to get your various event handlers to talk to each other. There's an advanced scheme that allows you to do this via an event-driven route, and this uses **listeners**. This is the scheme you'll use when you have large amounts of code and need to start making it hyper-efficient. For now though, you'll use shipDead as a flag that signifies that ship_mc is no more.

Creating a "game over" graphic

1. On the main Timeline, insert a new layer named text between the ship and actions layers.

2. Insert a dynamic text field in the center of the stage on the new layer. If you have any retro-looking pixel fonts, use one of those. If not, use any font that catches your eye (I'm using Sydnie). Set the text color to white, and make sure it's not selectable and doesn't have a border (via the Properties panel's Selectable icon and Show border around text icon, neither of which should be selected).

3. Inside this text field, click the Align center icon on the Properties panel, and then enter the text game over!! using italic font.

4. The TextField class associated with your text field doesn't have an onEnterFrame event, so to attach one to your text you need to make it into a movie clip (which does have this event). Select the text and press *F8* to make it a movie clip, and call it Game Text.

5. Using the Properties panel, call the instance overText_mc. You also want to name the text field instance inside this movie clip, so double-click the movie clip, select the text field, and name it overText_txt.

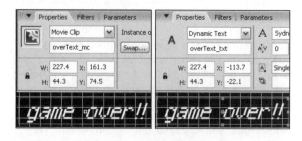

6. You can now start controlling this new clip. Return to the main Timeline and add the following lines to the initialization part of the script on frame 1 of the actions layer:

```
// Initialize
ship_mc.stop();
overText_mc.overText_txt.text = "";
shipPos = ship_mc._x;
shipDead = false;
speed = 10;
```

This new line uses dot notation to find the embedded text field gameText_txt and make it show no text. The next step is to add an onEnterFrame to gameText_mc that keeps looking out for the shipDead flag and responds to it accordingly.

7. Insert the following code at the beginning of the script:

```
overText_mc.onEnterFrame = function() {
  if (shipDead) {
  this.overText_txt.text = "game over!!";
    delete (this.onEnterFrame);
  }
};
```

This code attaches an onEnterFrame script to overText_mc. This checks the value of shipDead every frame. If it's true, then the if block will run, causing the overText_txt text to change to game over!!. The if block then deletes the onEnterFrame (because there's no reason to continue checking).

8. Test the movie again. You'll see that when you press the spacebar, the spaceship will flash and the game over!! text will appear. (You can add the obligatory "bloop-bloop-bloop-bloop-ping!" noise later if you feel the need.)

Note that if you try to publish the movie as it stands, the keys won't work until the user clicks the screen.

What happens when you press the spacebar is that the root Timeline sets the shipDead variable to true. The gameText_mc movie clip is constantly looking at this variable's status via the onEnterFrame check that's attached to it. As soon as it sees that it's true, it changes the text embedded inside it.

Here's the full listing:

```
1  overText_mc.onEnterFrame = function() {
2      if (shipDead) {
3          this.overText_txt.text = "game over!!";
4          delete (this.onEnterFrame);
5      }
6  };
7  ship_mc.onEnterFrame = function() {
8      if (Key.isDown(Key.LEFT)) {
9          this._x = this._x-speed;
10     }
11     if (Key.isDown(Key.RIGHT)) {
12         this._x = this._x+speed;
13     }
14     if (Key.isDown(Key.SPACE)) {
15         shipDead = true;
16         this.play();
17         delete (this.onEnterFrame);
18     }
19 };
20 // Initialize
21 ship_mc.stop();
22 overText_mc.overText_txt.text = "";
23 shipPos = ship_mc._x;
24 shipDead = false;
25 speed = 10;
```

Let's summarize how it works. It may be a good idea to see if you can explain the code to yourself before looking at your description.

- The initialization section starts at line 21. It causes the ship_mc clip to stop at frame 1 (its "I am alive" graphic appearance) and sets the game over!! text

overText_txt (which is embedded in overText_mc) to show no text. Finally, it sets the variables shipDead and speed to false and 10, respectively.

- There are two onEnterFrame scripts that run every frame. The first one is for overText_mc. This constantly looks for changes in the flag shipDead, and sets the text overText_txt to game over!! when it changes to true. When this happens, the script also stops checking for changes.

- The second script moves your ship via changes to its _x property, depending on whether the left and right keyboard arrow keys are pressed. It also checks for the spacebar being pressed, which you're using to simulate the ship being destroyed. This causes the ship_mc Timeline to start playing its death sequence. When this occurs, the script also sets shipDead to true to inform the rest of the code of its demise. It also stops itself from running any further.

> *Notice that the script wasn't written from line 1 down, but in the order that the script will actually run—initialization followed by the events. Also note that at the end of your animation, none of the code is left running.*

In addition to controlling the spaceship's position on the x-axis, you could just as easily control any other property of the movie clip. For example, using the rotation property, you could get the ship to rotate clockwise and counterclockwise in response to the arrow keys. You could also create a slider and use its position to vary the alpha property of a movie clip instance.

I mentioned earlier the alien hordes you'll need to create in order to complete your game. Each alien would need to have variables such as invaderPos, invaderDead, and firePhotonTorpedo. Controlling the properties of all your invaders individually is much simpler than you may imagine, as the next brief example will illustrate.

If you want to know more about advanced animation, games are a good way to do it. The skills used in creating Flash games are the same ones you use in creating advanced website interfaces. Due to the "Show us how to create a space invaders game!" feedback I got from the early editions of Foundation Flash, I created a simple Space Invaders–type game in Foundation ActionScript. Then I got requests for instructions on how to create a Flash version of a thousand games. In Flash Games Most Wanted, the author of this chapter takes the concepts shown here to their logical conclusion by writing a Flash version of the retro game Defender, complete with optimized game engine and dynamic backing soundtrack.

You can download the source files of either of these books from the friends of ED website (www.friendsofed.com) if you just want to have a look at the code—it's free, so take it while it's hot!

Armed as you are with your newfound knowledge of input text fields, dot notation, and sprite animation, you're now ready to implement the changes for your Smiler movie.

Making Smiler age-sensitive

If you don't have your fully functional version of Smiler saved, you can download a ready-made Smiler in the downloadable files for this book from the friends of ED website.

On the friends of ED website, you'll also find the finished FLA you'll be developing as smilerAge.fla, *and a more advanced version,* smilerAgeAdvanced.fla *(which shows how you can extend it a little).*

Guessing Smiler's age

First, you should quickly remind yourself what the requirements specification was:

- 1.1: Define a variable, age, with values between 1 and 99.
- 2.1: Input a numeric text entry from the user.
- 2.2: Assign this text entry to a variable called guess.
- 3.1: Create a new variable, difference, that's equal to age minus guess.
- 3.2: If difference is negative, make it positive.
- 3.3: Go to a frame number that's equal to difference in the Smiler animated movie clip.
- 4.1: If difference is 0, then stop. Otherwise repeat from 2.1.

Let's walk through this step by step.

The first thing you need to do is get Flash to come up with an age for Smiler that it can compare to the user's guess. It would be a good idea to make this a random value so that it's different for every run of the game. You can do this easily using Flash's Math.random() function.

Math.random() returns a number between 0 and 1. Because you require a number between 1 and 99, you'll multiply Math.random() by the maximum required number.

```
age=Math.random()*99;
```

This will return a number between 1 and 99 with decimal points. To force this to be a whole number, you use Math.floor(), which returns a rounded-down number.

```
age=Math.floor(Math.random()*99);
```

random *and* floor *are both methods from Flash's* Math *class. These and other methods, as well as constants (such as pi) are viewable in* ActionScript 2.0 Classes ➤ Core ➤ Math. *You'll be using some of these later.*

You want to generate the random number at the start of your game, during initialization, so that the age variable is populated, ready, and waiting for the user's guess.

1. In frame 1 of the actions layer in the existing Smiler movie, you already have the following ActionScript:

```
1  leftButton.onRelease = function() {
2      if (smilerFrame>1) {
3          smilerFrame = smilerFrame-1;
4          face.prevFrame();
5      }
6  };
7  rightButton.onRelease = function() {
8      if (smilerFrame<15) {
9          smilerFrame = smilerFrame+1;
10     }
11 };
12 face.gotoAndStop("neutral");
13 smilerFrame = 8;
14
```

You want to assign a new variable, age.

2. Delete the `smilerFrame = 8;` line and replace it with the following code:

```
age = Math.floor (Math.random ()*99);
```

Testing the movie won't make Smiler do anything new at the moment, but you've completed 1.1, so let's carry on with the rest of your specification.

- 2.1: Input a numeric text entry from the user.
- 2.2: Assign this text entry to a variable called guess.

3. You need to change your FLA so that it can now accept text input. Delete the left button and its associated text, better. Move the enter button and its text label to the bottom right, changing it so that it appears as shown:

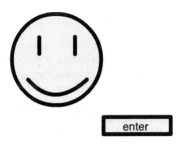

4. Change the instance name of the button to guessButton_btn. Make sure when you do this that you select the button and not the static text above it.

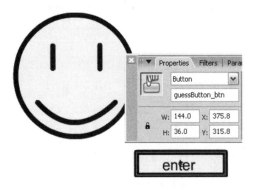

5. Add a new Input text field next to the enter button with properties as shown.

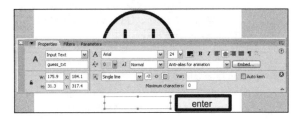

6. You also want to prevent the user from entering anything except numbers between 1 and 99, so set the maximum number of characters to 2 (in the Maximum characters area of the Properties panel) and click the Embed button so the user can only enter the digits 0 to 9, as shown:

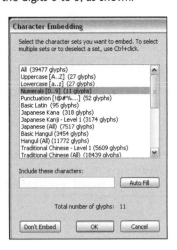

7. You could also do with some feedback from Smiler, so change the text above him to a dynamic text field. Give it an instance name of prompt_txt, and make sure it's not selectable. Enter the text prompt in it.

8. Delete the existing button scripts and add the following event handler for your new button, guessButton_btn. Now add an initialize comment and a new line after your age definition at the bottom of the script.

```
guessButton_btn.onRelease = function() {
  userGuess = Number(guess_txt.text);
  trace(userGuess);
};
// Initialize
face.gotoAndStop("neutral");
age = Math.floor(Math.random()*99);
prompt_txt.text = "Guess my age!";
```

A pretty big change—there are only two lines left from the original! So what does it do?

- The guessButton_btn.onRelease handler converts the user's guess into a number and traces it back to you.

- The last line causes the prompt text to appear with Guess my age! at the start of the game.

Not very clever so far.

In this step you'll cover 3.1.

9. 3.1: Create a new variable, difference, that's equal to age minus guess.

```
guessButton_btn.onRelease = function() {
  userGuess = Number(guess_txt.text);
  trace("your guess:"+userGuess);
  difference = age-userGuess;
  trace("you are out by:"+difference);
};
```

```
// Initialize
face.gotoAndStop("neutral");
age = Math.floor(Math.random()*99);
prompt_txt.text = "Guess my age!";
```

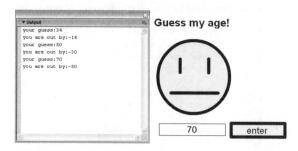

This time users can see the number they're inputting plus how far off they are, which is your variable difference.

Next up, 3.2 and 3.3.

- 3.2: If difference is negative, make it positive.

- 3.3: Go to a frame number that's equal to difference in the Smiler animated movie clip.

You want the Smiler movie clip to have 98 frames because that's the maximum amount you can be wrong by when you guess its age.

10. Inside the Smiler movie clip, add frames (using *F5*) to the left of the neutral keyframe to shift it up to frame 49. Then extend the layer to frame 98 by adding frames to the right of neutral, as shown in the following graphic. Finally, extend the eyes and face layers up to frame 98.

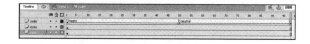

Add the following new lines:

```
guessButton_btn.onRelease = function() {
  userGuess = Number(guess_txt.text);
  trace("your guess:"+userGuess);
  difference = age-userGuess;
  trace("you are out by:"+difference);
  if (difference<0) {
    difference = Math.abs(difference);
  }
```

```
    face.gotoAndStop(difference);
};
face.gotoAndStop("neutral");
age = Math.floor(Math.random()*99);
prompt_txt.text = "Guess my age!";
```

This time, you'll see Smiler actually respond to your guesses by getting happier/sadder depending on how close you are to his age. Math.abs(difference) gives you the absolute value of difference—that is, the value as a raw number without a plus or minus. The number is always positive, so this line covers 3.2. gotoAndStop() converts this positive number into a frame number (notice that you're using a variable containing a frame number here rather than a label). This gives you 3.3.

Guess my age!

22

Almost there!

- 4.1: If difference is 0, then stop. Otherwise repeat from 2.1.

11. Add this code to do it:

```
guessButton_btn.onRelease = function() {
  userGuess = Number(guess_txt.text);
  trace("your guess:"+userGuess);
  difference = age-userGuess;
  trace("you are out by:"+difference);
  if (difference<0) {
      difference = Math.abs(difference);
  }
  if (difference == 0) {
    prompt_txt.text = "You got it!!";
```

```
    face.gotoAndStop("happy");
    face.onEnterFrame = function() {
        this._rotation =
this._rotation+➡
        rotationSpeed;
    };
  } else {
    face.gotoAndStop(difference);
    prompt_txt.text = "Nope. try➡
                    again...";
  }
};
    face.gotoAndStop("neutral");
    age = Math.floor(Math.random()*99);
    prompt_txt.text = "Guess my age!";
    rotationSpeed = 10;
```

Well, actually, there's a bit more that you need.

The first thing you added is an if that looks at whether difference is 0. If it is, you prompt the user with an appropriately upbeat message. You also add an onEnterFrame that makes the Smiler face do a little rotation trick to reward the user for getting the right answer. As part of this trick, you define a rotation speed at the end of the script.

> *The double equal sign (==) means "Check that the left side is equal to the right side." It doesn't make the difference equal 0, as a single equal sign (=) does. You should always use the double equal sign within an if condition; using a single equal sign instead is one of the most common mistakes in ActionScript.*

The code that contains the instructions of what to do when the user doesn't get it right is now in an else block of the if—if the user doesn't get it right, you continue doing much the same as you did last time.

And that's it. You've followed your top-down requirements specification, solved your problem, and finished your game. Here's the listing after it has been polished up and made a little more user-friendly.

```
guessButton_btn.onRelease = function() {
  userGuess = Number(guess_txt.text);
  difference = age-userGuess;
  if (difference<0) {
  difference = Math.abs(difference);
  }
  if (difference == 0) {
    prompt_txt.text = "You got it!!";
    face.gotoAndStop("happy");
    face.onEnterFrame = function() {
      this._rotation = this._rotation+➥
      rotationSpeed;
    };
  } else {
    face.gotoAndStop(difference);
    prompt_txt.text = "Nope. try again...";
  }
};
guess_txt.onSetFocus = function() {
    this.text = "";
};
//
//Initialize
face.gotoAndStop("neutral");
age = Math.floor(Math.random()*99);
prompt_txt.text = "Guess my age!";
rotationSpeed = 10;
```

You got rid of the trace() actions, added a little event handler that fires when the user clicks the text field ("gives it input focus"), and clears the last guess value.

You might want to give Smiler a bit more personality. For example, you could have a dynamic text box that displays a statement showing how Smiler feels about your last guess. If difference is greater than 30, it could say, "Miles away!" If the difference is less than 30, it could say, "Getting warmer!" And when the user guesses within 10 of the age, it could say, "Red hot!"

All this can be done by adding if and else actions that relate to the variable you've assigned to the text field. There are many other things that you can add to this program to make Smiler more intelligent, just using the commands and techniques you've now learned.

I've added something like this in the file smilerAgeAdvanced.fla. *Have a look at it if you want to see how to make Smiler's responses more appropriate.*

You've now reached the top of the intermediate learning slope. I haven't told you everything you need to know, but you now know all the basic principles and have had enough practice to allow you to quickly learn other structures that will increase your ability.

Case study

In this section, you're going to finish the case study by completing its ActionScript. By the end of this chapter, you'll have a fully functional website that's ready to be uploaded to the Internet.

1. Open your case study movie.
2. Select the keyframe on frame 1 of the actions layer and open the Actions panel. The code begins like this:

```
1  webButton.onRelease = function() {
2     toOpen = "open web";
3
4     if (userHasClicked == true) {
5        content_mc.play ();
6     } else {
7        content_mc.gotoAndPlay(toOpen);
8        userHasClicked = true;
9     }
10 };
```

At the moment, you can click any button more than once, and the chosen rectangle will close and reopen. You need to change the code a little so that repeated button clicks prevent any motion.

To initiate this, you need to change your if statements to do a few more crucial checks. You'll come to these in a moment. The first thing you need to do is store the previously opened page in a variable.

3. Add the following line of code (line 10) in between the last two curly brackets of the first bunch of code:

```
1  webButton.onRelease = function() {
2      toOpen = "open web";
3
4      if (userHasClicked == true) {
5          content_mc.play ();
6      } else {
7          content_mc.gotoAndPlay(toOpen);
8          userHasClicked = true;
9      }
10     lastOpened = toOpen;
11 };
```

Line 10 of the code creates a new variable called lastOpened that's set to the value stored in toOpen. This will be used in a moment.

4. Insert the code on line 10 in the corresponding position in each button section.

Now whenever a button is clicked, you store the accompanying frame label value. So when you click the webButton instance, lastOpened stores open web, or specifically, the value of toOpen.

You might be wondering here why both toOpen and lastOpened store the same value? It all relates to the new if condition that you're about to add. Let's look at it and then I'll explain it further.

5. Add the following code as shown:

```
1  webButton.onRelease = function() {
2      toOpen = "open web";
3
4      if (userHasClicked == true && toOpen != lastOpened)
5          content_mc.play ();
6      } else {
7          content_mc.gotoAndPlay(toOpen);
8          userHasClicked = true;
9      }
10     lastOpened = toOpen;
```

By adding an extra conditional, you're specifying that both conditions must be met for the code to run. If neither or only one of the conditions, say userHasClicked == true, is met, the else code statement is run.

The new condition added uses the not equals to operator. As you might have guessed, this is the exact opposite to the == operator, meaning that the condition is met only if the values toOpen and lastOpened aren't the same. The reason you've added this condition is to prevent a page being selected two (or more) times in a row.

Before you can test this, you need to add a second condition.

6. Amend the following line of code as shown:

```
1  webButton.onRelease = function() {
2      toOpen = "open web";
3
4      if (userHasClicked == true && toOpen != lastOpened)
5          content_mc.play ();
6      } else if (userHasClicked == false) {
7          content_mc.gotoAndPlay(toOpen);
8          userHasClicked = true;
9      }
10     lastOpened = toOpen;
```

Why are you doing this? In case you didn't notice, there was a flaw in your previous code. Every time toOpen and lastOpened were the same, the else statement was run by default, meaning that button clicks sent the playhead to the toOpen frame label, kind of defeating the purpose!

This new condition prevents this from happening by running the code only if userHasClicked == false. In the event that userHasClicked is true and a button is clicked, nothing happens. Your conditionals are quite clearly defined for both scenarios.

Now all the buttons require the same code.

7. Highlight all the conditional statement code (as shown from lines 4 to 9 here).

```
1  webButton.onRelease = function() {
2      toOpen = "open web";
3
4      if (userHasClicked == true && toOpen != lastOpened) {
5          content_mc.play ();
6      } else if (userHasClicked == false) {
7          content_mc.gotoAndPlay(toOpen);
8          userHasClicked = true;
9      }
10     lastOpened = toOpen;
```

8. Copy the selection using *Ctrl+C*.

9. Highlight the same code for each of the other button code sections and paste the copied code over it. Here's how all the code on frame 1 of the actions layer looks once it has been formatted:

```
webButton.onRelease = function() {
    toOpen = "open web";
    if (userHasClicked == true && toOpen ➡
    != lastOpened) {
            content_mc.play();
    } else if (userHasClicked == false) {
        content_mc.gotoAndPlay(toOpen);
        userHasClicked = true;
    }
    lastOpened = toOpen;
};
printButton.onRelease = function() {
    toOpen = "open print";
    if (userHasClicked == true && toOpen➡
    != lastOpened) {
        content_mc.play();
    } else if (userHasClicked == false) {
        content_mc.gotoAndPlay(toOpen);
        userHasClicked = true;
        }
    lastOpened = toOpen;
};
aboutButton.onRelease = function() {
    toOpen = "open about";
    if (userHasClicked == true && toOpen➡
    != lastOpened) {
        content_mc.play();
    } else if (userHasClicked == false) {
        content_mc.gotoAndPlay(toOpen);
        userHasClicked = true;
    }
    lastOpened = toOpen;
};
emailButton.onRelease = function() {
    toOpen = "open email";
    if (userHasClicked == true && toOpen➡
    != lastOpened) {
        content_mc.play();
    } else if (userHasClicked == false) {
        content_mc.gotoAndPlay(toOpen);
        userHasClicked = true;
    }
    lastOpened = toOpen;
};
userHasClicked = false;
```

10. Test the movie with *Ctrl+Enter* (*Cmd/Apple+Enter* on the Mac). Click a button more than once to see how the code has disabled the same page from closing and reopening.

That's it for the case study! Well done: you've built a complete portfolio website to display all your Flash and ActionScripting skills. You can now change the website content to display your own handiwork, and modify it by adding new pages or new content in the future. Once you're done, publish the website to the Internet for all to see.

Summary

In this chapter, you've explored the ActionScripting features that make Flash a powerhouse for sophisticated, powerful, web applications. Once you're comfortable with these principles, you can build the kind of websites you've dreamed of. I hope you've started to see that with ActionScript, the possibilities in Flash are infinite.

You saw that

- The top-down design approach is a great way to plan complex programming and ActionScripting tasks. The top-down approach can be summarized as

  - Defining the general problem to be solved.

  - Breaking the problem down iteratively into its smallest components.

  - Reassembling these components in a logical list of requirements.

  - Building solutions to each requirement; and testing, integrating, and testing again!

- Rudimentary user input can be captured using a simple input text field.

- Input text can be assigned to a variable and redisplayed in a dynamic text field.

- User input and variables can be manipulated with ActionScript. For instance, you used a big plus sign on a button to add together two numbers and display the result.

- Dot notation gives you a secure and flexible way of targeting named movie clip instances inside your movies.

- Dot notation gives you access to the hierarchy of movie clip Timelines implicit in every Flash movie.

- Movie clips have properties that you can target and modify using ActionScript, allowing you to alter a movie clip's appearance, behavior, and animation characteristics.

- Movie clip properties and behaviors can be modified based on user input and other movie events.

- Variables can be scoped and targeted using movie clip Timelines and dot notation.

- Code also has scope, which can be either "here" or "in the Timeline this code block is looking at."

Chapter 16

INTERMEDIATE ACTIONSCRIPT, PART 2

What we'll cover in this chapter:

- Fundamental concepts of top-down and bottom-up design
- Intro to advanced bottom-up design: class-based object-oriented (OO) design
- Top-down programming mind-sets as a starting point for learning advanced object-oriented coding
- The creation of a simple Flash game using almost everything you have learned in the book:
  - The bottom-up design mind-set
  - Frame actions
  - Nested timelines
  - Event handlers
  - Decision making

The real power of the current version of Flash over early versions is in its code structures. Flash allows proper coding techniques to be applied to ActionScript, but you have to be fairly advanced to appreciate it. Although you are not yet ready to write code in the new class-based style, this chapter will show you the bottom-up coding process, and it is a fairly short step from there to the new class-based style.

In this chapter, you'll tackle scripting in Flash and move on to writing bigger code listings.

First, though, consider the task of making a cup of your favorite instant coffee—no, I don't mean take a break; you've only started the chapter! I mean let's think about the process of making coffee.

Making coffee

First, let's think about how you'd analyze this in terms of the top-down approach that you considered in the previous chapter.

In top-down design, you take the problem and break it down into subproblems. As you keep breaking it down, you make the individual functional items smaller and more compact until you can start to see the solution in the subproblems because the subproblems become more and more manageable and easier to understand. Take this problem definition:

To make a cup of Café au Lait (coffee with milk) and sugar

First iteration:

1. Boil some water.
2. Have a cup ready with coffee and some sugar in it.
3. When the water has boiled, pour the water into the cup.
4. Stir mixture for 20 seconds and add milk.

Second iteration:

1.1 Fill the kettle full of water.

1.2 Connect the kettle to power, and switch on.

2.1 Get one teaspoon of sugar from the sugar bowl and transfer it to the cup.

2.2 Get one teaspoon of coffee from the jar and transfer it to the cup.

3.1 Wait until the kettle has boiled.

3.2 Pour water from the kettle into the cup.

3.3 Etc.

You're breaking things down until the problem is so basic that its components can be coded. A system based on this kind of analysis would yield a set of steps that carry out each stage of the task. A computer system developed in this way will usually consist of a series of carefully targeted, tightly constrained code elements—**procedures**—that each performs a small piece of the overall task. This approach is fine until you want the system to do something different—say, make a cup of lemon tea, or an iced coffee, or use a different brand of coffee. To reprogram the system to do this, you'd need to reengineer multiple elements in the system to allow them to perform a different task. The top-down method of deconstructing the problem tends to "hard-wire" the solution to the problem and make it less adaptable when your needs change.

A bottom-up cup of coffee

In bottom-up design, you try to look beyond the specific problem and analyze the nature of the building blocks that make up that problem. That means if you were looking at the process of making a cup of coffee in an object-oriented way, you'd ignore the brand of coffee, how hot the water needed to be, and how long you were supposed to stir the beverage. Instead, you'd think about the general processes involved, and try to conceptualize them.

The process of thinking from the bottom up is a little like being in an episode of one of those TV shows where fantastically wealthy, stylish, and attractive thirty-somethings agonize over their inner torment, questioning the meaning and content of every aspect of their existence. Well, maybe not *that* bad, but you *do* have to philosophize—what is making coffee all about?

The generalized answers to this question would be: it is a process that entails liquid and powder, switching things on and seeing when they're done and moving things from one container to another.

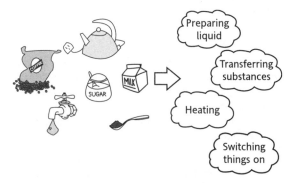

You're deconstructing the problem down into building blocks that are less specific to the components involved in the physical act of making a cup of coffee. You're not thinking about specific tasks anymore; you are thinking about general principles such as moving things from one container to another, liquid flowing, turning things on, and detecting when things have finished.

Once you can express the process in these generalized terms, you can start creating generic routines that embody these general principles. You might create, for example, a routine that describes the process called "prepare the liquid." This routine would outline how to prepare a liquid, but it wouldn't be tied to preparing any particular *type* of liquid. Instead, this routine would perform the basic process using the values you supply to it when you start that process. For instance, you might tell it the kind of liquid to use and the temperature the liquid should be.

The generic routines are flexible, and because you've distilled them down to the very essence of their functionality, they can be applied to a number of different tasks—making tea, making an iced drink, making a milkshake, and so on. The "prepare the liquid" routine is the same, but the details of an individual implementation of this process—making *this* cup of coffee or *this* iced tea—can be specified in each particular instance.

The "prepare the liquid" routine is one part of the solution to the overall "making a beverage" problem, and it acts in choreographed collaboration with the other generalized routines to achieve the overall aim.

The generalized routines are templates for carrying out each aspect of the task. When you perform a beverage-making task, you initialize **instances** of each of these templates and provide the **specific** information required to perform this *specific* task properly:

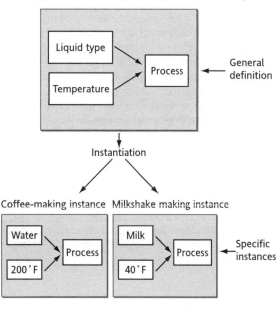

"Prepare the liquid" routine:

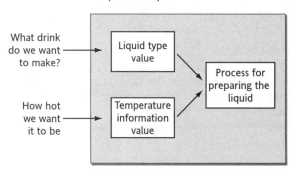

In one form of bottom-up code design, **object-oriented design**, the template is called a **class**. The class describes the essentials of a process or an item, and specifies the characteristics of the process that make it different from any other kind of process. The definition of the "prepare the liquid" class might include the following: the capacity to specify a type of liquid, a variable that describes the amount of liquid, and a variable that controls the prepared liquid's temperature. The functionality for carrying out the task and for coordinating activity with other routines is encapsulated in this class, but it is **very** general. That's a good thing, because you can apply it as the starting point to many problems. This kind of class is called a **super class**.

To turn this into a more specific problem-solving process, you extend the super class by making it more specific. To modify one process to make coffee, you specify the liquid as water and a temperature range of 200 degrees F. You can modify the same super class to use milk at a lower range of temperatures. The extended classes still don't have everything you need to make black coffee instead of espresso, or a strawberry milkshake instead of a chocolate one, but they are very close. All they are missing are **values.** These values or **properties**, when added to the classes, give you an individual cup of coffee the way you want it. The classes define methods of taking these values and working with them to provide real processes to form, in the case of our example, a **recipe** for which you specify **quantities** as well as the **methods** for making the raw materials into coffee.

> Notice that because our coffee and milkshake making structures share the same super class, they are both still structures for making a drink. The classes may be different, but they share the same super class.

This process is called bottom-up because you work from the general to the specific—you think about the specific aspects of your problem **last**. Unlike the top-down solution, in which you have to know **exactly** what you want at the start, in the bottom-up version, you start with a vague or abstract idea and build toward a more complete picture—in bottom-up you think from the bottom (general) up toward the more specific. The cool thing about this is that if your problem changes during the process, you don't really care—you can change the solution easily because it is just a set of **concepts**, which are easy to change.

> In real-world big programming jobs, the top-down approach requires that you define the full structure of the solution at the start. This is when you know the least about the practicalities of the problem, so you leave yourself open to having to start again because you missed something basic at the beginning.
>
> The bottom-up route allows you to step back and take an abstract view and add to it by extending, writing code from the start. As you extend, you understand the problem better. This time, problems you see on the way up are expected and act as signposts rather than hindrances—they tell you which way you need to extend the solution.
>
> This is why top-down design is rarely used in big projects, and when it is, it is only for the basic frameworks. Bottom-up is used when you are defining how to code up solutions because it is much more tolerant to changes in the understanding of the problem.
>
> The problem with top-down and bottom-up is that top-down seems to make more sense to our normal way of thinking—plan ahead and think of everything at the start. It works very well, but only for small projects. As your project get bigger, the bottom-up approach is necessary to manage the uncertainty caused by increasing complexity. The concepts of abstraction and generalization don't sound as useful as the straight-talking top-down process, though, and that's where problems start—bottom-up programming techniques (such as object-oriented programming) get labeled as difficult.

In case this seems a little Zen to you and you're wondering where the Flash programming comes in, here's a simple example, and real code.

Working with raw ActionScript

We won't ask you to type this example out (although you can). Instead, you'll simply walk through it so those of you who are feeling a little brave can start looking at ActionScript 2.0 classes. After the initial confusion most beginners have with object-oriented programming, you will find the Flash implementation fairly easy to get into—as long as you can type without making mistakes. It is *very* unforgiving if you get either spelling or case wrong.

The first thing to know is that Flash 8 Professional is geared more toward scripting than Flash 8 Basic, and you will do well to use that version if you have it. Flash 8 Professional has more document types than Flash 8 Basic, including the ActionScript File (external file with an .as extension), as shown in the New Document window (File ➤ New).

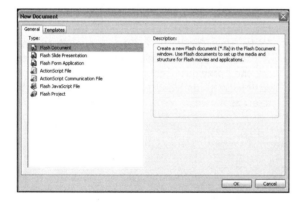

When you select an AS file in Flash Professional, you will enter a new authoring environment that is specifically designed for editing and creating code-only files. Gone are the timeline and stage views, and you can also close the panel docking areas if you want—you won't be using them, and they are grayed out in any case.

Flash Basic users can quit sulking because you can emulate the same big screen simply by increasing the size of the Actions panel's Script pane so that it occupies the same space. Here is the process for creating an AS file in the basic edition of Flash:

1. Open a new FLA.
2. Select frame 1 of the root timeline.
3. Create your script.
4. Select Export Script from the Actions panel menu. To load a previous AS file, select Import Script from the same menu.

Creating the super class

The super class is a general definition of the problem. Recall that the basic problem is this:

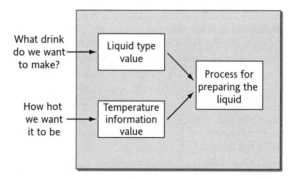

"Prepare the liquid" routine:

If you create a class for this, you would create an AS file something like this:

```
1  class DrinkTempProcess {
2      // Define properties and type
3      var liquid:String;
4      var froth:Boolean;
5      var temperature:Number;
6      // Define constructor
7      function DrinkTempProcess(arg_liquid:String, arg_froth:Boolean, arg_temperature:Number) {
8          // When a new drink instance is created...
9          liquid = arg_liquid;
10         froth = arg_froth;
11         temperature = arg_temperature;
12     }
13     // Create methods to solve the problem/define the process...
14     function processIngredients():String {
15         var doSomething;
16         doSomething = "I have changed the temperature of "+liquid+" to "+temperature+"DegC";
17         if (froth) {
18             doSomething = doSomething+", then frothed it";
19         }
20         return doSomething;
21     }
22 }
```

In this exercise, we are not trying to teach you object-oriented programming, but only the basics of how it is structured, and what a class actually looks like in Flash. If you are already a programmer in another discipline, you can pick up the basic Flash file structures and conventions from this example. If you are new to programming, don't worry too much about the exact nature of the code; instead concentrate on what each AS file is setting up as part of the solution, and how the FLA is using these building blocks.

We will describe the main features of this code (rather than go through it step by step), which are the following:

- The class name starts with a capital letter and is defined on line 1—DrinkTempProcess.

- The file is called DrinkTempProcess—that is, it has the same name as the class it is defining. It *must* be called this to work.

- The class defines its own properties (lines 3–5) and methods (lines 14 on). The properties are liquid, froth, and temperature. These are the parameters you have to define before you can process your drink. You will also have to answer the basic questions "What liquid are you using?", "Do you want it frothed?", and "What temperature do you want it?" The method defines the process you will use to make the *basic* drink.

- There is a **constructor** (lines 7–12). This is a function with the same name as the class (again, it **must** be the same, otherwise it will not work). This is the part that constructs an instance of your class DrinkTempProcess.

How does this all tie in with the "Prepare the liquid" diagram? Let's run it and see.

Preparing the liquid

If you are feeling confident, you can create the AS file yourself, but note that almost every part of it has to be typed in **exactly** as written, including spelling and case. If any part of it is wrong, the class will not work properly. We strongly recommend that you use our version of this file from the book's code download.

1. Create a new folder called drinkOOP somewhere on your hard drive.

2. If you are going to use our downloaded file, copy the file DrinkTempProcess.as into the drinkOOP folder. However, if you feel brave enough to type the code yourself, create a new AS file as described in the previous section "Working with raw ActionScript" and enter the following code precisely as shown:

Once you're done typing this hefty bit of code you can get Flash to check for errors by clicking the Check syntax *button:*

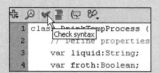

In class-based programming, this may catch errors that the Auto format *button misses, because not only does* Check syntax *check the current AS file, it also checks the whole class-based hierarchy and classes in other AS files that form part of your definition.*

3. Save the file as `DrinkTempProcess.as` in the `drinkOOP` folder. This is your super class definition.

4. Create a new FLA called `drinkTest01.fla`, and save it in the same folder as the super class definition. Select frame 1 of the timeline and add the following script (you can also use our completed file from the code download):

```
1 // test the Super Class...
2 testProcess1 = new DrinkTempProcess("water", false, 100);
3 testProcess2 = new DrinkTempProcess("milk", true, 4);
4 trace(testProcess1.processIngredients());
5
```

5. Test the FLA. Flash will pick up the class definitions, and will output the following:

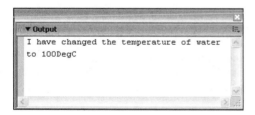

Flash is using your super class (well, at the moment it is just a class for reasons you will see in a moment) to create a solution to the basic problem—changing the temperature of a liquid. Here, you are getting Flash to do just that.

6. You can look at your class handling milk to form the basic process for a milkshake by altering line 4 as follows (change the 1 to a 2):

```
trace(testProcess2.processIngredients());
```

```
1 // test the Super Class...
2 testProcess1 = new DrinkTempProcess("water", false, 100);
3 testProcess2 = new DrinkTempProcess("milk", true, 4);
4 trace(testProcess2.processIngredients());
5
```

This time, Flash cooled the milk and frothed it.

You have the basic process of changing the temperature and using a straight or frothed liquid. If you think about it, that's the basic process you need to make all sorts of drinks: coffee, tea, cappuccino, or milkshakes.

The important point to notice here is not the code you used, but the fact that although you do not yet have a complete solution for making drinks, you are already writing code to solve it! You have a vague idea about what the core process of making a drink is, but that hasn't stopped you from creating and testing this vague idea in hard code. In the top-down process, you would have to fully define your problem before you could start programming, hope that you had covered everything, and also hope that coding would not uncover problems you hadn't thought of in the specification. That's a lot of hope, and in most cases, you can safely assume that Murphy's Law will come into play.

To make drinks rather than simply hot or cold liquids (frothed or otherwise), you need other ingredients. You need to *extend* your solution to include them. You do this by using the existing class `DrinkTempProcess` as a building block upon which you can add more specialized code to refine your solution.

Extending the solution

1. In the same way you created `DrinkTempProcess.as`, create another AS file, this time called `MakeDrink.as` (or use our download file). Save it in your `drinkOOP` folder when you are done.

```
class MakeDrink extends DrinkTempProcess {
    //properties...
    var solid:String;
    //constructor...
    function MakeDrink(arg_liquid:String, arg_froth:Boolean, arg_solid:String, arg_temperature:Number) {
        //pass to superclass...
        super(arg_liquid, arg_froth, arg_temperature);
        //create here...
        solid = arg_solid;
    }
    //methods...
    function makeIt():String {
        return processIngredients(liquid, temperature)+" and mixed in "+solid;
    }
}
```

This looks similar to the last class, but is different in a couple of ways:

- It refers back to the first class on line one with the word extends. This file uses the core from the basic class DrinkTempProcess and extends it toward the solution you want. By doing this, DrinkTempProcess becomes a super class because MakeDrink extends from it.

- You can see that MakeDrink extends DrinkTempProcess by adding a new property called solid. This is your solid ingredient. MakeDrink also creates a new method, makeIt. Notice that the code for this refers back to a method you saw in the super class, processIngredients—it is changing the basic method to heat/cool liquids by adding the solid ingredient into the mix—literally!

Let's give it a whirl.

2. Save both your AS files if either has an asterisk (*) on the tabs at the top.

3. Create a new FLA (or you can use our download file `testDrink02.fla`) and attach the following script to frame 1 of its timeline (as you did in "Preparing the liquid"). Save the FLA in your `drinkOOP` folder as `testDrink02.fla`.

```
// define our instances...
coffee = new MakeDrink("water", false, "ground coffee beans", 95);
milkShake = new MakeDrink("milk", true, "banana flavoring and sugar", 3);
cappuccino = new MakeDrink("water", true, "ground coffee beans", 80);
//
// now test them...
//
trace("To make an instance 'coffee'...");
trace(coffee.makeIt());
//
trace("\nTo make an instance 'milkShake'...");
trace(milkShake.makeIt());
//
trace("\nTo make an instance 'cappuccino'...");
trace(cappuccino.makeIt());
```

4. If you now test this FLA, you will see this:

```
▼ Output
To make an instance 'coffee'...
I have changed the temperature of water to 95DegC and
mixed in ground coffee beans

To make an instance 'milkShake'...
I have changed the temperature of milk to 3DegC, then
frothed it and mixed in banana flavoring and sugar

To make an instance 'cappuccino'...
I have changed the temperature of water to 80DegC, then
frothed it and mixed in ground coffee beans
```

This looks **much** more like a finished set of drinks! What did you do? The class MakeDrink extends the basic "make hot or cold liquid" class DrinkTempProcess. MakeDrink uses the DrinkTempProcess to create liquids at the right temperature and adds to them with its own method makeIt, which adds the other ingredients to make a drink!

Reviewing the solution

Some of you might be wondering how this relates to reality. What **real** problem would this actually solve?

The code is not really modeling how you would make drinks; it is the way a machine would make them—you can conceptualize, but in the end, code is for machines.

When they first build new vending machines that dispense cups of coffee and soup and such, they start with the core components—the heater/cooler that pours the basic ingredients—hot water or cold juice, etc—down a spout. They test this with a microcontroller containing code implementing something very like DrinkTempProcess.

> In real life, DrinkTempProcess *would itself extend other classes below it, and these classes would interface to the machine's hardware, so you have layers of classes of the form* hardware ➤ classes *that can talk to the hardware* ➤ DrinkTempProcess.
>
> *When* DrinkTempProcess *says it is frothing something, its super classes would use this to make a whisk move around at some point in the heating process.*

The class above DrinkTempProcess (by "above" we mean closer to the solution) adds other things to your hot and cold liquids to make drinks. You've used a class that is a simplified version of it—MakeDrink—which refers to the same hardware-specific classes to pour coffee into the drink at the right moment and so on, so our simple text messages will be converted to *real* drinks.

What are the instances of MakeDrink? They are not the actual beverages—coffee, milkshake, or cappuccino. They are—see if you can guess what they actually are before reading the next bit—**instructions** to create the actual beverages, structured as software instances. The **properties** of the MakeDrink class are **ingredients**, and the one method of it, makeIt is the **recipe** that works on the ingredients to make your drink.

When you click the cappuccino button on a machine, the drink machine will be configured by the cappuccino instance of MakeDrink, and you will get a *real* cappuccino. Object-oriented programming is not vague at all—

it's the way most machines behave when you press one of their buttons—from PCs and Macs, to the drink machine in the office.

What's the point of this? Why would you want to go through all this extra thinking and dip your toes into the world of object-oriented design? The answer is that object-oriented techniques result in solutions more robust, flexible, and easier to maintain and upgrade than other programming styles. Because you've designed the solution in terms of generalized and self-sufficient classes, you can reuse them in other tasks that have a similar element in them—a "preparing a bath" task could probably reuse the "prepare the liquid" class DrinkTempProcess. Furthermore, as each class communicates with other entities using interfaces, you can completely change the instructions inside a class and not affect the overall solution—provided that you keep the same interfaces. Each class and the instances that are derived from it can be reworked in isolation. Here, in essence, are the benefits of the object-oriented approach:

- Reusability
- Encapsulation—functionality embedded in a self-contained object
- Maintainability
- Extensibility
- Flexibility

The object-oriented approach helps you build solutions that can change as the world that they're modeling changes, and the strength of OO design lies in its ability to generalize. Generalized solutions based on these design principles are not locked into the problem you initially set out to solve because elements can be used elsewhere and changed when different problems arise.

What's this got to do with Flash and you as beginners, given that you can't yet write classes on your own? As a beginner, it's a Very Good Thing that you at least looked at the class-based coding stuff because

- It's the way Flash works. Here, you are just creating your own classes instead of relying on one created for you! The only difference between the movie clip class and MakeDrink is that Macromedia wrote the movie clip class. If the movie clip doesn't do exactly what you want it to do, you could make certain adjustments to it until it suited your needs better, or you could extend movie clip to make a class that does **Exactly What You Want**. You would do this in very much the same way as you made object-oriented programming drinks—it's not any harder. It is not that big of a leap in theory from this simple example to super classing movie clip to create your own Sprite class to write Flash video games with, or to write your own User Interface classes so you can make your websites out of already-built blocks.

- Macromedia already had the idea about already-built building blocks, and you probably already heard of them—they're called **components**. Knowing the basic framework of classes that underpin components will make you better at using them.

- You get the most out of Flash if you think in terms of classes. At the moment, you know there's a button class, and a movie clip class, a sound class, and more than 70 others! How will you ever get through them all? Simple—see them as the same thing. By adopting a class-based mind-set, you quickly see that all classes are essentially the same. As soon as you understand one ActionScript class in terms of real class-based thinking, you don't just understand that one class—you understand ActionScript. When you do that, you certainly won't be a beginner, nor will you be an intermediate; you will be an advanced user of Flash, soon to be a new Master of Flash.

- Even if you don't use the rigorous, code-based object-oriented structures, it helps to at least think in a general bottom-up way in Flash, rather than the more structured and formal top-down design way.

In the rest of this chapter, you will break away from pure class-based scripting and move to a more general design thought process. Rather than code using classes, you will use standard ActionScript but think in a bottom-up mind-set.

You are almost at the end of the **Foundation** part of your journey. You are an intermediate Flash user, and you have had a peek at the next mountain—it's a big one for sure. This is your starting point to that next mountain in the range. Think like a Master and you will become a Master, even if you don't yet have a Master's coat.

Flash and the built-in classes

Until now, your exposure to classes has been pretty limited, right? Wrong. As you probably already know from the last discussion, Flash is fully OO-based, so many of the elements you have already used in this book are classes. Typical classes in the Flash environment include video, sound, components, text, buttons, and of course, movie clips.

> *You can view a full list of Flash's predefined objects by using the Actions toolbox pane of the Actions panel and opening the ActionScript 2.0 Classes book. Try not to be too intimidated by the list because the number of these that you will use at the moment will be minimal.*

It will help you a great deal in the long run if you begin to think that ActionScript is object-oriented and begin to think of elements such as video, sound, text, buttons, and so on as classes, even if you do it without thinking too much about things like MakeDrink and super classing.

Let's explore the concept with a particular basic class that you're already really familiar with: **movie clips**.

A movie clip instance on the stage is essentially a specific named instance based on the movie clip class embodied in a symbol in the Library:

- Create an instance of (drag it out of the Library) these individual movie clip building blocks on the stage and, if necessary, give them instance names so that you can target them with ActionScript.

The movie clips must be **self-contained**. They must be able to solve their part of the problem by themselves, and they must be able to do this independently of whatever else is also going on in the movie.

The process works best in situations where there are multiple instances of a few very similar processes to be performed. You can illustrate this with a graphical effect in a Flash movie. A lot of computer graphic effects use a few basic rules that are applied many times over to give the illusion of complexity. Here, you'll see how a very simple movie clip with a single process can be replicated many times on the screen to create a much more complex-looking effect.

A movie clip object has standard, basic properties like size, position, and number of frames, and once you've built the individual instance by adding a few actions and frames of content to it, it can start to do things.

A class has a standard general structure. At its simplest level, it calculates a certain small but well-defined chunk of a solution (or movie), and it has well-defined interfaces that allow it to communicate with the other classes that deal with the other parts of the problem (movie). Remember that to follow the object-oriented route you have to

- Identify the basic elements of your problem in terms of what you can see happening (or what you **want** to happen in your movie).

- Identify what these basic building blocks **are** (conceptualize) and see whether you can generalize them into basic groups of building blocks so that each one builds on the previous one to extend your work toward the solution.

- Create movie clips in the Library that map to these basic groups and perform the functions associated with the group, thus making your movie clips your building blocks (rather than the classes in the last section). Instead of extending the movie clips, you can embed them into each other to create nested structures.

A simple mouse trail

The great thing about bottom-up design is that it allows you to play—you don't even need to have a high-level problem or task to solve. You can just say, "This effect looks interesting—let's break it down into its parts and see what we can build from them." You can use this as a creative thought process, and not necessarily as a logical, analytical problem-solving process. The reason for this is very simple: in Flash, your most common classes are not long-winded and obscure data elements—they're visual movie clips with animation and sound, which can be much more fun.

A mouse trail is a little group of characters or text that follows the mouse pointer. An effective mouse trail usually contains some very complex math, using things like inertia and trigonometry to calculate the pointer position and the relative position of the trail. By stopping and thinking about it, though, you'll realize that instead of using heavy math and shifting movie clips around behind the pointer, you could just use lots of static movie clips that *react* when the pointer moves over them. Basically, you're turning the problem on its head.

483

There are two stages to building a mouse trail: (1) building the basic movie clip object that you'll make multiple copies of later, and (2) integrating the multiple copies into the movie.

Creating the basic movie clip

The first thing to realize is that all those fancy mouse trails have one thing in common: the character furthest away from the pointer is *least* affected by what the mouse is doing now, and the closest is *most* affected.

In essence, you've abstracted the problem down to a generalization of the type of animation that's required to create the desired effect. The animation on any particular character should get weaker based on (1) increasing distance from the mouse, and (2) how long ago the mouse was near it—longer ago means weaker animation effect.

> *If you were embarking on a code-oriented solution, this would be the vague idea that would create your super class. This is similar to the way the vague idea that all drinks have a liquid brought to a well-defined temperature is the core part of its super class.*

The only thing you've encountered so far that's affected by the mouse is a button symbol, so maybe if you had loads of buttons all over the screen, you could make Flash do all the hard work for you. That's all you need to know. It seems pretty vague, but that's OK—it allows you more room to experiment.

1. Create a new Flash movie and change the background color to black using the Properties panel. Also make sure that the View ➤ Grid ➤ Show Grid and View ➤ Snapping ➤ Snap to Grid menu options are both selected.

2. Create a new graphic symbol and call it sy.circle. Inside it, create a circle with a blue stroke and fill. Give the circle a diameter of about 90 pixels, and center it using the Align panel.

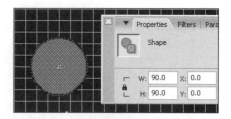

3. Create a movie clip and call it mc.circle. Change the name of the movie clip's default layer to circle.

4. Leave frame 1 of this movie clip empty, but add a keyframe in frame 2. Drag a copy of sy.circle into this keyframe, and center it on the stage at 0,0.

5. Use the Properties panel to select Alpha from the Color drop-down menu and give the circle a value of 70%:

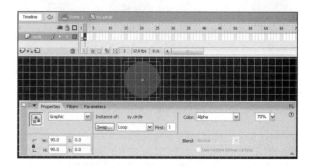

6. Add another keyframe at frame 20. In this frame, use the Color drop-down again, but this time, select Advanced and click the Settings button that appears to the right.

   The Alpha will already be set to 70% from before, but give the circle a red hue by moving the second Red slider (the one that's a number rather than a percentage) all the way up to 255:

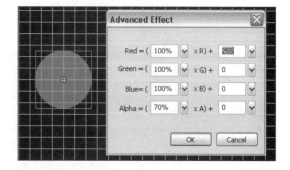

7. Using the Properties panel or Info panel, set the width and height of the circle to 1 and, if necessary, center the circle using the Align panel. Then create a motion tween from frame 2 to frame 20.

8. If you drag this movie clip onto the stage and test your movie, you'll see a circle that starts off big and blue and then gets smaller and red until it finally disappears.

You've now created your simple diminishing effect. Next, we need to change the clip so that it'll run through once when the mouse pointer passes over it and stop until the pointer goes over it again. The more recently the mouse pointer was near it, the bigger the circle will be. This continues for 20 frames, by which time the circle is so small it disappears. Your movie clip building block must somehow get the mouse input that will control its appearance and behavior. You could get it to look at how close the mouse is to it, but there is a simpler option to try first.

9. Duplicate sy.circle by selecting it in the Library window and clicking the menu icon on the top right of the Library panel and selecting Duplicate from the drop-down menu. Make the new symbol into a button via the Duplicate Symbol dialog box and call the button bu.circle.

10. The button should be totally transparent and the same size as the movie clip. In bu.circle, insert a keyframe in the Hit state, and delete the circle from the Up state. You now have a circular button that has no Up or Down state, but does have a Hit state, making it invisible but selectable:

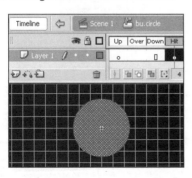

This clever little creation is called an **invisible button** in the world of Flash. Invisible buttons have been in popular use since version 4 of Flash, and although their halcyon days have passed, they are still a very useful way of creating a hit area for awkward assets (like text or small objects), and are commonly used for visual tricks such as the one we're in the process of making.

11. You want to add the invisible button and some simple actions to mc.circle, so go into mc.circle and add two new layers, one named actions and one named button:

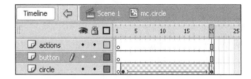

12. In the button layer, add the bu.circle symbol and center it. Then remove all the other frames from this layer so that the button only exists on frame 1. With the bu.circle button still selected, give it an instance name buCircle in the Properties panel.

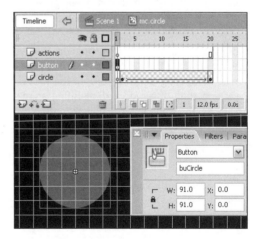

485

13. Type the following in frame 1 of the actions layer:

```
buCircle.onRollOver = function() {
    play();
}
stop();
```

You don't need to include a this reference on the second line (to give you this.play()) because your code is on the mc.circle timeline, and that's the timeline you want to stop.

14. Insert a keyframe in frame 20 of the actions layer and add gotoAndStop (1);.

That's it. You've created a movie clip that does the following:

- It waits at a blank first frame until it's rolled over.

- When it's rolled over by the mouse, it plays.

- When it has played once, it goes back to the blank first frame.

15. Drag an instance of mc.circle onto the stage and test your movie. You'll see a blank screen until your mouse happens to move over the button. As soon as this happens, a circle appears and gets smaller as time goes by until it disappears completely. That was the basic object you started out trying to create: an effect that diminishes based on either (a) time since it was started or (b) distance the mouse is away from it.

Notice that you haven't even thought how you're going to use this building block. You just wanted to create something that waited until the mouse was near and then displayed a diminishing animation. You've set aside the initial problem completely and concentrated on creating this building block.

When you created your super class, you did not consider the class that would eventually extend it. In the same way, you did not consider what you would use your movie clip building block for—you simply generalized the current problem.

Although you are not writing complex class-based code here, you are thinking about the problem in a class-based way, which is a good place to start. Flash is one of the few environments where you can work in a loosely object-oriented way like this, and that makes it a great application to start playing with advanced, industry-strength programming techniques without actually writing in a strict, code-centric manner. Because of this, Flash is a forgiving environment for creative people to move over to a structured programming style. As you add more code to your simple building blocks and see what other folks are doing, you will likely move toward the pure, class-based code. Some of you will only go part of the way, but some of you will travel all the way up that mountain.

Building the movie

The next step is to see if your simple movie clip animation, repeated many times, could be used to produce the complex behavior you're looking for.

1. Drag an instance of mc.circle onto the stage. Position it at the left edge of the stage with its registration point on a grid line as shown (don't worry about its vertical position):

We're now going to produce a line of duplicates. However, rather than use the standard Edit ➤ Duplicate or a command, we're going to use an advanced technique (aka a power tip).

2. Hold down the *CTRL* key (Option key for Mac) and drag on the mc.circle instance on the stage as if you were going to move it. As you drag, you'll notice that the cursor changes to a + symbol and a ghost outline appears. We are now dragging a new instance out from the previous. Oh—keep holding that mouse button and *CTRL*/Option key down.

3. Allow the dragged instance to snap to a grid line slightly offset right from the original and finally, release it (ensure it is roughly vertically aligned with the original):

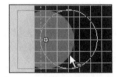

Phew! Now you can stretch those fingers again. The reason we had to do all that in one step is so that we can duplicate the whole step over and over. It'll save us from hard work in the long run.

4. Select Edit ➤ Repeat Duplicate to repeat the last step. Now you'll notice right away that a new instance has appeared alongside the last duplicate. If the duplicate didn't work for some reason, try the steps again.

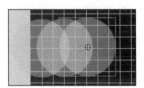

In essence, the step we "recorded" involved a couple of actions: creating a duplicate and positioning it. Note that every Repeat Duplicate continues from the previous one, so we get a staggered effect (and our line slowly builds).

By the way, the Repeat option from the Edit menu can be used to replicate many monotonous tasks in the same way.

5. Select Repeat Duplicate a number of times until the duplicates extend from the left side of the stage to the right:

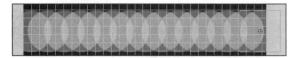

6. To ensure the movie clips are aligned correctly, use the Align panel's Align top edge button:

7. When you have a full row, select them all, press *F8* to convert the row into a new movie clip symbol, and call it mc.circle.row.

8. Continue adding rows above and below your starting row by dragging copies of mc.circle.row to the stage until you've filled the screen with a neat grid:

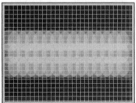

9. To ensure the rows are evenly spread, select them all and use the Align panel's Space evenly vertically button with the Align/Distribute to stage option switched on:

10. And now comes the moment of truth. Remember, you set the task of creating a trail that would start from wherever the mouse pointer was and gradually fade as the pointer moved away, or as time passed. Did you do it? There's only one way to find out—test that movie:

It seems to have worked perfectly. Cool. You can change the animation to be whatever you want—sparkling stars, jumping sheep—the possibilities are endless. The next step is to play and create!

Notice that in making this movie, all you've done is thought about an effect, decided what its most basic structure/building block was, and created a movie clip that does it. Then you made a more complex-looking effect by making lots of copies of the simple effect. Although this movie isn't truly object-oriented, the thinking behind it *is*. The visual effect you created is based on one button in one movie clip. One of the fundamental advantages of objects is that they're self-contained, and therefore reusable. What's more, because they are generalized solutions, they can be rearranged to fit new problems. A bit like classes—same concept, different level.

We'll now show you how small, seemingly obscure ideas and the theories behind them can be fleshed out in little experimental building blocks that grow slowly (aka the bottom-up approach).

Putting it all together

You're going to look at a simple memory game sometimes called "Concentration." The first thing you'll do is define the basic rules:

■ The player is presented with an even number of tiles with symbols on their faces. For each tile there is at least one other identical tile. All the tiles are positioned face down so their symbols aren't visible.

■ The player has to match each symbol with a matching symbol by turning a pair of tiles over each turn.

If the tiles match, the tiles are left face up. If the tiles don't match, the tiles are returned to their face-down state.

■ The game is over when all tiles are face up.

This game can be implemented using either a top-down or an object-oriented approach. If you try it using the top-down approach, you're guaranteed to end up with a bunch of if-then-else statements as long as your arm, and more variables than you would believe (we tried it just to make sure!).

Instead, let's look at it from a bottom-up approach.

Your first thoughts should be about what the fundamental objects of the game are. In this case, it's quite obvious—the only things being manipulated in this game are the **tiles**. If you can create a generalized tile object with an appropriate range of things it will do, you've cracked the whole game. What do you want the tile to be able to do?

At a guess, you'd want it to be able to do the following:

■ Be face down when it's unselected.

■ Turn face up when it's selected, and show the user and Flash its symbol.

■ Ask Flash when the current turn has finished. If the selected tile does not match the other selected tile, it must turn back to its initial state. If the selected tiles match, each tile must remain face up.

Notice that there are a few things you haven't defined as necessary to know, such as

■ How many tiles there are

■ How many different tile symbols there will be

■ How many tiles are face up

■ How many tiles are face down

You don't need to know these things because the object you're creating will represent only one tile. All these bits of information don't apply to one tile; they apply to many tiles working alongside each other. So, using the bottom-up design method, you'll first create the tile, and when that's working fine, you'll move on to the next step up and build the game timing and control building blocks—you won't think right now how you will do that.

But wait a minute . . .

Part of this definition sounds strangely familiar. The mouse trail you just created stays still when it's not selected, and then does something when it *has* been selected. This is a subset of the same sort of behavior you want for our tile. The only difference is that the mouse trail circles were all identical, but the tiles you want to create will be different. Can you reuse part of the previous exercise? It might be a good starting point.

Creating the tile

1. Start a new Flash movie. Using the Properties panel, change the movie background to a deep purple (the color we used has a hex value of #996699), and the dimensions to 800×800. Change the frame rate to 18 fps.

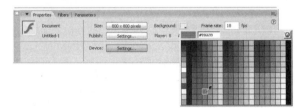

In the last exercise, you created a circle and a button that was the same size and shape as the circle to trigger the movie into action. You're going to do the same thing here.

2. Create a new graphic symbol and call it sy.tile.

3. Within sy.tile, create a tile shape by drawing a light blue rectangle (we used #99CCFF) with rounded corners and a black stroke. You could reuse the playing cards from earlier in the book, but remember to take the character off the front because you want them to be blank for now. Make your tile 80 pixels wide and 120 pixels high, and center it on the stage:

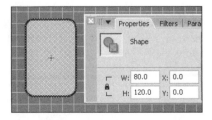

4. Use the Option menu from the Library panel to duplicate the symbol as a button, the same way you did in the last example. Call this symbol bu.transparent—the reason for this name will become clear in a moment.

5. Double-click to edit the newly duplicated symbol. Click and drag the button's Up state keyframe to the Hit state keyframe. This will make this an invisible button.

6. Now you need some pictures to go on the tiles. We've provided a set of graphics of fruit in the code download that you can use. To utilize our graphics, download tile game_graphics.fla, and use File ➤ Import ➤ Open External Library to load the library. Otherwise, feel free to come up with whatever you want. For this example, you'll use four different pictures: a tomato, an orange, a lemon, and a pear:

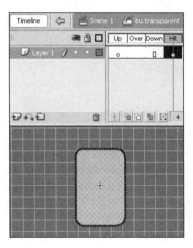

489

If you choose the easier of the two routes, drag the four graphic symbols from the external library into your own library: sy.fruit.tomato, sy.fruit.orange, sy.fruit.lemon, and sy.fruit.pear.

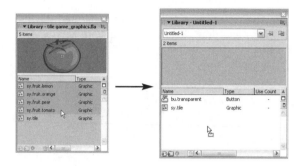

7. Create a new movie clip symbol and call it mc.tile.

We know that you'll need to have a button and an animation in this clip, so you'll put them in now.

8. Rename the first layer tile, then create a new layer and name it button. Because you have a button, you will also need to define its event, so let's add the layer to do that as well. Make a third layer on top and call it actions.

In the tile layer, you'll create an animation of the tile turning over, and to create this effect you'll use the same kind of illusion you implemented for the flipping face tween in Chapter 7.

9. In frame 1 of the tile layer, drag in a copy of sy.tile from the Library and center it. Add keyframes at frames 5 and 10.

10. The next thing is to create an animation of the tile flipping over. To do this, you'll make the tile get progressively shorter as it moves between frames 1 to 5, and then grow again until it's back up to its normal size in frame 10. This will give the illusion that the tile is flipping over. Click frame 5 and use the Properties panel (or the Info panel) to set the height (H) value of the graphic to 1. Center the graphic using the Align panel if necessary:

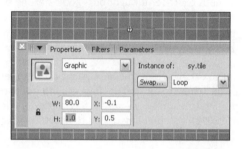

If you find that the value doesn't want to go to 1.0 exactly (it may change to 0.9 or 1.1 after you enter it), try changing the value you enter. For example, if you get 0.9, enter 1.1 instead, and it should start playing ball. Of course, this doesn't really matter—0.9 is still OK with us if it's OK with you!

11. Add two separate motion tweens between frames 1 and 5, and frames 5 and 10.

At the moment your flipping tile won't really seem very convincing as both sides look the same. After you've added a fruit picture to one side, the illusion will be complete.

12. Add a new layer between the tile and button layers and call it fruit. You want to make the fruit start to appear from frame 5 onward and grow until it's full size in frame 10.

13. Insert a keyframe in frame 10 of your fruit layer and drag a copy of one of your graphic symbols onto the stage—we're using the tomato symbol. Center your symbol and resize it until it fits nicely onto your tile:

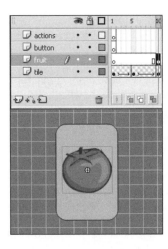

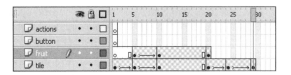

You don't need to reverse these frames—as you'll see, it looks fine if you play the movie clip.

19. If you were to do the same thing with the tomato animation, though, it would be the wrong way around. Click frame 5 on the fruit layer and again use the Edit ➤ Timeline ➤ Copy Frames menu option to copy it to the clipboard.

20. Click frame 24 on the same layer and paste the frame there. Then set up a motion tween between frames 20 and 24:

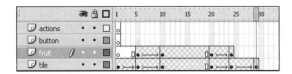

Now when you play back your movie clip, it should run through with no trouble.

You now have a tile that starts face down, flips face up, and then flips face down again. The next things you need are the actions.

14. Add a new keyframe at frame 5, copy the fruit from frame 10, and paste it in place into frame 5. Here's the trick: you want the tomato to be as thin as the tile at frame 5, so using the Properties panel, change the tomato's H value to 1, the same value as the tile, and then center it. At frame 5, you should now have a squashed tile and a squashed tomato over the top of it.

15. Create a motion tween from frame 5 to 10. Your animation should now give a convincing impression of a tile flipping over:

The tile should start off blank and shrink to nothing, before growing back to full size again with the tomato image on it.

16. Once the tile has flipped over, the next thing you'll want it to do is flip it back over to its face-down position. This motion would simply look like the animation you've created so far in frames 1 to 10, but in reverse. Create a new keyframe in frame 20 of your fruit and tile layers.

17. Select frames 1 through 10 on the tile layer and use the Edit ➤ Timeline ➤ Copy Frames menu option to copy them to the clipboard.

18. Click frame 20 of the tile layer and use the Edit ➤ Timeline ➤ Paste Frames menu option to paste the frames into the timeline:

Making the tile work

The tile should only flip when it's selected, so you need to incorporate a button into the movie clip to trigger this flipping.

The button will go into frame 1 of the button layer. This layer should have a single frame in it. Once the tile starts flipping, you don't want the user to be able to select it again because this could create problems later on in the game.

1. Drag the bu.transparent symbol from your Library onto the button layer, and center it on your existing tile. If you find it easier, you may want to hide and lock the other two layers by clicking the eye and lock icons on the timeline. Give it an instance name trans_btn.

491

The first thing you want the button to do when you click it is to start playing the movie clip, which you can achieve with some simple ActionScript.

2. Select frame 1 of the actions layer and add this script:

```
trans_btn.onRelease = function() {
  play();
};
stop();
```

This script will cause the tile to stay face down until it is clicked. As soon as the tile is clicked, it will begin its animation. Frame 1 is also the face-down point in the animation, and the place you will have to get back to when the card flips back over for an incorrect match. Let's label it: with frame 1 of the actions layer still selected, enter a frame label of facedown via the Properties panel.

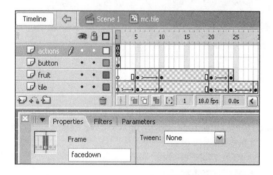

We'll finish with this movie clip's timeline a little later.

3. Go back to the main stage and drag a copy of your movie clip out from the Library. It doesn't matter where you place it because it's only there so you can test the movie.

4. Play your movie. The tile should stay blank until you click it, and then it will cycle through its animation and return to the face-down state. You should only be able to click it in the face-down state.

The next thing you need to do is to have the tile stop when it's face-up.

5. You'll need a little more than a stop action in this frame—you also want the tile to tell the user and Flash what symbol it has on it. The user bit is easy—they can see the picture on top of the tile—but telling Flash is a little more complicated. The questions that you should be asking are the following:

- Who or what do you tell?

- How do you tell it, and what does it need to know?

One of the fundamental things about creating bottom-up programs is that you have to know which parts of the program fit inside one movie clip, and which parts fit into another clip or into external code. This is a difficult concept to grasp at first, but if you think "What's the game doing? What can a tile do, and should it be able to do that?" it quickly becomes obvious that the pieces of a game—the tiles—should not be the **controllers** of the action. The rules, or a referee who knows the rules, should control the game.

The referee for this game will be the main timeline, so that will be in control. The tiles are just performing their specific actions and nothing more. This is because you need to be able to add as many tiles to the final game as you like. This is the beauty of bottom-up design: the tiles are just building blocks that you can plug into the program any number of times without having to recode them. They are **self-contained**.

As you know, the main timeline is called _root. Although using the root would be fine for your movie, it would stop your code from being truly general. Remember what we said earlier about building blocks being reusable? Well, to keep this reusability as open as possible, you don't always want to tie things to the main timeline. The way you can get around this is to give control of the movie clip to the next level up instead. By doing this, you'll be able to move the code around within the levels of a movie and still have it work. The name for the next level up in Flash is the *parent*. By telling the movie clip to talk to the parent level, you're keeping it as a separate portable object—wherever you place a tile in a movie hierarchy, this notation will ensure that it always talks to the next level up, irrespective of the name of that level's timeline.

That answers the first question—now you know you should be talking to the parent. What do you want to tell it? The parent needs to know what's on the tile, and in this case it's a tomato.

6. On frame 1 of the actions layer on the current timeline, add the following highlighted code to the button event handler block, so the ActionScript for the button looks like this:

```
trans_btn.onRelease = function() {
  _parent.buttonClick += 1;
  _parent.fruit = "tomato";
  play();
};
stop();
```

> *The second line of code above increments the variable* buttonClick *by 1 using the code shortcut* buttonClick +=1. *This is the equivalent of the statement* buttonClick = buttonClick +1. *This shortcut method can be used for incrementing a value by any number required (such as* buttonClick += 4).
>
> *Decrementing a variable is done in the same way using the minus operator. To decrement a value using the same shortcut method, use* buttonClick -= 1.

The next thing to do is test whether Flash can tell which fruit is on the tile.

7. Go back to the main movie timeline and draw a text field below the tile. Make the text field dynamic and nonselectable, and click the Show border around text button to make Flash draw a box around your text. Make sure the text color is different from your movie color's background, and finally, assign it the variable fruit by typing fruit in the Var field.

8. Test the movie.

   This time, when you click the tile, you'll see the tile communicating with the _parent, telling it what the variable fruit is:

You now have one tile working pretty well, but the game won't be much fun with only one tile! Now test it with multiple tiles, and see what sort of problems arise.

Using multiple tiles

You now need to start thinking how you want each tile to work when there is more than one tile on the stage.

1. Add three more tiles to your main stage to make a row of four in all. You can tidy up the row by using the Align panel.

2. Test the movie. Notice the following:

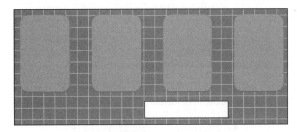

- Your text field won't change after you've selected the first tile because all the tiles are tomatoes.

- It's possible to flip more than two tiles.

- The first tile doesn't wait until the second tile has been flipped before it flips itself back around, so you'd have to be pretty quick to match a pair.

The first problem should sort itself out once you add different fruit symbols, so you don't need to worry about that.

For the second problem, you need to count the number of tiles that are now face up. If it's two or more, you shouldn't allow any other tiles to flip. To do this, you'll need a variable to count the number of tiles that have been flipped.

To fix the third problem, you'll need to wait until a second tile is face up and the person playing the game has had time to look at both tiles before the tiles are flipped back over. You must do a few other things before that becomes possible, so for now, simply add a stop(); to frame 10 of the actions timeline within mc.tile. This will make the tiles stay face up once they are turned.

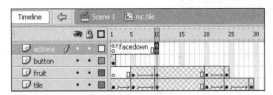

3. Click on frame 1 of the actions layer to view the ActionScript for the button. You've already told the parent and the ActionScript that the fruit on this symbol is a tomato. Now add the following line of highlighted code and another closing curly bracket (}) under the **play** action, so that your ActionScript for the button symbol looks like this:

```
trans_btn.onRelease = function(){
  _parent.buttonClick += 1;
  _parent.fruit = "tomato";
  if (_parent.buttonClick<=2) {
      play();
  }
}
stop();
```

You now know how many times a button has been clicked. You have also told Flash to stop allowing more tiles to be turned when more than two tiles have already been flipped. What you haven't yet done is create a button click variable on the main timeline, so let's do that now.

4. Add a new layer called actions on the main timeline. In frame 1 of it add the following script:

```
buttonClick = 0;
```

The last line of code that you attached to trans_btn checks if you've already clicked any two other buttons and, if so, instructs the program not to respond to any more button clicks. The beauty of tying buttonClick to the parent and not to each tile is that all the tile objects will look at the same variable. They don't need to know which other buttons have been clicked; they will respond as soon as any two buttons are clicked.

5. Test the movie to confirm this. You should see that

- Once you click a tile, it stays face up.

- You can turn tiles only if buttonClick is fewer than two. After that, they refuse to budge.

You can also check our version, tile_game_part1.fla, which has a text field set up to show you the value of buttonClick as well as fruit. Note that after clicking the second tile, buttonClick will still increase in value, but no tiles will respond—the play() in the if is no longer being executed.

fruit tomato
buttonClick 1

fruit tomato
buttonClick 2

fruit tomato
buttonClick 4

tile_game_part1.fla *is a test FLA that checks whether an important part of the final game works. When building complex Flash content, you will create lots of these. Many beginners look at big FLAs and think "How did they know that part would work?" The answer is that the test FLAs that were created along the way opened and checked parts of the inner workings so that code could be developed. In creating the tile game, for example, six or seven test FLAs were created along the way, each confirming a major milestone in the creation of working code. Without them, neither we nor anyone else for that matter could have created the game!*

If you get stuck in this or any other big FLA, save your work, and rename it as filename_partxx.fla. *Then open the code by either adding text fields or code that tests what you have done already, or stop the code at important points so that you can look at what is going on via the Debugger panel. Once you know what the problem is, go back to the original and continue from there. You will leave a trail of _partxx files (_part01, _part02, etc.) and these show your explorations from the main solution, solving minor problems that cropped up. Occasionally, you will come across a problem that can be solved in different ways, and you will create several partxxx files (_part1a, _part1b, etc.), each of which tries a different way.*

The important thing to realize is that not all the code you write will make it into the final FLA. As soon as you start to think "This isn't going to work," the temptation is to start adding lots of code to work around it, trying different routes in the same FLA. In the end, you have a single FLA that works, but you are no longer sure which bits of code actually work and which bits are just tests, so you don't delete anything! This makes it harder for you to continue, and it is the reason a lot of beginners don't write long scripts. It's not that long scripts are hard; it's just that the way they are written (if you don't use a system) makes them crash in on themselves under their own weight!

Getting the tiles to flip back correctly is a little more involved. You want to do the following:

- Keep the first tile flipped until a second is face up
- Decide whether the tiles match
- Flip both tiles back to face down or keep them face up based on whether they match

Hang on; the first part of that sounds a bit familiar: buttonClick already does that—it tells the main timeline how many buttons have been clicked so far. When that number is equal to 2, you know that the player has picked a pair, and the current turn is over whether they match or not—you can't pick anymore tiles.

The next part of your task is to make the tile stay face up until the referee says the current turn is over. You'll create a new variable called hadTurn to help you with that.

6. Back on the root timeline, name the existing layer the tiles are on tiles.

The first frame of the actions layer will set up the variables that apply to the whole game, and you'll insert a second keyframe that will actually control each turn.

7. Select frame 1 in the actions layer and add the following script, deleting what is there already (which will be buttonClick = 0):

```
function resetTurn () {

};
```

resetTurn is a function that you will run every time you want to start a new turn. What variables will you need? You would usually get out a pencil and paper and work it out, but we will tell you straight out for now.

You need one variable to tell Flash that the current turn has finished, and one variable to say how many buttons have been clicked so far—both of which have already been discussed:

```
buttonclick = 0;
hadTurn = false;
```

495

One to show what is on the last turned tile:

```
fruit = "";
```

One to show what's on the first tile:

```
fruit1 = "";
```

One to show what's on the second tile:

```
fruit2 = "";
```

And a final one to show if they match:

```
match = false;
```

If you add all these variables in your function, you get the following:

```
function resetTurn () {
    buttonclick = 0;
    hadTurn = false;
    match = false;
    fruit = "";
    fruit1 = "";
    fruit2 = "";
};
```

You still are not interested in the number of tiles and the number of different symbols there are on the tiles. They are not part of the problem even though they are part of the game. The important thing in this game is to find pairs, and it's this that determines our definition of the referee.

You'll start with a 4×4 playing board, which will include eight pairs—you'll eventually have four pairs of our four different fruits. This will be constant for every game, so this value will go in frame 1 of the actions layer on the main timeline. This frame is blank at the moment, but remember that you decided this frame would contain the variables that would be initialized only once for each game.

Add the following line at the end of the script to complete the game initialization:

```
function resetTurn () {
    buttonClick = 0;
    hadTurn = false;
    match = false;
    fruit = "";
    fruit1 = "";
    fruit2 = "";
};
pairs = 8;
```

That's your game initialization function; now it's time to set up your turn logic and initialize for a single turn.

8. Add a new keyframe at frame 2 of layer actions. In it, add the following code, which resets for a new turn. Note that although you defined the function resetTurn in frame 1, you did not run it. Frame 1 initializes the game and runs once. Frame 2 initializes the current turn and runs a number of times depending on how many turns it takes to complete the game.

```
resetTurn();
stop();
```

Now you're ready to start a new turn; how do you implement it? The main timeline is the referee of the game, and the referee watches the game closely. To "watch closely," Flash would have to look at every frame, and that implies an onEnterFrame script—but what to attach it to? Your script will not have to be attached to any particular movie clip, but it will be setting variables on the main timeline. How about attaching it to the main timeline itself, _root? _root is more like a movie clip timeline than you think—it is a movie clip. You may not be able to drag it from the Library, but it uses the movie clip class, which means it has the same properties and methods—and that means it has the same events as a movie clip. Understanding classes gives you some ideas that seem like little hacks and tricks to a non-class-savvy designer, but they are actually a consequence of knowing the class hierarchy well.

What is its instance name? Well, it's _root, but because you are actually on the main timeline, there is a better, more general name you can use—our old friend this. You want to attach it to this timeline, the one your code is on.

> *You can actually use nothing as well; just* onEnterFrame = function() { *(because you are outside a code block when you use* this, *and outside a code block,* this *is optional) but it tends to look a little odd having an event without an instance defined to attach it to—best to avoid that because it might confuse you later if you ever forget why you didn't add it!*

9. Add the following code to set up the event handler's block:

```
this.onEnterFrame = function() {
};
resetTurn();
stop();
```

You have defined your basic code for each turn, which will reset your variables for a new turn and stop. Some code will still be running, though—the code you will put in the onEnterFrame.

10. Each turn can be split into three sections:

- The first tile flipping over

- The second tile flipping over

- Checking the result

After the first tile click, you note what the first fruit is (i.e., you make fruit1 = fruit or make your first fruit equal to the fruit on the tile that has just been turned over). At the second click, you make fruit2 = fruit, but you also have to prevent any other tiles from being flipped over—each turn should only allow two tiles to be flipped. At the end of the second tile flip, you have to check whether the turn has been successful.

It is successful if the two fruits flipped over are the same, or fruit1 == fruit2. If that is the case, you have to cause the tiles to stay face up.

Otherwise, you have to make them return to the face-down state.

The variable that tells you whether the first or second tile has been turned over is buttonClick, so add the following:

```
this.onEnterFrame = function() {
    if (buttonClick == 1) {
       fruit1 = fruit;
    } else if (buttonClick == 2) {
      delete (this.onEnterFrame);
      fruit2 = fruit;
    }
};
resetTurn();
stop();
```

Note that you delete the onEnterFrame *at the end of tile flip 2. This is to stop the event from continuing to check when the turn is over. As you will see, the end of turn logic involves playing the timeline rather than running an event. This is a good example of mixing event-driven code and frame-based code—the event handler runs when the timeline is stopped, and stops when the timeline runs. When the timeline stops, Flash is still running something via the event handler—it is waiting for a change in the variables, and these will be caused by the buttons in the tiles.*

You moved up a level with this code—Flash is not just running timelines on simple button clicks, but is looking at internal changes caused by button events. You are now making Flash think about what the user clicked rather than simply doing a fixed goto. This is what makes the game seem a little more intelligent than a simple website button menu. Flash is looking for combinations of button clicks, and reacting differently to different sequences. This implies that Flash is making intelligent decisions.

Step 10 covers you for the two tile flips; you now need to check the result. After you set fruit2 to fruit1, the user's turn is over and you check the result.

The first thing you have to do is check whether the two fruit are the same:

```
if (fruit1 == fruit2) {
```

If they are, you have one less pair to find:

```
pairs -= 1;
```

As previously mentioned, this shortcut is used to decrement the variable pairs by 1.

Because the current turn found a match:

```
match = true;
```

Add the following code:

```
this.onEnterFrame = function() {
    if (buttonClick == 1) {
        fruit1 = fruit;
    } else if (buttonClick == 2) {
        delete (this.onEnterFrame);
        fruit2 = fruit;
        if (fruit1 == fruit2) {
            pairs -= 1;
            match = true;
        }
    }
};
resetTurn();
stop();
```

So by the match = true line, you know whether a match was made in the current turn. If a match was made, you need to see if that means the game has finished (that is, the last pair has been found) or if the user still needs to turn more tiles.

There are several ways you can do this part, some of which are very hard (and involve adding an ActionScript pause) and some of which are very easy (and involve simply jumping to two sections of the timeline—one for "Try Again" and one for "Game over, you've won."

Add the following lines to the listing so far:

```
this.onEnterFrame = function() {
    if (buttonClick == 1) {
        fruit1 = fruit;
    } else if (buttonClick == 2) {
        delete (this.onEnterFrame);
        fruit2 = fruit;
        if (fruit1 == fruit2) {
            pairs -= 1;
            match = true;
            if (pairs == 0) {
                gotoAndPlay("won game");
            }
        }
        play();
    }
};
resetTurn();
stop();
```

This last bit of code causes a branch in the timeline depending on what your onEnterFrame (the referee) sees. If it sees that the game has been won, it will go to a frame labeled won game. If it doesn't, you simply restart the timeline from this frame, frame 2. You still need to add these two frames, which you will do almost immediately, after this word from our sponsor.

> It is interesting to note that after the timeline is restarted, it is now acting dumb. You added the intelligent "gateway" that is the referee code that decides which of two outcomes the game is at and restarts the main timeline at two different points depending on what it sees. When that occurs, the referee is switched off (via the delete(onEnterFrame)), and you are back to the free-running linear timelines you looked at in the beginning of the book.
>
> You have actually mixed the two styles of creating Flash—the intelligent code, and the standard dumbly running timeline. You will see more of this throughout this game.

Completing the main timeline

You now need to complete the main timeline. If the main timeline simply continues playing from frame 2, you want it to eventually come back to frame 2 to start the next turn. You want it to run long enough for all the tiles to be flipped, and then you want to go back to frame 2 and start another turn.

1. Select frame 2 of layer actions and give it a frame label of start turn. At frame 10 of layer actions, add a keyframe. On it, add the following code:

   ```
   hadTurn = true;
   ```

   We place this further down the timeline to allow both tiles to be flipped. This frame tells the tiles that the turn is over. It is up to the tiles to find out if they need to turn back around (no match found) or stay face up (match found). You will look at this issue when you return to completing the tiles.

2. At frame 20, add another keyframe and give it a frame label of //end turn. The two forward slashes instruct Flash to add a comment rather than a label, the difference being that a comment is for our benefit and doesn't go into the final SWF (and so saves you a few bytes).

At frame 20, attach the following line of code:

```
gotoAndPlay("start turn");
```

3. Insert a keyframe on frame 50 of the actions layer, and add a keyframe at frame 30. Label the keyframe at frame 30 won game. Your actions layer should look like this:

When the timeline runs, it initializes the variables at frame 2 (using a function defined at frame 1), and then stops and runs a "referee script" that controls the player's turn, allowing the player to flip two tiles. If there is no match, the referee simply restarts the timeline. If this occurs, the timeline will turn hadTurn to true at frame 10, and jump back to frame 2 at frame 20. This will restart the referee—you start a new turn.

If the referee decides the game is won, you jump to frame 30 and start playing from there, bypassing the "next turn" loop. At the moment, nothing happens when you get there, so let's fix that.

4. Add a layer named finished and insert a keyframe in frame 50. Extend the layer tiles to frame 49. On frame 50 of the layer finished, add a suitable You did it!! message—don't worry if it's a bit basic right now, you can embellish it later.

5. Select frame 50 of the layer actions and add a stop(); action. Test your movie.

You'll be able to flip over a tile, and then Flash will wait for you to flip over another tile before continuing. When you've flipped over two tiles, Flash will start back at the beginning of the turn.

You can see what is happening by running our second text movie, tile game_part2.fla. buttonClick never increases beyond 2, and hadTurn changes from false to true for a short period after each pair has turned. When the turn is over, the fruit field and buttonClick are both reset to 0, and the referee is waiting for you to try again with another turn. The problem is that none of the tiles has flipped back over because they haven't been wired to do so.

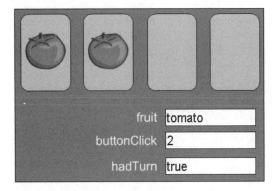

Adding the final touches

The only thing left to do is tell your tiles to stay face up when they are a pair, and you'll also put in a little animation to make them look different when they're matched.

Back in the movie clip, the crucial frame is frame 11. This frame is the brains behind the whole game because it decides what the tile is going to do after it has flipped face up. At the moment, it just looks for the root to tell it whether there are already two tiles turned over via buttonClick. It needs to start looking at hadTurn as well as match. If hadTurn is true, the tiles know that the current turn is finished. They know what they are required to do by looking at match. If the latter is true, they are a matching pair, and they should stay face up. Otherwise, they should flip back to the face-down position.

Sounds like a new problem, right? Well, not really—you want something like what the main timeline is already doing—a bit of code rather like the referee that causes a branch. This time you want to branch between two outcomes—a timeline that keeps the tiles face up, and one that flips them back over. It's the same problem as the one you just worked on in the main timeline!

> *The entire problem on both timelines is one of branching between two possible outcomes. If you used a more rigorous programming route, you would have written this branching code only once, either as a class or as some other encapsulated package. You won't in this exercise, but the important thing you should note is that the basic function of the tile is the same one as the umpire code below it!*

1. The main timeline works by having an onEnterFrame at the start of each turn. The only difference is that you are not controlling a complete turn, but a smaller part of it—a single tile flip that makes up part of a single turn. So the question is "Where does the onEnterFrame have to go on the tile timeline?", right? Wrong! If the problem is the same, you should really be asking where the branch point is this time because that is where the intelligent referee code needs to go. The tile will always do the same thing as it flips over, but once it has fully flipped face up, it can branch two ways—stay face up, or flip back. The branch point is when the tile is fully face up. More specifically, it's frame 10 on the tile timeline. Select frame 10 on the actions layer. This currently has a stop() on it.

   Change it to now read as follows:

   ```
   this.onEnterFrame = function() {
       if (_parent.match) {
           delete (this.onEnterFrame);
           gotoAndPlay("done");
       } else if (_parent.hadTurn) {
           delete (this.onEnterFrame);
           play();
       }
   };
   stop();
   ```

It's essentially a cut-down version of the referee but with different variables. If you have a matching pair, you go to a done frame, and this will run a bit of timeline that keeps the tiles face up. If you have had the current turn and there is no match, the tiles need to turn back over. All you have to do now is add those timeline animations.

2. Because frame 10 is the branching code, you should point it out as special. You can't call it a referee, so how about controller? Cool. Describes it perfectly—the code on frame 10 controls the tile timeline's branching intelligence. Select frame 10 and add a frame label of // controller, which is a comment to remind you of your code structure six months from now when you have completely forgotten about it all.

3. Add a keyframe at frame 30 and label it // down. This is the frame where the tile is back to face down, and is displayed if there was no match. The controller has simply restarted the timeline to show the "flip back" animation from frame 11 to 20. You are done for this turn when you get here and you want to go back to the start, so attach the following to frame 30:

   ```
   gotoAndPlay("facedown");
   ```

4. Add a keyframe at frame 40. Because you actually jump to this frame, Flash needs a label, so enter done as the label. You could simply add a "face up" graphic here, but instead you will have a five-frame victory animation. Add a keyframe at frame 50 and attach a stop() to it. This is the state of play at the end of this step:

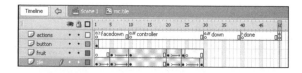

You need to add an animation for a match being found.

5. On the tile layer, insert a keyframe at frames 40 and 50. Select frame 10 in the fruit layer and right-click it to display the context menu. Select Copy Frames. Select frame 40 in the same layer, right-click it as before, and select Paste Frames. Finally, extend this layer to frame 50.

6. On the tile layer, use the Color drop-down in the Properties panel to set the Brightness of the tile in frame 50 to 100% and then put a motion tween between frames 40 and 50 to make it glow when a pair is found.

You can test this glow effect now by playing the movie and turning over two tiles. You can also see our work-in-progress version tile game_part3.fla.

It's time to add the rest of our fruit and get the game working fully.

7. You need a new tile graphic for each of the four fruits—the one that you've been using so far has a tomato on it, so rename mc.tile to mc.tile.tomato.

8. Duplicate this object three times in the Library, and name the copies mc.tile.lemon, mc.tile.orange, and mc.tile.pear.

We'll change the lemon movie clip now, and then you can go back and do the same to the orange and the pear clips. There are two things that you need to do to make the transformation complete: change all the pictures of tomatoes to lemons, and change the ActionScript that tells the timeline which fruit it is.

9. Start by locking all the layers except for fruit. You know that all the keyframes on this layer currently contain a tomato, and you need to change them even when they're squashed so much that you can't see them.

10. Click the first keyframe in frame 5, select the fruit (you will hardly be able to see it, but clicking in the center of the tile should select it), and use the Swap button on the Properties panel to change the tomato for sy.fruit.lemon.

11. Run through the rest of the keyframes in the animation and perform the same operation on each so that all the tomatoes are swapped for lemons.

Once you've done this to all five keyframes, your tomato will look like a lemon, but it will still think it's a tomato. So, you need to retrain it—luckily this isn't as hard as it sounds.

12. On the actions layer, select frame 1, and in the Actions panel change line 3 from

```
_parent.fruit = "tomato";
```

to

```
_parent.fruit = "lemon";
```

That's it. Now you just need to go back through the two fruit conversion stages for your pear and orange movie clips, and you're ready to make the game board. If you're feeling lazy, have a look at tile game_part4.fla.

13. Go back to the tiles layer of your main timeline and delete everything that's currently on the stage in that layer (lock the other layers to do this). Randomly place four of each different tile movie clip into the stage in a 4×4 grid. Use the Align panel to tidy up the tiles and get them into neat rows:

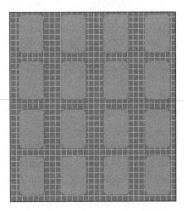

That's it. You're now ready to show off your first complete Flash game. Congratulations. Our final game is included in the code download for this chapter.

Possible improvements and modifications to your game

You're probably staring in disbelief at the title for this section. It's taken you long enough to get the game working, and there's *no way* you're going to change it now. At the back of your mind, though, there's a niggling little voice saying, "It would be nice if there were a few more fruits so I only needed one pair of each, and maybe a few more tiles, and while I'm at it, the victory screen could really do with improving." This section has been dictated by that voice.

- You can add as many tiles as you want, creating a 16×16 or even a 32×32 grid if your eyes are up to seeing tiles that small. All you have to do is change the initial value of pairs (in frame 1 of the main timeline's actions layer) to the number of pairs there are to find. This is actually a nice consequence of the way the game was built—the referee doesn't care how many tiles there are because it only looks at a single turn, and the tiles don't care how many other tiles there are—it just looks to the umpire via the variables it changes.

- You could make a timer or a turn counter to score each game.

- You could make a scoring system where the player scores 5 points for each correct tile, but loses 2 for each wrong tile.

- For those feeling really confident, you could figure out how to make the game deal a random set of tiles every time a new game is started. To do this, you would have to

  - Start with a blank stage.

  - Use ActionScript (via this.attachMovie() from the stage) to place tiles onto the stage in pairs and following the grid layout at runtime. You would probably need to use an array for Flash to know where it had already placed tiles as it does this.

> *If you want to get Flash to place the tiles randomly, you will probably need to use a* for *loop that runs eight times, and each time this should place two tiles of the same fruit.*

This game is more advanced than the simple mouse trail it's derived from. You can use it as the basis of other, even more advanced games. You could, for example, take the basic mc.tile and because it allows you to model a generalized playing card object, make some rather cool card games.

But what has this to do with website design? Websites and games are two branches of a tree called **interactivity**. There is an offshoot from the website branch that's very close to the game branch, and that offshoot is called **advanced website design**. Both use lots of clever bits of ActionScript to create their animations, interfaces, and effects. By learning simple games, you're priming yourself for the design and coding of complex sites.

> *There's another very basic reason for including games on a website. Web marketing studies have shown that games cause a visitor to return to a site even if the games have little to do with the site's subject matter.*

In particular:

- The way you mixed event handlers and timeline animation is no longer beginner stuff. You are no longer a beginner—you are well into intermediate.

- The way you solved two seemingly different problems (i.e., you found that a game turn is fundamentally the same as a tile flip) is an advanced concept. It's the type of thinking that will make classes and object-oriented programming seem like child's play once you have worked out the syntax.

The next chapter will start to look at website design and point you on your way. You've reached base camp one on the ActionScript Mount Everest, and armed with what you've learned so far and that little niggling voice that keeps on asking questions and tells you to try new things, the only way is up. Never lose sight of the main goal and keep having fun—it'll be worth it.

Summary

In this chapter, you've dipped your toes into the vast ocean that is object-oriented design and programming. You looked at the basic principles of the OO programming approach and seen how you can map this onto the movie clip objects you use in Flash.

You saw that

- Object-oriented design and programming delivers solutions that are

  - Reusable

  - Extensible

  - Flexible

- The key to OO design and programming is the ability to conceptualize the surface detail of a problem until you can define its absolutely essential components.

- A class defines the characteristics of one of those components—what it is, what it can do, what its characteristics are, and how it communicates with other components. The class is a template.

- An object is an individual instance built using the class template.

- In Flash, you can think of a named movie clip instance on the stage as an object. This object is derived from the original Library movie clip symbol. All instances of the symbol on the stage will share the same essential properties, but you can customize them so that their behavior and properties individualize them.

- Simple movie clip objects can be combined to produce complex effects.

In the next chapter, you're going to look at the considerations you need to take into account when you're designing your Flash site.

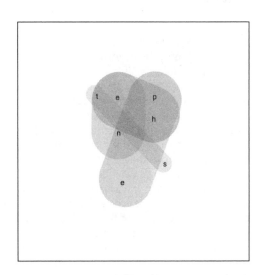

Chapter 17

HIGH-LEVEL SITE DESIGN

What we'll cover in this chapter:

- The principles of good design
- Website file structure and management
- Dynamic website design
- Recommended websites

At this point in the book, you can afford to congratulate yourself on your new status as a Flash programmer/designer. It has been a hard road, but it has been worth it. Before you rush off into the crowded world of web design, though, there are a couple more things to think about. So far, this book has been about the technical implementation of your ideas inside Macromedia Flash, but this chapter will run through some tips on what to do when you have that first spark of inspiration and how to make sure your ideas will work on the Web. This chapter will give you a rough guide to some of the dos and don'ts of designing for the Web, both by reminding you of some of the considerations discussed earlier in the book, and by drawing new ones to your attention. At the end of the chapter, Kris recommends some sites that will fire your imagination and get those designs flowing. First, I'm going to discuss some of the principles I follow when creating my designs.

The principles of good design

When I was in my early twenties, I worked on a design team that created VDU displays for nuclear power plants. The plant's operators would use the screens as their primary point of reference to see what was going on all over the plant. In an emergency, the reactor engineers had to be able to access the information they needed as quickly as possible, so the VDU displays had to present that information in a form they could understand immediately. It was important that the screens never showed too much information—just the relevant information that the engineer requested.

The rules I followed to resolve this project are just as important to the work I do today because now, as then, my projects have the same basic requirements: usability and clarity. Of course, websites have to be engaging, interesting, and entertaining as well, but that has more to do with the content than the design. Before users can be engaged, interested, and entertained by the content, they have to be able to *find* the content. There are sites out there that intentionally break the rules and are entertaining because of it, but the people who design those sites can get away with this because they're always aware of the rules they're breaking.

These principles, as important as they are for the usability of your site, won't bring you success on their own: originality is another defining feature of good web design. Sites that don't catch the eye and draw in the mind with good ideas and solid graphic design will get fewer visitors.

Flash is a cost- and bandwidth-effective design tool with loads of features that enable you to engage your visitors with compelling visuals and sound. One of the reasons that Flash is so prevalent on the Web is that is has such a high number of creative options, all of which are viewable with the small and simple Flash Player. However, viewers will leave your site if they've already seen it all before or are fed up with the two-minute download time. There's a fine line between multimedia and junk media, and designers must always be aware of which side they're on. In your design career, you must balance creativity with practicality—in this chapter, I talk about both.

File structure and file size

Whenever you create anything for the Web, you have to be aware—even if it's only in the back of your mind—of what the Web is and what it will do to your presentation as your files are downloaded or streamed. I talked about these issues in Chapters 13 and 14, "Optimizing" and "Publishing," but I'll reiterate some of the main points again here:

- Be aware of download times and optimize as much as possible to lower them.

- Differentiate between what's central to the message you're trying to get across and what's just eye (or ear) candy. If download times are an issue, you should know which parts of your movie should be the first to end up on the cutting room floor.

- Consider a multiple loadMovie download strategy to avoid a large initial download (see Chapter 14, "Publishing," for more details).

- Take special care with bitmaps and sound. Optimize them all individually and don't rely on the global export settings to do the job for you.

- When using video, consider making a number of Flash files in various sizes for different user bandwidths. Load these in with loadMovie.

- Choose your symbols carefully and use a "one symbol often" approach instead of using lots of symbols once.

- Remember that ActionScript-based "sprite" animation is particularly bandwidth friendly. It requires far fewer frames than the corresponding tween-based animations.

The chapters on optimizing and publishing explained how to structure your movies correctly, but I'll reiterate the main points because your increased understanding of ActionScript will help you understand the basis of more advanced solutions.

Preloaders

I introduced you to preloaders earlier. I work with three levels of preloader, so I'll give you a brief reminder of their varying degrees of complexity.

Basic: Timeline-based loader

I introduced this basic preloader in the "Optimizing" chapter. I recommend this option if you don't want to get your hands dirty with ActionScript or if you have a relatively simple and small SWF.

Intermediate: ActionScript-based loader

You can build a very efficient ActionScript preloader by looking at the _framesloaded and _totalframes properties of your movie. You can view these two properties of the main Timeline just like any other variable by using the Properties tab in the Debugger window.

You want to create a simple animation that keeps the user interested while the main site loads. You use ActionScript to stop playing the animation and display the main site once the movie properties _totalframes and _framesloaded are equal to each other. When these two values are equal, the whole of your SWF has been loaded.

Intermediate/advanced: Event driven loader

The most sophisticated (and efficient) preloader is one that uses the MovieClipLoader class. This inbuilt ActionScript class allows you to set up event handlers that will run when your content has loaded, and also when your content has loaded and is ready to be controlled by ActionScript. It also provides methods that can be used to create an efficient "percent loaded" type graphic.

Using the MovieClipLoader class is the best choice because event-driven code is also the fastest and most efficient way of handling preloading.

Intros

What you show during your preload is another major concern. A good intro (the animation that hides your preload) will draw the viewer into the main website, whereas a poor one is like a heavy rock band's drum solo—it goes on for *far* too long.

As a general rule, always have something interesting going on while the main site is loading. As I've said, the average Internet surfer won't stay long if you display a "please wait, loading" screen. Your intro must

- Show users what will be missed if they exit the site.
- Give an indication of the quality of the actual main website.
- Give viewers the option to skip past the intro if they want to.

Different types of websites require different intros. If you're creating a website advertising yourself as a website designer, you'll want to show off your technical ability and give the potential client a showcase of your advanced understanding of complex animation and graphic design ability. If you're designing an information service for a bank, however, you won't want to spend time showing fancy animations. Viewers of a site like that want to see the information they came to look at, and they want it *fast and clear*. They should be attracted to the site by a cool and slick Flash design, but once they decide to open an account, the route to the "Sign me up" page must just be a click away and free of overindulgent Flash animation and tricks. Making your design appropriate to your client and audience is a vital consideration.

Tailoring your designs

There are several constraints and features that you need to be aware of when building a website. Here are a number of checklist items that you should be aware of when you're ready to build your main site.

Timeframe

We all want to build the coolest Flash sites possible, but if you're doing this for a living, you need to think about how soon the site needs to be completed. A good, delivered-on-time site will always yield a satisfied customer, whereas a brilliant, cutting-edge site delivered three weeks late won't. Remember, it's very difficult to change a site once it's up, because people tend to get accustomed to the navigation and style. So be careful—unless, of course, the change is the client's idea and they're paying by the hour!

Style

The style you choose for the site is defined in part by the content and the impression that the client wants to get across to the viewer. When defining a style, be careful to choose one that's suited to the message rather than one that's easy to create in Flash. A lot of the time, the client already has a brief or advertising campaign that the site will be part of, so you should be flexible enough to incorporate your client's ideas and jump between styles.

Content

Unless you're creating a site based on a very specific brief for which the client provided all the site graphics and type, you'll have to find a way to hold the audience's attention long enough to get the site's message across. The coolest visual Flash interface will be ignored if it's not properly integrated with something interesting.

Navigation

The content of your site will greatly influence the navigation you create for it. In some (especially commercial) sites, there's often a route that you would prefer the visitor to take—the one that will most likely result in a sale or a click-through to your sponsor. Your navigation must make this route clear. Other sites are based around a central hub with numerous links going out to subtopics. With these sites, it's important that users can quickly access *any* area of the site, and as a general rule, they should be able to do it within two clicks.

Because there's no substitute for practical experience, I've included a walk-through of some site designs to illustrate the different methods of visualizing and creating a website.

Case study 1: online showcase

A few years ago (which equates to several decades in Flash years), I found a weathered poetry book dating back to Victorian England. Reading it, I was particularly taken by how different the thinking was from that of the 21st Century—whereas we live in an age in which everything is out in the open (especially on the Web), they had a much more closed and hidden society.

I decided to put an updated and fully interactive version of the book on the Web using all the new technology available to me. I wanted to create a website with the same look and feel of the book to give viewers a sense of the cultural and behavioral beliefs in that bygone world. But I wanted to present it via Flash animations.

Before I went into the Flash implementation, I had to have a very clear idea of what I wanted to create because I could see this being a very large project. I had to do two things:

- Create a set of storyboards and sketches that gave me a graphical direction and template
- Create the text, making sure that it matched the graphical style

Storyboarding

I had to define the look of the final website before I could begin. For the site to work, I knew it would have to be true to the original concept. I decided that the original book would play a part in the final look.

However, I had a problem: to navigate through a book, you turn pages. Going to a particular page is easy when you're holding the book because you can feel the paper's thickness—so you know if you want to go a point one-third of the way into the book, you just open

the book at one-third of its thickness. You can't do that with a 2D representation on a monitor. Here's the rough sketch that solved the problem:

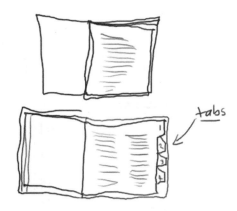

By looking at the way address books use tabs to help you quickly find a particular section of names—the Newmans and the Newton-Johns under "N," for example—I was able to create a 2D representation of a book that was still easy to navigate. Each tab would represent a chapter of the book.

To get the effect of old book pages, I used a cheap flatbed scanner to scan an image of a small notebook I'd carried with me in my coat pocket for close to a year. Then I got some newspaper that had faded to yellow in the sun and scanned that in too. I cobbled it all together in Photoshop so that it looked like this:

I now had an idea of what my open book would look like. The animated poems would appear in the page area as SWF files. Next, I needed to create my navigation tabs.

I also needed something to allow users to move between the individual pages of each chapter. I needed last page and next page buttons. I also needed a help button somewhere, so I sketched that in as well.

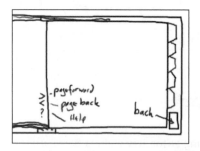

These sketches were created using a Wacom pen tablet. It's a quick way to make initial sketches, and it helps workflow because you can import the images directly into Flash (or whatever program you're using), rather than having to scan it and then fiddle with image resolution, color depth, and so on.

With my basic site structure worked out, I needed to make sure I could create a convincing set of tabs for navigation before I started devoting time to Flash programming. I went back into Photoshop to mock it all up.

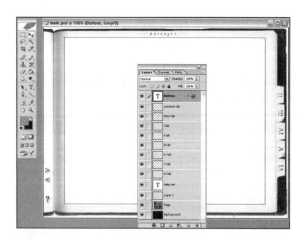

I put each tab on a separate layer to simulate the effect of a page being turned. I also used Adobe ImageReady, a web page preparation tool, and some JavaScript to create a simple HTML version of the book to see if the navigation was workable—and thankfully it was.

As you can see, removing tabs gives the impression that you've moved further into the book. Luckily, the fact that your virtual book still has the same number of pages left no matter how far into the book you are doesn't seem to kill the illusion.

By mocking up my ideas in Photoshop first, I proved to myself that the concept of a virtual book was a viable one before spending my time trying to get it working in Flash. As an added advantage, I now also had some bitmap images I could trace into Flash.

Content

The book would be called *Passages*, and it would be about the one journey we all make—the journey through life. Victorian society was full of double standards, and had a very rich upper class and a chronically poor underclass (maybe things haven't changed *that* much). Using this as a starting point, I wanted the book to liken an individual's lifetime to a child who's secretly in a rich man's mansion, seeing what's there and taking whatever he can.

Here are two initial storyboards done in Photoshop:

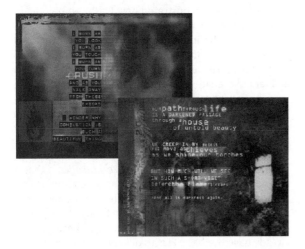

The pages were also made to turn with a simple tween animation, which you can see in this under-construction shot:

The first page is an introduction to the book, and the second is a poem called "crush." Both of these compositions are multilayer Photoshop files. By moving the individual layers around in real time, I gave myself a good idea of how the text should appear and how the individual elements should move. These shots show the last frame in each animation. There are approximately 40 animations for the whole *Passages* sequence, which follows your young thief through an entire lifetime using the metaphor of his trip through the mansion.

By now I had lots of images, sketches, and text, and I was ready to mold it into a site. Time to start looking at Flash.

Integration

The book had to look real. It had to have pages that turned. Contemporary native Photoshop files can be imported into Flash, but with such large file sizes, you're better off splitting the layers and exporting them as separate GIFs, PNGs, or JPEGs, as I did in this project. The separated Photoshop images were first converted to vectors and rebuilt as fully animated movie clips. Here's the final Flash symbol of the front of the *Passages* book, which is a fairly faithful reproduction of the original book's cover:

Here's the finished, open book in Flash. The whole book and associated animations come in at a little over 20K.

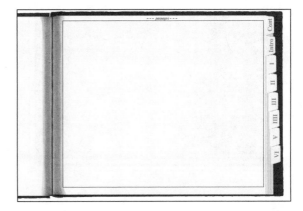

Next I built a simple intro to play as the book animations and graphics loaded. (The individual poems would come in as onLoad movie levels, using the loading manager I mentioned earlier.)

I wanted to introduce specific symbols to represent the themes of *Passages*: the Victorian ideas of life and mortality. For life, I chose a butterfly, and for mortality, I scanned in an image of a human spine from Gray's Anatomy. There were two advantages to this second choice: it was written in the Victorian period, and its engravings are royalty free—providing you don't copy the whole book. Neat.

> *New designers need to pay careful attention to issues of copyright and royalties to avoid getting themselves into unwanted, and perhaps costly, trouble.*

The butterfly appears in the introduction, and flits through the book as you turn certain pages. The image of the spine is shown as a recurring theme throughout the book as well.

figure 1a
Existence

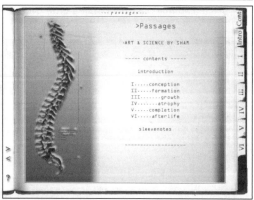

Summary

This case study demonstrated how Flash can be used in a creative way to make websites that are unlike anything else on the Internet. At its lowest level, *Passages* is nothing more than an online showcase of related Flash movies. However, by creating an overall style and ambience, the site will hopefully become much more than its individual components. I hoped users would forget that they're viewing a Flash website and become drawn into its strange and beautiful world—in the very way I was when I first found that old book.

The best thing about something like *Passages* is that it has no heavy ActionScript; it's all about basic artistic skills and ideas. Those of you who are coming into Flash from a Photoshop or graphic design background could create something like this now because you already have the basic Flash skills required to pull it off.

Mocking up the site and prototyping it in Photoshop and ImageReady was one of the most important parts of this site's creation. Flash doesn't have the tools to take in bitmaps and other scanned data in the same way Photoshop does, and for this reason a lot of professional designers use Photoshop for the initial design and storyboarding. Even when used in the simple ways shown here, Photoshop and Flash form the basis of a very powerful set of visualization tools for the designer—whatever he or she is designing.

Case study 2: my Flash home site interface

Designing your own home site is when you get to play. Some designers use it to show off and compete with other designers, but I think that's just asking for trouble—whenever another designer uses a new technique, you'll have to go one better. That kind of technological "arms race" isn't my idea of fun—I prefer to be creative.

The first example was all about design—how to get those vague ideas in your head onto a digital canvas by creating a plan and then animating the elements in Flash.

The next example looks at the sites that start as a folder full of half-finished ideas and uncompleted FLA files that you don't know what to do with—and then something in your head links them all together and an idea hits you out of nowhere.

Random idea #1

As I was driving down a busy highway, I noticed some large billboards by the side of the road. It put the idea in my head that sometimes size really "makes" a picture—wouldn't it be nice to have a browser that was as big as a billboard?

I decided I would try to do just that. But if you had a really big site, how would you see it all? The browser is way too small. Then I remembered a book called *Fahrenheit 451*, by Ray Bradbury. In it, cars moved so fast that the only way people could read the ads they drove past would be if the billboards were miles long and the images and text on them were stretched out to that length. At that speed, the stretched images would look normal. I decided to try and do the same with my site design: stretch it out horizontally into a really long billboard site.

I created a new movie, modified it to 2880 pixels by 600 pixels, and then set the publish width to 300% by 95%, just to see what would happen. It looks nice as a design concept because the user would have to scroll from left to right to get to the actual website at the end, where they would get an eye full of oversized logo (I've used one of mine as an example). Because this is a novel format (or will be until you all try it yourselves), the average web user will remember the first site that used it. As mentioned at the outset of this chapter, originality is an important component of your sites.

Random idea #2

Another thought was buzzing around my head at around the same time as I was thinking about the long billboard: my VCR was broken, so whenever I played anything on it, I got a horrible picture that was totally unviewable. It was the kind of snowy, fuzzed picture you get when you play a video that's a copy of a copy of a copy. In a funny way, though, I liked the mangled image on the screen. I imagined, somewhat dramatically, technology breaking out of our control and refusing to be mastered.

With this on my mind, I happened to walk past a shop that had a lot of TVs on at the same time in a four-by-four grid. No two screens showed exactly the same picture: one was brighter than the others, one was more red, one had a lower saturation, and so on.

I imagined the same effect in my browser window—separate "TV screens," each doing its own thing—and I decided to create this effect.

I used an array of little movies that sit on top of an underlying SWF, similar to the grid in the following graphic. If you read Chapter 8, "Masks and Masking," you'll no doubt have a good understanding of how this is done.

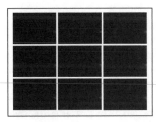

All I needed now was my broken VCR effect in each segment.

I built a set of little objects that randomly applied distorted noise effects to the underlying SWF. Remarkably, the whole thing worked! It looked a little bit like the video walls you still see in some bars or clubs that show one picture on a grid of TVs—each TV showing a separate square portion of the image.

I now needed something to tie my two media-related ideas—the billboard and the TV grid—together.

Integration

I don't know what made me put the television grid on the end of my billboard, but I did, and it worked. I was just playing around, putting this grid idea over other SWFs and looking at how it mangled everything up. I was just having fun. Even when the underlying SWF was motionless, there was still plenty of movement going on.

I needed a menu bar to really tie it all together, and I was still in love with the test patterns I mentioned earlier, so I created a row of rectangles that approximated the color bars. It's shown in grayscale here, but it's in fact the color progression you see on a color TV—white, yellow, cyan, green, magenta, red, and blue.

This menu bar is made up of little button objects that the user can press to navigate the site. The buttons wobble—when you press one, it expands and contracts and moves as though it were made of Jello. These wobblers are wrapped within a parent object called "menu." When one wobbler expands, the others contract (and vice versa) to preserve the overall length of the menu bar.

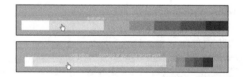

The menu bar buttons wobble with a delay so it looks a bit like a big plastic band, producing a bouncing effect that's fascinating and disorienting at the same time.

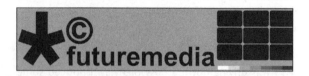

So here's my idea for my new Flash home site. You have to scroll in from left to right, going over the oversized billboard logo. Once you get to the far right end of the site and the mouse passes over the TV screens, they spring to life and play their test patterns and video noise until you click something. If you click a link to another website, you don't see it in a new window—it appears in the TV screens! Every now and again one of the screens gets a little brighter or loses synch or something, and the longer you leave the mouse still, the more pronounced the effect becomes.

The screens also display images even when the user hasn't clicked anything: little MTV-type animations, Japanese Manga cartoons, or grainy video footage taken from the cameras in missile nose cones during the first Persian Gulf war. I wanted to add things in those screens that are possibly *better* than the things the visitor came to see—I wanted my visitors to say "Never mind looking at the websites—missile command just showed up in the top-left corner! Quick—figure out the keys before it disappears!"

Summary

I hope that walking through these examples made you enthusiastic about creating your own innovative sites. Most of what you need to learn to achieve something like these sites is covered in the ActionScript chapters.

Don't overlook Flash as a tool for just trying out ideas. Maybe you'll start a collection of effects that you like but that have been done to death. You can take the best aspects of each and create something unique to use on your own site.

Most designers have a little box of collected effects, but unfortunately, some never change what they keep in it. The best designers are always on the lookout for new coding ideas. When they can offer a client the chance to be the first site to use a particular effect, they can ensure themselves a better chance of getting the job.

Dynamic websites

Even before Flash 8, building dynamic websites in Flash was fast becoming one of its key uses. In essence, Flash Basic 8 and Flash Professional 8 have significantly built up the dynamic armory and have cemented Flash as a prime tool for producing dynamic websites and applications.

Even though only some Flash users will grab hold of the dynamic beastie, it's well worth being aware of some of the considerations involved.

Case study 3: a dynamic visual guestbook

One night I had an idea to build a website guestbook that would build an archive of visitors' names. But unlike standard guestbooks, this archive would provide a visual representation of the visitors' names.

A dynamic site in Flash works by pulling in information (such as variables) from a data store, called a database, and displaying or processing the information in Flash. Usually, when fetching or sending information to or from the database, a server-side scripting language is used.

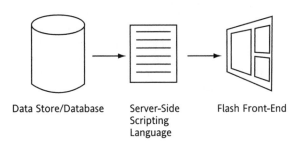

Data Store/Database   Server-Side Scripting Language   Flash Front-End

You might have already heard of a few server-side scripting languages such as PHP, ASP.NET, Java, or ColdFusion. Server-side scripting languages are beyond the scope of this book, but there are many different ways to develop your knowledge in this area. However, I'd advise that you get comfortable with ActionScript before attempting to integrate these languages with Flash.

For the guestbook, I decided to use a complex line-to-line structure to represent the names visually, a little like the way constellations are depicted in astronomy books. Each letter of the name would have a point, and two lines would connect one letter with the next. The first letter would start off the lines, the last letter would be the ending, and each letter would be randomly placed.

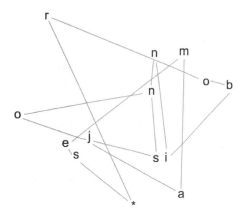

Rather than stick to a dull black-and-white canvas, I decided to incorporate a little color and different stroke widths. I came up with a set of simple rules to create some diversity:

- The color of each line is determined by the position in the alphabet of each letter of the user's name.
- The number of lines drawn is proportionate to the number of letters in the user's name.
- The stroke size and positioning of each letter is random, so no two names have the same visual representation.

All these factors are set using ActionScript in Flash, stored as variables, and then sent to the database for storage.

Given the stated rules, "Stephen" looks like this:

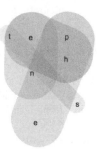

Once the user has seen his or her name in shapes, it's randomly placed with all the other "nameshapes" of previous visitors. The more people who sign the guestbook, the bigger the collective image will be, until all the layers are so thick that the stage is a mass of color and the guestbook needs to be cleared.

However, if I chose to clear the guestbook every month, an archive of all the previous months could be placed on display, forming a totally different image for each month. When a visitor views the guestbook, all the names and the visual information for each one are pulled from the database, and the composition is drawn in Flash.

If all this dynamic stuff sounds a little complicated, don't be put off. It's not an essential learning component for a designer (phew!). However, as you advance with ActionScript, you might also find yourself interested in learning other technologies. There's plenty of documentation available on the Web and in numerous books.

A number of books covering dynamic content technologies and their integration with Flash are available from the publisher of this very book, friends of ED. This includes Foundation PHP 5 for Flash, by David Powers, Foundation ASP.NET for Flash, by Ryan Moore, and Foundation XML for Flash, by Sas Jacobs.

If you really don't want to learn all this back-end stuff, fortunately there are programmers dedicated to making all this stuff happen. In this case, the communication between you and the back-end programmer is crucial. You must be sure that you both agree on naming conventions for variables and such, and you both need to understand how the two elements will tie together. (It goes without saying that you both will meet your deadlines, of course.)

Either way, dynamic sites are the next big thing, and Flash—Flash Professional in particular—has a lot of added functionality specifically designed for building dynamic web applications, so it pays to be familiar with some of the concepts involved.

Suggested sites

Now that you have a better understanding of how websites are created, the best place to start looking at Flash sites is the Web itself. As promised at the start of the chapter, here are some quick suggestions:

- www.presstube.com: This site is packed with loads of amazing linear and interactive animations. You might notice that most of the Flash files are published with the quality set to low, giving them an altogether different kind of texture.

- www.yugop.com: Yugop's creator, Yugo Nakamura, is always one step ahead of the pack, and his current pickings are better than ever. The creations on this site are truly amazing, and set the standard for other Flashers.

- www.levitated.net: This site contains a massive archive of beautiful Flash experiments showcasing the power of ActionScript combined with logic, written by Jared Tarbell among others. This site has all kinds of advanced elements, from basic interactivity to behavioral OOP (object-oriented programming). Many of the Flash files shown on this site are also available to download (be warned—this is advanced scripting).

- www.vectorama.org: This multiuser design pad allows a number of players to create a digital composition—working on the same canvas! Whereas the premise is to encourage collaboration with the other designers, this often turns sour, and the kill command comes in handy for destroying other people's hard work. For those of you who want to go out and imitate this site, be aware that it's built in both Flash and Director, and has a pretty hefty back-end too.

- www.friendsofed.com/fmc: Not a friends of ED plug at all, but a demonstration of how ActionScript can be used creatively to design some beautiful compositions. Many of the movies start simple, and with slight code changes, they progress, mutate, and develop.

- www.derbauer.de: This site is just amazing. These people really know how to put their images to use. The programmers and designers have created a slick, well-designed site. Even though the file sizes are large, the site is easy to navigate and is extremely interactive.

- www.banja.com: Great animations and a great game. Islands, treasures, pirates—the whole bit. Excellent interactivity and well-thought-out design that loads fast for such a large game.

- www.ferryhalim.com/orisinal: The lush graphics and simple addictive games here make this site a must-see. If you aspire to make games in Flash, look no further than here for some inspiration.

- http://demo.fb.se/e/v50/site: This is a commercial site with a fantastic use of video and interactivity in Flash. The fact that everything in sight can be interacted with makes the site very pleasing and tactile. Broadband is required for this hefty download.

- www.bit-101.com: This is the lplayground of Keith Peters, who regularly posts his Flash experiments and creations for others to marvel at and share. Most of the code available for download here is advanced ActionScript, so until you're confident enough to work out what's happening, you'll still be able to tweak the scripts and have fun.

Summary

The summary for this chapter is short and sweet:

- Learn
- Work
- Explore
- Plan
- Play

Great Flash design comes from continually honing your design and Flash skills, from innovation, and from trying things out as you go. Remember that time spent monkeying around with little movie clips and effects can pay dividends later.

In the final chapter, you're going to look at some other Flash areas that are ripe for exploration as you build your Flash future.

Chapter 18

FUTURESCAPE

What we'll cover in this chapter:

- Where to go next with your new Flash skills
- Using and improving your Flash skills
- Starting a career in Flash

Where next?

Flash has come a long way from being just a superb animation package. Flash is capable of producing fully functional web applications that are rich in graphics, sound, video, and interactivity. As a complete web application in its own right, Flash is rapidly becoming the web developer's tool of choice for creating a whole range of e-commerce, entertainment, and community sites. Flash can talk to web servers in a highly sophisticated way, meaning that (with ActionScript) dynamic content is within everyone's reach, and Flash has become integrated with other web standard technologies such as XML.

The latest version of Flash, Flash 8, has added a large number of features that make it the ideal tool for more creative endeavors. Real-time blending and filtering modes and video enhancements mean that you can use Flash as a multimedia platform for web-based art pieces or cool and immersive web designs.

As well as the additional graphic features, the Flash player enables you to create content that is fast as well as bandwidth-friendly via a drawing engine that can now handle bitmap graphics as well as it can handle vectors.

You've now learned the basic skills required for Flash competence. In the space of a few hundred pages, you've gone from a ground-level beginner making a mushroom grow, to an intermediate programmer coding interactive games and websites.

Mastering these new skills completely will keep you occupied for many months to come as you explore the full range of your powers. But before too long, you're going to want to do more. You'll be hungry for new knowledge and new skills, and you'll want to wring every possible design opportunity from Flash and from the Internet as a whole.

Using and improving your Flash skills

There are numerous Flash tutorial sites out on the Web, and most have beginners' sections. Most new Flash effects and interfaces seem to end up being deconstructed and presented as how-to tutorials within a very short time, so if there's a particular design effect you want to know more about, check out the Web first. Be sure to try the Macromedia newsgroups as well; these tend to provide a good way of picking up the knowledge of some of the older hands. My advice, though, is to check out the FAQs of these groups before asking questions of your own, as most beginner questions will have been covered.

Here are some good starting points for Flash resources on the Web:

- www.macromedia.com/support/flash
- www.friendsofed.com/forums
- www.flashmove.com
- www.flashmagazine.com
- www.ultrashock.com

Flash web design presents the user with a large number of different fields to look at. You only have to look at a few sites created by the Flash masters to realize that the variation in Flash sites is greater than that exhibited by any other web technology currently on view. From cartoon sites to futuristic-looking 3D sites, Flash has a large amount of the best of the Web covered. To give you an idea of some of the areas you may want to find out more about, I'm going to briefly introduce them to you now.

Flash site design

By far the easiest way to get noticed in the world of web design is to create your own site. Even if you're not a designer, you can create a site that sells you as one. By the time you've finished it, you will be a designer!

This is such a standard route into Flash design that it's almost a cliché; boy/girl meets Flash, boy/girl falls in love with Flash and creates something new and cool with it, boy/girl gets a job at <insert top web design house> based on their work.

The first thing that always happens at the end of the first attempt is the realization of how you could have done it all better. Usually, this realization comes hand in hand with a better understanding of ActionScript. That part of Flash may seem a little alien even now, but the only way to learn it is to use it often—it all starts to make sense when you finally revamp your clunky, bandwidth-heavy first site into your sleek, multiloading, quick and efficient version 2.0 site.

Flash games and toys

Getting noticed as a designer is hard work, and you need to find a way to get your skills recognized. One way to attract attention is by designing quality games, because games and toys can be a good way to hold a viewer's attention. You could add them to an existing site that's in need of new blood, or make them into a site in their own right where people can witness your Flash experimentation. If this is the area you're interested in, perhaps existing sites that need perking up with some Flash interaction would be willing to incorporate your work—if you give them enough of a nudge.

Check out http://ferryhalim.com/orisinal as a top example of the kind of interactive games you can create in Flash.

Flash cartoons

As a pure animation tool, Flash shouldn't be underestimated. Managing the timeline with the skills you've learned in this book can produce highly professional looking animations. You can generate drawings within Flash itself, scan in photos or drawings you've generated by hand to give a less computerized appearance to your work, or import work from other applications that give you more flexibility when creating your images (as you saw in the walk-through in the previous chapter).

The animation features of Flash are used in preliminary work for TV production, for mocking up commercials, and more recently, to produce content for the Sony PlayStation 2. Take a look at the Flash webisodes at www.s4studios.com, one of which is a Flash-animated trailer for Sony's "Twisted Metal: Black" game.

Alternatively, you can get noticed by becoming a Flash animator. Web animation is finally coming to the fore, given that bandwidth is creeping up and feature-length animations delivered across the Web are commonplace. See the following for some great examples:

- http://bs.brokensaints.com
- www.ninjai.com
- www.brackenwood.net

Using Flash with other software

In addition to using Flash in isolation, many designers use Flash in conjunction with other software, such as Macromedia's Multiuser Server included with Director. Using this application, designers can set up interactive sites—for example, enabling real-time multiuser online gaming and interaction—without having to learn new server-side scripting languages. Combinations such as this allow you to extend the use of Flash beyond whole web applications and into stand-alone programs.

Although Flash has its own drawing tools, there's a lot to be said for using programs such as FreeHand, Photoshop, and others to enhance the available options of Flash presentations. Many designers take this initial approach when designing their web projects. However, always make sure to optimize anything you bring into Flash because some of these image-manipulation applications aren't quite as web savvy as Flash can be.

Nevertheless, a sound understanding of Adobe Photoshop goes a long way toward helping create excellent Flash content.

Using sound effectively in Flash is another exciting area to investigate. Although creating sound can become very expensive, there are many entry-level options available—all you need is a good sound card as your main device, and shareware or freeware tracking and sequencing software.

3D in Flash

As some of the examples in this book—as well as many of the recommended sites—have shown, adding a 3D element to your work can achieve impressive results, and give your sites an extra edge over conventional Flash work. The applications available are well worth getting involved with; if a client wants a 3D version of their logo on their site, you want to make sure you're in the running for the job.

As the demands placed on websites increase and become more varied, 3D-rendering skills are becoming more desirable. Adding this ability to your impressive Flash résumé will do you no harm at all. Flash is well suited to the use of 3D images, and whether you're trying to make your name as a designer, or merely using Flash for fun, you'll find that using 3D objects will add to your success. Check out **Swift 3D** (www.swift3D.com)— a Flash-friendly 3D tool that can output SWF files, which you can then load in your movies.

Note that there's also a Swift 3D plug-in that works directly from the Flash interface. As of this writing, the plug-in is available for Flash MX 2004 only, but visit www.erain.com/products/Xpress for the latest information.

Advanced ActionScript-based Flash interface designs

ActionScript is now a major force in web programming, and now that you know the basics—more than just the basics in fact—thanks to this book, you'll no doubt be bursting to know what other possibilities are offered by this web wonder. Using ActionScript is a skill in itself, and knowledge of it will be a tremendous benefit to your designing. You saw in the later chapters of the book what effects can be achieved, but you've only seen the tip of the ActionScript iceberg. When you really flesh out your ability, the Flash designs you create will be sure to please and astound you. The sister book to this one, *Foundation ActionScript for Flash 8*, shows you how to create the home site of one of the authors of this book, a complete ActionScript-heavy website. See www.futuremedia.org.uk and/or the download page for the *Foundation ActionScript for Flash 8* book, where you can have a sneak peek of the files as soon as the book is published.

Dynamic content

With a good knowledge of ActionScript, you can go on to combine server-side architectures with Flash front-ends to create dynamic websites. You can pass data between the browser and web server using ActionScript in conjunction with a whole range of server-side scripting languages such as PHP and ASP/ASP.NET. You can also use a middleware package such as Macromedia ColdFusion. This is Macromedia's server back-end of choice for combining with Flash, and even closer integration of these products is expected in the future.

XML

Flash includes support for the eXtensible Markup Language (**XML**), which is already a web standard for disseminating data in a form that can be interpreted anywhere, on any device, and rendered according to the abilities of that device and the needs of the user.

Because XML tags can be used to tell a browser something *about* the included information rather than just *how to display it*, XML is taking off in a number of areas, including e-commerce, intelligent search engines, and wireless devices. Flash's ability to deal with XML data in ActionScript, coupled with the rich multimedia features that Flash is famous for, mean that Flash can be a powerful player in a world where XML and data-driven web applications are becoming ever more popular.

Flash is branching out into a whole new set of contexts—for all kinds of wireless and non-PC web devices, such as PDAs and cellular phones.

Starting a career in Flash

Flash has now become the standard for dynamic animation and sound on the Web. It follows, therefore, that it's also a discipline that can be used to form part of a career in web design. The question many people tend to ask is "How do you get your foot in the door?"

If you're so taken with Flash that you're considering attempting to earn a living as a Flash designer, you'll have to stop a moment and consider the following issues.

HTML

Most employers and agencies expect you to know something about HTML. This is something that's becoming less of a constraint as time passes and the majority of operations adopt site/HTML-creation packages like Macromedia Dreamweaver. However, a lot of Flash web design positions still require you to know HTML. Even if this isn't the case, I would be very surprised to find Flash positions that don't require an understanding of Dreamweaver. Some understanding of JavaScript is usually an advantage too, as ActionScript is based on JavaScript—good news for you, as it means there's less to learn to achieve competency.

Graphic design

Web design is an offshoot of a much wider discipline called graphic design. As a web designer, you won't be expected to get your pencils and paints out, but a knowledge of computer-based graphic design and layout packages is usually a distinct advantage—Adobe Photoshop is usually stipulated as a standard of competency. It's also worth your while to consider a point that the earlier chapters alluded to: with the ever-increasing competition for web surfers, your potential clients are going to take it for granted that you can produce a functional site. They're going to want something that's visually appealing *as well*—so your artistic skills need to be up to the job.

Getting in

As mentioned earlier, having an impressive home site is one of the best ways to get noticed on the Web. There are a number of well-known Flash designers who started out by building a killer home site. Having a cutting edge site doesn't necessarily mean that you have to be an ActionScript or 3D guru—there are plenty of other site styles that will appeal to users—humor, animation, innovation, and a distinctive style spring immediately to mind.

There are of course other, more stealthy ways into Flash design, and these seem to be the routes that most of us tend to end up following.

One of the things I would strongly recommend is that you build up a portfolio of work.

Although there's a fair demand for Flash designers at the moment, my feedback from design houses is that it takes a lot of interviews to find a designer who can actually create commercial-quality content. An applicant with a solid portfolio (much of which can include personal work, so don't get hung up with ideas of "you need a job to get a job") is the number one thing that's wanted.

As with all creative positions, a good portfolio counts for everything (a new designer who claims experience but has no portfolio to show for it will be sent to the back of the queue more quickly than a designer with an amazing portfolio and no clients). College courses and other web qualifications are also useful—but the portfolio is by far the main thing. Having a string of online URLs that you can add to every job application is a must.

Although your first few Flash sites may be more in the solid-but-dependable ballpark, it won't be long before you have a few sites that you're actually proud of. That's the time to start looking at full time **freelancing**. This is much easier to do now that the Web has really taken off, and there are a number of websites in America and Europe that will e-mail you with weekly lists of contract positions. Be aware that the market for this type of work is *very* competitive, and many jobs ask for Flash as part of a range of skills that increasingly include server-side technologies (or at the very least, XML and a knowledge of how to use it to communicate between Flash and other technologies). You'll also need to show sample URLs from your portfolio before you'll be taken seriously.

A good tip is to add Flash, HTML, Dreamweaver, Photoshop, and JavaScript to your résumé's list of key-words. If you choose this route, my advice would be to find a few websites that allow online resumes, and add links to your three best sites. You'll find that a lot of traditional employment agencies now scour such entries, and you sometimes find e-mails from agencies you've never worked with imploring you to get in touch about a contract!

Applying directly to web design houses is another option. However, unless you've already created a stir on the Web with your home site or other work, be prepared for a disappointing starting salary. There's a lot of money to be made from the Internet, but junior web designers seem to be seeing a minimal part of it. A lot of people may choose this option despite lack of initial pay because it can create a good body of work very quickly. If you work with the right company, the work can be very satisfying, and you can move up to more senior positions—or into freelance work, after a couple of years. There's much less uncertainty when starting out on this route than there is with freelancing, in which you may not be employed all year round (at least until you have a good freelance client list).

Flash farewell—for now

The end of this book is very much the beginning of your Flash career—whatever you choose to do with your new skills. You now have a platform of knowledge that will allow you to branch out into a variety of areas—all with their own pitfalls and possibilities. Flash is now a major force on the Web, and it's destined to increase its power and influence. There's an opportunity now to ride the crest of Flash's wave and make your mark in the world of web design. Don't rest on your laurels—practice the skills you have and search out new ones and new ways to apply them.

See you on the beach.

INDEX

X-Y-Z

friendsofed.com/forums

Join the friends of ED forums to find out more about our books, discover useful technology tips and tricks, or get a helping hand on a challenging project. *Designer to Designer*™ is what it's all about—our community sharing ideas and inspiring each other. In the friends of ED forums, you'll find a wide range of topics to discuss, so look around, find a forum, and dive right in!

- **Books and Information**

  Chat about friends of ED books, gossip about the community, or even tell us some bad jokes!

- **Flash**

  Discuss design issues, ActionScript, dynamic content, and video and sound.

- **Web Design**

  From front-end frustrations to back-end blight, share your problems and your knowledge here.

- **Site Check**

  Show off your work or get new ideas.

- **Digital Imagery**

  Create eye candy with Photoshop, Fireworks, Illustrator, and FreeHand.

- **ArchivED**

  Browse through an archive of old questions and answers.

HOW TO PARTICIPATE

Go to the friends of ED forums at **www.friendsofed.com/forums**.

Visit **www.friendsofed.com** to get the latest on our books, find out what's going on in the community, and discover some of the slickest sites online today!